CA Proficiency
Taxation 2 (NI)
2021–2022

CHARTERED
ACCOUNTANTS
IRELAND

Published in 2021 by
Chartered Accountants Ireland
Chartered Accountants House
47–49 Pearse Street
Dublin 2
www.charteredaccountants.ie

ISBN: 978-1-913975-11-1

Typeset by Deanta Global Publishing Services
Printed by eprint books limited, Dublin

Contents

PART ONE   INCOME TAX

PART TWO   CORPORATION TAX

PART THREE   CAPITAL GAINS TAX

PART FOUR   INHERITANCE TAX

PART SIX   VALUE ADDED TAX

Chartered Accountants Ireland *Code of Ethics*

Chartered Accountants Ireland's *Code of Ethics* applies to all aspects of a Chartered Accountant's professional life, including issues around taxation. The *Code of Ethics* outlines the principles that should guide a Chartered Accountant, namely:

- Integrity
- Objectivity
- Professional Competence and Due Care
- Confidentiality
- Professional Behaviour.

As a Chartered Accountant, you must ensure that the tax aspects of your professional life are in compliance with these fundamental principles. Set out in **Appendix 2** is further information regarding these principles and their importance in guiding you on how to deal with issues that may arise throughout your professional life, including giving tax advice and preparing tax computations.

Administration – Appeals, Enquiries and HMRC Powers

Learning Objectives

After studying this chapter, you will understand:

- The requirements for a valid appeal and the options open to taxpayers and HMRC.
- HMRC enquiries/compliance checks.
- HMRC information powers and inspection powers.
- Discovery assessments.
- Determinations.
- The penalty regime.
- Details of the rules for publishing deliberate tax defaulters and the Managing Serious Defaulters programme.

This chapter covers the additional administrative aspects of the UK tax system examinable at CA Proficiency 2. Under the cumulative knowledge principle, students are advised to recap on the administrative aspects of income tax, CGT, corporation tax and VAT covered at CA Proficiency 1 (or other studies).

1.1 Introduction

The UK self-assessment system is supported by a penalty regime that can apply to individuals and businesses who are not tax compliant. Interest may also be charged on the late payment of taxes. HMRC therefore regularly undertakes enquiries and discovery assessments on individuals and businesses. HMRC randomly selects individuals and businesses to enquire into on an ongoing basis or, where a particular risk has been identified, enquiries are conducted on a more structured basis. Campaigns can also be targeted at specific sectors where there are believed to be tax-compliance issues.

HMRC has a wide range of powers and vast sources of information at its disposal to enforce compliance with UK tax legislation. However, UK tax legislation also affords taxpayers certain important rights and safeguards, including the right to appeal.

1.2   The Appeals System

1.2.1   Overview

Disputes may arise between an individual, business or company and HMRC in respect of the tax treatment of a particular item, decision or view taken by HMRC or where a penalty has been imposed. In such circumstances, an appeal may be made by the taxpayer.

Where agreement cannot be reached between the taxpayer and HMRC, the taxpayer can appeal the decision and the case may be heard by the appropriate tax tribunal.

In the UK there is a two-tier system for appeals, consisting of the First-tier Tribunal (Tax) and the Upper Tribunal (Tax and Chancery Chamber).

Timeframes to lodge an appeal must be strictly adhered to. The **time limit** for appeal is 30 days from the issue of the relevant assessment, amendment, disallowance or demand.

The First-tier Tribunal is the starting point of the appeals process, after which appeals can be escalated to the Upper Tribunal then to the Court of Appeal and finally to the Supreme Court. The hierarchy of the appeals procedures is outlined in **Figure 1.1**.

FIGURE 1.1: THE APPEALS HIERARCHY FOR TAX MATTERS

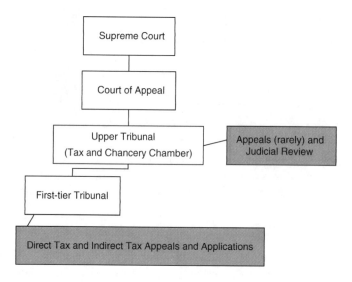

1.2.2   Right of Appeal

A taxpayer has the right to appeal against:

- any HMRC assessment to pay tax;
- a HMRC amendment to a self-assessment or a disallowance of a claim or election following an enquiry or discovery assessment (full or partial closure notice);
- a demand for documents made by HMRC;
- the imposition of a penalty or surcharge;

▣ the reason for undertaking a discovery assessment, i.e. the taxpayer may feel that the reasons cited by HMRC do not exist; or

▣ the decision of a discovery assessment

There is no right of appeal against:

▣ self-assessments – if HMRC has completed the tax liability calculation (i.e. a determination, see **Section 1.7**) because the taxpayer failed to submit a tax return on time, the submission of the actual self-assessment return by the taxpayer will automatically replace the determination. Therefore, there is no right to appeal a HMRC determination;

▣ an information notice (see **Section 1.4**); or

▣ an inspection notice (see **Section 1.5**).

1.2.3 Appeal Procedures

For HMRC decisions regarding **direct taxes** (income tax, capital gains, corporation tax, inheritance tax and stamp taxes) there are three options open to the taxpayer:

1. seek agreement with HMRC;
2. HMRC "internal review" – a taxpayer may request, or accept an offer from HMRC, to conduct an internal review, which would be carried out by a HMRC officer who is independent of the case; or
3. reject an offer of internal review and formally take an appeal to the Tribunal system.

Generally, where agreement cannot be reached between HMRC and the taxpayer, the taxpayer may be offered, or may request, an internal review. A HMRC internal review is, perhaps, the more cost-effective resolution for the taxpayer and HMRC as lower professional fees should be incurred. Once an internal review has been agreed to it must be concluded before an appeal to a Tribunal cannot be made.

If an internal review is agreed to, HMRC has 45 days to undertake it. On the conclusion of the review, the taxpayer has 30 days to either accept the outcome of the review or to send a "notice of appeal" to the Tribunal (in most cases this will be the First-tier Tribunal). The Tribunal will then inform the other party (normally HMRC as it is usually the taxpayer who will wish to appeal) that the notice of appeal has been received. If, after the 30-day period, neither action has been taken, the decision of the internal review is considered as final and the taxpayer has no further recourse.

Disputes regarding **indirect taxes** (including VAT) must be sent directly to the relevant Tribunal; that is, there is no scope for agreement or internal review.

1.2.4 Appeal to Tribunals

Categories of Cases

Once the Tribunal has received the taxpayer's notice to appeal and has informed the other party involved, the case is reviewed by the Tribunal to determine its complexity. There are four categories:

1. *Paper cases* – are dealt with by the First-tier Tribunal and apply to straightforward matters, such as fixed filing penalties. They are usually dealt with in writing and without a hearing.
2. *Basic cases* – are heard by the First-tier Tribunal and are usually dealt with at the close of a hearing with minimal exchange of documents before the hearing.
3. *Standard cases* – are heard by the First-tier Tribunal; they tend to have more detailed case management and are subject to more formal procedures than basic cases.

4. *Complex cases* – require lengthy or complex evidence or a lengthy hearing, involve a complex or important principle or issue, and may involve a large amount of money. Such cases will usually be sent directly to the Upper Tribunal.

The First-tier Tribunal (Tax)

The First-tier Tribunal (Tax) hears appeals made against decisions made by HMRC relating to tax. Appeals range from the relatively simple to complex areas across both direct and indirect tax.

The Tax Chamber is independent of HMRC and hears most of the appeals against decisions of HMRC in relation to tax. Appeals are heard by panels that are constituted according to the needs of the case and may be heard by legally qualified judges, non-legally qualified expert members or a mixture of the two.

Appeals may be brought against decisions of the First-tier Tribunal to the Upper Tribunal (Tax and Chancery Chamber) on a point of law.

The Upper Tribunal (Tax and Chancery Chamber)

The Upper Tribunal comprises judges and other members (non-legally qualified experts). Its main function is to hear appeals from the First-tier Tribunal (Tax) on points of law, however, there are occasions when cases may be referred directly to the Upper Tribunal. Typically, these would be matters giving rise to substantially complex issues regarding questions of law or judicial reviews.

Decisions of the Upper Tribunal are binding on the Tribunals and any affected public authorities. A decision of the Upper Tribunal may, however, be appealed to the Court of Appeal.

1.2.5   Appeal to the Court of Appeal and the Supreme Court

The First-tier Tribunal and the Upper Tribunal may confirm, reduce, or increase a disputed assessment. A Tribunal's decision on a matter of fact is final; however, either HMRC or the taxpayer may express dissatisfaction with the decision on a **point of law** and take the appeal further, to the **Court of Appeal** and ultimately to the **Supreme Court**.

The costs of taking an appeal to the courts can be extremely high, and an unsuccessful taxpayer may be required to pay HMRC's costs in defending the appeal as well as their own costs.

If the appellant disagrees with the decision of the Upper Tribunal and believes it made a mistake on a point of law, they may write to the Upper Tribunal to ask for permission to appeal. If permission is granted, the appeal moves to the higher court, i.e. the Court of Appeal. If permission is not granted, the appellant may ask the Court of Appeal directly for permission.

In a similar way, if the appellant disagrees with the decision of the Court of Appeal, they can obtain permission to appeal to the Supreme Court. Generally, permission will only be granted where there is an arguable point of law and it is of general public importance.

Prior to 1 January 2021, both Tax Tribunals, the Court of Appeal and the Supreme Court in the UK could also refer questions on tax matters to the Court of Justice of the European Union (CJEU). From 1 January 2021, following the end of the EU exit implementation period, the general ability to refer questions of European law to the CJEU ended. In the main, decisions made by the CJEU after this date are no longer binding on any UK court, though they may "have regard" to CJEU decisions if they feel they are relevant. In addition, the Supreme Court (and some other higher appeal courts) are free to depart from decisions of the CJEU made prior to 1 January 2021. There are some limited exceptions to this general rule. For example, the UK courts, including the Supreme Court, continue to be able to refer questions to the CJEU about the interpretation of the citizens' rights provisions in Part 2 of the EU–UK Withdrawal Agreement.

In addition, the position in Northern Ireland is more complicated due to the provisions of the Protocol on Ireland/Northern Ireland. Under the Protocol, the CJEU has jurisdiction with regards to the provisions within the Protocol relating to customs, technical regulations, VAT, and state aid. The European Commission can bring a direct infringement claim to the CJEU if it believes the UK to be in breach of the Protocol in these areas.

1.2.6 Postponement of Tax Pending an Appeal

Postponement of Payments

In the case of disputed amendments to self-assessments and disputed discovery assessments, the taxpayer may apply to HMRC, within 30 days, to postpone payment of all or part of the tax that has been assessed, pending settlement of the appeal.

Applications to **postpone payment** are subject to HMRC agreement. If HMRC refuses an application to postpone payment, the taxpayer may take the application to the Tribunal, within 30 days of HMRC's refusal. A postponement application is heard by the Tribunal in the same way as an appeal. The Tribunal's decision is final.

Any non-postponed part of the tax due on a disputed assessment is payable on the due date in the usual way. If the appeal is subsequently determined in the taxpayer's favour, any overpaid tax is refunded.

Interest on Postponed Payments

The postponement of the payment of tax pending an appeal does not impact on the date upon which interest will accrue. If the conclusion of the appeal is that the tax is due, late payment interest will be charged from the same date (i.e. when the tax should have been paid) as if there had been no appeal.

1.3 HMRC Enquiries and Compliance Checks

HMRC has substantial powers to ensure compliance with the tax legislation and carries out tax enquiries and compliance checks on an ongoing basis. If, during a tax enquiry, or outside the 12-month enquiry window, HMRC discovers that tax has been underpaid by a taxpayer due to the omission of profits or the excessive claiming of a relief, then it may issue a discovery assessment to recover the tax lost.

Tax enquiries and compliance checks can be conducted into any tax return submitted by a taxpayer, including, but not limited to, self-assessment and corporation tax returns, and those for stamp taxes, inheritance tax and VAT.

HMRC randomly selects tax returns for checking and enquiry as a matter of course. However, in recent years random checks have become less frequent. HMRC in most cases now selects tax returns where there is an identified tax risk, e.g. a taxpayer who regularly files their return and pays tax late or where HMRC's information sources suggest there may be an error or omission. Enquiries may be full enquiries (looking at the tax return as a whole) or may be limited to "aspect" enquiries (looking only at a particular item in the return, e.g. interest income).

In the course of an enquiry, HMRC may require the taxpayer to produce documents, accounts or any other information required (see **Section 1.5**).

HMRC does not need to have, or give, a reason for conducting an enquiry. Notably, it does not need to inform the taxpayer if they have been selected at random for enquiry. However, the taxpayer must be notified that an enquiry has been opened.

1.3.1 Notification of an Enquiry: Self-assessment Returns

HMRC must send written notice to the taxpayer that an enquiry is underway. Generally, this notification must be sent within 12 months of the date the return was filed or, if the return was filed late, within 12 months of the next "quarter day", i.e. 31 January, 30 April, 31 July, or 31 October. If after these 12 months have elapsed it is discovered that a full disclosure has not been made, HMRC may conduct a "**discovery assessment**" (see **Section 1.6**).

If the taxpayer **amended** the return after the due filing date, the enquiry 'window' extends to the quarter day following the first anniversary of the date the amendment was filed. Where the enquiry is not initiated within the period that would have applied had no amendment been filed, the enquiry is restricted to matters contained in the amendment.

Enquiries into partnership self-assessment returns are subject to the same timeframe, including amended returns. A notice to enquire into a partnership return is deemed to incorporate a notice to enquire into each individual partner's return.

Enquiries may also be made into stand-alone claims in self-assessment returns (e.g. for certain reliefs such as investment in a venture capital trust), provided notice is given by the HMRC officer by the later of:

- the quarter day following the first anniversary of the making or amending of the claim;
- 31 January after the end of the tax year, if the claim relates to that tax year; or
- the first anniversary of the end of the period to which a claim relates if it relates to a period other than that tax year.

1.3.2 Notification of an Enquiry: Company Tax Returns

The time span for which HMRC may give notice that it is enquiring into a stand-alone company tax return is 12 months from the date that the return was filed or, if the return was delivered late, within 12 months of the next "quarter day", i.e. 31 January, 30 April, 31 July or 31 October.

Where a company is a member of a group that is not small (as defined), the relevant time span is that the enquiry must be opened within 12 months from the statutory filing date. Broadly, a group will be a 'small group' if it satisfies at least two of the following conditions:

1. aggregate turnover is not more than £6.5 million net (or £7.8 million gross);
2. aggregate balance sheet total is not more than £3.26 million net (or £3.9 million gross);
3. aggregate number of employees is not more than 50.

'Net' refers to the aggregate after any set-offs or other adjustments to eliminate inter-group transactions; 'gross' is without those set-offs or other adjustments.

Generally, HMRC will conduct its enquiries under procedures set out in its enquiry manual. With many UK companies being family owned and run, it would not be unusual to find that HMRC would open an enquiry into the tax affairs of the directors/working shareholders at the same time.

1.3.3 During an Enquiry

Once an enquiry is underway, the taxpayer is not allowed to make any amendments to the return being investigated. A prompted qualifying disclosure is one that is submitted after notification of the HMRC enquiry has been received but before the enquiry physically commences (see **Section 1.8**).

At any time during the course of an enquiry the taxpayer may apply to the First-tier Tribunal to require HMRC to notify the taxpayer within a specified period that the enquiries are complete, unless HMRC can demonstrate that it has reasonable grounds for continuing the enquiry.

Disputes concerning a point of law can be resolved through litigation, if both sides agree, without having to wait until the whole enquiry is complete.

In situations where a return indicates an overpayment of tax and that a repayment is due, and this return is then subject to enquiry, any repayment may be postponed until the enquiry is complete. HMRC has discretion to make a provisional repayment, but there is no facility to appeal if the repayment is withheld until the enquiry is complete.

Where a taxpayer has engaged a tax agent or tax advisor to look after their tax affairs, HMRC will usually correspond with the agent regarding the enquiry into the tax affairs of their client. During the course of the enquiry, the taxpayer and/or its professional advisors will be asked to supply various documents and details relating to the queries raised by HMRC. In some circumstances a meeting may take place. Minutes of all such meetings would be taken and HMRC would normally request that the taxpayer sign a copy of these minutes as a verification of their content.

1.3.4   Partial Closure Notices

An enquiry is complete when HMRC issues a closure notice. However, it can issue a Partial Closure Notice (PCN) ahead of the final closure of an enquiry. HMRC tend to issue PCNs in enquiries where a taxpayer's tax affairs are complex or where there is avoidance or large amounts of tax at risk. These notices allow discrete elements of the enquiry to be closed and the relevant tax, interest, and penalty thereon to be collected in advance of full closure of the enquiry.

1.3.5   Conclusion of an Enquiry

At the conclusion of an enquiry, HMRC must issue a closure notice to the taxpayer informing them that the enquiry is complete, stating its conclusions and amending the self-assessment, partnership statement or claim (e.g. the amount of a loss relief claim) accordingly, if relevant.

The taxpayer has 30 days to either appeal the decision of the enquiry (see **Section 1.2**) or to amend the self-assessment, partnership statement or claim to give effect to HMRC's conclusions.

Once an enquiry is concluded, the taxpayer has an opportunity to make any other amendments to their tax return that could have been made had the enquiry not been initiated (amendments cannot be made while enquiries are in progress and such amendments may not have been within the scope of the enquiry). If HMRC is not satisfied with the taxpayer's amendment, it has 30 days in which to amend the self-assessment, partnership statement or claim.

If a claim has been disallowed but it does not affect the self-assessment, HMRC must advise the taxpayer of the extent to which it has been disallowed.

Once an enquiry has been completed, HMRC cannot make further enquiries into that particular return. In limited circumstances, HMRC may undertake a discovery assessment if it believes that there has been a loss of tax (see **Section 1.6**).

Any underpaid tax arising as a result of the enquiry must be paid within 30 days (of the closure notice), including interest and penalties (see **Section 1.8**). If a refund of tax is due, this will be paid by HMRC on foot of the amendments being submitted by the taxpayer.

1.4   HMRC's Information Powers

In recent years HMRC's powers have been significantly extended. It now has one set of information and inspection powers covering income tax, CGT, corporation tax, VAT, inheritance tax and stamp taxes, as well as PAYE, to ensure that taxpayers comply with their obligations, pay the right amount of tax at the right time and claim the correct relief and allowances.

HMRC usually **informally** request information and documents from taxpayers in connection with their tax affairs. If a taxpayer does not co-operate fully with an informal request, HMRC has statutory powers to request information and documents from taxpayers and/or relevant third parties.

HMRC must send a written "**information notice**" requesting documents and other information, such as appointment diaries, board minutes, correspondence, contracts, etc. An information notice can only be issued if the information and documents requested are "reasonably required" for the purpose of checking the taxpayer's tax position. An information notice may be issued to a taxpayer either with or without the approval of the First-tier Tribunal.

HMRC has the power to request and inspect documents held in a person's possession to explicitly include documents held on a computer or recorded electronically in any way. Anyone obstructing HMRC in the exercise of its powers, or failing to comply within a reasonable time, may be charged a penalty of £300.

1.4.1   Information Powers: Merchant Acquirers

HMRC can now issue information notices to card-payment processors, requiring them to provide bulk data on businesses accepting credit and debit card payments. The data provided, which covers the monthly totals paid to merchants, is of significant value in identifying businesses that do not declare their full sales. This also enables HMRC to better target compliance interventions (i.e. HMRC inspections and enquiries) at those who may be underpaying tax, as part of HMRC's attempt to minimise tax evasion and tax avoidance.

The type of information that can be requested includes information about credit, debit and charge card sales made by a retailer, and the retailer's name, address, VAT number (if available) and bank account details. It will not identify the details of the credit or debit cardholder, just the total sales made by particular businesses in each month. These are then used by HMRC to crosscheck against VAT registrations and business income declared on tax returns.

1.4.2   Information Powers: Third Parties

There are a number of rules and conditions regarding HMRC's powers to request information from third parties.

- Notice to a third party can be issued either with the agreement of the taxpayer or with the approval of the Tribunal unless the notice refers only to information or documents that form part of a person's statutory records and relate to the supply of services or supply, acquisition or importation of goods. Statutory records for this purpose are those primary business records that are required to be kept to ensure income and expenses are properly recorded.
- Where the Tribunal is satisfied that informing the taxpayer would prejudice the tax enquiry, it can approve the information request without the taxpayer having been informed.
- An authorised HMRC officer must agree to the notice before it is referred to the Tribunal.
- The taxpayer to whom the notice relates must receive a summary of the reasons for the third-party notice, unless the Tribunal believe it would prejudice the assessment or collection of tax.
- As with a notice to a taxpayer, the request must be "reasonably required" to establish the taxpayer's correct tax position.
- A third-party notice must name the taxpayer to whom it relates unless the Tribunal has approved the notice and disapplied this requirement.
- There is no right of appeal against a decision of the First-tier Tribunal to approve an information notice.
- Where an information notice was not approved by the Tribunal, the taxpayer may appeal to the Tribunal against the notice or any requirement therein, except a requirement to provide information or documents forming part of statutory records.

■ A right of appeal also exists for third-party notices and notices requiring information and documents about persons whose identities are not known, but only where it would be unduly onerous to comply with the notice or requirement.

■ On appeal, the Tribunal may confirm, vary, or set aside the notice or a requirement therein, and the Tribunal's decision is final.

1.4.3   Information Powers: Legal Professional Privilege

Tax advisors and auditors cannot be asked to provide information connected with their functions when this work comes within **legal professional privilege**. For example, a tax advisor does not have to provide access to their working papers used in the preparation of the taxpayer's return where the papers fall within the definition of "relevant communications", i.e. information and documents relevant to the case.

There are instances, however, when professional privilege does not apply. In a recent tax case, known as the *Prudential* case (*Prudential plc and another v. Special Commissioner of Income Tax and another* (2013)), it was held by the Court of Appeal that legal professional privilege did not apply to legal advice given by accountants. It was held that such privilege, outside the context of litigations, is applicable only in relation to advice from lawyers. Prudential plc appealed the decision to the Supreme Court. The Supreme Court, however, upheld the judgment and confirmed that legal advice given by non-lawyers does not enjoy the benefit of legal privilege.

1.5   HMRC's Inspection Powers

An authorised HMRC officer has the power to enter the business premises of a taxpayer whose liability is being investigated (by way of enquiry or discovery assessment) to inspect the premises, business assets and business documents that are on the premises. The power does not extend to any part of the premises used solely as a dwelling.

If an information notice has been issued (see above), the documents specified in that notice can be inspected at the same time. An authorised HMRC officer may take copies of, or make extracts from, inspected documents; and they may remove and retain inspected documents where it appears to be necessary, but must provide a receipt or copy where requested.

As with the information powers, the inspection must be "reasonably required" for the purpose of checking the taxpayer's tax position. HMRC will usually agree a time for the inspection with the taxpayer. However, an authorised HMRC officer can carry out the inspection at "any reasonable time" if either:

■ the taxpayer receives at least seven days' written notice, an "inspection notice"; or

■ the inspection is carried out by, or with the approval of, an authorised HMRC officer.

There is no right of appeal against an inspection notice. HMRC are also statutorily entitled to enter the premises of an "involved third party" to inspect the premises, business assets and relevant documents. Again, the inspection must be "reasonably required" for the purpose of checking the tax position of any period or class of persons. For example, a payroll-giving scheme operator may be considered a "third-party provider". HMRC are also entitled to enter premises for valuation purposes if this is reasonably required to check the tax position.

An officer may ask a Tribunal to approve an inspection. If the giving of the notice has been approved by the Tribunal then the notice must say so. Applications to the Tribunal to approve an inspection of a business are heard without the taxpayer being present. There is no right of appeal against a decision of the Tribunal to approve an inspection.

1.6   Discovery Assessments

Where, during an enquiry or after the 12-month enquiry window has lapsed, HMRC 'discover' that a taxpayer has omitted income or gains that should have been taxed, where the assessment is insufficient or the claiming of a relief excessive, then HMRC may issue a discovery assessment to the taxpayer. Discovery assessments are generally undertaken to **recover tax** that is due.

Discovery assessments can **only** be initiated where:

■ there has been "careless" or "deliberate" understatement by the taxpayer or their agent; or
■ at the time that an enquiry was completed or could no longer be made, HMRC did not have information available to it to make it aware of the loss of tax.

Discovery assessments **cannot** be raised if:

■ the return was made in accordance with prevailing practice at the time, e.g. where HMRC has changed its opinion on a certain matter, even if an error in the return resulted in tax lost; or
■ full disclosure was made in the return, unless there was a loss of tax due to careless or deliberate conduct, e.g. where income was returned in the incorrect position on the tax return.

The normal time limit for these assessments is four years from the end of the tax year in question, but it is increased to six years if there has been careless understatement and 20 years if there has been deliberate understatement. A taxpayer can appeal against a discovery assessment within 30 days of issue.

For discovery assessments, HMRC is bound by rules regarding what can be treated as "available". Information is **available** if:

■ it is contained in the taxpayer's return for the period (or for either of the two preceding/periods) or in any accompanying documents;
■ it is contained in a claim (e.g. a loss relief claim) made in respect of that period or in any accompanying documents;
■ it is contained in any documents produced in connection with an enquiry into a return (or claim) for the period or either of the two preceding periods; or
■ it is information, the existence and relevance of which could reasonably be expected to be inferred by HMRC from any of the above, or which was notified in writing by or on behalf of the taxpayer to HMRC. The information supplied must be sufficiently detailed to draw HMRC's attention to contentious matters, such as the use of a valuation or estimate.

These rules do not prevent HMRC from raising assessments in cases of genuine discoveries; but do prevent assessments from being raised due to HMRC's failure to make timely use of information or to a change of opinion on information made available.

1.7   Determinations

Where a return is not filed by the filing date, HMRC may determine the amount of tax due. This determination is replaced by the actual self-assessment when it is submitted, if done so within 12 months of the date of determination. A HMRC determination must be made within three years of the due date for the return.

Such a determination must be made to the best of HMRC's information and belief and is subsequently treated as if it were a self-assessment. This enables HMRC to seek payment of tax, including payments on account for the following tax year, and to charge interest.

1.8   The Penalty Regime

As noted above, a unified penalty regime applies to all taxes, although parts are still to be phased in over the next few years. This unified penalty regime covers failure to notify, late payment, late submission and incorrect returns or where inaccurate information or documents have been supplied. As the unified regime is being phased in, there are some variations that still exist across the different taxes. For example, the VAT default surcharge regime applies to late VAT payments and late returns rather than the unified late filing and late payment penalty regimes. An overview of the main principles that apply to the unified penalty regimes are outlined below. For example, a taxpayer will incur a penalty if they fail to notify HMRC that they are chargeable to tax, if they submit an incorrect return or if inaccurate information or documents are supplied.

It should be noted that there are proposed changes to penalties for late payment of tax and late submission of returns for income tax self-assessment (ITSA) and VAT. The changes introduce a points-based penalty regime that will apply from:

- 1 April 2022 for VAT;
- 6 April 2023 for ITSA, for those with business or property turnover in excess of £10,000 per year;
- 6 April 2024 for all other ITSA payers.

The detail of these new rules are beyond the scope of this textbook.

1.8.1   Penalties for Non-compliance: Overview

The main aspects of the penalty regime are:

- If a taxpayer can demonstrate to HMRC that they have taken "reasonable care" to correctly calculate their tax, they will not be penalised if they make an error.
- If they do not take reasonable care, errors will attract penalties – and higher penalties if the error is deliberate.
- Disclosing errors to HMRC early will substantially reduce any penalty due.
- Penalties can be charged where information declared to HMRC, e.g. a tax return or supplementary accounts submitted in support of a tax return, contains an inaccuracy that results in:
  - an understatement of a liability to tax;
  - a false or inflated statement of a loss;
  - a false or inflated claim to repayment of tax; or
  - a false or inflated claim for allowances and reliefs.
- Penalties can also be charged where tax has been under-assessed due to a failure to make a return (i.e. notify HMRC of chargeability) or where an error has been discovered but the taxpayer has not taken reasonable steps to inform HMRC.
- The inaccuracy must be "careless", "deliberate", or "deliberate and concealed" for a penalty to be incurred. The amount of the penalty depends on the potential lost revenue as well as the taxpayer's behaviour (i.e. careless, deliberate, or deliberate and concealed).
- Whether a taxpayer has taken "reasonable care" will be viewed in the light of their abilities and circumstances. For example, the same level of knowledge or expertise will not be expected from a self-employed and unrepresented individual as would be expected from a large multinational company; and a higher degree of care will be expected over large and complex matters than for simple straightforward ones.

■ If the information provided to HMRC contains more than one error or inaccuracy, a penalty can be charged for each error.

■ Taxpayers have the option to make prompted and unprompted disclosures to help reduce penalties.

■ HMRC will publish the names of tax offenders in certain circumstances.

■ For corporation tax purposes, the taxpayer is the company acting through its directors and officers.

■ In the case of deliberate inaccuracy that is found to be attributable to an officer of a company (which includes a director, secretary, or shadow director), both the company and the officer are liable for the penalty.

■ Appointing a tax advisor does not automatically mean that a taxpayer has taken reasonable care in the preparation of a return. The tax advisor should be competent and qualified, nevertheless the taxpayer still bears responsibility for the return and they are expected, within their ability and competence, to make sure that the return being signed is correct.

1.8.2 Potential Lost Revenue

Penalty charges are generally based on the additional tax (and subsequent additional national insurance contributions, if applicable) that are due as a result of correcting the error. This is known as the potential lost revenue (PLR). Depending on the level of error, the following penalties can apply:

■ careless behaviour (failure to take reasonable care) – maximum penalty: 30%

■ deliberate but not concealed behaviour (the inaccuracy is deliberate but there are no arrangements to conceal it) – maximum penalty: 70%

■ deliberate and concealed behaviour (the inaccuracy is deliberate and there are arrangements to conceal it)– maximum penalty: 100%.

Example 1.1
Peter is a sole trader and files his tax return for 2021/22 on time. The return shows his trading income to be £70,000. In fact, his trading income was £75,000. This oversight was due to carelessness.

HMRC's potential lost revenue is:
  £75,000 – £70,000 = £5,000 undeclared income
  PLR = £5,000 × 40% (income tax) + 2% (Class 4 NICs) = £2,100

Peter's error is "careless", so the maximum penalty is: £2,100 × 30% = £630.

1.8.3 Prompted and Unprompted Disclosures

The concept of prompted and unprompted disclosures aims to encourage taxpayers to voluntarily declare any errors or under-assessment in their tax affairs.

1. **Unprompted disclosures** are those where the taxpayer has no reason to believe that HMRC has discovered, or is about to discover, the inaccuracy or under-assessment. An unprompted disclosure can substantially reduce the penalty charged.

2. **Prompted disclosures** are those where an error has been admitted but it is in response to a HMRC investigation, such as a discovery assessment (see above). Taxpayers may receive a reduced penalty charge, but it is not as generous as for an unprompted disclosure.

For errors and inaccuracies considered to be "careless", if they are rectified within 12 months of the disclosure, further reductions are available. **Table 1.1** shows the mitigation of penalty charges by prompted or unprompted disclosures.

TABLE 1.1: MITIGATION OF PENALTIES – PROMPTED AND UNPROMPTED DISCLOSURES

Behaviour	Maximum penalty	Minimum penalty with unprompted disclosure	Minimum penalty with prompted disclosure
Careless	30%	0%	15%
Deliberate	70%	20%	35%
Deliberate and concealed	100%	30%	50%

(Students should note that the above table is **not** included in the Tax Reference Material supplied with the CA Proficiency 2 final examination.)

The reduced rates are the minimum penalty that can be imposed. Nevertheless, the reductions available, especially for unprompted disclosures, are significant. For instance, an unprompted disclosure of a "careless" error could have the penalty negated entirely.

When considering the actual penalty to be imposed, HMRC will consider the "quality" of the disclosure. HMRC consider the following three elements as primary when deciding on a reduced penalty:

1. the fact that the taxpayer has informed HMRC of their error. HMRC will take into consideration whether the disclosure was unprompted or prompted;
2. the fact that the taxpayer has made a full disclosure and explained how the error arose; and
3. the taxpayer has given reasonable help to HMRC to calculate the unpaid tax, including providing access to records.

Example 1.2

HMRC discovers an arithmetical error in Peony Ltd's tax return for the year ended 31 March 2022. The PLR is calculated to be £5,000. The return had been prepared by the company's financial controller and signed by its sole director, Dee. She had not checked the tax return before signing it and so was not aware of the error.

The company has been careless in the preparation of its tax return and was not able to disclose the error to HMRC before it was discovered. As the error was arithmetical, it was within Dee's competence and ability to find it. HMRC may impose a penalty of 30% of £5,000, i.e. £1,500, in addition to charging interest for late payment, although the penalty may be mitigated to 15% if a prompted disclosure is made. An unprompted disclosure is not possible as HMRC have already discovered the error.

1.8.4 Penalty Appeals

A taxpayer can appeal against:

- the fact that a penalty is being imposed;
- the amount of the penalty; and
- a decision by HMRC not to suspend a penalty and against conditions imposed by HMRC for suspension of penalties (see below).

For further information on the appeals procedures, see **Section 1.2**.

1.8.5 Suspended Penalties

Taxpayers who endeavour to improve their accounting systems (e.g. by keeping better records or using improved accounting systems so that payment and submission deadlines are not missed) to avoid errors or inaccuracies in reporting in the future, may escape a penalty charge. Conditions will be agreed and set with HMRC and if they are met the penalty will be cancelled. If they are not met, the penalty becomes payable. The period of suspension can be up to two years.

Only a penalty arising from the "careless" category, i.e. failure to take reasonable care, can be considered for suspension.

1.8.6 Failure to Keep and Preserve Records

The maximum penalty for failure to keep and preserve records for self-assessment returns in relation to any tax year is £3,000.

1.9 Publishing Details of Deliberate Tax Defaulters

In addition to recovering underpaid tax due, any interest thereon and a penalty tied to the potential lost revenue, legislation allows HMRC to publish the details of certain tax defaulters, including companies. A list of defaulters is published quarterly on www.gov.uk.

Deliberate tax defaults are: incorrect returns, failures to notify and certain VAT wrongdoings. This measure does not, however, apply to late filing or late payment penalties.

For HMRC to consider publication of a tax defaulters name and details, the following conditions must apply:

- a relevant penalty of the type set out above must be incurred;
- the taxpayer must be penalised for one or more deliberate defaults; and
- the amount of tax evaded must be greater than £25,000. In working out whether this threshold is reached, all tax that has been subject to a penalty for deliberate errors will be added together.

HMRC will not publish details where a full disclosure is made, either unprompted or prompted, and the taxpayer co-operates fully with HMRC, thereby receiving the maximum penalty reduction available.

In addition, the publishing of a tax defaulter's details follows a strict set of rules:

- All the penalty decisions underpinning the scheme can be appealed to an independent tribunal.
- No publication is possible until all appeals are concluded or opportunities to appeal have expired.
- The publication process is not part of the enquiry process.
- HMRC must publish within 12 months of the penalty becoming final and cease publishing that information 12 months thereafter.

If these criteria are met, HMRC will publish the details unless there are exceptional circumstances. HMRC are unlikely to decide not to publish because of a possible impact on the person's reputation, business interests or creditworthiness.

Taxpayers should therefore be encouraged to make a qualifying disclosure where possible, not only to achieve full penalty mitigation but also to avoid having their details published under this measure.

1.10 Managing Serious Defaulters Programme

HMRC's Managing Serious Defaulters (MSD) programme is aimed at closely monitoring the tax affairs of individuals and businesses, including companies, classed as "serious defaulters", i.e. where a "deliberate" or "deliberate with concealment" penalty has been charged. The key objective of the programme is to ensure that once a serious defaulter's taxes have been rectified that they remain tax compliant and are deterred from similar behaviour in the future.

The programme is not voluntary – HMRC will decide whether the serious defaulter's tax affairs warrant closer monitoring. It will advise the taxpayer in writing of their inclusion in the programme at the end of the relevant enquiry/compliance check. Where a full unprompted disclosure has been made, the defaulter will not be placed into the MSD programme, subject to having been given the maximum penalty reduction for deliberate behaviour.

The MSD programme applies to businesses and individual taxpayers who have been found to have made a deliberate understatement of any size, and applies the enhanced monitoring to all the defaulter's tax affairs and not just the area(s) from which the initiating behaviour originated.

In addition to the penalty for the original offence, for up to a five-year period afterwards, the taxpayer may be subject to additional monitoring, with the level and term of monitoring dependent on the seriousness of the offence.

HMRC will continue to check that returns are filed on time and that any tax due is paid on time, but there will also be regular reviews of the deliberate defaulter's tax affairs to check that any errors or failings have been rectified. There are a variety of measures HMRC may use to monitor a serious defaulter's tax affairs, which are beyond the scope of this textbook. The MSD programme is in addition to the rules which allow the publishing of details of deliberate defaulters.

Questions

Review Questions
(See Suggested Solutions to Review Questions at the end of this textbook.)

Question 1.1

Explain briefly how HMRC enquiries work in respect of individual tax returns. If a taxpayer has an issue with a HMRC enquiry that cannot be settled by agreement with HMRC, what options are open to the taxpayer?

Question 1.2

Petra Mirren, a new client of your practice, called you recently for some advice in relation to her company, Mirren Marketing Consultancy Ltd, which provides marketing consultancy services to local businesses. The company's tax compliance work was previously carried out by a small 'one-man band' in the local area who is not a Chartered Accountant.

It is now early July 2022 and only yesterday Petra received a letter from HMRC informing her it had opened an enquiry into the company tax return for 31 March 2021, which had been filed online by the local accountant on 10 June 2021. The Inspector of Taxes has asked for detailed analysis of a number of items. Upon inspection you identify an underpayment of corporation tax of £22,000. Mirren Marketing Consultancy does not pay corporation tax in instalments.

Petra knows the return was late but said she had been told there would be no penalty as this was the first time this had happened. "This letter that I have received, has the company anything to worry about? I assume every company receives a letter like this now and again."

Requirement

Write to Petra addressing the following issues:

- The implications for the company of the £22,000 underpayment of corporation tax.
- Advise what action the company should take in the context of the letter from HMRC and the underpayment.
- Assess if it is correct that no late filing penalty will be payable for the late submission of the 2021 corporation tax return.

Question 1.3

It is early May 2021 and you are Seana Williams, a recently qualified Chartered Accountant working in the tax department of Smith & Co., a medium-sized accountancy practice in Newry. You have just received a telephone call from a client, Denis O'Connor, the majority shareholder of O'Connor & Co. (architects).

"Hi Seana, I hope you are well. I'm calling about a notice I received yesterday from HMRC. O'Connor & Co. is to be visited for a VAT inspection for the period 1 January 2020 to 31 March 2021. The visit was to take place at our premises on 1 August 2021. However, I've just had a call from the HMRC Inspector who will be carrying out the inspection. She said she intended to inspect my home as well and also 'casually' mentioned that she intends asking O'Connor & Co's customers to provide information related to the VAT returns as part of the inspection! She says she's allowed to do this – hold on, I wrote this bit down, here it is. Apparently, paragraph 2 of Schedule 36 Finance Act 2008 allows it? Is that right? I really do not want our customers being involved or my home being searched. Is there anything we can do to avoid it?"

Requirement

Advise Denis if HMRC is able to ask the company's customers for information and what action he should take as a result of the proposed inspection of his home.

Residence, Domicile and Deemed Domicile

Learning Objectives

After studying this chapter you will understand:

- The concepts of residence, domicile and deemed domicile and be able to apply these to someone's individual circumstances.
- The implications of residence, domicile and deemed domicile for income tax.
- The remittance basis of taxation for income tax.

2.1 Introduction

The extent to which an individual is liable to UK income tax/capital gains tax (CGT) depends on three criteria:

1. residence;
2. domicile; and
3. deemed domicile.

Residence is based on physical presence in the UK, whereas domicile is dependent upon an individual's permanent homeland. The concepts of residence, domicile and deemed domicile are important because an individual's status will determine whether the person is liable to UK income tax/CGT in respect of the income/chargeable gains in the tax year. The source of the income/chargeable gain is also important, i.e. whether the income/chargeable gain arises in the UK, such as rental income from a UK property, or whether it arises overseas, such as the disposal of a property in Spain. This is dealt with in more detail in **Section 2.5** (income tax implications) and **Chapter 17** (CGT implications).

This chapter considers the concepts of residence, domicile and deemed domicile that apply to income tax and CGT. (The concepts of residence and domicile set out in this chapter are also relevant for inheritance tax, but students should note that the concept of **deemed domicile** set out in this chapter only applies to income tax and CGT – different deemed domicile rules apply for inheritance tax purposes (see **Chapter 22, Section 22.3.1**).)

2.2 The Statutory Residence Test

The statutory residence test (SRT) is used to determine an individual's tax residence status. For tax purposes, the UK is England, Scotland, Wales and Northern Ireland, and includes its territorial waters and its designated continental shelf. It does not include the Isle of Man or the Channel Islands.

2.2.1 Overview of the Statutory Residence Test

The SRT comprises three components:

1. the automatic overseas test;
2. the automatic UK test; and
3. the sufficient ties test.

The three tests are generally considered in the order given above. However by default, if someone is present in the UK for more than 183 days in a tax year, they will satisfy the **first automatic UK test** and as a result will be UK resident and none of the automatic overseas tests will be met. If, for a given tax year, an individual meets any of the automatic overseas tests, they will be treated as non-UK resident for the tax year in question. The automatic overseas test is therefore the next test to be considered if the 183 days default test is not met.

If none of the automatic overseas tests are met, then the automatic UK tests are considered. An individual is UK resident if any of the automatic UK tests applies.

If an individual does not satisfy either the automatic overseas tests or the automatic UK tests, recourse is made to the sufficient ties test. The individual will be considered UK resident if they have sufficient UK ties for the tax year combined with the relevant number of days spent in the UK.

It is therefore necessary to work through the tests systematically in order to determine whether an individual is non-resident or resident in the UK.

Note that an individual's residence is determined for each tax year separately, i.e. residency status must be re-assessed each tax year and an individual's status will depend upon the facts and circumstances in that tax year. An online tool is available on the HMRC website to enable individuals to assess their residence status under the SRT. Provided the correct details are inputted, the result of the online tool can be relied upon should the person's residence status be later enquired into by HMRC. However, HMRC will not be bound by the results where the information provided did not accurately reflect the facts and circumstances of the individual.

2.2.2 Automatic Overseas Tests

An individual will be treated as non-resident if any of the three automatic overseas tests are met. These are as follows:

1. **First automatic overseas test** – the individual was resident in the UK for one or more of the preceding three tax years but, in the relevant tax year, they spent fewer than **16 days** in the UK.
2. **Second automatic overseas test** – the individual was not resident in the UK for any of the preceding three tax years and spent fewer than **46 days** in the UK in the relevant tax year.
3. **Third automatic overseas test** – in the relevant tax year the individual **works full time overseas** for "sufficient hours" without any "significant breaks" and, during that tax year:
   (a) has fewer than 31 UK "work days" (considered as working more than three hours per day in the UK); and
   (b) spends fewer than **91 days** in total in the UK.

"Sufficient hours" is considered to be an average of at least 35 hours per week. "Significant break" is a period of more than 30 days during which the individual did not work for more than three hours, and this was not due to periods of annual leave, sick leave or parenting leave.

The tests require the individual to count the number of "days spent in the UK". These are explained in detail in **Section 2.2.6**.

Example 2.1

Meg is considering whether she meets the third automatic overseas test in respect of her work in Germany in the 2021/22 tax year. Meg visited the UK for a four-week holiday in May 2021. During this break in the UK, she worked six hours on four of the days. Meg is employed by the same German employer since 2020/21. On average, throughout 2021/22 she worked for 38 hours per week.

The key facts are:

▣ Meg has worked full-time overseas in 2021/22 as she has, on average, worked in excess of 35 hours per week in 2021/22, with no significant breaks of more than 30 days.

▣ Meg has fewer than 31 UK work days in 2021/22 as she only worked more than three hours per day in the UK for four days in 2021/22.

▣ Meg only spent 28 days in the UK in 2021/22 in total.

Based on the above analysis, Meg is non-resident in the UK in 2021/22 under the third automatic overseas test.

If the individual does not meet any of the automatic overseas tests, the next step is to consider the automatic UK tests.

2.2.3 Automatic UK Tests

An individual will be considered resident in the UK if any of the three automatic UK tests are met.

1. **First automatic UK test** – the individual spends at least **183 days** in the UK in the tax year.
2. **Second automatic UK test** – the individual **has a home in the UK** for all or part of the tax year and there is at least one period of **91 consecutive days** (at least 30 days of which fall within the tax year in question) when an individual has a home in the UK in which they spend a "sufficient amount of time" (at least **30 days** during the tax year), **and either the individual has**:
   ● no overseas home, **or**
   ● an overseas home or homes in each of which they spend no more than 30 days.
3. **Third automatic UK test** – the individual **works full time in the UK** for any period of **365 days** with no "significant break" and:
   (a) all or part of that work period falls within the tax year;
   (b) more than 75% of the 365-day period are UK work days (i.e. more than three hours work per day in the UK); and
   (c) at least one day (which falls in both the tax year and the 365-day period) is a day on which they do more than three hours of work in the UK.

"Significant break" has the same meaning as for the third automatic overseas test (see above).

HMRC guidelines offer examples to illustrate the practical considerations of the tests. The following examples have each been adapted from these examples.

Example 2.2 First automatic UK residence test

Lucas has lived in Austria all his life. On 1 July 2021 he took a holiday to Northern Ireland, during which time he met a partner. After dating for one week, they decided to get married and so Lucas never returned to Austria.

Lucas will be considered UK tax resident in 2021/22 as he has spent more than 183 days in the UK in the 2021/22 tax year. From 1 July 2021 to 5 April 2021, he will have spent over nine months in the UK.

> **Example 2.3 Second automatic UK residence test**
> Stan has lived in Australia all his life. In June 2021 he takes a holiday in London and likes it so much he decides to emigrate to the UK. He spends the next few months preparing for the move. He sells his Australian house (his only home) on 10 January 2022 and arrives in the UK on 25 January 2022. He finds a flat in London and moves in on 1 February 2022. The London flat is now his only home and he lives there for a year.
>
> There is a period of 91 consecutive days, falling partly within tax year 2021/22 (the period starting on 1 February 2022), when Stan has a home in the UK and no home overseas (it does not matter that the period when these conditions are met is in fact longer than 91 days). During tax year 2021/22, Stan is present in his UK home on at least 30 days. As Stan does not meet any of the automatic overseas tests, he is resident under the second automatic UK test for the tax year 2021/22.

> **Example 2.4 Third automatic UK residence test**
> Henri travels to the UK on 1 July 2020 to start a new job on the following day. His posting finishes on 1 July 2021 and he leaves the UK on 6 August 2021. Over the 365-day period to 30 June 2021, Henri calculates that he worked full time in the UK and has not taken a significant break from his UK work during this period. Part of the period of 365 days falls within the tax year 2020/21 and part falls within the tax year 2021/22.
>
> Over the period of 365 days ending 30 June 2021, Henri works for over three hours on 240 days, 196 (80%) of which are days when Henri worked for more than three hours in the UK. At least one day when Henri does more than three hours' work in the UK falls within the tax year 2020/21; therefore, Henri is resident in the UK under the third automatic UK test for the tax year 2020/21.
>
> There is also at least one day when Henri does more than three hours' work in the UK within the tax year 2021/22, so Henri also meets the third automatic UK test for that year.

2.2.4 The Sufficient Ties Test

If the individual does not meet any of the automatic overseas tests or any of the automatic UK tests, the "sufficient ties test" must be used to determine whether the individual is resident or non-resident in the UK. Essentially, the "sufficient ties test" is seeking to establish the level of connection (the number of ties) an individual has to the UK. If sufficient ties are recognised, then the individual is considered resident in the UK when this is combined with the required number of days in the UK. The ties considered are:

- a "family tie";
- an "accommodation tie";
- a "work tie";
- a "90-day tie"; and
- a "country tie" (only applicable if an individual was UK resident for one or more of the preceding three tax years).

The test distinguishes between individuals who were resident in the UK in any of the three preceding tax years ('leavers'), and those who were not ('arrivers'). Basically, if you were resident in one or more of the previous three tax years there is a greater chance of being classed as resident in the current tax year, compared to someone who was not resident in any of the three preceding tax years.

Number of Ties

Residency status is determined by the number of days spent in the UK and the number of ties that must apply. The more days an individual has spent in the UK, the fewer number of ties are needed to be treated as UK resident, and vice versa. The table below shows the number of ties required to be considered resident or non-resident.

SUFFICIENT TIES TABLE – STATUTORY RESIDENCE TEST

Days spent in the UK	Arrivers	Leavers
Fewer than 16 days	Always non-resident	Always non-resident
16–45 days	Always non-resident	Resident if at least 4 ties apply
46–90 days	Resident if 4 ties apply	Resident if at least 3 ties apply
91–120 days	Resident if at least 3 ties apply	Resident if at least 2 ties apply
121–182 days	Resident if at least 2 ties apply	Resident if at least 1 tie applies
183 days or more	Always resident	Always resident

Definition of UK Ties

Family Tie An individual will be considered to have a "family tie" for the tax year if any of the following are UK resident for tax purposes for that year:

- his or her husband, wife or civil partner (unless separated);
- his or her partner (if they are living together as husband and wife or as civil partners);
- his or her child, if aged under 18.

Accommodation Tie An individual has an "accommodation tie" for a tax year if he or she has a "place to live" in the UK and "it is available to them for a continuous period of 91 days or more" during the tax year, and either:

- they "spend one or more nights there" during the tax year; or
- "if it is at the home of a close relative they spend 16 or more nights there".

"Place to live" can include a holiday home or a temporary retreat. The property, therefore, does not have to be owned. "Close relative" includes parent, grandparent, brother, sister and children or grandchildren aged 18 or over.

Gaps of 15 days or fewer in the availability of the accommodation will count towards the continuous period of availability.

Work Tie An individual will be treated as having a "work tie" if they work in the UK for "at least 40 days in the tax year (whether continuously or intermittently)". A work day is the same definition as used elsewhere in the SRT, i.e. where more than three hours of work is undertaken.

90-Day Tie This tie is met if an individual spends more than 90 days in the UK in one or both of the preceding two tax years.

Country Tie An individual has a "country tie" if he or she has spent more days in the UK than in any other country during the tax year. The country tie only applies to individuals who were resident in one of the previous three tax years.

Sufficient Ties Test – Examples

Example 2.5

Carmen, who is single and has no children, was born in Italy. Her mother was born in Belfast and so Carmen often comes to Belfast to visit her relatives.

She arrives in Belfast on 1 May 2021 and stays with her grandmother as she does not own a house in Northern Ireland. She has been asked to fill a full-time role teaching Italian for the period from 5 May 2021 to 31 August 2021. She will return to Italy on 8 September 2021 and will commence her final year at Rome University on 15 September 2021.

Carmen has not been UK resident in any of the previous three tax years and has spent less than 90 days in the UK in each of the previous two tax years.

Explain whether Carmen is UK resident for the tax year 2021/22.

1. Consider the **automatic overseas test** – Carmen does not meet any of the automatic overseas tests.

2. Consider the **automatic UK test** – Although Carmen has been in the UK for over 30 days in the tax year (she has been in the UK for 130 days), she does not have a home in the UK whereas she does in Italy. She also does not meet any of the automatic UK tests.

3. Consider the **sufficient ties test** – Carmen has spent 130 days in the UK in the 2021/22 tax year and must therefore meet the criteria for at least two ties to be considered UK resident.
   (a) *Family tie* – Carmen does not have a husband, civil partner, partner or child who is UK resident. The family tie is not met.
   (b) *Accommodation tie* – Carmen has a "place to live" in the UK. She stays at the home of a close relative (her grandmother) for 16 or more nights. Therefore the accommodation tie is met.
   (c) *Work tie* – Carmen is taking up a full-time post and will work for at least 40 days in the UK in the tax year. The work tie is also met.
   (d) *90-day tie* – Carmen has not spent more than 90 days in the UK in one or both of the preceding two tax years, so this tie is not met.
   (e) *Country tie* – As Carmen was non-UK resident for one or more of the preceding three tax years, i.e. she is an arriver, we do not need to consider this tie.

So, Carmen meets two ties and will therefore be treated as UK resident in the 2021/22 tax year.

Example 2.6

Joe, a bachelor with no children, decided to take a year off work to travel the world. He finished work on 1 April 2021 and left the UK on 1 June 2021 to commence his travels with a tour of the Rockies.

He spent no more than 30 days in each country until he arrived in Austria, where he has an apartment. He spent two months there (February and March 2022) before continuing to tour Europe. He returned to the UK on 1 June 2022. While Joe was away he rented out his UK home.

Joe has always been UK resident, up to and including the 2020/21 tax year.

Explain whether Joe is UK resident for the 2021/22 tax year.

1. Consider the **automatic overseas test** – Joe has been in the UK for 56 days in the 2021/22 tax year. He is not going to work full time overseas. Therefore, he does not meet any of the automatic overseas tests.

2. Consider the **automatic UK test** – Although Joe has been in the UK for more than 30 days, he has a home in Austria where he has spent over 30 days. Joe does not meet any of the automatic UK tests.

3. Consider the **sufficient ties test** – Joe has spent 56 days in the UK in the 2021/22 tax year and must meet at least three ties to be considered UK resident.

   (a) *Family tie* – Joe does not have a wife, civil partner, partner or child who is UK resident. The family tie is not met.

continued overleaf

(b) *Accommodation tie* – Joe does have a "place to live" in the UK and has lived in it during the tax year; however, as he is renting it out while he is away it is not available for a continuous period of 91 days or more. The accommodation tie is therefore not met.

(c) *Work tie* – Joe does not work for at least 40 days in the UK in the tax year, meaning this tie is not met.

(d) *90-day tie* – Joe has spent more than 90 days in the UK in both of the preceding two tax years. The 90-day tie is met.

(e) *Country tie* – Joe has spent 56 days in the UK in the tax year, but he has spent more time in Austria (60 days). The country tie is therefore not met.

Joe satisfies only one tie and is therefore treated as non-UK resident in the 2021/22 tax year as at least three ties are required where someone has been in the UK for 56 days.

2.2.5   The SRT – Summary

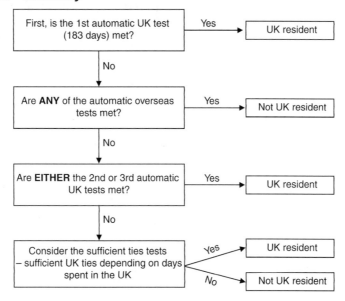

2.2.6   Meaning of "Day Spent in the UK"

All of the SRT tests require an individual to count the number of days they have spent in the UK in the particular tax year. The general rule is that if you are in the UK at the end of the day, i.e. midnight, then that is considered a day spent in the UK.

2.2.7   Split Year Treatment

Typically, if a person is deemed to be UK resident under the SRT they are treated as resident for the full tax year. However, in certain circumstances it is possible to split the tax year into two parts – one part where the individual is treated as UK resident, and the other where they are treated as non-UK resident. This is referred to as 'split year treatment' (SYT).

Leaving the UK

For those leaving the UK, SYT applies in the current tax year if the individual is:

- UK resident for the current tax year (i.e. the tax year being considered for SYT); and
- UK resident for the previous tax year (whether or not it is a split year); and

- non-UK resident in the following tax year; and
- leaves part way through the current tax year because:
  - they are starting full-time work overseas; or
  - they are accompanying a partner overseas; or
  - they cease to have a home in the UK.

Example 2.7: SYT Case 1 (adapted from HMRC example)

Amanda has been living in the UK since she was born and is UK resident for tax purposes. She has worked in the media industry for five years and lands herself a job as a reporter on a three-year contract based in India. She moves there on 10 November 2021 and lives in an apartment provided by her new employer. She works full time overseas from 10 November 2021.

She returns to visit her family over the Christmas period for two weeks and does not work while she is here.

Amanda remains working in India throughout the tax year 2022/23, again only returning for a two-week period over Christmas.

Amanda is eligible for SYT for tax year 2021/22 because:

- she was UK resident for the current tax year (2021/22);

- she was UK resident for the previous tax year (2020/21);

- she is non-UK resident in the following tax year (2022/23); and

- she has left the UK to start full-time work overseas.

For Amanda, in 2021/22 she will be UK resident from 6 April 2021 to 9 November 2021 and non-UK resident from 10 November 2021 to 5 April 2022.

Arriving in the UK

For those arriving in the UK, SYT applies in the current tax year if the individual is:

- UK resident for the current tax year (tax year being considered for SYT);
- non-UK resident for the previous tax year; and
- arrives in the UK part way through the tax year because:
  - they are starting to have a home in the UK only; or
  - they are starting full-time work in the UK or ceasing to have full-time work overseas; or
  - they are returning/relocating to the UK with their partner.

Example 2.8: SYT Case 4 (adapted from HMRC example)

Olan has been working for his employer in Germany for the last five years. He had no UK ties and was not resident in the UK. On 1 June 2021, Olan moves to the UK to look for work here. He rents out his flat in Germany on a two-year lease, from 27 May 2021.

He arrives in the UK and stays in temporary accommodation while he finds a flat to rent. He signs a 12-month lease on a flat in London on 1 July 2021.

He starts UK employment on 22 July 2021 and remains in the UK for a further two years.

Olan receives SYT for 2021/22 as:

- he is UK resident for the current tax year (2021/22);

- he is non-UK resident for the previous tax year (2020/21);

- he arrives part way through the current tax year; and

- he only has a home in the UK when he arrives in the UK in the tax year.

For Olan the overseas part of the tax year will end on 30 June 2021 and the UK part of the tax year will start on 1 July 2021, the day he started to have his only home in the UK.

2.3   Domicile

The concept of domicile is one of general and common law, having evolved through the court system and not being legislatively defined. In broad terms, unlike residency, an individual can only ever have one domicile at any one time. Domicile is distinct from nationality or residence and, as already noted, it is one of the criteria used to determine UK income tax/CGT liability.

There are three kinds of domicile:

1.   domicile of origin;
2.   domicile of choice; and
3.   domicile of dependency.

Four general points regarding domicile require special attention:

1.   A person cannot be without a domicile.
2.   A person cannot possess more than one domicile at any time.
3.   An existing domicile is presumed to continue until it is proved that a new domicile of choice has been acquired.
4.   Even if someone is not UK domiciled, they may be UK deemed domiciled (see **Section 2.4**).

The following factors can be relevant when considering an individual's domicile intentions; permanent residence; business interests; social and family interests; ownership of property; the form of any will made, burial arrangements and so on. This is not an exhaustive list, but it does illustrate the many different criteria that should be considered.

2.3.1   Domicile of Origin

An individual has a domicile that is acquired at **birth** and is known as the domicile of origin. It is either the domicile of the individual's father or, if the father is predeceased or the parents are not married, it is the domicile of the mother. Importantly, there need be no connection between an individual's place of birth and their domicile of origin.

As stated above, it is not possible to have more than one domicile. Thus. the domicile of origin subsists until it is displaced by a new domicile, either of choice or of dependency. Domicile of origin is characterised by two main factors, namely: its permanence; and the large burden of proof required to displace it.

2.3.2   Domicile of Dependency

The domicile of dependency refers specifically to dependent persons, i.e. children less than 16 years old or incapacitated persons. The dependant's domicile is determined by the domicile of the person on whom they are dependent. If, before the age of 16, the domicile of the parent from whom the child has taken their domicile changes, then the child's domicile will also change and follow that of the parent.

2.3.3   Domicile of Choice

A domicile of choice is the domicile that any independent person, i.e. an individual of legal capacity not dependent for his or her domicile upon another person, may acquire for themselves by a **combination of residence and intention**.

To acquire a domicile of choice, an individual must establish a physical presence in the new jurisdiction and have an intention to reside there permanently. The individual must sever all ties with the country of his or her former domicile and settle in the new country with the clear intention of making his or her permanent home there indefinitely.

A domicile of choice can be abandoned; in which case the domicile of origin will be reinstated unless, and until, it is replaced by a new domicile of choice.

2.4   Deemed Domicile

For UK income tax and CGT purposes, there are two ways that an individual can be deemed UK domiciled for the tax year despite having a domicile of origin, choice or dependency elsewhere:

1. The 'long-term UK resident' rule – if the individual has been resident in the UK for at least 15 of the 20 tax years immediately before the relevant tax year. Such individuals, however, will not be deemed UK domiciled under this rule if:
    (a) the individual is not UK resident for the relevant tax year; and
    (b) there is no tax year beginning after 5 April 2017 and preceding the relevant tax year in which the individual was UK resident.

    Under this deemed domicile rule, deemed domiciled status is only shaken off if someone leaves the UK and there are at least six tax years as a non-UK resident in the 20 tax years before the relevant tax year.

    > **Example 2.9 Deemed domicile: long-term UK resident rule**
    > Agi has a Polish domicile but works in the UK and is UK tax resident. She has lived and worked in the UK since 29 July 1997 but has always intended to return home to Poland. Under her common law domicile, Agi would not be UK domiciled. However, the '15 out of 20' rule means that she is deemed to be domiciled in the UK for both income tax and CGT purposes in 2021/22.

2. The 'formerly domiciled resident' rule – if the individual:
    (a) was born in the UK;
    (b) had a UK domicile of origin; and
    (c) was resident in the UK in the relevant tax year.

    If an individual is deemed UK domiciled under either of these rules, they are not able to claim the remittance basis (see **Section 2.6** and **Chapter 17, Section 17.5**).

    > **Example 2.10 Deemed domicile: formerly domiciled resident**
    > Shane was born in the UK and had a UK domicile of origin. In 2011 he emigrated to Australia, acquiring an Australian domicile of choice. Shane's employer seconded him to the UK on 6 April 2021 for one year. As a result, Shane is UK resident in 2021/22. As Shane was born in the UK, had a UK domicile of origin and was UK resident in 2021/22, he is deemed to be domiciled in the UK for both income tax and CGT purposes in 2021/22.

2.5   Impact of Residence, Domicile and Deemed Domicile on Income Tax

As we have seen, the whole question of whether an individual is liable to UK income tax, and to what extent, relies on residence, domicile and deemed domicile. In summary, there are four possible situations. An individual can be either:

- ■ UK resident and UK domiciled;
- ■ UK resident but non-UK domiciled (though deemed UK domiciled);

■   UK resident but non-UK domiciled (and not deemed UK domiciled); or
■   Non-UK resident (domicile is irrelevant).

The 'arising basis' means that the income that is subject to UK tax is the income that has arisen or accrued in the tax year. The 'remittance basis' means that the income that is subject to UK tax is the income that has been remitted to or brought into the UK in the tax year. Remittance income is always taxed as non-savings income.

2.5.1   UK Resident and UK Domiciled

An individual who is UK resident and UK domiciled is liable to UK income tax on their **worldwide personal income**, irrespective of where it is earned and whether or not it is remitted to the UK, i.e. all income is taxed on the arising basis. The remittance basis is never available.

2.5.2   UK Resident but Non-UK Domiciled (though deemed UK domiciled)

An individual who is UK resident and non-UK domiciled (though deemed UK domiciled) is also liable to UK income tax on his or her **worldwide personal income**, irrespective of where it is earned and whether or not it is remitted to the UK, i.e. all income is taxed on the arising basis.

Even though such individuals are not UK domiciled, they are not able to use the remittance basis by virtue of their UK deemed domicile status.

2.5.3   UK Resident but Non-UK Domiciled (and not deemed UK domiciled)

An individual who is resident but not domiciled in the UK (and not deemed UK domiciled) can be taxed in one of two ways for UK income tax purposes:

1.   their worldwide income is automatically subject to UK tax (similar to individuals who are both resident and domiciled/deemed domiciled in the UK) on the arising basis; or
2.   they can be taxed on the "remittance basis", in which case their overseas income is subject to UK income tax only if it is actually remitted to the UK (i.e. it is brought in, used or enjoyed in the UK). This may be automatically available or claimed. Any UK source income is also subject to UK tax as normal on the arising basis.

2.5.4   Non-UK Resident

An individual who is not resident in the UK is only liable to income tax on income that arises in the UK, e.g. UK property income, UK employment income, UK interest, dividends from UK shares. Overseas income is exempt from UK tax.

Non-UK Resident – Access to Allowances
In general, non-resident individuals are not entitled to allowances (such as personal allowance, blind person's allowance, married couple's allowance and so on), but the following exceptions to the rule can claim allowances:

■   from 1 January 2021, any non-resident individual who is a UK national;
■   citizens of the European Economic Area (EEA), i.e. the European Union plus Iceland, Liechtenstein and Norway;
■   individuals resident in the Isle of Man and the Channel Islands;
■   current or former Crown servants and their widows or widowers;

- former residents who have left the country for health reasons; and
- nationals and/or residents of a country with which the UK has a double taxation treaty (DTT) (see **Section 2.7**).

The impact of the residence and domicile status on UK income tax liability is summarised in the table below.

Status	UK Income	Overseas Income
UK resident and UK domiciled	Taxed – pay UK income tax on UK income on arising basis in tax year.	Taxed – pay UK income tax on overseas income on arising basis in tax year.
UK resident and non-UK domiciled (though deemed UK domiciled)	Taxed – pay UK income tax on UK income on arising basis in tax year.	Taxed – pay UK income tax on overseas income arising in tax year.
UK resident and non-UK domiciled (and not deemed UK domiciled)	Taxed – pay UK income tax on UK income on arising basis in tax year.	Taxed – pay UK income tax on overseas income automatically under arising basis or "remittance" basis.
Non-UK resident	Taxed – pay UK income tax on UK income on arising basis in tax year.	Overseas income is exempt from UK income tax.

The treatment of overseas income is dealt with in more detail in **Chapter 5, Section 5.2**. See **Chapter 17** for the specific implications of residence, domicile and deemed domicile for CGT purposes. Note also that in scenarios where foreign income/gains are taxed in two jurisdictions, double tax relief is available if the individual is UK resident – see **Section 2.7**.

> *Example 2.11*
> Anna is UK resident but not UK domiciled or deemed UK domiciled for income tax/CGT purposes. She has overseas property income of £25,000 per annum and remits £10,000 of this property income to the UK each tax year.
>
> If she is taxed on the arising basis, she will include £25,000 in her UK income tax computation. If she is taxed on the remittance basis, she will include £10,000 in her UK income tax computation.

The legislation provides detailed provisions to identify what can be counted as a remittance. In essence, in this context a remittance is the "use or enjoyment" in the UK of income earned overseas. This covers overseas income spent in the UK or cash brought into the country, and includes property or services acquired in the UK with overseas income. Assets and personal effects, such as clothes, jewellery, etc. costing less than £1,000 are excluded.

An exemption was also introduced for remittances of foreign income or gains to the UK for the purposes of commercial investment in qualifying UK businesses. A qualifying investment is basically a purchase of shares (the purchase must be of newly issued shares in the company and not a purchase of shares from another existing shareholder) or where a loan is provided to a company. There is no limit to the amount of remittances that qualify for this relief. This is known as business investment relief – the detailed rules of which are beyond the scope of this textbook.

2.6   Overseas Income – The Remittance Basis

As the table above shows, the overseas income of an individual who is **UK resident but non-UK domiciled** (and not deemed UK domiciled) may be taxed either on the arising basis or the remittance basis. There are rules to determine what basis applies as set out below. These rules focus on the remittance basis in the context of foreign income and the loss of an individual's personal allowance, but the rules can apply equally to foreign gains that are remitted to the UK and, where the remittance basis is claimed, result in the loss of an individual's capital gains annual exemption (see **Chapter 17**).

2.6.1   Overseas Income Automatically Taxed on the Remittance Basis

No formal claim is required for the remittance basis of taxation to be applied in three instances. See **Chapter 17, Section 17.5.1**.

Example 2.12

Pierre is UK resident but French domiciled and he is not deemed UK domiciled. He has lived in the UK for the past 10 years and earns property income of £12,000 from a property he rents out in France in tax year 2021/22. He has no other income outside the UK and he remits all except £1,000 of the income into the UK.

Pierre will automatically be taxed on the remittance basis of tax, i.e. he will be taxed on the £11,000 he uses/enjoys in the UK rather than being taxed on the £12,000 that arises in the tax year. No formal claim is required for Pierre to have his overseas income taxed on the remittance basis. Double taxation relief may be available.

Example 2.13

Selena is UK resident but American domiciled and she is not deemed UK domiciled. She has lived in the UK for the past 12 years and earned dividend income of £122,000, in 2021/22, from shares she owns in a company listed on the New York Stock Exchange. She has no other income outside the UK. In December 2021, she remits £115,000 of the income for a deposit to purchase a property in London.

As Selena's unremitted amount is £7,000 (i.e. more than £2,000) she will not be automatically entitled to the remittance basis. Unless a formal claim is made for the remittance basis to apply, Selena will be subject to UK income tax on £122,000. Double taxation relief may be available.

In situations where the remittance basis is automatically applied, the taxpayer is allowed to keep their entitlement to UK personal tax allowances and UK CGT annual exemption and is not required to file a tax return. They are also exempted from the remittance basis charge (RBC) (see **Section 2.6.3**).

2.6.2   Overseas Income Taxed on the Remittance Basis but Formal Claim Required

If a taxpayer is not automatically taxed on the remittance basis, they will automatically be taxed on the arising basis. If they want to be taxed on the remittance basis, they will have to make a formal claim for that tax year. The formal application is made to HMRC using the self-assessment system.

Example 2.14

If Pierre, from **Example 2.13**, had overseas property income of £12,000 and had remitted only £3,000 into the UK, then he would automatically be taxed on the arising basis as he would have £9,000 of unremitted overseas income, i.e. greater than £2,000 unremitted. This means he would have £12,000 overseas property income in his UK income tax computation.

If he wanted to be taxed on the remittance basis and have only £3,000 of his overseas income subject to UK tax, he would have to make a **formal claim** to be taxed on the remittance basis.

Where a formal claim is made, certain personal tax allowances are withdrawn. They include: the basic personal allowance, age-related allowances, blind person's allowance, tax relief for married couples and civil partners and relief for life insurance premiums. The CGT annual exemption is also withdrawn.

The withdrawal of allowances and reliefs is made under UK domestic law; however, if an individual is resident in the UK and is also resident in another treaty country (dual resident), then the treaty may provide that the individual retains the UK allowances/reliefs above. For example, the UK/Ireland double taxation treaty contains such a provision, whereas the UK/USA treaty does not.

2.6.3   The Remittance Basis Charge

When an individual has to make a formal claim in order to have their overseas income/gains taxed on the remittance basis, they may be subject to the remittance basis charge. The remittance basis charge (RBC) is an annual tax charge in respect of overseas income and gains left outside the UK. It is in addition to any UK tax due on either UK income and gains or overseas income and gains remitted to the UK. The amount of the RBC depends upon how long the individual has been resident in the UK (see table below).

A taxpayer will pay the RBC if:

- they make a **claim** to use the remittance basis; and
- they are **resident in the UK** in the year that they make their claim for the remittance basis and are **aged 18 or over** at the end of the tax year; and
- they are long-term residents in line with the table below.

Long-term residence status	RBC
Individual has been resident in the UK for at least 7 of the previous 9 tax years	£30,000
Individual has been resident in the UK for at least 12 of the previous 14 tax years	£60,000

When ascertaining the number of tax years an individual has been resident for this purpose, all the tax years when they were resident in the UK, even if they were under 18 years of age in those years, are counted. For example, an individual who is over 18 years of age during the tax year and has been **resident in the UK for seven out of nine years immediately preceding the year of assessment** will only be able to use the remittance basis if they pay the RBC of £30,000 for the year.

The charge does not apply in situations where the remittance basis is available without a formal claim.

The RBC (whether £30,000 or £60,000) is administered and collected through the self-assessment system. It should be noted that the full RBC applies irrespective of whether the individual was present in the UK for the whole of the year or only part of the year. In other words, the RBC cannot be pro-rated for those entering or leaving the UK during a tax year.

If a taxpayer does not wish to pay the RBC, they can choose not to claim the remittance basis. They will then be taxed on the arising basis instead and will pay UK tax on their worldwide income. The decision is made on a year-by-year basis.

It is important to note that the remittance basis can only be claimed on overseas income/gains – income/gains earned in the UK are always taxable on the arising basis.

Example 2.15

Paulo is domiciled in Italy but has been resident in the UK since 2011/12. He is not dual resident for tax purposes. In 2021/22 he earned £55,000 from his UK employment and £20,000 gross interest from overseas investments. He remits £5,000 of the overseas interest into the UK in the tax year. Determine whether Paulo should claim the remittance basis or not (ignore any overseas tax paid and the personal savings allowance).

Paulo has unremitted overseas income of £15,000. As this exceeds £2,000, he is automatically taxed on the arising basis. In order to be taxed on the remittance basis, he would have to make a formal claim.

Arising basis – automatic		**Remittance basis – formal claim required**	
	£		£
Salary	55,000	Salary	55,000
Overseas interest	20,000	Overseas interest	5,000
Total income	75,000	Total income	55,000
Personal allowance	(12,570)	Personal allowance	–
Taxable income	62,430	Taxable income	55,000
£37,700 × 20%	7,540	£37,700 × 20%	7,540
£24,730 × 40%	9,892	£17,300 × 40%	6,920
		RBC	30,000
Tax liability	17,432	Tax liability	44,460

Note: if Paulo formally claims the remittance basis, he loses his entitlement to the personal allowance. The RBC of £30,000 applies because Paulo has been resident in the UK for more than seven of the previous nine tax years.

Paulo would be better off not making a formal claim to be taxed on the remittance basis as he would save UK income tax of £27,028.

Example 2.16

Martha is 42 years old and resident in the UK in 2021/22. Her unremitted foreign income for that year is £250,000. Martha's residence status for the preceding years was as follows:

2012/13 and 2013/14 – non-UK resident
2014/15 to 2020/21 – UK resident

Martha has been resident in the UK for seven of the preceding nine tax years and therefore has to consider whether to make a claim for the remittance basis. She will have to pay the £30,000 RBC if she decides to claim the remittance basis in 2021/22.

If, instead, Martha had been resident in the UK from the 2009/10 tax year (i.e. 12 out of the previous 14 tax years), the RBC would be £60,000 in the 2021/22 tax year.

The RBC represents tax paid in advance on income arising abroad but not yet remitted to the UK. When a taxpayer makes a claim for the remittance basis, they must nominate how much of their foreign income (and/or foreign gains for capital gains tax purposes) the RBC (whether £30,000 or £60,000) is in respect of. When the "nominated" amounts are remitted, they are not taxed again; however, un-nominated income and gains are deemed to be remitted first.

2.7   Double Taxation Relief

As we have seen, UK income tax arises on the worldwide income of UK residents, whether on the arising basis or the remittance basis, and on the UK income of non-residents. Due to domestic tax laws, income may, on occasion, be taxed in two countries:

■   first, in the country where the income arises; and
■   secondly, in the country where the taxpayer resides.

In order to eliminate this double tax charge, double taxation relief may be given. It should be noted that double taxation relief is only provided in the UK where the individual is UK resident. Relief can be obtained in one of three ways:

1.   under the provisions of a double taxation treaty;
2.   as credit relief (also known as "unilateral relief") under a double taxation treaty or in its own right; or
3.   as deduction relief.

2.7.1   Double Taxation Treaties

Relief can be provided under a double taxation treaty (DTT) in two main ways:

■   **Exemption relief** – where income is only taxable in the country of residence, e.g. the UK/ Ireland DTT states that interest income is taxable only where the individual is resident under the DTT.
■   **Credit relief** – which reduces UK income tax by the amount of overseas tax paid. The maximum relief cannot exceed the UK tax on the same income.

2.7.2   Unilateral Relief

Where there is no DTT in place, relief for double taxation may be given as unilateral relief. The relief is the lower of:

■   the overseas tax paid; or
■   the UK tax on that source of income.

To determine the UK tax on that source of overseas income, two calculations must be carried out: the UK income tax calculation including the overseas income and the UK income tax calculation without the overseas income. The difference between these calculations will be the UK tax on that source of income. Essentially the overseas income is treated as the 'top slice' of income, i.e. considered after dividends.

No refund can be given in the UK for any excess foreign tax paid. However, relief for excess foreign tax on overseas trading income may be possible; see **Chapter 5, Section 5.2.3**.

Note that overseas income is always included gross in an income tax computation, i.e. inclusive of any foreign tax paid.

2.7.3   Deduction Relief

Deduction relief reduces overseas income in the tax computations by any overseas tax suffered. This is not usually as generous as credit relief and so is usually only claimed instead of credit relief if there is no UK tax liability (e.g. due to loss relief) to set off.

Questions

Review Questions
(See Suggested Solutions to Review Questions at the end of this textbook.)

Question 2.1

Hank is a US citizen seconded to work in the UK for just over two years. He first arrives in the UK on 19 May 2020 and leaves on 10 October 2022 and takes no significant breaks from his UK employment. During the secondment he does not leave the UK. On 11 October 2022 Hank returns to his employment in the US.

Hank returns to the UK for 10 days in November 2022 to see some friends he met during his secondment. He also visits London for six days in December 2022 to do some Christmas shopping.

Requirement
What is Hank's residence status for each relevant tax year?

Question 2.2

Sheila is an Australian citizen. She is an architect but has been out of work for several months. Sheila's husband, Mark, has recently been seconded to London. The secondment is set to last for two years from March 2020. Mark will be UK resident during this time.

Sheila's brother, John, who lives in Edinburgh, has asked her to help him design the plans for his new house, which he hopes to build later that year. Sheila agrees to help John and travels to Edinburgh where she spends from 20 June to 25 September 2021 helping John with the plans for his house before returning home to Australia. Sheila lives with John and his family during her time in the UK.

Sheila has never been UK resident

Requirement
What is Sheila's residence status for the tax year 2021/22? (Assume that none of the automatic UK or overseas tests apply to Sheila in 2021/22.)

Question 2.3

Sean has lived in Belfast for several years and has been UK resident since his arrival. He runs a successful chain of internet cafés in Belfast and has plans to open several more cafés in the Republic of Ireland (RoI). In 2021/22, as part of his plans to expand into the RoI, he buys an apartment in Dublin and spends a lot of his time there overseeing the plans for the new cafés.

Sean's family are UK resident and remain resident in the UK while he is away setting up the new cafés. Sean travels back to Belfast once a month for the weekend and also returns for a few days in September, staying in his family home each time. His total time in the UK in 2021/22 is 52 days.

Requirement
What is Sean's residence status for the tax year 2021/22? (Assume that none of the automatic UK or overseas tests apply to Sean in 2021/22.)

Question 2.4

Mr Harris is an American citizen and is not resident in the UK. He is married to Sue-Ann and has the following sources of income in the 2021/22 tax year:

	£
Net UK property income (Note 1)	36,000
US dividends	4,000

Note:

1. £9,000 tax was deducted at source by the UK lessee. (Rental income paid to a non-resident landlord must have income tax at basic rate deducted (see **Chapter 5, Section 5.3**).)

Requirement

Calculate Mr Harris's UK income tax liability for the 2021/22 tax year. Would the answer have been different if Mr Harris were a French citizen?

Question 2.5

Apply the statutory resident test to determine whether the following persons are or are not UK resident in the tax year 2021/22:

(a) Janet spends 10 days in the UK in 2021/22. She was previously resident in the UK in 2018/19.
(b) Paul comes to the UK in July 2021 and stays until March 2022, renting an apartment in Belfast. Paul was not resident in the UK in a previous tax year.
(c) In the tax year 2021/22, Victor works full time in Paris. He spends his summer holidays (three weeks of July 2021) in the UK, working five hours per day. He was resident in the UK in 2019/20.
(d) Christine comes to the UK in mid-November 2021. She buys a house in the UK on 1 February 2022, which she lives in as her home. This house is her only home and she stays in the UK for a number of years. Christine has never had an overseas home. She was not resident in the UK in a previous tax year.
(e) Terry spends 35 days in the UK in 2021/22. He was previously resident in the UK in 2017/18.
(f) Margaret comes to the UK on 22 November 2021 and begins full-time employment (eight hours per day) from 1 December 2021 to 30 November 2022. During that time she obtains holidays of 25 days.
(g) Ned loses his full-time job in the UK in March 2021. He remains unemployed in the UK and moves to Italy on 1 September 2021 and starts work full time the next day. He was resident in the UK in all previous tax years. He purchases an apartment in Italy shortly after he arrives, which he lives in as his home. Ned does not return to the UK during the remainder of 2021/22 and returns to the UK permanently on 10 April 2022, when he starts a new full-time job. Ned does not have a home in the UK.

Part One
Income Tax

Income Tax: Recap

Learning Objectives

■ This chapter is an overview of the cumulative knowledge of income tax required at CA Proficiency 2. Students should refer to their CA Proficiency 1 or other studies to understand the level of cumulative knowledge required and the necessary technical details in more depth.

■ The following have been introduced as a result of Finance Act 2021:
  ● new super-deduction/special rate deduction rules for companies (see **Section 3.5.4**);
  ● the temporary extended loss carry-back rules (see **Section 3.6**).

Chartered Accountants Ireland's *Code of Ethics* applies to all aspects of a Chartered Accountant's professional life, including dealing with income tax issues. Further information regarding the principles in the *Code of Ethics* is set out in **Appendix 2**.

In addition, **Appendix 3** examines the distinction between tax planning, tax avoidance and tax evasion, which can arise in relation to all taxes, including income tax.

Students are reminded that it is their responsibility to ensure that they have the necessary **cumulative knowledge** of income tax from CA Proficiency 1 or other studies. This chapter is a recap of key income tax topics covered at CA Proficiency 1 and is not a substitute for detailed understanding of the cumulative knowledge required at CA Proficiency 2.

Students should also review this chapter to note changes resulting from Finance Act 2021, which you will need to be aware of for your CAP 2 studies. For income tax these changes are:

■ changes to income tax bands (see **Section 3.1.2**);
■ introduction of new super-deduction capital allowance and a special rate first-year allowance (see **Section 3.5.4**);
■ the temporary extension of loss carry-back rules for losses incurred in tax years 2020/21 and 2021/22 (see **Section 3.6.2**).

3.1 The Income Tax Computation

3.1.1 Classification of Income

Income tax is payable by:

■ adults, on their own income and on their share of the income of a partnership; and
■ children, if they have sufficient income to pay tax.

Some persons and organisations are generally **exempt** from income tax.

One key income tax consideration is that the rules for the computation of taxable income tax depend on the source of the income; different rules apply to different sources. The different types of income are set out in the table below in accordance with the Income Tax (Trading and Other Income) Act 2005:

Classification of income	Type of income
Trading income – profits of trades, professions, and vocations	Non-savings
Employment income – income from employment and pensions	Non-savings
Savings income – income from savings, including interest	Savings
Investment income – income from investments, including dividends	Dividend
Property income – profits of property businesses, e.g. rental income	Non-savings
Miscellaneous income – e.g. post cost cessation receipts, income from royalties	Non-savings

Each source of income has different rules and treatment for computing income tax, so recognising where an individual's income has come from is fundamental to the computation.

A broad distinction is also made between non-savings, savings, and dividend income. This distinction is important as it determines the order in which income tax is charged – income tax is charged first on non-savings income, then on savings income and finally on dividend income.

There are also a number of exempt sources of income; recap on these from your CA Proficiency 1 or other studies.

If a taxpayer is in receipt of foreign income, whether it is overseas employment income, trading income, property rental income or investment income, there are implications for UK income tax (see **Chapter 5, Section 5.2**).

The income tax computation involves a number of stages and different calculations that follow in a logical sequence. The following sections provide an overview only of each of the steps involved.

3.1.2   Income Tax Rates and Bands

UK income tax operates by using tax bands that correspond to different rates of income tax. Specific tax bands (or thresholds) and their corresponding tax rates apply to the three categories of income: non-savings, savings, and dividend.

Non-savings Income
The tax rates that apply to non-savings income in 2021/22 are:

	Income band	Tax rate
Personal allowance	£0–£12,570	0%
Basic rate	£12,571–£50,270	20%
Higher rate	£50,271–£150,000	40%
Additional rate	Over £150,000	45%

Savings Income

For savings income, the same tax bands and rates apply as for non-savings income, except that there is a "starting limit" of £5,000 for which a 0% rate applies, but only if the individual's taxable non-savings income is less than £5,000. If taxable non-savings income is greater than £5,000, then the savings income is subject to the same rates as non-savings income.

A "personal savings allowance" may be available for savings income earned. This personal savings allowance allows up to £1,000 a year of a basic rate taxpayer's savings income to be tax-free; for higher rate taxpayers the annual threshold is £500. The personal savings allowance is not available to additional rate taxpayers.

The amount of personal savings allowance depends on an individual's adjusted net income. The table below shows the amount of the personal savings allowance an individual is entitled to for 2021/22, depending on whether they are a basic, higher, or additional rate taxpayer.

Tax rate	Income band (adjusted net income)	Personal savings allowance
Basic rate: 20%	Up to £50,270	Up to £1,000
Higher rate: 40%	£50,271–£150,000	Up to £500
Additional rate: 45%	Over £150,000	Nil

Dividend Income

For dividend income the same tax bands apply as for non-savings and savings income. However, the rates of tax applying to dividends are 7.5%, 32.5% and 38.1%. A £2,000 dividend allowance is also available. Therefore, in 2021/22 up to £2,000 of income earned from dividends will be tax-free, regardless of the individual's level of income. Dividend income in excess of the allowance is taxed at the following rates: 7.5% (basic rate band), 32.5% (higher rate band) and 38.1% (additional rate band).

Standard Personal Allowance

An individual may be entitled to a number of allowances that will help reduce the amount of their income that will be subject to income tax.

All individuals are entitled to the standard personal allowance, which is simply the amount of income, from any source, that income tax is not payable on. For 2021/22 the standard personal allowance is £12,570.

The standard personal allowance is reduced for individuals with an "adjusted net income" that exceeds £100,000. For every £2 above the £100,000 threshold, the personal allowance is reduced by £1. This calculation will continue until the personal allowance is reduced to nil, i.e. if an individual has adjusted net income of £125,140 or more they lose their entitlement to the personal allowance.

The personal allowance is also modified by eligibility to claim the marriage allowance or the blind person's allowance. Recap on this from your CA Proficiency 1 or other studies.

3.1.3 Income Tax Computation

The tax legislation, specifically the Income Tax Act 2007 (ITA 2007), details how income tax should be calculated. The calculation steps are outlined below as an overview of the whole process.

STEP 1	Identify "total income" for each source ("component") of income: non-savings, savings income, and dividend income. The gross income from each component is added up separately in the personal income tax computation.
STEP 2	Deduct from total income any specified reliefs (see **Sections 3.6** and **3.10**) the taxpayer is entitled to, such as various trade loss reliefs, to give "net income".
STEP 3	Deduct from net income any allowances the taxpayer is entitled to, such as the personal allowance and blind person's allowance (see **Section 3.10.4**). The personal allowance is deducted from the non-savings component of income first, then savings income and finally dividend income. These may need to be restricted (e.g. if income is greater than £100,000). This amount is referred to as "taxable income".
STEP 4	For each component amount calculated in Step 3, calculate tax at the applicable rates. Before calculating tax on savings income, the personal savings allowance must be considered (basic rate taxpayer: £1,000 @ 0%; higher rate taxpayer: £500 @ 0%). When calculating the tax on the dividend component, the dividend allowance covering the first £2,000 of dividends is taxed at 0%.
STEP 5	Add together the component amounts calculated in Step 4.
STEP 6	From the total calculated at Step 5, deduct any tax reductions that the taxpayer may be entitled to, such as married couples allowance, tax reducers (see **Chapter 5**) or the basic rate tax reduction available for rented residential finance costs (see **Section 3.9.3**).
STEP 7	To the amount calculated at Step 6, add additional tax charges that may apply, such as tax retained on annual payments (recap from your CA Proficiency 1 or other studies).
STEP 8	Finally, income tax deducted at source (e.g. PAYE) is subtracted to get **tax payable**, which is the balance to be settled. The result is the taxpayer's income tax liability/(refund) – the income tax that is due to be paid or refunded for that particular tax year.

Details of the calculation of the different sources of income, and the rules and restrictions around the various reliefs, allowances, and reductions, are dealt with briefly in subsequent sections (but see *Taxation 1 NI 2021–2022* for full details). **Chapter 5** of this textbook deals with the taxation of overseas income and where each source of overseas income fits within the income tax computation.

The pro forma computation overleaf shows the layout of the calculation, indicates where the component amounts should be placed and systematically works through the computation.

	Non-savings Income £	Savings Income £	Dividend Income £	Total £
Gross income:				
Trading income	xx			xx
Property income	xx			xx
Employment/pension income	xx			xx
Savings and investment income:				
Bank/building society interest		xx		xx
National Savings & Investment a/c interest		xx		xx
UK dividends			xx	xx
Step 1 Total income	xxx	xxx	xxx	xxx
Less: specified reliefs	(xx)	(xx)	(xx)	(xx)
Step 2 Net income	xxx	xxx	xxx	xxx
Step 3 Taxable income	xxxx	xxxx	xxxx	xxxx
Step 4 Income tax:				
Non-savings income:				
£ × 20%				xxxx
£ × 40%				xxxx
£ × 45%				xxxx
Savings income:				
£ × 0% (Starting limit for savings income and personal savings allowance, if available.)				0
£ × 20%				xxxx
£ × 40%				xxxx
£ × 45%				xxxx
Dividend income:				
Up to £2,000 dividend allowance × 0%				0
£ × 7.5%				xxxx
£ × 32.5%				xxxx
£ × 38.1%				xxxx
Step 5 Total				xxxx
Step 6 Less: tax reducers and/or basic rate tax reduction for property finance costs				(xxx)
Step 7 Add: additional tax				xxx
Step 8 Less: tax deducted at source				(xxx)
Step 9 Less: double taxation relief (see **Chapter 2**, **Section 2.7**)				(xxx)
Result Income tax liability/(refund)				**xxx**

3.2 Trading Income

Income tax is charged on profits or gains arising from any trade, profession, or vocation. Individuals liable to income tax are sometimes referred to as being self-employed.

It is important to establish whether an activity constitutes a trade, as specific rules apply as a result. In some instances, a profit or sale may be taxed as capital income (as opposed to trading income) and be subject to the capital gains tax (CGT) rules (see **Part Three**).

This section recaps the types of activity that are subject to income tax, the specific tax rules for the commencement and cessation of a trade, the computation of taxable trading income and the specific tax rules that apply to partnerships.

3.2.1 "Trade", "Profession" and "Vocation"

Where the activity carried on by an individual falls within the definition of a trade, profession, or vocation, then the income from that activity will be subject to income tax.

The term "trade" is not fully defined in tax legislation. Therefore, the interpretation of whether a trade exists or not is left largely to the courts. In the legislation, "trade" is taken to include "any venture in the nature of trade". The question of whether or not a trade is carried on is a question of fact rather than a point of law.

The term "profession" is not defined in tax legislation. Examples include teachers, doctors, opticians, accountants, and journalists.

In tax case law the word "vocation" has been compared with a "calling". Judgments in various tax cases have held that a bookmaker, dramatist, jockey, and an author are all vocations.

3.2.2 "Badges of Trade"

The "badges of trade" are a set of six rules drawn up in 1955 by the UK Royal Commission on the Taxation of Profits and Income. They are used to help decide whether or not a trade exists. The six badges are as follows:

1. The subject matter of the realisation
2. The length of the period of ownership
3. The frequency or number of similar transactions by the same person
4. Supplementary work on or in connection with the property realised
5. The circumstances that were responsible for the realisation
6. Motive.

Recap on the "badges of trade" from your CA Proficiency 1 or other studies.

3.2.3 Basis of Assessment of Trading Income

Although each tax year runs from 6 April to 5 April, individuals who operate a trading business may not prepare their financial statements to 5 April – creating a problem in terms of reporting income and the calculation of tax. The basis period rules therefore 'link' the "period of account" for a business (i.e. the accounting year/period end for which financial statements are prepared) with the appropriate tax year.

The basis period, for an ongoing trading business, **will be the 12-month period of account ending during the tax year**. Income, profits, etc. that fall in the basis period are considered when calculating income tax for the associated tax year, even if some of the months of that basis period fall outside the tax year.

The basis period is also affected by the date of commencement and cessation of a trade and by any change in accounting date; each of these is subject to specific rules as outlined in overview below.

Overlap Profits

Overlap profit is the amount of profit in an accounting period that is taxed in two successive tax years. Overlap profits can occur:

- in the opening years of a business; or
- on a change of basis period following a change of accounting date.

To ensure that the business is taxed over its life on the actual taxable profits made, "overlap relief" is provided.

Relief for overlap profits may be given on a change of accounting date (which should be recapped from your CA Proficiency 1 or other studies). The additional overlap profits will then be available for relief at a future change in accounting date or on the cessation of the trade.

On the cessation of a trade any overlap profits that remain unrelieved are deducted from the profit falling to be taxed in that tax year (or they are added to any loss). In these circumstances other "loss reliefs" may be available; see **Section 3.6**.

A record should be kept of both the amount of the overlap profit and its overlap period on a time basis (i.e. the number of months).

Commencement of a Trade

The date of commencement of a trade determines the accounting period for the business, which in turn determines the basis period of assessment for the business. There are special basis period rules for the first three tax years after commencement of the business.

- **First tax year** The tax year during which the trade commences. The basis period year is the tax-adjusted result (taxable trading profit/loss) **from the date of commencement of the trade to the end of the tax year** (i.e. the following 5 April). If the period of account(s) of the business does not coincide with the tax year, then the tax adjusted result is arrived at by time apportionment.
- **Second tax year** The basis period depends on the position in the second tax year. There are three possibilities:
  - if the accounting date falling in the second tax year is at least 12 months after the start of trading, the basis period is the **12 months to that accounting date**; or
  - if the accounting date falling in the second tax year is less than 12 months after the start of trading, the basis period is **the first 12 months of trading**; or
  - if there is no accounting date falling in the second tax year (because the first accounting period is a very long one that does not end until a date in the third tax year), the basis period for the second tax year is the **tax year itself** (i.e. 6 April to the following 5 April).
- **Third tax year** The basis of assessment depends on whether an accounting date falls in the second tax year:
  - if the accounting date does fall in the second tax year, the basis period for the third tax year is **the accounting period ending in the third tax year**; or
  - if the accounting date does not fall in the second tax year, the basis period for the third tax year is the **12 months to the accounting date ending in the third tax year**.

For later tax years, apart from the year in which the trade ceases, the basis period is the **accounting period ending during the tax year**. This is known as the current year basis of assessment.

There are also specific rules which must be considered if there is change in accounting date. Recap on these and the detailed basis period rules from your CA Proficiency 1 or other studies.

Cessation of a Trade

The cessation of a trade results in the application of rules that override the normal basis period rules outlined above:

1. If the trade commences and ceases in the same tax year, the basis period for that year is from **the date of commencement to the date of cessation**.
2. If the trade ceases in the second tax year, then the basis period for that year runs **from 6 April at the start of the second tax year to the date of cessation**.
3. If the trade ceases in the third or later tax year, the basis period runs from **the end of the basis period for the previous year to the date of cessation**.

3.3 Computation of Taxable Trading Income

An individual carrying on a trade prepares accounts based on commercial and accounting principles to arrive at their net profit/(loss) for a particular year. However, the net profit/(loss) per the statement of profit or loss (SOPL) in the accounts **is not the tax-adjusted result** (either a taxable profit or a relievable trading loss).

The adjustments needed to arrive at the tax-adjusted trading result are:

1. Start   Net profit/(loss) per the SOPL
2. Add   • Expenses included in the SOPL that are not allowable for tax purposes.
                 • Income which is a taxable trading profit but is not included in the SOPL.
3. Deduct   • Profit/income included in the SOPL that is not taxable as trading income.
                 • Expenses not included in the SOPL that are tax deductible.
                 • Capital allowances.
4. Result   Tax-adjusted profit/(loss) for income tax purposes.

Deductible expenditure is referred to as "allowable expenditure" for tax purposes; **non-deductible expenditure** is "disallowable expenditure" (or "addbacks") for tax purposes.

The tax legislation provides that trading profits of a business are to be calculated in accordance with generally accepted accounting practice (UK GAAP). However, the cash basis may be chosen in certain circumstances (this is beyond the scope of this textbook).

3.3.1 The Adjustment Process – Overview of Key Principles for Allowable and Disallowable Items

When calculating the tax-adjusted profit/(loss) for income tax purposes, there are two fundamental principles:

1. If an item is of a capital nature, it must be disallowed.
2. Even if an item is of a revenue nature, it may still be specifically disallowed by the legislation.

3.3.2 Capital Receipts versus Revenue Receipts

Capital receipts and expenditure are not subject to income tax as they are usually accountable under capital gains tax. When deciding, for income tax purposes, whether a receipt is capital or revenue, the following general rules apply:

- Capital receipt – from the sale of fixed capital (assets that form part of the permanent structure of a business/assets that have an enduring benefit), e.g. income from the sale of land, buildings, machinery or motor vehicles.
- Revenue receipt – from the sale of circulating capital (assets acquired in the ordinary course of a trade and sold), e.g., the groceries in a supermarket.

Overall, there are five basic principles:

1. Income from the sale of the assets of a business are, prima facie, capital receipts.
2. Income received as compensation for the destruction of the recipient's profit-making apparatus are capital receipts.
3. Income in lieu of trading receipts are of a revenue nature.
4. Income made in return for the imposition of substantial restrictions on the activities of a trader is a capital receipt.
5. Income of a recurrent nature is more likely to be treated as a revenue receipt.

Recap on the detailed rules for capital and revenue from your CA Proficiency 1 or other studies.

Expenditure "Wholly and Exclusively" for the Purposes of the Trade
Unless it is covered by a specific statutory provision, expenditure is only allowable in computing profits if it is revenue in nature and is "wholly and exclusively" for the purposes of the trade.

Expenditure is, therefore, not tax deductible if it is not for trade purposes or if it reflects more than one purpose (duality of purpose). Relief is available for the business element of expenditure only; any private proportion of expenses is not tax deductible. Where payments are to or on behalf of an employee, the full amounts are deductible, but the employee is taxed under the benefit in kind rules.

The tax treatment of common expenses was covered in your CA Proficiency 1 or other studies and should be revisited.

3.3.3 Trading Income Allowance

A trading income allowance of £1,000 is available for small amounts of trading income, but not to businesses carried on in partnership. This allowance is applied to an individual's gross trading receipts (relevant income).

Where an individual's relevant income for the tax year does not exceed the £1,000 trading income allowance, there is no charge to tax and no requirement to complete a self-assessment.

Where an individual's relevant income exceeds the £1,000 trading income allowance, the individual can elect to use an alternative method of calculating income. Under this method the charge to tax is on the excess of relevant income over £1,000. As a basic rule, an individual would not elect to use the alternative method of calculating income if their allowable trading expenses are more than £1,000.

3.3.4 Simplified Expenses

Certain items of expenditure often have a business and private element. To claim the relevant deduction, the taxpayer must calculate the actual expenditure incurred and apportion it between business and non-business use, supported by detailed records. Simplified expenses is therefore a method to claim for particular items of business expenditure. It allows all unincorporated businesses, irrespective of size, to choose to use flat-rate expenses for particular items of business expenditure, namely:

- business use of cars etc.;
- business use of home; and
- private use of business premises.

Recap on the detailed rules from your CA Proficiency 1 or other studies.

3.4 Partnerships

A partnership (defined as the relationship which subsists between persons carrying on a business in common with a view of profit) is regarded as a single unit for the purposes of determining tax-adjusted profits. However, for the purposes of tax assessment, each partner's share of the joint profits is treated as personal to that partner. Commencement and cessation rules apply to each partner individually when they enter or leave the partnership.

The partnership must prepare a partnership self-assessment. The "nominated partner" is responsible for ensuring the partnership's tax return is prepared and submitted to HMRC. Each partner will also prepare an individual self-assessment.

3.4.1 Calculation of Tax-adjusted Trading Result

Once the partnership's tax-adjusted trading result has been computed it is shared between the partners according to the profit-sharing arrangements for that accounting period. This allocation cannot create or increase a loss for a partner. Any "notional" loss calculated in this way must be re-allocated to the other partners.

The general approach is to calculate the partnership's profit, then to tax each partner as if they were a sole trader running a business equal to their share of the partnership.

Recap on the detailed rules for partnerships from your CA Proficiency 1 or other studies.

3.5 Capital Allowances

As set out earlier, capital expenditure is not deductible for income tax purposes. This rule equally applies for corporation tax purposes. Instead, businesses and companies can claim capital allowances on certain types of asset which allows the business or company a deduction against the tax-adjusted trading result for the net cost where those assets are employed for the purpose of the business or company. As a general principle, capital allowances cannot be claimed in the period that a company or business ceases to trade.

Capital allowances are operated through the use of "pools" with the cost of qualifying assets added to the specific "pool", depending on the nature of the asset. A business or company obtains relief for its capital expenditure by reducing the value of the pool in accordance with specific rates and rules. The reduction in the pool value (i.e. the capital allowance) is included as a deduction from the tax-adjusted trading result (profit/(loss)).

Capital allowances for both companies and unincorporated businesses are calculated for accounting periods.

3.5.1 Plant and Machinery

There is no statutory definition of plant and machinery for the purposes of capital allowances. The principal test suggested by case law is whether the asset in question is functional to the operation of the business, as distinct from the setting in which the business is carried on. Recap on this area from your CA Proficiency 1 or other studies.

For buildings/structures, including assets that are incorporated into the building/structure, the general rule is that expenditure does not qualify as expenditure on "plant". However, over the years case law and capital allowances legislation have made exceptions to this rule in certain instances. Recap on this from your CA Proficiency 1 or other studies.

3.5.2 Annual Investment Allowance

The annual investment allowance (AIA) is available to all businesses and offers 100% capital allowances, up to a specified annual limit, on plant and machinery. It can be claimed against both the main pool and special rate pool additions (see below). The AIA cannot be claimed in respect of cars (lorries, vans and trucks are not defined as cars) and some other assets.

The AIA limit is £1,000,000 for expenditure incurred between 1 January 2019 and 31 December 2021. The AIA limit will fall to £200,000 after that date. As a result, the rules that apply where there is a change in the AIA limit may need to be considered if a company or business has an accounting period spanning 31 December 2021; recap on these from your CA Proficiency 1 or other studies.

If the accounting period of the business or company is greater than or less than 12 months, the AIA is proportionately reduced or increased. The AIA is available to assets that would have been included in the main pool and also to certain categories of assets that would have qualified for the special rate pool. Any proceeds on the disposal of assets that qualified for AIA will therefore be taken to one of those pools.

3.5.3 First-year Allowance

If an asset is purchased and it qualifies for the first-year allowance (FYA), then the full cost of the asset can be deducted in arriving at the tax-adjusted trading profits of a business.

The main types of asset on which 100% FYA is available are:

1. new and unused electric cars or zero-emission cars (i.e. those with CO_2 emissions of 0g/km) acquired on or after 1 April 2021; and
2. new, zero-emission goods vehicles.

Where the FYA is not claimed in full, the balance of expenditure is transferred to the main pool (see below). An FYA is not reduced pro rata in a short period of account, unlike AIAs and annual writing down allowances (WDAs).

3.5.4 Super-deduction Capital Allowance and Special Rate First-year Allowance

For expenditure incurred from 1 April 2021 until 31 March 2023, companies investing in certain qualifying new assets will be able to claim:

- a **130% super-deduction capital allowance** on qualifying plant and machinery (including lorries and vans) that would ordinarily qualify for the 18% main rate WDA; and
- a **50% first-year allowance** for qualifying special rate assets that would ordinarily qualify for the 6% rate WDA (referred to as the 'special rate allowance' or 'SR allowance').

Example 3.1 Super-deduction

A company with a 31 December accounting period end incurs £2 million of capital expenditure in May 2021. Ordinarily, this would qualify for the 18% main rate WDA but the company can now claim the super-deduction. It will receive a deduction of £2.6 million (i.e. £2 million × 130%).

If, instead, the company had incurred the expenditure in February 2021 it would have been able to claim the AIA of £1 million, and the £1 million balance would have received WDAs of £180,000 (i.e. £1 million × 18%). The difference in capital allowances in the first year would be £1,420,000 (£2.6 million – £1 million AIA – £180,000 WDAs), saving corporation tax at 19% of £269,800.

Example 3.2 Special rate allowance

A company with a 31 December accounting period end incurs £2.1 million on integral features in June 2021.

As the expenditure qualifies as a special rate asset, it is possible to claim the SR allowance. The company is also permitted to allocate the AIA to all or some of the expenditure on the asset, so the AIA and SR allowance can be used together on different parts of the asset. It can claim the AIA on £1 million of the total spend and the SR allowance on the remaining £1.1 million (a deduction of £550,000 (£1.1 million × 50%)).

If, instead, the company had incurred the expenditure in February 2021 it would have been able to claim the AIA of £1 million, and the £1.1 million balance would have received WDAs of £66,000 (i.e. £1.1 million × 6%). The difference in capital allowances in the first year would be £484,000, saving corporation tax at 19% of £91,960.

Both allowances are available for **companies only** and not for unincorporated businesses (such as sole traders or partnerships).

The **plant and machinery must be new and unused**, i.e. not second-hand. Cars are excluded from qualifying for either relief.

Plant and machinery expenditure which is incurred under a hire purchase or similar contract must meet additional conditions to qualify for the super-deduction and special rate relief (which are beyond the scope of this textbook).

If an accounting period straddles 1 April 2023 (when the scheme comes to an end), the rate of the super-deduction should be apportioned based on days falling prior to 1 April 2023 over the total days in the accounting period. This is calculated as follows:

1. divide the number of days in the accounting period before 1 April 2023 by the total number of days in the period;
2. multiply this ratio by 30%; and
3. add 100%.

For example, if qualifying expenditure is incurred in a chargeable period ending on 31 December 2023, the relevant percentage of the super-deduction is calculated as:

$$(90/365 \times 30\%) + 100\% = 107.4\%$$

This rate would then be applied to any expenditure incurred in the period qualifying for the super-deduction, which would only include qualifying expenditure incurred in that part of the accounting period falling before 31 March 2023. Expenditure not qualifying for the super-deduction would be eligible for the AIA or the 18% WDA.

This apportionment exercise only applies to the super-deduction and not to the SR allowance.

Disposals

Where assets on which either of these reliefs were claimed are disposed of, there will be a balancing charge on disposal. The disposal rules mean that it will therefore be vital to track and be able to trace expenditure on which either of these reliefs has been claimed.

The calculation of the balancing charge is different depending on which relief was originally claimed.

For the super-deduction, the disposal proceeds of the asset are treated as balancing charges (taxable profits) and not as proceeds to be taken to the main rate pool.

If only part of the original expenditure was claimed as a super-deduction and part was claimed by other capital allowances, the rules treat only part of the disposal receipt as a balancing charge. In such cases, only the relevant proportion of the proceeds that related to the part that qualified for the super-deduction is treated as a balancing charge.

Example 3.3

A company has a 31 December accounting period end. Expenditure of £2 million on computer equipment is incurred by a company in August 2021. The company decides to sell the computer equipment in December 2024 for £750,000.

For the year ended 31 December 2021 the company is entitled to a super-deduction of £2.6 million against taxable profits in the year, saving corporation tax of £494,000 (£2 million × 130% × 19%).

For the year ended 31 December 2024, the company disposes of the assets for £750,000. This triggers a balancing charge of £750,000 equal to the disposal proceeds, which increases taxable profits by the same amount for the period. No relevant proportion calculation is required as the whole of the assets (i.e. the computer equipment) upon which a super-deduction was claimed were disposed of.

Additional rules apply if the disposal takes places in a period that ends before 1 April 2023 or that straddles 1 April 2023. This is to ensure companies do not abuse the super-deduction and SR allowance by disposing of an asset shortly after acquisition.

Where the disposal takes place in a chargeable period that ends before 1 April 2023, the balancing charge is multiplied by 1.3. Where the disposal takes place in a period that straddles 1 April 2023, the balancing charge is multiplied by a factor calculated as follows:

1. divide the number of days in the accounting period before 1 April 2023 by the total number of days in the period;
2. multiply this ratio by 0.3; and
3. add 1.

For example, for a 12-month accounting period ending 30 September 2023, the factor would be 1.15 ((182/365 × 0.3) + 1). The balancing charge is then multiplied by this factor.

For disposals of assets which qualified for the SR allowance, a balancing charge also arises but this is calculated differently to reflect that the original allowance was for 50%. The balancing charge will be equal to relevant proportion of the proceeds.

The relevant proportion is calculated by:

1. dividing the amount of expenditure on which a SR allowance was claimed by 2 (to compensate for the fact that the original allowance was only 50% of the qualifying cost);
2. dividing the amount from 1. by the total expenditure on which capital allowances were claimed (either as a SR allowance, a first-year allowance or within a pool);
3. multiplying the amount from 2. by the disposal value of the asset to give the balancing charge. Any remaining disposal proceeds are taken to the special rate pool.

In simple terms, where the whole asset qualified for the SR allowance, the balancing charge will be equal to 50% of the disposal proceeds. The remaining 50% of the proceeds is taken to the special rate pool.

Example 3.4

A company with a 31 December accounting period end acquires a special rate asset in July 2021 for £2.5 million. AIA of £1 million and SR allowance on the remaining £1.5 million is claimed.

The company disposes of the asset in August 2024 for £500,000. The relevant proportion is equal to:

(SR expenditure ÷ 2) / total expenditure (£1.5 million ÷ 2) / £2.5 million) = 30%

Step 3 is then to apply the disposal proceeds of £500,000 to get the balancing charge. The balancing charge is therefore £150,000 (£500,000 × 30%). The balance of the disposal proceeds of £350,000 (£500,000 – £150,000) is then taken to the special rate pool.

3.5.5 Research & Development Allowance

A R&D allowance (RDA) of 100% is available on capital expenditure incurred on R&D activities. R&D expenditure includes all expenditure incurred for carrying out (or providing facilities for carrying out) R&D. For example, RDAs are available for the cost of building or refurbishing R&D facilities and the cost of plant, machinery, fixtures, or fittings to support R&D activities but not land or dwelling houses. RDA is available for businesses of all types. However, R&D tax relief on revenue expenditure (see **Chapter 8, Section 8.3**) is only available to companies.

3.5.6 Structures and Buildings Allowance

Building expenditure does not generally qualify for capital allowances, however, the structures and buildings allowance may provide relief for expenditure on the construction of commercial property that does not qualify for capital allowances as either plant and machinery or as an integral features.

The allowance is available on all contracts for construction work entered into on or after 29 October 2018. Relief is available at a fixed rate of 3% per annum on a straight-line basis.

3.5.7 The Main Pool

The majority of plant and machinery expenditure will fall into the main pool. The main pool comprises all items of plant and machinery, including cars with CO_2 emissions of 50g/km or less, but it does not include assets that are part of the special rate pool, assets that are used for both business and personal use or assets that have been elected as short-life assets (see below).

When an individual buys an asset that falls into the main pool, it will increase the size of the pool; when assets are disposed of, the value of the main pool is decreased by the proceeds from the disposal (restricted to original cost).

Where the sale proceeds are not at arm's length (as they would be in a sale between unrelated parties) or where there are no sale proceeds (e.g. due to a takeover or to the gifting of a business asset for personal use), the market value is used as the deemed proceeds.

Writing Down Allowance

The writing down allowance (WDA) of 18% is an annual allowance to reflect the wear and tear of plant and machinery. Unlike the AIA and the FYA, which are applied to the cost price of the equipment, WDAs are applied on a reducing balance basis. The WDA is calculated on the cost price of the plant and machinery less any capital grants received in the first period. The WDAs in subsequent periods are calculated based on the opening tax written down values (TWDVs) plus current-period additions, less current-period disposals.

To qualify for the WDA, an asset must be owned by the individual and in use "wholly and exclusively" for the purposes of the individual's trade, profession, or employment at the end of the period.

When plant is sold, the proceeds (limited to the original cost) are removed from the main pool. Where the trade is continuing, the pool balance remaining will continue to be written down on an annual basis by WDAs, even if there are no assets left, unless the balance falls below £1,000.

Where an accounting period is less than 12 months, the WDA must be pro-rated.

Balancing Allowances and Balancing Charges

To adequately capture profits and losses in disposals of fixed assets qualifying for capital allowances, the capital allowances system uses balancing charges and balancing allowances to reflect any profit or loss on the disposal (i.e. sale) of an asset.

A balancing allowance arises when the sales proceeds of an asset are less than its tax written down value (a loss on disposal).

A balancing charge arises when the sales proceeds (restricted to original cost) of an asset are greater than its tax written down value (a profit on disposal).

The main scenario where balancing allowances and charges can arise is when business or company ceases to trade. For this reason, there is an option to treat certain assets as short-life assets (see below).

3.5.8 The Special Rate Pool

The special rate pool contains capital expenditure on:

- long-life assets;
- integral features of a building; and
- cars with CO_2 emissions greater than 50g/km.

The WDA applied to the special rate pool is 6% per annum; therefore, a pro-rated adjustment is required for long or short periods of account.

The AIA can apply to all assets in the special rate pool except for cars. An individual can decide how to allocate the AIA in the most tax-efficient manner. A business should therefore prioritise the use of its AIA limit against qualifying special rate pool expenditure (which would otherwise only attract 6% WDA) rather than to main pool expenditure (18% WDA). Expenditure in excess of the AIA is added to the special rate pool and will be eligible for WDA in the same period in which the expenditure is incurred.

Long-life Assets

Long-life assets are assets with an expected working life of 25 years or more. For expenditure to fall within the long-life asset rules, total expenditure in the accounting period must be more than £100,000 (reduced proportionately for accounting periods of less than 12 months).

If an individual spends less than this on long-life assets, the expenditure is not treated as long-life assets and may fall into the main pool.

Integral Features

"Integral features" are certain fixtures and fittings seen as essential to a building and which have a longer average economic life than other plant and machinery. These therefore attract capital allowances at a lower WDA rate of 6%. Integral features include:

- electrical systems (including lighting systems);
- hot- and cold-water systems;
- space-heating systems, powered systems of ventilation, air cooling or air purification, and any floor or ceiling comprised therein;
- lifts, escalators and moving walkways; and
- external solar shading.

3.5.9 Commercial Property Acquisitions including Fixtures

Special rules apply where a business acquires a commercial property that includes existing fixtures. The purchaser can only claim capital allowances on fixtures if the following two conditions are satisfied:

1. the seller of the building must have previously claimed capital allowances on the relevant items, i.e. their cost has been allocated to a capital allowances pool; and
2. the vendor and purchaser must jointly elect to fix the value of the fixtures under what is known as a section 198 Capital Allowances Act 2001 claim.

If either of the above conditions is not met, the new purchaser and any subsequent purchaser cannot make a claim for the relevant fixture.

3.5.10 The Single Assets Pool

Private-use Assets

This rule generally only applies to capital allowances in the context of unincorporated businesses. An asset that has mixed use and is used privately by a trader is dealt with in a single asset pool and the capital allowances are restricted. The allowance is calculated as normal and is then reduced by the private element. Only the business use proportion of the WDAs is allowed as a deduction from trading profits; however, the full annual allowance is deducted when arriving at the tax written down value at the end of each period.

An asset with some private use by an employee suffers no such private use restriction. The employee may instead be taxed on the benefit in kind instead, so the business receives capital allowances on the full cost of the asset.

When an asset in a single asset pool is sold, a balancing allowance/charge will always arise, depending on the proceeds received.

Cars

Cars that have an element of private use by the owner of an unincorporated business must be kept in the single asset pool.

The WDA on the single asset pool will be 18% if CO_2 emissions range from 1–50g/km; and 6% if emissions are over 50g/km. A 100% first-year allowance is available for zero-emission cars (see **Section 3.5.3**).

3.5.11 Short-life Assets

Where an asset is acquired and is likely to be disposed of within eight years from the end of the accounting period in which it was bought, it is considered a "short-life" asset. Short-life asset treatment cannot be claimed for motor cars or plant used partly for non-business purposes. Provided an election is made to treat the asset in a single asset pool instead of the main pool, a balancing charge or allowance arises on its disposal.

If the asset is not disposed of within this time period, its tax written down value is added to the main pool at the end of that time.

3.5.12 Disclaim of Capital Allowances

Where the capital allowances claim for a particular year of assessment exceeds the assessable profits from the trade or profession, it will give rise to a trade loss. In this situation an individual does not have to claim the full capital allowances to which they are entitled and can make a partial claim instead. This would reduce any trade loss and result in a higher tax written down value brought forward (increasing the WDA in future years).

A trader should therefore consider whether it is beneficial to claim capital allowances in the period and, if so, whether a full or partial claim should be made. Issues to consider include whether the individual has sufficient income in the period to utilise the trade loss without wasting their personal allowance and the fact that by disclaiming capital allowances in the current period, the business or company may be forfeiting AIAs as a result (as these can only be claimed in the accounting period of expenditure).

3.5.13 Additional Aspects

Date of Purchase of Assets
For capital allowances purposes, expenditure is generally deemed to be incurred when the obligation to pay becomes unconditional (provided this is within four months). This will usually be the date of the contract, e.g. where payment is due a month after delivery, then the date of delivery is relevant.

However, if the amount is due more than four months after the obligation to pay becomes unconditional for capital allowance purposes, then the expenditure is instead deemed to be incurred when paid.

Capital Grants
The qualifying cost for capital allowance purposes is the net cost, i.e. total cost minus grant receivable.

Hire Purchase
Assets acquired under a hire-purchase contract are deemed to be incurred at the time they are brought into use. Capital allowances are available on assets acquired under hire-purchase agreements. The business/company will also be able to claim the interest charge as a tax-deductible trading expense.

Finance-leased Assets
Where an individual leases an asset on a finance lease, no capital allowances can be claimed on the capital expenditure. However, in the accounts of the business the asset will be depreciated over its life. In accordance with general accounting practice, the depreciation as well as the interest being

charged by the lessor will be debited to the statement of profit or loss for the period are both allowable expenditures.

VAT
The qualifying cost of plant and equipment for capital allowance purposes is the actual expenditure incurred on the plant or equipment. This will be the cost of the plant or equipment exclusive of VAT, where the VAT paid on acquisition is recoverable by the individual because they are VAT registered. If, however, a business that is not registered for VAT acquires plant or equipment outright, the VAT element of the purchase price represents a cost and the total cost, including VAT, can be claimed as a capital allowance.

3.6   Loss Relief

This section briefly discusses the tax implications of a tax-adjusted trading loss being incurred by an individual or partner in a partnership and how such a trading loss can be used to reduce their tax liability. Recap on this topic from your CA Proficiency 1 or other studies. Students are reminded that the loss relief rules for companies, covered in **Chapter 7, Section 7.9** in overview, differ to these rules.

3.6.1   Relief for Trading Losses

When a tax-adjusted trading loss (hereafter referred to as a trading loss) is calculated for a business, traded by an individual alone or in partnership, income tax relief may be available for trading losses in the following ways:

1. by offsetting the losses against other (general) income in the same year and/or the previous tax year (subject to the cap on income tax reliefs, see **Chapter 4, Section 4.3**);
2. a temporary extension of the loss carry-back rules is available for losses arising in the 2020/21 and 2021/22 tax years, which allows the trading loss of a sole trader or a partner to be carried back three years rather than the normal 12 months, but only against trading profits;
3. by carrying forward the losses against subsequent (future) profits of the same trade (not capped);
4. where the losses occur in the early years of a trade, by carrying them back against other income from the previous three tax years on a FIFO basis (subject to the cap on income tax reliefs, see **Section 4.3**);
5. by offsetting the losses against capital gains (see **Part Three**) of the same or preceding tax year (subject to the cap on income tax reliefs, see **Section 4.3**); or
6. by carry back in a "terminal loss" situation, i.e. where a trade ceases, enabling the loss incurred in the final 12 months of trading to be carried back against trading profits from the same trade in the previous three tax years on a LIFO basis.

3.6.2   Relief Under Extended Loss Carry-back Rules

A temporary extension of the loss carry-back rules is available for losses arising in the 2020/21 and 2021/22 tax years, which allows the trading loss of a sole trader or a partner to be carried back three years rather than the normal 12 months. (A similar temporary extension applies to companies, see **Chapter 7, Section 7.91**.)

The losses can only be offset against trading profits and are carried back against later years first. The amount of trading losses that can be offset against trading profits in the previous 12 months is unlimited. After this, the maximum amount of trading losses that may be carried back against trading profits of the earlier two years is capped at £2 million for each tax year. There is, therefore, a separate cap of £2 million for losses in 2020/21 and another £2 million cap for losses in 2021/22.

Prior to claiming this extended carry back, the trader or partner must first make a claim against net income for either the year of the loss and/or the previous year (i.e. under bullet point 1 in **Section 3.6.1**). If no such claim is possible (for example, because the trader has no income in the current or previous tax year), it is still possible to make a claim under the extended loss carry-back rules for the earlier two years.

Example 3.5

An individual trader's profits, losses and other income are as follows:

	2017/18	2018/19	2019/20	2020/21
	£	£	£	£
Trading profits/(losses)	1,200,000	1,200,000	500,000	(3,000,000)
Employment income	50,000	50,000	60,000	70,000

The trader makes a claim under section 64 of ITA 2007 to set the 2020/21 loss against general income of both the year of the losses (£50,000) and the previous year (£550,000). The cap on relief for trading losses against general income applies (see **Section 4.3**). Therefore, only £50,000 of the employment income in each of the 2020/21 and 2019/20 tax years can be relieved.

The remaining part of the 2020/21 losses, up to a maximum of £2,000,000, is available to carry back to set against trading profits of 2018/19 and 2017/18 (in that order) under the extended loss relief rules. It is not possible to offset the trading losses against the employment income in the 2018/19 and 2017/18 tax years, as only trading profits can be relieved.

In summary, losses are set against:

1. £50,000 of the employment income in 2020/21 (subject to the cap on trading loss relief against general income).
2. £550,000 in 2019/20 (£500,000 against trading profits which is not restricted by the cap on relief against general income. Only £50,000 of the employment income can be offset as this is subject to the cap.)
3. £1,200,000 of trading profits in 2018/19.
4. £800,000 of trading profits in 2017/18 (loss restricted as the £2 million cap applies).
5. £400,000 of the loss remains available to be claimed to carry forward and set against trade profits in future years.

3.6.3 Cessation of Trade to Incorporate

If a business is transferred to a company, i.e. incorporated, any unrelieved loss of the sole trader/ partnership can be carried forward and set-off against the first available income received from the company by way of salary, dividends, interest, etc.

The consideration for the transfer of the business must be wholly or mainly in the form of shares (at least 80%), which must be retained by the seller throughout any tax year in which the loss is relieved.

Practical tip: an individual should choose whichever loss relief saves tax at the highest tax rate – but they need to be careful to consider the potential wasting of other reliefs, such as personal allowances, etc. and the rate of saving achieved by the loss claim.

3.7 Employment Income

Employment earnings are generally understood in monetary terms but can also include benefits or 'perks'. For income tax purposes, such non-monetary benefits must be converted to a cash equivalent. Income tax computations must deduct allowable expenses incurred by an employee in the performance of their work – there are rules established to decide if such expenses are deductible from employment income. Each of these areas is looked at in overview in this section.

First it is important to understand the distinction between general employment income (sometimes referred to as "general earnings") and "specific employment income". General earnings are an individual's employment earnings plus the cash equivalent of any (taxable) non-monetary benefits and include:

- salary/wages;
- directors' fees;
- bonuses and commission;
- non-monetary benefits in kind etc;
- round-sum expense allowances;
- payments on commencement of employment (e.g. inducement payments).

Specific employment income is dealt with in detail in **Chapter 6**.

"Net taxable earnings" or "net earnings" are both defined as employment income less any allowable expenses or deductions.

3.7.1 Employment Status

The distinction between an employee and a self-employed person is not set out in tax legislation. Whether an individual is employed or self-employed is an important question for tax purposes as there are many differences in the way in which they are taxed.

Employees are taxed under PAYE with income tax and Class 1 national insurance contributions (NICs) being deducted from payments made to them. Class 1 and Class 1A NICs are also payable by their employers. By contrast, the self-employed pay income tax and Class 2 and 4 NICs directly to HMRC under self-assessment. (See your CA Proficiency 1 or other studies in relation to the PAYE system and NICs.)

Some important consequences that arise from this are:

1. the NIC liability of a self-employed individual is much lower than that of an employee;
2. the rules allowing tax relief for expenses are generally more relaxed for self-employed individuals;
3. self-employed individuals have a cash-flow advantage in the timing of their payments compared with employees who are taxed at source under PAYE; and
4. if there has been an incorrect classification, the "employer" may find that he has additional income tax, NIC, penalties and interest to pay.

Contract of Service versus Contract for Service
Case law has determined that an employee is a person who has a contract of service with his employer; a self-employed person will provide services under a contract for services. A contract can be written, oral, implied or a combination of these.

Sometimes, the distinction between an employee and a self-employed person is not entirely clear, and accordingly the issue has been the subject of a number of cases. Initially, try to establish the terms and conditions of the engagement, which can normally be determined from the contract between the person and the client or employer. Next, any other relevant facts should be considered. No one single factor is decisive in itself; it is necessary to look at the circumstances as a whole.

Where the evidence is evenly balanced, the intention of the parties may then decide the issue. HMRC provides an online tool, the Employment Status Indicator (ESI), to check the employment status of an individual or a group of workers.

Recap from your CA Proficiency 1 or other studies on the main factors that determine whether a person is an employee or self-employed.

3.7.2   Basis of Assessment of Employment Income

The general earnings (excluding non-monetary benefits in kind) of a UK tax resident (see **Chapter 2, Section 2.2**) individual, are taxed in the year of receipt, i.e. when the income is received. Assessment is therefore on the "arising basis", i.e. in the tax year in which the income is earned.

General earnings are treated as "received" on the earlier of:

- the date the payment is actually paid; or
- the date the employee becomes entitled to the payment.

In the case of directors, general earnings are "received" on either the earlier of the dates as above, or on the earlier of:

- the date the remuneration is credited in the company's accounts; or
- the end of the accounting period during which the remuneration is determined; or
- the date the remuneration is determined if that is after the end of the accounting period.

Benefits in Kind

Non-monetary benefits in kind are "received" in the tax year in which it is provided to the employee. A monetary value needs to be calculated.

Pensions

State pension is taxable on the total amount received (or accrued) in the tax year, irrespective of the date when the payment is received.

3.7.3   Computation of Taxable Employment Income

Lump Sum Payments

Lump sum payments fall under the general earnings category and as such are taxed on the arising basis. There are a variety of lump sum payments, the terms of which need to be understood.

Restrictive Covenant Payment

A restrictive covenant is a lump sum payment made in return for an undertaking by an employee to restrict their conduct or activity in some way. Such payments are fully taxable as general earnings.

Commencement or Inducement Payments

Payments made to an individual as an incentive to take up an employment ('golden hellos' or 'golden handcuffs') are generally treated as advance pay for future services of employment and are therefore taxable as general earnings.

"Gardening Leave"

If a payment is made to an employee where notice has been given but not worked, the employee continues to be employed until the end of the notice period and the payment is taxable as general earnings.

Allowable Deductions from Employment Income

For an expense to be deductible from an employee's or director's employment income, it must be shown that it was incurred for "qualifying travel" or "wholly, exclusively and necessarily in performing the duties of the office or employment". The latter test is extremely difficult to satisfy in practice.

Qualifying Travel Expenses

Income tax relief is not available for an employee's normal commuting costs. However, employees are entitled to relief for travel expenses, at full cost, incurred while travelling in the performance of their duties or to/from a place they have to attend in the performance of their duties (so long as their attendance at a particular workplace does not last/is not expected to last, more than 24 months). Tax relief is available for travel accommodation and subsistence expenses incurred by an employee who is working at a temporary workplace on a secondment expected to last up to 24 months.

Other Allowable Deductions

Certain other expenditure is specifically deductible in computing net taxable earnings:

- Contributions to registered occupational pension schemes;
- Subscriptions to certain professional bodies if relevant to duties;
- Payroll giving to charities; and
- Mileage allowance relief where an employee uses his or her own car for business travel.

Round-sum Expense Allowance

In general, a round-sum expense allowance advanced to an employee to be disbursed at their discretion is taxable general earnings.

Expenses not Reimbursed by Employer

If an employee incurs legitimate allowable employment expenses for which they are not reimbursed by their employer, tax relief can still be available on a claim to HMRC.

3.7.4 Tax Treatment of Benefits in Kind

Some expense payments and benefits are treated as taxable remuneration. Benefits provided to an individual (including their family or household members) are taxed on the cash equivalent of the benefit, which is generally the cost to the employer of providing the benefit, less any amounts made good by the employee. If benefits are provided in-house, the value for tax purposes is generally the additional marginal cost to the employer. There are also a number of non-taxable payments and benefits.

Note, however, that there are special rules for valuing certain benefits, such as share options, company cars, fuel for private use in company cars, living accommodation, etc. Recap on the main benefits taxable on all employees and directors and the calculation rules from your CA Proficiency 1 or other studies

3.8 Savings and Investment Income

Where an individual has money on deposit in a bank, savings income, i.e. interest, may be earned on that money. Similarly, an individual may have purchased shares in a company and if that company decides to pay a dividend to its shareholders, dividend income will have been earned and will need to be taxed accordingly. The treatment of overseas savings and investment income is covered in **Chapter 5, Sections 5.2.1** and **5.2.2**.

In simple terms, savings income is interest. The main types of savings income include interest from a bank or building society account or a credit union account.

If an individual owns shares in a company, they may receive dividends from the company throughout the year. Such income is taxed as dividend income.

3.8.1   Basis of Assessment and Computation of Savings and Investment Income

General Rules

The amount of savings and investment income taxable for a tax year is the amount arising in that year. Income arises when it is paid or credited. Accrued income not yet paid or credited is ignored.

Personal Savings Allowance

The personal savings allowance depends on an individual's "adjusted net income". Adjusted net income is total taxable income before deducting the personal allowance and after certain other tax reliefs.

There is an important interaction between the personal savings allowance and the dividend allowance (see below). When determining the amount of the personal savings allowance (if any), it is necessary to consider if the adjusted net income includes dividend income. If dividend income is included, that income is treated as if it is chargeable at the higher or additional rate, even if it is within the £2,000 dividend allowance.

The personal savings allowance is available in addition to the savings income starter rate, increasing the amount of savings income that could be received tax-free to £6,000.

Dividend Allowance

All individuals, regardless of their level of earnings, are entitled to the tax-free dividend allowance, which means that no tax will be payable on the first £2,000 of dividend income.

Dividend income covered by the dividend allowance will still count towards an individual's basic or higher rate bands. It will therefore affect the rate of tax that is payable on dividends received in excess of the £2,000 allowance.

3.8.2   Exempt Savings and Investment Income

Certain investment and savings income is exempt for investors resident and domiciled in the UK (see **Chapter 2, Sections 2.2** and **2.3**). The main types of exempt income include:

1.   interest and dividend income from individual savings accounts;
2.   interest and terminal bonuses under Save As You Earn schemes;
3.   interest awarded as part of an award of damages for personal injury/death; and
4.   dividends on ordinary shares in a venture capital trust (see **Chapter 4, Section 4.4**).

Recap on exempt savings and investment income from your CA Proficiency 1 or other studies.

3.9   Property Income

Property income of individuals is categorised as non-savings income. The rules for property income of companies are dealt with in overview in **Chapter 7**. An individual taxpayer with UK property income is treated as if they are operating a UK property business; therefore, the rules and calculations are broadly the same as for trading income, subject to some specific considerations.

Property income and property expenses are consolidated to give a single profit or loss figure on which income tax is assessed on the default cash basis or on the accruals basis (see below). Overseas property income is covered in **Chapter 5**, **Section 5.2.4** and is broadly treated as a separate property business to any UK property business the taxpayer may also have.

Students should recap on the detailed property income rules from their CA Proficiency 1 or other studies. The additional aspects of property income included at CA Proficiency 2 are covered in **Chapter 5**, **Section 5.3** (non-resident landlords scheme) and **Section 5.4** (furnished holiday lettings).

3.9.1   Basis of Assessment of UK Property Income

The profits of UK property income are computed for each tax year and each tax year's profit is taxed in that year. That is, for the 2021/22 tax year, property income profits from 6 April 2021 to 5 April 2022 are taxed. Property income profits or losses are computed on the default cash basis (where property receipts do not exceed £150,000) or on the accruals basis (i.e. UK GAAP) where property receipts exceed £150,000.

3.9.2   Computation of Taxable Property Income

Property Income Allowance

A £1,000 property income allowance is available for individuals with gross receipts from property of £1,000 or less. Where an individual's property income for the tax year does not exceed the £1,000 property income allowance, there is no charge to tax and no requirement to complete a self-assessment.

Where an individual's property income exceeds the £1,000 property income allowance, the individual can elect to use an alternative method of calculating property income. Under this method the charge to tax is on the excess of property income over £1,000. As a basic rule, an individual would not elect to use the alternative method of calculating property income if their allowable property expenses are more than £1,000.

Computation of Profits

Property income includes not only the agreed rents but also the taxable portion of any premium paid by a tenant. If more than one property is being let, the income and deductible expenses for each property are pooled together to calculate a total profit or loss for the tax year.

The pro forma computation shows the layout of the property income calculation. It does not include all potential expenses that are allowable as deductions against property income, but it does include the most common.

PRO FORMA TAXABLE PROPERTY INCOME COMPUTATION

	£	£
Rental income	X	
Lease premium received (income element)	X	
		X
Less: expenses:		
Rent payable	X	

Rates/council tax	X	
Gas/electricity/waste disposal costs paid by landlord and not reimbursed by tenant	X	
Finance/mortgage interest costs (subject to restriction, see below)	X	
Accountancy fees	X	
Legal fee re. lease renewal	X	
Travel costs to and from the property	X	
Replacement furniture relief (where a dwelling house is let)	X	
Capital allowances (where a commercial property is let)	X	(X)
Property income profit/(loss)		X

3.9.3   Allowable Deductions from Property Income

As property income rules broadly follow trading income rules, any qualifying costs incurred by the property business can be deducted to reduce the tax liability. The "wholly and exclusively" rule is the main rule applied to property income. The following are some of the main costs deductible from the gross property income:

- rent payable on the property;
- rates, council tax and ground rent;
- gas, electricity, waste disposal if paid for by the landlord;
- cost of insurance, maintenance, and management of the property;
- accountancy fees for rental accounts and rental records;
- legal fees for renewal of a short lease (50 years or less);
- for commercial property – capital allowances on plant and machinery (see **Section 3.5**);
- travel costs to/from let properties;
- irrecoverable rent;
- replacement furniture relief for replacement of certain items in a dwelling house;
- fixtures that are considered 'integral' to the property as repairs to the property.
- finance costs in respect of the purchase or renovation of **commercial property**. The rules for finance costs in relation to residential property are different (see below). (Note also that there are separate rules for the deductibility of finance costs for corporation tax purposes (see **Chapter 7, Section 7.5.4**).)

Recap on pre-letting expenses, expenses between lettings and other expenses deductible from property income from your CA Proficiency 1 or other studies.

Finance Costs/Mortgage Interest in Relation to Residential Property

The amount of tax relief available for finance costs (mortgage interest on loans to acquire or renovate the rental property) in respect of UK and overseas residential property businesses is not deductible as a property expense. Instead relief is available as a reduction at basic rate only (at Step 6 of the income tax computation in **Section 3.1.3**). Capital repayments in respect of loans are not deductible.

The basic rate tax reduction is the lower of:

1. the finance costs in the tax year plus any finance costs brought forward; or
2. the property business profits in the tax year (after any brought-forward losses); or
3. the individual's adjusted total income exceeding an individual's personal allowance (after losses and reliefs and excluding savings and dividends income).

3.9.4   *Property Income Losses*

Losses from a UK property business can be carried forward indefinitely to be used against future UK property profits for the same UK property business. For a property business that has more than one property, the net profit or loss is computed for each one separately for the particular tax year. The profits/losses are then aggregated to arrive at the total UK profit/loss for the tax year. The treatment of overseas property business losses is covered in **Chapter 5**, **Section 5.2.4**.

Losses on favoured lettings, i.e. properties let at less than market value, are not allowed. Expenses are only permitted up to the level of income on such lettings.

3.10   Deductions on Income, Allowances and Reliefs

Students should recap on the detailed rules for deductions, allowances and relief from their CA Proficiency 1 or other studies. A brief reminder of the main points is given below.

3.10.1 *Qualifying Reliefs*

In the income tax computation, total income has qualifying reliefs deducted (at Step 2 of the income tax computation in **Section 3.1.3**) to arrive at "adjusted net income".

Relief for Eligible Interest
Interest charged on certain loans is eligible for income tax relief – by deducting the interest paid from the total income to give net income for a particular tax year. Relief should be deducted from non-savings income first, then savings income and lastly dividend income.

The following are the main types of loan eligible for this relief:

- loan to purchase an interest in a partnership;
- loan to buy ordinary shares in, or to lend money to, a close company (see **Chapter 9**);
- loan for the purchase of shares in an employee-controlled company;
- loan for the purchase of equipment and plant and machinery for a partnership; and
- loan for the purchase of equipment and plant and machinery by an employee for use in their employment.

There are additional conditions to be met in respect of each of the above. Tax relief for eligible interest is one of the reliefs affected by the cap on certain income tax reliefs (see **Chapter 4, Section 4.3**). If there is excess eligible interest in a tax year because there is either insufficient taxable income to cover it or the cap restricts its use, this cannot be carried back or forward and is therefore effectively wasted.

Annual Payments
Relief for annual payments is given by deducting the annual payments from total income to give net income for the tax year.

Gifts of Shares or Land to Charity
Gifts of qualifying investments to a UK charity are eligible for income tax relief as a qualifying relief by deducting the amount gifted from total income to give net income for the tax year in which the gift is made.

3.10.2 Pension Contributions

The government incentivises saving through pensions by offering tax relief to individuals who pay contributions to their pension schemes. Where an individual is an employee, contributions are paid into their work/occupational pension scheme, with the employer also contributing on the employee's behalf. Self-employed individuals (or employees that are not in an occupational scheme), can contribute to a personal pension scheme.

Income Tax Relief on Registered Pension Schemes
Income tax relief on an individual's contributions to a registered pension scheme is dependent on the rate of income tax paid by the individual: a basic rate taxpayer will receive relief at 20%; a higher rate taxpayer's relief will be 40%; and an additional rate taxpayer's relief will be at 45%. Thus, relief for pension contributions is given at an individual's marginal rate of tax (the highest rate of tax they pay).

Basic rate tax relief is generally deducted at source. If the person is a higher rate taxpayer, the relief operates by increasing the upper limit of the basic rate tax band (£37,700 in 2021/22) by the individual's gross contributions. If the person is an additional rate taxpayer, both the upper limit of the higher rate band (40%) and the basic rate band is increased by the gross pension contribution.

For occupational pension schemes only, an alternative method of administering the relief is available whereby the individual's (the employee's) gross contributions are deducted from their gross pay, i.e. before PAYE is deducted. This arrangement is referred to as a "net pay arrangement".

Annual Allowance
The annual allowance is a 'ceiling' on the amount of pension contributions (an individual's and an employer's, if applicable) that can benefit from the tax relief. It does not restrict the amount of tax relief; instead, it applies a charge, the "annual allowance charge", when the annual allowance has been exceeded. In effect, the charge reverses the relief on the excess amount over the annual allowance so that if the amount paid into a pension exceeds the annual allowance it does not mean the relief is restricted to the annual allowance. The annual allowance in 2021/22 is £40,000. However, this tapers away for certain high earners where adjusted income is above £240,000 (see **Chapter 4, Section 4.2**).

Any unused annual allowance in a tax year in which the individual is a scheme member can be carried over and added to the next tax year's annual allowance, up to a maximum of three tax years.

If an individual's gross contributions in a tax year (including any from an employer) exceed the annual allowance, the excess contributions are liable to income tax (the annual allowance charge), which is calculated on the individual's marginal tax rate.

Lifetime Allowance
There is no limit on the amount of benefits an individual can be paid from a pension scheme; however, the amount that can be accrued in a pension 'pot' without suffering income tax is subject to the lifetime allowance. Like the annual allowance, the lifetime allowance operates by applying a charge (the lifetime allowance charge) for payments received that exceed the limit. The lifetime allowance from 2021/22 to 2025/26 is £1,073,100. Recap on the detailed rules for the pensions lifetime allowance from your CA Proficiency 1 or other studies.

Retirement Benefits

Unless retiring due to ill health, pensions will not normally be allowed to be paid out of a pension scheme until the individual member reaches normal pension age (55). All or part of the pension fund can be taken to provide pension benefits at any time from age 55 onwards. It is therefore possible to receive a pension and still continue to work.

A tax-free lump sum payment of up to 25% of the lower of the fund value or the lifetime allowance can be paid out of the scheme.

Pension income is taxable as non-savings income and is taxed through the PAYE system.

3.10.3 Gift Aid Donations and Payroll Giving Scheme

Charitable donations made under gift aid are paid net of basic rate tax, i.e. giving basic rate tax relief when the payment is made. Gift aid donations attract relief at the donor's marginal rate of tax by extending the taxpayer's basic rate band by the grossed-up amount for higher rate taxpayers; and by extending both the basic rate and higher rate bands if they are an additional rate taxpayer (i.e. similar to the way tax relief on pension contributions is given). The charity is then able to claim the taxpayer's basic rate relief from HMRC. Note: sufficient tax must be paid by the donor to cover the basic rate repayment to the charity.

Under the payroll giving scheme, charitable donations may be deducted from gross employment earnings before tax is calculated. The employer must obtain HMRC approval to operate the scheme. The employer passes the donation on to the approved charity.

3.10.4 Personal Allowances

Personal allowances are deducted from net income (see **Section 3.1.3**). The standard personal allowance is recapped at **Section 3.1.2**.

Blind Person's Allowance

If a taxpayer is registered as blind, the blind person's allowance can be claimed. This is in addition to the standard personal allowance and is £2,520 for 2021/22. A claim can also be made in the tax year before registration if blindness can be proved in that year.

Marriage Allowance

The marriage allowance lets an individual transfer £1,260 in 2021/22 of his or her personal allowance to their husband/wife/civil partner. For a couple to benefit from the marriage allowance, the lower earning spouse/civil partner must have an income of £12,570 or less. The higher earning spouse/civil partner must have income between £12,571 and £50,270.

3.11   Administration and Procedures

Income tax in the UK is administered via the self-assessment system for tax, whereby an annual tax return is filed. Students are advised to revisit the detailed self-assessment rules from their CA Proficiency 1 or other studies and to also review the Corporation Tax Self-Assessment rules for companies covered in overview in **Chapter 7**.

Income Tax Reliefs – Additional Aspects

4.1   Introduction

The cumulative knowledge of reliefs from CA Proficiency 1 was briefly covered in overview in **Chapter 3, Section 3.10**. This chapter focuses on additional aspects of income tax reliefs in UK tax legislation. **Sections 4.1** and **4.2** each build on topics first covered at CA Proficiency 1, while the remainder of the chapter focuses on the various tax-advantaged venture capital schemes in UK tax legislation designed to encourage individuals to invest in higher-risk trading companies that would otherwise struggle to raise money to help them grow and develop.

4.2   Pensions Annual Allowance Tapering Rule

As covered in detail at CA Proficiency 1 (and briefly covered in overview in **Chapter 3, Section 3.10.2**), the annual allowance is a 'ceiling' applicable in each tax year on the amount of pension contributions (an individual's and an employer's, if applicable) that can benefit from pensions income tax relief. It does not restrict the amount of tax relief; instead, it applies the **annual allowance charge** when the annual allowance has been exceeded by the amount of the pension contributions. The annual allowance limit for the tax year 2021/22 is £40,000.

However, the annual allowance for certain high earners is reduced on a tapering basis. For every £2 of adjusted income (broadly total taxable income before reliefs and allowances) above £240,000, an individual's annual allowance is reduced by £1 until it falls to a minimum level of £4,000. This means that a taxpayer with adjusted income in 2021/22 of £312,000 or more has an annual allowance of £4,000.

4.3 Cap on Certain Income Tax Reliefs

UK legislation includes a cap on certain income tax reliefs. The cap limits the relief(s) available in that tax year to the **greater** of:

- £50,000; or
- 25% of the individual's adjusted total income for the tax year.

4.3.1 Adjusted Total Income

Adjusted total income (ATI) is the income calculated specifically for the purposes of the cap on certain reliefs. There are three steps to calculate ATI:

1. Aggregate all income sources, i.e. trading income, employment income, savings income, etc., to give **total income**; then
2. deduct any relevant pension contributions, i.e. gross amounts of personal pension contributions; then
3. add back any charitable donations made through payroll giving.

The purpose of the adjustments is to ensure that the income calculated, and on which the cap will be based, takes into account deductions made before or after tax has been paid. The cap is applied to the year of the claim, hence it must be calculated on a tax-year-by-tax-year basis.

4.3.2 Summary of Reliefs Impacted

To the extent that they can be relieved by individuals against **general income**, the main reliefs affected include the following:

- trade loss relief against general income in the current year or carried back to the previous tax year;
- early trade loss relief; and
- qualifying loan interest.

Each of the above reliefs were covered in detail on the CA Proficiency 1 course and should be revisited.

It is important to note that trading losses that have been generated by overlap relief are not subject to the cap. In addition, there is no restriction on losses that are carried back and set against profits of the same trade. Similarly, no restriction applies to trading losses carried forward against profits of the same trade. This is because losses in these situations are being set against the same type of income.

4.4 The Venture Capital Trust Scheme

The venture capital trust (VCT) scheme is designed to encourage individual **indirect equity** investment in unquoted trading companies. The scheme offers generous tax reliefs (both income tax and CGT) to individual investors who invest directly in a VCT company that then itself invests in high-risk, unquoted companies. The individual investor therefore spreads the risk.

4.4.1　VCT Scheme Reliefs

Individuals can invest a maximum of £200,000 per annum in new ordinary VCT shares in a tax year, attracting income tax relief at 30% on their taxable income as a tax reducer, providing the shares are held for five years.

VCT income tax relief is always given in the tax year in which the investment is made; there is no carry back or carry forward facility. The relief must be claimed on the individual's tax return and must be claimed within four years after the 31 January following the tax year of the investment. For qualifying investments made in 2021/22, the deadline would therefore be 31 January 2027.

Dividends received from VCT shares are exempt from income tax in respect of shares acquired within the permitted £200,000 maximum.

Investors in VCT shares are exempt from CGT on any gains made on the disposal of the VCT shares within the permitted £200,000 maximum. Losses on VCT share disposals within the permitted £200,000 maximum are not allowable losses; hence only losses on disposals above the permitted limit can be used in the usual way and these do not attract any special relief (see **Chapter 16, Section 16.7**).

4.4.2　Conditions of the VCT Scheme

There are no special conditions for the investor except that they must be over 18 years old and subscribe on their own behalf for new ordinary shares in VCTs. There are, however, stringent conditions to be met by the VCT and the company it invests in to avail of the generous tax reliefs.

VCT Conditions

The main conditions to be met by the VCT itself are:

- it must be listed on a regulated UK or EU market;
- its income must come "wholly or mainly" from shares or securities;
- at least 70% of its investment must be shares in "qualifying holdings" (broadly unquoted companies carrying on qualifying trades in the UK);
- no single holding can amount to more than 15% of its total investment shares; and
- it must distribute (i.e. pay out in dividends to shareholders) at least 85% of its income from shareholdings and securities.

HMRC's approval of the VCT for the scheme may be withdrawn if it ceases to satisfy these conditions.

Investee Company Conditions

The main conditions for the company being invested in, the investee, by the VCT are:

- it must have fewer than 250 full-time employees at the date of issue;
- its gross assets must not exceed £15 million prior to, nor £16 million after, the investment;
- it must not have raised more than £5 million in venture capital schemes in the 12 months ending on the date of the investment; and
- the money invested by the VCT must be used by the recipient company wholly for the purpose of the company's qualifying trade within two years.

A VCT can invest up to 15% of its money in a single company. Each company can receive up to £5 million of VCT or other tax-efficient funding in any 12-month period, with a cap of £12 million over its lifetime (£20 million for knowledge-intensive companies).

The company must exist for the purpose of carrying on a "qualifying trade" or be the parent company of a trading group whose business as a whole meets the scheme's rules. The company must also have a permanent establishment in the UK. Most trades qualify, provided they are conducted on a commercial basis with a view to making profits. A trade will not qualify if one or more excluded activities together are a "substantial part" of that trade (broadly more than 20%).

The main excluded activities are:

- dealing in land and financial instruments (including property letting and development);
- financial activities;
- providing legal or accountancy services;
- leasing or letting assets on hire;
- receiving royalties or licence fees;
- farming, market gardening, or forestry;
- operating or managing hotels, guesthouses, hostels, nursing, or residential care homes.

4.4.3 Withdrawal of the Relief

The VCT scheme income tax relief can be withdrawn if:
- the shares in the VCT are disposed of within five years of issue (this only applies to the 30% relief; the exemption on dividends is not subject to the minimum holding period); or
- HMRC's approval of the VCT is withdrawn within five years of issue.

As the relief is a tax reducer relief, the withdrawal of the relief must be made at the same rate of tax as when it was provided. Where the relief is clawed back, additional tax will be due for the tax year in which the relief was originally claimed.

4.5 The Enterprise Investment Scheme

The Enterprise Investment Scheme (EIS) is broadly similar to the VCT scheme except that it targets **direct equity** investment in higher risk, unquoted trading companies. As with the VCT scheme, generous reliefs (income tax and CGT) are available that recognise the commercial risk involved in such investments. The various CGT reliefs for the EIS are dealt with in detail in **Chapter 20, Section 20.3**.

4.5.1 Conditions of the EIS

As with the VCT scheme, extensive conditions are required to be met for a company and an individual investor to qualify for EIS relief.

Individual Investor Conditions
The main conditions for the investor to qualify are:

- they must subscribe in cash for new shares in the company;
- they cannot be "connected" to the company, i.e. they cannot be an employee or own more than 30% of the ordinary share capital, voting rights or rights available on winding up the company. With regard to connection, rights owned by a spouse or "other connected person" are included.

Investee Company Conditions

For the company being invested in, the main conditions are:

- it must be an unquoted trading company (which can include companies listed on the London Stock Exchange's Alternative Investment Market);
- the funds raised must be used by the company (or by a 90% subsidiary) in carrying out "qualifying trading activities" (see **Section 4.4.2** for definition);
- it must not be a 51% subsidiary (or be under the control) of another company;
- it must have fewer than 250 full-time employees on the date of issue;
- its gross assets must not exceed £15 million prior to, nor £16 million after, the investment;
- it must not have raised more than £5 million in Venture Capital Schemes (the VCT scheme, EIS or Seed Enterprise Investment Scheme) in the 12 months ending in the date of investment; and
- the money raised by the EIS share issue must be used for the purpose of the trade either within two years of the issue of the shares or within two years from the commencement to trade.

4.5.2   EIS Income Tax Relief

An individual investor can invest up to £1 million in new ordinary shares in an EIS company in a tax year and obtain relief at 30% against their taxable income as a tax reducer, providing that the shares are held for at least three years. Unlike the VCT scheme, the investment can be carried back and treated as if invested in the prior tax year. The carry back is subject to the caveat that the amount carried back plus any amount already subscribed in that prior year does not exceed the threshold for that earlier year.

For example, if £40,000 is subscribed in 2021/22, this could be carried back to 2020/21. However, if £990,000 had already been subscribed in 2020/21, only £10,000 can be carried back from 2021/22. Relief must be claimed within four years after the 31 January following the tax year of the investment.

4.5.3   Withdrawal of the Relief

The EIS income tax relief can be withdrawn if:

- the shares are no longer eligible shares;
- the individual is no longer a qualifying individual;
- the company is no longer a qualifying company;
- the company has failed to comply with the time limits for employing the money raised by the issue;
- the subscriber disposes of his or her shares within three years;
- the subscriber receives value from the company or a connected person within three years;
- the company purchases any of its own shares from a member who has not had relief within three years; or
- the subscriber disposes of any share capital or securities of the company to a person connected with the company.

As the income relief is a tax reducer relief, the withdrawal of the relief must be made at the same rate of tax as when it was provided. Where the relief is clawed back, additional tax will be due for the tax year in which the relief was originally claimed.

Although the company must be unquoted when the EIS shares are issued, there is no withdrawal of relief if the company subsequently becomes listed (unless there were arrangements in place for the company to be listed at the time of issue).

4.6   The Seed Enterprise Investment Scheme

The Seed Enterprise Investment Scheme (SEIS) is also designed to incentivise **direct equity** investment in new, smaller, start-up, higher risk, unquoted trading companies by offering substantial tax breaks to the investor. The SEIS is broadly similar to the EIS except that it targets relatively new companies that are in need of investment in order to kickstart their businesses. As with the EIS, generous reliefs (income tax and CGT) are available that recognise the commercial risk involved in such investments. The various CGT reliefs for SEIS are dealt with in detail in **Chapter 20**, **Section 20.4**.

4.6.1   SEIS Income Tax Relief

An individual investor can invest up to £100,000 in new SEIS ordinary shares in a tax year and obtain relief at 50% against their taxable income as a tax reducer, providing that the shares are held for at least three years. The increased inherent risk in investing in new start-up companies is reflected in a higher rate of income tax relief than for the EIS – 50% rather than 30%.

Like the EIS, the investment can be carried back and treated as if invested in the prior tax year again subject to the caveat that the amount carried back plus any amount already subscribed in that prior year does not exceed the threshold for that earlier year.

4.6.2   Conditions of the SEIS

As with the EIS, extensive conditions are required to be met for a company and an individual investor to qualify for SEIS relief.

Individual Investor Conditions
The main conditions for the investor to qualify are broadly similar to those for the EIS. However, an SEIS investor is allowed to be an employee of the company as long as they are also a director. In addition, there must be no:

- related investment arrangements (broadly where the investment is part of a reciprocal arrangement);
- linked loans to the investor or their associates which are linked to their subscription for shares; or
- tax avoidance, hence the subscription must be made for genuine commercial reasons and not as part of a scheme or arrangement the main purpose or one of the main purposes of which is the avoidance of tax.

Investee Company Conditions
The operation of the SEIS is also very similar to the EIS, though it is designed for much smaller companies, therefore the conditions are largely the same just that the scale is reduced. The following conditions must be met by the company being invested in:

- it must have less than 25 full-time employees;
- the total value of its assets must not exceed £200,000 before the share issue;
- the maximum it may raise under the scheme is £150,000;
- it must be less than two years old;
- it must carry on a genuine new trade;
- it must not be controlled by another company;
- the funds raised must be used by the company (or by a 90% subsidiary) in carrying out "qualifying trading activities" (see **Section 4.4.2** for definition) ;

- the company must not have previously raised money under either the EIS or VCT scheme, i.e. SEIS relief must be claimed as the priority; and
- the money raised by the EIS share issue must be used for the purpose of the trade either within three years of the issue of the shares or within three years from the commencement to trade.

Once a company has claimed SEIS, it can only seek EIS or VCT investment if at least 70% of the SEIS funds have been spent in its qualifying business.

4.6.3   Withdrawal of the Relief

The SEIS relief can be withdrawn in the same circumstances as for the EIS relief.

Questions

Review Questions
(See Suggested Solutions to Review Questions at the end of this textbook.)

Question 4.1

Jenna had employment income of £260,000 in 2021/22. She made gross pension contributions of £70,000 in 2021/22 and has unused annual allowance brought forward from the previous three years of £35,000.

Requirement
Calculate Jenna's annual allowance limit for 2021/22 and any annual allowance charge she may be required to pay.

Question 4.2

In 2021/22 Cathy's employment income is £650,000 and she has £200,000 of trading losses from her share of the losses from a partnership in which she is a partner. Cathy does not have an occupational pension with her employer but does contribute to a personal pension scheme.
  In 2021/22 she made gross contributions of £40,000 to her personal pension (her pensions annual allowance was £45,000 including £41,000 carried forward from the previous three years).
  Cathy wishes to make a claim for loss relief to set the trading loss in 2021/22 against her other income.

Requirement
Calculate how much of the £200,000 trading loss Cathy can use in 2021/22 in addition to the amount of tax saved as a result.

Question 4.3

Jonathan subscribed £100,000 for new ordinary shares in a VCT company in May 2021. Jonathan's income tax liability, before any relief for the VCT investment, is £50,000.

Requirement
Calculate Jonathan's income tax liability. What would the position be if his tax liability in the 2021/22 tax year was £20,000 before his VCT investment was taken into consideration?

Overseas Income and Additional Aspects of Property Income

Learning Objectives

After studying this chapter, you will be able to:

- Determine and calculate the UK income tax payable on income received by UK resident individuals from overseas sources, specifically savings, dividend, trading and property income from the Republic of Ireland (ROI).
- Explain the non-resident landlords scheme.
- Explain the tax treatment of furnished holiday accommodation.

5.1   Introduction

In this chapter we focus on the income tax treatment of various sources of overseas income. As the UK's nearest geographical overseas jurisdiction, the Republic of Ireland (ROI) is referred to but the rules set out in **Section 5.2** equally apply to those sources of income from other overseas territories. The implications of residence, domicile and deemed domicile for the taxation of overseas source income is set out in the table in **Chapter 2, Section 2.5**.

This chapter also covers the tax implications of a non-resident individual landlord receiving rent from a property in the UK and finishes by examining the special tax treatment afforded to furnished holiday accommodation.

5.2   Overseas Income

5.2.1   Overseas Savings Income

Overseas savings income is interest received by a UK resident individual from a non-UK bank, building society or other financial institution, e.g. from a bank account held in the ROI. Interest may also be paid from an overseas company to a UK resident individual.

If the **arising basis** of taxation applies, overseas savings income is taxed in the same way as UK savings income, i.e. at 0% for the starter rate band, 20% for the basic rate band and so on. The personal savings allowance may also be available.

Where the **remittance basis** applies because the individual is not UK domiciled or deemed UK domiciled, all income from the relevant source is treated as if it were non-savings income. It is then taxed in the same way as other non-savings income, i.e. at 20% for the basic rate band, 40% for the higher rate band and 45% for the additional rate band. The remittance basis and arising basis were covered in **Chapter 2, Sections 2.5** and **2.6** and should be revisited.

Whether the arising basis or the remittance basis applies, if the overseas savings income has already suffered tax deducted at source or a withholding tax and has thus been paid net of tax, it must be included in the income tax computation gross with double tax relief considered later (see **Chapter 2, Section 2.7**).

5.2.2 Overseas Dividend Income

Overseas dividend income is dividend income received by a UK resident individual from non-UK resident companies. Its treatment is similar to overseas saving income, with the distinction being between the arising basis and the remittance basis.

Thus, if the **arising basis** of taxation applies, overseas dividend income is taxed in the same way as UK dividend income, i.e. at 7.5% if it falls within the basic rate band; at 32.5% for the higher dividend rate band; and at 38.1% for the additional rate band. The dividend allowance of £2,000 applies in all instances.

Where the **remittance basis** applies because the individual is not UK domiciled or deemed UK domiciled, the overseas dividends are taxed as non-savings income and the 20% basic rate, 40% higher rate or 45% additional rate applies instead. The remittance basis and arising basis were covered in **Chapter 2, Sections 2.5** and **2.6** and should be revisited.

If the overseas dividend income is subject to dividend withholding tax (DWT) in the paying company's 'home' country, it should be considered whether a double taxation treaty (DTT) exists between the UK and that country. If a DTT does exist, under the double tax relief rules any DWT that has been paid will be deducted from the UK liability, up to the limit of the UK tax suffered (see **Chapter 2, Section 2.7**). As the dividend will have been received net of DWT, it must be included gross in the income tax computation.

Some DTTs have provision whereby an individual can apply for an exemption to the DWT before it is deducted. For example, the ROI has DWT of 25% on the gross dividend at the time of payment. However, residents in other EU Member States or residents of a country with a DTT with the ROI can apply for exemption from this Irish DWT. As the UK has a DTT with the ROI, no Irish DWT should be suffered by a UK resident receiving ROI dividends. As a result, double tax relief is not a consideration as the dividend will be received gross.

Example 5.1

A UK resident individual who is non-UK domiciled and not deemed UK domiciled, and who claims the remittance basis, receives an overseas net dividend of £25,000 in the 2021/22 tax year. The dividend is received net of withholding tax paid at 25%. The individual remits the £25,000 dividend to their UK bank account. The individual is a higher rate taxpayer.

The overseas dividend that is remitted would be taxed as follows:

	£
Dividend remitted to the UK	25,000
Add: withholding tax suffered	8,333
Gross dividend for UK purposes	33,333
UK dividend income tax @ 40%	13,333
Less: withholding tax (Note)	(8,333)
Tax payable	5,000

Note: Full relief on the overseas DWT paid is available as the overseas rate is lower than the UK rate.

5.2.3 Overseas Trading Income

Overseas trading income is trading income received by a UK resident individual from a business conducted wholly or mainly outside the UK. Profits of an overseas trade are computed under the same rules as for UK trades (see **Chapter 3** for a brief recap).

If the **arising basis** of taxation applies, overseas trading income is taxed in the same way as UK trading income, i.e. the 20% basic rate, 40% higher rate or 45% additional rate applies. The trading income allowance may also be claimed.

Where the **remittance basis** applies because the individual is not UK domiciled or deemed UK domiciled, overseas trading income is still taxed as non-savings income. The remittance basis and arising basis were covered in **Chapter 2**, **Sections 2.5** and **2.6** and should be revisited.

Where the UK resident individual is also subject to taxation overseas on the profits of the overseas trade, double tax relief should be considered (see **Chapter 2**, **Section 2.7**). Should the foreign tax paid not be fully relieved in the UK, upon the making of a claim within four years of the end of the accounting period in which the excess foreign tax arises, the excess foreign tax can be carried forward without limit, or carried back to the previous three accounting periods on a LIFO basis. It may then be offset against UK income tax chargeable on income from the same qualifying overseas trade.

If a trading loss arises in the overseas trade of a UK resident individual, that loss may be used either against the person's other foreign income in the same tax year or it can offset against foreign trading income from the same trade by way of carry-forward or under the terminal loss relief rules (see **Chapter 3**, **Section 3.6**). It cannot be carried back.

An individual who is not UK resident is not liable to UK tax on the profits of trades carried on wholly abroad unless they have a "permanent establishment" in the UK.

A permanent establishment would include a fixed base, e.g. a shop, a place of management, a branch office or a construction site lasting over six months (as per the UK/ROI double taxation treaty). For example, if a ROI resident individual owns a shoe shop in the centre of Belfast, they will be taxed in the UK on profits from the permanent establishment, i.e. the shoe shop, but they will also be taxed on this income in the ROI as that is where they are resident. Relief will be available under the UK/ROI DTT to reduce the Irish income tax liability by any UK income tax suffered on the same profits from the shoe shop i.e. the double tax relief is not provided in the UK but in the country of residence.

5.2.4 Overseas Property Income

Overseas property income is property income received by a UK resident individual from a property not located in the UK, including the ROI. A UK resident individual who receives rents and other property income from abroad is treated as carrying on an overseas property business. Profits of an overseas property business are computed under the same rules as for UK property business (see **Chapter 3**, **Section 3.9** for a brief recap).

If the **arising basis** of taxation applies, overseas property income is taxed in the same way as UK property income (as non-savings income), i.e. the 20% basic rate, 40% higher rate or 45% additional rate applies. The trading income allowance may also be claimed.

Where the **remittance basis** applies because the individual is not UK domiciled or deemed UK domiciled, overseas property income is still taxed as non-savings income. The remittance basis and arising basis were covered in **Chapter 2**, **Sections 2.5** and **2.6** and should be revisited.

If an individual has both UK and overseas property income, they would be treated as two separate property businesses.

Where a UK resident individual makes a profit on an overseas property rental business, say in the ROI, relief will be given in the UK for any Irish tax paid in respect of the ROI property profit under the double tax relief rules. However, the amount of double taxation relief available will be limited to the UK tax on the ROI property rental profit (see **Chapter 2, Section 2.7**).

Losses on overseas property businesses are ring-fenced and can only be used against current-year overseas property profits and the excess carried forward against further overseas property income only.

5.3   The Non-resident Landlord Scheme

Individuals who are not UK resident under the statutory residence test (see **Chapter 2**) and who receive rental income from a UK property must be treated under the non-resident landlord (NRL) scheme. Basically, under the scheme the rental income is taxed at source at the basic income tax rate of 20% and the landlord's property income is received net.

To operate the NRL scheme, a non-resident landlord has a representative, either their tenant or collecting agent, designated as the "prescribed person" by HMRC. The prescribed person is required to make the requisite payments (20% income tax on rental payments to the non-resident landlord) direct to HMRC. A tenant who pays more than £5,200 per year (or the proportionate equivalent for a shorter period) is automatically the prescribed person; tenants who pay less than that amount do not have to operate the scheme unless requested to do so by HMRC.

The prescribed person is entitled to be indemnified by the landlord for such payments and to retain from the payments sufficient sums to meet their obligations to HMRC. The income tax due, less certain allowable expenses and deductions (see **Chapter 3, Section 3.9.3**), must be paid on a quarterly basis. The prescribed person must provide the non-resident landlord with an **annual certificate** on form NRLY showing details of tax deducted and paid, **by 5 July after the year end**.

Non-resident landlords will then set the tax deducted against their UK tax liability through their self-assessment.

Non-resident landlords can apply to HMRC to be excluded from the scheme and to receive their UK property income gross. HMRC must be satisfied that the non-resident landlord will comply fully with the self-assessment provisions, and that the following points are met:

1.   their UK tax affairs are up to date;
2.   they have never had any obligations in relation to UK tax; or
3.   they do not expect to be liable to UK tax for the tax year in which the application is made; and
4.   they undertake to comply with all their future UK tax obligations.

The landlord has the right to appeal against a refusal of their application or a withdrawal of previous approval.

Example 5.2
Derek is Irish tax resident and lets out an apartment in Belfast. He lets the apartment through a letting agency, which deducts tax on his quarterly rental income under the non-resident landlord scheme. In 2021/22, Derek has agreed a quarterly rental amount of £4,500. The letting agency charges a 10% fee on the gross rents. Derek incurred expenditure of £7,800 for repairing the property (all allowable expenditure) in 2021/22 and also paid £400 in accountancy fees in the tax year.

continued overleaf

Under the NRL scheme, how much will be paid in income tax?

Rental income per quarter	£4,500
Less: letting agent fee	(£450)
Net rental income	£4,050
NRL scheme (20% of net rents)	£810

Annual amount paid by the letting agent to HMRC: £810 × 4 = £3,240

When Derek prepares his property income computation for inclusion in his self-assessment tax return, he will calculate his tax liability as follows:

Rental income		£18,000
Less: expenses:		
Letting agent fee	£1,800	
Repairs	£7,800	
Accountancy fees	£400	(£10,000)
Property income profits		£8,000

The £8,000 property income profit will be fully covered by the personal allowance of £12,570. Therefore, no income tax will be due.

Derek will be due a refund of £3,240 from HMRC as he will be able to claim a credit in respect of the tax already paid by the letting agent.

Derek would not claim the £1,000 property income allowance as his rental expenses in 2021/22 are more than this amount.

5.4 Furnished Holiday Home Lettings

Furnished holiday homes (FHH) lettings are subject to favourable tax rules whereby the letting is treated as if it were a **trade** rather than under property income rules. This means that although the income is taxed as income from a property business, some of the more generous provisions that apply to actual trades also apply to FHHs.

The default basis for calculating profits and losses for FHH lettings is the simplified cash basis. However, where gross rental receipts exceed £150,000, an accruals basis must be used. This threshold is reduced proportionately where the FHH letting is not carried on for the whole of the tax year.

The income tax rules for FHHs are:

1. any finance costs incurred in respect of an FHH are not restricted in the same manner as with residential properties, meaning relief is not restricted to basic rate only;
2. the favourable tax rules apply to FHHs located in the UK or any state in the EEA; (the 27 EU Member States plus Iceland, Liechtenstein and Norway);
3. loss relief may only be offset against income from the same FHH business;
4. capital allowances are available on furniture, equipment and fixtures (relief is only available under the replacement furniture rules for other let residential properties);
5. the income qualifies as relevant earnings for pension relief (see **Chapter 3**, **Section 3.10**);
6. the basis period rules for trades do not apply; the profits or losses on an FHH must be computed for actual tax years (6 April–5 April);
7. on disposal/gift of an FHH property, the various CGT reliefs for traders, such as rollover relief (see **Chapter 16**, **Section 16.11.3**), gift relief (see **Chapter 16**, **Section 16.11.4**) and business asset disposal relief (see **Chapter 19**, **Section 19.1**), apply if the relevant conditions are met.

To qualify as an FHH, the property must be **furnished** accommodation and run on a **commercial basis with a view to the realisation of profit**. The property must also satisfy the following three conditions:

1. *Availability condition* – the accommodation is available for commercial letting as holiday accommodation to the general public for at least 210 days in the year.
2. *Letting condition* – the accommodation is commercially let as holiday accommodation to the public for at least 105 days in the year. The 105-days test can be met by making an election to average periods of occupation of any or all FHHs owned by the taxpayer. However, an averaging election must be made separately for properties in the UK and properties in an EEA country.
3. *Pattern of occupation condition* – during a 12-month period, not more than 155 days fall during periods of longer-term occupation. "Longer term" is a continuous period of more than 31 consecutive days during which the accommodation is in the same occupation, unless there are abnormal circumstances.

It is possible that a property could qualify as an FHH in one year but fail to qualify in the next year as the property was not actually let for enough days. In such cases the taxpayer can elect to treat the property as continuing to qualify as an FHH for the first year in which the letting condition is not met and, if necessary, the next year as well.

To qualify, the individual must have had a genuine intention to meet the letting condition in each year. This election must be made by the anniversary of 31 January following the first tax year in which the failure occurs.

If a landlord has both FHH lettings and other lettings, it is necessary to keep separate rental accounts to reflect the fact they are two separate property businesses. This is to clearly identify the profits and losses treated as trade profits and losses.

Questions

Review Questions
(See Suggested Solutions to Review Questions at the end of this textbook.)

Question 5.1

Laura is UK resident and domiciled and has the following income in 2021/22:

UK trading income	£165,000
UK bank interest	£500
Overseas bank interest	£1,000 (gross)

Overseas tax is paid at a rate of 15% in respect of the overseas interest.

Requirement
Calculate Laura's UK income tax liability for 2021/22.

Question 5.2

Sarah owns and lets three properties. In 2021/22 these give rise to the following property profits and losses for tax purposes:

	Profit/(Loss)
Flat in Hackney, London	(£2,000)
Apartment in New York	£20,000
Villa in Tuscany*	(£5,500)

* Not a furnished holiday home letting.

Sarah has no other income and she is UK resident and domiciled. Sarah is considering meeting the conditions for the Tuscany property to be a furnished holiday home letting.

Requirement
(a) Calculate Sarah's income tax for 2021/22.
(b) Set out for Sarah the conditions that must be satisfied in order for the Tuscan villa to be a furnished holiday letting and recalculate her 2021/22 income tax as if it did qualify as such in 2021/22.

Question 5.3

Marc is UK resident and domiciled. He had the following sources of income in 2021/22:

UK trading income	£65,000
UK bank interest	£2,500
Overseas trading income	£20,000

Marc paid foreign tax of £9,000 in respect of his overseas trade.

Requirement
Calculate Marc's income tax for 2021/22.

Employment Income – Additional Aspects

6.1 Introduction

This chapter mainly focuses on the income tax treatment of **specific employment income** within UK tax legislation. The more general rules around the taxation of employment income were covered on the CA Proficiency 1 course and should be revisited (see also **Chapter 3, Section 3.7** for a brief recap).

First it is important to understand the distinction between general employment income (sometimes referred to as "general earnings") and "specific employment income". The distinction is recognised in the Income Tax (Earnings and Pensions) Act 2003 (ITEPA 2003) and is broadly split as follows:

■ **General earnings** are an individual's employment earnings plus the cash equivalent of any (taxable) non-monetary benefits.
■ **Specific employment income** includes:
- payments on termination of employment, such as non-statutory redundancy payments or ex-gratia or compensation payments on retirement or dismissal; and
- share-related income.

6.2 Payments on Termination of Employment

Lump sum payments made on the termination of employment, often known as 'golden handshakes', are taxable under the normal general employment income rules where they are treated as payment for employment services rendered. Such payments can include payment for work performed prior to the termination of employment, a terminal bonus paid as part of the final payment to the employee and based on work performed as an employee or payments in lieu of notice.

Where the payment does not fall within those general rules, it is taxable under special rules, subject to an exemption for the first £30,000 (section 401 ITEPA 2003), i.e. as specific employment income. Amounts in excess of the first £30,000 are taxable as earnings. From 6 April 2020, an employer must pay Class 1A national insurance contributions (NICs) at 13.8% on the excess over £30,000; employee's Class 1 NICs are not payable.

Generally, where the employee is entitled to receive the payment, whether implicit (by custom or practice) or explicit (actual written documentation), it is taxable under PAYE as earnings.

Where a payment is made by way of compensation for breach of the employment contract, it falls under the special rules (i.e. first £30,000 exemption). It should also be noted that statutory redundancy is not taxable, but it does use part of the exempt £30,000 threshold.

6.2.1   Payment in Lieu of Notice and Compensation for Loss of Office

All payments in lieu of notice (PILONs), whether contractual or not, are treated as taxable earnings and are therefore subject to income tax.

Employers must identify the amount of basic pay the employee would have received if they had worked their notice period, even if the employee leaves the employment part way through that notice period. The amount of pay that the employee receives for their notice period is referred to as the post-employment notice pay (PENP) and this amount is fully taxable as earnings and is not eligible for the £30,000 exemption. Any payment in excess of the PENP counts towards the £30,000 exemption.

Example 6.1

Alice has a monthly salary of £5,000 and is required to give a notice period of three months. In 2021/22 Alice was dismissed without notice and given a termination payment of £25,000, the equivalent of five months' salary.

Alice's PENP is £15,000 (£5,000 per month × 3 months). This £15,000 is taxable as earnings. The remaining £10,000 falls within the £30,000 exemption and will be tax-free.

Example 6.2

George has an annual base salary of £40,000 and a notice period of three months. In 2021/22 George's contract is terminated with immediate effect but he is given a termination payment of £35,000, comprising £20,000 as compensation for loss of office and £15,000 as a non-contractual PILON.

George's PENP is £10,000 (£40,000 per annum/12 × 3 months). This £10,000 is taxable as earnings. The remaining £25,000 is a non-contractual payment, which is in excess of the PENP and therefore falls within the £30,000 exemption and will be tax-free.

Example 6.3

Helena was made redundant in May 2021. She received £5,000 statutory redundancy pay and £18,000, under the terms of her contract, as a PILON (which was equivalent to three months' salary). Her contract required a three-month notice period. She also received £36,000 as compensation for loss of office; this was not a contractual entitlement.

Confirm the treatment of each type of income and calculate the total taxable income.

1. The statutory redundancy payment of £5,000 is exempt.
2. The PILON of £18,000 is equivalent to her PENP and is therefore fully taxable.
3. The compensation for loss of office is entirely ex-gratia, meaning that the £30,000 exemption is available – although it will be reduced by the statutory redundancy payment.

Total taxable income is:

	£	£	£
PILON/PENP			18,000
Compensation for loss of office		£36,000	
Less: exemption	£30,000		
Less: statutory redundancy	(£5,000)	(25,000)	
		11,000	11,000
			29,000

6.2.2 Redundancy Payments

Payments in respect of genuine redundancy (where the post originally held no longer exists, etc.) are taxable under the special rules and the first £30,000, including any statutory redundancy, is exempt from income tax. As noted earlier, although statutory redundancy itself is not taxable, it does use part of the exempt £30,000 threshold.

6.2.3 Exempt Payments

Certain termination payments may be completely exempt (rather than only up to the £30,000 limit). Such payments include payments on the accidental death of the employee or on account of injury or disability.

Where the payment is in the nature of a compensation payment made in respect of an employee's injury or disability and the disability or injury prevents the employee from carrying out the duties of their employment, the payment is potentially fully exempt from both income tax and NICs.

For the exemption to apply there must be an identified medical condition that prevents the employee from carrying out their duties at the time that the employee terminates their employment, and the payment must be made only on account of that disability. However, the medical condition does not need to have resulted from some failure, omission or commission of the employer and can be completely unrelated to the employment.

6.2.4 Miscellaneous

Payments and other benefits provided in connection with the termination of employment (or a change of terms of employment) are taxable in the year in which they are received. For this purpose, "received" means when it is paid or when the recipient becomes entitled to it (for cash payments) or when it is used or enjoyed (for non-cash benefits). Non-cash benefits are taxed by reason of their cash equivalent.

HMRC regards payments notionally made as compensation for loss of office, but which are made on retirement or death (not accidental death, which is exempt), as lump sum payments under the unapproved pension scheme regime and, therefore, taxable in full. An employee may, on leaving or at some later date, accept a limitation on their future conduct in return for a payment (restrictive covenant). In these circumstances, the payment is taxable in full as general earnings.

If the termination package is a partly exempt one and exceeds £30,000, then the exempt limit is allocated to earlier benefits and payments. In any particular year, the exemption is allocated to cash payments before non-cash payments.

Unfair dismissal payments are eligible for the £30,000 exemption. Employees have an obligation to report termination settlements to HMRC by 6 July following the end of the tax year. No report is required if the settlement is entirely cash.

6.3 Share-related Income

Shares and share options are a way of remunerating, rewarding or incentivising employees and directors. Share options arise when employees or directors are granted an option to acquire shares in the company or its parent company, at a fixed price, at some time in the future. The CGT treatment of share schemes is covered in **Chapter 18, Section 18.3**.

6.3.1 Share Schemes

When directors and employees acquire shares (and securities) in their employing company, income tax may be chargeable as specific employment income. For example, where:

■ A director or an employee is given shares or is sold shares for less than their market value, the employee is liable to income tax on the difference between the market value and the amount (if any) the individual paid for the shares.

The difference between market value and the amount paid may also be subject to NICs, but only where the shares represent readily convertible assets (i.e. are readily convertible into cash). This includes shares quoted on any recognised stock exchange and those where private trading arrangements exist before their acquisition (e.g. the imminent sale of a company whose shares have been acquired). It also includes where the issuing company is not entitled to a corporation tax deduction in respect of the shares awarded. Where the shares are readily convertible assets, Class 1 (employer and employee) NIC may be due. In addition, PAYE would apply. Where shares are not readily convertible assets, no NIC is due.

■ The employee has an option to acquire shares, the employee is liable to income tax on the difference between the market value of the shares when the option is exercised and the cost of the shares when the option is granted.

Example 6.4

Malcolm works for Sparks plc. He is granted a share option in consideration of services in his employment at a time when the shares are worth £1 per share. The option entitles Malcolm to acquire 1,000 shares at £2 per share. Four years later Malcolm exercises the option, pays £2,000 and acquires 1,000 shares which, at the time he acquires them, have a market value of £5,000 (£5 per share).

There is no liability to income tax in respect of the grant. However, Malcolm will be subject to income tax on £3,000 when the option is exercised. That is, he will be liable to tax on the difference between the market value of the shares when the option is exercised (£5,000) and the cost of the shares to him (£2,000).

To minimise or avoid the liability to income tax, there are a range of tax-efficient schemes approved by HMRC under which an employer may grant employees a stake in the business.

Table 6.1 below provides a summary of the main HMRC-approved share option schemes.

TABLE 6.1: SUMMARY OF HMRC-APPROVED SHARE SCHEMES

	Operation of Scheme	**Tax Treatment**
Save As You Earn Scheme (SAYE)	● Employee makes regular monthly investments up to £500 into special accounts. ● Investments are made for three or five years. ● A tax-free bonus is added to the account by way of interest. ● At withdrawal, employee can take money in cash or buy ordinary shares in the employing company under options granted when the employee started to save. ● The price that will have to be paid to exercise the options is fixed from the start. ● The option price must be at least 80% of the market value of the shares at the date the option is granted. ● Scheme must be open to all employees and all full-time directors on similar terms.	No income tax charge on the purchase of the shares using the employee's savings. (See **Example 6.5**).

Company Share Option Plans (CSOP)	● Employer may offer a CSOP under which employees are granted options on shares. ● There must be no discount offered on the shares i.e. share price must equal the market value at the time of the granting of the options. ● The tax exemption is lost if option is exercised earlier than three years or later than ten years after the grant. ● CSOPs do not have to be open to all employees/directors so key employees can be rewarded.	No income tax on either the grant of the option or on the profit arising from the exercise of the option between three and ten years after the date of grant of the option or on the disposal of the shares.
Enterprise Management Incentives (EMI)	● EMIs are intended to encourage experienced people to 'take the plunge' and leave established careers in large companies for riskier jobs in similar start-up or developing firms. ● The exercise of the options must take place within ten years of the granting of the option. ● Key employees can be selected and granted options over shares worth up to £250,000 at the time of the grant, in a three-year period. ● The employee must spend at least 25 hours each week or, if less, 75% of their working time working as an employee for the company whose shares are subject to the EMI option or for a qualifying subsidiary (known as the 'working time condition').	● No income tax or NICs are chargeable on either the grant or exercise of the options under an EMI scheme, provided the exercise price is the market value of the shares at the date of the grant. ● If options are granted at a discount, the discount is subject to income tax at the date of exercise. ● When someone sells shares acquired via EMI options, they may qualify for business asset disposal relief (BADR), provided the share options were granted at least two years prior to the date of disposal or the date the company ceased trading and the options are exercised within 10 years of grant. Unlike the normal conditions for BADR, there is no need for the option holder to own 5% of the share capital. The other conditions for BADR must still be met, i.e. the trading test and the officer/ employee test.
Share Incentive Plans (SIPs)	There are four ways you can get shares under SIPs: 1. **Free shares** – employee can be given up to £3,600 of free shares in any tax year. Employer must offer 2. **Partners** a minimum amount to each employee on similar terms **hip shares** – employee can buy shares out of salary before tax deductions up to the lower of either £1,800 or 10% of income for the tax year. 3. **Matching shares** – employer can give up to two free matching shares for each partnership share bought by employee. 4. **Dividend shares** – employee may be able to buy more shares with the dividends received from free, partnership or matching shares.	If SIP **free, partnership or matching** shares are kept in the plan for five years, no income tax or NICs are due on their value. No income tax is due on **dividend** shares if they are kept in the plan for at least three years.

Example 6.5

Sinead works for Spencer plc and is offered the opportunity to take part in its HMRC-approved SAYE option scheme. The share price was £4.25 at the time the SAYE scheme launched and the maximum discount of 20% was applied, so the option price was set at £3.40.

Sinead decides to save £8.50 a week and after three years in the SAYE scheme she has saved £1,224. She has the opportunity to buy Spencer plc shares at the option price of £3.40, despite the fact that the current share price is £10 per share.

Sinead can buy 360 shares. No income tax is due on the purchase of the shares.

Questions

Review Questions

(See Suggested Solutions to Review Questions at the end of this textbook.)

Question 6.1

How much of the following income would be taxable as employment income in 2021/22?

(a) £100,000 wholly ex-gratia payment received on termination of a job in the Civil Service.
(b) £5,000 received due to legal claim as a result of being hit by a passing car while carrying out duties of employment.
(c) £50,000 paid by employer's health insurance to employee who lost an arm in a factory accident and cannot return to work.
(d) Shares worth £2,400 granted to an employee by their employer for nil consideration.
(e) Shares worth £2,400 given to an employee by their employer via a HMRC-approved share incentive plan (SIP).

Question 6.2

Nuala Casey, a director of a company, was discharged from her employment contract on 30 September 2021. She received £90,500 compensation for breach of contract (this was not a contractual entitlement) and her salary from 6 April 2021 to date of discharge on 30 September 2021 was £33,750 gross (PAYE paid £7,300).

In June 2021, she also exercised her Enterprise Management Incentive scheme share options (which she was granted in 2016). She immediately sold and received £50,000 for the shares. The options cost £42,000 when she exercised the grant (which was the market value of the shares).

Requirement
Calculate Ms Casey's income tax liability for the tax year 2021/22.

Question 6.3

Mr Houghton retired from Liver Ltd on 30 June 2021 after 18 years' service. As a token of their appreciation, the board of directors of Liver Ltd voted him a lump sum of £65,500. This was not provided for in his contract of employment, but every employee who had previously retired from the company in the last six years had received a similar payment.

Mr Houghton had been paid a gross salary of £20,000 and PAYE of £7,000 was deducted to the date he retired in the tax year.

He was also able to exercise 20,000 tax-advantaged/approved share options that had been granted to him four years earlier under a HMRC-approved scheme (net gain arising was £30,000) and 5,000 share options under the same scheme granted to him 18 months ago (net gain arising £5,000).

Requirement

Calculate Mr Houghton's income tax liability for the tax year 2021/22.

Question 6.4

Gráinne Foley is an employee of Super Pizza, a fast-food restaurant chain. She has been employed by the company for 15 years and eight months and was made redundant on 6 April 2021. Grainne's notice period was one month. As part of her redundancy package she received the following:

Lump sum from approved pension fund	£8,000
Pay in lieu of notice (2 months' salary)	£1,200
Company car	£22,500
Compensation payment	£41,000

Gráinne also received dividends on shares she holds in a share incentive plan of £1,000, which were reinvested in shares in the relevant company.

Requirement

Calculate Gráinne's liability to income tax for the year 2021/22, assuming she had no other income.

Part Two

Corporation tax

Corporation Tax: Recap

Learning Objectives

This chapter is an overview of the cumulative knowledge of corporation tax required at CA Proficiency 2. Students should refer to their CA Proficiency 1 studies to understand the level of cumulative knowledge required and the necessary technical details.

In addition, the following areas are on the CA Proficiency 2 syllabus and will be new to you:

- The impact of residence on determining the beginning and end of an accounting period.
- The impact of residence/non-residence on the chargeability to UK corporation tax.
- Group payment arrangements for companies paying corporation tax instalment payments.
- The treatment of miscellaneous income.
- Where management expenses/surplus management expenses fit into the pro forma corporation tax computation.
- Additional adjustments to be considered in calculating the tax-adjusted trading result.
- The CT61 process.
- Qualifying charitable donations paid by investment companies.
- An overview of other types of distribution by companies.
- The corporate capital loss restriction rule applicable from 1 April 2020.
- Anti-avoidance rules for trading losses.
- The temporary extended loss carry-back rules for companies (as a result of Finance Act 2021).

Chartered Accountants Ireland's *Code of Ethics* applies to all aspects of a Chartered Accountant's professional life, including dealing with corporation tax issues. Further information regarding the principles in the *Code of Ethics* is set out in **Appendix 2**.

In addition, **Appendix 3** examines the distinction between tax planning, tax avoidance and tax evasion, which can arise in relation to all taxes, including corporation tax.

Students are reminded that it is their responsibility to ensure that they have the necessary **cumulative knowledge** of corporation tax from CA Proficiency 1 or other studies. This chapter is a recap of key corporation tax topics covered at CA Proficiency 1 and is not a substitute for detailed understanding of the cumulative knowledge required at CA Proficiency 2.

Students should also review this chapter to note the following changes resulting from Finance Act 2021, which you will need to be aware of for your CAP 2 studies:

■ the temporary extension of loss carry-back rules for companies (see **Section 7.9.1**).

7.1 Overview and Accounting Periods

Corporation tax is calculated by applying the relevant corporation tax rate to the company's taxable total profits (TTP). The financial year for corporation tax commences on 1 April and ends on the following 31 March. Corporation tax rates are fixed for financial years.

Corporation tax is payable by and levied on the profits of a company (defined as any "body corporate" or unincorporated association). Therefore, the computation of corporation tax requires the analysis of profits between the various sources of income and chargeable gains.

UK companies are required to prepare and file statutory accounts with Companies House in respect of the period of account. Companies report their liability to corporation tax to HMRC via the corporation tax self-assessment procedures and each company must calculate its own liability.

7.1.1 Accounting Periods

HMRC will issue a notice specifying the accounting period (usually 12 months) for which it considers a corporation tax return is due. While the corporation tax accounting period would normally follow the statutory period of account, there are specific rules that determine the date of commencement and cessation of a corporation tax accounting period.

Corporation tax is assessed on the TTP arising in the company's accounting period. Ordinarily this is the period for which the company makes up its accounts (the "period of account"), but an accounting period for corporation tax cannot exceed 12 months.

Commencement of the Accounting Period
For corporation tax purposes, the first accounting period of a company begins whenever the company comes within the charge to UK corporation tax. A company may come within the charge to UK corporation tax in one of several ways. Recap on these from your CA Proficiency 1 or other studies.

In addition, at CA Proficiency 2, it should be noted that a company not resident in the UK, which is carrying on a trade outside the UK, may become UK resident. In which case, its first accounting period will start on the day it becomes UK resident. A non-resident company may also be within the charge to UK corporation tax on certain of its income streams (see **Chapter 11, Section 11.2** for more details).

The End of the Accounting Period
An accounting period runs for a maximum of 12 months from its start but will end earlier if the company's own period of account is less than 12 months. A new accounting period starts immediately after the end of the previous accounting period (unless the accounting period ended because the company ceased to be within the charge to corporation tax). An accounting period can also end when certain other events happen. Recap on these from your CA Proficiency 1 or other studies.

In addition, at CA Proficiency 2, it should be noted that the end of an accounting period also occurs when:

■ the company begins to be resident in the UK; and
■ the company ceases to be resident in the UK.

The residence of companies is dealt with in detail **in Chapter 8, Section 8.2**.

Companies that Prepare Accounts for a Period of Less than 12 Months

For periods of account of less than 12 months that have resulted from a change in the normal annual accounting date of the company, HMRC has no special powers. However, when seeking to amend the accounting date of a company, the relevant company law conditions must be met.

For example, if a company has prepared a 12-month set of accounts to 31 December 2020, then an eight-month set of accounts to 31 August 2021 followed by a 12-month set of accounts to 31 August 2022, corporation tax is simply payable for each of the three accounting periods.

Companies that Prepare Accounts for a Period Exceeding 12 Months

As the maximum length of an accounting period is 12 months, where a company prepares a set of accounts for a period exceeding 12 months, this "period of account" must be divided into tranches, each a maximum of 12 months long. The first accounting period will always be at least 12 months long.

Each of the split periods will require the preparation of a separate company tax return and have separate due dates for the payment of corporation tax. There is only one filing deadline, however, which is normally 12 months after the end of the second period of account. Recap on the rules for the calculation of corporation tax where a company prepares accounts for a period of account more than 12 months from your CA Proficiency 1 or other studies.

7.2 The Charge to Corporation Tax

Corporation tax is assessed on the profits of companies for accounting periods. The question of whether, and how, a company is to be charged to corporation tax depends on whether or not it is resident in the UK. In the case of a company resident in the UK, the charge to corporation tax is imposed on all its income wherever arising and its chargeable gains wherever the assets were situated. The residence of companies is dealt with in detail in **Chapter 8, Section 8.2**.

Chapter 11 deals with the taxation of non-resident companies, as well as the area of double taxation relief (in situations where a UK resident company has a source of income or gains taxable both in the UK and in another country).

7.3 Rate of Corporation Tax

The main rate of corporation tax for single companies with a full 12-month accounting period for financial years 2020, 2021 and 2022 is 19%, chargeable on total taxable profits (TTP) irrespective of company size.

From financial year 2023 (i.e. from 1 April 2023), however, the rate of corporation tax will depend on a company's level of profits. The main rate will increase to 25% for a company with profits above £250,000. For companies with profits of £50,000 or less the rate will remain at 19%. Companies with profits between these limits will be charged at 25% but will be able to claim marginal relief (so the overall effective rate will fall between 19% and 25% depending on the amount of marginal relief available).

If a company produces accounts for a period of less than 12 months, TTP is still taxed at the main rate applicable to the relevant financial year(s).

If a company's accounting period straddles two financial years and the rate of corporation tax for each year is different, its TTP must be apportioned on a time basis for each year and the corporation tax rate for each financial year applied. HMRC reserves the right to amend this general rule if a more accurate and fairer estimate can be applied to the split between the financial years.

7.4   Payment of Corporation Tax

A small or medium-sized company's corporation tax is due and payable nine months and one day after the end of the accounting period. However, "large" companies are required to pay their corporation tax liabilities in up to four quarterly instalments. The number of quarterly instalment payments a company needs to make depends on the length of the accounting period and the number of related 51% group companies on the last day of the previous accounting period. Recap on the rules for related 51% group companies from your CA Proficiency 1 or other studies.

The following is an overview of the corporation tax instalment rules:

1. Determine if the company is "large" in the current period (i.e. divide the £1.5 million limit by the number of related 51% group companies on the last day of the previous accounting period. The company is large if the augmented profits (taxable total profits plus franked investment income (dividends received from shareholdings of 50% or less)) are greater than this threshold.
2. If the company is "large" in this period (but was not in the previous period), quarterly instalments will only be due in this period if augmented profits exceed £10 million. The £10 million threshold is also divided by the number of related 51% group companies at the end of the previous period.
3. If the threshold in 2. is not exceeded or if the corporation tax liability is less than £10,000, instalment payments are not required. If this threshold is exceeded and the company has a corporation tax liability in excess of £10,000, calculate the instalment payments using the following formula:

$$\frac{3 \times \text{corporation tax liability}}{\text{No.of months in accounting period}}$$

Each of the above limits of £10,000, £10 million, and £1.5 million are reduced where the accounting period is less than 12 months.

If the company is required to make instalment payments in the period, set out the due dates of each instalment.

Companies that are "very large" – one whose augmented profits exceed £20 million adjusted for the number of related 51% group companies at the end of the previous accounting period and if the company has an accounting period of less than 12 months – have different instalment deadlines. Recap on the due dates for corporation tax instalments from your CA Proficiency 1 or other studies.

7.4.1   Interest

If a company pays its corporation tax liability after the due date, then it will be charged late payment interest, calculated from the day after the normal due date until the effective date of payment. For companies required to pay in instalments, the position is considered after the due date for each instalment on a cumulative basis and the interest position is calculated by HMRC after the company submits its corporation tax return.

If a company has overpaid corporation tax, it may make a repayment claim and it will also be entitled to interest on the repayment.

Interest paid on underpayments of corporation tax is deductible for corporation tax and any interest received on overpayments is taxable as non-trade interest paid/received under the loan relationship rules (see below).

7.4.2 Penalties

Penalties can arise where a company fails to pay the correct corporation tax instalments. The penalty is an amount not exceeding twice the amount of interest charged on any unpaid amount in respect of the total liability of the company for its accounting period. Recap on the detailed rules for instalment payments from your CA Proficiency 1 or other studies.

7.4.3 Group Payment Arrangements

Group payment arrangements is additional material at CA Proficiency 2. Given the potential uncertainties over the tax liabilities of individual group members (see **Chapter 12**) and, until such time as all relevant group relief and other claims have been determined after the end of the accounting period, HMRC permits arrangements whereby instalments can be paid by one nominated company in the group and subsequently allocated among the group in line with their eventual individual final liabilities. This is particularly efficient from an interest perspective as often the final liabilities in groups are dependent on group relief allocations.

Companies that can enter into a group payment arrangement are a parent company and any 51% subsidiaries, i.e. any company of which it is the beneficial owner of more than 50% of the ordinary share capital. The 51% subsidiaries of those subsidiary companies, and so on, can also be included in the group.

7.5 Computation of Taxable Total Profits

The basic rule for the calculation of taxable total profits (TTP) of companies is that, apart from certain special provisions relevant only to companies, it is computed in accordance with income tax principles. However, capital allowances due to trading companies are treated as trading expenses for corporation tax purposes and not as a deduction from the assessable income as in the case of income tax (see **Chapter 3**).

There are a number of differences in treatment for certain items when computing a company's tax-adjusted profits from its statement of profit or loss for an accounting period. Recap on these from your CA Proficiency 1 or other studies.

The pro forma corporation tax computation is set out overleaf before being analysed in overview later in the chapter.

7.5.1 Adjustments in Arriving at the Trading Result

The tax-adjusted trading profits are arrived at after making a number of adjustments after capital allowances have been deducted, but before relief for unutilised trading losses carried forward from the same trade (see **Section 7.9**). When adding back expenses or making deductions, include an explanation of the tax treatment separately in the computation.

The starting point when calculating the tax-adjusted trading result is always the profit/(loss) before tax as calculated in the statement of profit or loss. In arriving at the adjusted trading profit/(loss) the following steps should always be considered:

1. Look out for receipts or income that are not taxable and deduct non-trading income and gains taxed under other rules.
2. Add back any expenses not properly associated with the trading activities.

TYPICAL COMPANY LIMITED
Corporation Tax Computation
for the 12-month accounting period to 31 March 2022

	£	£
Trading income:		
Tax-adjusted trading profits (see **Section 7.5.1**)	X	
Losses forward under section 45 CTA 2010 (see **Section 7.9**)	(X)	
		X
Property income (see **Section 7.5.3**)		X
Miscellaneous income (see **Section 7.5.2**)		X
Surplus non-trade loan relationship credits (see **Section 7.5.4**)		X
Chargeable gains (see **Section 7.5.5**)		X
"Total profits"		X
Deduct: management expenses/surplus management expenses carried forward (see **Chapter 8**, **Section 8.5**)		(X)
Deduct: surplus non-trade loan relationship debits (see **Section 7.5.4**)		(X)
Deduct: losses carried forward under section 45A CTA 2010 (see **Section 7.9**)		(X)
Deduct: qualifying charitable donations (see **Section 7.7**)		(X)
Deduct: Group/consortium relief (see **Chapter 12**, **Sections 12.1.2** and **12.1.3**)		(X)
Taxable total profits (TTP)		X
Corporation tax @ 19%		X

Deduction of Non-trading Income and Gains Taxed under other Rules
When a source of income or profit is not taxable as trading income or is exempt from corporation tax, it is deducted in the adjustment of trading result computation and then treated accordingly. The main types of income or profit include, but are not limited to, the following:

- *Interest received* Once deducted it is generally taxed under the loan relationship rules (see **Section 7.5.4**).
- *Property income/rents* Taxed as property income after deducting allowable expenditure (see **Section 7.5.3**).
- *Dividends received from other companies* Should be exempt from UK corporation tax (see **Section 7.8.2**).
- *Profit on disposal of fixed assets* If capital allowances have been claimed, broadly you should deduct the proceeds in the capital allowances computation. If the asset is also a chargeable asset, then compute the chargeable gain/loss position (see **Section 7.5.5** and **Chapter 13**, **Section 13.3**).

Add-back of Expenses not Properly Associated with Trading Activities

When an expense falls to be disallowed, it is added back in the adjustment of trading result computation. The following is a summary of expenses commonly disallowed.

1. Expenses or losses of a capital nature, includes:
    - Depreciation.
    - Loss on sale of fixed assets (if capital allowances have been claimed, broadly you should deduct the proceeds in the capital allowances computation. If the asset is also a chargeable asset, remember to compute the chargeable gain/loss position.
    - Purchase of fixed assets and improvements of a capital nature.
    - Amortisation of goodwill unless it is allowable under the corporate intangibles regime (see **Chapter 8, Section 8.4**).
2. Expenses not wholly and exclusively for the purposes of the trade or business, includes:
    - Rental expenses (though these may be allowable against property income).
    - Political donations – never allowed.
    - Qualifying charitable donations – added back and then allowed later as a deduction from total profits (see **Section 7.7**).
    - Fines, etc. related to tax (however, see the position in respect of interest paid/received in respect of corporation tax (see **Section 7.4.1**).

There are also specific rules in respect of different categories of expenditure. Recap on the treatment of certain specific items and the treatment of provisions from your CA Proficiency 1 or other studies.

At CA Proficiency 2, the following adjustments also need to be considered when calculating the tax-adjusted trading result:

- Where a car is leased, a disallowance of 15% of the leasing costs will apply where the CO_2 emissions of the car are greater than 50g/km.
- Research and development (R&D) expenditure – see **Chapter 8, Section 8.3**.
- Payments for intangible assets – see **Chapter 8, Section 8.4**.
- Key person insurance – where there is a personal benefit to a key person policy and the premiums are paid on behalf of a participator or an associate of a participator of a close company (see **Chapters 9** and **10**), the amounts are disallowed for corporation tax and will result in the participator being taxed on the premiums paid as a distribution, i.e. a dividend (see **Section 7.8.1**). If the participator, or their associate on whose behalf the premiums are paid, is an employee or director of the company, then the premiums will be allowable for corporation tax as they will be taxed on the individual personally as a benefit in kind.
- Delayed payment of royalties to a related party – a special rule applies where a royalty:
    - is payable by a company to, or for the benefit of, a 'related party' and is accrued in the accounting period; and
    - it is not paid within 12 months of the end of the accounting period in which it is accrued; and
    - its receipt is not at some time fully taxable on the recipient.

In such circumstances, the royalty will only count as deductible when it is actually paid and should therefore be added back in the corporation tax computation for the period in which it is accrued.

Section 835 CTA 2009 sets out four cases in which A (a natural person or a legal entity, including a company) is a related party of B (a company). The four cases are:

1. where A is a company and either A or B controls/has a major interest in the other;
2. where A is a company and both companies are under the control of the same person;
3. where B is a close company and A is either a participator/an associate of a participator in B or is a participator in a company that has control of B (see **Chapters 9** and **10**); or
4. where A and B are companies within the same group (see **Chapter 12**).

■ Transfer pricing adjustments – see **Chapter 14**. Note that transfer pricing adjustments may also arise in other elements of the computation of taxable total profits as the rules apply to all transactions between connected parties, not just the sale of goods. Thus, transfer pricing adjustments may also need to be made in relation to royalties and loan relationships.

■ Employee share schemes – the costs of setting up employee share schemes and employee share ownership trusts are capital expenditure and, therefore, would not be an allowable deduction in computing taxable profits under ordinary principles. This would include any initial amount settled to bring a trust into existence. However, specific statutory deductions are given for the costs of setting up the following approved schemes:
  ● share incentive plans;
  ● savings-related share option schemes; and
  ● company share option plans.

These specific statutory deductions are given for the accounting period in which the expenditure is incurred, except where the scheme is approved more than nine months after the end of that period. In that case, the expenditure should be disallowed for the period of payment, and allowed instead in the period in which the scheme is finally approved.

If a scheme has been used to grant options or transfer shares before the date of approval, the costs of setting up the scheme are not allowable.

An employer's expenditure in meeting the incidental costs of running an employee share scheme for the benefit of its employees is revenue expenditure and therefore is allowable as a deduction in calculating taxable trading profits.

A company is also entitled to claim a corporation tax deduction on an employee's share option when the employee exercises it. The deduction claimable is the value of the shares under option at the date of exercise less the exercise price.

If the relevant accounts contain a share-based payment calculated in accordance with GAAP, this does not qualify for a corporation tax deduction and should be added back.

Share schemes and their income tax treatment are covered in **Chapter 6, Section 6.3**. The CGT treatment of share schemes is covered in **Chapter 18, Section 18.3**.

7.5.2 Miscellaneous Income

The treatment of miscellaneous income is additional material at CA Proficiency 2. Sections 979–981 of CTA 2009 charge corporation tax on the income of a company that is not already taxable under other corporation tax provisions. Income treated as miscellaneous income includes, but is not limited to:

■ any payment for a service where there is an agreement that the service would be provided for a reward;
■ any income that is not otherwise taxable and which is received under an agreement or arrangement;
■ any payment for the use of money that is not interest or is not within the loan relationships legislation (see **Section 7.5.4**).

7.5.3 Property Income

Companies are charged corporation tax on income arising from the letting of land and property, wherever situated. Income generated from land and property in the UK is aggregated into one "UK property business". Income from all land and property outside the UK is combined into the company's "overseas property business".

Property business profits/(losses) are computed in accordance with generally accepted accounting principles. Corporation tax is charged on the net income arising during the accounting period on an accruals basis. The cash basis, which applies to individual landlords by default, does not apply and is not available to companies.

Landlords of residential property can deduct the actual costs incurred on replacing furnishings in the company's accounting period. This relief is available for domestic items, including furnishings, appliances and kitchenware provided for the use of a lessee in a dwelling-house.

Interest is excluded from a property income computation; however, relief is instead obtained as a non-trading "debit" under the loan relationship rules (see **Section 7.5.4**).

Should a company receive or pay a premium in respect of a short lease (a lease of less than 50 years), the premium will be treated partly as a capital under the CGT rules (outside the scope of this textbook) and partly as income. Recap on the calculation and treatment of this from your CA Proficiency 1 or other studies in addition to allowable deductions/expenses in calculating property income of companies.

Property Income Losses

If a property company, carried on commercially, incurs losses in an accounting period on its rental business, these losses can be set against the company's total profits for the same accounting period. The treatment of property income losses was dealt on the CA Proficiency 1 course and should be revisited.

7.5.4   Loan Relationships

A loan relationship arises when a company lends or borrows money. This can either be:
- a creditor relationship (where the company lends or invests money); or
- a debtor relationship (where the company borrows money or issues securities).

Interest paid and related expenses (debits) or interest received (credits) by a company is relieved/taxed on the accruals basis. From a corporation tax standpoint, it is imperative to distinguish whether a loan relationship is trading or non-trading.

At CA Proficiency 2, students must also be aware of the corporate interest restriction rules and how they impact on the deductibility of trade and non-trade interest paid by a company (see **Chapter 12, Section 12.5**).

Trading Loan Relationships

Broadly, where a company either owes or is due monies for the purposes of its trade which arises under a loan relationship, then it is within the trading loan relationship rules. Any resultant credits and debits are included as trading receipts and expenses within the trading income computation and no adjustments are required.

If the company is the lender, it is very difficult for it to fall within the trading loan relationship regime unless the loans were entered into in the course of activities forming an integral part of its trade. The latter situation is only likely to be the case for companies in the financial sector.

Non-trading Loan Relationships

If a loan relationship does not have a trading purpose it will be a non-trading loan relationship. In such cases, any non-trade loan relationship debits must first be added back in the adjustment of trading profits. Any non-trade loan relationships credits must also be deducted in the adjustment of trading profits. This is followed by a separate 'pooling' exercise.

Note that if a company is an investment company (see **Chapter 8**, **Section 8.5**) which does not carry on a trade, there is no requirement to add back the non-trade interest paid and/or to deduct non-trade interest received initially as these have not been included in the trading result (because there is no trade). However, the pooling exercise referred to must still be completed to arrive at the net non-trading loan relationship result.

Pooling Exercise

Once the various adjustments to the trade result are made, a 'pooling' exercise is carried out where non-trading loan relationship debits and credits are combined to result in a net deficit or surplus. If a surplus results, it is taxable as "surplus non-trade loan relationship credits" and must be included in the calculation of total profits for corporation tax purposes (see the pro forma computation). If a deficit results, the company has a choice as to how it uses this (see **Section 7.9**).

7.5.5 Computation of Chargeable Gains

A corporation tax computation also includes chargeable gains of companies, net of any current-year or carry-forward capital losses (subject to the loss-restriction rule). Where a chargeable gain accrues to a company in an accounting period or arises on a gain transferred to the company under section 171A Taxation of Chargeable Gains Act 1992 (TCGA 1992) by another capital gains group member, the chargeable gain is included in the company's TTP. The gain calculated is after deducting both allowable capital losses in the current accounting period and those brought forward from previous years (see **Section 7.9.1**). Chargeable gains in the context of companies and groups of companies is dealt with in detail in **Chapter 13**.

The main category of disposals that will be relevant to companies will be the disposal of land and property, goodwill (acquired or created before 1 April 2002) and shareholdings. Companies may also dispose of assets that fall under the chattels rules (see **Chapter 16, Section 16.9**).

Basic Computation

The basic calculation for companies is broadly computed in accordance with normal CGT principles, with four important exceptions:
1. A company does receive the CGT annual exemption.
2. Companies are able to avail of indexation allowance (but up to 31 December 2017 only).
3. For assets acquired pre-31 March 1982, a company has a choice between using the original base cost of the asset (and any related costs of acquisition and enhancement expenditure incurred prior to that date) or the 31 March 1982 value can be used, if higher.
4. A company pays corporation tax, not capital gains tax, on a chargeable gain.

Capital Losses

The above basic calculation could result in a capital loss, for which see **Section 7.9.1**.

Substantial Shareholdings Exemption

The substantial shareholdings exemption (SSE) is additional material at CA Proficiency 2. It is an important exemption and is dealt with in detail in **Chapter 13**. In essence, the SSE, subject to all the relevant conditions being fulfilled, will result in there being no chargeable gain on the disposal of shares (or an interest in shares) held by a company in another company. As such, it should always be considered where a company disposes of shares. Gains on the disposal of shares that do not qualify for the SSE should be included in the corporation tax computation and are subject to corporation tax in the usual way.

7.6 Income Tax on Annual Payments

Banks, building societies, etc. are not required to deduct income tax from interest paid, i.e. this source of income is paid gross. A company, however, must deduct 20% basic rate income tax when making certain relevant payments. The deduction of income tax by the company must follow the CT61 process (see below), which is additional material at CA Proficiency 2. Certain annual interest may be paid without deduction of tax. Recap on these rules from your CA Proficiency 1 or other studies.

Prior to 1 June 2021, payments made by a UK company or a UK permanent establishment of an overseas company to an EU-associated company were exempt from UK withholding tax. To qualify, the UK company had to own at least 25% of the shares in the recipient (or vice versa), or a third company had to directly hold at least 25% of the shares in both. From 1 June 2021 this no longer applies and withholding tax will be charged on interest payments to EU-associated companies, unless reduced under the terms of a double tax treaty.

7.6.1 CT61 Process

Form CT61 must, potentially, be completed a maximum of five times during an accounting period, namely on four defined quarter dates plus the date coinciding with the end of the accounting period (if this differs to one of the normal calendar year quarter-ends). Thus, a company with a year ended 31 March 2022, may have to complete CT61s for the quarters ending 30 June 2021, 30 September 2021, 31 December 2021, and 31 March 2022. If a company's year end is different from any of these, it will have five return periods. For example, for a company with a year end of 31 January 2022, the return periods would be:

- 1 February 2021 to 31 March 2021;
- 1 April 2021 to 30 June 2021;
- 1 July 2021 to 30 September 2021;
- 1 October 2021 to 31 December 2021; and
- 1 January 2022 to 31 January 2022.

The return for each period and any tax is due 14 days after the end of the return period. For example, the return for the quarter to 31 March 2022 would be due by 14 April 2022. Interest, at the current rate of 2.6% per annum, is charged on any overdue or underpaid amount. Penalties can also arise for late submission.

7.6.2 Credit for Tax Suffered

If a company receives a payment from which UK income tax has been deducted, the grossed-up amount is included within the company's corporation tax computation in that accounting period.

If a company both makes and receives payments from which it deducted income tax and had it deducted, respectively, then as well as completing the relevant CT61 form for the period in which the various payments were made, the company must also consider the net income tax position at the end of the accounting period. If the tax suffered on income exceeds the tax deducted from amounts paid net, then this excess is reclaimed by subtracting it from the company's corporation tax liability.

7.7   Qualifying Charitable Donations

A payment made to a charity by a company may be a qualifying charitable donation (QCD) if certain conditions are met (beyond the scope of this textbook). QCDs include:

■ cash donations; and
■ gifts of shares quoted on a recognised stock exchange; and
■ gifts of UK land or buildings.

For cash donations, the amount paid to charity is first added back in the adjustment of trading profits and then deducted from total profits in arriving at taxable total profits for the chargeable accounting period in which the donation is made.

For gifts of shares or UK land/buildings, it is the market value at the date of the gift that is treated as a QCD. Again, these are first added back and then later deducted from total profits.

Under section 1300(5) CTA 2009, QCDs made by a company are deducted from the company's total profits for the period after any other relief from corporation tax, other than group relief/consortium relief (see **Chapter 12**).

The amount of the deduction is limited to the amount that reduces the company's TTP for the period to nil. This may result in the company's QCDs being wasted. Recap on the treatment of QCDs from your CA Proficiency 1 or other studies.

At CA Proficiency 2, students must also understand that if a company has an investment business, excess QCDs can be carried forward as management expenses (see **Chapter 8, Section 8.5**) and that it may also be possible for group/consortium companies to relieve excess QCDs (see **Chapter 12**).

7.8   Distributions

7.8.1   *Distributions Paid by UK Companies*

For corporation tax purposes, no deduction is allowed in computing income from any source for dividends or other distributions paid by a company.

For corporation tax purposes, the distribution rules also apply whenever cash or assets are passed to the company's members or where certain interest and benefits are paid to, or on behalf of, participators/associates of participators by close companies (see **Chapters 9** and **10**). These will have been included in the statement of profit or loss and will therefore have to be added back in the company's corporation tax computation.

However, where the payment relates to a member/participator who is an employee or director of a close company, the payment is taxed as employment income and is thus deductible for corporation tax.

Distributions can take a variety of forms and include, but are not limited to:

1. Dividends paid by a company.
2. Any distribution out of assets in respect of shares (except any part that represents a repayment of capital).
3. Sale or transfer of assets by a close company at undervalue to a non-working participator/associate of a participator may be treated as a distribution.
4. Interest payments in excess of a normal commercial rate of return paid to a non-working participator/associate of a participator which may be treated as a distribution.

5. Certain expenses incurred by a close company in the provision of benefits for a non-working participator/associate of a participator which may be treated as a distribution.
6. Company purchase of own shares – if the conditions for the capital treatment are not met (see **Chapter 21**).

Points 3-5 inclusive are covered in more detail in **Chapter 10**.

7.8.2 Distributions Received by UK Companies

Due to a wide range of exemptions, most dividends received by UK companies are likely to be exempt from corporation tax. Such dividends must therefore be deducted from the adjustment of trading result.

Dividends received from non-group companies are referred to as franked investment income (FII). The concept of FII is only relevant when calculating augmented profits for the purpose of the instalment payment rules for corporation tax (see **Section 7.4**).

The dividend exemption rules, and how they work, depend on whether the recipient company is a "small company" or a "large company". Recap on these rules from your CA Proficiency 1 or other studies.

7.9 Corporate Loss Relief

The following table is a brief overview only of some of the different types of losses of a single company. It is recommended that students recap on the detailed rules for company loss relief from their CA Proficiency 1 or other studies.

In addition, Finance Act 2021 temporarily extended the loss carry-back rules for companies, of which you will need to be aware of for your CAP 2 studies. At CA Proficiency 2, students must also be familiar with the group and consortium loss relief rules – see **Chapter 12**.

SUMMARY OF LOSS RELIEFS

Type of Loss	Current Year	Carry Back	Carry Forward*	
			Pre-1 April 2017	Post-1 April 2017
Trading loss	• Set off against profits before QCDs • 'All or nothing' claim – partial claims not permitted	• Carried back against total profits of the previous 12 months before QCDs*** • A current-year claim must be made before the excess trading loss is carried back • 'All or nothing' claim	Carried forward against future trading profits of the same trade in the same company	Carried forward against total profits in the company**

Non-trade loan relationship deficits	Set off against profits before QCDs in preference to trading and property losses – **can be tailored**, hence a partial claim is possible	• Carried back against non-trade loan relationship surpluses of previous12 months • 'All or nothing' claim • Losses can be carried back even if a current-year claim not made	[Beyond scope of this textbook]	Carried forward against total profits of the company**
UK property losses	Mandatory set off against profits before QCDs in preference to trading losses– **cannot be tailored**, hence a partial claim is not possible	Cannot be carried back	[Beyond scope of this textbook]	Carried forward against total profits of the company**
Management expenses (in relation to investment companies; see **Chapter 8, Section 8.5**)	Mandatory set off against profits before QCDs in preference to trading losses – **cannot be tailored**, hence a partial claim is not possible	Cannot be carried back	[Beyond scope of this textbook]	Carried forward against total profits of the company**

*The use of losses carried forward is subject to the relevant deductions allowance of £5 million (adjusted, if necessary, for periods of less than 12 months). Note that the deductions allowance that applies to the offset of carried-forward losses is a group-wide threshold (see **Chapter 12** for further detail on group relief).

These losses can also be surrendered as group relief/consortium relief (see **Chapter 12).

*** For accounting periods ending between 1 April 2020 and 31 March 2022, the period over which trading losses can be carried back is extended from 12 months to three years. A maximum of £2 million can be carried back against total profits before QCDs of the two earlier years (see **Section 7.9.1**).

7.9.1   *Temporary Extension to Loss Carry-back Rules for Companies*

Where a trading loss arises to a company in an accounting period ending between 1 April 2020 and 31 March 2022, the period over which trading losses can be carried back is extended from 12 months to three years. Companies will have to consider whether to make the extended carry-back claim and obtain the refund at the corporation tax rate of 19%; or keep the losses and obtain relief at (up to) 25% from 1 April 2023.

Losses must be carried back in order, with set-off against profits of the most recent year before earlier years. For example, for a company with a 31 December 2021 year end, the losses would be carried back first to 31 December 2020, then to 31 December 2019 and finally to 31 December 2018 (assuming the company has profits in those periods to utilise the losses).

The rules operate differently depending on whether the claim is being made by a standalone company or a company which is part of a group. The definition of a group for these purposes is largely based on the group relief rules, i.e. 75% ownership.

Extended loss carry-back claims must generally be made by the company in its tax return; however, claims below a *de minimis* limit of £200,000 may be made outside of the company's tax return. This rule may be useful in accelerating claims for tax repayments where losses are expected but the tax return is not yet finalised.

In calculating whether or not a claim is *de minimis*, a company must apply the following assumptions:

- any available claims in relation to capital allowances of the period (or any other claim or relief that would result in an increase in the amount of the loss) are made by the company;
- the company does not surrender any losses as group relief;
- the maximum permissible loss carry-back claims are made by the company.

It is only the amount of losses carried back to the two earlier periods which must be compared with this limit when assessing whether or not a claim is *de minimis*.

Standalone Companies

For standalone companies, the carry back of losses from the current accounting period to the previous year remains unchanged and is uncapped, as is the case under the normal rules. However, after carry back to the prior year, a cap applies to the carry back of the trading losses to the two earlier periods. Under the cap, the maximum amount of losses that may be carried back to the earlier two years is:

- £2 million for losses arising in accounting periods ending between 1 April 2020 and 31 March 2021; and
- £2 million for losses arising in accounting periods ending between 1 April 2021 and 31 March 2022.

This is regardless of the number of accounting periods falling within each of those 12-month periods. The losses being carried back is offset against total taxable profits before QCDs.

Example 7.1

A Ltd has a trading loss of £3,300,000 in the year to 31 December 2021. Profits of previous periods are:

31 December 2020	£1,100,000
31 December 2019	£1,750,000
31 December 2018	£1,250,000

Current rules which allow £1,100,000 of the current-year trading loss to be carried back to 31 December 2020 remain unaffected and therefore uncapped.

The temporary extension would allow A Ltd to carry back £1,750,000 (limited to the profits of the period) of the trading loss to 31 December 2019 and £250,000 (limited to unused amount of the £2,000,000 losses cap available for carry back) of the loss to 31 December 2018.

As the claim for the two earlier periods exceed the *de minimis* limit of £200,000 it must be made in the company's tax return. The remaining £200,000 of the trading loss will be carried forward for relief in future periods.

Example 7.2

X Ltd has trading losses (before capital allowances) of £500,000 for its accounting period ended 31 December 2021. It also has available capital allowance WDAs of £50,000 and a fellow group company with profits of £125,000 to which it could surrender losses as group relief.

The company's profits for the year ended 31 December 2020 were £225,000.

The profits of the prior accounting period must be relieved, leaving trading losses of £275,000. The losses could be increased by claiming the capital allowances for the 2021 period which would bring the losses available for relief to £325,000.

A surrender of losses to the fellow group company would reduce the available losses to £200,000 (within the *de minimis* level) but, as group relief notices of surrender may subsequently be withdrawn, that is not taken into account in determining the available amount.

X Ltd will therefore not be entitled to make a *de minimis* claim and must claim any extended loss carry back in its company tax return.

Group Companies

Where a company which is part of a group makes a non-*de minimis* claim (broadly, one exceeding £200,000), a group cap applies. This means that the claim can only be made where it, together with all other claims (including *de minimis* claims) made by the company and other members of the same group, does not exceed £2 million.

In addition to the cap, extra reporting requirements apply where a non-*de minimis* claim is being made. In such cases, a nominated company from the group must submit a loss allocation statement to HMRC showing how the £2 million cap has been allocated.

The group cap and the reporting requirements will not be triggered if all companies in the group only make *de minimis* claims.

As is the case for standalone companies, the extended loss carry-back claims must be made in a return, unless the claims are below the *de minimis* limit of £200,000.

Example 7.3

Five companies (A, B, C, D and E) make up a group for the purposes of the temporary extension rules. In the accounting period ending 31 March 2021, the companies have trading losses remaining, after carry back to the previous 12-month accounting period, as follows:

Company A	£150,000
Company B	£150,000
Company C	£200,000
Company D	£200,000
Company E	£1,500,000

Companies A, B, C and D have losses below the *de minimis* threshold and so are able to make claims in advance of submitting their returns for the accounting period.

Company E has up to £1,500,000 of losses to relieve. Since this amount exceeds the *de minimis* threshold, the group cap applies. A claim can only be made by E Ltd up to a maximum of £2 million after considering any claims made by other group companies. In addition, Company E must submit its claim in its return alongside an allocation statement (if it is the nominated company) showing all claims made within the group. The other claims total £700,000, meaning the group cap applies to restrict the amount Company E can relieve to £1,300,000.

7.9.2 Capital Losses

As noted earlier, a company is charged to corporation tax on its chargeable gains. The quantum of chargeable gains is reduced by any capital losses of the same period, as well as any unrelieved capital losses brought forward. It is not possible to carry back capital losses or to set such losses against other income, except in certain circumstances. Capital losses can only be set against chargeable gains of the current period or carried forward to set against future chargeable gains.

From 1 April 2020, capital losses carried forward for offset against future chargeable gains are also subject to the loss restriction rule. Recap on the loss restriction rule from your CA Proficiency 1 or other studies.

From 1 April 2020, the £5 million deductions allowance must be shared between carried-forward capital and income losses. The proportion of the allowance allocated to capital losses is referred to as the "chargeable gains deductions allowance". The amount of chargeable gains that can be relieved with carried-forward capital losses is restricted to 50% where they exceed the chargeable gains deductions allowance. Effectively, the maximum carried-forward capital losses that can be used against current-year capital gains is equal to:

■ the company's chargeable gains deductions allowance, plus
■ 50% of the current-year gains that exceed the chargeable gains deductions allowance.

Capital losses (both current-year and carried-forward losses) cannot be group-relieved. However, a group can achieve a similar result by netting-off its gains and losses by utilising the election in section 171A TCGA 1992 (see **Chapter 13**). A group of companies has only one deductions allowance.

Where a share disposal by an investing company meets the conditions for the substantial shareholdings exemption (SSE), the disposal of such shares is deemed not to be a chargeable gain. Thus, in the circumstances where a capital loss would otherwise arise, no capital loss is created for the investing company because the entire transaction is exempt from corporation tax. In this scenario, a capital loss can be created by breaking one of the conditions for the exemption which applies automatically when its conditions are satisfied. See **Section 7.5.5** and **Chapter 13, Section 13.2**.

Example 7.4

Prospero Ltd is a stand-alone company. In its accounting period ending 31 March 2022 the company has a chargeable gain of £12 million. The company has a capital loss carried forward at 1 April 2021 of £16 million and wishes to claim the maximum possible relief in 2022. The company has no other losses carried forward.

The company will pay corporation tax in 2022 as follows:

	£	
Chargeable gain		12,000,000
Less: capital loss carried forward (Note)	(8,500,000)	
Taxable total profits		3,500,000
Corporation tax @ 19%		665,000

Loss Memo	£
Capital loss brought forward	16,000,000
Utilised in 2022	(8,500,000)
Loss carried forward	7,500,000

Note: capital loss carried forward = £5 million deductions allowance + 50% of the remaining £7 million.

7.9.3 Anti-avoidance – Trading Losses

These anti-avoidance measures are additional material at CA Proficiency 2. The availability of unused trading losses carried forward is potentially valuable. If a company makes profits from its trade or has other sources of income against which the trading loss can be used under section 45A CTA 2010, it will not pay corporation tax until all the trading losses carried forward are utilised. Therefore a company with unused trading losses could be an attractive target for takeover by another company – the intention being to ensure that the loss-making company's trade is made profitable by the new shareholders (e.g. by transferring existing business to the loss-maker) and utilising the trading losses to offset against these newfound trading profits, thus reducing or eliminating its tax liability. This is called 'loss buying' or 'loss shopping'.

Anti-avoidance Test
Anti-avoidance rules are in place to limit the ability to do this type of planning. There are provisions to disallow the carry forward of trading losses incurred before a change in ownership of a company's shares. A change in ownership occurs when another company acquires more than half of a company's ordinary share capital. Only direct ownership changes are considered for this rule.

However, direct changes of ownership of more than 50% are ignored if the company concerned was a 75% subsidiary of the same parent company both before and after the change. The legislation is contained in sections 673–675 CTA 2010. The disallowance will apply if there is a change in the ownership of a company and either:

1. there is a "major change in the nature or conduct of a trade" carried on by the company within any period of five years (beginning no more than three years before the change in ownership) in which the change of ownership occurs (i.e. three years before or up to five years after the date of the change in ownership); or
2. at any time after the change in ownership, the scale of the activities in a trade carried on by the company has become small or negligible (and before any significant revival of the trade).

The provisions are designed to discourage the practice of purchasing shares in a company to obtain the benefit of accumulated trading losses carried forward.

In applying the provisions to the accounting period in which the change of ownership occurs, the part of the period occurring before the change of ownership and the part occurring after the change are treated as separate accounting periods. Apportionments are to be made on a time basis except where, to HMRC, it appears that that method would work unreasonably or unjustly.

A company that newly joins a corporation tax group for group relief purposes (see **Chapter 12**) is also treated as a change in ownership. However, for this rule to apply, neither 1. nor 2. above are required. Under this rule, any pre-acquisition trading losses cannot be surrendered as group relief for offset against group profits for a period of five years after the change in ownership.

Major Change in the Nature or Conduct of a Trade
A "major change in the nature or conduct of a trade" includes:

"(a) a major change in the type of property dealt in, or services or facilities provided in, the trade, or
(b) a major change in customers, outlets or markets of the trade."

Such a change will be regarded as occurring even if the change is the result of a gradual process that began outside the three-year period.

There have been a number of cases that have dealt with the meaning of a "major change in the nature or conduct of a trade" that provide some guidance on how these rules are to be interpreted and applied in practice.

Cases where it was held that there had been no major change in the nature or conduct of the trade, include:

- A company that had sold its products directly to customers, mainly wholesalers, then commenced to do the same through distribution companies.
- A company ceased to slaughter pigs and manufacture meat products and, for a temporary period of 16 months, distributed the same products manufactured by its parent company. After the 16-month period it recommenced slaughtering and manufacturing meat products.
- A company operating a dealership in one make of vehicle switched to operating a dealership in another make which served the same market.

Cases where it was held that there had been a major change in the nature or conduct of the trade, include:

- A company that carried on a business of minting coins and medallions from precious metals purchased its principal supplier's entire stock of gold and then purchased gold directly from wholesalers. This resulted in substantial increases in stock levels.
- A company that operated a retail chain of shops, changed its promotional policy by discontinuing the issue of trading stamps and reducing prices. The change resulted in a substantial increase in turnover.
- A company that changed from providing a service to being instead a primary producer.

In addition, HMRC's *Statement of Practice 10/91* also provides useful guidance.

7.10 Self-assessment and Administration

7.10.1. Notification, Filing and Amendment of Company Tax Returns

Companies are obliged to notify and report their liability to corporation tax to HMRC under the Corporation Tax Self-Assessment (CTSA) regime. It is the responsibility of the company to inform HMRC, in writing, within three months from when it comes within the charge to corporation tax; this is normally satisfied by completing and submitting form CT41G.

If a company fails to notify HMRC, then it will assume that the first accounting period will run for 12 months from the date of incorporation, which may or may not be the actual position.

A company that has not received a company tax return or notice to file must inform HMRC if it becomes chargeable to tax within 12 months from the end of the relevant accounting period. Penalties can arise for failure to notify and these are calculated based on the potential lost revenue to HMRC that could have arisen due to failure to notify (so this could be calculated on the basis of the corporation tax liability in the first accounting period). No penalty will be charged if the company has a reasonable excuse for failure to notify. The level of penalty will depend on how the failure to notify arose, and how HMRC became aware of it. Recap on this from your CA Proficiency 1 or other studies

Company tax returns must include a declaration by the person making it that, to the best of their knowledge and belief, the return is correct and complete. A complete company tax return should include:

1. completed form CT600;
2. any appropriate supplementary pages;
3. a copy of the relevant full statutory accounts;
4. a tax computation showing how the figures on the CT600 have been derived from the statutory accounts.

All companies and organisations are required to file their company tax return online in iXBRL format. A company tax return is due for filing online with HMRC by the due date, being the last day of whichever of the following periods is the last to end:

1. Within 12 months of the end of the accounting period.
2. If the company's statutory accounting period lies between 12 and 18 months, then 12 months from the end of the accounting period.
3. If the company's statutory accounts are for a period longer than 18 months, then 30 months from the beginning of that period.
4. Within three months of receiving a notice to deliver (where the notice has been forwarded late to the company).

Directors of UK companies are required to file statutory accounts with Companies Registry/ Companies House for every 12-month accounting period. In general, the corporation tax accounting period follows the statutory accounting period but, as set out earlier, for corporation tax purposes there are specific dates at which an accounting period will begin or end and these can differ from those for the statutory accounts.

If the statutory period of account is greater than 12 months, it is divided for corporation tax purposes into 12-month tranches and a residue period. The filing date for both returns is 12 months after the end of the period of accounts. However, there will be two deadlines for payment of corporation tax, providing the instalment payment rules do not apply.

A company can amend its return at any time within 12 months of the return's filing deadline (not the actual filing date) to make any amendments to the return. This could be, for instance, to revise a loss relief claim, amend a capital allowances claim, or correct an error. This time limit is not extended if a return is delivered late. If a return is delivered more than 12 months late, no amendment to the return can be made.

HMRC has nine months from the actual date of filing a return to correct any obvious errors in it. HMRC may also amend anything else in the return that the officer has reason to believe is incorrect in light of information available to the officer.

7.10.2 Penalties

If the company's tax return is filed within three months after the due date, it will incur a flat rate penalty of £100. The penalty rises to £200 after this and is increased to £500 and £1,000 where the failure occurs for a third successive time.

If a company fails to deliver a return within 18 months of the end of an accounting period (or a later filing date, if applicable), then the penalty becomes 10% of the unpaid tax at that date if it remains undelivered within two years of the due date, rising to 20% thereafter. These tax-geared penalties are in addition to the flat-rate penalties already incurred.

7.10.3 Company Records

A company must keep all business records and accounts until the latest of:

1. six years from the end of the relevant accounting period;
2. the date that any enquiries are completed; or
3. the date after which enquiries may not be commenced.

The maximum penalty for failing to preserve records is £3,000 per chargeable accounting period. See also **Chapter 1** for other administrative aspects for companies, including HMRC enquiries and amendment of company tax returns.

Corporation Tax: Miscellaneous Additional Aspects

8.1 Tax Transparency and Accountability Measures

The area of tax continues to attract attention globally, with public and media interest in the tax position of large multinationals of particular interest as 'tax transparency' and accountability remains high on the agenda of many governments. Over the last decade or more, the UK has introduced specific measures focusing on tax transparency and accountability: senior accounting officer's responsibilities, publication of large businesses' tax strategy and country-by-country reporting.

8.1.1 Duties of Senior Accounting Officers of Qualifying Companies

The senior accounting officer (SAO) legislation applies to certain large companies and is a measure targeted at the tax accountability of large businesses. Although all companies have an obligation to deliver correct and complete tax returns, compliance with this obligation can be compromised if the company's tax accounting arrangements are not fit for purpose. These arrangements range from how a company accounts for its business transactions, to how it works out its final tax liability. The SAO provisions apply to the tax accounting arrangements in place for the calculation of various taxes including, but not limited to, corporation tax, VAT, PAYE, and stamp taxes.

The legislation addresses the potential 'accountability gap' by making the SAO of a qualifying company responsible for ensuring that appropriate tax accounting arrangements are in place. In many cases the SAO will be the chief financial officer of the company or group.

Qualifying companies for this provision are generally UK incorporated companies, with either:

- turnover of more than £200 million, or
- a relevant balance sheet total of more than £2 billion,

in the preceding financial year, either alone or when results are aggregated with other UK companies in the same group.

The SAO is the director or officer with overall responsibility, as appropriately delegated, for the company's financial accounting arrangements. The company will judge who best fits this definition; in most cases it will be evident from established governance arrangements.

The SAO must take reasonable steps to ensure that the company establishes and maintains appropriate tax accounting arrangements. They must also provide HMRC with a certificate stating that the company has appropriate tax accounting arrangements or, if it does not, provide an explanation as to why not. The certificate must be submitted no later than the end of the period for filing the accounts for the financial year.

Penalties may arise for failure to comply with this legislation, as follows:

- a penalty of £5,000, assessable on the SAO, for failure to comply with the main duty of taking reasonable steps to ensure that the company establishes and maintains appropriate tax accounting arrangements;
- a penalty of £5,000, again assessable on the SAO, for failure to provide a certificate or providing an incorrect certificate; or
- a penalty where a company fails to notify HMRC of the name(s) of the person who was the SAO throughout the financial year.

8.1.2   Large Businesses' Tax Strategy

The requirement for certain large companies to publish their tax strategies online and free of charge to the public is a measure targeted at the tax transparency of large businesses.

The legislation applies to qualifying companies, which are defined as:

- UK-registered companies, partnerships, and permanent establishments of groups with turnover of £200 million or more, or gross assets of £2 billion or more, on the last day of the previous financial year; or
- multinational businesses with any operations (regardless of size) carried out through UK companies or permanent establishments that have consolidated turnover of €750 million or more.

For the purpose of this measure, a qualifying group comprises two or more relevant bodies, where one or more relevant body in the group is the 51% subsidiary of another relevant body in the group.

The legislation affects stand-alone companies, partnerships, and groups. Companies that are part of a UK group or a UK subgroup at the end of that group's previous financial year are not considered qualifying companies.

Minimum Information Requirements

The legislation requires the company to prepare and sign-off the company's UK tax strategy. HMRC's view is that board-level approval is likely to be required to satisfy this requirement. It must then be published on the internet, available to the public free of charge for a year. The minimum information that must be made publicly available in respect of UK tax is:

- The company's approach to risk management and governance arrangements in relation to UK tax.
- The company's attitude towards UK tax planning so far as it affects UK tax.
- The level of risk that a company is prepared to accept in relation to UK tax.
- The company's approach towards its dealings with HMRC.

There is no requirement for publication of the amounts of taxes paid (although this is a requirement for qualifying companies under the country-by-country reporting rules, see **Section 8.1.3**).

Publication Requirements
A company's tax strategy should be published for the first time before the end of the first financial year commencing after 15 September 2016. For example, for a company with a December year-end, the first year caught by these new rules was 31 December 2017.

If the company was a qualifying company in the previous financial year it must publish its tax strategy before the end of the current financial year and not more than 15 months after the day on which its previous tax strategy was published. Once published, the strategy must remain there until replaced with the following year's version.

It can be published as a separate document or a self-contained part of a wider document and does not need to be called a 'strategy' but can be referred to as a 'policy'. It must remain accessible to the public, free of charge for the period until the next year's strategy is published. The responsibility to ensure preparation and publication rests with the head of the group or subgroup.

If there are any stand-alone UK subsidiaries of a foreign group, these are treated as separate subgroups, i.e. that company would need to publish its own tax strategy.

Penalties
Penalties apply to the entity or group for failure to publish a tax strategy within the prescribed period that meets the legislative requirements, or for not making the strategy publicly available for the prescribed period. Penalties are assessed on the head of the group or subgroup.

The following penalties for non-compliance apply:

- Up to a maximum of £7,500 where the strategy is not published before the end of the accounting period or not publicly available for at least a year from publication.
  A warning notice will be issued for non-publication on or after the first day of non-publication. This allows 30 calendar days for publication; a penalty will apply from day 31 onwards.
- A further penalty of up to £7,500 if the strategy remains unpublished six months after the end of the accounting period.
- A further £7,500 per month thereafter until the strategy is published.

These penalties are subject to the normal appeals process. No penalty will arise if a business has a reasonable explanation for its failure to publish and if it remedies that failure without unreasonable delay.

In addition, companies should not discount the reputational risk of not complying with the legislation. Reputational damage could have a greater financial impact than any penalty imposed by the legislation.

8.1.3 Country-by-country Reporting

Country-by-country (CbC) reporting was introduced as part of the OECD's Base Erosion and Profit Shifting (BEPS) project to provide participating tax authorities, including the UK, with an overall picture of the worldwide position on the profit and tax paid by multinational enterprises (MNEs) operating in their jurisdiction. This legislation is another measure aimed at tax transparency.

Information reported under the UK's CbC legislation is designed to enable HMRC to make a more informed assessment of where tax risks lie. HMRC has stated that it intends to use CbC reports as part of its risk-assessment process for cross-border transactions, principally between members of a multinational group.

Qualifying Entities

An entity is required to submit a CbC report for any period, if it is part of an MNE group, and the MNE group meets the following criteria:

1. it has two or more enterprises that are resident for tax purposes in different jurisdictions; and
2. it had consolidated group revenue of €750 million in the previous period.

In the UK, where an MNE group meets these criteria, the CbC obligations are imposed on the UK ultimate parent entity (UPE). If there is no UK UPE, the obligations fall on the highest entity in the group that is UK resident for tax purposes or has a permanent establishment in the UK. This is referred to as the "UK entity" (UKE).

Filing a CbC Report

A UK UPE must file a CbC report in respect of every period it is in scope. A UKE must file a CbC report when:

- "the UPE of the group is resident for tax purposes in a country that does not require it to file a CbC report; or
- the UPE of the group is resident for tax purposes in a country that either has entered into an international agreement which allows for exchange of information (like the Multilateral Convention for Mutual Administrative Assistance in Tax Matters) but has not entered into specific arrangements to exchange CbC reports; or
- HMRC has notified the UK entity that exchange arrangements with the country in which the UPE is tax resident are not operating effectively".

UPEs and UKEs are required to notify HMRC for each period covered by a CbC report. The deadline for notification is the end of the period to which the report relates.

Exceptions to the Need to Report

An exception to the need to report can be granted if the information the UKE would be required to file has already been filed, either in a CbC report already received by HMRC or one that has been filed with a jurisdiction that will exchange the report with HMRC.

The exception to report must be applied for by the UKE. When applying, the UKE must inform HMRC, by the filing deadline, which entity in the MNE group has filed the CbC report and the date the report was filed.

Content of the Report

A CbC report must be filed in XML format, which allows it to be validated and provides a common medium for exchange between the countries adopting CbC reporting rules.

For each country (i.e. tax jurisdiction) in which the MNE group carries on its business, the report must show:

- the amount of revenue, profit before income tax and income tax paid and accrued; and
- the total employment, capital, retained earnings and tangible assets.

Administration and Penalties

The deadline for filing CbC reports is 12 months after the end of the period to which the CbC report relates. CbC reports must be filed online through the secure HMRC portal, and the MNE will need to register online to do so.

The reporting and notification requirements are supported by a penalty regime in the event that an entity does not provide its CbC report or notification on time without a reasonable excuse for the failure, or knowingly supplies incorrect information.

An initial penalty of £300 can be charged for failure to comply with the filing obligation. Following notification of this initial penalty, if the failure continues a further penalty of £60 can arise for each subsequent day. A £3,000 penalty can be charged for an inaccuracy in a CbC report.

8.2 Residence of Companies

8.2.1 The Incorporation Test

The most important factor in determining a company's liability to corporation tax (or other UK taxes) is the company's residence. The starting point for determining if the company is UK resident is the **incorporation test**. That is, is it incorporated in the UK, i.e. does it have a UK Companies House/Companies Registry number. However, if a company is not UK resident under this test it may still be UK resident under the "central management and control test".

8.2.2 Central Management and Control Test

The concept of central management and control in relation to the residence of a company has evolved from case law. The earliest case that dealt with company tax residence is *Calcutta Jute Mills Co. Ltd v. Nicholson*, which established that residence is located where a company's centre of control is located. The most important subsequent case is *de Beers Consolidated Mines v. Howe* (1906), in which it was held that a company's residence is where its real business is carried on, which is where the central management and control actually abides.

The central management and control test was further endorsed in *Bullock v. Unit Construction Co. Ltd* (1959). This case emphasised the point that central management and control is a question of fact and that it is not necessarily located where it appears to be located, e.g. where the board of directors hold its meetings. These principles were reaffirmed by the Court of Appeal in 2006 in the case of *Wood v. Holden*.

A 2009 case, *Laerstate BV v. HMRC*, also examined this concept and provides a useful indication of factors a court will look at to determine residence:

- Whether the board meets regularly on strategy/policy?
- Is documentation tabled?
- Are there minutes accurately reflecting the discussions?
- Are all meetings held and documents signed outside the UK?

These and other UK court decisions determined that one of the key factors in determining where a company is resident is where it is **managed and controlled**. The following are factors considered by the UK courts in determining the centre of the company's management and control and, therefore, its place of residence:

- Where are the questions of important policy determined?
- Where are the directors' meetings held?

- Where do the majority of the directors reside?
- Where are the shareholders' meetings held?
- Where is the negotiation of major contracts undertaken?
- Where is the head office of the company?
- Where are the books of account and the company books (minute book, share register, etc.) kept?
- Where are the company's bank accounts?

As you can see, control is generally determined by reference to where the directors hold their meetings and whether real decisions affecting the company are taken at those meetings. In each case, one needs to look at the facts to determine where the company is actually managed and controlled from.

In summary, a company is resident in the UK if it is incorporated in the UK, i.e. it has a UK Companies House/Companies Registry number. If it is not incorporated in the UK it will be resident in the UK if it is centrally managed and controlled in the UK.

8.2.3 Implications of UK Residence

A company resident in the UK is chargeable to corporation tax on all its profits wherever the income arises. This includes the results of foreign branches, although double taxation relief will be available for any corporation tax or equivalent paid in another jurisdiction (see **Chapter 11, Section 11.3**). A company can however elect into the foreign branch exemption regime to exempt the results of all of its branches from UK corporation tax (see **Chapter 11, Section 11.1.1, Overseas Branches**). Corporation tax is also payable on the disposal of chargeable assets, irrespective of where the asset was situated and whether or not the proceeds were received or transmitted to the UK. Again, double taxation relief will be a consideration.

8.2.4 Non-resident Companies

A non-resident company is chargeable to UK corporation tax if it carries on a trade in the UK through a permanent establishment (PE). If it has a PE, then it will be chargeable on its trading income, income from property and on any chargeable gains arising on the disposal of assets situated in the UK and which are used for the purposes of the PE trade.

A PE is a fixed place of business (or a dependent agent) through which the company carries out, either wholly or partly, its business in that country.

Profits of UK property businesses, other UK property income and profits of loan relationships that the non-resident company is a party to for the purpose of the property business or generating the income are also subject to UK corporation tax.

It should be noted that a non-resident company which does not carry on a trade in the UK through a PE remains chargeable to income tax at the basic rate (currently 20%) on any other UK income that it may have. See **Chapter 11, Section 11.2** for more on the taxation of non-resident companies.

If a non-resident company also pays tax in another country on the transactions it has been taxed on in the UK, double tax relief is **not available** against its UK corporation tax liability because the company is not UK resident.

8.2.5 Dual Resident Companies

It is sometimes the case that a former non-resident company, having become UK resident (or vice versa), may be deemed under the domestic law of the foreign jurisdiction to continue to be resident in that jurisdiction. In this scenario, the company has dual residence and the terms of the relevant double taxation treaty have to be examined. Double taxation treaties will generally contain a 'tie-breaker' clause to determine in which country the company is "treaty resident" for tax purposes. These tie-breaker clauses are beyond the scope of this textbook.

8.3 Research and Development Tax Relief

8.3.1 Overview

Relief is available for capital research and development (R&D) expenditure incurred by a company via the capital allowances regime and for revenue R&D expenditure through the various tax reliefs available. The definition of R&D for tax purposes follows its definition under UK GAAP.

Capital Expenditure
For capital expenditure, relief may be claimed on providing facilities to carry out R&D. This includes buildings used for R&D purposes, but not any land element. See **Chapter 3** for more on the calculation of capital allowances.

Revenue Expenditure
Enhanced tax relief for revenue R&D can only be claimed on "relevant" R&D, i.e. R&D related to the trade carried on by the company or from which it is intended that a trade be carried on. It should be noted that the various reliefs which follow are only available to companies.

8.3.2 Qualifying Company

Tax relief for qualifying expenditure on R&D may be claimed by companies of all sizes, though the level of tax relief is more generous for small and medium-sized entities (SMEs), as defined, than it is for large companies or groups – hence, there are two 'regimes' for the relief. There is no minimum level of qualifying expenditure in order for relief to be available.

8.3.3 Qualifying R&D Revenue Expenditure

While the definition of R&D follows that under UK GAAP (and specifically IAS 38 *Intangible Assets*), HMRC recommends that the Department for Business, Energy & Industrial Strategy guidance tests must also be applied. In essence, a project will qualify as an R&D project if it is carried on in the field of science or technology, and it is undertaken to extend knowledge and to address scientific or technological uncertainties.

Qualifying revenue expenditure is similar (but not identical) under the SME and "large" companies R&D tax relief regimes. However, under both regimes, the expenditure must meet the following conditions and, *inter alia*:

1. must not be capital in nature (capital expenditure may qualify for 100% R&D capital allowances instead, as set out earlier);
2. must be attributable to relevant R&D that is either directly undertaken by the company or on its behalf; and
3. must be incurred on staffing costs (to include salaries and wages (but not redundancy payments), employer's NIC, employer's pension fund contributions (but not non-cash benefits in

kind), consumable or transformable materials, software, externally provided workers, utilities (such as power, water and fuel), subcontracted R&D expenditure and on payments to participants in clinical trials.

Where R&D activity results in goods or services sold in the normal course of a company's business, the cost of consumable items reflected in those goods or services does not qualify for relief. Qualifying expenditure on consumable items is limited to the cost of only those items fully used up or expended by the R&D activity itself and which do not go on to be sold as part of a commercial product e.g. a prototype.

One difference between the SME and "large" company R&D regimes is that SMEs can claim an **enhanced deduction** on 65% of qualifying subcontracted R&D costs, but only where the company and the subcontractor are not connected (or where an election has not been made under section 1135 CTA 2009 to treat the company and the subcontractor as connected). If the company is connected to the subcontractor or an election to be treated as connected is made, the company can claim SME R&D tax relief on the lower of:

- the payment that it makes to the subcontractor; or
- the relevant expenditure of the subcontractor, as long as the whole amount of the subcontract payment is brought into account in determining the subcontractor's profit in accounts drawn up under GAAP within 12 months of the end of the claimant company's accounting period for which the relief is claimed.

"Connected" has the meaning given by section 1122 CTA 2010. Broadly, a company is connected with another company if:

- the same person has control of both; or
- a person has control of one company and a person connected with them has control of the other; or
- a group of two or more persons has control of each company, and the groups consist of the same persons.

For claims under the "large" company regime, the expenditure on R&D contracted to other persons is generally not allowable. However, it can be qualifying expenditure if it is revenue expenditure on relevant R&D and the company contracts for work to be directly undertaken by a qualifying body (generally a non-taxable body such as an educational establishment or a charity) or an individual or a partnership (each member of which is an individual).

R&D tax relief claims (including claims for the payable tax credit) should be made by the company in its corporation tax return for the relevant accounting period. A company has a two-year time limit from the end of the relevant accounting period to make an R&D claim.

8.3.4 R&D Tax Relief: SMEs

For the purposes of the relief, an SME is defined as a company that has either:

- turnover of €100 million or less; or
- a balance sheet total of €86 million or less;

and has fewer than 500 employees. (Note that the turnover and net assets limit are correctly denoted in euro.)

Calculation of Enhanced Deduction

An SME, as defined, can qualify for a total deduction from its trading profits of 230% of its qualifying R&D expenditure. The qualifying expenditure must be such that it would have been allowable as a deduction in computing the taxable profits of a trade carried on by the company.

Where the company has a trading loss in an accounting period in which it also claims relief under the SME R&D tax relief regime, the company may (instead of any loss relief that it may be entitled to) surrender the loss for a cash payment of 14.5% of the surrenderable loss for the chargeable period. For accounting periods starting on or after 1 April 2021, this is subject to a cap which is linked to the company's total PAYE and NIC costs.

The tax relief is claimed as an adjustment to the trading income computation. The qualifying expenditure is first added back and then the enhanced deduction later made at 230%. The SME regime has an upper limit of €7.5 million per R&D project. Should qualifying costs exceed that amount, the excess may be claimed under the R&D regime for "large" companies.

Example 8.1

Tiny Ltd, an SME for R&D purposes, spends £165,000 on qualifying R&D revenue in its accounting period ended 31 March 2022. In calculating taxable trade profits for the year to 31 March 2022 the total deduction for R&D will be:

$$£165,000 \times 230\% = £379,500$$

If the £165,000 has already been deducted in arriving at the company's adjusted trading result, an additional deduction of £214,500 should be deducted for corporation tax purposes.

Impact of Grants Received

Often an SME may claim and receive grant aid in relation to an R&D project. This can affect whether an R&D claim is possible under the regime for SMEs or that for "large" companies, even if the company meets the R&D SME definition.

If the grant received towards the project is notified 'state aid', then a claim is not possible under the SME regime. This is because state aid would then be obtained twice on the same expenditure. Instead, the company would be required to claim under the "large" company regime (see **Section 8.3.5**). In such a case, the grant aid received **is not deducted** from the expenditure qualifying for relief under the "large" company regime. 'Notified state aid' is state aid that has been notified to, and approved by, the European Commission. From 1 January 2021, following the end of the implementation period, EU control ceased to apply to any state aid granted by the UK unless it affects any trade between Northern Ireland and the EU that is subject to the Protocol on Ireland/Northern Ireland. As a result, state aid rules typically do not apply from 1 January 2021. A new subsidy control system is due to be implemented in the UK, the detail of which has yet to be finalised.

If the grant received towards the project does not constitute notified state aid, then a claim is still possible under the SME regime providing the remaining conditions are met. In this case the grant received **is required to be deducted** from the qualifying expenditure, with 230% relief available on the net amount.

Calculation of Payable Tax Credit for Loss-making Companies

As noted earlier, if a company makes a claim for R&D tax relief under the SME regime and has a trading loss, then the company may claim a payable tax credit. The company effectively surrenders the whole or part of this loss in return for the payable tax credit. Should the company choose to claim the payable tax credit instead of relief for the trading loss in the usual way (see **Chapter 7, Section 7.9** and **Chapter 12**), the surrenderable loss is the lower of:

- the unrelieved trading loss; or
- 230% of the qualifying R&D expenditure.

The payable tax credit is calculated as 14.5% of the surrenderable loss for the period.

Cap on the Payable Tax Credit

For accounting periods beginning on or after 1 April 2021, the payable tax credit is subject to a cap, which is based on the PAYE and NIC that the company is required to pay for its own employees, plus any PAYE and NIC of connected companies. The NIC total includes both employer and employee contributions.

The cap restricts the maximum credit which can be claimed to £20,000 plus three times the company's "relevant expenditure on workers", being the total of:

- the company's own total PAYE and NIC liabilities for the period (note: this is for the entire company and not just the PAYE and NIC of workers associated with its R&D activities); **PLUS**
- where the company makes payments to connected companies for providing it with subcontractors or externally provided workers (EPW) used towards qualifying R&D activities, the PAYE and NIC paid by the connected company in providing those subcontractors or EPW; **LESS**
- any PAYE or NIC incurred by the company in providing EPW or subcontractors to connected companies for the purposes of their R&D activities (to avoid double-counting as the connected company will include these costs in calculating its own cap).

The £20,000 is proportionately reduced for accounting periods of less than 12 months.

A company is exempt from the cap if:

- its employees are creating, preparing to create or managing intellectual property (patents, trademarks, copyrights, design rights, etc.); and
- it does not spend more than 15% of its qualifying R&D expenditure on subcontracting R&D to, or the provision of EPW by, connected persons including those connected by election under section 1135 CTA 2009 (see **Section 8.3.3**).

The exemption is targeted at companies which have low PAYE and NIC liabilities but are nevertheless themselves engaged in genuine, substantial R&D activities.

Example 8.2

Innova Ltd has been trading for several years and recently completed the period of account ending on 31 March 2022. The company's draft corporation tax computation currently denotes an adjusted tax loss of £1,742,000 before a claim for R&D tax relief. You review the R&D revenue expenditure incurred and note that £800,000 qualifies under the legislation and that Innova Ltd is an SME.

Prepare the adjusted corporation tax computation and outline how relief is obtained by a company incurring a loss and also making a claim for R&D relief. The company's PAYE and NIC bill for the period is £100,000. No payments were made to or from connected companies for subcontractors or externally provided workers.

Innova Ltd – corporation tax computation for the accounting period ended 31 March 2022

	£
Adjusted tax loss before R&D relief	(1,742,000)
Add: qualifying R&D expenditure	800,000
Deduct: claim for R&D relief £800,000 @ 230%	(1,840,000)
Adjusted tax loss	(2,782,000)

continued overleaf

Innova Ltd has made a trading loss of £2,782,000 in its accounting period ended 31 March 2022.

This loss is available to carry back against total profits under section 37(3)(b) CTA 2010, or to carry forward under section 45A CTA 2010, for use against the company's future profits arising from the same trade. Alternatively, the company may surrender the lower of its unrelieved trading loss of £2,782,000 and 230% of qualifying R&D expenditure (£1,840,000) for a repayable R&D tax credit. The level of tax credit claimable would therefore be £266,800 (14.5% × £1,840,000). This is subject to the PAYE cap. However, as the cap is equal to £320,000 (£20,000 + (3 × £100,000)), there is no restriction and the full £266,800 can be claimed.

Losses available for carry back, for offset in the current year against other income or for carry forward would be as follows:

	£
Loss (as above)	2,782,000
Less: surrendered	(1,840,000)
Remaining losses	942,000

The decision whether to surrender £1,840,000 of the loss and claim the R&D payable credit, or to not surrender the losses, should be discussed with the company directors – particularly considering that the difference in the rate of relief for the losses surrendered of £1,840,000 is 4.5% (i.e. main corporation tax rate of 19% – 14.5% rate of relief for tax credit). The increase in the rate of corporation tax to 25% from 1 April 2023 would also be a relevant consideration.

8.3.5   R&D Tax Relief: "Large" Companies

A company not meeting the definition of an SME for R&D purposes, or one meeting the SME definition but in receipt of state aid, or one meeting the SME definition but having exceeded the SME €7.5 million upper limit for a project can instead claim under the R&D tax relief rules for "large" companies.

Arriving at the costs of what qualifies as R&D expenditure for "large" companies is almost identical to that for SMEs, except where subcontracted costs are concerned (see **Section 8.3.4**).

"Large" companies receive a taxable R&D expenditure credit (RDEC) on qualifying costs incurred. The RDEC is treated as **a taxable receipt** in calculating the adjusted trading result of the trade for the accounting period, which is why it is sometimes called the 'above the line credit'. The company will also receive a **credit against its tax liability** of the same amount. This credit is equal to 13% of the company's **qualifying R&D expenditure** incurred.

If the company's corporation tax liability is **lower** than the RDEC or, if the company claiming the RDEC **incurs a trading loss** in the period, the company is entitled to claim a payable credit (subject to a number of adjustments, which are beyond the scope of this textbook).

Example 8.3
Conan Ltd is a "large" company with the following results for the year to 31 March 2022.

	£
Turnover	7,500,000
R&D expenditure	(750,000)
Other expenditure	(5,750,000)
Net profit	1,000,000

continued overleaf

Conan's net profit represents fully taxable profits for corporation tax purposes. Its RDEC would be calculated as follows:

	£	£
Turnover		7,500,000
R&D expenditure	(750,000)	
13% RDEC (£750,000 × 13%)	97,500	(652,500)
Other expenditure		(5,750,000)
Taxable total profits		1,097,500
Corporation tax (Note)		111,025
Profit after tax		986,475
Note: Corporation tax calculation		
Corporation tax: £1,097,500 @ 19%		208,525
Deduct: RDEC		(97,500)
Net corporation tax payable		111,025

8.4   The Corporate Intangibles Regime

A special corporation tax regime has been in place since 1 April 2002 that applies to a company's expenditure on intangible fixed assets (IFAs). IFAs are a company's 'intellectual property' and include items such as patents, copyrights, trademarks, and goodwill. Patent royalties are also within the scope of this regime and fall to be taxed on the accruals basis.

IFAs acquired or created prior to 1 April 2002 are not generally within the corporate intangibles regime and are instead treated as capital gains assets (they are typically referred to as 'pre-FA 2002' assets). The corporate intangibles regime applies to expenditure on the creation, acquisition, and enhancement of IFAs (including abortive expenditure), as well as expenditure on their preservation and maintenance, on or after 1 April 2002.

In addition, pre-FA 2002 IFAs acquired on or after 1 July 2020 from related parties (but not a related party that is a fellow capital gains group company) are also brought within the corporate intangibles regime. Ordinarily, this would mean that tax relief is available on the amortisation or impairment of such assets under the corporate intangible rules; however, there are a series of anti-avoidance measures which mean that (in most cases) while the assets will be within the scope of the regime, no tax relief will be available for any amortisation or impairment.

Companies generally obtain tax relief on expenditure on IFAs within the corporate intangibles regime through their amortisation policy, as long as this is in accordance with UK GAAP.

The company can, if it chooses, apply instead a fixed irrevocable rate allowance of 4% per annum, effectively writing-off the IFA over 25 years. A company would generally only elect to do so where the 4% election would accelerate relief, e.g. the amortisation policy under the relevant accounting standard is to write-off the IFA over a period of time in excess of 25 years. Or, where no accounting amortisation is available, a company can choose the 4% election.

In this regime, the loss or gain on the disposal of an IFA asset within the regime is either taxable (for income and profits on disposal) or deductible (for expenses (including amortisation) and losses on disposal). There is also a form of rollover relief available in the situation where an IFA is disposed of for more than the original cost and the disposal proceeds are reinvested in newly acquired IFAs. The amount by which the disposal proceeds exceed the original cost may be rolled over against the cost of the new IFA assets. However, the clawed back amortisation cannot be rolled over, only the profit on the original cost of the goodwill.

Example 8.4

Dapper Ltd purchased a business inclusive of a trading copyright on 1 April 2016. The copyright element cost £400,000 and is being amortised over 10 years. The company's accounting period end is 31 March.

During the 31 March 2022 period the company sells the business and copyright. The copyright element is sold for £850,000. Any income profit on the sale of the copyright could be rolled over against reinvestment in new intangible assets. However, the clawed back amortisation cannot be rolled over, only the profit on the original cost of the copyright.

To date the company has received corporation tax relief on the copyright totalling £200,000 in its last five accounting periods (as the company is not entitled to claim amortisation in the period of disposal). The tax written down value, which also equates to its accounting value, is £200,000. Therefore, the taxable receipt on the copyright is £650,000 (£850,000 – £200,000). However, the amount on which rollover relief can be claimed is £450,000 (£850,000 – £400,000).

The accounts of the company will include taxable profit of £650,000. If rollover relief is claimed, the £450,000 that qualifies should be deducted in the adjusted trading profit computation. This means that the company will be taxed on the clawed back £200,000 amortisation as a trading receipt.

Under the regime, gains and losses relating to IFAs used in a company's business are generally taxed as revenue items. Expenditure is a 'debit' and income a 'credit'. The actual tax treatment of these debits and credits depends on whether the assets are held for trading purposes, a property business, or a non-trading purpose.

8.4.1 Treatment of Goodwill

Relief is potentially available for goodwill in one of two ways depending on when it is acquired.

Goodwill Acquired before 8 July 2015

Relief is available for amortisations of relevant assets, including certain goodwill (see definition later), acquired before 8 July 2015, but only where the relevant asset was not received from a related party individual or partnership. For the purposes of this rule, the term "related party" is defined as a participator or associate of a participator in a close company (see **Chapters 9** and **10**). This rule applies to transfers to both UK close limited companies and to non-UK resident companies that would be categorised as a close company if they were resident in the UK.

Overall, this measure prevents corporation tax relief being available for goodwill where a company acquires internally generated goodwill and customer-related IFAs from related individuals on the incorporation of a business.

For the purpose of this provision, relevant assets include the following assets acquired before 8 July 2015:

1. goodwill;
2. an IFA consisting of information relating to customers, or potential customers, of a business;
3. an IFA consisting of a relationship (whether contractual or not) between someone carrying on a business and one or more customers of that business;
4. an unregistered trademark or sign used in the course of a business; or
5. a licence or other right that relates to an asset within items 1 to 4.

Goodwill Acquired on or after 1 April 2019

Companies that acquire goodwill (and certain other customer-related intangible assets) on or after 1 April 2019 only receive relief where:

■ they acquire the goodwill (or customer-related assets) as part of a business; and
■ other qualifying intellectual property (IP) is also acquired as part of the acquisition.

The categories of qualifying IP assets include patents, registered designs, copyright, and design rights. Relief is given at a fixed rate of 6.5% per annum (restricted for periods of less than 12 months) on the lower of:

■ the cost of the goodwill (or customer-related assets); or
■ six times the amount of the qualifying IP.

If no qualifying IP assets are acquired as part of the transaction, no relief is available for the relevant assets, including any goodwill. This measure is therefore targeted at IP-intensive acquisitions by companies.

Again, relief is not available for internally generated goodwill and customer-related IFAs in a related party incorporation.

Goodwill acquired prior to 1 April 2019 continues to be subject to the tax treatment prevailing at the time it was acquired.

Example 8.5

On 1 July 2021, Innovate Ltd purchased a business from an unconnected third party. The purchase included copyright (£50,000), design rights (£75,000) and goodwill (£800,000). The intangible assets acquired are being amortised in the company's accounts over 10 years in accordance with IAS 38 *Intangible Assets*. The company's accounting period end is 31 March.

Copyright

£50,000/10 × 9/12 = £3,750 amortisation in the company accounts. No adjustment is required to the company's corporation tax computation in 2022 as the company obtains relief via its amortisation policy. The company will therefore obtain a deduction for the full £3,750 amortised in the 2022 period.

Patent

£75,000/10 × 9/12 = £5,625 amortisation in the company accounts. No adjustment is required to the company's corporation tax computation in 2022 as the company obtains relief via its amortisation policy. The company will therefore obtain a deduction for the full £5,625 amortised in the 2022 period.

Goodwill

£800,000/10 × 9/12 = £60,000 amortisation in the company accounts. Add-back of £60,000 required in the company's corporation tax computation in 2022 and relief to be calculated in accordance with the rules for relevant assets acquired on or after 1 April 2019.

Relief is given at a fixed rate of 6.5% on the lower of:

■ the amount of the relevant asset, i.e. £800,000; or
■ six times the amount of the qualifying IP, i.e. £50,000 + £75,000 = £125,000 × 6 = £750,000

Therefore, the maximum goodwill that qualifies as a relevant asset is £750,000.

In 2022, the company should obtain a corporation tax deduction of £36,563 (£750,000 × 6.5% × 9/12). This should be deducted in its calculation of trading profits.

Debits and credits on the disposal of relevant assets (including goodwill) that do not qualify for corporation tax relief as set out in this section are deemed to be a non-trading debit or credit and dealt with in accordance with the loan relationship rules (see **Chapter 7, Section 7.5.4**).

8.4.2 Trading Debits and Credits

Debits and credits in respect of assets held for the purposes of a trade are dealt with in the normal trading income computation as expenses and receipts of that particular trade. If they relate to a property business, then they are dealt with as property income.

8.4.3 Non-trading Debits and Credits

Non-trading debits and credits on intangible assets are initially grouped together and netted-off against each other. If there is a resultant net gain, then it is assessable under the catch-all "miscellaneous income" provisions (see **Chapter 7, Section 7.5.2**).

If there is a net "loss", then the company has a choice about how it wishes to relieve this loss, i.e. either to group-relieve the loss or to set it against the company's total profits of that accounting period. Any unutilised loss is carried forward to the next accounting period and treated as if it were a non-trading debit of that period.

Gains or losses on the disposal of IFAs not within the corporate intangibles regime continue to be dealt with under the CGT regime and will either be chargeable gains or allowable capital losses.

8.4.4 Rollover Relief for IFAs

As previously mentioned, there is a form of rollover relief available in the situation where an IFA within the corporate intangibles regime is disposed of for more than the original cost and the disposal proceeds are reinvested in newly-acquired IFAs. The amount by which the disposal proceeds exceed the original cost (not the tax written down value) may be rolled over against the cost of the new IFA. In this situation, the company is taxed as if the disposal proceeds of the old IFA and the cost of the newly acquired IFAs are both reduced by this excess. Relief is further restricted where not all of the net proceeds from the IFA are reinvested.

The reinvestment must occur in the period 12 months before to three years after the time the old IFA is realised. Claims for the relief must be made within four years after the later of either the end of the accounting period of disposal of the old IFA, or the acquisition of the new IFA.

Relief is also available where the reinvestment occurs in a group company (see **Section 8.4.5**).

Example 8.6

Taking **Example 8.4**, assume Dapper Ltd thereafter purchases a business with a trading copyright costing £900,000 during the 2023 period. This qualifies for IFA rollover relief as the entire proceeds were reinvested.

The rollover relief which can be claimed is £450,000 (£850,000 – £400,000). Therefore, the £450,000 trading profit in the corporation tax computation is not subject to corporation tax and should be deducted. The company will still be subject to corporation tax on the clawed-back £200,000 amortisation as a trading receipt.

The £450,000 is rolled over against the base cost of the new IFA, which is reduced for tax relief amortisation purposes to £450,000 (£900,000 purchase price less £450,000 rollover relief).

8.4.5   Groups

A company may be part of an IFA group for the purposes of the corporate intangibles regime. This can give important benefits to the companies within the group, namely that IFAs can be transferred from one group company to another without triggering a taxable receipt. In addition, taxable receipts on disposal of IFAs can also be rolled over inter-group. The definition of an IFA group mirrors that of a capital gains group (see **Chapter 13, Section 13.4** for examples).

Broadly, companies are in an IFA group where:

- at each level, there is a 75% direct holding; and
- the top company has an effective interest of at least 51% in the group companies.

A company can only be a member of one IFA group. Assets classified as IFAs under the corporate intangibles regime can be transferred between members of the IFA group on a tax-neutral basis. This is similar to the rule that applies under section 171 TCGA 1992 for chargeable assets taxed under the capital gains tax regime, where the companies are part of a capital gains group (see **Chapter 13, Section 13.5**).

In general, a transfer of an IFA from one member of the group to another is deemed to be for a consideration of such amount that neither a gain nor a loss accrues. This relief applies as a result of section 775 CTA 2009. The IFA group is effectively treated as one taxpayer so that the original taxable receipt or loss does not arise until the asset is sold outside the group or the company holding the asset leaves the group.

In particular, this means the transferee inherits the transferor's tax written down value for the IFA, and all such debits and credits that have been brought into account are treated for this purpose as though they had been brought into account by the transferee. **Relief for transfers of IFAs between IFA group companies (UK to UK only) is granted automatically and is compulsory, i.e. an election is not required**.

Non-UK resident companies are included within an IFA group and, provided there is no loss to HMRC, the tax-neutral IFA transfer is possible within a worldwide group of companies. For example, it may be possible to make a tax-neutral transfer of an IFA to a non-UK resident company with a branch or agency in the UK.

However, where a transfer of an IFA is made to a non-UK resident company that is not within the charge to UK corporation tax, the transfer of the IFA is deemed to take place at market value – meaning corporation tax can arise for the transferring company should a taxable receipt be deemed to occur (a loss may also occur depending on the market value of the IFA and its tax written down value).

For transactions occurring in accounting periods ending on or after 10 October 2018, if a UK resident company (or a UK branch of a non-UK resident company) transfers an IFA to a group company resident in an EU/EEA state that is not within the charge to UK corporation tax and a taxable receipt is deemed to occur, the relevant corporation tax payable can be deferred, either in whole or in part, by entering into a corporation tax payment plan. Deferral is possible only in cases where the transfer would otherwise have been on a tax-neutral basis under section 775 CTA 2009. See **Chapter 13, Section 13.5** for more details of the process involved.

Example 8.7

Again, taking **Example 8.4**, assume that Dapper Ltd instead of selling the copyright for its market value of £850,000 transferred it on a tax-neutral basis to its 100% UK resident subsidiary.

The tax written down value of the copyright at that point is £200,000. The recipient company can claim tax relief on the remaining amortisation. It is treated, for all intents and purposes, as if it had always owned the copyright.

> **Example 8.8**
>
> Now assume that Dapper Ltd has a 100% UK subsidiary that reinvests in a patent at a cost of £900,000 in 2023.
>
> As the entire proceeds were reinvested inter-group, the rollover relief that can be claimed is £450,000 (£850,000 – £400,000). This is rolled over against the base cost of the new intangible owned by the subsidiary, which is reduced for tax relief amortisation purposes to £450,000. That is, the gain on an IFA disposed of by Dapper is rolled over against the purchase of the IFA made by its subsidiary, the companies being together in a corporate intangibles group.
>
> Therefore the £450,000 trading profit in the corporation tax computation is not subject to corporation tax and should be deducted. Dapper Ltd will still be subject to corporation tax on the clawed back £200,000 amortisation as a trading receipt.

8.4.6 Degrouping Charges on IFAs

A degrouping IFA charge may arise where a company leaves a group and there has been an earlier transfer to it of an IFA within the corporate intangibles regime on a tax-neutral basis in the previous six years. The rules are modelled on the capital gains degrouping rules, as they are aimed at the same potential problem.

The broad effect is to recognise the profit or loss deferred on the earlier tax-neutral disposal if the IFA in question leaves the group other than by a direct disposal of the IFA. The company leaving the group makes a deemed disposal and reacquisition of the IFA at market value immediately after the time it acquired the IFA from another group company at the date of the original transfer. This is known as a degrouping charge.

The event that triggers a degrouping adjustment is a company ceasing to be a member of a group; but the amount of the gain or loss is determined by reference to the previous tax-neutral transfer in the previous six years. Although the calculation of any gain or loss on disposal is calculated by reference to the market value of the IFA at the time immediately following the disposal by a group member to the transferee company, the taxable credit or deductible debit resulting is treated as though it arose immediately prior to the transferee company leaving the group.

However, like the rules for degrouping charges on chargeable assets (see **Chapter 13, Section 13.7**), where a company leaves the group as a result of a disposal of shares by another group company, any degrouping charge is made by way of an adjustment to the consideration taken into account for calculating the gain or loss on the disposal of shares. A consequence of this is that if the substantial shareholdings exemption (SSE) (see **Chapter 13, Section 13.2**) applies to the share disposal, it will also apply to the degrouping intangibles charge.

In such circumstances, the IFAs that would have been subject to a degrouping charge will remain at their tax written down value and continue to attract relief as they did prior to degrouping.

Should the SSE not be available on the share disposal, the degrouping charge remains taxable on the company leaving the group. In this scenario, the amortisation deduction for the period that the company leaves the group will also need to be adjusted to reflect an acquisition cost based instead on market value at the time of the original transfer.

If two or more related 51% group companies that would form a group by themselves leave the main group at the same time, the degrouping adjustment does not apply to any IFA transfers that have taken place between those related 51% group companies. However, if one of these companies subsequently leaves the sub-group, there may be a degrouping adjustment on that occasion, again subject to the potential for the SSE to be available. Full or partial reallocation of the taxable credit is possible between group members. In addition, the departing company may of course invest in new IFAs and defer the gain via a claim for rollover relief.

> **Example 8.9**
> Following on from the scenario in **Example 8.7**, Dapper Ltd sells the shares in its subsidiary in the 2023 accounting period. The subsidiary is deemed to have realised and reacquired the IFA for its 2022 market value of £850,000. That gives rise to a taxable credit of £650,000, representing the excess of the market value at the time of the transfer (£850,000) over the tax written down value at that time (£200,000).
>
> However, no taxable trading debit will arise if Dapper is able to meet the conditions for the SSE on the disposal of the shares. Instead, the subsidiary leaving the group continues to receive tax relief on the intangible as it did prior to degrouping and there is no change to the tax written down value at that time.

8.5   Investment Companies

A company that is in the business of holding and managing investments is taxed as an investment company. The key feature is that, for tax purposes, allowable expenses in respect of investment activity are limited to those required for investment management. These are referred to as management expenses.

An investment company is defined in the legislation as "any company whose business consists **wholly or partly** in the making of investments." The meaning of business is taken from case law, but broadly there must be some active behaviour carried on by the company in relation to the investments. Therefore, a company that carries on a substantial trading activity and a small investment business will still be able to claim relief for management expenses.

8.5.1   Management Expenses

Management expenses include all expenses relating to the management of a company's investment business. Expenses that are directly related to a particular source of income must be deducted from that income source, e.g. letting expenses are deductible against property income, and costs associated with financing will be deductible as trade or non-trade deficits. If a company carries on both an investment business and a trading activity within the same entity, the expenses must be allocated on a just and reasonable basis.

Items of a capital nature cannot be claimed as management expenses.

Investments are not held for a business or other commercial purpose if they are held directly/indirectly in consequence of, or in connection with, any arrangements for securing a tax advantage. In addition, no deduction is allowed in so far as the expenses are otherwise deductible from total profits, or in calculating any component of total profits.

Expenditure on appraising and investigating investments will, in general, be revenue in nature. However, the process of appraisal will eventually reach the stage where the company will decide which, if any, companies it is seeking to acquire. Expenditure up to the point at which a decision is made to acquire a particular investment will generally be non-capital. Similar considerations apply where it is a disposal rather than an acquisition that is being considered.

Once it has been decided to purchase/dispose of an investment, any costs incurred after that point will be costs of the acquisition/disposal and therefore capital. An abortive acquisition or disposal is no different, in terms of the nature of expenditure, from a successful acquisition/ disposal.

The following table shows types of expenditure that are either allowable or disallowable as management expenses.

Allowable expenditure	Disallowable expenditure
■ Costs, such as keeping the investment company share register, printing annual accounts and holding annual shareholder meetings.	■ Professional fees in respect of land held as investments (fees for managing/protecting such assets would be allowable).
■ Costs incurred in respect of stock exchange quotations.	■ Cost of appraising investments (a general appraisal of the market would not be disallowed, and work on a potential new investment would not be disallowed until such point as a firm decision to acquire the investment is made).
■ Maintenance and repair costs in respect of premises used by the investment company.	■ Brokerage, commissions, and stamp duty in respect of investments.
■ Payments in respect of an HMRC-approved retirement scheme.	■ Costs of raising capital (but will qualify as a non-trade loan relationship deficit).
■ Directors' and employees' remuneration (subject to being a reasonable expense of managing investments and the 9-month rule for accruals).	■ Capital expenditure.

An investment company is also subject to the self-assessment regime for corporation tax and is subject to the same administrative rules.

8.5.2 Utilisation of Management Expenses

Management expenses are first deducted against a company's total income. Therefore, it does not matter if the company also carries on trading activity as relief for management expenses is not restricted to investment or non-trading activity. The deduction is mandatory and must be made before any other deductions from total profits.

Where management expenses cannot be fully utilised against a company's total profits (known as 'excess management expenses'), they can be surrendered as group relief or carried forward and treated as having been incurred in the next period until such time as they are fully utilised.

From 1 April 2017, where management expenses are carried forward to a future period, it is not necessary to allow a deduction for the carried-forward management expenses before other deductions from total profits. Instead, the order of offset is more flexible. Any surplus carried forward is also deducted from total profits of the next period. In cases where management expenses are group relieved, there is a requirement for the surrendering company to use these against its own income sources first (i.e. only excess management expenses can be group relieved).

Companies with investment business that have excess qualifying charitable donations can carry those excess charitable donations forward as management expenses (see **Chapter 7, Section 7.7**).

8.5.3 Capital Allowances

Capital allowances are available in respect of capital expenditure incurred for the purpose of the company's investment business (see **Chapter 3**).

Questions

Review Questions

(See Suggested Solutions to Review Questions at the end of this textbook.)

Question 8.1

A long-standing client comes into your office to discuss their future business plans. Peter Dorman and his wife, Angela, are the directors and shareholders of Gourmet Ltd, a UK company specialising in producing gourmet ready-meals.

They have carried out some market research and as a result are planning to expand into an overseas market by setting up a new company. This company will purchase the plant and premises in the overseas country for production of the company's products, which will then be sold in that country.

The shares in the new company will still be owned by Peter and Angela, who will be the only directors. They will appoint a local manager to operate the plant, appoint suppliers and recruit staff. However, Peter and Angela will be wholly responsible for any strategic decisions such as those involving finance, investment, and marketing strategy. They will make these decisions from the UK.

Requirement

Explain, with supporting analysis, whether the new company will be considered resident in the UK for corporation tax purposes. If you consider the new company will be UK resident, state the deadline for informing HM Revenue & Customs that the company is within the charge to corporation tax.

Question 8.2

It is January 2023, and you are the newly appointed financial controller of a UK stand-alone company. When recruited, it was made clear to you that some of your duties would involve tax compliance in order to minimise the cost of taking professional advice. One of your first projects is to review the draft corporation tax computation for the year ended 31 March 2022 which was prepared by your predecessor.

The company, Comtech Ltd, has its own R&D department and, when reviewing the draft corporation tax computation, you noted that no claims for R&D tax relief have been made. You mention this in passing to the finance director who asks you to prepare a memo outlining the key aspects of the UK R&D tax relief scheme and the potential amounts that the company could claim tax relief on for the 2022 period only, including providing explanations of your calculations and the overall tax saving available.

Comtech's turnover for the year ended 31 March 2022 was £34.6 million (which equates to roughly €40 million) and it has 55 employees. The total reported in its statement of financial position was £48 million (roughly €55 million).

You have reviewed the draft computation and are satisfied that, aside from any potential claim for relief on R&D expenditure, no other adjustments to the draft taxable total profits figure of £1,828,925 is required.

The R&D team is tasked with developing new and innovative products for the company to bring to market, so its work directly links to the trade of the company and, in its particular field, Comtech is considered a 'blue skies' industry leader.

At a meeting with the head of the R&D department, it is established that the revenue costs of running the R&D department in 2022 were as follows:

	£
Gross wages	212,567
Redundancy payments	4,250
Employer's NIC	27,209
Pension scheme contributions	15,000
Company car benefit in kind	7,825
Consumable items (used up as part of R&D process)	22,425
Power, water, and fuel	8,762
Software	4,933
Rates	25,655
Professional fees*	12,250
	340,876

*During the period, the R&D department subcontracted some of its work to a specialist laboratory nearby, at a cost of £12,250. The laboratory is not connected to the company.

Having reviewed the above costs you do not identify any tax disallowable items.

Requirement
(a) Prepare a memo to the finance director outlining the UK R&D regime, including details of the amount of relief potentially available and the conditions for claiming the relief.
(b) Assuming the activities of the R&D department qualify as R&D as defined by tax legislation, calculate the maximum amount of tax relief available to the company under the UK R&D regime. Outline for the finance director the tax saving to be achieved by making the R&D claim and any other relevant recommendations.

Question 8.3

The finance director of Feed Specialists NI Ltd (FSNI) recently left the company. Since his departure the shareholders of the company, Peter and Annette have identified a major error in the corporation tax return for FSNI for the year ended 31 March 2021 (which was submitted to HMRC on time) relating to the company's claim for SME R&D tax relief.

This has resulted in the corporation tax liability for the period being understated. The submitted corporation tax computation included a claim for R&D tax relief on revenue expenditure of £750,000. The correct qualifying R&D expenditure was £75,000. Peter and Annette have discussed the matter and they agree that, as the finance director probably included an additional zero in the computation by mistake, the error was not deliberate and thus they do not need to disclose the error to HMRC. They also believe that as the corporation tax return for FSNI for the year ended 31 March 2021 was submitted on time, and the HMRC enquiry window has now closed, this treatment should be fine. You may assume that all other aspects of the company's R&D tax relief claim were correct except for the amount of qualifying expenditure.

Requirement
(a) Advise Peter and Annette on how they should deal with the error identified in FSNI's corporation tax return for the year ended 31 March 2021 (include a calculation of the underpayment).
(b) Outline how the HMRC penalty regime operates, and the different penalties potentially payable in this situation.

Question 8.4

You have recently taken on a new client Solar Heating Ltd. At a recent meeting, the finance director mentioned that it is planning to incur R&D expenditure of around £525,000 in the accounting period ending 30 September 2021.

You have reviewed the planned expenditure and are satisfied that it qualifies under both the SME and large company R&D tax relief regimes; though the company meets the definition of SME for these purposes.

Solar Heating has been offered a grant of £50,000 (which was received before 1 January 2021 and is notified state aid) by Invest NI towards this expenditure. Although the finance director is tempted by this, she asks you to carry out some calculations to ensure the company is minimising the cost to the company (after R&D tax relief) before it signs the letter of offer.

Requirement
(a) Calculate the net cost to the company (after R&D tax relief) of the planned R&D project if the company:
  (i) signs the letter of offer and receives the grant; and
  (ii) does not sign the letter of offer and does not receive the grant.
(b) Advise the company what action it should take as a result if the company wishes to minimise its R&D spend on this project in 2022.

Question 8.5

You have recently attended a meeting with Mr Tweedy, the finance director of Matador Ltd, a trading company that is a client of your firm. At the meeting, the following issues were discussed:

■ Matador is planning to acquire the trade and assets of a competitor company, Warp Ltd, in April 2022. Based on current projections, it is estimated that the value of a patent included in the acquisition is £240,000. Mr Tweedy has confirmed that the patent will not be amortised in the accounts, but he understands the company can make an election to claim tax relief in respect of the patent; it is his intention that Matador will make this election.

■ Mr Tweedy has also informed you that Matador sold a registered patent used in the company's trade in June 2021. The proceeds of sale were £200,000, and the written down value (for tax and accounting purposes) at the time of sale was £90,000. The patent had been purchased exactly two years prior to the disposal date from Max Ltd (an unrelated company). The cost of the patent was £150,000.

■ Mr Tweedy is aware of a way to reduce any corporation tax liability arising on the disposal of the patent if the new Warp patent is acquired in April 2022, but he is unsure of how this works in practice. Matador prepares accounts to 31 March each year.

It is March 2022. You and a tax partner in your firm are due to telephone Mr Tweedy to discuss the above matters.

Requirement
Prepare a briefing note on the following:

(a) calculate any potential relief available for the disposal of the patent in June 2021 and any corporation tax that may arise on its disposal;
(b) calculate the annual writing down allowance and tax relief available, assuming the relief is applied and the writing down election is made;

(c) state briefly how the above calculations would be affected if the new patent acquired as part of the Warp acquisition is valued at £170,000 and not £240,000.

(Your note should be brief, in bullet-format, and does not need to include details of time limits or practicalities of making any of the claims and elections mentioned above, but should include any conditions that must be satisfied.)

Question 8.6

Investco Ltd is a small company under the dividend exemption rules. It reported the following results for the accounting period ended 31 March 2022 in its management accounts:

	£
Investment income	
UK dividend income	25,000
Bank interest (received gross)	3,000
Rental income	12,000
Total investment income	40,000
Expense	
Directors' remuneration	12,000
Appraisal costs of identified target	1,750
Shareholder meeting costs	2,240
Rent of office	3,000
Repairs to office door	500
Total expenses	(19,490)
Net profit per management accounts	20,510

The company also had a chargeable gain of £5,000 that has not yet been reflected in its accounts.

Requirement
Calculate the corporation tax payable for Investco Ltd for the accounting period ended 31 March 2022.

Close Companies

Learning Objectives

After studying this chapter you will understand:

- The definition of a close company.
- An overview of the tax rules that apply to close companies and their shareholders.

9.1 Meaning of Close Company

A close company is a UK resident company that is under the control of:

- five or fewer participators; or
- any number of participators who are also directors.

A company will not be a close company if it is non-UK resident. Control is the ability to exercise, or entitlement to acquire, direct or indirect control over the company's affairs, including the ownership of over 50% of the company's share capital, voting rights and distributable income or assets in the event of the winding up of the company.

Many UK private companies are close companies, whereas publicly quoted companies tend not to be close companies. As many private companies are close companies, the specific tax provisions that relate to close companies must be considered. Certain companies that under the above definitions would be regarded as close companies are not actually considered close companies (these are beyond the scope of this textbook).

9.2 Definitions

These definitions are based on those in Part 10 CTA 2010.

9.2.1 "Participator"

A "participator" is any person having a share or interest in the capital or income of the company and also includes:

1. a person who possesses, or who is entitled to acquire, share capital or voting rights in the company;
2. a "loan creditor" of the company (this is a creditor to the company because of money lent to the company or a capital asset sold to the company. A normal bank would not, however, be regarded as a loan creditor);

3. any person who has a right, or is entitled to acquire a right, to a share in the distributions of the company including any amounts payable to loan creditors by way of premium on redemption; and

4. any person who is entitled to secure that income or assets, either at present or in the future, will be applied directly or indirectly for his benefit.

Future entitlement includes anything which the person is entitled to do at a future date, or will at a future date be entitled to do.

9.2.2 "Control"

A person is regarded as having control of a company if he exercises, is able to exercise, or is entitled to acquire, direct or indirect control over the company's affairs and, in particular, if the person possesses or is entitled to acquire:

1. more than 50% of the company's issued share capital;
2. more than 50% of the company's voting share capital;
3. more than 50% of the company's income if it were distributed (excluding rights as a loan creditor); or
4. more than 50% of the company's assets in a winding up.

Importantly, if two or more persons together satisfy any of the conditions, they are deemed to have control. Therefore, in determining if an individual satisfies any of the above tests, the rights and powers of his associates and any company over which he, or he and his associates, have control, are attributed to him.

9.2.3 "Associate"

An "associate" of a participator means:

1. A relative of the participator (i.e. spouse or civil partner, parents or grandparents, child or grandchild, brother or sister).
2. A partner of the participator.
3. A trustee of a settlement established by the participator or a relative.
4. If the participator has an interest in any shares or obligations of a company which are subject to any trust, the trustees of any settlement concerned.

9.2.4 "Director"

In order to be regarded as a director, a person need not actually have the title director. A "director" includes a person:

1. occupying the position of director by whatever name called; or
2. in accordance with whose directions or instructions the directors are accustomed to act; or
3. who is a manager of the company or otherwise concerned in the management of the company's trade or business and who, as beneficial owner, is able to control at least 20% of the company's ordinary share capital (either directly or indirectly).

Example 9.1

Shares in Alphabet Ltd, a UK resident company, are held as follows:

	Status	Shareholding
Mr A	Director	10%
Mrs A		2%
Mrs C (Mr A's aunt)		2%
Mrs B		10%
B Ltd (Shares in B Ltd held 50% each by Mr and Mrs B)		5%
Mr J (Mrs B's cousin)		4%
Mr D	Director	10%
Mrs D		2%
Ms D (Mr and Mrs D's daughter)		2%
Mrs E (Mr D's sister)		2%
Mr F		6%
Mr G		5%
Other shareholdings		
(unrelated parties all holding < 5%)		40%
		100%

Is Alphabet Ltd under the control of five or fewer participators?

Shares held by Mr A:		
Mr A	10%	
Mrs A	2%	12%
Shares held by Mrs B:		
Mrs B	10%	
B Ltd	5%	15%
Shares held by Mr D:		
Mr D	10%	
Mrs D	2%	
Ms D	2%	
Mrs E	2%	16%
Mr F		6%
Mr G		5%
		54%

In determining the shares controlled by each participator, shares held by associates are included. While spouses, children, siblings and parents are included as associates, shares held by cousins or aunts are not included.

Alphabet Ltd is under the control of five or fewer participators and is, therefore, a close company.

9.3 Consequences of Close Company Status

A company controlled by a small group of persons can arrange its affairs to enable those persons to avoid tax. The rationale for the special tax rules for close companies is to deal with the fact that closely held companies can, generally, take decisions in such a way as to minimise tax. These would not be feasible for a publicly quoted company.

Without the close company rules, it is likely that more individuals would incorporate, although incorporation may become less attractive given the future increase in the rate of corporation tax from 1 April 2023. The top income tax rate is currently 45% (plus either employee's NIC or self-employed Class 2 and Class 4 NICs), while the corporation tax rate for the financial year 2021 is 19%. Therefore, at the 19% rate of corporation tax, incorporation could possibly save money. However, the close company status provisions may make incorporation significantly less attractive, as they:

- extend the meaning of "distributions" to encompass certain benefits, excessive interest and transfers at undervalue that may be disguised distributions of profit to the shareholders or their families; and
- impose tax in respect of certain loans made to shareholders that would otherwise represent the extraction of profits without the payment of tax by the shareholders (section 455 being the legislative basis of the rule).

The detailed operation of these negative consequences is set out in **Chapter 10**.

Questions

Review Questions
(See Suggested Solutions to Review Questions at the end of this textbook.)

Question 9.1

X Ltd has 1,000 issued shares of £1, held as below:

Trustees of A's settlement	449
Mrs A (settlor)	60
Ten other shareholders	491
Total issued ordinary shares	1,000

The ten shareholders are not associated with each other or with A or Mrs A and none of them hold more than 50 shares.

Requirement
Determine if X Ltd is a close company.

Question 9.2

In a trading company, issued ordinary shares carry one vote each but 'A' ordinary shares do not confer any voting rights. The shareholders are as below:

	Ordinary shares	'A' ordinary shares
A	280	
Wife of A	100	
B (brother of A)	10	
Trustees of A's settlement	40	
Company X (controlled by A)	80	
	510	
Mrs C (daughter of B)	20	
10 other equal holdings	470	500
Total issued shares	1,000	500

The shares carry equal rights to dividend.

Requirement

Determine if the company is a close company.

Question 9.3

The authorised and issued share capital of Company Y is £1,000 in the form of 1,000 ordinary shares of £1 each, held as below.

A	200
B	100
C	50
D	50
E	40
Company Z	99
Other shareholders	461
Total issued ordinary shares	1,000

A, B and C are directors.

The issued capital of Company Z is £100 in the form of 100 ordinary shares of £1 each, held by:

F (son of E)	60
G	40
Total issued shares	100

The shareholders in Company Y, other than Company Z, are all individuals and none are related or otherwise associated. No 'other shareholder' holds more than 50 shares.

Requirement

Determine if the company is a close company.

Close Companies: Disadvantages

Learning Objectives

After studying this chapter you will understand:

■ The holistic tax implications for close companies of expenses, excessive interest and loans to participators (and their associates), and transfers at undervalue.

10.1 Disadvantages of Close Company Status

The disadvantages of close company status are as follows:

1. Certain **expenses** paid by a close company on behalf of participators/associates of participators are treated as distributions.
2. **Interest** payments made by a close company to participators/associates of participators that are in excess of a normal commercial rate of return may be treated as a dividend.
3. There is a potential tax payable by close companies when making **loans** to participators or their associates. Loans to participators or their associates that are subsequently **written off** will be assessable to income tax in the hands of the individuals.
4. Transfers at undervalue by close companies can result in the capital gains tax base cost of the share of shareholders in a close company being adjusted; or the undervalue charged as a distribution on participators or as employment income on employees.

There are also inheritance tax implications where a close company makes a transfer of value (see **Chapter 28, Section 28.1**).

10.2 Certain Expenses for Participators and their Associates

Any expenses incurred by a close company in providing benefits or facilities of any kind for a non-working participator, or a non-working associate of the participator, are treated as a distribution. Where an item is treated as a distribution, the expense is disallowed in the company's corporation tax computation.

The following expense payments are not treated as distributions:

1. Any expense made good to the company by the participator/associate of a participator.
2. Any expense incurred in providing benefits or facilities to working directors or employees as such expenses are already assessable as benefits in kind.

3. Any expense incurred in connection with the provision for the spouse, children or dependants of any director or employee of any pension, annuity, lump sum or gratuity to be given on his death or retirement.

Example 10.1

Mr A holds 2% of the ordinary share capital of X Ltd, a close company. Mr A is not an employee or director of X Ltd.

X Ltd pays the rent on Mr A's house of £3,000 per annum. The amount is charged each year in X Ltd's accounts under rental expenses.

As X Ltd is a close company and Mr A is a participator, the expense will be treated as a distribution. Accordingly, the £3,000 will be disallowed to X Ltd in arriving at its taxable total profits and will also be treated as a distribution in the hands of Mr A (i.e. Mr A will be treated as receiving a dividend of £3,000. This will be taxed accordingly).

10.3   Excessive Interest

A participator, or an associate of a participator, may lend money to the close company and charge interest on that loan. Interest payments made by a close company to non-working participators/associates that are in excess of a normal commercial rate of return may be treated as a dividend. Any excess is thus not deductible for corporation tax and should be added back in the corporation tax computation. If the payment is to an employee or director of the company, the interest is deductible for corporation tax purposes and is instead taxed on the employee's/director's employment income as a benefit in kind.

The allowable element of the interest paid by the company is subject to a late payment rule that prevents a corporation deduction being obtained where the interest is accrued and paid more than 12 months from the end of the relevant accounting period.

Any allowable element of the interest paid to the participator/associate (who is not an employee or director) is taxable on them under the income tax rules for savings income.

Interest payments by participators/associates to companies on overdrawn loan accounts that are below the normal commercial rate may be classed as a distribution or as a benefit in kind and taxable as employment income, depending on the status of the recipient. However, at all times the employment income treatment takes precedence over the distribution treatment.

Example 10.2

Mr X owns 100% of X Ltd and has lent the company £100,000. He charges the company 10% interest annually. The amount is charged each year in X Ltd's accounts under 'Interest paid'. The commercial rate of interest on such a loan would be 5%.

As X Ltd is a close company and Mr X is a participator, the excess interest of £5,000 will be treated as a distribution. Accordingly, the £5,000 will be disallowed to X Ltd in arriving at its taxable total profits. It will also be treated as a distribution in the hands of Mr X (i.e. Mr X will be treated as receiving a dividend of £5,000 for income tax purposes). When paying the interest to Mr X, X Ltd will be required to deduct 20% basic rate income tax and follow the CT61 procedure (see **Chapter 7, Section 7.6.1**).

10.4   Loans to Participators and their Associates

Where a close company makes a loan to an **individual** who is a participator or an associate of a participator, the company will be required to pay tax in respect of the amount of the loan at the rate of 32.5% (section 455 CTA 2010). The section 455 tax is due for payment on the lower of:

- the loan balance outstanding at the end of the accounting period; or
- the loan balance outstanding nine months and one day from the end of the accounting period.

Any section 455 tax forms part of the company's corporation tax liability for the period and is due on the relevant date.

There are **three exceptions** to the above, that are **not** treated as loans to participators:

1. Where the business of the company is or includes the lending of money and the loan is made in the ordinary course of that business.
2. Where a debt is incurred for the supply of goods or services in the ordinary course of the business of the close company, unless the credit given exceeds six months or is longer than the period normally given to the company's customers.
3. Loans made to directors or employees of the company if:
    (a) the amount of the loan, together with all other loans outstanding made by the company to the borrower (or his spouse), does not exceed £15,000; **and**
    (b) the borrower works full time for the company; **and**
    (c) the borrower does not have a "material interest" in the company (broadly defined as more than 5% of ordinary share capital). If the borrower subsequently acquires a material interest, the company is required to pay corporation tax in respect of all the loans outstanding from the borrower at that time.

When the loan, or part of the loan, is repaid by the participator /associate or if it is released or written off, the section 455 tax, or a proportionate part of it, is refunded to the company provided a claim is made within four years of the end of the accounting period in which the repayment is made or the release or writing-off occurs. However, the tax is not refunded with interest. A refund of section 455 tax cannot be reclaimed until nine months and one day after the end of the accounting period in which the loan is repaid (or partially repaid), released or written off.

Depending on the timing of the repayment, the company can either:

- complete an amended return for the accounting period in which the loan was made (provided the amended return is submitted within the 12-month period); or
- write to HMRC with the appropriate details, or complete HMRC's iForm for claiming the repayment.

Example 10.3

ABC Ltd, a close company, made interest-free loans to the following shareholders in the accounting period to 31 March 2022. The company does not pay corporation tax in instalments. Assume the loans are still outstanding on 1 January 2023.

	£
Mr A (director owning 10% of the share capital)	
Loan made 29 June 2021	16,000
Mr B (director owning 4% of the share capital)	
Loan made 31 October 2021	10,000
Mr C (director owning 20% of the share capital)	
Loan made 31 December 2021	8,000

continued overleaf

What are the tax consequences for the company, assuming that no other loans had been made to the three individuals in the past? You may also assume that Mr A and Mr B work full time for the company.

The company will be required to pay corporation tax in respect of the loans to Mr A and Mr C at 32.5% of the outstanding amount, calculated as follows:

	£
Mr A	16,000
Mr C	8,000
	24,000 × 32.5% = £7,800

The loan to Mr B is not subject to this provision as:

1. Mr B is a director who works full time for the company, and

2. he does not have a "material interest" in the company, and

3. the loan is less than £15,000.

This tax of £7,800 must be paid over to HMRC on or before 1 January 2023 (nine months and one day after the accounting period end). The tax will be repaid (or partially repaid) by HMRC nine months and one day after the end of the accounting period in which the loans have been repaid (or partially repaid) by the shareholders. For example, if the loans were repaid to the company by Mr A and Mr C in the accounting period ended 31 March 2023, the section 455 tax would be repaid by HMRC to the company no earlier than 1 January 2024.

10.4.1 "Bed and Breakfast" Rule

In the past, HMRC perceived avoidance behaviour to be taking place by participators and close companies seeking to exploit the legislation by what was known colloquially as the "bed and breakfasting" of loans to participators. Loans would be repaid by the accounting period end date, or in the nine months between the end of the accounting period, to prevent the section 455 charge becoming due and payable. The participator would then, very shortly after the repayment, redraw the money (or a greater amount). The participator had therefore only lost the use of the money for a very short period – and in many cases never intended the repayment to be lasting. In addition, other loans may be repaid after the section 455 tax has been paid on them, so that a section 455 repayment relief claim can be made. Again, the participator very shortly afterwards would have redrawn the money with the same result, i.e. the participator still had the funds but had also reclaimed the tax.

To tackle such behaviour, the '30-day rule' was introduced. This provision is a mechanical rule that applies where, within any 30-day period:

■ repayments totalling £5,000 or more are made (before or after the end of the accounting period); and
■ new loans totalling £5,000 or more are made (after the end of the first accounting period).

In this situation, the repayments are matched to repaying the new loans (rather than any earlier loans) to the extent that the repayment does not exceed the new loan.

Example 10.4
Mr Alf Bett owns 100% of the shares in ABC Limited. The company's accounting period ends on 31 March and it does not pay corporation tax in instalments.

On 25 May 2021 the company lends Mr Bett £6,000; on 29 March 2022 he repays the loan. On 3 April 2022, during the new accounting period, the company makes a new loan to him of £6,000. This is still outstanding at 1 January 2023.

continued overleaf

> The legislation matches the repayment of £6,000 in March 2022 against the new loan. Therefore the loan made on 25 May 2021 is still treated as outstanding and section 455 tax of £1,950 (£6,000 × 32.5%) will therefore be due on 1 January 2023.

10.5 Write-off of Loans to Participators

Where a company makes a loan to a participator and subsequently releases or writes it off, the shareholder is deemed to receive a distribution, i.e. a dividend, at the time of writing off the loan as a debt is released. The participator will be treated as though their total income for the year in which the release, or writing off, occurs is increased by the amount released or written off. In other words, it is treated as a dividend in his or her hands. If the individual is also an employee, there is potentially a double charge to tax – once as a dividend, and once as employment earnings. To prevent this, priority is given to taxing the write off as a dividend for income tax purposes. However, no similar treatment exists for national insurance purposes. This means that the income, while treated as a dividend for income tax purposes, is still taxed as earnings for national insurance purposes and Class 1 NICs (both employer's and employee's) may be due on the amount written off.

In addition, the section 455 tax already paid by the company is not available for offset against any additional tax arising in the hands of the individual. The company can, however, reclaim the section 455 tax paid, subject to the procedure, conditions and time limits for same already outlined.

Example 10.5

Assume that in **Example 10.3** Mr A repays his loan of £16,000 on 1 February 2023 and at the same time the company writes off the loan to Mr C.

What are the tax consequences for the company and the shareholders?

Company

The company will be repaid the tax on Mr A's loan, i.e. £5,200 (32.5% × £16,000) but only after 1 January 2024, i.e. nine months and one day after the end of the accounting period in which repayment occurred (being 31 March 2023).

Shareholders:

There are no tax consequences for Mr A.

Mr C, however, will be assessed as receiving gross distribution income of £8,000. This amount will be subject to income tax at the dividend rate, and this charge will take precedence over any employment income tax charge. Class 1 NICs will potentially also be payable on the loan write off. Tax will also be repaid on Mr C's loan. The company will also not be entitled to a corporation tax deduction for the £8,000 written off to the statement of profit or loss.

10.6 Transfers at Undervalue by Close Companies

10.6.1 Corporation Tax Implications for the Company

Where a company transfers a chargeable asset to any person other than by way of a bargain made at arm's length, section 17 TCGA 1992 treats them as having sold the asset at market value and, therefore, corporation tax will arise on any chargeable gain on the basis of deemed market value being substituted for the undervalue proceeds. A capital loss can arise on the basis of market value, which can be used in the usual way (see **Chapter 7, Section 7.9.1**). HMRC are likely to very carefully scrutinise the market value utilised in such transactions.

The transferee of the asset is treated as having acquired the asset at market value. If the transfer took place at undervalue, the transferee will have a capital gains tax base cost that is higher than the amount they paid for the asset. However, generally speaking, such transfers are only likely to occur between persons connected to the company as the company is unlikely to be willing to suffer a chargeable gain or to forego a capital loss to give a third party a tax benefit.

10.6.2 CGT Implications for the Participator

A transfer at undervalue by a company to another company or individual, be they connected to the company or not, will also reduce the value of the company's shares. Put simply: if a company with assets worth £100,000 sells them for £20,000, the value of a 100% shareholding will be reduced by £80,000; the value of a 75% shareholding would be reduced by £60,000.

Section 125(1) TCGA 1992 restricts the advantage a shareholder may have gained if a close company transfers assets at undervalue in a bargain made other than at arm's length. The acquisition cost of the shares is reduced by an appropriate proportion of the difference between the market value of the asset and any consideration paid for it. The appropriate proportion is calculated by allocating the difference between the shareholders in proportion to their shareholding in the company. If the apportioned undervalue is greater than the shareholder's acquisition cost, the acquisition cost is reduced to nil. In situations where the transferee is a company and the transfer of the asset is covered by section 171 TCGA 1992 (see **Section 13.5**) then section 125 does not apply. In addition, a transfer at undervalue is also likely to be a transfer of value for inheritance tax purposes if the company is a close company (see **Chapter 28**, **Section 28.1**).

10.6.3 Exceptions for Transfers at Undervalue by Participators

There are exceptions built into the legislation to ensure a taxpayer is not taxed twice on transfers of an asset at undervalue where the transferee is a participator/associate of a participator in the company, or where they are an employee (including a director).

Distribution Exception
Under section 125(4) TCGA 1992 Case 2, if the transferee is a participator or an associate of a participator in the company and the transfer is treated as a distribution under the close company rules, then section 125(1) does not apply and the base cost of the shares is not adjusted.

Employment Income Exception
Under section 125(4) Case 3, if the transferee is an employee of the company and the undervalue is treated as their employment income, then section 125(1) does not apply and the base cost of the shares is not adjusted. The undervalue is thus taxed under income tax as employment income, resulting in both income tax and NIC liabilities. Note that this treatment takes precedence where the transfer at undervalue is made to a participator who is also an employee or director.

Example 10.6
In March 2006, Mrs Donnelly buys 5,000 out of the 50,000 shares issued in Happy Holidays Ltd, a close company, for £50,000. In September 2013, Happy Holidays Ltd sells a caravan site with a market value of £800,000 to an unconnected person at a price of £500,000. In December 2021, Mrs Holland sells her 5,000 shares for £300,000. She is not an employee of the company. What are the consequences of these transactions?

The acquisition cost of Mrs Holland's shares is reduced by a proportionate part of the transfer at undervalue. Mrs Holland owns 5,000 out of the 50,000 issued shares. The undervalue is £300,000 (market value of £800,000 less the consideration paid of £500,000), thus the proportion by which the base cost of her shares is reduced is 10% of the undervalue, being £30,000. The revised base cost of her shares is therefore £20,000 (£50,000 less £30,000, the proportion of the undervalue), meaning she will have a chargeable gain on the disposal of her shares in December 2021 of £280,000 (£300,000 less the revised base cost of £20,000) and not £250,000.

continued overleaf

If the company had sold the caravan to Mrs Donnelly for the above amount, as she is a participator in the company the base cost of her shares would not have been adjusted (in accordance with section 125(4) Case 2). Instead, the sale at undervalue would have been taxed on her as a distribution, paying income tax at a maximum rate of 38.1%.

If Mrs Donnelly had been a participator and an employee/director of the company, again the base cost of her shares would not have been adjusted, this time under section 125(4) Case 3. Instead, as an employee of the company, the employment income rules would take precedence and the sale at undervalue would be taxed on her as employment income instead of as a distribution at a maximum rate of 47%.

Questions

Review Questions

(See Suggested Solutions to Review Questions at the end of this textbook.)

Question 10.1

(a) State the tax effect on a close company arising out of a loan made to a participator in that company. Indicate the circumstances in which the loan would have no tax consequences for the company.

(b) Size Ltd is a close company and has the following adjusted profits for the year ended 31 March 2022:

	£
Property income	30,000
Trading income	100,000
Deposit interest	3,000
	133,000

Calculate Size Ltd's corporation tax liability for the year ended 31 March 2022.

Question 10.2

Close Ltd is a family-owned distribution company. Results to 31 March 2022 are as follows:

	£	£
Gross profit	50,000	
Other income (Note 1)	10,000	
		60,000
Depreciation	15,000	
Salaries	10,000	
Rent and rates	1,000	
Sundry (Note 2)	1,100	(27,100)
Net profit		32,900

Notes

1. Other income:

	£
Bank interest	8,500
Capital grants	1,500
	10,000

2. Sundry:

	£
Miscellaneous office expenses	300
Expenses of majority shareholder's brother Y who does not work for Close Ltd paid to him on 01/07/2021	800
	1,100

Capital allowances due are £4,000.

Requirement
(a) Compute the corporation tax payable.
(b) Explain the tax treatment of the expenses paid for Y.

Question 10.3

Maxi Ltd, a family-owned company, deals in farm machinery. The results for the year ended 31 March 2022 were as follows:

	£	£
Sales		6,300,000
Opening stock	1,100,000	
Purchases	5,650,000	
	6,750,000	
Closing stock	1,450,000	
		(5,300,000)
		1,000,000
Less: Expenses		
Administration	220,000	
Financial	200,000	
Distribution and sales (Note 1)	270,000	
Depreciation	100,000	(790,000)
Trading profit		210,000
Loss on sale of plant (Note 4)	(20,000)	
Profit on sale of building (Note 2)	1,480,000	
Rents (Note 3)	200,000	
		1,660,000
Net profit		1,870,000

The directors have a policy of not paying dividends.

Notes
1.   The following items were included in distribution and sales:

	£
Entertainment	
Entertaining customers	6,000
Entertaining suppliers	5,000

Staff Christmas party	10,000
Christmas gifts for suppliers	900
Cost of MD attending trade fair in London	850
	22,750

2.   The building, which was sold in October 2021, had been acquired in 1970 for £2,000. It was valued at £50,000 on 31 March 1982. The building was located on a site on which planning permission had been granted for the construction of a shopping centre. Proceeds received for the building were £1.5 million. Legal fees of £18,000 were incurred in connection with the disposal. Indexation allowance from March 1982 to 31 December 2017 was 110%.

3.   On 1 June 2021, the company re-let its investment property under a 20-year lease. A premium of £50,000 was received on the sub-letting. This premium is included in property income in the statement of profit or loss.

4.   Total capital allowances for the year were agreed at £50,000.

Additional information
In June 2021 the managing director (and principal shareholder) borrowed £550,000 from the proceeds from the sale of the building to purchase a new residence for himself in his own name.

    Maxi Ltd has £210,000 of trading losses forward which arose in the period ended 31 March 2017.

Requirement
Calculate the corporation tax payable by Maxi Ltd. The CGT consequences arising from the granting of the lease may be ignored.

Question 10.4

Servisco Ltd, a closely held firm of management consultants, had the following income for the year ended 31 March 2022:

	£
Professional income	430,000
Property income	100,000
Bank deposit interest	50,000
Chargeable gains before adjustment	86,400

The company had a loss forward of £9,000 on its professional activities from the year ended 31 March 2017.

    The company received dividends of £17,500. £10,000 of these dividends were from another UK company in which Servisco has a minor shareholding. The remaining £7,500 gross dividend was from a company resident in the Republic of Ireland, in which Servisco Ltd holds 7.5% of the shares, and was received on 1 April 2021.

Requirement
Compute the company's corporation tax liability for the year ended 31 March 2022.

Question 10.5

Machinery Ltd was incorporated in the UK on 1 June 1970 and since that date has been engaged in providing machinery to companies.

The founder members of the company were Mr Vincent Duffy and his wife Julie and the company was formed to take over their existing business which they previously conducted in partnership. Mr and Mrs Duffy have actively encouraged members of their immediate family and other relatives to take up employment within the company and have endeavoured to ensure that the control of the company remains, as far as possible, within the family.

The company's statement of profit or loss for the year ended 31 March 2022 showed the following results:

		£	£
Sales			1,660,000
Stocks at 31/03/2022		450,000	
Stocks at 01/04/2021		(360,000)	(90,000)
			1,750,000
Purchases			(805,000)
Gross profit			945,000
Less:	Depreciation	59,790	
	Rent	79,710	
	Light and heat	17,500	
	Distribution costs	39,000	
	Bank and loan interest	65,000	
	Motor expenses (all vans)	44,300	
	Sundry expenses	13,000	(318,000)
	Net profit from trading		626,700
Add:	Bank deposit interest	10,000	
	Rents from let property		
	(after allowable deductions)	50,000	60,000
	Profit for year		686,700

The shareholdings and loans made to the company as at 31 March 2022 were:

	Ordinary £1 shares	Loans made (@ interest rate)	Interest paid £
V. Duffy (director)	3,000	£4,000 @ 15%	600
Mrs J. Duffy (director)	1,250	£5,000 @ 12%	600
Trustees of settlement made by V. Duffy	2,900	£5,000 @ 15%	750
Executors of the will of J. Duffy deceased (father of V. Duffy)	2,000	£5,000 @ 15%	750
D. O'Connell (director)	2,750	£5,000 @ 15%	750
Mrs K. Moran (aunt of V. Duffy)	500	–	–
L. T. Smith (director)	2,100	£10,000 @ 13.21%	1,321
Louise Hare (company secretary)	3,000	£3,000 @ 5.5%	165
Paul Hare (husband of V. Duffy's sister)	2,500	£3,000 @ 6%	180
	20,000		5,410

Notes
1. V. Duffy is an executor of his father's will.
2. The loan interest was paid in addition to bank interest of £59,590, thus reconciling with the amount shown in the statement of profit or loss.
3. For the accounting period ended 31 March 2022, capital allowances were £10,700.
4. None of the shareholders are related except as shown above.
5. The share capital at 1 April 2021 was the same as at 31 March 2022.
6. The commercial rate of return is deemed to be 6%.

Requirement
Compute the corporation tax liability of the company for the accounting year ended 31 March 2022.

Question 10.6

Tax Advisors Ltd, a professional services company, had the following sources of income and charges for the year ended 31 March 2022:

	£
Trading income	100,000
Interest income	100,000
Qualifying charitable donations paid	(60,000)

Requirement
Calculate the corporation tax payable by Tax Advisors Ltd in respect of the above figures.

11

Non-resident Companies

Learning Objectives

After studying this chapter you will understand:

- The residence rules for companies resident in the UK.
- The tax treatment of a non-resident company.
- The principles of double tax relief.

11.1 Introduction

You will recall from **Chapter 8** that a company incorporated in the UK is automatically UK tax resident. In addition, a company centrally managed and controlled in the UK is also regarded as resident in the UK. Most companies in the UK are UK resident and are therefore liable to UK corporation tax on all their profits, irrespective of where the income arises or wherever the assets (classed as chargeable gains) are situated. This is known as the worldwide basis of taxation. The remittance basis of taxation is not available to companies or branches of companies and is only available to individuals (see **Chapter 2, Section 2.6** and **Chapter 17, Section 17.6**).

If a non-UK resident company were to move its central management and control to the UK, it would thus become UK resident. However, the jurisdiction of its incorporation may determine that it also remains resident in that other country. In this situation, the company becomes a dual-resident company, and the relevant double taxation treaty and any specific tiebreaker clause needs to be examined in such situations.

A company that is regarded as resident in another country under the terms of a double taxation treaty may, therefore, have its income exempt from UK corporation tax. See **Section 11.2** for the UK tax position of non-resident companies

11.1.1 UK Companies Trading Overseas

A UK company may trade overseas through a variety of different structures, each with differing tax implications.

Overseas Subsidiaries

Where a UK company expands into international markets, it may establish a separate subsidiary company in the foreign country. Often the foreign subsidiary is managed and controlled in that foreign country and is, therefore, not UK resident. Such foreign subsidiaries of UK companies are non-resident in the UK and are only liable to UK corporation tax as a non-resident company, as detailed later. Foreign subsidiaries typically do not generate UK profits (as they are established to generate foreign profits) and, therefore, in most cases no UK tax is payable by the foreign subsidiary. Foreign tax is likely to arise in the overseas jurisdiction.

Overseas Branches

Alternatively, the UK company may establish a branch in the foreign country. The profits of the foreign branch will be included with the year end results for the UK company and are chargeable to UK corporation tax as a UK resident company is subject to corporation tax on the worldwide basis as set out earlier. The foreign branch profits may or may not be assessed to tax in the foreign country, depending on the taxation rules in the foreign country. Where foreign tax is payable, this will normally be available for deduction by credit relief against the element of the UK corporation tax assessed on the branch profits, thereby providing double taxation relief.

UK corporation tax legislation allows companies with overseas branches to exempt the results (both profits and losses) of all of its overseas branches from UK corporation tax. This would mean that no double tax relief (see **Section 11.3**) would be available as branch profits would not be subject to UK corporation tax. Companies are able to opt into this exemption regime, and any such election is irrevocable. This election has effect from the start of the next accounting period after the election is submitted.

This election should be considered if additional UK corporation tax arises when branch profits are subject to additional UK corporation tax. The most relevant scenario for Northern Ireland companies is those who have a branch presence in the Republic of Ireland. Such branch companies pay only 12.5% Irish corporation tax on their Irish branch trading profits. However, an additional 6.5% (19% UK rate −12.5% Irish rate) corporation tax arises in the UK because those branch profits are also taxable in the UK despite full double taxation relief being available.

In this scenario, the additional UK corporation tax of 6.5% would be saved by entering into the foreign branch exemption election.

In a scenario where the Irish branch is loss-making, an additional saving of 6.5% arises on branch losses relievable in the UK. In loss-making scenarios where additional relief is available in the UK, the foreign branch exemption would be resisted.

11.1.2 *Foreign Investment into the UK*

Where a foreign company establishes an operation (e.g. factory in the UK), the operation may be run by a company in the group. This company may be a UK-resident company established specifically to run the UK operation. Sometimes, for international tax planning reasons, a non-resident company is used (see **Section 11.2**). Alternatively, a UK branch operation may instead be set up as part of the non-resident company structure.

11.2 Non-resident Companies

A non-resident company is chargeable to UK corporation tax if it carries on a trade in the UK through a permanent establishment (PE). A PE is a fixed place of business through which the business of the company is wholly or partly carried on; **or** it can be where an agent has, and exercises, authority to do business on behalf of the company. Examples of a fixed place of business include a branch, workshop, factory or office.

If the non-resident company does carry on a trade in the UK through a PE, corporation tax will be charged on:

1. any trading income arising directly or indirectly through or from that PE;
2. any income, wherever arising, from property or rights used by, or held by or for that PE, e.g. income from patent rights held by the branch;
3. chargeable gains accruing on assets situated in the UK used for the purpose of the trade of the PE; and
4. profits of UK property businesses, other UK property income and profits of loan relationships that the non-resident company is a party to for the purpose of the property business or generating the income.

Income from sources *within* the UK that are not subject to corporation tax (as set out above) are instead subject to **income tax** at the basic rate (currently 20%) on any UK income. If tax has been deducted at source from such income, the tax payable is limited to that amount.

Therefore the difference between a non-resident and a resident company is that any profits not attributable to the UK branch, e.g. foreign interest and foreign trading income, are not liable to UK tax. In addition, a non-resident company is not generally entitled to double tax relief in the UK for any foreign tax paid, as it is not UK resident.

11.3   Double Taxation Relief

As we have seen, UK resident companies are liable to UK corporation tax on worldwide income. Due to domestic tax laws, the company may, on occasion, be taxed in two countries on the same income:

- in the country where the income arises; and, also,
- in the country where the company is resident.

To eliminate this double tax charge, double taxation relief may be given in the country of residence. Relief can be obtained in one of three ways:

1. under the provisions of a double taxation treaty;
2. as credit relief (also known as 'unilateral relief') under a double taxation treaty or in its own right (i.e. via UK domestic legislation); or
3. as deduction relief.

11.3.1   Double Taxation Treaties

Relief can be provided under a double taxation treaty (DTT) in two main ways:

1. **Exemption relief** – where income is only taxable in the country of residence.
2. **Credit relief** – which reduces the UK corporation tax by the amount of overseas tax paid.

The maximum relief obtained cannot exceed the UK corporation tax on the same income.

11.3.2   Unilateral Relief

Where there is no DTT in place, relief for double taxation may be given as unilateral relief. This relief is the lower of:

- the overseas tax paid; or
- the UK corporation tax on that source of income.

The relief available is calculated on a source-by-source basis. The basic rule is that the relief available is the lower of the UK corporation tax due on that source of income and the foreign tax suffered. Note that overseas taxable income is always included gross in a corporation tax computation, i.e. inclusive of any foreign tax paid.

Double taxation relief will not be a consideration where a foreign dividend is received that meets one of the dividend exemption tests (see **Chapter 7, Section 7.8.2**), or where the profits of a foreign branch are not subject to UK corporation tax due to the foreign branch exemption. If an overseas dividend is not exempt, relief for foreign tax paid can be claimed. Overseas dividends received by a UK resident company may have suffered withholding tax. Withholding tax is generally recoverable (subject to the limit for unilateral relief) but not in cases where the dividend is exempt from UK corporation tax.

In addition, as dividends are paid out of post-tax profits, the dividend will also have suffered what is called 'underlying tax'. A credit for underlying tax can only be claimed when a company holds directly, or indirectly, at least 10% of the voting power of the company paying the dividend, or is a subsidiary of such a company. Where a dividend is paid by a non-resident company to a UK resident company, there is a cap for the underlying tax. The calculations of this cap and relief for underlying tax are beyond the scope of this textbook.

11.3.3 Surplus Foreign Tax

Generally there is no relief in a scenario where the foreign tax paid is greater than the UK corporation tax liability on that income. However, where surplus foreign tax arises on the profits of a non-exempt foreign branch whose profits of the overseas permanent establishment are subject to corporation tax in the UK, surplus unrelieved foreign tax (after double tax relief) may be **carried forward** to the next accounting period or **carried back** to accounting periods beginning in the previous **three years**.

The carry forward is indefinite, (unless the permanent establishment ceases to exist), though the surplus unrelieved foreign tax can only be set against corporation tax due on profits from the same permanent establishment.

The carry back is on a **LIFO basis**, starting with later years first. The time limit for a claim is **four years** from the end of the accounting period in which the surplus unrelieved foreign tax arose or, if later, one year after the foreign tax was paid.

Questions

Review Questions

(See Suggested Solutions to Review Questions at the end of this textbook.)

Question 11.1

Shed-It Limited is a manufacturing company based in Newry and a client of your practice. Shed-It does not pay corporation tax in instalments. Stephanie Adams, the finance director, telephones you requiring advice on a possible expansion of Shed-It's activities.

Shed-It wants to expand into the Republic of Ireland as it believes there is a market for the company's products there. The board is undecided if these activities should be operated through a branch of Shed-It (the company does not currently have any overseas branches) or a 100%-owned Irish resident subsidiary company, Shed-It (Ireland) Ltd. The board is aware that the rate of corporation tax in the ROI is much lower (12.5%) and is keen to keep its overall corporation tax liability as low as possible. However, projections prepared show that this Irish trading activity is likely to be loss-making, at least initially.

Requirement

Write a letter to the finance director of Shed-It outlining the exposure to UK corporation tax and any other relevant tax factors if Shed-It:

(a) establishes a branch in the Republic of Ireland; or
(b) sets up a 100% wholly-owned subsidiary in the Republic of Ireland.

Question 11.2

Prudent Limited, a UK resident company has the following income for the year ended 31 March 2022:

	£
Adjusted trading profits from UK business	1,400,000
Profits from an overseas branch	450,000
Taxable total profits	1,850,000
Withholding tax on overseas branch profits (@ 15%)	

Requirement

Calculate the UK corporation tax payable, with or without an irrevocable election that profits from all of its overseas branches are exempt from UK corporation tax.

Group Relief and Consortia Relief

12.1   Introduction

For corporation tax purposes, the percentage shareholding that one company has in another often determines the taxation consequences.

The main types of relationship for tax purposes (based on the degree of share ownership) are:

1. Related 51% group companies
2. 75% subsidiaries
3. Consortia
4. Capital gains groups (see **Chapter 13**).

12.1.1   Related 51% Group Companies

For corporation tax purposes, two companies are related 51% group companies only if they are members of a "51% group". A "group" of companies for this purpose means a group headed by a company, irrespective of where it is resident. Dormant companies are not counted.

As outlined in **Chapter 7**, the number of related 51% group companies can determine the limits to be applied for determining if a company is required to pay corporation tax in instalments.

A 51% relationship exists where there is an entitlement to at least 51% of the share capital, voting rights, income or net assets on a winding up.

A company is another company's related 51% group company in an accounting period if it is a related 51% group company for **any part** of the accounting period. This rule applies to each of two or more related 51% group companies even if they are related 51% group companies for different parts of the accounting period.

12.1.2 Group Relief

While related 51% group companies are based on more than 50% shareholding/control, special rules apply to situations where the share ownership reaches 75%.

For corporation tax purposes, two companies are members of a "group" for group relief purposes where one is a direct/indirect 75% subsidiary of the other, or both are 75% subsidiaries of a third company. In this context, for one company to be a 75% subsidiary of another, the holding company must have at least 75% of the ordinary share capital. However, if the company is not also entitled to at least 75% of the distributable income of the subsidiary **and** entitled to at least 75% of the net assets of the subsidiary on a winding up, group relief may be denied when there are unusual financing structures in a subsidiary so that, for example, the parent is entitled to less than 75% of profits.

For two companies to be in a group, there has to be a 75% effective interest. Hence, if company H owns 90% of company A, which in turn owns 80% of company B, then B **is not** in a group with H as H only has an effective interest of 72% of B (being 90% of 80%). Nevertheless, A and B **are** in a group for group relief purposes as they have a 75% relationship. Note that a company can be a member of more than one group for 75%-group relief purposes. In this example, A and B also form a group together, therefore A is a member of two groups.

However, it should be noted that the group relief rules **cannot** be circumvented by trying to use company A as a conduit. For example, if B transfers losses to A, these cannot in turn be transferred by A to H, or vice versa.

A group-relief group may include non UK-resident companies. Furthermore, while losses may generally only be surrendered between UK-resident companies, group relief can, in certain circumstances, be available to UK branches or permanent establishments of overseas non-UK companies or to UK holding companies of certain overseas non-resident subsidiaries.

In addition, a non-UK resident company that does not have a UK branch or UK permanent establishment but which is carrying on a UK property business that comes within the charge to corporation tax can also be regarded as a UK member of a group of companies for group relief purposes. This means that both profits and losses of such non-resident companies can be group-relieved to other members of the group. This is, however, dependent on whether or not relief has already been claimed elsewhere for the same loss (i.e. whether relief for the loss has already been obtained in the local territory of the non-resident company).

12.1.3 Consortium Relief

A company is owned by a consortium if:

1. at least 75% of its ordinary share capital is owned by companies (known as members of the consortium), none of whose shareholding is less than 5%, and each member of the consortium is entitled to at least 5% of any profits available for distribution and at least 5% of any assets on a winding up; **or**
2. if a trading company is a 90% subsidiary of a holding company and is not a 75% subsidiary of any company apart from the holding company and, as a result of 1, the holding company is owned by a consortium, then that trading company is also owned by the consortium.

Although a consortium can be established with non-UK resident companies, losses generally cannot be surrendered to or from a non-UK resident company under the consortium relief rules.

12.1.4 Capital Gains Groups

Companies are in a capital gains group if, at each level, there is a 75% holding and the top company has an effective interest of at least 51% in the group companies. Compare this with the effective 75% direct and indirect interest required for "group-relief groups".

Thus, if company S holds 80% of company T, which in turn holds 80% of U, which in turn holds 80% of V, which in turn holds 80% of W, then:

- S, T, U and V are in a capital gains group (since S has an effective 51.2% interest in V, being 80% × 80% × 80%);
- but S only has a 40.96% effective interest in W (80% × 80% × 80% × 80%), so W is not part of this capital gains group.

For group relief purposes, the groups would be S and T, T and U, U and V, and finally V and W. Therefore, losses from S can be surrendered to T (and vice versa), but the losses from S cannot flow onwards to U, despite T being part of both groups. Only losses arising in T could be surrendered to U (or vice versa).

In contrast with the position for group relief outlined above, it is only possible to be part of one capital gains group. See **Chapter 13** for more on capital gains groups.

12.2 Intragroup Payments

Certain payments made by companies are generally required to be made under deduction of income tax at the standard rate (see **Chapter 7, Section 7.6**).

A UK company is not required to deduct tax at source from intragroup interest and royalty payments where the other company is either:

1. UK resident; or
2. if non-resident, the company operates a UK permanent establishment (though see the rules for royalty payments to non-residents covered in CA Proficiency 1).

Inter-company interest can be accrued in the year to obtain tax relief.

If interest is being paid by a UK company to a company not resident in the UK and without a UK permanent establishment, basic rate income tax (currently 20%) must be deducted and the CT61 procedure outlined in **Section 7.6.2** followed. However, the recipient company can apply to HMRC to have the interest paid gross without deduction of tax.

12.3 Group Relief for Losses

12.3.1 Introduction

The group relief provisions mean that companies within a 75% group (see **Section 12.3.6**) can transfer current-period and most carry-forward losses to other group companies within the group. They can then be offset against taxable profits to reduce the group's overall corporation tax liability.

Generally, losses may only be surrendered between UK-resident companies. In certain circumstances group relief is available to UK branches of overseas companies (see **Section 12.3.9**) and losses of EEA overseas subsidiaries may be group-relieved to its UK holding company (see **Section 12.3.8**).

12.3.2 Current-period Losses

The type of eligible current-period losses that can be group-relieved include:

1. trading losses; or
2. surplus non-trade loan relationship deficits.

The total amount of these losses may be surrendered by the surrendering company, even if it has other taxable profits in the same accounting period against which these losses could be set.

Furthermore, the surrendering company may also surrender, in the following order:

3. excess qualifying charitable donations;
4. excess UK property business losses;
5. excess management expenses; and
6. excess non-trading losses on intangibles.

Capital losses can never be surrendered as group relief (however, see **Chapter 13**, **Section 13.5.1**). The amount of "excess" available for group relief in categories 3–6 inclusive refers to amounts in excess of a profit-related tax threshold. This threshold is the surrendering company's taxable profits before any losses are set off (including brought forward losses).

The surrendering company surrenders to the claimant company/companies (i.e. the profit-making companies), which must set the losses against taxable total profits of the same chargeable accounting period.

Any losses claimed under group relief cannot be carried back, carried forward or given to another group member by the company which has received these via group relief.

The offset against taxable total profits is made after qualifying charitable donations and any current-year or brought-forward losses. However, the offset is made before losses brought back from a future period, i.e. losses carried back do not displace group relief already claimed.

Where the surrendering company's and claimant company's accounting periods are not coterminous, **both** the profits and losses must be apportioned so that only the results of the **overlap** period are relevant. The apportionment is generally calculated on a time basis, unless another method provides a more "just and reasonable" result. In addition, where a company joins or leaves a group part way through an accounting period, group relief is restricted to the part of the period where the companies were part of the group.

12.3.3 Carry-forward Losses

Most losses carried forward (see **Chapter 7, Section 7.9**), with the exception of pre-1 April 2017 losses, can also be surrendered to other group members. However, in such cases the loss restriction rule should be considered. The loss restriction applies to all types of losses carried forward, including the use of capital losses. As a result, companies with profits in excess of the relevant deductions allowance are not able to reduce profits wholly to nil by using relief for carried-forward losses. Where a company is a member of a group, the £5 million deductions allowance is shared (on a pro-rata basis if necessary) amongst the group members as they see fit.

In addition, the deductions allowance that may be used by a group member is restricted so that where a company is a member of one group and an 'ultimate parent' of another, it is only able to use a share of the allowance from the group of which it is a member. This is designed to prevent groups from acquiring new members to increase the amount of the deductions allowance available.

Group surrender of carry-forward losses is denied to the extent that the company carrying the loss forward has the capacity to use the losses carried forward against its own profits. Relief is also denied where the surrendering company has no assets capable of producing income at the end of the period.

For the purpose of the deductions allowance, a group means two or more companies where:

- one company is the "ultimate parent" of each of the other companies; and
- is not the "ultimate parent" of any other company.

A company is the ultimate parent of another if it is the parent of that other company and no company is the parent of both companies.

A company is the parent of another company if:

- that other company is its 75% subsidiary; and
- it is beneficially entitled to at least 75% of any profits available for distribution to equity of that other company; or
- it would be beneficially entitled to at least 75% of assets in the event of a winding up of that other company.

Example 12.1: Definition of group for deductions allowance

Company A owns 100% of the shares in Company B, and Company B owns 100% shares in Company C.

Here, A is the ultimate parent; B is a 75% direct subsidiary; and C is a 75% indirect subsidiary. The "group" therefore comprises companies A, B and C for the purposes of the deductions allowance.

A and B cannot form a separate group because, while A is the ultimate parent of B, it is also the ultimate parent of C.

B and C cannot form a separate group because, while B is the parent of C, it cannot be the ultimate parent as A is the parent of both B and C.

It follows that there will be a single group deductions allowance to be shared amongst A, B and C.

The deductions allowance is allocated to companies that are members of the group by a nominated company. The nomination must be made by all the companies in the group that are within the charge to corporation tax and must state the date the nomination takes effect. The nomination must be signed by an "appropriate person" on behalf of each company. An "appropriate person" is a proper officer of the company or another person who has the authority of the company to act on its behalf.

Nominations cease to have effect when:

- a new group allowance nomination takes effect; or
- the nomination is revoked in writing by an appropriate person of a group company, or
- the nominated company ceases to be a company within the charge to UK corporation tax or ceases to be a member of the group.

The nominated company is responsible for submitting a group deductions allowance allocation statement for each of its accounting periods for which it is the nominated company. This statement must be received by HMRC before the first anniversary of the filing date of the nominated company's corporation tax return for the accounting period to which the statement relates.

A revised group allowance allocation statement can be submitted for an accounting period of a company that is or was the nominated company.

Example 12.2

Parker Ltd is a member of a large group and had trading profits of £10 million in the year ended 31 March 2022. A deductions allowance of £1 million has been allocated to Parker Ltd for the accounting period.

Advise Parker Ltd of the maximum value of carried-forward losses that can be claimed from the group.

Parker Ltd can claim up to £5.5 million of carried-forward losses, being:

Deductions allowance	£1 million
50% × (profits (£10 million) – deductions allowance (£1 million))	£4.5 million
Maximum group relief claim	£5.5 million

> **Example 12.3: Deadline for submitting group allowance statement**
> Company A is a member of a group and prepares accounts to 31 March every year. In its accounting period ended 31 March 2022 it is nominated by all the other companies that are members of the group and the nomination takes effect from 1 October 2022.
>
> Company A must submit a group allowance allocation statement for its accounting period ended 31 March 2022 (the nominee's accounting period).This must be done before 31 March 2024.

12.3.4 Method of Relief

The maximum relief that can flow from one company to another is the lower of:

1. the available loss of the surrendering company (after deducting any prior surrenders for the overlapping period); or
2. the available total profits of the claimant company (after deducting any prior claims for the overlapping period).

A detailed illustration of the calculation of the relief is given in **Example 12.4** below.

The surrendering company is given some flexibility as regards both the method of relief and the amount to be relieved. To this extent, it may surrender current-period trading losses and surplus non-trading loan relationship deficits **before** setting them against its other profits for the period of the loss **and** it can choose the quantum of its losses that it wishes to surrender. As set out in **Section 12.3.2**, only the excess of the remaining types of loss for which group relief is available can be surrendered. Carry-forward losses can only be group-relieved after the surrendering company has made all possible current-year claims for those carry-forward losses This is also subject to the group's relevant deductions allowance.

The aim of group relief is to ensure that no company in the group is unnecessarily exposed to making payments of corporation tax in instalments. Overall the quantum of corporation tax across the group will remain the same irrespective of how the group loss is relieved, as each company is subject to a 19% rate of corporation tax in FY 2021 and FY 2022. Group relief will take on added importance when the main rate of corporation tax increases to 25% from 1 April 2023.

Claimant Company
A company's 'available total profits' are its total profits after all possible deductions for the current period **except** amounts carried back from later periods **less** the amount of previously claimed group relief for that period.

The claimant company may claim maximum relief or part of the surrendering company's surrenderable amounts. The claimant company is therefore assumed to use its own current year losses or losses brought forward to determine the maximum amount of group relief it may claim. This is a theoretical calculation as HMRC is effectively restricting the availability of the losses to be claimed.

So, the profits available for offsetting group-relieved losses are calculated **after all other reliefs for the current period are claimed**, including surplus non-trade deficits on loan relationships. However, group relief is given **before** relief for any amounts brought back from later periods. It should also be remembered that if a company has qualifying charitable donations, these are allowed as deductions from the company's total profits – but only after group relief.

Example 12.4

The following companies are in a group:

Company	Accounting period	
A	12 months to 31/12/2022	Profit £72,000
B	6 months to 30/06/2022	Profit £5,000
C	12 months to 30/09/2022	Current-year trading loss £120,000

Company B claims from company C, which has not previously surrendered any of its losses.

C's "available loss for the overlapping period" is the same as its loss for the overlapping period. This is because there have been no prior surrenders of C's losses. It is calculated as:

$$6/12 \times £120,000 = £60,000$$

B's "unrelieved available profits for the overlapping period" is also the same as its "available profits for the overlapping period". This is because it has made no prior claims. It is calculated as:

$$6/6 \times £5,000 = £5,000$$

The amount that can be surrendered/claimed is the lower of these, i.e. £5,000.

A then claims from company C, which has made a prior surrender. The calculations are as follows:
The overlapping period is nine months ended 30 September 2022. C's "loss for the overlapping period" is:

$$9/12 \times £120,000 = £90,000$$

C's "available loss for the overlapping period" is this amount less the "amount of any prior surrenders attributable to the overlapping period".

Step 1

B's claim from C involves part of C's surrenderable amount for the accounting period ended 30 September 2022.

Step 2

The amount of B's claim, £5,000, is treated as being for the overlapping period in that claim, which is six months ended 30 June 2022.

The common period of the overlapping periods in B's claim and A's claim is six months ended 30 June 2022. The whole of the £5,000 is apportioned to that common period.

Step 3

The total, £5,000, is the "amount of any prior surrenders attributable to the overlapping period".

So C's "available loss for the overlapping period" is £90,000 less £5,000 which is £85,000.

A's "unrelieved available profits for the overlapping period" is the same as its "available for the overlapping period". This is because it has made no prior claims. It is:

$$9/12 \times £72,000 = £54,000$$

If there was another company in the group and A had already claimed group relief from this company for the same overlapping period, the amount of this would have to be deducted from the £54,000.

However, there have been no prior claims and, therefore, the amount that can be surrendered/claimed is the smaller of £85,000 and £54,000, which is £54,000.

Method of Claim

A claim for group relief is generally made on the claimant company's tax return, but there must also be a notice of consent given by the surrendering company. In order to amend a claim, the claimant company must withdraw the original and submit a new claim. All such claims must be made no later than:

1. the first anniversary of the filing date for the accounting period of the claim; or
2. 30 days after either the completion of an enquiry into the return, the amendment of a self-assessment or settlement of an appeal against an amendment.

There is also the facility for group-wide claims/surrenders to be made. It should be noted that no payment is required by the claimant company to the surrendering company in respect of the group relief transferred. However, any such payment, up to the level of the actual loss surrendered, is ignored for corporation tax purposes.

12.3.5 Examples

Example 12.5

A Ltd owns 80% of B Ltd. The following are the results for the year ended 31 December 2022:

	A Ltd	B Ltd
	£	£
Relevant trading profit/(loss)	10,000	(25,000)
Net credit on loan relationships	8,000	6,400

Calculate the corporation tax payable by each company.

	£	£
		B Ltd
Trading income		–
Net credit on loan relationships		6,400
Loss relief (section 37(3)(a) CTA 2010)		(6,400)
Taxable total profits (TTP)		NIL

	A Ltd
Trading income	10,000
Net credit on loan relationships	8,000
Total	18,000
Group relief (section 99 CTA 2010)	(18,000)
TTP	NIL

Loss Memo	£
Relevant trading loss for y/e 31/12/2022	25,000
Utilised by way of:	
section 37(3)(a) against B Ltd	(6,400)
section 99 against profits of A Ltd	(18,000)
Losses to be carried forward under section 45A	600

Example 12.6

C Ltd owns 90% of D Ltd and 90% of E Ltd. The following are the results for the year ended 31 March 2022. Both C Ltd and D Ltd were "large" for instalment purposes in the previous accounting period. The companies have been in a group since 31 March 2000.

	C Ltd	D Ltd	E Ltd*
	£	£	£
Relevant trading profit	500,000	90,000	200,000
Net credit on loan relationships	6,000	12,000	23,000
Property income	30,000	10,000	18,000
Chargeable gain	110,000	–	–
Qualifying charitable donation	(5,000)		

* E Ltd has a trading loss of £594,000, which was carried forward from the accounting period ended 31 March 2021.

continued overleaf

Calculate the corporation tax payable by each company after maximum utilisation of any group relief available.

In questions of this type, one should begin by looking at the position in the absence of any group relief.

	C Ltd	D Ltd	E Ltd
	£	£	£
Trading profit/(loss)	500,000	90,000	200,000
Net credit on loan relationships	6,000	12,000	23,000
Property income	30,000	10,000	18,000
Chargeable gain	110,000	–	–
Qualifying charitable donations	(5,000)		
TTP	641,000	112,000	241,000
Corporation tax rate	19%	19%	19%

	C Ltd	D Ltd	E Ltd
	£	£	£
TTP (before group relief)	641,000	112,000	241,000
Less: section 45A CTA 2010			(241,000)
Less: section 99 CTA 2010	(353,000)	(12,000)	
TTP after group relief	288,000	100,000	-
Corporation tax rate × 19%	54,720	19,000	-

The limit for quarterly instalments must be calculated first. There were three related 51% group companies in the group at the end of the previous accounting period; therefore the limit is £1,500,000/3, i.e. £500,000. It is important to note that a company can only surrender carried-forward losses that it is unable to deduct from its own profits during that accounting period. This means that E Ltd must first use the carried-forward losses against its own taxable profits before surrendering any remaining losses to C Ltd or D Ltd. It would appear that the losses of E Ltd can be surrendered in any manner as each company is paying corporation tax at 19%. However, because the instalment payments limit is £500,000, C Ltd Ltd would be required to pay its corporation tax in instalments as its augmented profits before any group relief is greater than £500,000. Therefore it will be critical to reduce the level of its TTP to at least £500,000.

In this example, because the amount of carried-forward losses being used does not exceed £5 million, relief for the trading loss carried forward by E Ltd is not restricted by virtue of the deductions allowance.

Example 12.7: Corresponding accounting period
F Ltd owns 100% of G Ltd. F Ltd's results for the year ended 31 August 2022 show a trading loss of £12,000 and it has no other income.

G Ltd has had the following results for the two years ended 30 November 2021 and 2022:

	Year ended	
	30 Nov 2021	30 Nov 2022
	£	£
Trading income	16,000	10,000

For the year ended 30 November 2021, the overlap period would be 1 September 2021 to 30 November 2021 (although technically apportionment should be in days, we shall work in months for simplicity).

continued overleaf

	£
G Ltd (profits 3/12 of £16,000)	4,000
F Ltd (losses 3/12 of £12,000)	(3,000)

Thus G Ltd could make a group relief claim for £3,000 against its profits.

For the year ended 30 November 2022, the overlap period would be 1 December 2021 to 31 August 2022.

	£
G Ltd (profits 9/12 of £10,000)	7,500
F Ltd (losses 9/12 of £12,000)	(9,000)

Thus G Ltd could make a group relief claim for £7,500 against its profits.

The unutilised loss of £1,500 (£12,000 − £3,000 − £7,500) is available for relief in the normal way (either carry back/carry forward, etc.). The deductions allowance does not need to be considered in this example as the loss being utilised is not a loss carried forward.

12.3.6 Qualifying Group

To avail of group relief in the relevant accounting period, the profit-maker must be in the same "75% group" as the loss-maker. This condition is satisfied in relation to two companies if one company holds, directly or indirectly, not less than 75% of the ordinary share capital of that company, or if the companies are 75% subsidiaries of another company. Groups can include all companies whether UK resident or not. However, under general rules, the loss of a foreign company cannot be transferred and relieved in the UK, and vice versa, except as set out in **Sections 12.1.2, 12.3.8** and **12.3.9**.

A company may establish the 75% holding by aggregating any ordinary shares held directly in that company and also those held indirectly through the medium of a third company. This is illustrated further in the following examples of qualifying loss groups.

Examples of Qualifying 75% Loss Group for UK Group Surrenders

1. Where the loss-maker is a 75% subsidiary of the profit-maker, or vice versa:

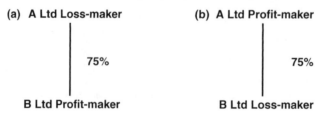

2. Where both are 75% subsidiaries of a third company:

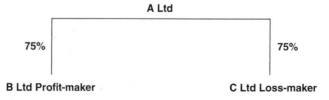

3. By establishing a 75% relationship through the medium of a third company – A Ltd owns 100% of C Ltd and 50% of B Ltd and C Ltd also owns 30% of B Ltd.

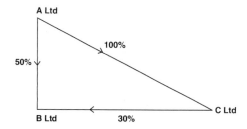

A Ltd, B Ltd and C Ltd are all members of the same 75% loss group.

12.3.7 General Considerations

1. In a qualifying group, relief may be passed upwards, downwards or sideways.
2. It is permissible for two or more profit-makers to avail of relief from any one loss-maker.
3. It is not necessary for the profit-maker to make a claim for the full amount of the loss-maker's loss, i.e. the claim may be tailored to suit the individual company's needs. It is not necessary for the profit-maker to make a payment to the surrendering company when claiming group relief.
4. Even if the relationship between the companies is less than 100%, all of the loss may be grouped as long as the companies form a group-relief group.
5. The rule in group relief that requires that losses of the surrendering company must first be applied in reducing other profits arising in the accounting period of the loss, only applies to carry-forward losses. The surrendering company may, for current-period losses only, choose to be liable to corporation tax on any trading or non-trading loan relationship profits of the period, while surrendering the full amount of the loss sustained in the period. However, losses in categories 3–6 in **Section 12.3.2** must be set first against any current-period income sources the company may have. Therefore it is only the excess, unused amounts of these losses that are available for surrender.
6. It is vital to remember that, before availing of group relief, the profit-maker concerned must claim all other reliefs, except set-off of losses for a subsequent accounting period.
7. Group relief is only available where the accounting period of both the loss-maker and profit-maker corresponds wholly or partly. Where they correspond partly (overlap period), the relief is restricted on a time-apportionment basis.
8. Generally, group relief claims must be made no later than the first anniversary of the filing date for the accounting period of the claim.
9. The loss-maker must give formal consent for the surrender of the loss.
10. Payments to the loss-maker by the profit-maker for availing of the losses are ignored for corporation tax purposes, provided they do not exceed the amount of the loss surrendered, i.e. no tax deduction is available to the profit-maker in respect of the payment and the receipt by the loss-maker is not taxable.
11. The group deductions allowance and the allocation of group relief should be done in the most tax-efficient manner. This will generally mean ensuring no company in the group is unnecessarily exposed to instalment payments of corporation tax.

12.3.8 Worldwide Groups

Groups can be established by including companies not resident in the UK. However, generally, the losses of a foreign company cannot be group relieved in the UK; nor can a UK company surrender losses to a non-resident company.

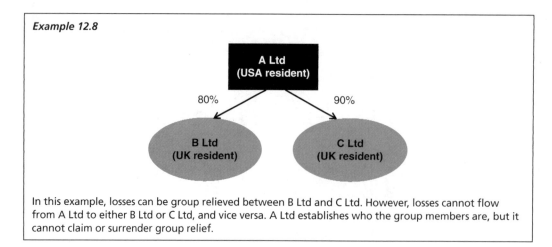

Example 12.8

In this example, losses can be group relieved between B Ltd and C Ltd. However, losses cannot flow from A Ltd to either B Ltd or C Ltd, and vice versa. A Ltd establishes who the group members are, but it cannot claim or surrender group relief.

12.3.9 Overseas Losses of EEA Resident Subsidiaries

Under UK tax legislation, a "qualifying overseas loss" may be surrendered for group relief purposes to a UK parent company if the losses are incurred by EEA subsidiaries and certain conditions are met. The EEA comprises all EU Member States plus Iceland, Liechtenstein, and Norway.

Anti-avoidance legislation prevents relief for such losses where the amount would not qualify for group relief but for any relevant arrangements, or the amount would not have arisen to the non-resident company but for any relevant arrangements and the main purpose, or one of the main purposes, of the relevant arrangements was to secure group relief.

To qualify for the relief, the surrendering company must be chargeable to tax under the law of an EEA state. Relief is available where either:

1. the surrendering company is a 75% subsidiary of the claimant company and the claimant company is resident in the UK; or
2. both the surrendering company and the claimant company are 75% subsidiaries of a third company that is resident in the UK.

The losses to be surrendered must meet the following conditions:

- the equivalence condition – the loss is a type of loss eligible for group relief;
- the EEA tax loss condition – the loss arises under the laws of the EEA state;
- the qualifying loss condition – the loss has not been, or cannot be, used in the current accounting period, or has not been carried back or carried forward by the company or a third party; and
- the precedence condition – the loss cannot be relieved in an intermediate holding company that is not resident in the UK, nor in the same territory as that in which the surrendering company is resident.

The qualifying loss condition essentially makes sure that relief is only available in the UK for only the surplus unused EEA loss.

Once it has been established that a loss exists under the above conditions it must be recalculated using UK rules. The maximum loss that can be surrendered is the recalculated EEA loss. The usual group relief rules for coterminous accounting periods and the amount that the claimant company can claim then apply. Given the strict conditions that apply before a loss can be surrendered, it will only be in limited circumstances where an EEA loss can be group-relieved.

It should be noted that these rules still apply as they are incorporated into UK legislation; however, it is possible that post-Brexit they could be amended or even repealed. As yet, no changes have been signalled.

Example 12.9
X Ltd is resident in France. It's corporation tax computation for the accounting period ended 31 March 2022 includes the following components:

	£
Trading loss	425,000
Non-trade interest paid	175,000
Property income	100,000
Unrelieved EEA loss	500,000
UK recalculation:	
Trading loss	425,000
Surplus non-trade loan relationship debit	<u>175,000</u>
Potential loss available for group relief	600,000
Property income	100,000

The UK recalculation shows that, potentially, all £600,000 could be surrendered as group relief, leaving the £100,000 property income subject to corporation tax in France. However, under the rules a loss only meets the qualifying loss condition to the extent that relief cannot be given for any period.

In the EEA, £100,000 of either the foreign trading loss or the foreign surplus non-trade loan relationship debit is relieved against the foreign property income. This amount does not meet the qualifying loss condition. Therefore the amount available for relief in the UK is £500,000, although it would still need to be shown that the loss has not been used in the current accounting period, or carried back or carried forward by the company or a third party before it can qualify.

12.3.10   UK Permanent Establishments of Non-resident Companies

Losses may be transferred to a UK permanent establishment (PE) of a non-resident company by a UK group member (and vice versa) if the following conditions are satisfied:

- if a profit had arisen in the UK PE it would have been subject to UK corporation tax (and would not be exempt under a double tax treaty); and
- no part of the loss is relievable or allowable, in any period, against non-UK profits of any person for the purposes of any foreign tax.

The effect of such surrenders is that the loss of the UK PE is treated as relievable in the foreign territory in preference to relief in the UK.

If the non-resident company is established in the EEA, losses of its UK PE may be surrendered provided that they are not actually used against the non-UK profits of any person in any period. If the losses are subsequently used against non-UK profits, any UK group relief claimed is withdrawn.

12.4   Consortium Relief for Losses

12.4.1   Definition of a Consortium

If it is the case that a company is not a group member because it fails the 75% test (meaning group surrenders are not possible to or from that company), it should instead be considered if a consortium exists, which can provide consortium relief for losses.

As set out earlier, a consortium company is:

- a company that is **not** a 75% subsidiary of any company; and
- **at least** 75% of its ordinary shares are owned by companies, **each** of which owns **at least** 5%.

This is known as '**consortium condition 1**'. The company owned by the consortium members is referred to as a consortium-owned company; the companies holding the shares are known as consortium members. '**Consortium condition 2**' – broadly, where a consortium-owned company meeting consortium condition 1 is itself the parent of a 90% trading company – scenarios are outlined in **Section 12.4.3**. A consortium can also be established by "link" companies, but these provisions are beyond the scope of this textbook.

12.4.2 Consortium Relief

Consortium relief is a variation of group relief where losses of a UK consortium-owned company can be surrendered to UK consortium members and vice versa. A surrender is also possible from a non-UK resident company carrying on a trade in the UK through a PE where a consortium relationship exists.

The surrender of losses for consortium relief is different to group relief because it is in proportion to the consortium member's interest in the consortium company. Remember, for group relief purposes once the group members have been established, potentially all the loss can be surrendered (subject to certain conditions being satisfied).

Note that the group relief rules outlined in **Section 12.3.9**, which allow relief for losses of overseas EEA subsidiaries, do not apply to consortium situations.

Example 12.10

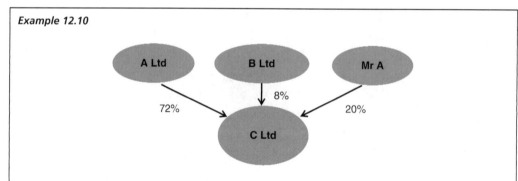

Assume that A Ltd is UK resident and B Ltd is resident in Ireland.

In this example, C Ltd is a consortium-owned company as at least 75% (in this case 80%) of its shares are owned by companies A Ltd and B Ltd, the consortium members. In addition, no single company owns 75% of the shares (as that would make the companies group members) and no single company holds less than 5% of the shares. It is irrelevant that the remaining 20% of the shares are held by an individual, Mr A.

The effect of consortium relief is that a loss of C Ltd is available to the UK resident consortium members. 72% of that loss could be transferred to A Ltd. No losses can be transferred to B Ltd because it is not UK resident; and no losses can be transferred to Mr A because he is an individual. And finally, losses cannot be transferred between A Ltd, B Ltd and Mr A.

C Ltd is owned, to the extent of 72%, by one UK resident company, which owns at least 5%. However, to determine whether a consortium exists we include the shares owned by B Ltd, even though B Ltd cannot receive or surrender losses under the consortium relief rules.

12.4.3   Consortium Condition 2

Consortium relief may also be available if 'consortium condition 2' applies, that is where:

■   there is a consortium holding company; and
■   that holding company has a 90% trading subsidiary that is not a 75% subsidiary of any company apart from the holding company; and
■   as a result of 'consortium condition 1', the holding company is owned by a consortium.

When a consortium-owned company is a holding company in this way, losses can flow directly between the 90% trading subsidiary/subsidiaries and the consortium members, based on the amount of the 90% trading subsidiary's loss, multiplied by the consortium member's interest in the consortium-owned company.

A consortium member's interest is taken as the lowest percentage of the following factors:

■   ownership of ordinary share capital;
■   entitlement to profits available for distribution to equity holders;
■   entitlement to assets distributable to equity holders on a winding up; or
■   the proportion of the voting power that is directly possessed by the consortium member.

Losses can flow to or from the consortium members and the holding company. Again, all of the companies must be UK resident. A surrender is also possible from a non-UK resident company carrying on a trade in the UK through a PE.

Under consortium condition 2, the consortium-owned holding company and the consortium-owned trading company also form their own group for group relief purposes. Where there is a possibility of a group surrender and a consortium relief surrender, group relief takes priority. It is therefore deemed that any group relief claims that the consortium-owned holding company or 90% trading company could make within that group have been made. Therefore it is the net loss that may be surrendered to the consortium members in the relevant proportions.

Example 12.11

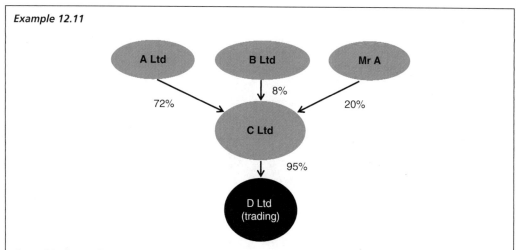

If D Ltd had a trading loss of £100,000 and C Ltd had no taxable total profits, 72% of D Ltd's loss (i.e. £72,000) could be surrendered to A Ltd. Note that it is the consortium member's interest in the holding company (C Ltd) that is relevant here – the loss is not further apportioned based on the holding company's interest in the trading subsidiary.

If C Ltd had other income of £50,000, a deemed group relief surrender from D Ltd to C Ltd of £50,000 would be made. Of the remaining £50,000, 72% (i.e. £36,000) could be surrendered to A Ltd. However, in both scenarios, if A Ltd's profits are below the maximum surrender possible, then only this amount can be surrendered as consortium relief.

12.4.4 Deemed Current-year Claim

Where a consortium-owned company has a loss and has other income, it is also deemed that a current-year section 37(3)(a) CTA 2010 loss relief claim is made first by the company **before** consortium relief is computed. Note that this differs to group relief, which does not require the surrendering company to make a current-year claim first in respect of either trading losses or surplus non-trade loan relationship deficits. It is therefore the consortium-owned companies' net loss after any current-year claim that is available to the consortium members. The current-year claim is only a notional claim – while it does restrict the maximum loss available under consortium relief, it does not actually have to be made by the company.

12.4.5 Available Amounts

Consortium Condition 1

If the consortium-owned company is loss-making, the maximum consortium relief available is the lower of:

- the consortium-owned company's loss, multiplied by the consortium member's interest in that consortium; or
- the consortium member's available profit.

Consortium Condition 2

If the 90% trading subsidiary of a consortium-owned holding company is loss-making, the maximum consortium relief available is the lower of:

- the consortium-owned 90% trading subsidiary's loss, multiplied by the consortium member's interest in that consortium; or
- the consortium member's available profit.

If the claimant company is a consortium-owned company, the maximum consortium relief available is the lower of:

- the consortium-owned company's profit, multiplied by the consortium member's interest in that consortium; or
- the consortium member's available loss.

The consortium relief rules also contain provisions that mirror the group relief rules where the claimant company and surrendering company do not have coterminous accounting periods and where companies have recently become consortium-owned or consortium members part-way through an accounting period.

The types of losses that can be surrendered as group relief and the rules and restrictions that apply to them also apply to consortium relief.

12.4.6 Administrative Aspects

The group relief administration rules and time limits also apply to consortium relief claims.

Example 12.12

H Ltd owns 65% of K Ltd, I Ltd owns 25% of K Ltd and J Ltd owns 10% of K Ltd. Thus K Ltd is a consortium-owned company whose consortium members are H Ltd, I Ltd and J Ltd.

The results for the year ended 31 March 2022 were as follows:

	H Ltd	I Ltd	J Ltd	K Ltd
	£	£	£	£
Trading profit/(loss)	780,000	80,000	1,000	(63,000)
Net credit on loan relationships				13,000

H Ltd paid corporation tax in instalments in prior years.

Calculate the corporation tax liability for all four companies, assuming that it would be more efficient to relieve as much as possible of the loss in K Ltd to H Ltd. Assume H Ltd's only related 51% group company is K Ltd.

Solution

It would be more efficient for H Ltd to claim consortium relief of 65% on the £63,000 loss as this would reduce its taxable total profits to below £750,000, the limit at which it must make instalment payments of corporation tax. However, for consortium relief purposes, the amount available for surrender **must** be reduced by the potential current year claim by K Ltd against its other income sources.

Therefore the consortium relief that may be claimed by H Ltd, I Ltd and J Ltd is:

H Ltd	The lower of:	
	(£63,000 − £13,000) × 65% = £32,500	
	£780,000	£32,500
I Ltd	The lower of:	
	(£63,000 − £13,000) × 25% = £12,500	
	£80,000	£12,500
J Ltd	The lower of:	
	(£63,000 − £13,000) × 10% = £5,000	
	£1,000	£1,000

So, the consortium members' corporation tax liabilities are:

H Ltd – Corporation Tax	£
Profits	780,000
Consortium relief	(32,500)
Taxable total profits (TTP)	747,500
Corporation tax: £747,500 @ 19%	142,025
Liability (due on or before 1 January 2023)	

I Ltd – Corporation Tax	£
Profits	80,000
Consortium relief	(12,500)
TTP	67,500
Corporation tax: £67,500 @ 19% (due on or before 1 January 2023)	12,825

continued overleaf

J Ltd – Corporation Tax

Profits	1,000
Consortium relief	(1,000)
TTP	Nil

K Ltd has unused losses to use in the current period and then carry-forward of £17,000 (being £63,000 − £32,500 − £12,500 − £1,000).

12.5   The Corporate Interest Restriction Regime

The OECD's Base Erosion and Profit Shifting (BEPS) project is an initiative to tackle the issue of multinational enterprises 'shifting' profits between companies, often in groups, to minimise tax liabilities resulting in the erosion of a countries tax base. The UK's Corporate Interest Restriction (CIR) legislation implements BEPS Action 4 recommendations to limit excessive tax relief for net interest and related costs. Ultimately, the aim is that a company only obtains a corporation tax deduction for finance costs commensurate with the extent to which its activities are subject to corporation tax in the UK.

The CIR should be considered in the context of all UK resident companies liable to corporation tax. However, groups with less than £2 million of net UK interest expense and other financing costs per annum are not be subject to the restriction and have no reporting requirements. This £2 million *de minimis* limit is adjusted for periods of less than 12 months.

12.5.1   Operation of the CIR

The CIR potentially applies where there is a 'worldwide group' (based on IFRS consolidation rules) (see **Section 12.3.8**), consisting of an 'ultimate parent' company and any consolidated subsidiaries. An ultimate parent with no consolidated subsidiaries is referred to as a "single-company worldwide group". In most cases the ultimate parent will have at least one consolidated subsidiary and is referred to as a "multi-company worldwide group". It is the ultimate parent's accounting period that is considered when calculating the CIR. However, groups can nominate one company (the reporting company) to file the CIR return for the whole group.

The aim of the legislation is to restrict a group's deductions of **net** interest and similar financing costs (its 'tax-interest') to an amount relative to the group's activities that are already taxed in the UK. In calculating this amount, any borrowings from third parties are taken into account.

The Steps for Calculating the CIR
There are two methods for calculating the interest allowance (the restriction) of a group's tax-interest deductions:

1. the fixed ratio method – limits the tax-interest deduction to 30% of the **UK** group companies' tax-EBITDA (i.e. taxable earnings before tax, interest, depreciation and amortisation); or
2. the group ratio method – limits the tax-interest deductions by calculating the proportion of net group interest expense (excluding interest on related party debt) as a percentage of the tax-EBITDA of **all** group companies. This percentage is then applied to the **UK** tax-EBITDA.

The fixed ratio method is the default method; the group ratio method must be elected for (although this election can be revoked).

The group ratio method can potentially result in a higher restriction limit, i.e. higher than the 30% fixed rate, but it is capped at 100%. Similarly, if the calculation results in a negative result or if group EBITDA is zero, it is also set to 100%.

Once the method for calculating the interest allowance is decided upon, the modified debt cap must then be considered. This debt cap is a further potential restriction, capping the interest or debt allowance at the level of the group's 'net group-interest expense', i.e. its worldwide net debt costs **excluding** any inter-company finance costs. The UK companies in the group will therefore suffer a disallowance of tax-interest deductions where the **aggregate UK net tax interest expense** (ANTIE) in the accounting period exceeds its **interest capacity** for the period. This excess is referred to as the 'total disallowed amount', which can be allocated to the UK companies in any way (generally so that a company can avoid having to pay corporation tax instalments).

The interest capacity is calculated as the greater of:

- the interest allowance for the accounting period, plus unused interest allowance from earlier periods; or
- £2 million (on a pro-rata basis if necessary).

Any unused interest allowance can be carried forward for up to five years. This means that disallowed interest can be "reactivated" if there is sufficient interest allowance in a subsequent period. Disallowed interest can be carried forward indefinitely.

Example 12.13

An overseas parent company has a £10 billion loan from an external unconnected source on which it pays interest of £200 million. The overseas parent lends £200 million to its 100% UK subsidiary company, which pays £50 million in interest to its overseas parent. The UK subsidiary company itself holds 100% of the shares in a non-UK trading company.

The tax-EBIDTA of each company is:

	£m
Overseas parent	350
UK company	100
Non-UK trading company	100
Total group tax-EBIDTA	550

The group is a worldwide group and as the UK holding company has net interest expenses of over £2 million (being £50 million) it is subject to the CIR rules.

Using the fixed ratio method, the interest allowance is 30% of the UK company's tax-EBITDA, i.e. 30% × £100 million = £30 million.

Using the group ratio method, the interest allowance is:

$$\frac{\text{Group net qualifying interest expense}}{\text{Group tax} - \text{EBITDA}} \times 100$$

$$\frac{£200 \text{ million}}{£550 \text{ million}} \times 100 = 36.36\%$$

Therefore the group would elect to use the group ratio method as this gives a higher allowance. The modified debt cap would then need to be considered. As this is £200 million in this case, the interest allowance is not further restricted and remains at 36.36% of £100 million.

The UK company's interest capacity for the period is 36.36% × £100 million = £36,360,000 Therefore the excess of £13,640,000 would be disallowed.

12.5.2 Administration

The CIR rules contain special filing requirements that are in addition to the company's usual obligations under the corporation tax self-assessment regime. If a group is not subject to an interest restriction, there is no filing obligation. However, if a group is subject to an interest restriction in a period of account or it wishes to apply any unused interest allowance from a previous year in a later period, it must:

- appoint a reporting company; and
- file an interest restriction return for the period within 12 months of the period end.

An amended interest restriction return can be filed up to 36 months after the end of the relevant period of account. The filing responsibility for the interest restriction return falls on the reporting company which will normally be appointed by the group. The CIR regime has its own set of penalty rules for late filing and errors in returns etc.

Questions

Review Questions
(See Suggested Solutions to Review Questions at the end of this textbook.)

Question 12.1

B Ltd has the following results for year ended 31 March 2022:

	£
Tax-adjusted trading profits (i.e. after current year capital allowance claim)	170,000
Bank deposit interest	4,000
Property income	20,000

Unutilised trading losses brought forward from the year ended 31 March 2017 amount to £16,000. Z Ltd is a 100% trading subsidiary of B Ltd. During the year ended 31 March 2022, it incurred tax-adjusted trading losses of £96,000. It also had taxable interest income of £20,000.

Requirement
Compute B Ltd's corporation tax liability for the year ended 31 March 2022 after allowing for any group relief for losses of Z Ltd.

Question 12.2

A Ltd owns 80% of B Ltd's issued share capital and 75% of C Ltd's issued share capital. Results for year ended 31 March 2022 were:

	A Ltd	B Ltd	C Ltd
	£	£	£
Trading profit/(loss)	(90,000)	56,000	48,000
Net credit from loan relationships	1,000	2,000	3,000
Property income	20,000	25,000	2,000
Trading losses forward (from the accounting period ended 31 March 2017)	(4,000)	–	(26,000)

Requirement

Calculate the corporation tax payable by each company for the year ended 31 March 2022.

Question 12.3

Queen Ltd has two wholly-owned subsidiaries, Pawn Ltd and Rook Ltd. All three are trading companies. Accounts for the year to 31 March 2022 show the following results:

	Queen Ltd	Pawn Ltd	Rook Ltd
	£	£	£
Gross operating profit	297,463	81,000	47,437
Less: depreciation	12,000	10,000	16,000
Entertaining (customers)	1,350	1,200	1,650
Administration	73,650	61,110	107,373
Interest	11,150	10,720	3,000
	98,150	83,030	128,023
Net profit/(loss) before investment income	199,313	(2,030)	(80,586)

Notes

1. Rook Ltd was incorporated and commenced to trade on 1 April 2021.
2. (i) Interest is analysed as follows:

	Queen Ltd	Pawn Ltd	Rook Ltd
	£	£	£
Accrued 1 April 2021	(1,250)	–	–
Paid	10,000	9,000	2,750
Accrued 31 March 2022	2,000	1,720	250
Interest on overdue PAYE	400	–	–
	11,150	10,720	3,000

 (ii) Pawn Ltd has used its loan to purchase 7% of the share capital of Bridge Ltd, whose income consists mainly of property income from commercial properties. The interest paid by Queen and Rook is trade-related, unless otherwise identified.

3. (i) On 1 September 2021, Queen Ltd received a dividend of £9,000 from a French company in which it has a 20% shareholding. This dividend has not been included in the profit figures above.

 (ii) Queen Ltd also received deposit interest gross of £23,846, which is not included in the profit figures above.

4. Capital allowances

	Queen Ltd	Pawn Ltd	Rook Ltd
	£	£	£
	7,375	3,000	5,627

5. Pawn Ltd had trade losses brought forward of £80,000 from the accouting period ended 31 March 2021. Queen Ltd intends to pay a dividend of £10,000 on 9 June 2022.

Requirement

(a) Compute the corporation tax liabilities (if any) of each of the three companies for the year ended 31 March 2022, on the assumption that all available reliefs are claimed to the benefit of the group as a whole.

(b) State the tax consequences for the company of paying the dividend of £10,000.

(c) State the amount of any losses available to carry forward at 31 March 2022 for each company.

(d) State the due date of payment of any corporation tax payable.

Company Chargeable Gains

13.1 Chargeable Gains Liable to Corporation Tax

13.1.1 UK-resident Companies

UK-resident companies are liable to corporation tax in respect of all chargeable gains wherever they arise. As such, gains on disposal of foreign assets by a UK resident company are liable to UK corporation tax, although double tax relief may be available.

13.1.2 Non-resident Companies

A non-resident company is, generally, only liable to corporation tax if it carries on a trade in the UK through a permanent establishment. In addition, from 6 April 2020, non-resident companies will pay corporation tax on profits of UK property businesses, other UK property income and profits of loan relationships that the non-resident company is a party to for the purpose of the property business or generating the income. The chargeable gains which are assessable are those accruing on the disposal of assets situated in the UK used for the purposes of the trade of the permanent establishment.

Non-resident companies are also subject to tax on direct and indirect disposals of UK land and property under the non-residents capital gains tax regime (but which are beyond the scope of this textbook).

13.2 Exemption from Tax on Disposal of Certain Shareholdings

There is an exemption from corporation tax for any gain arising when a company disposes of the whole or any part of a substantial shareholding in another trading company (or in the holding company of a trading group). This exemption is known as the substantial shareholdings exemption (SSE). When the conditions for the SSE are met, the exemption automatically applies, meaning any gains are exempt from corporation tax with any capital losses arising not relievable.

13.2.1 The Main Exemption

The SSE legislation is set out in Schedule 7AC TCGA 1992. It contains a main exemption, which is discussed below, and two secondary exemptions (which are beyond the scope of this textbook).

The main exemption is contained in Schedule 7AC paragraph 1. It states that a gain accruing to a company (the "holding company") on a disposal of shares in another company (the "subsidiary") is not a taxable gain if the requirements in relation to the substantial holding and the subsidiary company are satisfied.

Substantial Shareholding Requirement

The first requirement, in paragraph 1, in relation to the shareholding itself is that the holding company must have held a "substantial shareholding" in the subsidiary throughout a 12-month period in the six years before the disposal takes place.

The meaning of "substantial shareholding" in this context is set out in paragraph 8 and is a holding of shares in the subsidiary company by virtue of which the holding company:

1. holds at least 10% of the company's ordinary share capital;
2. is beneficially entitled to at least 10% of the profits available for distribution to equity holders of the company; and
3. would be beneficially entitled on a winding up to at least 10% of the assets of the company available for distribution to equity holders.

As only a 10% holding of shares is required, it is not technically correct to use the terms "holding company" and "subsidiary". The legislation uses the terms "the investing company" and "the company invested in". For ease of understanding, this section will continue to refer to holding companies and subsidiaries, but bear in mind that only a 10% shareholding is required to qualify for SSE.

Subsidiary Company Requirement

The first point to note is that there is no requirement for the subsidiary company to be UK resident. The key requirement is that the company being sold must have been a "qualifying company" throughout the 12 months prior to the disposal (paragraph 19). A "qualifying company" is a trading company or the holding company of a trading group or subgroup. The terms "trading company" and "trading group" require some consideration in this context. Paragraph 20 refers to a trading company as "a company carrying on trading activities whose activities do not include to a substantial extent activities other than trading activities". A "trading group", under paragraph 21, is a group:

> "(a) one or more of whose members carry on trading activities, and
> (b) the activities of whose members, taken together, do not include to a substantial extent activities other than trading activities".

The SSE will not be available if HMRC can show that there is a substantial element of non-trading activities in a company or group. "Substantial", for these purposes, is not defined in the legislation but is generally taken to be 20% and can relate to a percentage of turnover, assets or management time.

This is the same test used for holdover relief and business asset disposal relief (see **Chapter 16, Section 16.11.4** and **Chapter 19, Section 19.1**). Trading groups often assume that there will be no difficulty in falling below the 20% test when looking at non-trading activities. The problem is that HMRC's interpretation of "non-trading activities" may differ from that of the group or its advisors. Non-trading activities can include items such as the making of intercompany loans.

There are two instances where the company being sold must also be a qualifying company immediately **after the sale**:

1. where the share disposal is to a person connected to the investing company; or
2. when the trade has been transferred into a new company within the previous 12 months.

"Connected", for these purposes, takes the definition in section 1122 CTA 2010, which deals with companies under common control (greater than 50%).

Example 13.1

Holdco Ltd, an investment company, owns 100% of the shares in Tradeco Ltd, a qualifying trading company. Holdco Ltd is a holding company with no other investments and has held the shares for five years. Holdco sells the shares in Tradeco Ltd to an unconnected third party, realising a gain of £10 million.

As Holdco satisfies the substantial shareholding requirement and Tradeco Ltd is a trading company at the time of the disposal, the gain on the disposal of shares satisfies the requirements for the main exemption in paragraph 1 of Schedule 7AC TCGA 1992 and is thus exempt from corporation tax.

Example 13.2

Owner Ltd, a UK trading company, has owned 100% of Irish Ltd, a trading company resident in the RoI, for the last 10 years. Acquisition Ltd wishes to acquire Irish Ltd. This disposal by Owner Ltd will generate a profit of £5 million. Due to the availability of SSE, Owner Ltd will pay no corporation tax on this gain.

Conversely, if Owner Ltd incurred a capital loss on the disposal, this is not a qualifying capital loss for corporation tax purposes and is thus disregarded as a loss. As the company being sold is an Irish resident company, the Irish tax implications will need to be considered.

The SSE therefore means that even if Owner Ltd is required to pay corporation tax in Ireland on the disposal of the shares in Irish Ltd, as the gain is exempt in the UK double tax relief does not arise.

13.3 Method of Taxation

Where, for an accounting period, chargeable gains accrue to a company, the chargeable gain is calculated by comparing the gross sale proceeds, net of incidental costs of sale, with the allowable items of expenditure, to include the original cost of the asset (or the value at 31 March 1982 if held at that time and this is a higher amount), any enhancement expenditure and any incidental costs of acquisition.

As well as the allowable expenditure, a company may also deduct an "indexation allowance" against the allowable expenditure. This allowance is intended to reflect the "time value of money" associated with the allowable costs and is calculated by reference to the period of ownership up to the date of sale.

Indexation allowance is calculated by multiplying the indexation factor by the original cost of the asset or any enhancement expenditure. The indexation factor is calculated as:

$$\frac{RD - RI}{RI}$$

where:

RD = Retail Price Index (RPI) at the date of disposal (for assets disposed of before 1 January 2018) or the RPI for December 2017 (for assets disposed of on or after 1 January 2018). and

RI = RPI for the month in which the expenditure (original cost or enhancement expenditure) was incurred.

The indexation factor is always expressed as a decimal and is generally **rounded to three decimal places** (although this does not apply where the asset being disposed of is shares and the shares were acquired after 31 March 1985).

Indexation allowances for companies are frozen from 31 December 2017. Disposals of chargeable assets on or before this date still attract full indexation allowance; but for disposals on or after 1 January 2018, indexation allowance is only available on assets acquired before that date and is only calculated up to 31 December 2017. Therefore, if a company acquires a chargeable asset on or after 1 January 2018, no indexation allowance will be available on its future disposal.

Note that when computing a company's chargeable gain, any **indexation allowance available cannot create a loss**, i.e. the indexation allowance is limited to the amount required to reduce the gain to nil, **or increase a capital loss**. See also the rules for capital losses recapped at **Chapter 7, Section 7.9.1**.

Example 13.3

X Ltd prepares accounts to 31 March each year. In the year ended 31 March 2022, the trading profit was £20,000. During that year, the company sold an asset for £17,000 which it had bought the previous year for £10,000. The indexation factor up to 31 December 2017 was a figure of 0.04. The company had a capital loss brought forward of £1,000.

X Ltd year ended 31 March 2022

	£
Trading profit	20,000
Chargeable gain (Note)	5,600
Taxable total profits	25,600

	£
£25,600 @ 19%	4,864

Note:
Chargeable gain

	£	£
Proceeds		17,000
Cost	10,000	
Indexation (0.04 × £10,000)	400	
		(10,400)
Gain		6,600
Capital loss b/fwd		(1,000)
Chargeable gain		5,600

As the amount of losses brought forward being used does not exceed £5 million, relief for the capital loss carried forward is not restricted by virtue of the deductions allowance.

13.4   Capital Gains Group: Introduction

A company may be part of a group for capital gains purposes – a capital gains group. This can give important benefits to the companies within the group, namely that chargeable assets can be transferred from one group company to another without triggering a chargeable gain, i.e. on a no gain/no loss basis. There are several other benefits which are outlined later.

Companies are in a capital gains group where:

1.   at each level, there is a 75% holding; and
2.   the top company has an effective interest of at least 51% in the group companies.

The 75% definition is similar to the rules for group relief (see **Chapter 12**), but for a capital gains group only 75% of the ordinary shares is needed and not 75% of distributable profits nor 75% of assets on a winding up.

The capital gains group regime also has slightly different rules for sub-subsidiaries. To be part of the group, the direct relationship must be at least 75%, but the indirect relationship need only be above 50%, i.e. at least 51% effective indirect control. In **Chapter 12** we saw that a company can be a member of more than one group for group relief of losses. However, a **company can only be a member of one capital gains group.**

The various reliefs available in a capital gains group can also apply to assets situated outside the UK and which are used in or for the purposes of a trade carried on in the UK **and** the company is a 75% subsidiary of a UK resident company.

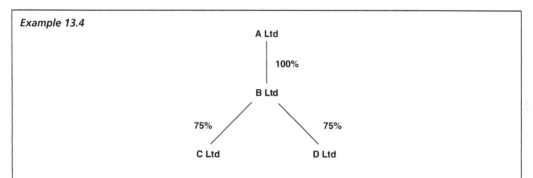

Example 13.4

A, B, C and D form a capital gains group.

If A, C and D are UK resident and B is non-resident in the UK (and has no branch in the UK), A, B, C and D still form a capital gains group but the reliefs applying on transfer of assets between group members only apply to transfers between A, C and D. However, if B had a UK branch and if the asset was used by the UK branch, even if it is situated outside the UK, then a transfer of the asset between B and A, C or D would qualify.

The distinction between a group for loss relief purposes and for capital gains purposes is that the top company **must have an effective** 75% direct or indirect interest for **group relief** purposes; whereas capital gains groups only require an effective 51% indirect interest, although direct relationships must be a minimum of 75%.

Example 13.5

X Ltd takes over 80% of the ordinary share capital of A Ltd. The new structure is as follows:

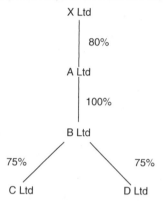

While X does not directly or indirectly own 75% of the ordinary share capital of C or D Ltd, all the companies X, A, B, C and D are members of the one capital gains group. This is because B, C and D are clearly 75% subsidiaries of A, and A itself is an effective 75% subsidiary of X. It should be noted, however, that all of the above companies do not form a single group for loss relief purposes, i.e. X, A, B, and A, B, C, D groups form separate groups for loss relief purposes, i.e. X is not common to both these groups.

A company can only be a member of one capital gains group. Where the conditions qualify so that it would appear that a company could be a member of two or more groups, it is the link to the principal company that determines to which group it belongs.

Example 13.6

A capital gains group exists.

If the non-UK resident company has a UK branch operation, capital assets can be transferred between Y Ltd and the UK branch of X Ltd without crystallising an immediate gain, or vice versa. However, if an asset were transferred by Y Ltd to the head office of X Ltd, then Y Ltd is liable to corporation tax on its chargeable gain.

This is an example of a capital gains group structure incorporating a non-resident company.

13.5 Disposal of Capital Assets within a Capital Gains Group

In general, a transfer of a chargeable asset from one member of the group to another is automatically deemed to be for a consideration of such amount that neither a gain nor a loss accrues. This relief applies as a result of section 171 TCGA 1992.

The capital gains group is effectively treated as one taxpayer so that a chargeable gain does not arise until the asset is sold outside the group or the company holding the asset leaves the group.

Non-UK resident companies are included within a capital gains group and, provided there is no loss to HMRC, the no gain/no loss transfer is possible within a worldwide group of companies. For example, it may be possible to make a no gain/no loss transfer to a non-UK resident company with a branch or agency in the UK.

Example 13.7: UK-resident companies

X Ltd owns a building which it bought for £1 million, nine months ago. It disposes of it to its parent Y Ltd when it is worth £1.525 million. Therefore, a gain of £0.525 million arose.

Normally this gain would be included in the profits of X Ltd. However, the section 171 rule ensures that the asset moves at no gain/no loss, i.e. its cost of £1 million.

Consequently, X Ltd has no chargeable gain and Y Ltd's base cost is £1 million.

Relief for transfers of chargeable assets between capital gains group companies (UK to UK only) is granted automatically and is compulsory. Therefore an election is not required.

However, where a transfer of a chargeable asset is made to a non-UK resident company that is not within the charge to UK corporation tax, the transfer of the chargeable asset is deemed to take place at market value. This means that corporation tax can arise for the transferring company (should a chargeable gain be deemed to occur).

For transactions occurring in accounting periods ending on or after 10 October 2018, if a UK resident company (or a UK branch of a non-UK resident company) transfers a chargeable asset to a group company resident in an EU/EEA country that is not within the charge to UK corporation tax, the relevant corporation tax payable can be deferred, either in whole or in part, by entering into a corporation tax payment plan. Deferral is possible only in cases where the transfer would otherwise have been on a tax-neutral basis (under section 171) but for the non-UK residence of the EU/EEA company. Under the corporation tax payment plan, the corporation tax that arises on the transaction can be deferred in whole or in part.

The transferring company must make an application (which must contain certain details) to enter into the corporation tax payment plan within nine months after the end of the accounting period in which the relevant transfer took place.

The deferred tax is due in six equal instalments as follows:

(a) the first instalment is due nine months and one day after the end of the relevant accounting period; and

(b) the remaining five instalments are due on each of the first five anniversaries of that day.

The deferred tax carries interest from the normal due date for payment of corporation tax as if the corporation tax payment plan had not been entered into. Each time a payment is made, it must also include any interest payable on it.

This deferral mechanism applies not just to corporation tax on capital gains but also on transfers of intangible assets (see **Chapter 8, Section 8.4.5**).

If certain events occur at any time after a corporation tax payment plan is entered into by a company, the outstanding balance of the deferred tax is due on the next due date for payment of the next instalment of that tax. The events are:

(a) the company becoming insolvent or entering into administration;

(b) the appointment of a liquidator in respect of the company;

(c) an event under the law of a country or territory outside the UK corresponding to (a) or (b);

(d) the company failing to pay any amount of the deferred tax for a period of 12 months after the date on which it is due; and

(e) the company ceasing to be within the charge to corporation tax.

If certain trigger events occur during the instalments period, all of the outstanding remaining tax deferred will become immediately due. A trigger event occurs if:

(a) the transferee ceases to be resident in an EEA state and does not become resident another EEA state; or

(b) the company and the transferee cease to be members of the same group; or

(c) the transferee disposes of the asset that is the subject of the payment plan.

13.5.1 Capital Losses

As noted in **Chapter 12**, capital losses cannot be included in a group relief surrender. However, under section 171A TCGA 1992, members of a capital gains group can elect for the chargeable gain or capital loss arising on disposal of an asset that is sold outside the group to be treated as if it had been transferred (either wholly or partially) between them immediately before its "outside" disposal. In this situation, the chargeable gain or allowable loss (either wholly or partially transferred) is deemed to belong to the transferee company.

A section 171A election must be made within two years of the end of the accounting period in which the disposal took place and can be for a percentage of the transaction if required. Partial transfers of gains or losses are therefore possible. Only current-year chargeable gains or capital losses can be transferred under this election.

The objective of this election is to ensure that capital losses or other losses arising in capital gains group companies fully, or partially, mitigate the gain arising, and that no company in the group is unnecessarily exposed to the instalment payment rules. This would be beneficial in circumstances where the transferee company had capital losses of its own (either carried forward or in the same period) which are unused and which would be available for offset against the deemed chargeable gain transferred under a section 171A election. From 1 April 2023 it will also be useful to transfer a capital gain from a company which is paying a lower rate of corporation tax to a company which is subject to a higher rate.

13.5.2 Pre-entry Losses

Companies that anticipate a future gain on the disposal of an asset may seek to acquire a company with capital losses forward. The asset with the gain could be transferred, before the sale, into the company with the losses forward so that the losses forward could be used to shelter the gain. UK anti-avoidance legislation restricts this type of planning in respect of "pre-entry losses".

The term 'pre-entry losses' refers to losses accruing to the company on actual disposals of chargeable assets before entry to a group which triggered a capital loss. Anti-avoidance provisions prevent the use of pre-entry losses. While the provision ensures that these losses cannot be used subsequently by a group that had no previous commercial connection with the company when those losses accrued, that company will be allowed to use those losses itself in the same way that it could have, had it never entered the group.

Pre-entry losses that actually accrued to the company before it joined the group can be set against:

1. gains on assets disposed of after entry but which were held by the company before entry;
2. a gain arising on the disposal of an asset that was acquired from a non-group member and which has been used for the purpose of the company's trade; or
3. gains on assets disposed of before joining the group.

Post-entry realised capital losses can be offset under the normal rules.

13.5.3 Rollover Relief

Provided certain conditions are fulfilled, a company may claim that a chargeable gain arising on the disposal of a business asset (the "old asset") may be "rolled over" against the cost of acquiring a replacement business asset (the "new asset").

In this scenario, the disposal of the old asset is deemed to give rise to neither a gain nor loss, and the cost of the new asset is reduced by the actual gain that would have arisen but for the rollover relief. In essence, the chargeable gain is "deferred" until such time as the new asset is disposed of (subject to the possibility of a further rollover claim being available).

Full rollover relief is only available provided **all of the disposal proceeds** (not just the chargeable gain) are applied in acquiring the new asset. Any proceeds not reinvested, i.e. the excess cash, fall to be taxed immediately (provided the amount retained is less than the gain) and the cost of the new asset is reduced by the amount of the gain that was not immediately chargeable.

The conditions which must be satisfied in order for a company to make a rollover claim are:

1. both the old and new asset must be within one of the qualifying classes of assets but do not need to fall within the same category (see below);
2. the old asset must have been used only for trade purposes throughout the period of ownership and the new asset must be used only for trade purposes; and
3. the new asset must be acquired during the period beginning one year before and ending three years after the date of disposal of the old asset.

The classes of assets include, *inter alia*:

(a) land, buildings and fixed plant and machinery;
(b) ships, aircraft and hovercraft;
(c) satellites, space stations and spacecraft.

However, for companies (unlike individuals), the list does **not** include **goodwill** or **quotas** as these assets are incorporated within the intangible assets regime for companies. The rules apply where a company, which is a member of a group, disposes of an asset used in its trade at a time when it is a member of the group, and another company acquires an asset at a time when it is a member of the same group within the period of one year before and three years after the first asset is disposed of. A joint claim must be made by the two companies. Rollover relief and group rollover for intangible fixed assets is dealt with in **Chapter 8, Section 8.4.4**.

13.5.4 Holdover Relief

Where the new asset is a "depreciating asset" (an asset with an expected life of 60 years or less at the time of acquisition), the chargeable gain arising on the disposal of the old asset **cannot** be rolled over and is **not** deducted from the cost of the new asset. Instead, the chargeable gain is "held over" or "temporarily deferred" until it becomes chargeable (crystallises) on the earliest of the following three dates:

1. the date on which the new asset is disposed of;
2. the date on which the new asset ceases to be used in the trade; or
3. the 10th anniversary of the acquisition of the new asset.

The most common types of depreciating assets (which are also qualifying assets for rollover relief purposes) are fixed plant and machinery, and leases where the term of the lease is for 60 years or less. It should be noted that, if a company were to purchase a non-depreciating asset (within the relevant class) prior to the expiration of the earliest of the above three dates, then it could "convert" the temporary "held-over" gain into a "rolled-over" gain by making a claim to do so.

13.5.5 Group Rollover Relief

Rollover relief is also available within a capital gains group. If a group member disposes of an asset which is eligible for capital gains rollover (or indeed, holdover) relief, then it can treat all the group members as a single entity for claiming such relief (provided, of course, that all relevant conditions are met).

Thus, if other group members acquire a relevant asset within the qualifying period (one year before the disposal or three years afterwards) then the company making the disposal may match the acquisition for rollover/holdover relief purposes. For it to be effective, both the acquiring company and the disposing company must make the claim.

Example 13.8

In October 2021, A Ltd sells a warehouse for £700,000 realising an indexed gain of £252,000. B Ltd, which is part of the same capital gains group as A Ltd, pays £2 million in May 2021 for the purchase of a new factory. A joint claim for rollover relief can be made by A Ltd and B Ltd which means:

1. the £252,000 indexed gain on the sale of the warehouse is not chargeable in A Ltd;
2. the base cost for capital gains purposes of the factory for B Ltd becomes £1,748,000 (i.e. £2 million less the rolled over gain of £252,000).

It should be noted that assets transferred intragroup on a no gain/no loss basis **are not available** to be matched for rollover/holdover relief purposes. See **Chapter 16, Section 16.11.3** for more on rollover relief. Note that rollover relief in the context of a company is deducted **after** deducting any available indexation allowance.

13.6 Disposal of Capital Assets Outside the Group

If there is a disposal of an asset by a member of a capital gains group to a person outside the group, and the asset had been acquired by the company making the disposal from another group member, then the period of ownership for the purpose of calculating indexation allowance (if relevant) is arrived at **by reference to the length of time the asset had been owned by the group as a whole.** Of course, if the asset had originally been acquired prior to 31 March 1982, then either the original cost or the market value at that date will form the base cost for indexation purposes. Indexation will run from 1 April 1982 to the date of sale, but is only available up to 31 December 2017 for assets disposed of on or after that date.

Example 13.9

A Ltd and Y Ltd are UK resident members of a capital gains group. Both companies prepare accounts to 31 December each year. Y Ltd acquired an asset in 1973 at a cost of £10,000 and transferred it to A Ltd in August 1985. On 31 December 2021, A Ltd sold the asset to a non-group company for £200,000. The market value of the asset at 31 March 1982 was £60,000. Indexation factor is 1.80 up to 31 December 2017.

When the asset was disposed of by Y Ltd to A Ltd in 1985, no gain arose to Y Ltd (i.e. it transferred under the no gain/no loss rules).

A Ltd has a disposal in the year ended 31 December 2021 of an asset with a base cost of £60,000 (i.e. 31 March 1982 valuation as this is higher).

Computation of A Ltd's liability

	£	£
Proceeds		200,000
Base cost (market value at 31/03/1982)	60,000	
Indexed @ 1.80 (up to 31 December 2017 only)	108,000	
		(168,000)
Chargeable gain		32,000

13.7 Company Leaving Group: Anti-avoidance Measure

Where a company ceases to be a member of a group of companies within six years of an intragroup transfer, and at that time still owns that asset, a capital gain or loss may arise. This is known as a degrouping charge.

The chargeable gain is calculated by deeming that the asset was, in effect, sold and immediately reacquired by the company leaving the group at its market value at the time of its original acquisition from the other member of the group, i.e. **the gain (or loss) arising on the original transfer between the group members is triggered.** Indexation allowance is applied by reference to that date and not by reference to the date the company actually leaves the group. While the gain is calculated as at the date of the original intragroup transfer, it is not charged on the company leaving the group, but on the company selling the shares in the accounting period in which the company leaves the group. The cost of future disposals of the asset in question by the company leaving the group will, of course, be the market value attributed to the earlier transfer.

Rollover relief cannot be claimed on such degrouping gains.

Where a company leaves a group as a result of a disposal of shares by a group company, any degrouping charge is made by way of an adjustment to the consideration taken into account for calculating the gain or loss on the disposal of shares. A consequence of this is that any exemption or relief that may apply to the share disposal, such as the substantial shareholdings exemption (SSE) (see **Section 13.2**), will also apply to the degrouping charge.

No chargeable gains degrouping charge is made in respect of an asset that has been transferred between two companies belonging to the same sub-group, if those companies leave the group together.

Section 171A TCGA 1992 (election to re-allocate gain or loss to another member of the group) can also apply to a standalone degrouping gain or loss if this has not been exempted by the SSE.

Example 13.10

Groups Ltd acquired a freehold property for £100,000 in the 1990s. In December 2014, when the market value of the property was £460,000 and indexation to date was £26,000, Groups Ltd transferred the property to it's 100% subsidiary, Just Ltd, for £375,000. Just Ltd leaves the group on 1 June 2021. Both companies prepare accounts to 31 July.

Calculate the chargeable gains arising in respect of the above transactions. Assume Groups Ltd cannot claim the substantial shareholdings exemption on the disposal of Just Ltd's shares.

Solution

2014: No chargeable gain arises as the transfer was to another group member on a no gain/no loss basis.

2021: Gain on Groups Ltd would be calculated as:

	£	£
Gross proceeds (market value)		460,000
Cost	100,000	
Indexation	26,000	
		126,000
Chargeable gain		334,000

This is chargeable on Groups Ltd in the year ended 31 July 2021. Note that £375,000 paid by Just Ltd is irrelevant; full market value must be used as the companies were connected at the date of the original transaction. The degrouping charge is added to the proceeds that Groups Ltd receives for the sale of Just Ltd's shares. As the substantial shareholdings exemption is not available, the degrouping chargeable gain is subject to corporation tax at 19%, being the corporation tax rate for the accounting period ended 31 July 2021.

Questions

Review Questions

(See Suggested Solutions to Review Questions at the end of this textbook.)

Question 13.1

It is April 2026 and a longstanding client comes into your office to discuss a proposed transaction. Paul Kelly is the managing director of Kelly Cars Group Limited, a UK company that acquired 100% of the shares in Kelly Luxury Cars GmbH in 2006. Kelly Luxury Cars GmbH is a German company specialising in sourcing and importing luxury cars from Europe for wealthy customers. Both companies have always been trading companies.

Kelly Cars Group Limited sold 95% of the shares of Kelly Luxury Cars GmbH on 25 June 2021 for a significant profit. The new owners of Kelly Luxury Cars GmbH converted the company to an investment company when they bought the shares.

Kelly Cars Group Limited held on to the remaining 5% of the shares for sentimental reasons. However, the company has now been approached by the same buyers and is in negotiations to sell the remaining 5% by the end of May 2026.

Requirement

Explain, with supporting analysis, whether the sale of the 95% shareholding in Kelly Luxury Cars GmbH in June 2021 qualified for the substantial shareholdings exemption (SSE). Advise whether the sale of the remaining 5% (for a profit) in May 2026 will qualify for SSE.

If the remaining 5% is to be sold at a loss, consider what recommendation you might make to the company.

Question 13.2

You are a tax senior in a mid-sized Belfast practice. One of the clients recently assigned to you is the Solar Group. Solar is a trading company that has four wholly-owned trading subsidiaries – Neptune Ltd, Venus Ltd, Saturn Ltd and Mercury Ltd. At a recent meeting with the managing director you discussed the group's tax affairs. The managing director is keen for the group's corporation tax affairs to be finalised as soon as possible and is anxious to know what the group's liability is for the year ended 31 March 2022. All companies in the group prepare accounts to 31 March and none paid corporation tax in instalments in 2021.

During the year ended 31 March 2022, Solar and its subsidiaries had the following results:

▨ Solar made a trading profit of £67,550 and has unused capital losses carried forward from earlier years of £200,000.

▨ Neptune made a trading profit of £47,087. At 31 March 2017 it had trade losses available to carry forward of £75,000.

▨ Venus made a trading profit of £72,680 and also made a chargeable gain of £55,260. At 31 March 2021 it had capital losses to carry forward of £47,000.

▨ Saturn made a trading profit of £112,559, as adjusted for tax purposes, before deducting capital allowances. The capital allowances for the period are £29,766.

▨ Mercury made a trading loss of £9,236 before deducting capital allowances of £37,257. At 31 March 2017, the company had trade losses available to carry forward of £27,073.

You have been provided with the following additional information:

1. It is the intention to sell Saturn and an offer of £300,000 has been received from an interested party, Y Ltd. It is almost certain that this offer will be accepted within the next week. Y Ltd intends to inject additional funding into Saturn to assist them in purchasing additional freehold property and fixed plant and machinery and so expand Saturn's trade.

    The original cost of Solar's investment in Saturn in June 1997 was £55,000. Indexation allowance from 1997 to 31 December 2017 is 65%. The principal assets of Saturn are its freehold property and goodwill which has been created over a number of years. The property was originally bought by Solar in February 1981 for £40,000 and transferred to Saturn in March 2017 when its value was £230,000.

    Its current value is £350,000 and, in March 1982, the property was worth £50,000. Assume indexation allowance from February 1981 to March 2017 is 100%, from March 1982 to March 2017 is 107% and from 1982 to 31 December 2017 is 122%.

2. Due to Neptune's continued expansion, it requires larger business premises. Solar therefore plans to transfer to Neptune a suitable freehold property that it no longer requires and which it currently rents out. If sold to an unconnected third party, a capital gain of £100,000 would arise.

    Neptune, in turn, proposes to sell the property it currently occupies outside the group. This property was acquired from Solar 10 years ago. X Ltd, an unconnected third party, has been identified as a possible purchaser. A capital gain of approximately £250,000 will be realised from the sale.

3. As part of the future marketing strategy of the group it has been decided to acquire a new company, Mars Ltd. Mars has significant trading losses, in excess of £500,000, which are proving attractive to the Solar Group. The board intends to focus on substantially different products aimed at new customer types and markets.

Requirement

The board of directors would like you to draft a report providing information on the following specific areas:

(a) The group's corporation tax liability for the year ended 31 March 2022, making use of all available claims and elections and advising on the due date for payment of any tax liabilities arising.

(b) Advice in relation to the tax implications of the proposed sale of shares in Saturn, in particular:

    (i) the amount of the capital gain arising in respect of the sale of Solar's shareholding in Saturn and whether the substantial shareholdings exemption will be available;

    (ii) any other tax implications arising from Saturn leaving the group.

(c) Advice in relation to the proposed transfer of the freehold property from Solar to Neptune and the sale by Neptune of its current property, in particular:

    (i) the tax implications arising out of the proposed transfer as part of Neptune's expansion plans;

    (ii) mitigating the gain arising on the sale of Neptune's property.

(d) Acquisition of Mars – advise the board on the availability for relief after acquisition of the trading losses that exist in this company.

Transfer Pricing

14.1 Introduction

Transfer pricing often occurs in transactions between connected businesses where the price does not reflect the true commercial cost of the transaction. In other words, the transaction price is not at arm's length, i.e. the agreed price is not the same or similar to that which it would have been if the transaction had taken place between unrelated parties. This can give an unfair tax advantage to the connected parties, which the UK transfer pricing legislation seeks to prevent by adjusting the tax computation of the advantaged UK party.

The OECD publishes transfer pricing guidelines that set out different methods of calculating prices consistent with the arm's length principle. The UK's transfer pricing legislation, which is contained in the Taxation (International and Other Provisions) Act 2010, makes reference to these principles.

14.2 The Basic Rule

The basic rule is that where there is a non-arm's length transaction between two parties and either one of the parties or an individual connected to one of the parties was "directly or indirectly participating in the management, control or capital" of the other party then, for tax purposes, the transaction is considered to have been made at arm's length. This is sometimes referred to as the 'participation test' and seeks to remove any UK tax advantage.

Such transactions are not restricted to intercompany sales or purchases of goods/services. As a result, transfer pricing adjustments can be made in relation to common intercompany transactions such as management charges, royalty payments, corporate intangibles (e.g. patents) and loan relationships. The rules do not apply, however, to chargeable assets for capital gains tax purposes.

The rules also apply irrespective of the geographic location of the parties involved, meaning that transactions within the UK as well as cross-border transactions are caught. In reality, the rules impact less on transactions within the UK as the parties will usually pay the same rate of corporation tax (though note the change in corporation tax rates which will apply from 1 April 2023 (see **Chapter 7**, **Section 7.3**)). However, transfer pricing adjustments still need to be considered as any adjustments could result in a company being exposed to the instalment payment rules for corporation tax.

The transfer pricing rules only require adjustments to be made in the relevant tax calculations, i.e. the corporation tax computation and return. This means that the parties involved can charge what they wish in their financial statements, although financial reporting standards may require a related party disclosure.

14.2.1 Key Definitions

The key terms referred to in the transfer pricing rules are:

- direct participation – in the control of a company or a partnership;
- indirect participation – when a person has:
  - future rights to control;
  - rights are being exercised under their instruction or for their benefit; or
  - they are major participants in the company.
- major participants – two people in control of a company, each with at least 40% share of rights in the company.
- control – the power to direct the company by means of shareholdings (generally at least 51%), voting power or powers conferred by documents regulating the company. The participation test can therefore be applied to cases where one company controls another, or both companies are controlled by the same person(s). It can also apply in the case of joint ventures where the 40% test is met.
- connected persons – includes spouses/civil partners, siblings, lineal descendants (children, grandchildren, etc.). It also extends to relatives (siblings and lineal descendants) of spouses and spouses of relatives.

14.3   UK Tax Advantage

A transfer pricing adjustment is only made where, as a result of a non-arm's length transaction (or series of transactions), a UK tax advantage has been gained. This tax advantage is considered to have arisen if either:

1. a **lower** non-arm's length transaction price is taken into account in calculating the chargeable profits, i.e. taxable profits are reduced; or
2. a **higher** non-arm's length transaction price is taken into account in calculating any losses, i.e. a larger loss results or a loss is created.

Cross-border transactions, where one of the parties is not subject to UK tax, can often result in a UK tax advantage. However, as set out earlier, transactions within the UK can also result in a tax advantage.

14.4   Corresponding Adjustments

Non-arm's length transactions that result in a UK tax advantage mean that one party has reduced its UK tax liability, while the other may have paid more tax than they would have done if an arm's length price had been paid. If the disadvantaged party is also UK tax resident and has paid more UK income or corporation tax than it would otherwise have had, a claim can be made for the arm's length price to be used in computing its taxable profits. This adjustment is known as a 'corresponding' (or compensating) adjustment.

Claims for corresponding adjustments must be made to HMRC within two years after the potentially advantaged party has filed its relevant tax return showing the transfer pricing adjustment.

Example 14.1

X Ltd sells goods to its Y Ltd at a price of £250 per unit. The arm's length price would have been £380. During the accounting period ended 31 March 2022, X Ltd sold 10,000 of these items to Y Ltd.

A transfer pricing adjustment is made on the basis that the arm's length price was received. As a result, X Ltd's taxable income for corporation tax is increased by £1,300,000 (10,000 × £130) and any profit is increased (or a loss reduced or turned into a profit). X Ltd has gained a tax advantage as its profit was originally understated. Y Ltd is the disadvantaged party.

Y Ltd can adjust its allowable expenditure, increasing it by £1,300,000 to reflect the arm's length price. The difference in its calculation of taxable profits or losses is the corresponding adjustment, meaning either a lower profit (or a profit turned into a loss or a higher loss).

X Ltd is therefore taxed as if it had received £380 for each item and Y Ltd is taxed as if it had paid £380.

14.5 Exemptions

There are important exemptions in the legislation for dormant companies and small- and medium-sized enterprises (as defined).

14.5.1 Dormant Companies

Companies that were dormant, either for the whole of an accounting period that ended on 31 March 2004 or for the three months ending on 31 March 2004, are exempt from the transfer pricing requirements as long as they continue being dormant.

14.5.2 Small and Medium-sized Companies

In general, small or medium-sized enterprises (SMEs) are exempt from the transfer pricing rules. (There are exceptions to this rule, but these are beyond the scope of this textbook.) A company will be an SME for these purposes where it has:

- less than 250 employees, and either:
  - less than €50 million turnover; or
  - less than €43 million balance sheet total.

Note that this definition of SME differs to its definition for the purpose of the SME R&D tax relief regime (see **Chapter 8, Section 8.3.4**).

14.6 Advance Pricing Agreements

Transfer pricing adjustments are part of the UK's corporation tax self-assessment regime. It is therefore each company's responsibility to ensure that all transfer pricing adjustments are made when calculating its corporation tax position for an accounting period. If the necessary adjustments are not made or are made incorrectly, this can result in interest on late payment or underpayment of corporation tax, and/or penalties for errors and omissions. To mitigate against this possibility, companies can enter into an advance pricing agreement (APA) with HMRC. APAs usually cover complex cross-border transactions.

An application for an APA must be made in writing to HMRC and should set out the transactions to be covered, the basis for needing a transfer pricing adjustment and how the company has calculated the arm's length price and proposes to deal with these transactions.

14.7 Transfer Pricing Methods

As noted at the outset, the UK legislation specifically refers to the OECD's guidelines when calculating prices in line with the arm's length principle. Two methods are proposed:

1. traditional transaction methods; and
2. transactional profit split methods

The OECD's guidelines also contain guidance on how to select the most appropriate transfer pricing method according to the circumstances of the case. The detail of these methods is beyond the scope of this textbook.

14.8 Administrative Issues

14.8.1 Record-keeping

It is the responsibility of the company to retain all records and documents relating to the transfer pricing, e.g. communications and agreements between parties, tax computations, adjustments and so on.

14.8.2 Penalties

If a company does not retain the appropriate records and documents, a penalty of up to £3,000 can be charged.

If the transfer prices are found to not be at arm's length and the company's behaviour is held to have been careless or deliberate in setting a non-arm's length price, a penalty can be charged for an incorrect return (see **Chapter 1**).

Example 14.2: HMRC example
A group of companies charge a service charge of 8% for services provided between them. HMRC determine that it should have been 12%–16%. The company cannot show that they considered whether 8% was arm's length, or there is documentation that states that 8% is arm's length without any supporting evidence. A penalty would arise.

Question

Review Question
(See Suggested Solution to Review Questions at the end of this textbook.)

Question 14.1

Shane Delaney has been in business for over 40 years running his 100%-owned company, Delaney Electrics (UK) Ltd (Delaney UK), which provides electrical engineering services to some major clients in the public and private sector. Delaney UK is not an SME for transfer pricing purposes. Shane also holds 100% of the shares in an Irish resident trading company, Delaney Electrics (Ireland) Ltd (Delaney Ireland), which was set up to tender for Irish public sector contracts and which also provides electrical engineering consultancy services to clients of Delaney UK and Delaney Ireland.

The statement of profit or loss for Delaney UK, for the accounting period ended 31 March 2022, is outlined below.

Delaney UK had total trading income of £500,000 and property income of £67,000 in the 18-month accounting period ended 31 March 2021.

Shane has decided that on 31 March 2024, Delaney UK will cease to trade. As the business is being run down in the period up to its cessation, Delaney UK is projected to have the following results in the next two 12-month accounting periods:

Accounting period	31 March 2023	31 March 2024
Adjusted trading (loss)/profit	£ 60,000	(£ 1,792,000)
Property income	£ 75,000	-
Interest received	£ 70,000	-
Chargeable gains	£ 175,000	-

Delaney Electrics (UK) Ltd
Statement of Profit or Loss for the year ended 31 March 2022

	Note	£	£
Turnover			7,145,000
Cost of sales	1		(4,754,500)
Gross profit			2,390,500
Operating expenses:			
Wages and salaries	2	1,272,456	
Legal and professional fees	3	25,400	
Depreciation	1	155,250	
Amortisation	4	12,000	
Repairs and maintenance	5	34,222	
Insurance	6	25,780	
Rent and rates		145,000	
Audit fees		16,500	

Taxation compliance fees		15,450	
Bad debts	7	49,000	
Bank charges		2,150	
Sundry expenses	8	25,222	
			(1,778,430)
Other income and expenses:			
Rental income	9	40,000	
Dividend income	10	60,000	
Profit on disposal of patent	11	185,000	
Management charge	12	100,000	
Bank interest payable	13	(28,245)	
			356,755
Profit before tax			**968,825**

Notes:

1. Cost of sales includes depreciation of £25,000, which relates to plant and machinery bought under finance lease agreements.

2. Wages and salaries include a payment of £23,000 to a former manager of the company. £6,000 of this was a statutory redundancy payment, while £17,000 was an ex-gratia payment. The manager worked in a division of the company that closed in December 2021. He was the only employee of this division made redundant as he was not happy to move to another division of the company.

3. Legal and professional fees include:

Fees re. HMRC corporation tax enquiry (Note 8)	£3,559
Legal fees re. case against supplier for faulty goods	£12,500
Legal fees re. issue with tenants of leased commercial premises (Note 9)	£5,000

4. Company policy is to amortise goodwill over a 10-year period. The goodwill was originally acquired in 2016.

5. Repairs and maintenance include:

   (a) Repairs to plumbing and heating system in commercial premises costing £3,465 (see Note 9);

   (b) Extending the trading premises of the company – building new staff bathrooms, changing areas and showers costing £20,000.

6. Insurance includes:

Key person insurance policy – the policy is in respect of Shane's wife who is not employed by the company	£6,200
Public liability insurance	£5,500
Insurance for leased-out commercial premises (see Note 9)	£2,375
Insurance for directors' motor vehicles owned by company	£3,300

7. At the end of the accounting period, the general provision for bad debts was £20,000 (31 March 2021: £30,000). The remainder of the bad debt provision is calculated in accordance with IFRS.
8. The following amounts are included within 'other expenses':
    (a) Penalties following the closure of the HMRC enquiry of £3,500. Corporation tax interest payable to HMRC following the closure of the enquiry of £2,500;
    (b) New division opening party and gifts totalling £2,045. The total cost of the new division opening party includes:
        - £500 for drinks and food for customers and suppliers;
        - £500 to a local celebrity to sing at the event
        - £1,045 in gifts of branded hoodies to suppliers and customers. Each branded gift cost £35.
    (c) Motor lease charges paid in respect of two BMW cars during the year ended 31 March 2022. The details of each lease are outlined below:

	Lease cost	CO_2 emissions (g/km)	Date of lease
BMW i3	£5,500	31	1 May 2021
BMW 6 Series Coupe	£7,650	110	1 June 2021

9. Rental income is received in respect of the lease of commercial property to an unconnected company.
10. The dividend income was received from ordinary shares in an Irish company. Delaney UK is not a small company for the purpose of the dividend exemption rules.
11. The company sold patent rights used in its trade for £260,000 in December 2021; it had been bought for £150,000 in October 2012. By the time of their sale, these patent rights had been written down to £75,000. In July 2021 the company bought copyrights for use in its trade for £290,000.
12. The management income of £100,000 was received from Delaney Ireland for cross-referrals of clients from Delaney UK. The income did not take into account commission payable by Delaney Ireland to Delaney UK, which would have made the arm's length price £200,000.
13. The bank loan interest is payable on a bank overdraft used for working capital requirements of the company.
14. Capital allowances for the year ended 31 March 2022 are £92,324.

Requirement

(a) Calculate the taxable total profits, before any potential claim for loss relief, for Delaney Electrics (UK) Limited for the year ended 31 March 2022.

Provide a brief explanation as to why an adjustment does or does not arise in calculating the total taxable profits in respect of **each** of the items referred to in Notes 1–13 (inclusive). Assume the company makes all beneficial claims and elections to mitigate or defer corporation tax where necessary.

(b) Using the projected results for 2023 and 2024, calculate the revised taxable total profits of Delaney Electrics (UK) Limited for the 2021–2023 accounting periods inclusive, and briefly explain how the projected trading loss arising in 2024 is used.

Taxation of Directors/Shareholders

Learning Objectives

After studying this chapter you will understand:

- The calculation of tax for company directors as a direct result of holding a directorship.
- The different ways of extracting cash from a company and the tax implications for both the company and the recipient.

15.1 Introduction

Many UK companies, particularly in Northern Ireland, are family-owned and managed. In family companies, the directors are also likely to be shareholders. As a consequence, directors of family companies often have control over their own remuneration packages and should consider the tax effects of such packages on both the company and on themselves.

Legislation is in place to prevent directors from arranging their remuneration in such a way as to avoid taxation. One example of this is in relation to national insurance contributions (NICs). Class 1 NICs are calculated by reference to the earnings period. This means that an employee in receipt of a monthly salary has their NICs calculated for each month in isolation (in contrast to the calculation of their income tax liability, which is carried out on a cumulative basis).

Example 15.1

Rhonda's gross monthly salary for 2021/22 is £2,000. In March 2022, she receives a bonus of £5,000 on top of her normal salary. The primary Class 1 NICs are calculated as follows:

April 2021 – February 2022	£
Gross salary	2,000
Less: primary threshold	(797)
Earnings on which NICs are due	1,203
Class 1 NICs due @ 12%	144.36

Monthly NICs liability for the 11 months from April to February is, therefore, £144.36. So the total for the period is £144.36 × 11 = £1,587.96.

continued overleaf

March 2022	
	£
Gross salary	2,000
Bonus	<u>5,000</u>
Total earnings for period	<u>7,000</u>
Class 1 NICs due (£4,189 − £797) @ 12%	407.04
Class 1 NICs due (£7,000 − £4,189) @ 2%	<u>56.22</u>
Total Class 1 NICs due	463.26
Rhonda's total annual NICs are therefore £1,587.96 + £463.26 = £2,051.22.	

As can be seen from this example, Rhonda's NIC liability in March 2022 is increased as the gross earnings for that period are in excess of the upper earnings limit for the month of £4,189. This is an area that could be exploited by directors with control over their remuneration – they could structure their salary in such a way as to utilise the upper earnings limit to restrict their exposure to primary Class 1 NICs.

For this reason, directors are subject to the **annual** earnings basis for the purposes of calculating their primary Class 1 NICs liability. This has the effect of calculating their NICs on a cumulative basis, so that they only benefit from the lower 2% rate of NICs when their total annual salary (including bonuses and other similar payments) exceeds the upper earnings limit.

Example 15.2

Using the same details as **Example 15.1**, this time assume Rhonda is a director and so subject to the annual earnings basis. The primary Class 1 NICs are calculated as follows:

April 2021 – March 2022

	£
Gross annual salary (£2,000 × 12)	24,000
Bonus in March 2022	<u>5,000</u>
Total annual earnings	29,000
Less: primary threshold	<u>(9,568)</u>
Earnings on which NICs are due	<u>19,432</u>
Class 1 NICs due @ 12%	<u>2,331.84</u>

Note: none of the earnings have been charged at 2% as the annual earnings are less than the annual upper earnings limit of £50,270. As a result, the total NICs charge for the year has been increased by £280.62.

15.2 Tax on Remuneration

As stated above, when a director who is also a shareholder of a company is planning their own remuneration strategy, they will want to consider the taxation impact on both the company and themselves. There is no point in saving £3,000 in income tax on profits extracted if the company is exposed to an additional corporation tax liability of £5,000 as a result.

The first consideration when developing a remuneration strategy is the level of profits to be extracted. It may be more tax-efficient to retain most of the profits within the company, where they will be subject to corporation tax at a maximum rate of 19% (though note the changes being introduced from 1 April 2023 (see **Chapter 7, Section 7.3**)), rather than extracting them and exposing them to income tax at rates of up to 45% before any national insurance cost is considered.

Income tax rates and bands are an annual tax and can be revised annually. Also, if profits are retained this will increase the value of the company, and so the value of the shareholdings in the company. This will increase any chargeable gain on the future disposal of those shares, but such a disposal may qualify for business asset disposal relief (see **Chapter 19, Section 19.1**) and/or be exposed to lower CGT rates than if an extraction was made now, which could be taxed at up to 47% (45% income tax plus 2% NICs).

However, it will be the case that most directors will need to extract some level of profit to fund their living expenses; the rest of this section will consider the various ways in which this may be achieved.

15.2.1 Salary or Dividend

When profits are extracted by way of salary, NICs will be charged at the secondary rate (currently 13.8%) on the company and at the primary rate (currently 12%) on the recipient (2% on earnings in excess of the upper earnings limit). The recipient will also be exposed to income tax at up to 45% of the gross salary. The total cost of the salary, i.e. gross salary plus secondary NICs, will be an allowable deduction for corporation tax purposes.

When profits are extracted by way of dividends, no NICs are payable by either the company or the recipient. Income tax is restricted to a maximum of 38.1% after deducting the available level of the £2,000 dividend allowance that applies to the first £2,000 of dividend income received. However, dividends are not an allowable deduction for corporation tax purposes, as they must be paid out of the distributable reserves of the company.

Therefore, when determining the most tax-efficient method of profit extraction, the effect of corporation tax and NICs must be considered. As dividends are not deductible for corporation tax purposes, this means that they are not automatically more tax-efficient than salary payments.

Example 15.3

Rory is the director/shareholder of Mill Ltd. The company's taxable profit for the year ended 31 March 2022 is £600,000 and Rory would like to extract £50,000 by way of either a bonus or dividend. Rory's salary from the company is £150,000 in the 2021/22 tax year. (*Note:* no personal allowance is available to Rory as his income is in excess of £125,140). Rory receives no other dividends.

Extraction by way of bonus:

Mill Ltd		£	£
Profits			600,000
Less: remuneration (Note 1)			(50,000)
Taxable total profits (TTP)			550,000
Corporation tax:	£550,000 @ 19%		(104,500)
Profits after tax			445,500
Secondary NICs	£43,937 @ 13.8%	6,063	
Total tax charge		110,563	

continued overleaf

Rory

Gross salary			43,937
Primary Class 1 NICs	£43,937 @ 2%	879	
Income tax	£43,937 @ 45%	19,772	
Total tax/NICs		20,651	(20,651)
Income after tax			23,286
Total tax		131,214	
Effective rate of tax	(£131,214/£600,000) × 100		21.87%

Extraction by way of dividend:

Mill Ltd

TTP			600,000
Corporation tax:	£600,000 @ 19%		(114,000)
Total tax charge			
Profits after tax			486,000
Profits after dividend	£486,000 − £50,000		436,000

Rory

Gross dividend		50,000	
Less: dividend allowance		(2,000)	
Taxable dividend		48,000	
Income tax @ 38.1%		18,288	(18,288)
Income after tax			31,712
Total tax		132,288	

The effective rate of tax ((£132,288/£600,000) × 100) is 22.05%

Note:
1. This amount includes the gross salary of the director together with the employer's secondary NIC (13.8%). To calculate the gross salary, this needs to be divided by 113.8 and multiplied by 100. Therefore, £50,000 x 100/113.8, i.e. £43,937.

As can be seen in **Example 15.3**, because corporation tax is 19% and the rate of income tax is 38.1% for an additional rate taxpayer, the effective rate of tax between dividends and salary/bonus is very close, especially when dealing with an additional rate taxpayer.

Example 15.4

Thomas is the director/shareholder of Soap Ltd. The company's taxable profit for the year ended 31 March 2022 is £300,000 and Thomas would like to extract £40,000 by way of either a bonus or dividend. Thomas's salary from the company is £52,000 for the 2021/22 tax year and he receives no other dividends.

Extraction by way of bonus:

Soap Ltd		£	£
Profits			300,000
Less: remuneration			(40,000)
TTP			260,000
Corporation tax	£260,000 @ 19%	49,400	(49,400)
Profits after tax			210,600
Secondary NICs (Note 1)	£35,149 @ 13.8%	4,851	
Total tax charge		54,251	
Thomas			
Gross salary			35,149
Primary Class 1 NICs	£35,149 @ 2%	703	
Income tax	£35,149 @ 40%	14,060	
Total tax/NICs		14,763	(14,763)
Income after tax			20,386
Total tax		69,014	
Retained profits			228,386
Effective rate of tax	(£69,014/£300,000) × 100		23.00%

Extraction by way of dividend:

Soap Ltd		£	£
TTP			300,000
Corporation tax	£300,000 @ 19%	57,000	(57,000)
Profits after tax			243,000
Profits after dividend	£243,000 − £40,000		203,000
Thomas			
Gross dividend		40,000	
Less: dividend allowance		(2,000)	
Taxable dividend		38,000	
Income tax @ 32.5%		12,350	(12,350)
Income after tax			27,650
Total tax		69,350	

The effective rate of tax ((£69,350/£300,000) × 100) is 23.12%.

Note:

1. Secondary NICs includes the gross salary of the director plus the employer's secondary NIC (13.8%). To calculate the gross salary, divide salary by 113.8 and multiply by 100 (£40,000 × 100/113.8 = £35,149).

As can be seen from the above examples, it is necessary to carry out detailed calculations to determine the most tax-efficient method. This is especially important where income straddles tax rate bands, where an individual may be exposed to the high-income child benefit charge, or where a loss of personal allowances is possible if income exceeds £100,000. The following should also be considered:

1. Dividends are not earnings and so the level of tax-relievable pension contributions that a director may make will be restricted if their remuneration is mainly in the form of dividends (contributions of up to £3,600 may be made irrespective of earnings). It may be possible to reduce the impact of this restriction on the growth of a pension pot by making a company contribution on behalf of the director. Indeed, this can be a very tax-efficient form of remuneration for directors/shareholders of family companies.
2. A small salary should always be paid to protect entitlement to contributions-related social security benefits, such as the state pension.
3. The company must have sufficient distributable reserves to cover any proposed dividends.
4. If the director is employed under an "explicit" employment contract then the national minimum and living wage must be considered.
5. The relevant paperwork for the dividend must be completed, including minutes of any meeting approving the dividend and any dividend vouchers. If a shareholder waives their entitlement, the dividend waiver document should also be prepared at that time.

15.2.2 Benefits in Kind

A limited company is a separate legal entity from its directors. This means that where a director meets personal expenditure with company funds, there will be a benefit in kind that will be charged to tax and NICs on the director as employment income. The taxation of benefits in kind is studied at CA Proficiency 1; however, there are certain items that tend to apply more specifically to company directors.

Where a company meets the personal expenses of a director, these are taxable expense payments. The payments should be included on the director's Form P11D and subject to income tax. Class 1 NICs will also be payable and should be collected through the payroll. The company will pay Class 1A NICs at 13.8%. The taxable amount may be reduced where there is legitimate business use.

Example 15.5
Cora is a director of Firefly Ltd and the company pays her home telephone bills. Cora is the subscriber. The total amount paid in 2021/22 was £800, including line rental of £100. Cora has determined that about 10% of the calls made from her home telephone were business calls relating to Firefly Ltd's trade (and has evidence for this). What is the PAYE/NICs treatment?

PAYE Income Tax
The full amount of line rental plus 90% of the cost of calls (i.e. the private portion) should be declared on form P11D. Income tax will therefore be charged on an amount of £730.

NICs
No Class 1A NICs are due as the company is meeting Cora's personal expenditure rather than providing a benefit. Class 1 NICs are however due and will be collected by putting an amount equal to the full line rental, plus 90% of the cost of calls through the payroll. The total amount on which Class 1 NICs are therefore due is £730.

Care should be taken to ensure that any company credit cards used by a director are not used for personal expenditure, as this would give rise to a taxable expense charge.

Assets transferred by the company to the director will give rise to a taxable benefit in kind, which should be reported on Form P11D. Such a transfer will **also** be subject to income tax and Class 1A NICs.

Certain payments or transfers made by a "close" company to a participator are, for income tax purposes, treated as distributions in the hands of the participator (see **Chapter 10**). When the participator is also a director or employee, such payments/transfers will instead be taxed as employment income.

Example 15.6

Serenity Ltd is a family-owned and managed company. The shareholders are Neil (who has a shareholding of 40%), his sister Carol (who has a shareholding of 40%) and his brother David (who has a shareholding of 20%). Both Neil and Carol are directors in the company. David is not a director or employee of the company.

Serenity Ltd pays the rent on each of the shareholders' houses. As Neil and Carol are directors of the company, they will be subject to an income tax charge based on the benefit in kind rules for the provision of living accommodation. The company is entitled to a corporation tax deduction for expenses treated as a benefit in kind.

As David is not an employee of the company, the rent paid on his house will be taxed as a distribution in his hands under the rules relating to participators. The company is **not** entitled to a corporation tax deduction for expenses treated as a distribution.

15.2.3 Loans to Participators

Loans by a close company to a participator (including directors) can give rise to a potential charge on the company under section 455 CTA 2010 (see **Chapter 10**). The recipient, if a director, may also be treated as having received a beneficial loan under the benefit in kind rules, rather than a distribution, and taxed accordingly. It should be noted that such a loan can arise where a director's current account in the company becomes overdrawn. Even where no charge arises under section 455 CTA 2010 (e.g. where the overdrawn amount is repaid within nine months of the accounting year-end), there may still be a taxable benefit in kind.

Repayment of section 455 tax is only given for genuine repayments as opposed to instances where the loan is repaid and shortly there after drawn down again (see **Chapter 10**).

Example 15.7

Peter is a full-time working director of Bap Ltd, in which he has a shareholding of 60%. Bap Ltd prepares its accounts to 31 December. On 6 May 2021, Peter purchased a painting for £15,000. As he had insufficient funds, he borrowed this amount from the company. On 5 March 2022, he repaid the £15,000 to the company.

As the amount borrowed is repaid within nine months of the year end, there is no charge under section 455 CTA 2010.

However, the loan is subject to the benefit in kind rules as it is "interest free and is more than £10,000", and Peter will be charged income tax on the cash equivalent on the loan. Bap Ltd will also have a Class 1A NICs liability in respect of the loan.

15.3 Pensions

Pension contributions can be a very tax-efficient form of remuneration for directors. They qualify for tax relief on personal contributions in the same way as other employees, but may also have the option of more significant employer contributions made by the company.

The tax relief available on pension contributions was covered at CA Proficiency 1 and should be revisited, but it is worth mentioning here that a company contribution into a director's pension scheme is a deductible expense for corporation tax, provided it is wholly and exclusively for the purposes of the trade and is paid in the accounting period. Such contributions may also be subject to the 'spreading' provisions (covered at CA Proficiency 1). When determining whether a company contribution is excessive (thereby failing the wholly and exclusively test), the complete remuneration package and pattern of profit extraction by the director will be taken into account.

As pension funds benefit from tax-free growth, extracting profits in this way can be a more tax-efficient method than taking a salary or dividend. However, it is only really useful for those who can afford to lock the profits into their pension pot until they retire. Also, it must be remembered that the funds eventually available to draw down from the pension will depend on the performance of the fund investments and may also be affected by changing legislation.

The annual allowance for pension contributions for an individual for the 2021/22 tax year is £40,000. However, the annual allowance for those earning above £240,000 is reduced on a tapering basis. An individual's annual allowance reduces by £1 for every £2 of adjusted income above £240,000, subject to a minimum annual allowance of £4,000. Therefore, individuals who earn more than £312,000, their annual allowance will reduce to £4,000 (i.e. £40,000 less £36,000, being £72,000/2). It is also possible, if certain conditions are met, to carry forward unused allowance from the previous three tax years to offset any excess in the current year.

The annual allowance limit is the maximum level at which an individual can benefit from tax relief. The contributions can be made by either the individual or their employer. Any contributions in excess of the available annual allowance limit are subject to income tax on the individual. Tax relief is available for gross personal contributions up to the higher of £3,600 or 100% of relevant earnings.

The lifetime allowance (the amount an individual can save in a pension scheme) is currently £1,073,100 and will stay at this level until 2025/26. An individual can protect their pension pot and keep a higher lifetime allowance, but by doing so they would not be able to make further pension contributions. Any pension pots that exceed the lifetime allowance are also subject to a tax charge. The rate of tax on pension savings above the relevant lifetime allowance depends on how the money is paid. The rates are as follows:

- 55% if the money is received as a lump sum; or
- 25% if the money is received any other way, e.g. pension payments or cash withdrawals.

15.4 Other Issues

15.4.1 Timing

It may be the case that the total remuneration payable to a director in respect of an accounting period will not be finally determined until the accounts have been prepared and the profits have been assessed. Also, remuneration may be credited to a director's loan account rather than being paid in cash.

For directors, the date of payment of remuneration for the purposes of PAYE/NICs will be the **earlier** of:

- the date the payment is made;
- the date the director becomes entitled to be paid;
- the date the payment is credited in the company accounts or records;
- the date the remuneration is fixed or determined.

In the case of profits extracted by way of dividend, the date of payment for the purposes of calculating the income tax charge is the date of the dividend as stated in the board minute declaring the dividend and the supporting documentation (i.e. dividend voucher). It is important that this documentation is properly maintained, especially where a dividend is being credited to a director's current account rather than being paid out.

15.4.2 Limits on Remuneration

It should be remembered that remuneration, like any other trading expense, must be incurred wholly and exclusively for the purposes of the trade. HMRC may disallow a deduction for corporation tax purposes where they regard the remuneration as excessive.

15.4.3 Personal Liability

If PAYE/NICs are not properly deducted in respect of remuneration paid to a director, then the director may be personally liable to pay the tax if he knew of the failure to deduct or account for the tax.

Questions

Review Questions
(See Suggested Solutions to Review Questions at the end of this textbook.)

Question 15.1

To recognise the increased contribution by one of its directors, Clara, over the past year, a company has decided to reward her with an additional gross payment of £100,000 to be paid before the end of the current tax year 2021/22. Clara's gross salary for the year was £130,000.

Requirement
Calculate the tax implications to the company and Clara of making this payment, either as a bonus or as a dividend. Conclude which is more tax-efficient overall.

Question 15.2

It is March 2022 and you have just had a meeting with your clients, Mr and Mrs Andrews, who are both in their early fifties. At the meeting you discuss a number of issues. However, it is apparent that they would like some immediate advice in respect of the strategy for their remuneration by their company.

They each hold 50% of the shares in Andrews Transport Ltd (ATL) being 50 shares each and have done so since the company was incorporated in 1978.

The current total value of the company is £3 million. Annual pre-tax profits are in the region of £250,000. Most of the value of the company is in goodwill, current assets and motor vehicles, although there is also spare cash of £750,000. The cash has accumulated as no dividends have been paid by ATL over the years. Distributable reserves in ATL currently amount to over £1 million.

Currently Mr Andrews is paid £100,000 per annum by the company, and Mrs Andrews is not paid anything in respect of the secretarial services she provides to the company. Mr Andrews has been a full-time director of the company since 1978, while Mrs Andrews has never been an employee or director of ATL.

They have two children who are currently at university and who also work part time for the company. The children are not paid by the company, but are rewarded by Mr Andrews himself, who also pays their college expenses. Several years ago the company set up a Revenue-approved pension scheme to provide Mr Andrews with a pension. However, the actual contributions made to the scheme have been relatively low and the projected pension on his retirement is quite small.

Mrs Andrews has no company pension and Mr Andrews is concerned that his expected pension will not be sufficient to meet their needs.

Requirement

Draft a letter to Mr and Mrs Andrews dealing with the current remuneration structure and the various options for remunerating them from the company. In your letter include suggestions for potential savings. There is no requirement for detailed calculations.

Part Three
Capital Gains Tax

Capital Gains Tax: Recap

Learning Objectives

This chapter is an overview of the cumulative knowledge of capital gains tax (CGT) required at CA Proficiency 2. Particular attention should be paid to private residence relief, lettings relief, rollover relief and holdover/gift relief (**Section 16.11**) as these areas have been specifically added to the CAP 2 Competency Statement.

Students should refer to their CA Proficiency 1 or other studies to understand the level of cumulative knowledge required and the necessary technical details.

Chartered Accountants Ireland's *Code of Ethics* applies to all aspects of a Chartered Accountant's professional life, including dealing with CGT issues. Further information regarding the principles in the *Code of Ethics* is set out in **Appendix 2**.

In addition, **Appendix 3** examines the distinction between tax planning, tax avoidance and tax evasion, which can arise in relation to all taxes, including CGT.

Students are reminded that it is their responsibility to ensure that they have the necessary **cumulative knowledge** of CGT from CA Proficiency 1 or other studies. This chapter is a recap of key CGT topics covered at CA Proficiency 1 and is not a substitute for detailed understanding of the cumulative knowledge required at CA Proficiency 2.

16.1 Basic Charge to CGT

There are three basic elements that must exist before the provisions relating to the taxation of capital gains come into operation:

1. there must be a chargeable disposal,
2. of a chargeable asset,
3. by a chargeable person.

16.1.1 Disposal

For a CGT liability to arise, a disposal of a chargeable asset must take place or must be deemed to take place. The **main** situations in which a disposal occurs are:

- on the sale of an asset or part of an asset (part disposal – see **Section 16.3.2**);
- on the gift of the whole or part of an asset; and
- on the transfer of an asset to a trust or a corporate body.

Certain disposals are exempt from CGT (subject to certain conditions). As a general rule CGT is not triggered on death. Chargeable assets held on death are, however, revalued to their market value as at the date of death.

A chargeable disposal occurs at the date of the unconditional contract or the date that the condition is satisfied on a conditional contract. A contract can be written or verbal.

16.1.2   Chargeable Assets

Chargeable assets for CGT purposes include all forms of property, whether situated in the UK or not. The basic rule is that any capital asset of an individual or company is a chargeable asset unless it is specifically exempt from CGT or corporation tax on chargeable gains.

The **main** exempt assets include:

- motor cars;
- certain chattels (see **Section 16.9.2**, Rule 1.);
- certain wasting chattels (see **Section 16.9.1**);
- a taxpayer's principal private residence (subject to conditions) (see **Section 16.11.1**) which may also qualify for lettings relief (see **Section 16.11.2**).

16.1.3   Chargeable Persons

CGT is charged on gains accruing by individuals, business partners, trustees and personal representatives of a deceased person. The CGT territoriality rules which specifically determine chargeability are discussed in **Chapter 17**. Companies are also chargeable persons but are assessed to corporation tax on chargeable gains and not to CGT (see **Chapter 13**).

16.2   Rate of Tax, Date of Payment and Returns

16.2.1   Rates of CGT

CGT is charged by reference to fiscal years of assessment for individuals, i.e. for relevant transactions within the tax year ending 5 April. Individuals must calculate their total taxable income to be able to apply the correct CGT rate.

1. Calculate taxable income by deducting any tax-free allowances due.
2. Identify how much of the basic rate band (BRB) is already being used against taxable income. The maximum BRB for 2021/22 is £37,700.
3. Allocate any remaining basic rate band first against gains charged at 18% (for residential property) and then against gains charged at 10%.
4. Any remaining gains above the basic rate band are charged at 20% or 28% (for residential property).

The rates of CGT for gains on residential property disposals, irrespective of location, are 18% for those in the BRB and 28% thereafter after deducting private residence relief (see **Section 16.11.1**) and lettings relief (see **Section 16.11.2**).

16.2.2   Date of Payment

The UK self-assessment regime also applies to CGT. CGT due must generally be paid in full on or before 31 January following the end of the relevant tax year. For example, the CGT due on a chargeable gain or gains arising during 2021/22 falls due for payment on or before 31 January 2023. However, where the disposal relates to residential property, payment must be made within 30 days of the date of disposal. A similar deadline applies to the reporting of the gain (see **Section 16.2.3**).

If the taxpayer receives the disposal proceeds in instalments over a period of 18 months or more, they may choose to make a claim to pay the CGT liability by way of interest-free instalments. It is also possible for the taxpayer to elect to pay by instalments where gift relief is not available (see **Section 16.11.4**). Recap on the rules for payment by instalments from your CA Proficiency 1 or other studies.

16.2.3   Returns

A return of most chargeable gains must be made within the self-assessment income tax return filing deadline for individuals. Taxpayers are normally not required to complete the CGT pages of their tax return if **both** the following conditions are satisfied:

1. the total disposal proceeds from the tax year do not exceed four times the amount of the annual exemption (£49,200 for 2021/22); and
2. the total chargeable gains for the tax year do not exceed the annual exemption (£12,300 for 2020/21 to 2025/26).

As chargeable gains are reported to HMRC under self-assessment, the self-assessment regime equally applies to CGT. (Students are reminded that the detailed operation of self-assessment is cumulative knowledge previously covered on the CA Proficiency 1 course and is thus beyond the scope of this textbook.).

From 6 April 2020, UK tax residents must report and pay CGT on all residential property disposals within 30 days of the date of completion of the disposal (rather than by 31 January following the end of the tax year in which the sale is made). A similar deadline applies to non-UK resident individuals who dispose of UK property (both residential and commercial), either directly or indirectly (for example, through the disposal of shares in a company that itself holds UK property).

16.3   Computation of Gain or Loss

In summary, taxable gains are the net chargeable gains (after current-year capital losses) of the tax year reduced by unrelieved losses brought forward from previous years and the annual exemption.

The capital gain/loss is the difference between:

1. the consideration for the disposal of the asset, or the deemed consideration after deducting certain incidental costs of disposal; and
2. the cost of acquisition of the asset or its market value if not acquired at arm's length, certain incidental costs of acquisition and enhancement expenditure incurred for the purposes of enhancing the value of the asset (and which is reflected in the nature or state of the asset at the time of disposal).

Review from your CA Proficiency 1 or other studies the different items that may fall within each category.

The pro forma computation overleaf shows the layout and calculation of CGT in 2021/22 for individual taxpayers.

CAPITAL GAINS TAX COMPUTATION FOR 2021/22

	£	£
Sales proceeds (or market value)	X	
Less: incidental costs of sale	(X)	
		X
Deduct allowable costs:		
Original cost of asset	X	
Incidental costs of acquisition	X	
Enhancement expenditure	X	
		(X)
Gain		X
Deduct: reliefs available (if any – see **Section 16.11** and **Chapter 19**)		(X)
Deduct: capital losses (if any – see **Section 16.7**)		(X)
Deduct: annual exemption (see **Section 16.3.1**)		(X)
Taxable chargeable gain		X
CGT payable: taxable gain at 10%/18%/20%/28%		X

16.3.1 Annual Exemption

Every individual (but not companies) is entitled to an annual exemption, which is available for offset against the "taxable" gains of the particular tax year after deduction of capital losses (if any). The annual exemption cannot be carried forward and thus any excess over the taxable gains is lost. The annual exemption for 2021/22 is £12,300 and will remain as such up to and including 2025/26 (for 2020/21 it was also £12,300).

16.3.2 Part Disposal

Where a portion of an asset is sold, the sale proceeds are easily quantified but it is necessary to calculate how much of the original cost of the asset is allowable as a deduction in computing the chargeable gain or allowable loss arising on the part disposal.

For assets other than shares (see **Chapter 18, Section 18.1.2**), this is calculated as the proportion of the original cost of the asset that the value of the part being disposed of bears, at the time of disposal, to the market value of the whole asset. The formula is:

$$\text{Original cost} \times \frac{A}{(A+B)}$$

where A is the gross proceeds/market value of the part disposal (i.e. before deducting incidental costs of disposal) and B is the market value of the portion of the asset retained.

"Small Disposal" Proceeds of Land
A special relief may be claimed where the part disposal qualifies as a "small disposal" of land. Review the conditions for this claim and how it works from your CA Proficiency 1 or other studies.

16.3.3 Application of Market Value

Normally, where a disposal is at arm's length and the consideration is known in money terms, the consideration paid is accepted for CGT purposes. In certain circumstances the market value of an asset is substituted as deemed proceeds in lieu of the actual consideration paid for the disposal. The main circumstances where this will occur are:

1. where there is a transaction between connected persons (see **Section 16.6**).
2. where a disposal is not made at arm's length (e.g. a gift); or
3. where the consideration is not valued in money terms or is a barter transaction.

16.3.4 Specific Computational Rules

Enhancement Expenditure
Where enhancement expenditure has been incurred on an asset, the cost, and each subsequent item of enhancement expenditure, is treated as a separate asset for the purposes of CGT.

Valuation Rule for Quoted Shares and Unit Trusts
For CGT purposes, the method of valuation of shares, securities and strips is to use the middle figure (between the lowest and highest) of the closing prices of the day.

Disposals before 31 March 1982
For disposals of assets acquired before 31 March 1982, the gain or loss arising is always calculated with reference to the market value as at 31 March 1982. All acquisition and enhancement costs incurred on or before 31 March 1982 are irrelevant for CGT purposes for individuals as they will be replaced by the asset's market value on 31 March 1982.

16.4 Married Couples and Civil Partners

A husband and wife, or each member of a civil partnership, are separate persons for CGT purposes and their gains or losses are computed separately.

16.4.1 Disposal by One Spouse to the Other

A disposal of an asset from one spouse to the other does not give rise to a CGT liability where the spouses are living together. The asset is deemed to have passed from one to the other at a value which gives rise to a no gain/no loss position.

16.4.2 Jointly Held Assets

Where a couple disposes of an asset that has been held in their joint names, any chargeable gain arising is apportioned between them in accordance with their respective beneficial interests in the asset at the time of the disposal.

16.5 Partnerships

An asset owned by all the partners is a "partnership asset". Rollover relief may be available where a partner disposes of a qualifying asset (see **Section 16.11.3**).

Dealings in partnership assets are treated as dealings by the individual partners and not by the firm. Each partner has to be considered to own a fractional share of each partnership asset, rather than an interest in the partnership as a whole.

Chargeable gains or allowable losses accruing on the disposal of partnership assets are therefore apportioned among the partners in accordance with their capital profit-sharing ratio. Recap on the remaining rules for partnerships in the context of CGT from your CA Proficiency 1 or other studies.

16.6   Connected Persons

16.6.1   Meaning of Connected Person

Where there is a transaction between "connected persons", the consideration is deemed to be the open market value (unless specifically overwritten, as in the case of spousal/civil partner transfers). The following, amongst others, are the main categories of connected persons:

1.   Relatives – includes spouses, etc. (but subject to the inter-spousal/civil partner no gain/no loss rule; see **Section 16.4.1**), brother, sister, parent, grandparent, children and grandchildren;
2.   Trustees – a trustee of a settlement is connected with:
     (a) the settlor (i.e. the person who created the trust);
     (b) any person connected with the settlor; and
     (c) any company connected with the trust.
3.   Partners – a person is connected with any person with whom he is in partnership, and with the spouse or civil partner or a relative of any individual with whom he is in partnership.
4.   Company – a company is connected with another person if that person has control of the company or if that person and the persons connected with him together have control of the company. Companies under common control are also connected persons.

Recap on the other categories of connected person from your CA Proficiency 1 or other studies. See also the rules for losses when a disposal is made to a connected person (**Section 16.7.4**).

16.7   Losses

Losses are computed in the same manner as gains. In general, a loss is an allowable loss if, had there been a gain on the disposal of the assets, the gain would have been a chargeable gain.

Relief for capital losses cannot be claimed unless they are notified to HMRC within four years from the end of the tax year in which the losses were incurred. The annual exemption and losses should be used in the most beneficial way possible, i.e. set against any gains taxed at the higher CGT rate of 28%, followed by gains taxed at 20%, then gains taxed at 18% and finally against gains taxed at 10%.

16.7.1   Current-year Capital Losses

Allowable losses arising must be set-off against chargeable gains accruing in the same year of assessment, even if this wastes all or part of the annual exemption. Current-year capital losses may be set against gains in any way to maximise tax relief. To the extent that there is an unutilised balance, the capital losses unutilised must be carried forward and set-off against chargeable gains arising in subsequent years.

16.7.2   Capital Losses Carried Forward

Capital losses carried forward by a taxpayer will be automatically offset against capital gains arising in a later period, but can only reduce the gains to the level of the annual exemption. This offset is automatic and preserves the annual exemption (in contrast with current-year capital losses).

16.7.3   Carry Back of Losses

The general rule is that capital losses cannot be carried back to earlier years. An exception to this rule is losses that accrue to an individual in the tax year in which they die. Such losses may be carried back and set against gains of the three years of assessment preceding the year of assessment in which the individual died. These losses are offset against the later years first only to the extent that those net gains exceed the annual exemption for the year in which they arise.

16.7.4   Losses between Connected Persons

Losses realised by a person on the disposal of an asset to another person with whom they are connected may only be set-off against any chargeable gains realised by them on the disposal of an asset to the same connected person.

16.7.5   Personal Representatives

Personal representatives of a deceased person are liable to CGT on any disposal made by them during the administration period of the estate. They are entitled to the annual exemption for the year of death and the following two years.

16.7.6   Losses on Assets Qualifying for Capital Allowances

If a capital loss accrues on the disposal of an asset on which capital allowances have been claimed (e.g. machinery used in a business), this capital loss may be restricted with reference to any capital allowances claimed. This would have the effect of reducing the capital loss to nil, but it can never turn a loss into a gain.

16.7.7   Losses on Chattels

As recapped in **Section 16.9.2 Rule 1**, where a chattel is disposed of for gross proceeds of £6,000 or less and original cost was also £6,000 or less, the transaction is **exempt** from CGT. As it is exempt, a capital loss cannot therefore arise.

16.8   Negligible Value Claims

Where an asset becomes worthless, a negligible value claim may be made to crystallise a capital loss even though the asset has not been disposed of. Where a claim is made, a disposal is deemed to take place and the asset is immediately reacquired for consideration equal to the value specified in the claim. The effect of a claim is to trigger a capital loss, even though a disposal has not actually taken place.

The capital loss that arises can be claimed in that year, or in either of the two preceding tax years provided that the asset was of negligible value in the relevant year also. Once allocated to a year, it is treated as a capital loss for that year. There is no requirement to make a claim within a specified time of the asset having become of negligible value.

16.9   Chattels

A chattel is an item of "tangible movable property". A wasting chattel is an asset with a remaining life of less than 50 years and such assets are generally exempt from CGT. Plant and machinery are wasting chattels unless fixed to premises and immovable. A non-wasting chattel has a remaining life of more than 50 years and is not generally exempt from CGT.

16.9.1   Wasting Chattels and Capital Allowances

There is an exception to the general rule that wasting chattels are exempt from CGT – wasting chattels used in a business and eligible for capital allowances are not exempt. Such wasting chattels are treated as non-wasting chattels and subject to the rules below.

16.9.2   Non-wasting Chattels – Rules

There are three special rules to be aware of for non-wasting chattels and for wasting chattels used in a business and eligible for capital allowances:

- *Rule 1: exemption relief* If a non-wasting chattel is sold for gross proceeds of £6,000 or less and the base cost was also £6,000 or less, then any gain/loss is exempt from CGT.
- *Rule 2: restricted loss relief* If the disposal consideration is £6,000 or less and the base cost is more than £6,000, a loss arises. Any such loss is restricted by replacing the proceeds with deemed proceeds of £6,000 with the effect of reducing the allowable capital loss. This rule cannot turn a loss into a gain, instead the loss would be reduced to nil.
- *Rule 3: marginal relief* If the gross proceeds exceed £6,000 and the base cost is less than £6,000, an individual may be able to avail of marginal relief. The chargeable gain is restricted to the lower of:
  (a)   the gain itself, or
  (b) $5/3 \times$ (gross proceeds – £6,000).

16.9.3   Disposal as Part of a Set

Since the chattel exemption can be quite beneficial, taxpayers may try to abuse this relief by selling off parts of a set of chattels individually, with each sale being less than £6,000, thereby qualifying for the exemption. A set of chattels are chattels which are essentially similar and complementary, and where their value taken together would be greater than their total individual value, e.g. a set of four antique chairs, a set of two candlesticks, etc. There is anti-avoidance legislation to counter this. Review the anti-avoidance rule for sets of chattels from your CA Proficiency 1 or other studies.

16.10 Wasting Assets (Not Chattels)

If a wasting asset is not a chattel, then it is **not exempt** from CGT. The main types of non-chattel wasting assets are intangible assets, fixed plant and machinery or options and leases. However, intangible assets acquired or created on or after 1 April 2002 and disposed of by companies are subject to the corporate intangibles regime (see **Chapter 8, Section 8.4**).

As its name implies, the original cost of the asset wastes away over time. Generally, the allowable cost is reduced on a straight-line basis in proportion to the total length of ownership. The chargeable gain is calculated by comparing the disposal proceeds with the unexpired part of the asset's cost at the disposal date.

16.11 CGT Reliefs

The following is a summary overview of the main CGT reliefs. Students should review the details of these reliefs from their CA Proficiency 1 or other studies. See also **Chapter 19** and **Chapter 20, Section 20.1** for additional understanding of these reliefs required at CA Proficiency 2.

16.11.1   Principal Private Residence Relief

Provided certain conditions are met, any gain on the disposal by an individual of their PPR is exempt. Note, this is an exemption relief and not a deferral relief. PPR relief is deducted from the gain arising on the disposal as follows:

	£
Gain on property	X
Less: PPR relief	(X)
Chargeable gain	X

A PPR is an individual's only or main principal private residence and includes a dwelling house and any surrounding land that is for their own occupation and enjoyment as its garden or grounds up to half a hectare.

Full Exemption

A chargeable gain arising on the disposal of a PPR will be wholly exempt if the owner has occupied the whole of the residence throughout the entire period of ownership as their only or main residence.

Where the residence has been occupied for only part of the period, or only part of the property has been occupied as a residence then the relief available is restricted.

Partial Exemption

If occupation of the PPR has been for only part of the period of ownership, the proportion of the gain that is exempt from CGT is given by the formula:

$$\frac{\text{Period of occupation post 31 March 1982}}{\text{Total period of ownership post 31 March 1982}} \times \text{Total gain}$$

This formula is further adjusted if only part of the property has been occupied as the owner's PPR (see below).

Period of Occupation

There are two types of period of occupation: **actual occupation** (where the individual resides in the property as their only or main residence); and **deemed occupation** where periods of absence are treated as periods of occupation for the purposes of the formula above.

Deemed periods of occupation include:

1. where the individual has resided in a property as their only or main residence at some point in time during the ownership period, then from 6 April 2020 the last nine months will always be treated as a period of occupation. This is known as the final-period exemption. In some cases it can be 36 months (but only for certain limited categories of individuals such as disabled persons or residents of care homes);
2. certain other periods of absence provided that:
    (a) the taxpayer had no other exempt PPR at the time; and
    (b) there is a period of actual physical occupation both at some time before and after the period of absence.
    Therefore, subject to (a) and (b) above, deemed periods of occupation are:
    (i)   any period (or periods) of absence, for any reason, up to a total of 36 months;
    (ii) any periods of absence during which the taxpayer is working abroad; and
    (iii) a total of up to four years of absence during which the taxpayer is working elsewhere in the UK (employed or self-employed) such that they could not occupy their PPR.

More than One Residence

Where a person has more than one residence (owned or rented), they may elect for one of the properties to be regarded as their main or sole residence by giving notice to HMRC within two years of commencing occupation of the second residence. For the election to be valid, the individual must actually reside in both properties.

In the absence of an election, HMRC will impose a ruling as to which house is to be treated as the PPR of an individual with more than one residence.

Married Couples/Civil Partnerships

Where a husband and wife or civil partners live together, only one residence may qualify as the main residence for PPR. Where they each owned one property before the marriage/registration of the civil partnership, a new two-year period for electing which property is to be treated as their main residence commences on their marriage/registration.

Business Use

If part of a residence is used exclusively for business purposes throughout the period of ownership, PPR relief will not be available on the portion of the gain relating to this part of the property. In addition, the last nine months (36 months in some cases) of deemed occupation will not apply to this portion.

16.11.2   Lettings Relief

PPR relief is extended to a gain accruing, up to a certain limit, while the property is let to tenants as residential accommodation. From 6 April 2020, this is only available where the tenant or tenants share occupation with the owner of the property. This extended relief is known as "lettings relief". PPR relief should be deducted from the gain first and takes priority over lettings relief.

Lettings relief may be available to cover some or all of the gain not covered by PPR but is restricted to the lower of:

1. the gain accruing during the letting period of shared occupancy with the owner;
2. the part of the gain which is exempt under the PPR provisions; or
3. £40,000.

16.11.3   Rollover Relief and Depreciating Assets

If an individual disposes of a business asset a chargeable gain may crystallise. Where the individual reinvests the proceeds into a replacement asset within a fixed timeframe, they can make a claim to defer the chargeable gain. Rollover relief is therefore relief for the replacement of business assets used in a trade. This relief is also available for companies.

Provided certain conditions are met, an individual may claim that a chargeable gain arising on the disposal of a business asset (the old asset) may be 'rolled over' against the cost of acquiring a replacement business asset (the new asset).

The disposal of the old asset is deemed to give rise to neither a gain nor a loss and the cost of the new asset is reduced by the gain that would have arisen but for the rollover relief. The chargeable gain is therefore "deferred" until such time as the new asset is disposed of (subject to the possibility of a further rollover claim being available).

Full or partial relief is available, depending on the circumstances.

- Full rollover relief is only available where all the net disposal proceeds are applied in acquiring the total cost of acquisition of the new asset.
- Partial rollover relief is where not all the disposal proceeds are reinvested. The amount not reinvested falls to be taxed immediately.

In both instances, the cost of the new asset is reduced by the amount of rollover relief claimed. It also not possible to specify or tailor the amount of rollover relief to be claimed.

The conditions that must be met before a rollover claim can be made are:

1. Both the old and the new assets must be within one of the specified classes of assets, which include (but is not limited to):
   ■ land, buildings and fixed plant and machinery;
   ■ ships, hovercraft, aircraft, satellites, space stations and spacecraft;
   ■ goodwill falling within the CGT regime.
2. The old asset must have been used only for trade purposes throughout the period of ownership and the new asset must be taken into and used immediately in the trade.
3. The new asset must be acquired during the specified period beginning 12 months before and ending 36 months after the date of disposal of the old asset.

Claims for the relief must be made within four years after the end of the tax year (or accounting period for companies) in which the later of the disposal of the old asset or the acquisition of the new asset took place.

It is possible to make provisional claims for rollover relief if it is intended that a purchase of a qualifying asset will take place within the specified period.

Depreciating Assets

A depreciating asset is fixed plant and machinery not forming part of a building, or an asset that has a predictable useful life not exceeding 60 years from the time it is acquired (for example a short-term lease of 60 years or less).

Where the new replacement asset is a depreciating asset, the chargeable gain arising on the disposal of the old asset cannot be rolled over and is not deducted from the base cost of the new asset. Instead, the chargeable gain is 'frozen' until it becomes chargeable (crystallises) on the earliest of the following three dates:

1. the date on which the new depreciating asset is disposed of;
2. the date on which the new depreciating asset ceases to be used in the trade; or
3. the tenth anniversary of the acquisition of the new depreciating asset.

16.11.4   Gift Relief/Holdover Relief

Section 165 Gift Relief – Business Assets

When a qualifying business asset is gifted for nil consideration, the transferor receives no proceeds from the transaction. For CGT purposes, the disposal is treated as a disposal at market value as the transaction is not at arm's length. A chargeable gain may crystallise, which means that the taxpayer, in the absence of any gift relief, could find themselves having to pay CGT in respect of the gift but not having received any proceeds with which to fund it.

Section 165 gift relief is a form of deferral relief for certain business assets. Where a gain arises on a gift of a business asset, the gain may be 'held over'. Both the transferor and transferee must jointly elect for the gain on the gift to be held over and claims must be made within four years from the end of the tax year of disposal.

Where gift relief is claimed, the taxable capital gain is deferred by deducting the gift relief obtained from the base cost of the asset in the hands of the recipient.

Under section 165 gift relief, gifts must be business assets and one of the following:

1. An asset used in the business carried on by the transferor or by the transferor's "personal trading company", as defined.
2. Shares/securities of trading companies or holding companies of trading groups where:
    (a) the shares are unlisted; or
    (b) the shares are in the transferor's personal trading company.
3. Agricultural land and buildings used for a farming trade that would qualify for IHT agricultural property relief (see **Chapter 25, Section 25.2**).

Section 165 Gift Relief – Restricted Cases

There are two instances where gift relief will be restricted (i.e. when full gift relief is not available): sales at undervalue, and gifts of shares in a personal trading company.

Sales at Undervalue

The rule in this instance is that the "excess proceeds", i.e. the amount of the proceeds exceeding the original cost of the asset, is taxed immediately and the difference between the gain before relief and this taxable amount qualifies for gift relief and is deferred.

Gifts of Shares in a Personal Trading Company

If the gift is of shares in a personal trading company, and the company has any non-business chargeable assets (such as investments) at the date of the gift on its statement of financial position, the gain eligible for gift relief is restricted. Gift relief is only available on that part of the gain represented by the proportion of chargeable business assets (CBA) to total chargeable assets (CA), calculated as:

$$\text{Qualifying gain} \times \frac{\text{Market value of CBA}}{\text{Market value of CA}}$$

Market values of the assets as per the statement of financial position at the date of the gift are used for these purposes.

CBAs are assets that are typically used in the business, e.g. goodwill, factory premises, plant and machinery, etc. However, goodwill will be neither a CBA nor a chargeable asset if it was acquired or created on or after 1 April 2002, as in those cases goodwill is treated as an intangible fixed asset under the corporate intangibles regime (see **Chapter 8, Section 8.4**).

Chargeable assets are CBAs plus any non-business chargeable assets (e.g. investments). This would include, for example, rental properties and quoted shares held as investments.

Mixed Use (Business and Non-business Use)

As for rollover relief, gains on assets (other than shares) with mixed use must be apportioned. Only the gain relating to the business portion may qualify for gift relief.

Instalment Payments

For certain assets gifted where gift relief is not available (i.e. non-business assets), CGT may be payable in 10 equal annual instalments, if elected. The CGT instalment option is available for land and buildings, shares in unquoted companies (e.g. investment companies) and shares in quoted companies where the donor has control before the gift. Such instalments are interest-bearing.

Territoriality Rules

Learning Objectives

After studying this chapter you will understand the UK's territoriality rules in the context of CGT and specifically:

- The application of the residence, domicile and deemed domicile rules for CGT purposes.
- The remittance basis of taxation.
- The application of the rules on temporary non-residence.
- The application of the rules for non-residents directly or indirectly disposing of UK property.

An individual's exposure to UK CGT generally depends on their residence and domicile status. The concepts of residence, domicile and deemed domicile were dealt with in detail in **Chapter 2**. Take the time now to review these important concepts.

It should be noted that the terms "residence" and "domicile" have the same meaning for CGT as they have for income tax and inheritance tax, but that the definition of deemed domicile is different for CGT and income tax purposes compared to inheritance tax (see **Chapter 22, Sections 22.3.1** and **22.3.2**).

17.1 Deemed Domicile – 6 April 2017 Rebasing

For CGT purposes only, individuals becoming deemed UK domiciled in 2017/18 under category 1 of the deemed domicile rules (see **Chapter 2, Section 2.4**) may be able to 'rebase' the original base cost of their non-UK situs assets to the market value as at 6 April 2017 when calculating the gain or loss on the disposal of that asset. This is subject to the following conditions:

- the individual made a claim for the remittance basis and the remittance basis charge applied in 2016/17 or an earlier year;
- the individual was UK resident in 2017/18;
- for 2017/18, and each subsequent year up to and including the year the disposal is made, the individual is deemed UK domiciled under category 1 of the deemed domicile rules (see **Chapter 2, Section 2.4**);
- the individual has not become domiciled in the UK;
- the asset was held on 5 April 2017;
- the disposal occurred on or after 6 April 2017; and
- the asset was not situated in the UK at any time from 16 March 2016 to 5 April 2017.

Rebasing can be considered on an asset-by-asset basis and, on disposal, an election can be made for rebasing not to apply to that asset. The main benefit of rebasing is that the base cost of the asset is uplifted to its market value at 6 April 2017, which may result in either a lower gain or higher capital loss.

17.2 Double Tax Relief

Where a UK resident individual makes a capital gain on the disposal of a foreign asset and foreign tax is paid on that transaction, relief can be claimed against the UK CGT liability.

There are general provisions relating to the making of arrangements with governments of territories outside the UK for avoiding double taxation known as double taxation agreements. The purpose of a double taxation agreement is primarily to avoid the incidence of double taxation by limiting the taxing rights of each contracting state.

Relief for foreign tax suffered on gains that are chargeable to CGT (or corporation tax) in the UK may be obtained under the terms of a double taxation agreement between the UK and the relevant overseas territory. Under the terms of an agreement, it may be the case that the gain is only taxable in one of the contracting states (i.e. the state of residence or the state in which the gain arose).

Where double taxation remains, i.e. where both states retain the right to tax the gain under the agreement, it is generally the case that the agreement will provide relief which, in the case of UK residents, invariably takes the form of a credit for the foreign tax against the UK tax liability on the profits or gains concerned.

If the overseas territory does not have a double taxation agreement with the UK, the taxpayer can still avail of "unilateral relief".

Unilateral relief (sometimes known as credit relief) is the lower of:

1. the UK tax on the foreign gain; or
2. the foreign tax suffered.

Unilateral relief reduces the UK CGT charge and is the most widely used form of double tax relief.

If there is no double taxation agreement and unilateral relief is not claimed, the foreign gain, net of foreign tax, is charged to UK CGT, i.e. the foreign tax is treated as an additional cost in the CGT computation (expense relief). This treatment may be appropriate if there is no UK tax to shelter, perhaps because the gain has been reduced by losses or other deferral reliefs.

When calculating the CGT liability where there are foreign gains, the annual exemption is allocated first against UK and foreign gains on which no double taxation or unilateral relief is being claimed, and then against gains on which relief is being claimed, beginning with the gain that has been subjected to the lowest effective rate of foreign tax.

17.3 Residence Condition is Met

17.3.1 UK Assets

A person is chargeable to UK CGT on gains arising on the disposal of UK assets if the residence condition is met in the year of assessment. The residence condition is, in the case of an individual, that the individual is resident in the UK under the statutory residence test for the year in question (see **Chapter 2, Section 2.2**). Losses arising on the disposal of assets are allowable losses available for set-off (see **Chapter 16, Section 16.7**).

17.3.2 Foreign Assets

A UK domiciled or deemed domiciled individual who is resident in the UK is chargeable to UK CGT on an arising basis on **worldwide** chargeable gains arising on the disposal of assets.

Therefore, an individual who is resident in the UK and is UK domiciled or deemed domiciled is taxable in the UK on gains arising anywhere in the world, regardless of whether or not the proceeds of any foreign asset disposals are remitted to the UK. Losses arising on the disposal of worldwide assets are again allowable losses available for set-off.

The special rules in relation to individuals with a foreign domicile and who are not deemed UK domicile (see **Section 17.5**) are discussed below. In essence, such individuals resident in the UK may, in certain instances, only be liable to UK CGT on foreign gains to the extent that the proceeds are remitted to the UK, i.e. be able to apply the remittance basis of tax. Such individuals will always be liable to UK CGT on gains arising in the UK. Where the remittance basis is not automatically available or is not elected for, the individual is assessable on foreign gains on an arising basis. See also the rules applying to overseas losses for individuals taxed under the remittance basis.

It is therefore important to determine if a gain is a UK gain or a foreign gain.

17.3.3 Location of Assets

CGT legislation contains rules for determining the location (or situs) of assets. These rules are particularly relevant to an individual who is UK resident but is not UK domiciled or deemed UK domiciled for UK CGT purposes and who is availing of the remittance basis (see **Section 17.5**).

Accordingly, it is important for an individual to establish the situs of their assets and if gains were realised from the disposal of assets that were in fact situated outside the UK. The following specific rules apply:

1. Rights or interests in **immovable** or **tangible movable property** or **chattels** are situated where the property is situated.
2. In general, **debts** (secured or unsecured) are situated in the UK if the creditor (i.e. the person is owed the money) is resident in the UK. This is only really relevant to inheritance tax as simple debts owed to an individual are not a chargeable asset for UK CGT purposes.
3. **Shares or securities** issued by a government, governmental authority or municipal authority are situated in the country where that authority is established.
4. **Other registered shares and securities** are situated where they are registered and, if registered in more than one register, where the principal register is situated.
5. **A ship** or **aircraft** is situated in the UK if, and only if, the owner is resident in the UK.
6. **Goodwill** of a business is situated at the place where the trade, business or profession is carried on.
7. **Patents, trademarks** and **registered designs** are situated in the country where they are registered.
8. **Copyrights** and **licences** to use any copyrights, patents, trademarks or designs are situated in the UK if the rights derived from them are exercisable in the UK.

Note that the assets in categories 6–8 are treated instead under the corporate intangibles regime where they are disposed of by a company who acquired, enhanced or created the relevant asset on or after 1 April 2002 (see **Chapter 8, Section 8.4**).

The above rules for determining situs of assets also apply when considering where an asset is situated for IHT purposes.

17.3.4 Split-year Basis

As set out in **Chapter 2, Section 2.2**, if an individual is UK resident under the statutory residence test (SRT) then they are generally considered resident for the entire tax year, even if they arrived in or left the UK during the tax year. This means that all disposals of chargeable assets, irrespective of situs, are subject to UK CGT subject to the remittance basis rules for non-UK domiciled individuals (who are not deemed UK domiciled for UK CGT purposes).

However, if during a tax year an individual arrived in or left the UK, then the split-year residence rules may apply and they may be assessed only on gains arising after they arrived in the UK or before they left the UK, as applicable. Certain conditions have to be met, which are beyond the scope of this textbook.

In respect of the individual's non-resident part of the split year, the taxation rules for non-residents should also be considered (see below).

17.4   Residence Condition is Not Met

The general rule is that an individual who is non-resident in the UK is not subject to UK CGT. There are, however, three exceptions to this rule that you should be aware of at CA Proficiency 2:

1. A non-resident person or company carrying on a business in the UK through a branch or agency (or permanent establishment in the case of a company) is chargeable to UK CGT (or corporation tax) on gains arising from assets in the UK that are used for the purposes of the UK business. Capital losses are also allowable.
    Note: rollover relief may be available where the replacement asset is situated in the UK (rollover relief was covered in detail at CA Proficiency 1, and see also the overview in **Chapter 16, Section 16.11.3**).
2. Gains arising under anti-avoidance provisions for temporary non-residents (see **Section 17.9**). Losses arising during the period of temporary non-residence are also allowable.
3. Gains arising to non-resident individuals who are either directly or indirectly disposing of UK land or property are subject to UK CGT, despite being non-resident (see **Section 17.10**). Losses arising under these rules can be set against any chargeable gains arising to the non-resident individual.

17.5   The Remittance Basis

Only certain non-domiciled individuals who are not deemed UK domiciled for UK income tax and CGT purposes are permitted to automatically avail of the generous remittance basis of taxation. The remittance basis means that a resident, non-domiciled individual who is not deemed UK domiciled for UK income tax and CGT purposes is taxable on foreign gains only to the extent that the proceeds are remitted (i.e. taken back) to the UK. UK gains are fully taxable irrespective of the remittance position. Recap on the rules for deemed domicile for income tax and CGT from **Chapter 2, Section 2.4**.

Under the rules, there is a **basic assumption** that a resident but non-UK domiciled individual who is not deemed UK domiciled for UK income tax and CGT purposes is taxed on foreign chargeable gains on the arising basis of taxation **unless** they make a claim for the remittance basis of taxation to apply, or the remittance basis is automatically available (see **Section 17.5.1**).

Special rules apply where the individual is regarded as a long-term resident of the UK. Such individuals are required to pay a "remittance basis charge" in addition to any tax on sums remitted into the UK if they wish to claim the remittance basis of taxation in relation to their income and/or gains. This applies only if they have been UK-resident for at least seven of the preceding nine tax years.

17.5.1   Remittance Basis of Taxation with No Claim Required

No formal claim is required for the remittance basis of taxation to be applied in three instances:

1.   Where the unremitted income or gains arising overseas is less than £2,000. The £2,000 is the net unremitted income or gains for the year.

> **Example 17.1**
> Pierre is UK resident but French domiciled. He has lived in the UK for the past 10 years and makes a capital gain in France of £120,000 (€145,000) in the tax year 2021/22. He has no other income or gains outside the UK and he remits £119,000 of the proceeds on the sale to the UK.
>
> Pierre will be taxed automatically on the remittance basis of taxation as his unremitted proceeds from the gain of £1,000 are less than £2,000.

2.   Where:
     (a)   the individual has no UK income or gains; and
     (b)   no remittances of any foreign income or gains have been made; and
     (c)   the individual has been resident in the UK for fewer than seven out of the preceding nine years or is under 18 years old.

> **Example 17.2**
> Pierre's sister, Marie, is a student living in the UK since mid-2017. She is aged 21. She has no UK income or gains, but does have a small amount of French savings on which she receives interest. She has not made any remittances to the UK.
>
> Marie can have the benefit of the remittance basis of tax without having to make a formal claim as she meets conditions (a), (b) and (c).

3.   Where:
     (a)   the individual has no UK income or gains other than taxed investment income not exceeding £100; and
     (b)   no remittances have been made; and
     (c)   the individual has been resident in the UK for fewer than seven out of the preceding nine years, or is under 18 years old.

If either of the above three cases applies, the individual is still entitled to UK personal allowances (subject to the relevant conditions being met) and the CGT annual exemption. This is not the case if a formal claim for the remittance basis is made as it is not automatically available.

17.5.2   Remittance Basis of Taxation with a Formal Claim Required

Where the remittance basis is not automatically available, a formal claim must be made. In such cases, certain allowances are withdrawn, including the CGT annual exemption (£12,300 for 2021/22) and any UK personal allowances (see **Chapter 2**, **Section 2.6**).

17.6   Remittance Basis Charge

A non-domiciled individual who is not deemed UK domiciled for UK income tax and CGT purposes and who is over 18 years of age during the tax year may, if electing to use the remittance basis, also have to pay the remittance basis charge (RBC) in addition to full UK CGT on any UK gains and UK CGT only on foreign gains remitted. The RBC is payable if the individual is long-term UK resident, i.e. has been **resident in the UK for at least seven out of nine years immediately preceding the year of assessment**. Such individuals will only be able to use the remittance basis if they pay the RBC for the year. The RBC is not payable where the remittance basis is available without a formal claim being required.

A long-term UK resident non-domiciled individual (who is not deemed UK domiciled for UK income tax and CGT purposes) and who is not automatically entitled to the remittance basis has a choice as to whether they wish to be assessed on their foreign income and gains on the remittance basis of taxation, or on the arising basis of taxation. If they do not claim the remittance basis and so do not pay the RBC, or if they do claim but do not pay the applicable RBC, they will be assessed to UK tax on their worldwide income and gains on the arising basis.

A non-domiciled individual who is not UK deemed domiciled for CGT purposes and who arrived in the UK in 2014/15 (or earlier) will need to pay the RBC of £30,000 if they wish to have the benefit of the remittance basis of taxation in 2021/22.

In 2021/22, if the non-domiciled individual who is not deemed UK domiciled for UK CGT purposes arrived in the UK in 2009/10 (or earlier), the increased RBC of £60,000 will be payable as they will be have been UK resident for 12 of the previous 14 years immediately preceding the year of assessment, assuming the remittance basis of taxation is selected. The £30,000 or £60,000 charge is in addition to any tax due on the foreign income and gains remitted to the UK. Such individuals will also pay UK CGT on any UK gains arising as these remain taxable under the arising basis.

An individual with a foreign domicile who is not deemed UK domiciled for UK CGT purposes and who pays the £30,000 or £60,000 RBC is known as a "remittance basis user".

The RBC is a charge on **nominated unremitted income and gains** rather than a standalone charge. The foreign domiciled individual can nominate any amount of income or gains. The nominated amounts are then charged to tax as if they were taxed on an arising basis. They cannot be charged to tax again if they are subsequently remitted to the UK. Unremitted income and gains that the individual may have are deemed to be "remitted" **before** nominated income and gains.

If the RBC payment is paid directly to HMRC from an overseas account it is not treated as a remittance of tax and there is no UK liability on it. If the individual were to remit £30,000 or £60,000, to the UK **and** then use that money to pay the RBC, this latter remittance would be taxable in the UK.

The RBC is administered and collected through the self-assessment system and normal filing and payment dates apply. When considering whether the additional RBC charge is applicable, the individual will need to look back over the last 14 tax years, the 14th year being the tax year before the year of the potential claim.

It should also be noted that the RBC applies irrespective of whether the individual is resident in the UK for the whole of the year; there is no pro rata reduction for those coming to or leaving the UK part-way through a tax year, i.e. in situations where split year basis is available.

17.6.1 Summary: Claims for Remittance Basis

An individual who is UK resident and non-domiciled (and who is not deemed UK domiciled for UK income tax and CGT purposes) who wishes to pay tax under the remittance basis:

1. must make a claim to have access to the remittance basis, if not automatically entitled to it;
2. must have been resident in the UK for that tax year;
3. must pay the RBC if they are long-term UK resident (£30,000 if they have been resident in the UK for at least seven out of the preceding nine tax years, or £60,000 if resident in the UK for at least 12 out of the preceding 14 tax years);

4. will lose their UK personal allowances; and

5. will lose the UK CGT annual exemption.

The remittance basis is only available in respect of foreign income and chargeable gains (i.e. gains accruing on the disposal of assets situated outside the UK). The consequences in points 1–5 are in addition to any UK CGT payable. Double tax relief should also be considered where appropriate.

17.7   Overseas Losses

Losses on foreign assets are allowable losses if the individual is taxed on their worldwide gains on an arising basis, e.g. the individual is UK resident.

Where a foreign domiciled individual who is not deemed UK domiciled for UK CGT purposes claims the remittance basis of taxation and is not automatically entitled to it, relief for losses on foreign assets is only available if they make an election to do so.

This election must be made in the first year when the remittance basis is claimed, even if there are no foreign gains or losses realised in that year. If no election is made, foreign losses of that year and future tax years will **not be** allowable losses, even if the individual is later taxed on an arising basis (unless they accept that they are domiciled in the UK). The election must be submitted to HMRC within four years of the end of the tax year in question.

If an election has been made then, in a tax year in which the remittance basis applies, special ordering rules apply to determine how gains are to be relieved by losses. These are beyond the scope of this textbook.

17.8   Meaning of Remittances

HMRC guidance on what constitutes a remittance is very widely drawn and it would be very easy to inadvertently remit monies to the UK for these purposes. There are also a number of exemptions and a special relief for money remitted into the UK in order to acquire shares in, or make a loan to, a qualifying trading company (business investment relief). These rules are beyond the scope of this textbook.

17.9   Temporary Non-residents

A person who is a "temporary non-resident" may be chargeable to CGT on gains accruing during their period of absence from the UK, i.e. while non-UK resident. This is anti-avoidance legislation designed to cover the situation where the individual crystallises their unrealised gains whilst temporarily abroad (i.e. temporarily residing outside the UK). In the absence of this rule, the taxpayer could escape UK CGT by simply leaving the UK for a relatively short time and realising any gains on their chargeable assets during their period of non-UK residence. However, before considering if this rule applies, the exceptions which impose CGT on non-resident individuals, i.e. categories 1 and 3 in **Section 17.4**, should first be considered when a chargeable asset is disposed of while non-resident.

In essence, where an individual has left the UK and subsequently returns, they are chargeable to CGT on gains arising during their absence on the disposal of assets they **owned prior to their departure** if:

■ following a residence period (i.e. a full tax year or a split year) where the individual has a sole UK residence, one or more residence periods occur for which they do not have sole UK residence;

- in four or more of the seven tax years immediately preceding the year of departure the individual had either:
  - sole UK residence for the tax year; or
  - the year was a split year that included a residence period for which the individual had sole UK residence, and
- the period of non-residence is five years or less.

Note: this anti-avoidance rule does not therefore apply to assets acquired while non-UK resident.

The gains arising in their year of departure are taxable in that year under the normal rules; while the gains arising during their absence from the UK, under the temporary non-resident rules, are deemed to arise and be taxed in the tax year of their return to the UK, unless these are otherwise taxable under categories 1 and 3 in **Section 17.4**.

The individual will be able to claim the annual exemption for the year of departure and the year of return but, in general, will not be able to avail of annual exemptions during the period of non-residence unless these are otherwise taxable, under categories 1 and 3 in **Section 17.4**.

If, instead, losses are made during the period of non-residence, then these losses are allowable and will be set-off against the gains arising in the year of return, providing all of the above conditions for the temporary non-resident rule are met. If the gain has already been taxed in another country in the year that it arises and is then taxed in the UK in the year of return, relief for double taxation should be considered (see **Section 17.2**).

Therefore, if an individual who has always lived in the UK wishes to become non-resident to avoid paying UK CGT on assets owned at the date of departure, they must remain resident outside the UK for at least five years. However, consideration should also be given to whether the gain is already caught under categories 1 and 3 in **Section 17.4**.

Example 17.3

Richie Rich owns 40% of the shares in TeleUK Ltd. The shares cost him £200,000 in 2002/03. He lived in the UK from birth until he emigrated in October 2020. He sold the shares for £500,000 in December 2021 and realised a gain of £300,000.

During February 2021 he sold other shares making a loss of £10,000. He had also acquired these shares during 2002/03.

On 20 April 2023 he sold a UK commercial investment property, which he had acquired in December 2020, realising a gain of £100,000.

He returned to live in the UK in August 2025.

Solution

Date of departure: October 2020
Date of return: August 2025

As Richie Rich returned to the UK within five years the gains arising in the non-resident period on assets which were owned at the time of departure are taxable in the year of return.

	£
2021/22	300,000
2020/21	(10,000)
Total chargeable gains 2025/26	290,000

Note: the gain on the UK property in 2023/24 does not come into charge on his return to the UK as it was acquired after Richie had left the UK and was disposed of during a tax year in which he was non-resident. However, as the asset is UK land it would be subject to tax under the NRCGT rules (see **Section 17.10.2**).

17.10   Non-residents CGT on UK Land and Property

There are two special regimes that impose CGT on non-residents directly or indirectly disposing of UK land and property (both residential and commercial). These regimes together are known as the non-residents CGT (NRCGT) regime.

17.10.1   6 April 2015 – NRCGT on Disposals of UK Residential Property

Non-resident persons directly disposing of UK residential property interests on or after 6 April 2015 pay UK CGT on such disposals. UK commercial properties and indirect disposals are not caught by this legislation (however, see **Section 17.10.2**).

Definition of UK Residential Property Interest
A UK residential property interest is any interest in UK land or property that has consisted of or included a dwelling. However, this only applies to ownership periods on or after 6 April 2015.

In the legislation, a dwelling is "any property used or suitable for use as a dwelling, or in the process of being constructed or adapted for this use." Land that at any time is, or is intended to be, "occupied or enjoyed" as a garden or grounds (including any building or structure on it) is also taken to be part of the dwelling.

The legislation does include some specific exemptions from the definition of a dwelling, but these are beyond the scope of this textbook.

Definition of Non-resident Person
"Non-resident" is defined as not UK resident for tax purposes, depending on the category the non-resident "person" falls into. The legislation is widely drafted and applies to the following categories:

■   non-resident individuals;
■   personal representatives of non-residents who have died;
■   any non-residents who are partners in a partnership.

The legislation also provides for an exemption from the legislation for certain institutional investors and for other categories of non-residents to be caught by the rules, which are beyond the scope of this textbook.

Calculation of NRCGT Gains and Losses
There are three possible approaches to the calculation. Non-resident persons can choose the most tax-efficient method for their particular circumstances, so each of the three calculations must be carried out to determine the most favourable approach to take.

Method 1 – Standard Default Approach
The standard approach for calculating the gain is to use the market value as at 5 April 2015, unless the property was acquired after 5 April 2015 but before 5 April 2019, in which case the property's market value at the date of its acquisition is used.

Step 1.   Establish the value of the property as at 5 April 2015 (known as "rebasing").
Step 2.   Calculate the difference between the value on 5 April 2015 and the value on the date the property is disposed of.
Step 3.   Deduct any costs of improving the property incurred after 5 April 2015 and the legal cost of selling the property.

The following examples are taken from the HMRC guidance, *Capital Gains Tax for non-residents* (www.gov.uk).

Example 17.4: HMRC example of the standard default approach
Rebasing calculation – gain from 5 April 2015 to disposal:

Disposal proceeds	£1,250,000
Incidental disposal costs	£30,000
Net disposal proceeds	£1,220,000
Market value at 5 April 2015	£1,000,000
Enhancement costs	£0
Total cost	£1,000,000
Gain over period from 5 April 2015 market value	£220,000

An election can be made for the rebasing to 5 April 2015 not to apply. This then allows either method 2 or method 3 below to be used for calculating the gain/loss if either would result in a lower gain or a loss. See **Section 17.10.3** for more on this election.

Method 2 – Straight-line Time-apportionment Approach
A simple straight-line time apportionment of the whole gain made over the period the property was owned can be carried out instead, with only the element of the apportioned gain/loss falling after 6 April 2015 being taxable/relievable.

Example 17.5: HMRC example of straight-line time apportionment
Total ownership 65 months, period from 6 April 2015 to disposal was 14 months, 21.53% (14/65 × 100) of ownership relates to period from 6 April 2015 to disposal.

Disposal proceeds	£1,250,000
Incidental disposal costs	£30,000
Net disposal proceeds	£1,220,000
Acquisition cost	£750,000
Incidental costs of acquisition	£40,000
Enhancement costs	£0
Total acquisition cost	£790,000
Gain over entire period of ownership	£430,000
Time-apportioned post-5 April 2015 gain 21.53%	£92,579

Method 3 – Gain Over Whole Period of Ownership Calculation
The non-resident person can decide not to make an apportionment, particularly if they want to establish a capital loss on the property disposal. Further apportionments can also be made to reflect any non-residential use of the property.

Example 17.6: HMRC example of gain over whole period of ownership	
Disposal proceeds	£1,250,000
Incidental disposal costs	£30,000
Net disposal proceeds	£1,220,000
Acquisition cost	£750,000
Incidental costs of acquisition	£40,000
Enhancement costs	£0
Total acquisition cost	£790,000
Gain over period of ownership	£430,000

Clearly, in the scenario used in **Examples 17.4** to **17.6**, the straight-line time-apportionment approach would be chosen by the non-resident person to calculate the gain/loss. Therefore this individual would be required to elect for rebasing to 5 April 2015 not to apply.

Rates and Exempt Amounts

The rates of CGT, and whether or not the annual exemption is available depends on what category the non-resident falls into (see above).

For individuals, individual partners in a partnership and personal representatives of a deceased non-resident, the following apply:

■ Rate of CGT is 18% or 28%, depending on the level of other UK source income or chargeable gains in the tax year of disposal.
■ CGT annual exempt amount available.

Note that the 18% rate is not available to the personal representatives of a deceased person. The CGT annual exempt amount is available to the personal representatives of a deceased person in the year of death and the following two tax years.

For the treatment of NRCGT losses, see **Section 17.10.3**.

17.10.2   6 April 2019 – NRCGT on Direct and Indirect Disposals of UK Land

Non-resident persons **directly or indirectly** disposing of UK "land property" (including commercial property) on or after 6 April 2019 pay UK CGT on such disposals. This regime does not apply if the relevant disposal is already subject to UK CGT because the UK land disposed of was used in a UK branch or agency by the non-resident person (see **Section 17.4**, category 1).

The legislation also includes some specific exemptions from these rules and for certain non-residents; these are beyond the scope of this textbook.

Definition of Non-resident Person

"Non-resident" is defined as not UK resident for tax purposes and is identical to the definition set out in **Section 17.10.1** for direct disposals of UK residential property on or after 6 April 2015. Again, the legislation also provides for other categories of non-residents to be caught by the rules, which are beyond the scope of this textbook.

Indirect Disposals of UK Land

A non-resident person will be chargeable to UK CGT on indirect disposals where:

- the non-resident person disposes of an interest in a company (UK resident or non-UK resident); and
- that disposal is of an asset that derives at least 75% of its gross asset value from UK land; and
- the non-resident person making the disposal has a "substantial" indirect interest in the UK land (which broadly means they have an investment of at least 25% in the company being disposed of at any point in the **two years** prior to the disposal).

When establishing if the non-resident person has a "substantial" indirect interest, the rights and interests of persons who are connected with them must also be taken into account. For these purposes, a person is connected to:

- their spouse or civil partner;
- their lineal ancestors, e.g. siblings;
- their lineal descendants;
- the lineal ancestors or descendants of their spouse or civil partner.

However, a person is not automatically connected to their business partners or to the spouses or civil partners of business partners.

Effectively this measure treats the whole or part of the share disposal by the non-resident person as an indirect disposal of UK land subject to UK CGT. This means that business asset disposal relief, which is potentially available on certain disposals of shares in personal trading companies (see **Chapter 19, Section 19.1**), is not available where the whole or part of the share disposal is treated as an indirect disposal of UK land under this regime. However, a trading exemption may be available in certain cases, the conditions for which are beyond the scope of this text.

Example 17.7

Mark and Sarah (who are not connected with one another and are not married) are resident in Ireland. Together they own the entire share capital of an Irish resident company. Mark owns 80% of the shares and Sarah owns 20%. In June 2027, the company is sold for £2 million. At that time the company owned 20 acres of valuable commercial land in Belfast valued at £1.8million, which was acquired in June 2020.

Mark makes a gain on the disposal of his shares of £1,520,000. Sarah makes a gain of £380,000. Neither gain meets the conditions for the trading exemption in respect of indirect disposals.

The disposal of Mark's shares is treated as an indirect disposal of UK land because:

- he disposed of his interest in the company; and
- more than 75% of the gross asset value of the company (in this case 90% – £1,800,000/£2,000,000) was derived from UK land; and
- he held 80% of the company, which is a substantial investment.

Sarah is not treated as having made an indirect disposal of UK land as she did not hold a substantial indirect investment (as her shareholding was below 25%). Mark and Sarah will also need to consider their Irish CGT position on this transaction. Even if Irish CGT is also payable by Mark, double tax relief in the UK would not be available against his UK CGT liability as Mark is not UK resident.

Calculation of NRCGT Gains and Losses

The computational rules that follow apply to both direct and indirect disposals of UK land, as previously defined.

If the asset was acquired on or after 6 April 2019, the relevant gain or loss is calculated under normal principles.

If the asset was acquired before 6 April 2019, there are three methods that can be applied if the asset is UK residential property as set out in **Section 17.10.1**. For direct disposals of commercial property, mixed-use property and indirect disposals on or after 6 April 2019, two methods can be applied as set out below. Again, the non-resident person can choose the most tax-efficient method for their particular circumstances, so both calculations must be carried out to determine the most favourable approach to take.

Method 1 – Standard Default Approach
The standard default approach for calculating the gain is to use the market value as at 5 April 2019 in place of the original base cost of the asset.

Step 1. Establish the value of the asset as at 5 April 2019 (known as "rebasing").
Step 2. Calculate the difference between the value on 5 April 2019 and the value on the date the asset is disposed of.
Step 3. Deduct any costs of improving the asset incurred after 5 April 2019 and any costs of selling the asset.

Example 17.8: HMRC example of standard default approach
A non-resident person directly disposes of a UK commercial property that was acquired before 6 April 2019.

Rebasing calculation – gain from 5 April 2019 to disposal:

Disposal proceeds	£1,000,000
Incidental disposal costs	£50,000
Net disposal proceeds	£950,000
Market value at 5 April 2019	£800,000
Enhancement costs	£0
Total cost	£800,000
Gain over period from 5 April 2019 market value	£150,000

Method 2 – Whole Period of Ownership Calculation (the 'retrospective' method)
The non-resident person can elect not to rebase to the 5 April 2019 value, particularly if they want to establish a capital loss on the property disposal. In this case the whole period of ownership can be used to calculate gain/loss if either would result in a lower gain or a higher loss. (See **Section 17.10.3** for more on this election.)

However, if the election is made in respect of an indirect disposal of UK land any loss arising as a result of the election is not an allowable loss.

Example 17.9: HMRC example of whole period of ownership calculation
The details are the same as in **Example 17.8**.

Disposal proceeds	£1,000,000
Incidental disposal costs	£50,000
Net disposal proceeds	£950,000
Acquisition cost	£1,000,000
Incidental costs of acquisition	£10,000
Enhancement costs	£0
Total acquisition cost	£1,010,000
Loss over period of ownership	£60,000

Clearly, in the scenario used in **Examples 17.8** and **17.9**, the whole period of ownership calculation approach would be chosen by the non-resident person, which would result in a NRCGT loss (see **Section 17.10.3**). Therefore this individual would be required to elect to apply Method 2.

Rates and Exempt Amounts
The following rules apply for direct disposals:

■ Rate of CGT is 10% or 20% for direct non-residential land and property disposals and 18% or 28% for residential land disposals (depending on the level of other UK source income or chargeable gains in the tax year of disposal).
■ CGT annual exempt amount is available.

For indirect disposals:

■ Rate of CGT is 10% or 20% (depending on the level of other UK source income or chargeable gains in the tax year of disposal).
■ CGT annual exempt amount is available.

Note that the 10% and 18% rates are not available to the personal representatives of a deceased person. The CGT annual exempt amount is available to the personal representatives of a deceased person in the year of death and the following two tax years.

17.10.3   NRCGT – General Points

Double Taxation
As the non-resident person is resident in another territory, it is likely that the transaction will also be taxed outside the UK. Where the gain is taxed in two territories, **double taxation relief is not available** in the UK as the non-resident person is not UK resident. However, double taxation relief may be available in the overseas territory as double taxation agreements generally provide that tax paid by a non-resident in the source country will be credited against tax paid in the country of residence.

NRCGT Losses
Losses arising on NRCGT disposals can only be offset against NRCGT gains of the non-resident either in the tax year of disposal or in subsequent tax years. Where a non-resident individual dies, NRCGT losses can be claimed against NRCGT gains in the three tax years preceding death, setting the NRCGT losses against NRCGT gains in later years first.

If the non-resident person becomes UK resident, any unused NRCGT losses become general capital losses and are not ring-fenced. Likewise, if a UK resident becomes non-resident, any unused UK land or property capital losses become NRCGT losses and can only be set-off against future NRCGT gains.

These rules apply to NRGT losses under both of the NRCGT regimes set out above.

Administration
NRCGT disposals must be reported to HMRC within 30 days of completion of the property transaction, even if there is no NRCGT to pay. So, if the property was conveyed on 1 July 2021, the reporting deadline is 31 July 2021.

Each property liable to NRCGT must be notified **separately** to HMRC. Notification is made by completing a special online NRCGT return form, regardless of whether or not the non-resident person is registered with HMRC for UK tax through self-assessment.

Unless a non-UK resident person is within the UK self-assessment regime, the NRCGT return should include an assessment of any tax due. Payment of the NRCGT is due within 30 days.

If the non-resident person is already registered in the UK for self-assessment, they can defer the payment of their NRCGT liability and pay any NRCGT owed as part of their normal self-assessment the following 31 January after the tax year of disposal.

If the individual wishes to elect to not rebase to the relevant market value (at either 5 April 2015 (**Section 17.10.1**) or 5 April 2019 (**Section 17.10.2**), this election must be made in the non-resident's self-assessment return. If no election is made, the default rebasing rules apply.

An election is irrevocable if made in the non-resident's self-assessment return. If it is made in a return relating to the 30-day payment on account rules, the election may be withdrawn.

The normal self-assessment penalties apply if the non-resident person:

- reports the disposal late;
- submits the NRCGT online return late; or
- the payment deadline is missed.

A penalty will also arise if the information on the NRCGT online return form or the self-assessment return is inaccurate. The usual penalty regime for errors applies (see **Chapter 1**); and interest is payable as normal on any late or underpaid payments.

Principal Private Residence Relief

If the non-resident individual lived in the property as their main home, principal private residence (PPR) relief may apply to all or part of the gain on its disposal. (PPR relief was covered in detail at CA Proficiency 1; see also the overview in **Chapter 16, Section 16.11.1**).

A non-UK resident will only receive PPR relief on a UK residential property disposal if:

- they, or their spouse/civil partner, were living in the UK for that tax year; or
- they, or their spouse/civil partner, stayed overnight at the property at least 90 times in the tax year (the 90-day rule).

If the property was only owned for part of the year, the 90 days are time apportioned in line with the period of ownership. If the 90-day rule is not met, the non-resident person will be counted as away from the property for that tax year. The normal rules for absence and lettings reliefs are unaffected.

Questions

Review Questions

(See Suggested Solutions to Review Questions at the end of this textbook.)

Question 17.1

You arrive into work on a Monday morning in mid-January to find the following email from a client, Jessica Arnold:

To: An Accountant
From: Jessica Arnold
Date: 10 January 2022 at 19.58pm
Subject: Help!

Dear An Accountant,

I'm hoping you remember me; I was a client of your practice some years ago before I emigrated to Brisbane, Australia, and I need help with some tax issues.

I'm back in Northern Ireland, briefly, for a month-long visit from Oz, where I moved to from Armagh in June 2018. I only went on a year-long secondment originally, but a week after arriving I met my husband, who was born here, and extended my stay indefinitely after getting married. We have just had our second child.

I'm here in Belfast for two weeks and we are hoping to move back permanently in early December of this year. We are hoping to have sold our flat in Australia by then, which we bought when we got married.

The plan is that the proceeds of that sale will help towards a down payment on a wee house in Holywood. Our estate agent is very positive and expects me to make a gain on the flat of around £80,000.

Another useful source of funds to help us start a life in Northern Ireland will be the proceeds from the sale of a painting I inherited from my favourite Aunt Delilah in January 2014. I got £750,000 for the painting at an auction last October. I couldn't believe it as the probate value had only been £520,000. Apparently the artist has a huge following in Oz!

I'm a bit worried, though, that these transactions may create UK tax issues for me. Can you advise?

Best wishes,
Jessica

Requirement
Assess whether the temporary non-residence rules for capital gains tax apply to the above transactions. What practical advice would you give Jessica?

Question 17.2

Sophia has been UK resident since 6 April 2008 but has a Belgian domicile of origin. She sold a foreign, residential investment property during 2021/22, resulting in a chargeable gain of £220,600 and remitted £25,000 of this to the UK during the year. Sophia is employed in the UK and has employment income of £90,000. She had no other sources of income during the tax year and paid no capital gains tax in Belgium.

Requirement
(a) Assess, with comparative calculations, if Sophia should make a claim to use the remittance basis in 2021/22 in respect of the above chargeable gain. Include calculations of the UK capital gains tax under each scenario and address any other relevant considerations.
(b) If Sophia had been UK resident since 6 April 2001, outline what difference this would make to her UK CGT position.

Question 17.3

It is February 2022. Catarine Martinique is financial director of a successful UK company and has telephoned you about a taxation matter she needs assistance on. Catarine was born in France but has lived and worked in the UK since 6 April 2008. Her only source of income is her £70,000 salary from her employer. Catarine did own an apartment in Paris but never generated any income from it and recently sold it (on 1 January 2022) for a profit of £472,600. No French tax is payable on the disposal due to several generous reliefs available in France. A month later Catarine transferred £240,000 from that disposal to her UK bank account to use as a down payment on a luxury holiday property near Lough Erne. The remaining £232,000 she intends to leave untouched in her French, high-interest savings account.

Requirement
Draft a letter to Catarine assessing, with comparative calculations, whether she should make a claim to use the remittance basis in 2021/22 in respect of the chargeable gain on the Parisian property.

A calculation of the CGT liability under each option is required, including any other relevant tax considerations. You should assume Catarine has made no other disposals in 2021/22 and that she is an additional rate taxpayer.

Question 17.4

It is April 2022 and you are a Tax Senior in a medium-sized practice based in Newry. Your client Annette Stewart has telephoned you about a taxation matter she needs assistance on. Annette has lived and worked in Australia since she left school at 18 and hasn't been back in the UK since she got married in Perth six years ago.

On 6 February 2022 Annette sold her holiday home in Lough Erne, Enniskillen for net proceeds of £650,000, she hasn't used it in six years and never lived in it. Annette bought the house on 6 December 2012 for £425,000. Annette read somewhere that the 5 April 2015 value of the property is important. The valuation she obtained established that the value at that date was £360,000.

Annette's only source of UK income is rental income on an investment property that uses up her basic rate band every year. She asks you to advise on any UK capital gains tax issues that arise in relation to this property. Annette doesn't need any advice on the Australian side of things as the transaction is exempt there.

Requirement
Draft a letter to Annette to address the following matters:

(a) Assess if a liability to UK capital gains tax arises on the disposal of the Lough Erne property by Annette.

(b) If Annette is liable to UK capital gains tax, calculate the chargeable gain arising using the most tax-efficient method. Calculate Annette's UK capital gains tax liability (if any) assuming she made no other disposals in 2021/22.

Question 17.5

You are working on the 2021/22 self-assessment calculations of a new client of your practice, Stefan Roux. Stefan became UK tax resident in 2020/21 when he married his UK-born wife Maria and he remains UK resident in 2021/22.

Stefan is French domiciled and intends to return to France to live there in a few years. He is a higher rate taxpayer.

During 2021/22, Stefan disposed of an investment property he owned in the Dordogne, making a gain of £125,000. Stefan advised you when preparing his draft self-assessment that he wished to claim the remittance basis as he has not made any remittances to the UK in respect of this disposal, nor does he plan to.

On preparing the 2021/22 accounts for Stefan's sole trade business, you note a large unexplained lodgement of £75,000 into the sole trade's UK account in June 2021; just a few weeks after his property disposal.

When you ask Stefan what this refers to he gives a Gallic shrug and winks, saying "It may or may not be from the sale of my Dordogne house" and then seems to suggest you should ignore what you found and prepare his self-assessment as if there had been no remittances.

Requirement
(a) Explain the tax implications of the £50,000 lodgement from the sale of the Dordogne property. Detailed calculations are not required.
(b) What action should you take given your suspicions that the lodgement is from the Dordogne disposal?

Shares and Series of Transactions

18.1   Introduction

Shares present special problems when attempting to compute gains or losses on disposal.

Where a taxpayer disposes of shares or securities in a company (hereafter referred to as "shares") which they have built up over a period of time, the calculation of the gain or loss arising on a disposal of some of the shares cannot be undertaken until one establishes the base cost of the shares being sold. The shares were purchased at different times at different costs. Thus, a set of share identification (**share matching**) rules are used to **match disposals with acquisitions**.

The share-matching rules are only applied when there is a pot of shares of the same class in the same company.

Example 18.1

Joe bought the following shares in X Ltd:

1,000 in January 1996 for £2,000

1,000 in January 2007 for £8,000

If he sells, say, 1,200 shares today, how would his base cost be determined? To determine the chargeable gain, Joe needs to work out which shares out of the two original holdings were actually sold.

If Joe purchased 1,000 ordinary shares and 1,000 preference shares in X Ltd, then each would be dealt with separately and the share matching rules do not apply as each class of share is distinguishable.

18.1.1   The General Rule

The general rule is that disposals of shares by individuals are matched against acquisitions of the **same class** of shares in the **same company** in the following strict order:

1.   Acquisitions made on the **same day** as the day of disposal.

2.   Acquisitions made during the **following 30 days.** If there is more than one acquisition, then on a 'first in first out' (FIFO) basis – also known as the 'bed and breakfast' rule (see **Section 18.1.3**).

3.   Shares forming the **share pool** "section 104 holding" – this holding will contain all the shares of the same class in the same company that were acquired before the date of the current disposal and which have not been matched at either 1. or 2. above.

Example 18.2

Jeremy had the following disposals and acquisitions of ordinary shares in Razor Plc:

Number of shares	Date	Acquisition/Sale
1,900	06/04/2020	Bought
800	09/09/2021	Bought
1,100	09/09/2021	Sold
180	30/09/2021	Bought
1,200	01/03/2022	Sold
950	23/03/2022	Bought

Set out how the disposals will be matched against the various acquisitions.

The disposal of 1,100 shares on 9 September 2021 is first matched with the 800 shares bought on the same day, leaving 300 shares to be matched. Then the residue is matched against the shares purchased within 30 days (180 shares) on 30 September 2021 (point 2 above), leaving 120 shares still to be matched. These 120 shares are finally matched against the section 104 holding (point 3 above), leaving a balance of 1,780 shares in this holding as at 9 September 2021.

Sold:	9 September 2021	1,100
Bought:	9 September 2021 – same-day rule	(800)
Bought:	30 September 2021 – 30-day rule	(180)
Bought	Share pool	(120) Leaves 1,780 in share pool

The disposal of the 1,200 shares on 1 March 2022 are first matched against the shares purchased within 30 days (as there were no shares bought on the same day), leaving a balance of 250 shares. Finally, these shares are matched against the section 104 holding (point 3 above), leaving a balance of 1,530 shares in this holding going forward.

Sold:	1 March 2022	1,200
Bought:	23 March 2022 – 30-day rule	(950)
Bought:	Share pool	(250) Leaves 1,530 in share pool

18.1.2   Section 104 Holding (TCGA 1992)

The "section 104 holding" pooling arrangements eliminate the need to keep detailed records of the date and costs of each individual share acquisition. All that is required is to have a record of both the **number of shares** in the section 104 holding and the **total allowable expenditure,** i.e. the cost of the shares in the holding. The only potential modification required to the section 104 holding will be to replace the acquisition cost of shares purchased before 31 March 1982 with the market value of those shares as at that date, if the disposal is made by an individual. If the disposal is made by a company, remember that two calculations must be carried out (see **Chapter 16**).

Example 18.3
Brian had made the following acquisitions over the years in Arnold Plc.

Number of shares	Cost £	Date
1,000	1,000	01/01/1978
3,200	5,600	01/01/1988
3,000	6,000	01/01/2004
2,400	7,200	01/01/2022
9,600	19,800	

The shares had a market value of £1.36 per share as at 31 March 1982 and Brian had made no disposals throughout the period.

The section 104 holding as at 1 January 2022 will be built up as follows:

Acquired	Number	Allowable Expenditure
01/01/1978	1,000	1,360 (MV)
01/01/1988	3,200	5,600
01/01/2004	3,000	6,000
01/01/2022	2,400	7,200
Section 104 holding as at 01/01/2022	9,600	20,160

Average price per share as at 1 January 2022 is £2.10.

All that is required to be carried forward is the holding of 9,600 and its associated costs of £20,160. This principle can be demonstrated by the following worked example.

Example 18.4
Following on from the last example, Brian sold 4,000 shares in Arnold Plc on 27 March 2022 for £11,000. He made no further acquisitions within the next 30 days. Calculate Brian's CGT liability for 2021/22. He has already fully utilised his basic rate band but has made no other chargeable disposals in the year.

Since there were no acquisitions on the same day or within 30 days of the sale on 27 March 2022, the sale is matched with the section 104 holding as follows:

		Allowable Expenditure £
Section 104 holding cost b/fwd	9,600 shares	20,160
Allowable expenditure: £20,160 × $\frac{4,000}{9,600}$		(8,400)
Section 104 holding cost c/fwd	5,600 shares	11,760

Calculation of chargeable gain:

	£
Proceeds	11,000
Allowable cost	(8,400)
Gain	2,600
Less: annual exemption	(2,600)
Assessable	nil

As can be can be seen in **Example 18.4** above, where a part disposal of shares takes place the legislation provides that this is calculated as being the proportion of the number of the shares being disposed of bears, at the time of disposal, to the number of shares as a whole. The formula is, therefore:

$$\text{Original cost} \times \frac{A}{(A+B)}$$

where A is the number of shares being sold, and B is the number of shares remaining.

Contrast this with the part disposal formula for other assets as set out in **Chapter 16, Section 16.3.2**.

18.1.3 Anti-avoidance – the "Bed & Breakfast" Rules

The requirement to match share disposals first with acquisitions on the same day, and then with acquisitions within 30 days, is an anti-avoidance measure. It is designed to prevent taxpayers benefiting from the creation of artificial losses and was introduced to remove the tax benefits of such transactions. The transactions involved are commonly referred to as "bed & breakfast" transactions. Typically, an individual would dispose of shares to trigger either a capital loss or a capital gain, but would acquire the shares back within a short timeframe as their long-term intention is to retain the shares.

Any gain was typically calculated so as to be sheltered by the annual exemption and the new shares would have a higher base cost for a future sale. Clearly, such a transaction was purely for tax reasons and not commercial reasons.

Example 18.5: Acquisition within 30 days of disposal

Harry owns 1,000 shares in X Ltd, which he originally purchased in 2005 at £5 each. On 30 December 2021, the shares are quoted at £1 each. Harry does not wish to sell his 1,000 shares as he believes they will rise in price in the future but, at the same time, he wishes to claim loss relief for the paper loss which he has suffered. He cannot do this unless he has a realisation, i.e. a disposal.

Accordingly, he arranges to sell his 1,000 shares at £1 each on 30 December 2021 on the understanding that his stockbroker will re-purchase 1,000 shares two or three days later. Harry will thereby realise a capital loss of £4,000 on the disposal which, in the absence of the anti-avoidance provisions, would be available to set-off against any gains in 2021/22. He will also still own 1,000 shares in X Ltd when he buys them back at a favourable price a few days later.

The legislation prevents this arrangement by providing that, as the disposal and reacquisition of the same class of shares takes place within 30 days, then the disposal is not matched with the acquisition in 2005 but is instead matched with the acquisition that takes either on the same day as, or within 30 days of, the sale, i.e. £1 per share. This greatly restricts, and may even eliminate, the capital losses arising. If the share price has not really altered in the short period between the sale and purchase, these rules mean that no gain or loss will be triggered.

18.2 Bonus Issues and Rights Issues

18.2.1 Bonus Issues (Scrip Issues)

For CGT purposes, a bonus issue is treated as a reorganisation of share capital. As its name implies, a bonus issue occurs when a company issues "free" shares to its existing shareholders, in direct proportion to their existing holding. So a "1 for 10" bonus issue would give each shareholder (of that class of share) one additional share for every 10 that they previously held **at no extra cost**; hence it is a reorganisation of the share capital.

All previous acquisitions fall within the section 104 holding, thus all that is required is to add the number of bonus issue shares to the carried forward share column and no cost to the carried forward allowable cost column – in essence, reducing the average value per share.

Example 18.6

In **Example 18.4**, Brian had a carried forward section 104 holding of 5,600 shares in Arnold Plc with an allowable cost of £11,760 as at 27 March 2022. If the company had made a "1 for 8" bonus issue on 6 June 2022, then the resultant section 104 holding would become:

	Number of shares	Allowable Expenditure
		£
Section 104 holding b/fwd	5,600	11,760
Bonus issue (06/06/2022)	700	nil
Section 104 holding c/fwd	6,300	11,760

Example 18.7

Rianna had made the following acquisitions in Games Plc.

Date	Number of shares	Cost £
01/01/1980	2,600	2,600
04/10/1986	1,000	2,000
11/09/2000	600	1,800
02/03/2004	1,800	4,200

The market value of the company's shares as at 31 March 1982 was £1.50 per share. On 1 July 2008, the company made a "1 for 6" bonus issue. Rianna sold 2,100 of her shares for £2.00 per share on 1 November 2021. She had no further acquisitions in the following 30 days. Calculate the chargeable gain arising on this latter sale, assuming that she has already utilised her annual exemption for 2021/22.

As the disposal on 1 November 2021 cannot be matched with any acquisition on the same day or the following 30 days, it must be matched with the section 104 holding.

Date	Number of shares	Cost £
01/01/1980	2,600	3,900 (MV)
04/10/1986	1,000	2,000
11/09/2000	600	1,800
02/03/2004	1,800	4,200
Section 104 holding b/fwd	6,000	11,900
01/07/2008 Bonus issue (1 for 6)	1,000	0
Section 104 holding as at 01/07/2008	7,000	11,900
01/11/2021 – sold 2,100 shares	(2,100)	
Allowable expenditure = 2,100/7,000 × £11,900		(3,570)
Section 104 holding as at 01/11/2021	4,900	8,330

continued overleaf

Chargeable gain:	
Proceeds (2,100 shares at £2 per share)	4,200
Allowable cost	(3,570)
Chargeable gain	630

Note: the average price of the section 104 holding after bonus issue on 1 July 2008 was £1.70 per share, being £11,900 divided by 7,000 shares.

18.2.2 Rights Issue

A rights issue occurs where a company offers its existing shareholders a right to buy extra shares at a price. Generally, the shares are offered in proportion to the existing shareholding and the price is usually set at a competitive rate compared to the open market value at that time. The company is offering shares at competitive rates to existing shareholders instead of going to the market for fresh capital investment.

A shareholder, having been offered the rights issue, will effectively have three options, namely:

1. to buy the shares being offered;
2. to not buy the shares, but instead sell the "rights" to buy the shares; or
3. do nothing and ignore the rights issue.

Depending on the option they choose, the CGT treatment will be different.

Option 1 – Buy the Shares
In this situation, the CGT treatment is similar to that for bonus issue shares except that the allowable cost column will have to incorporate the price paid for the shares.

Example 18.8
Continuing with the last example, let us assume that Games Plc had made a rights issue of "1 for 6" at a price of £1.40 on 1 July 2008 (instead of the bonus issue). If Rianna had purchased her entitlement to her shares, she would have purchased 1,000 shares at a cost of £1,400. In this situation, her section 104 holding would have become:

Date	Number of shares	Cost £
01/01/1980	2,600	3,900 (MV)
04/10/1986	1,000	2,000
11/09/2000	600	1,800
02/03/2004	1,800	4,200
Section 104 holding b/fwd	6,000	11,900
01/07/2008 rights issue (1 for 6) @£1.40/share	1,000	1,400
Section 104 holding as at 01/07/2008	7,000	13,300

Note: the average allowable cost per share is now £1.90 (£13,300/7,000).

Example 18.9

David had the following acquisitions of shares in Newbury Plc:

Date	Number of shares	Cost £
01/01/1977	2,000	2,000
04/01/1989	1,000	2,500
11/09/2000	600	1,800

The market value of the company's shares as at 31 March 1982 was £1.60 per share. On 1 September 2021, the company made a "1 for 9" rights issue at a price of £1.50 per share. David took up his shares. David sold 1,000 of his shares for £2.20 per share on 1 December 2021. He had no further acquisitions in the following 30 days. Calculate the chargeable gain arising on this latter sale, assuming that David had already utilised his annual exemption for 2021/22.

Once again, the disposal cannot be matched with same day or next 30-day acquisitions. Hence, the disposal must come from the section 104 holding.

Date	Number of shares	Cost £
01/01/1977	2,000	3,200 (MV)
04/10/1989	1,000	2,500
11/09/2000	600	1,800
Section 104 holding b/fwd	3,600	7,500
01/09/2021 rights issue (1 for 9) @ £1.50/share	400	600
Section 104 holding as at 01/09/2021	4,000	8,100
01/12/2021 – sold 1,000 shares	(1,000)	
Allowable expenditure = 1,000/4,000 × £8,100		(2,025)
Section 104 holding c/fwd at 01/12/2021	3,000	6,075
Chargeable gain:		
Proceeds (1,000 shares @ £2.20 per share)		2,200
Allowable cost		(2,025)
Chargeable gain		175

Option 2 – Sell the Rights to Buy the Shares

In this scenario, the taxpayer does not buy the shares but rather is selling the "right" or "option" to buy the shares. This process is known as "sale of rights nil paid", the tax treatment of which is beyond the scope of this textbook.

Option 3 – Ignore the Rights Issue

In this scenario, there will be no CGT implications as nothing has been bought or sold.

18.3   CGT Treatment of Employee Share Options

As set out in **Chapter 6**, share options are a common feature in the remuneration packages of company executives. They usually consist of the right to subscribe at a specified price for a specified number of shares in the employer company during a specified period of time. The following sections deal with the CGT treatment only of employee share options. The income tax treatment of share options was covered in **Chapter 6** and should be revisited. Students will recall that a different tax treatment applies depending on whether the share option scheme is approved or unapproved.

18.3.1 Approved Share Option Schemes

There are a number of employee approved share option schemes, namely, the SAYE scheme, the Company Share Option Plan (CSOP), the Share Incentive Plan, and Enterprise Management Incentives (EMI).

Broadly, the position can be summarised as follows:

- There is no income tax charge on the grant of the option.
- There is no income tax charge on the exercise of the option.
- The shares obtained on foot of the option are instead within the CGT regime and not the income tax regime, and have a base cost equal to the sum paid for them.

For each of the specific schemes, there are conditions to be met in order for the above tax treatments to be applied (see **Chapter 6**).

Example 18.10

John works for ABC Plc. On 1 January 2007, he received options under the company's share option plan over 1,000 shares in the company exercisable at any time within the following five years at the market price of the shares at 1 January 2007. The option scheme was approved by HMRC. The market value of the shares as at 1 January 2007 was £10 per share. On 31 March 2008, John exercised his option and acquired the 1,000 shares for the sum of £10,000.

On 1 January 2022, John sold the shares for £30,000.

Because the share option scheme was approved by HMRC, and because there was no discount on the market value of the shares at the time of grant of the option, neither income tax nor CGT was chargeable at the time of grant or exercise of the option.

Accordingly, on 1 January 2022, John is treated as having a CGT disposal in respect of his shares. His base cost in that computation is £10,000. The sale proceeds are £30,000, so John has made a chargeable gain of £20,000.

18.3.2 Unapproved Share Option Schemes

Broadly, an employee is subject to income tax on the exercise of an unapproved share option and this is based upon the market value of the shares obtained, less the amount paid for the shares and less the amount (if any) which has been paid at the time of the granting of the option. Where the shares are also readily convertible assets, i.e. are readily convertible into cash, Class 1 NICs (both employer and employee) would be charged. In such cases, the income tax and NIC would be collected via PAYE.

For CGT purposes, any amount which has been assessed to income tax must be taken into account in determining the CGT liability. An individual cannot be subject to tax twice on the same gain. Therefore, the base cost for CGT purposes will take into account the amount paid by the individual plus the amount which has been subject to income tax at the time of exercise/grant of the option.

A taxpayer acquired shares after exercising an option. The shares are later sold. The pro forma computation is:

Proceeds	X
Less: cost of shares on exercise	(X)
Less: charge to income tax on exercise	(X)
Chargeable gain/loss	X

Example 18.11

Patrick is granted an option in 2013 by his employer, XYZ Plc, to subscribe for 1,000 £1 ordinary shares at a price of £1 each at any time in the following eight years. He is granted this right by reason of his employment at a time when the shares are valued at £3 each. Patrick exercised the option during December 2021 when the shares were worth £10 each.

There is no income tax suffered at the time of the granting of the option.

At the date of exercise Patrick is subject to income tax through the PAYE system on the uplift in the value of the shares, i.e. £10 less price paid of £1 = £9 per share. Specific employment income is £9 × 1,000 = £9,000.

CGT: Patrick's base cost of the shares is £10,000 (i.e. £1,000 actual cost + £9,000 subject to income tax). If Patrick sold the shares immediately for £10,000 on exercising his option, then he would have a no gain/no loss situation for CGT.

18.4 Treatment of a Series of Transactions between Connected Persons

Where a person disposes of assets by means of a series of transactions to one or more connected person(s) (see **Chapter 16, Section 16.6**) through a series of linked transactions (rather than in one transaction), and:

- the aggregate market value of the asset acquired as a whole is greater than the combined total of their separate values when acquired singly; then
- all of the acquisitions are treated as if they were acquired in one single transaction for a consideration equal to their aggregate market value (when acquired in a single transaction); and
- that revised aggregate market value is then apportioned rateably to each transaction for the purposes of determining the consideration for which each disposal is deemed to have taken place.

Transactions are linked if they occur within six years of each other.

Example 18.12

George and Jimmy are brothers. George has three sets of rare antique Cuban stamps. He gifts them to Jimmy in three separate transactions as follows:

Date of gift		£
01/05/2019	Set 1 market value (on individual basis)	5,000
01/06/2020	Set 2 market value (on individual basis)	10,000
01/07/2021	Set 3 market value (on individual basis)	15,000
		30,000

The market value of the three sets, if disposed of together, is £40,000.

continued overleaf

For the purpose of computing George's CGT liability (if any) on the disposals, the aggregate £40,000 market value will be apportioned rateably to the three transactions as follows:

Revised consideration

£

Set 1: $\dfrac{5,000}{30,000} \times 40,000$ 6,667

Set 2: $\dfrac{10,000}{30,000} \times 40,000$ 13,333

Set 3: $\dfrac{15,000}{30,000} \times 40,000$ 20,000

40,000

George's liability to CGT would then be computed by reference to the increased consideration for each of the three disposals separately. The non-wasting chattels rules would then be applied when calculating the CGT position on each transaction (see **Chapter 16, Section 16.9.2**).

Questions

Review Questions
(See Suggested Solutions to Review Questions at the end of this textbook.)

Question 18.1

Mark had the following transactions in Magnet plc:

Purchase date		No. of shares acquired	Cost
			£
05/10/2001	Purchase	1,500	8,000
10/04/2004	Purchase	2,800	10,000
18/03/2006	Rights issue, 1 for 2 held @ £1.50 per share	2,150	3,225

Disposal date	No. of shares	Proceeds
		£
29/07/2021	2,500	30,000

Requirement
Assuming Mark is an additional rate tax payer, calculate his CGT liability in respect of the above disposal, assuming he has fully used his capital gains tax annual exemption, and state the due date for payment of the CGT.

Business Asset Disposal Relief and Investors' Relief

Learning Objectives

After studying this chapter you will understand:

■ The operation of business asset disposal relief and its interaction with the other CGT reliefs.
■ The operation of investors' relief.

19.1   Business Asset Disposal Relief

Business asset disposal relief (BADR) (previously referred to as entrepreneurs' relief) is available in respect of gains on qualifying business disposals by individuals. The relief reduces the effective rate of CGT on such disposals to 10% (rather than the standard CGT rate of 20%), up to a lifetime limit of £1 million.

Note: on the whole, BADR applies on the disposal of a business and not on the disposal of individual business assets (except in very limited circumstances).

19.1.1   "Qualifying Business Disposal"

For BADR, any kind of disposal which gives rise to a chargeable gain will qualify for relief if the relevant conditions are met. Such disposals can include an outright sale, a gift, a transfer (e.g. at undervalue) and certain capital distributions, e.g. a distribution received from a company purchase of its own shares where the capital treatment is met and the relevant conditions for BADR are satisfied (see **Chapter 21**).

A "qualifying business disposal" includes:

1. a "material" disposal of business assets; and
2. a disposal "associated" with a relevant "material" disposal.

Each of these two conditions are discussed in detail at **Section 19.1.4**. First, we will consider how BADR works in principle.

19.1.2   Operation of BADR

BADR applies so that any gain qualifying for the relief is simply charged to tax at 10%.

Example 19.1

During May 2021, Margaret sells her retail shop business for £650,000. The chargeable gains arising were £250,600, all of which qualifies for BADR. Margaret had no other disposals in 2021/22 and her full lifetime limit is available.

	£
Gains	250,600
Less: annual exemption	(12,300)
Taxable gain	238,300
CGT @ 10%	23,830

As noted above, there is a threshold limit for each individual on chargeable gains on which BADR may be claimed. This is a lifetime limit of £1 million. Therefore, an individual can claim BADR on more than one occasion, provided the overall lifetime limit is not exceeded. It should be carefully checked if a taxpayer has already used their lifetime limit against previous transactions.

In determining the rate of CGT charged on other non-BADR gains, gains qualifying for BADR and investors' relief (see **Section 19.2**) are deemed to be set against any unused basic rate band before those other non-BADR gains.

Example 19.2

Siobhan has previously used £500,000 of her lifetime BADR limit. In 2021/22, her taxable income, after all allowable deductions and the personal allowance, is £21,535. In May 2021, Siobhan realises a chargeable gain of £300,000 on the disposal of a business. In December 2021, she sells another business, realising further chargeable gains of £700,000. Both disposals qualify for BADR (subject to sufficient of her lifetime limit being available). Siobhan has no allowable losses to set against these gains. None of the gains relate to residential property.

The £300,000 gain realised in May 2021 is subject to the £1 million lifetime limit for BADR, of which Siobhan has previously used £500,000. Consequently all of the gain will qualify for BADR. The annual exemption will be used against the later gain as it is exposed to a higher rate of CGT.

May 2021 Disposal

	£
Gains	300,000
Less: annual exemption	–
Chargeable gain	300,000
CGT payable: £300,000 (qualifying for BADR) @ 10%	30,000

Only £200,000 of the £700,000 gain realised by Siobhan on the disposal of a further business in December is chargeable at the 10% rate of CGT. While Siobhan's taxable income is £16,165 below the basic rate band (£37,700 − £21,535), the £500,000 of gains charged at 10% is taken into account in priority to other gains in determining whether total income and gains exceed the basic rate band. So the remaining £500,000 gain, less the annual exemption, is charged at the higher rate of 20%, as none of the gain relates to residential property.

continued overleaf

December 2021 Disposal

	£
Gains	700,000
Less: annual exemption	(12,300)
Chargeable gain	687,700
CGT payable:	
£200,000 (qualifying for BADR) @ 10%	20,000
£487,700 @ 20%	97,540
Total	117,540

It should be noted that the taxpayer can choose to offset the annual exemption in the most beneficial way. In this case, it is clearly more beneficial to use this against the element of the gain taxed at 20%.

19.1.3   Losses and BADR

If a qualifying business disposal would be such that both chargeable gains and allowable losses are created, it is the "net qualifying gains" on which BADR is given.

The annual exemption and losses on gains not qualifying for BADR may be deducted from gains in whatever way is most beneficial, i.e. set against gains taxed at 28% in the first instance.

Example 19.3
Niall makes a chargeable gain of £90,000 in October 2021 which qualifies for BADR. He makes further chargeable gains on the disposal of various quoted shares during 2021/22 of £26,390. Niall also has a current-year loss of £10,000 on the disposal of various quoted shares. The quoted shares do not qualify for BADR or investors' relief (see **Section 19.2**). His taxable income for 2021/22, after all deductible tax reliefs and the personal allowance, is £27,700. Niall claims BADR where possible.

	BADR	Non-BADR	Total
	£	£	£
Gains qualifying for BADR	90,000		90,000
Other gains		£26,390	26,390
Less: capital losses		(10,000)	(10,000)
Less: annual exemption		(12,300)	(12,300)
Taxable gains	90,000	4,090	94,090
CGT:			
Gain qualifying for BADR @ 10%	9,000	–	9,000
£4,090 @ 20%	–	818	818
Total	9,000	818	9,818

Note that the gain qualifying for BADR has used up the remaining £10,000 of the basic rate band when determining the CGT rate to be applied to other gains. Note also, that the capital losses and annual exemption are set against the gains not qualifying for BADR, as this is the most tax-efficient utilisation.

19.1.4   Categories of Qualifying Business Disposals

Material Disposal of Business Assets
There are certain conditions which must be met for a gain to qualify for BADR. The disposal must be "material", and be one of the following:

1. A disposal of the **whole or part of a business** (or a share in a partnership), as a going concern, which has been owned by the individual throughout the period of two years ending on the date of the disposal. The assets within this business must be used in the business, e.g. goodwill.

OR

2. A disposal of **one or more assets after the business has ceased** provided that:
    - the assets had been in use for the purposes of the business at the date of cessation;
    - the business was **owned** by the individual throughout the period of two years ending on the date of cessation; **and**
    - the **date of cessation** is within **three years** prior to the date of the disposal.

OR

3. A disposal of shares or securities in a company which has been the individual's **personal trading company** and of which the individual has been an employee or officer, and these conditions are met either:
    - throughout the period of two years ending on the date of the disposal, **or**
    - throughout the period of two years ending with the date on which the company ceases to be a trading company and that date is within the period of three years ending with the date of the disposal.

Under 1. and 2. above, it should be noted that BADR is only given in respect of "relevant business assets". These are assets used for the purpose of the business and, hence, investments or shares will not qualify. A business under 1. above will qualify for BADR if it is a trade, profession or vocation conducted on a commercial basis with a view to making a profit. This does not include property letting businesses (taxable as property income) but does include the business of commercial letting of furnished holiday accommodation (taxable as trading income) in the UK or the EEA.

Under 3. above, an individual's "**personal trading company**" is a trading company in which the individual holds at least 5% of the company's ordinary shares **and** that holding also has an entitlement to at least 5% of the voting rights in the company in addition to entitling the holder to 5% of the company's distributable profits and 5% of the assets available to equity holders on a winding up. **Note:** the definition of "trading company" is the same for gift relief and BADR (see **Chapter 19**). However, the definition of "personal trading company" is **not** the same for both reliefs.

Associated Disposals

It may be the case that a person carries on a business through a company or partnership but personally owns some or all of the assets which that business uses (for example, the building which is used as the trading premises). The disposal of an asset owned personally by an individual may qualify for BADR if it can be "associated" with a relevant "material" disposal. Three general conditions must be satisfied:

1. the individual must make a "**material**" disposal of either the whole or part (at least 5%) of their interest in the assets of a **partnership** or the **shares** in a company; and
2. the associated disposal is made as part of the **withdrawal** of the individual from participation in the business of the partnership or the company; and
3. the assets are **in use** in the business throughout the period of two years ending with the earlier of the dates of "material" disposal of business assets or the cessation of the business of the partnership or company.

Example 19.4

A company director of X Ltd, who owns the factory premises from which the company operates its business, sells the premises at the same time as he sells his 10% shareholding in the company; the sale of the premises may be treated as an associated disposal and so qualify for BADR. If the director only held 3% (i.e. below 5%) of the shares in the company, neither the shares nor the associated disposal of the premises would qualify for BADR.

The "associated" disposal rule does not extend to disposals associated with a material disposal by a sole trader. It is also important to note that BADR is restricted where:

- the asset has only been used in the business for part of its ownership period;
- the asset has not been fully used in the business;
- the individual has not been involved in the business for the whole of the ownership period of the asset; or
- the individual has charged the company or partnership rent for the use of the asset, e.g. a property they own personally.

Disposals of Goodwill to Related Companies

BADR is not available on most disposals of "the reputation and customer relationships associated with a business" (i.e. its goodwill) where the consideration received for the disposal is in the form of cash or debt. This measure sits alongside a measure that restricts a corporation tax deduction being obtained by a company when goodwill is acquired from a related party on incorporation (see **Chapter 8, Section 8.4**).

Both measures are aimed primarily at incorporations whereby the proprietor(s) of a business sell it to a close company to which they are related in order to extract funds at what is, effectively, 10% rather than the normal rates of income tax and national insurance contributions. As consideration in such incorporations is in the form of cash or debt, proprietors can draw this down tax-free from the company, having only paid a 10% rate of CGT upfront. The inability to claim BADR on goodwill can therefore apply to incorporations where there is a sale of a business to a close company in which the previous owner of the sole trade or partnership will be a shareholder. Such gains are charged at the normal rates of CGT (subject to other reliefs being, potentially, available). A claim for BADR, however, is still possible if the individual holds shares or voting rights in the acquiring company that are less than 5% of the company's total ordinary share capital or rights.

A close company, in this context, has its usual meaning (see **Chapter 9**). A related party takes the meaning in Part 8 CTA 2009, in particular section 835(5), where it is broadly defined as a participator or associate of a participator in a close company. This means anyone with a share or interest in the capital or income of the company, or their spouse/civil partner, parent/child or remoter, brother/sister or partner.

19.1.5 How to Claim BADR

BADR must be claimed by the individual on or before the first anniversary of 31 January following the end of the tax year in which the qualifying business disposal took place. For example, if the disposal took place during 2021/22, then the claim must be made by 31 January 2024.

19.1.6 Interaction with other CGT Reliefs

BADR is applied after the following reliefs:

- Rollover relief – replacement of business assets relief, if claimed (see **Chapter 16, Section 16.11.3**).
- Incorporation relief (if no election is made to disapply) (see **Chapter 20, Section 20.2**).

- Gift relief (if claimed) (see **Chapter 16, Section 16.11.4**).
- EIS deferral relief/SEIS reinvestment relief, if claimed (see **Chapter 20, Sections 20.3** and **20.4**).

Chapter 20, Section 20.6 deals with the interaction of BADR with the above CGT reliefs in more detail.

In some instances, it may be preferable not to claim BADR and/or the reliefs above with a view to utilising the annual exemption and available losses.

Example 19.5

On 5 November 2021, Anita sold her pharmacy to her daughter Kerry. Anita owned has owned the pharmacy since 2011. The chargeable assets on disposal were goodwill and the freehold shop. Details are as follows:

	Cost £	Market Value £
Goodwill	Nil (the goodwill was not purchased)	100,000
Shop	40,000 (purchased January 2011)	150,000

Kerry paid Anita £40,000 for the goodwill and £60,000 for the shop.

Anita made a claim for BADR, and Anita and Kerry made a joint election for gift relief. Anita made no other gains or losses in 2021/22 and has already fully utilised her basic rate band. This is Anita's first lifetime claim for BADR.

Anita's CGT position:	£	£
Goodwill:		
Market value	100,000	
Less: cost	(0)	
Gain	100,000	
Less: gift relief	(60,000)	
Chargeable gain (excess proceeds rule)	40,000	40,000

Anita's CGT position:	£	£
Shop:		
Market value	150,000	
Less: cost	(40,000)	
Gain	110,000	
Less: gift relief	(90,000)	
Chargeable gain (excess proceeds rule)	20,000	20,000
Chargeable gains after gift relief		60,000
Less: annual exemption		(12,300)
Taxable gain		47,700
CGT @ 10%		4,770

continued overleaf

Kerry's base cost position:	£
Goodwill:	
Market value	100,000
Less: gift relief (joint election)	(60,000)
Revised base cost	40,000
Shop:	
Market value	150,000
Less: gift relief (joint election)	(90,000)
Revised base cost	60,000

Note: stamp duty land tax and inheritance tax should also be considered in such a transaction. No stamp duty land tax will arise on the goodwill as goodwill is not a stampable asset. Stamp duty land tax will not arise on the property as the consideration is £60,000, being less than the £150,000 zero-rate threshold for non-residential property.

19.2 Investors' Relief

Investors' relief is designed to provide a financial incentive for individuals to invest in shares in unlisted trading companies over the long term where they are not connected with the company. Often a connection with the company is not appropriate or practical for outside investors.

The relief applies a 10% rate of CGT to gains on the disposal of qualifying shares in unlisted trading company held by individuals. Qualifying shares must be newly issued to the individual on or after 17 March 2016, and have been held for a period of at least three years starting from 6 April 2016. Gains that qualify for the relief are subject to a lifetime limit of £10 million (note that this limit is separate from the limit applying to BADR).

The qualifying shares must:

■ be new shares – they must have been acquired by the person making the disposal on a subscription for new consideration;
■ have been issued by the company on or after 17 March 2016;
■ be in an unlisted trading company or an unlisted holding company of a trading group.
■ have been held continually for a period of three years before disposal, starting from 6 April 2016.

The claimant must be an individual, other than an employee or officer of the company. Unlike BADR, there is no requirement to hold 5% of the shares, voting rights, etc. The relief only applies to new shares issued for genuine commercial purposes; and it is restricted so that it does not apply to investors where those connected with the investor are officers or employees of the company.

However, a "relevant employee" can qualify for the relief, subject to all the remaining conditions being met. A "relevant employee" is one who becomes an unremunerated director of the company, or a connected company, following the subscription of qualifying shares. An unremunerated director must never have been previously involved with the issuing company and must not have previously received disqualifying payments. This is aimed at 'business angels' who may work closely with a company after their investment.

In addition, an individual who subsequently becomes an employee of the company more than 180 days after the shares are issued, where there was no reasonable prospect that they would become an employee at the time of the share issues, is also a "relevant employee".

In situations where the investor receives value in the period of one year before to three years after the date that the shares are issued, the shares become excluded and do not qualify for the relief. Any claim for investors' relief in respect of a disposal must be made on or before the first anniversary of the 31 January following the tax year in which the disposal is made. For example, if the disposal took place during 2021/22, the claim must be made by 31 January 2024.

Given the conditions for the relief, the earliest that a claim for investors' relief could be made was 6 April 2019, i.e. for disposals from the tax year 2020/21 onwards.

Questions

Review Questions

(See Suggested Solutions to Review Questions at the end of this textbook.)

In **Questions 19.1–19.9** (inclusive), calculate the effect of BADR assuming that no earlier BADR claim has ever been made and that the annual exemption and basic rate band are otherwise utilised.

Question 19.1

Anthony disposed of his trading business, which he had owned for five years, in May 2021, crystallising a gain of £900,000.

Question 19.2

Geraldine sold her trading business making a gain of £120,000 in December 2021, having commenced to trade on 2 February 2020.

Question 19.3

Denis disposed of his trading business on September 2021, having owned it for 10 years. He received £1,150,000 and made a gain of £1,030,000. He has made no previous claims for BADR. Denis has already used his annual exemption.

Question 19.4

Donald sold a residential property in January 2022 which he has let unfurnished to the same tenant since April 2007, crystallising a gain of £240,000.

Question 19.5

Brian ceased his trading business, which he had owned for 20 years, on 20 June 2021. Over the last five years Brian operated the business from three separate premises. He realised a gain of £360,000 on the sale of one property during August 2021 but made a loss of £90,000 on the sale of another business property during December 2021. In June 2022, he disposed of the remaining business property making a gain of £72,000. Assume the rules and the rates in 2022/23 are the same as the rules in 2021/22. He has made no previous claims for BADR.

Question 19.6

Thomas owns 4% of a UK trading company and has owned these shares for the past three years. He sells the shares in March 2022, crystallising a gain of exactly £300,000. Thomas is an employee in the company throughout this time and is a higher-rate taxpayer.

Question 19.7

Terry sold his trading business in May 2020, realising gains of £630,000, having owned and operated this business for many years. In June 2020, Terry purchases a 10% share in a trading company and becomes a working director. He accepts an offer for sale in July 2022 for his shares, realising a gain of £1 million. Assume the rules and the rates in 2022/23 are the same as the rules in 2021/22 and that Terry has already used his annual exemption.

Question 19.8

Patricia ran a shoe shop for a number of years until she decided to cease trading on 30 April 2021. She did not sell the business but sold the premises in April 2022.

Question 19.9

Marie retires as a partner from her accountancy partnership on 30 June 2021. She realises capital gains on the disposal of her share of the trading premises of £150,000, and gains of £40,000 for the disposal of goodwill sold to an unconnected third party.

Question 19.10

You attend a meeting with your client, James Devlin, in April 2022. James has recently retired and on 15 March 2022 he sold his 40% shareholding in the company, Devlin Communications Ltd, an independent mobile phone shop, for £85,100. James had held these shares since the company was incorporated, when he subscribed for 100 £1 ordinary shares, which he paid for in full. James was appointed as a full-time director of the company on 1 April 2011.

James also owned a shop in Dungannon from which the company had always traded, having originally bought it as an investment on 1 April 2009 for £125,000. Devlin Communications Ltd started trading when it was incorporated on 1 April 2011 and from that date onward traded solely from the shop. James charged rent of £1,575 per month for the use of the shop from that date. A full commercial rent would have been £2,250 per month.

The shop was subsequently sold by James for £475,000 on 31 March 2022, as Devlin Communications Ltd was moving to larger premises and they no longer needed to rent the property.

Note: James is an additional rate taxpayer and the company is a trading company. The shares and Dungannon property are the only assets he has ever owned.

Requirement
Prepare a report to James dealing with the sale of the shares and the building that considers the following:

(a) The capital gains tax payable by James as a result of the above transactions. You should identify any potential claims/relief(s) James could avail of to reduce his chargeable gains on the disposals, state why the disposals qualify for any claims/reliefs you are proposing and outline the saving to be achieved.

(b) The due date for payment of the capital gains tax arising, together with the time limit(s) which apply to any claims/reliefs you consider available to mitigate the gain.

Question 19.11

In February 2021, Michael sells his entire holding of shares in Grafton Ltd, an unlisted trading company, for £10,600,000. Michael does not work for the company. He subscribed for the shares in March 2017 for £400,000.

Michael has made no previous claims to the relief nor any other capital disposals in the 2021/22 tax year and is an additional rate taxpayer.

Requirement

Assuming the disposal qualifies for investors' relief, calculate the CGT on the disposal.

Capital Gains Tax Reliefs

20.1 Additional Understanding: Principal Private Residence Relief, Rollover Relief and Gift Relief

Students are reminded that principal private residence (PPR) relief, rollover relief and gift relief are all cumulative knowledge from the CA Proficiency 1 course and should be revisited. These topics were summarised in **Chapter 16, Sections 16.11**. This section introduces additional points of understanding required at CA Proficiency 2 level in addition to this cumulative knowledge.

20.1.1 Principal Private Residence Relief

PPR and Residence
A residence is only capable of qualifying for PPR if located in a territory in which the individual, or their spouse/civil partner, is resident. If it is located in a different territory to their territory of residence, the individual must also meet the "day count test" in relation to residence (see **Chapter 17, Section 17.10.3**).

If a couple wishes to elect a non-resident property as their PPR, this too will only be capable of qualifying for PPR if located in a territory in which the individual or their spouse/civil partner is resident. Again, where it is located is in a different territory, the individual must meet the "day count test".

After a period of absence, a non-resident individual must meet the 90-day occupation test in respect of the property for the absence relief to apply to that property.

PPR Restriction

There is no PPR relief available where a property (or interest therein) was purchased with a view to resell to make a gain. This restriction also extends to expenditure subsequently incurred wholly or partly for the purposes of realising a gain on the disposal.

Interaction with Section 260 Gift Relief

PPR relief is denied where there is a related claim to gift relief under section 260 TCGA 1992 (see **Section 20.1.3**).

Business Use of PPR

Where a PPR is also used for business purposes. the apportionment between business and residential use must be undertaken on a just and reasonable basis, e.g. number of rooms in use, floor area, etc. Each case is judged on its own merits and facts.

The part used for trade purposes may qualify for relief as the replacement of a business asset (rollover relief) or business asset disposal relief (see **Chapter 19, Section 19.1**) if the conditions in each instance are met.

20.1.2 Rollover Relief

Rollover Relief and Residence

A person who is resident in the UK can roll over a gain from the disposal of qualifying assets against the acquisition of new qualifying assets wherever they are situated. If all other conditions for relief are met, HMRC will not deny relief where a person has ceased to be resident in the UK when the new qualifying assets are acquired.

A person who is not UK resident but who is chargeable on gains from the disposal of qualifying assets of a branch or agency (or, in the case of a company, of a permanent establishment) in the UK can only roll over gains into the acquisition of further UK branch or agency assets.

Rollover Relief – Groups of Companies

Rollover relief is also potentially available within a capital gains group of companies (see **Chapter 13**). If a capital gains group member disposes of an asset that is eligible for rollover relief, it can treat all the group members as a single entity for claiming such relief (provided, of course, that all the remaining conditions are met).

Thus, if another group member acquires a relevant asset within the qualifying period (12 months before the disposal or 36 months afterwards), the company making the disposal may match the acquisition for rollover relief purposes.

The acquiring company must be a member of the capital gains group at the time of acquisition and the disposing company must be a member of the group at the time of sale. However, there is no requirement for them both to be a member of the group at the same time. For it to be effective, both the acquiring company and the disposing company must make a joint claim for the relief to apply.

It should be noted that assets transferred intragroup on a no gain/no loss basis *cannot* **be matched for rollover relief purposes.**

20.1.3 Gift Relief

Gift Relief Anti-avoidance

Gift relief is only available if the transferee is resident in the UK at the time of the gift. If the transferee is an individual who becomes non-resident in the UK in any of the **six tax years**

following the year of the gift, and before disposing of the asset transferred, then the gain held over is chargeable on them as if it arose immediately before they became non-resident in the UK.

Section 260 Gift Relief

Gift relief is also available on gifts that are immediately chargeable to inheritance tax (IHT) (section 260 TCGA 1992), e.g. most gifts into trusts (see **Chapter 24**). The transfer will be regarded as chargeable to IHT, even if it falls within the IHT nil rate band, and is covered by the IHT annual exemption or qualifies for an IHT relief, such as business property relief.

This form of gift relief is available for all asset types, meaning the asset does not have to be one of the specified qualifying business asserts for section 165 gift relief (see **Chapter 16, Section 16.11.4**). Section 260 gift relief is also available in full even if the asset gifted is shares in a personal trading company – for which section 165 gift relief would be restricted by virtue of chargeable non-business assets.

No joint election is required if the asset is gifted into a trust and section 260 gift relief is claimed. Section 260 gift relief claims must also be made within four years from the end of the tax year of disposal.

If both section 165 gift relief and section 260 gift relief are available on the same transaction, section 260 gift relief takes priority.

20.2 Transfer of a Business to a Limited Company

Many individuals commence self-employment as a sole trader/partnership as to do so has relatively lower costs and more beneficial loss reliefs than corporate entities. As the business grows and expands, it may well be that the decision is made to incorporate and form a limited company. This will create a separate legal entity. This has become more prevalent in recent years due to the relatively low rate of UK corporation tax; however, this may change from 1 April 2023 when the rate will increase to above 19% for companies with taxable profits in excess of £50,000. The cessation of the sole trade/partnership business will result in adjustments in respect of capital allowances, income tax consequences and also potentially crystallise a CGT liability on the chargeable assets that are transferred to the limited company.

The implications of the incorporation of a sole trade business include the following:

- A cessation of the sole trade/partnership business for income tax purposes.
- The former proprietor/partner of the sole trade/partnership becomes an employee of the new company and is subject to income tax and Class 1 NICs.
- Class 1 NICs will be payable by the company, whereas the sole trader will have been subject to Class 2 and Class 4 NICs.
- A disposal of the sole trade assets (including goodwill) for CGT purposes will arise on their transfer to the new company.
- The new company will be subject to corporation tax, whereas the sole trader will have been subject to income tax on the profits of the business.

As the business owner and their limited company (i.e. the company in which they are the majority shareholder) are separate legal entities, the transfer of business assets from a sole trade to a new company on incorporation is a chargeable event for CGT purposes. The transfer is deemed to take place at full market value as it is a transaction between connected parties. In the absence of any reliefs, the taxpayer would potentially incur a CGT liability without having received any monies for the transfer with which to fund the payment of the tax.

This is obviously an undesirable situation and would perhaps discourage individuals from incorporating their businesses, even where it makes very sound commercial sense. It is for this reason that "incorporation relief" is available where a sole trade or partnership business is transferred to a company in return for consideration, either wholly or partly, in the form of shares. Where all of the conditions for this relief are met it is applied **automatically**, without the need for the taxpayer to make a formal claim.

20.2.1 Incorporation Relief (section 162 TCGA 1992)

The **conditions** for incorporation relief are:

1. the sole trade business must be transferred as a going concern;
2. all of the assets (except cash) of the business must be transferred to the company;
3. the transferor must receive shares in the new company as consideration.

Full incorporation relief will be available where the only consideration for the transfer is shares.

Partial relief is available where only part of the consideration is in shares, in this case only part of the chargeable gain is held over. The held over gain is the ratio that the value of the shares bears to the total consideration (including any non-share consideration, such as loans or cash). This means that where cash or loan stock is provided as part consideration, then a percentage of the gain will be immediately taxable. Cash has the advantage that it can be left on a director's loan account and the director/shareholder can withdraw it, tax-free, from the company at any time.

Incorporation relief applies in priority to business asset disposal relief (BADR). Therefore, if full incorporation relief is available, BADR cannot be claimed. However, where part of the gain is chargeable, BADR can be claimed on that proportion of the chargeable gain.

Calculation of the Relief

Incorporation relief on gains arising is calculated as follows:

$$\text{Incorporation relief (i.e held-over gain)} = \frac{\text{Value of shares issued}}{\text{Total consideration}} \times \text{Whole gain}$$

Incorporation relief is another form of deferral relief, as the **held over gain is deducted from the base cost of the shares received, i.e. the gain is deferred**. Note, it is the base cost of the shares that is reduced this time, not the assets transferred as with gift relief (under section 165 – see **Chapter 16, Section 16.11.4**; or section 260 – see **Section 20.1.3**).

Sometimes it is preferable for the taxpayer that incorporation relief does not apply. The taxpayer therefore has the choice of opting out of this automatic relief and can elect that incorporation relief should not apply. Alternatively, the taxpayer could purposely ensure that the above conditions are not met, e.g. by not transferring all the assets into the company or not receiving any consideration in shares, so that incorporation relief will not apply. A taxpayer may prefer for incorporation relief not to apply where they have sufficient annual exemption and/or capital losses to cover any gain, and/or the rate of tax payable now is potentially less than what it may be in future years.

The deadline for electing to disapply section 162 relief is the first anniversary of the 31 January after the end of the tax year of incorporation. For example, if someone incorporates on 25 March 2022, they must elect to disapply section 162 relief by 31 January 2024.

20.2.2 Transfer of Liabilities to the New Company

Where business liabilities (e.g. bank loans, trade creditors) are taken over by a company on the transfer of a business to that company, then ordinarily this is treated as paying non-share consideration to the former proprietor and the deferred gain would be only be due partial incorporation relief and reduced accordingly.

Example 20.1

Market value of the assets was £1 million and incorporation included consideration in the form of shares and trade creditors taken over of £100,000. Total value of consideration is £1 million. Share value is £900,000 (£1 million – £100,000 = £900,000 of shares) as trade creditors are treated as consideration other than shares (same as cash consideration). Full incorporation relief would not be allowed as the deferral would be diluted by the formula:

900,000/1,000,000 (total value of shares/total value of the consideration).

However, by concession, HMRC do not treat such liabilities as part of the consideration for the transfer if the other conditions of section 162 TCGA 1992 are satisfied. This means that there is no restriction and full rollover relief is still available even if the sole trade's trade creditors are taken over by the company. Relief is also not precluded by the fact that some or all of the liabilities of the business are not taken over by the company.

Example 20.2

Following on from the example above, assuming all other conditions are met, the concession says that full incorporation relief would be permitted as the total value of shares equals the total value of the consideration (900,000/900,000).

It should be noted that the concession only applies in establishing whether the relief is available. It has no bearing in determining the net cost of the shares.

If, by contrast, liabilities which are not business liabilities (e.g. a personal income tax bill) are taken over by the company, these are treated as consideration other than in the form of shares, so that an immediate CGT charge arises on part of the gain.

Example 20.3

Martin commenced business as a pipe-laying civil engineer on 1 January 1997. On 31 December 2021, he transfers his business to MMH Pipes Ltd in consideration for the issue of 20,000 shares of £1 each fully paid in that company, and £65,000 in cash. The value of the 20,000 shares is £450,000. Martin is a higher rate taxpayer.

At the date of transfer, the statement of financial position of the business was as follows:

		£
Assets:	Premises	150,000
	Plant and machinery	12,000
	Stock	20,000
	Debtors	40,000
	Goodwill	200,000
		422,000
Liabilities:	Trade creditors	75,000
	Capital and reserves	347,000
		422,000

continued overleaf

On 31 December 2021, the assets and liabilities of the business are as follows:

	Chargeable gains	Market value 31 Dec 2021
	£	£
Premises	50,000	200,000
Plant and machinery*	–	15,000
Stock	–	25,000
Debtors	–	50,000
Goodwill	100,000	300,000
	150,000	590,000
Less: liabilities: trade creditors		(75,000)
	150,000	515,000

* No single item cost more than £6,000, or had a market value more than £6,000, on 31 December 2021.

All assets and liabilities are taken over by the new company MMH Pipes Ltd.

The market value of the assets is £515,000. The cash received is £65,000. Therefore, applying the HMRC concession, the shares are worth £450,000.

The chargeable gains arising on the disposal of the business to MMH Pipes Ltd are as follows:

		£
Total chargeable gains		150,000
Incorporation relief:	$\frac{450,000}{515,000} \times 150,000$	(131,068)
Gains chargeable in 2021/22 before annual exemption		18,932

CGT is payable as follows:

	£
Gain on premises:	
£50,000/£150,000 × £18,932	6,311
CGT @ 10% (Note)	631
Gain on goodwill:	
£100,000/£150,000 × £18,932	12,621
Less: annual exemption	(12,300)
Taxable gain	321
CGT @ 20% (Note)	64

Total CGT payable is therefore £695 (£631 + £64).

Note: The transfer of the sole trade on incorporation would qualify for BADR; however, as goodwill is specifically excluded for qualifying for BADR on an incorporation, it is necessary to keep this separate when determining the CGT payable. The premises is taxed at 10% (as BADR is available) and the goodwill is subject to tax at 20% as Martin is a higher rate taxpayer. As the goodwill is subject to tax at a higher rate, the annual exemption should be set against this gain.

The allowable base cost of the shares is £450,000 less £131,068 = £318,932. Plant and machinery is a wasting chattel, however, as it is used in a trade and capital allowances could have been claimed, it is treated under the non-wasting chattels rules. In this case, as both the proceeds for each item and the cost of each did not exceed £6,000, the transaction is exempt under rule 1 (see **Chapter 16, Section 16.9.2**).

20.2.3 Gift Relief or Incorporation Relief?

If incorporation relief does not apply (or is not desirable), then the option of claiming section 165 gift relief (see **Chapter 16, Section 16.11.4**) on chargeable business assets such as goodwill, business premises, etc., is still available. Transferring all the assets of the business, including property, into the company could have high tax costs, e.g. stamp duty land tax and a potential double tax charge on the subsequent disposal of the property by the company (i.e. corporation tax on the chargeable gain within the company and then tax on the individual on the future extraction of the net proceeds). The use of gift relief under section 165 TCGA 1992 gives greater flexibility than incorporation relief under section 162 TCGA 1992, by allowing capital gains planning to be dealt with on an asset-by-asset basis. The main disadvantage of gift relief is that the base cost of the assets in the hands of the transferee company is the former sole trader's original base cost, rather than their market value at the date of transfer (i.e. under gift relief the base cost = market value less held over gain). The base cost of the shares will also be low, typically £1, as the trade is "gifted" to the company. Where incorporation relief is claimed, the base cost of assets transferred to the company is their market value at the date of transfer. It is the base cost of the shares that is reduced in value by any held over gain.

Example 20.4

Michael commenced business on 1 July 2001. On 1 October 2021, he transferred the business, comprising the assets set out below, to Comptech Ltd in consideration for the issue of 10,000 shares of £1 each fully paid in that company and £20,000 in cash. The value of the 10,000 shares was £140,000. The value of the assets transferred was £160,000 at the time of the transfer. Michael is a higher rate taxpayer.

At the date of transfer, the balance sheet of the business was as follows:

		£
Assets:	Premises	25,000
	Plant and machinery	10,000
	Stock	6,000
		41,000
Liabilities:	Capital and reserves	41,000

	Chargeable gains £	Market value 1 Oct 2021 £
Premises	80,000	105,000
Plant and machinery*	–	7,000
Stock	–	8,000
Goodwill	40,000	40,000
	120,000	160,000

* No single item cost more than £6,000, nor had a market value of more than £6,000 on 1 October 2021.

The market value of the assets is £160,000. The cash received is £20,000; therefore, the shares are worth £140,000.

		£
Total chargeable gains		120,000
Incorporation relief:	$\dfrac{140,000}{160,000} \times 120,000$	(105,000)
Gain chargeable in 2021/22 before annual exemption		15,000

continued overleaf

CGT is payable as follows:

	£
Gain on premises:	
£40,000/£120,000 × £15,000	5,000
Less: annual exemption	(5,000)
Taxable gain	0
Gain on premises:	
£80,000/£120,000 × £15,000	10,000
Less: annual exemption	(7,300)
Taxable gain	2,700
CGT @ 10% (Note)	270

Total CGT payable is therefore £270.

Note: The transfer of the sole trade on incorporation would qualify for BADR; however, as goodwill is specifically excluded for qualifying for BADR on an incorporation, it is necessary to keep this separate when determining the amount of CGT. The premises is taxed at 10% (as BADR is available) and the goodwill is subject to tax at 20% as Michael is a higher rate taxpayer. As the goodwill is subject to tax at a higher rate the annual exemption should be set against this gain first and then any remaining annual exemption set against the gain on the premises.

The goodwill has no base cost as it was not acquired. Plant and machinery is a wasting chattel, however, as it is used in a trade and capital allowances could have been claimed, it is treated under the non-wasting chattels rules. In this case, as both the proceeds for each item and the cost of each did not exceed £6,000 then the transaction is exempt under rule 1 (see **Chapter 16, Section 16.9.2**).

On 1 January 2022, Michael sold the whole of his shareholding in Comptech Ltd for £220,000. His chargeable gain is computed as follows:

	£	£
Proceeds		220,000
Deduct: cost of acquisition	140,000	
Less: incorporation relief claimed	(105,000)	
		(35,000)
Chargeable gain before annual exemption		185,000
Less: annual exemption		(12,300)
Taxable gain		172,700
CGT @ 20% (Note)		34,540

Total CGT payable is therefore £270.

Note: BADR is not available as Michael has not held the shares for a period of two years.

20.3 Enterprise Investment Scheme Shares

As set out in **Chapter 4, Section 4.5**, the Enterprise Investment Scheme (EIS) aims to incentivise investments in qualifying companies. The EIS regime provides income tax and CGT reliefs for qualifying individual investors who subscribe in cash for qualifying new shares in qualifying companies. This section examines the two CGT reliefs potentially available for EIS shares (the income tax relief for EIS investments and the qualifying conditions were covered in **Chapter 4, Section 4.5** and should be revisited).

20.3.1 EIS Deferral Relief

As seen earlier, a chargeable gain is capable of being deferred in certain circumstances (transfers of business to a limited company on incorporation, gifts of assets, rollover/holdover relief, etc.). For the aforementioned reliefs to be available, the assets broadly have to qualify as business assets. However, reinvestment into new EIS shares can give rise to a relief available for any type of capital gain, not just gains on the disposal of business assets.

A "deferral" of the gain is possible on **any** gain where an amount of money equal to a maximum **gain** (or less) is used to subscribe for eligible new shares under the rules of the EIS. It should be noted that it is not necessary to reinvest the whole proceeds – all that is required is to **reinvest the gain**.

While it is possible for the taxpayer to also obtain income tax relief on a subscription for EIS shares, this is not a pre-condition in order to obtain CGT EIS deferral relief. Also the taxpayer can choose to restrict the amount of relief being claimed where this is beneficial (say to leave sufficient gains to utilise their annual exemption, capital losses etc.). Importantly, unlike income tax EIS relief, EIS CGT deferral relief has no cap.

In summary, the amount deferred is the lower of:

- the gain;
- the amount invested in EIS shares; or
- the amount specified in the claim.

The subscription for EIS shares must take place in the period starting 12 months before or ending 36 months after the date that the chargeable disposal has taken place. In addition, the taxpayer must be UK resident.

The effect of the relief is to 'freeze' the gain. **Note:** the base cost of the new shares is **not** reduced by the deferred gain.

The deferred gain becomes chargeable on:

1. the disposal of the EIS shares (although the taxpayer would have the option to defer again by subscribing for further EIS shares);
2. the taxpayer becoming non-resident within three years of the issue of the shares; or
3. the shares ceasing to be eligible.

A claim for EIS deferral relief must be made before the fifth anniversary of 31 January following the tax year in which the EIS shares were issued. Therefore if a taxpayer wishes to make a claim for EIS deferral relief in 2021/22, the deadline for the claim is 31 January 2028.

20.3.2 Disposals of EIS Shares

A gain on the sale of EIS shares is exempt from CGT if the following conditions are met:

1. the shares are held for three years from the date of issue, and
2. income tax relief was obtained on the original subscription for the shares.

A loss on EIS shares is always allowable but is restricted by the amount of income tax relief given and not withdrawn. EIS capital losses also qualify as a loss on disposal of shares in accordance with the provisions set out at **Section 20.5**. However, such a loss is not subject to the cap that applies for certain income tax reliefs (see **Chapter 4, Section 4.3**).

20.4 Seed Enterprise Investment Scheme Shares

As set out in **Chapter 4, Section 4.6**, the Seed Enterprise Investment Scheme (SEIS) operates in a similar manner to the EIS but is instead targeted at qualifying individual investors who subscribe in cash for qualifying new shares in new, qualifying SEIS companies. This section examines the two CGT reliefs potentially available for SEIS shares (the income tax relief for SEIS investments and the qualifying conditions were covered in detail in **Chapter 4, Section 4.6** and should be revisited).

20.4.1 SEIS Reinvestment Relief

SEIS reinvestment relief exempts gains on disposals of assets reinvested into new, qualifying SEIS shares from CGT. The relief provides for an exemption from CGT of 50% of the gains reinvested, with the maximum gain that can be treated as exempt being £50,000. This differs from EIS deferral relief because that relief is a deferral relief only; whereas reinvestment into SEIS shares is an exemption relief.

In summary, the amount of the available SEIS expenditure that is exempted from CGT is the lower of:

- the gain;
- the amount reinvested on which SEIS income tax relief is claimed; or
- the amount specified in the claim.

As the maximum amount on which SEIS income tax relief can be claimed is £100,000 per tax year, the maximum available expenditure is £100,000. The maximum gain that can be treated as exempt is therefore £50,000.

SEIS reinvestment relief must be matched with the year in which SEIS income tax relief is obtained. Therefore, if SEIS income tax relief is treated as carried back to the previous tax year, SEIS reinvestment relief will only be available in that year.

As SEIS reinvestment relief only provides 50% relief of the gain up to a maximum of £50,000, the balance of the unrelieved gain may then qualify for EIS deferral relief.

Two notable differences exist between EIS deferral relief and SEIS reinvestment relief:

1. While it is possible for the taxpayer to obtain income tax relief on a subscription for EIS shares, this is not a pre-condition in order to obtain EIS deferral relief. However, SEIS reinvestment relief cannot be obtained unless the conditions are met for SEIS income tax relief to be claimed and it is claimed. This is because SEIS reinvestment relief is a CGT exemption relief, whereas EIS CGT deferral relief simply defers the gain to a later point in time.
2. SEIS reinvestment relief is capped at 50% of the gain up to a maximum of £50,000, whereas there is no upper limit on EIS deferral relief.

Claims must be made before the fifth anniversary of 31 January following the tax year in which the SEIS shares were issued. Therefore, if a taxpayer wishes to make a claim for SEIS reinvestment relief in 2021/22, the deadline for the claim is 31 January 2028.

> **Example 20.5**
>
> Catherine sells an asset in June 2021 for £200,000 and realises a chargeable gain (before exemption) of £80,000.
>
> If Catherine makes qualifying investments of at least £80,000 in SEIS shares in 2021/22, and all other conditions are met, then £40,000 of the gain will be completely free from CGT (being 50% of the gain). She does not need to invest the whole £200,000 sale proceeds in order to get full exemption.
>
> If Catherine makes qualifying investments of only £20,000 in SEIS shares in 2021/22, £10,000 of her gain will be exempt from CGT (provided all conditions are met) and she will be liable to CGT on a chargeable gain of £70,000 on the disposal of the asset in June 2021.
>
> The remaining £70,000 chargeable gain will still be eligible for any other CGT reliefs that are available, and allowable losses and the CGT annual exempt amount can be set-off against it in the normal way. It should also be noted that Catherine may also be able to claim EIS deferral relief on the remaining £70,000 of the gain, subject to the necessary conditions being met.

20.4.2 Disposals of SEIS Shares

A gain on the sale of SEIS shares is exempt from CGT if the following conditions are met:

1. the shares are held for three years from the date of issue; and
2. income tax relief was obtained on the subscription for the shares.

A loss on SEIS shares is always allowable but is restricted by the amount of income tax relief given and not withdrawn. SEIS capital losses also qualify as a loss on disposal of shares in accordance with the provisions set out at **Section 20.5**. Such a loss is not subject to the cap that applies for certain income tax reliefs (see **Chapter 4, Section 4.3**).

20.5 Losses on Disposals of Certain Shares

As a general rule, capital losses are restricted for set-off against capital gains only (see **Chapter 16, Section 16.7**). The only exception to this is in relation to share loss relief, where, in certain circumstances, allowable capital losses on shares in unlisted trading companies are eligible for income tax relief as an alternative to CGT relief. These provisions can be found in Chapter 6 ITA 2007, section 131 onwards.

This relief can prove very valuable as it can provide relief for the capital loss against income, which might otherwise be taxed at 45% (if the individual was an additional rate taxpayer), compared to the maximum 28% CGT saving available by setting the loss against a chargeable gain on a residential property disposal.

20.5.1 The Relief

Where an individual incurs an allowable loss on the disposal of qualifying shares, they may claim to set that loss against their total income for:

- the year in which the loss was incurred, and/or
- the preceding year.

Relief is only allowed in respect of a disposal of shares where the shares were originally acquired by way of **subscription** for money or money's worth. This is distinct from shares purchased from others or acquired by gift or inheritance.

The taxpayer may therefore be able to reduce their income tax liability where they have allowable capital losses available following:

1. a disposal of shares at arm's length (e.g. on a sale to an unconnected buyer);
2. a distribution in a liquidation; or
3. on a claim that the shares have become of negligible value (see **Chapter 16, Section 16.8**).

The year the losses are available for tax relief will depend upon the date of disposal or, if the loss arises from a claim for negligible value, on the date the claim is made and the deemed disposal date chosen by the claimant.

20.5.2 Method of Relief

Relief may only be claimed for the full amount of the loss (partial claims cannot be made). Hence it is not possible to restrict the loss relief claim for the year to the amount required to reduce the taxpayer's income to the level of personal allowances or reliefs, or to maximise relief at the additional rate or higher rate of income tax.

Losses arising on shares in a qualifying trading company that are neither EIS nor SEIS shares are subject to the individual's cap (that applies to certain income tax reliefs) for that tax year (see **Chapter 4, Section 4.3**).

A capital loss for which relief is given against income is not also available for relief under the CGT provisions. The balance of the unused capital losses, if any, can be deducted from chargeable gains in the normal way.

Example 20.6

Mr Bloggs subscribed £20,000 in 1997 for shares in a company making seating. The business failed in July 2021, with the shares becoming worthless. Mr Bloggs made a negligible value claim in respect of the shares in August 2021 and claimed an allowable capital loss of £20,000 for 2021/22 from the deemed disposal of shares.

If all conditions for the relief are met, Mr Bloggs may claim to set the allowable capital loss on the shares either against chargeable gains in the normal way, or against his total income for 2021/22 or 2020/21, subject to his overall cap on income tax reliefs in each of those tax years.

This relief has to be claimed within one year of 31 January following the end of the tax year in which the loss was made. Thus, an allowable loss in 2021/22 has to be claimed on or before 31 January 2024. The claim must specify the year for which relief is claimed. Where a claim is to be made for both years, then it is necessary to specify which year takes priority.

20.5.3 "Qualifying Shares"

"Qualifying shares" must either be:

- shares that already qualify for EIS/SEIS relief, although these reliefs need not be claimed; or
- ordinary shares in a qualifying trading company.

There are strict conditions as to what a qualifying trading company is, although these conditions are similar to those of a qualifying company under the EIS/SEIS regimes. **The detailed provisions of the definition of qualifying trading company and this relief are outside the scope of this textbook.**

20.6 Interaction of Reliefs

This section examines how the various CGT business reliefs interact with business asset disposal relief (BADR) (see **Chapter 19**, **Section 19.1**).

20.6.1 Rollover Relief

A taxpayer should consider if it would be more beneficial to claim BADR or rollover relief, or potentially both, where the relevant conditions for each are met.

BADR is only available on the disposal of the whole or part of a business and not on the disposal of individual assets. Rollover relief is typically relevant where there is a sale of an individual business asset and the individual continues to carry on the business.

If it is possible to claim both reliefs, an individual may wish to claim BADR instead of rollover relief in order to crystallise a gain taxable at 10%, or to utilise capital losses and the CGT annual exemption.

If both reliefs are claimed, rollover relief applies before BADR. This would apply, for example, where some proceeds have not been reinvested so that rollover relief does not cover the whole of the gain. In this case, BADR will apply to the gain left after rollover relief has been applied. However, the gain must be a qualifying business disposal for BADR.

20.6.2 Gift Relief

A taxpayer should consider if it would be more beneficial to claim BADR or gift relief, or potentially both, where the relevant conditions for each are met. This would only apply, for example, where some proceeds have been received, i.e. there has been a sale at undervalue or a share disposal has been restricted by virtue of the company having chargeable non-business assets.

Where a gain is eligible for both gift relief and BADR and a claim is made for both, gift relief is applied first. BADR is only available on the disposal of the whole or part of a business and not on individual assets.

Alternatively, it may be beneficial to claim neither in situations where the gain is covered by the annual exemption and/or losses.

20.6.3 Incorporation Relief

Since incorporation usually involves the disposal of all or part of a business, BADR can usually also be claimed on incorporation. Incorporation relief is applied in priority to claiming BADR. As noted in **Section 20.2.1**, it is possible to elect not to avail of incorporation relief.

If both reliefs are claimed, BADR will be applied to any gain remaining after incorporation relief, e.g. where consideration is not wholly in the form of shares and only partial incorporation relief is available as a result.

However, it should be noted that there are restrictions on claiming BADR in respect of goodwill gains arising on incorporation (see **Chapter 19**, **Section 19.1.4**).

20.6.4 EIS Deferral Relief

If EIS deferral relief is tailored so that the full gain is not covered by the relief, BADR may be available on any unrelieved amounts remaining.

Gains that are eligible for BADR but which are instead deferred into EIS qualifying investments can still benefit from BADR when the gain becomes chargeable later (in one of the three circumstances outlined in **Section 20.3.1**), subject to the normal conditions for BADR applicable at the time of the first disposal.

20.6.5 SEIS Reinvestment Relief

SEIS reinvestment relief exempts the gain, and so takes priority over BADR. BADR may be available on any unrelieved amounts remaining.

Questions

Review Questions
(See Suggested Solutions to Review Questions at the end of this textbook.)

Question 20.1

It is mid-November 2021 and you are working on the file of your client, Áine Taylor, who runs a manufacturing business as a sole trader. The factory used in the business was acquired in November 1998 for £500,000, but due to recent growth in orders is now too small to cope with demand, even though the business has been working night shifts as well as day shifts.

Áine has therefore been considering her options and has decided to sell the factory and move to new premises. An offer of £1,500,000 was accepted from a local property developer for the existing factory on 8 November 2021.

She has recently been to see you to discuss her options. She is open to whether the business will lease new factory premises or purchase new factory premises. Furthermore, she has recently been approached by a friend to invest in her company, Shoe Manufacturer Ltd, which needs some additional cash to fund expansion into a new market. Áine is very keen to ensure that she takes advantage of any available reliefs to reduce/defer any tax liability arising on sale of the factory.

Áine has not made any other capital disposals in the 2021/22 tax year and is an additional rate taxpayer. For the purposes of the question, assume that business asset disposal relief is **not** available.

Requirement
Write a letter to Áine that covers the following topics:

(a) Calculate the tax payable on sale of the factory, state the date that the tax is due and the type of tax that is payable.
(b) Explain rollover relief and how it could be used to defer any tax payable on the sale of the factory.
(c) Explain how an investment in Shoe Manufacturer Ltd could be used to defer any tax payable on the sale of the factory. Assume that Shoe Manufacturer Ltd is a "qualifying company" for the purposes of relevant relief and that it is not a new company.

Question 20.2

Mark sold an asset in July 2021 which generated a capital gain on sale of £88,300. He is interested in reinvesting the money from the sale into new qualifying Enterprise Investment Scheme (EIS) shares but wants to know the maximum investment he should make.

Mark had capital losses of £28,000 carried forward at 6 April 2021. He owns no other capital assets and you can assume that he is a qualifying EIS investor and the company is a qualifying EIS company.

Requirement
(a) Outline how EIS reinvestment relief operates; and
(b) State the maximum amount of EIS reinvestment relief that Mark should claim after claiming all available reliefs.

Question 20.3

Denise sold an asset in October 2021, resulting in a capital gain of £84,000. She is interested in reinvesting the money from the sale into new qualifying Seed Enterprise Investment Scheme (SEIS) shares.

Denise had capital losses of £35,000 at 6 April 2021 and has a capital loss of £10,000 from a disposal in June 2021. Denise owns no other capital assets and you can assume that she is a qualifying SEIS investor and the company is a qualifying SEIS company.

Denise wishes to use the minimum amount possible of her capital losses carried forward as she expects to need these in 2022/23.

Requirement
State the maximum amount of SEIS reinvestment relief that Denise should claim in 2021/22.

Question 20.4

James invested £35,000 into EIS shares on 1 November 2019 and received EIS income tax relief. He is a qualifying investor and the company is a qualifying EIS company.

James sold his EIS shares in the company on 31 March 2022 for £10,000.

Requirement
(a) Calculate the capital loss arising.
(b) What would the capital loss be if the shares had been sold on 31 March 2023?
(c) State how both capital losses can be used.

Question 20.5

Simone Stafford started a sole trade business making her own beauty products. The demand for her products and services has increased so much that Simone decided to transfer the business to a new company, Stafford Beauty Ltd on 1 January 2022 when it was worth £250,000.

In return for her sole trade, Simone received 1,000 shares worth £100,000 and cash of £150,000. The gain on incorporation was £80,000 (£50,000 on a property, £30,000 in respect of goodwill). Simone made no other disposals for CGT purposes in the 2021/22 tax year and owns no other assets.

Requirement
Calculate the CGT payable by Simone on incorporation of her business and the base cost of her shares in Stafford Beauty Ltd. You should assume Simone is a higher rate taxpayer.

Acquisition by a Company of its Own Shares

Learning Objectives

After studying this chapter you will understand:
- The tax rules relating to a company's purchase of its own shares, including:
  - knowledge of the income tax treatment; and
  - the conditions for CGT treatment to apply.

21.1 Overview

A company may be legally able to buy back its own shares. A company might do this if a shareholder wishes to dispose of shares and the other shareholder(s) do not want to, or cannot afford to, buy the shares and want to ensure the shares are not sold to an unknown third party. The purchase of shares by a company is governed by companies legislation in the UK.

For tax purposes, a company purchase of its own shares is treated as either an income distribution or a capital disposal as the shareholder, whose shares are being bought back, is disposing of the relevant shares.

21.2 Income Distribution – Dividend Treatment

Where an individual sells shares back to the original company for more than the original subscribed share capital, the default treatment is that any excess is treated as an income distribution for tax purposes

As a result, the recipient is treated in the same way as a recipient of ordinary dividends under the income tax rules (as covered in CA Proficiency 1; and see also **Chapter 15**). The dividend (distribution) is treated as income when calculating the shareholder's income tax liability, after deduction of the £2,000 dividend allowance, if available. The £2,000 dividend allowance is deducted against the first £2,000 of dividend income. Any dividends received over the £2,000 dividend allowance are taxed at the following rates:

- 7.5% on dividend income within the basic rate band;
- 32.5% on dividend income within the higher rate band; and
- 38.1% on dividend income within the additional rate band.

However, the £2,000 tax-free allowance is deemed to use up £2,000 of the relevant income tax band. The individual will also have a CGT calculation to carry out as the disposal of shares is also a chargeable disposal of a chargeable asset. However, the same "profit" cannot be taxed twice under tax legislation and, as the distribution is taxed under the income distribution route, the proceeds received from the share disposal are reduced by the amount subject to income tax as a distribution. If the shares were subscribed for at more than nominal value, a capital loss would arise. If shares were subscribed for at nominal value, a no gain/no loss position position for CGT would result; while if the shares were subscribed for at a price greater than the nominal value, a capital loss for CGT purposes would arise.

Example 21.1

Philip and his brother set up ABC Limited in April 2008 for £1 per share nominal value. The issued share capital was 1,000 shares. The shareholding was split 50:50.

In September 2021, Philip decided to sell his shares back to the company for £1.75 per share. A market valuation of the company was undertaken. What is the tax treatment of Philip's disposal? Ignore the dividend allowance.

Income tax calculation – distribution

	£
Proceeds	875.00
Less: nominal value (500 × £1)	(500.00)
Excess distribution	375.00
Taxed as a dividend	375.00

CGT calculation

	£
Proceeds	875.00
Less: amount taxed as income	(375.00)
	500.00
Less: base cost	(500.00)
Capital gain	0.00

If Philip originally subscribed for his shares at a price of £3 per share, the calculations would be as follows:

Income tax calculation – distribution

	£
Proceeds	875.00
Less: nominal value (500 × £1)	(500.00)
Excess distribution	375.00
Taxed as a dividend	375.00

CGT calculation

	£
Proceeds	875.00
Less: amount taxed as income	(375.00)
	500.00
Less: base cost	(1,500.00)
Capital loss	(1,000.00)

Overall, Philip has realised a loss of £625, i.e. he bought 500 shares at £3 and sold them for £1.75. This has been reflected as an income distribution of £375 and a capital loss of £1,000.

21.3 Capital Disposal – CGT Treatment

Where certain **conditions** are met, the excess distribution noted above will be treated as a capital disposal subject to CGT, instead of an income distribution subject to income tax (in this case, only a capital gains calculation needs to be carried out rather than an income and a capital gains calculation as was the case above under **Section 21.2**). Once the conditions are met, the treatment of the transaction as capital is **automatic**.

The rules governing a capital distribution are found in section 1033 CTA 2010 and, where the relevant conditions are met, apply automatically on two occasions:

1. Payments made by an **unquoted trading company or an unquoted holding company of a trading group** on the purchase or redemption of its own shares, provided certain conditions are met. For these purposes, shares dealt in on the Unlisted Securities Market or the Alternative Investment Market (AIM) are treated as unquoted.
2. Where the payments from the company are used by the shareholder wholly or mainly to discharge an IHT liability arising as a result of a death. The company must, in this instance, also be an unquoted trading company or an unquoted holding company of a trading group (see below).

21.3.1 Unquoted Companies

Where an unquoted trading company or an unquoted holding company of a trading group buys back its own shares from a UK shareholder in order to benefit its trade, the payment made to the shareholder is, subject to certain conditions being met, not to be treated as an income distribution but instead will be a capital disposal falling under the CGT provisions. Therefore, the purchase of shares by the company will be treated as a disposal of shares by the shareholder and normal CGT rules will apply.

For the purposes of this legislation, a company is classed as a trading company if it is "wholly or mainly" trading, i.e. trading activities constitute at least 51%. This is a different test to the trading company test for business asset disposal relief (see **Chapter 19**), gift relief (see CA Proficiency 1) and the substantial shareholdings exemption (see **Chapter 13**). The trading company test for the purpose of these reliefs requires non-trading activity to be less than 20%.

Conditions for CGT Treatment

The following conditions must **all** be met in order for CGT treatment to apply to the buy back of shares by such a company:

1. The trade must not consist of dealing in shares, securities, land or futures.
2. The main objective of the repurchase must **not** be one of avoidance of tax. It must be for bona fide commercial reasons.
3. The repurchase must be wholly or mainly for the benefit of the trade. The "benefit to the trade test" will be satisfied where any of the following apply:

    (a) a dissident or disruptive shareholder is bought out;
    (b) the proprietor wishes to retire to make way for new management;
    (c) an outside investor who provided equity wishes to withdraw his investment; or
    (d) a shareholder dies and his personal representatives do not wish to retain his shares.

    Note: this list is not exhaustive.
4. There are also various conditions that must be satisfied by the vendor:

    (a) They must be resident in the UK, as determined by the statutory residence test (see **Chapter 2**), when the shares are bought back. This ensures that the vendor is within the charge to UK CGT.

(b) The vendor (or their spouse) must have owned the shares throughout a **five-year period** ending with the date of the buy-back. The period of ownership of a spouse living with a vendor at the date of the buy-back is aggregated with that of the vendor. (Five years is reduced to three years if acquired on death and the ownership of the deceased can also be taken into account.)

(c) Where the vendor's shareholding (and that of their **associates**) in a company is not fully purchased, redeemed or repaid, then the vendor and his associates must as a result of the purchase have their interest in the company's share capital substantially reduced, i.e. reduced to 75% or less of their interest before the disposal. This test is considered in two ways, first looking at the shareholding, and secondly looking at their share in the profits of the company. Associates include spouses, minor children, controlled companies, trustees and beneficiaries and, if the company is a member of a group, then the whole group is treated as one for these purposes.

(d) After the transaction, the vendor **must not** be connected with the company or any company in the same 51% group.

For these purposes, a person is "connected" with a company if they directly or indirectly possess, or are entitled to acquire, more than 30% of the ordinary share capital, the issued share capital and loan capital, the voting rights of the company or the assets for distribution on a winding up.

Any shares repurchased by the company are cancelled and not re-issued. This is particularly important when assessing condition (c) above as the issued share capital of the company is reduced by the amount of shares bought back.

Example 21.2

Karen owns 1,500 shares in Winddrops Ltd, a UK unquoted trading company which has issued share capital of 5,000 shares. If all other conditions are met, can the buyback be treated as a capital disposal if the company buys back 400 shares from Karen?

Solution

	Winddrops Ltd Total Shareholding	Karen's Shareholding
Pre-repurchase	5,000	1,500
Repurchased and cancelled	(400)	(400)
Post-repurchase	4,600	1,100

Karen originally held 1,500 shares (out of the issued share capital of 5,000 shares) which amounted to a 30% interest in Winddrops Ltd. After the repurchase, this dropped to 1,100 shares (out of the reduced issued share capital of 4,600 shares) which is a 23.9% shareholding. Karen's shareholding has dropped by 6.1%, which amounts to a decrease of 20.3% (6.1%/30%). This is not enough to meet the test at 4(c) above as the repurchase must reduce her shareholding by at least 25%. The transaction would therefore be treated as an income distribution.

Assuming all other conditions were met, if the company had repurchased 484 shares the repurchase would be a capital distribution and CGT rules would apply. Karen's interest has to reduce by at least 25%; therefore, her 1,500 shares must be reduced to 1,016 shares or less.

	Winddrops Ltd Total Shareholding	Karen's Shareholding
Pre-repurchase	5,000	1,500
Repurchased and cancelled	(484)	(484)
Post-repurchase	4,516	1,016

Karen's interest of 1,016 shares amounts to a shareholding of 22.5% in the company which means that Karen's interest has dropped by 25% (30% $\times$ 75% = 22.5%).

Example 21.3

Doyle Books Ltd has an issued share capital of 100,000 £1 ordinary shares, of which Emmett holds 20,000 shares (i.e. a 20% shareholding). If Emmett sells 5,000 shares to Doyle Books Ltd, the company's issued share capital is reduced for tax purposes to 95,000 shares, of which Emmett holds 15,000, a fraction of 15/95ths or 15.79% shareholding.

	Doyle Books Ltd Issued Share Capital	Emmett's Shareholding	%
Pre-repurchase	100,000	20,000	20%
Repurchased and cancelled	(5,000)	(5,000)	
Post-repurchase	95,000	15,000	15.79%

Thus, although Emmett has sold 25% of his original holding, Emmett's percentage holding has been reduced by only 21% ((20% − 15.79%)/20%), and the buyback will not qualify for CGT treatment and it will be treated as an income distribution.

To achieve a reduction of 25%, Emmett would need to sell 5,890 shares.

	Doyle Books Ltd Issued Share Capital	Emmett's Shareholding	%
Pre-repurchase	100,000	20,000	20%
Repurchased and cancelled	(5,890)	(5,890)	
Post-repurchase	94,110	14,110	15%

Note: remember that the vendor must not be connected with the company or group company after the sale, i.e. the vendor and the vendor's associates must not, after the sale of the shares, be entitled to more than 30% of the capital, voting rights or assets on a winding up of the company. In addition, where the vendor maintains a shareholding in the company that is not small (i.e. more than 5%), it can be difficult to demonstrate that the "trade benefit" condition has been met.

21.3.2 Payments for Inheritance Tax

As noted above, where the whole of the payment (apart from any amount used to pay CGT arising) is applied by the recipient in discharging a liability for inheritance tax (IHT) charged on a death, and where it is so applied within a period of two years after the death, and the IHT so paid could not otherwise have been paid without undue hardship, then the payment may be treated as a capital disposal and CGT will apply. In this instance, there is no requirement to meet certain of the conditions as set out above, i.e. the benefit of trade test and the vendor conditions test; however, the company must be an unquoted trading company or an unquoted holding company of a trading group.

21.4 Other Aspects

21.4.1 Clearance Procedure

An advance clearance procedure is available under section 1044 CTA 2010, whereby the company can set out the precise reasons for the buy back and provide HMRC with all relevant information to enable them to determine if all of the conditions for the CGT treatment are met. HMRC have 30 days to reply to the clearance application. It is recommended that this clearance procedure is used.

21.4.2 HMRC Notification

After the company makes the payment to the shareholder it must file a return to HMRC within 60 days, giving details of the payment and the circumstances surrounding it and, in particular, justifying the application of the CGT treatment to the transaction. The return must be made even if HMRC have confirmed that the capital treatment will apply to the payment under the advance clearance procedure.

21.4.3 Other Issues

There is no corporation tax deduction for the company, irrespective of whether the repurchase is treated as an income distribution or as a capital disposal. This also applies to any expenses incurred in buying back the shares.

Where a company acquires any of its shares (by purchase, bonus issue or otherwise), it is not treated for tax purposes as acquiring an asset. As a result of acquiring or holding the shares the company is not treated as being a member of itself, hence the shares are cancelled.

The company will pay 0.5% stamp duty on the consideration paid for the acquisition of the shares (see **Chapter 29**). No reliefs are available to reduce or remove the resulting stamp duty charge, which must be paid within 30 days of the transaction.

The CGT treatment is generally more beneficial than the income tax treatment, due to the comparatively low CGT rates of 10% and 20% when shares are sold (compared to the maximum income tax rate of 38.1% on a distribution).

Careful consideration should always be given to determining the most tax-efficient treatment for the individual. However, it is likely to be the case that the CGT treatment will be preferred if the 10% rate of CGT applies or where business asset disposal relief or investors' relief (see **Chapter 19**, **Section 19.1**) can be claimed, or where the taxpayer is an additional rate taxpayer.

If the CGT treatment is not the most tax-efficient route (if, say, the income distribution route would tax the transaction at 7.5%, i.e. the basic rate of dividend tax), then it may be necessary to break one of the conditions for capital treatment, given that this is automatic if all the relevant conditions are satisfied.

Example 21.4

Harry and Peter, two UK resident individuals and additional rate taxpayers, set up Super Friends Ltd in 1992 to sell electronic equipment. Harry owns 80% of the shares, while Peter owns 20%. The company has been very profitable and now has revenue reserves of £2 million. Harry believes that the success of the company is due totally to his efforts. He believes that Peter does not really contribute to the success of the company and is more interested in his golf handicap. There have been a number of acrimonious board meetings and, as a result, Harry has decided to buy Peter out. Peter is happy to dispose of his shares provided that he receives £1 million (being the market value of his shareholding) and pays the least amount of tax on the disposal.

If Harry were to buy the shares, he would need £1 million of funds. As Harry does not have that amount of cash, he would have to either borrow the money (which would have to be repaid) or get money from the company (on which he would be liable to income tax, e.g. salary or dividend, etc.).

If Super Friends Ltd bought back the shares from Peter, then Harry would own all the shares, without having to find the cash to actually buy the shares. Peter will be liable to income tax on the cash received from Super Friends Ltd in excess of the amount he contributed for the shares. However, if he satisfies the conditions, he will be liable to CGT on the gain, and not income tax.

continued overleaf

Checklist of conditions:

1	Trading company?	Yes
2	Will the acquisition benefit the trade?	Yes, there is disagreement between shareholders
3	Is the main purpose of the buy-back the avoidance of tax?	No, genuine exit of a shareholder from the business
4	Is Peter resident in the UK in 2021/22?	Yes
5	Has Peter owned the shares for five years?	Yes
6	Is Peter selling all his shares, or at least substantially reducing his shareholding?	Yes, he is selling all his shares
7	Confirm Peter is not connected with Super Friends Ltd after the disposal?	Yes, confirmed

As all the conditions have been satisfied, Peter will be liable to CGT on the disposal of the shares to Super Friends Ltd.

As Peter is disposing of shares in his personal trading company, he should be able to avail of BADR and thus pay CGT at a maximum of £100,000 (assuming his annual exemption is otherwise utilised), i.e. at a rate of 10%.

Note: the cost of the shares was not provided but would obviously be deducted from the proceeds before applying the 10% BADR rate. This compares with the figure of £381,000 (38.1%, ignoring the dividend allowance) that he would have had to pay if he had received the £1 million as an income distribution (as his marginal income tax rate is 45% and again ignoring the original subscription price paid for the shares).

Questions

Review Questions
(See Suggested Solutions to Review Questions at the end of this textbook.)

Question 21.1

Andrew Jameson is 63 years old and is a 75% shareholder in Andrewstones Limited, an unquoted trading company. He has lived and worked in the UK all his life. His 30-year-old son, John, holds the remaining 25% shareholding. Andrew is considering retiring from the business to make way for new blood and thus give his son control of the company. His son does not have the cash to buy his shareholding and does not wish to enter into a claim for gift relief. Therefore the most suitable option is for the company to buy back Andrew's shares as he does not want the shares to go outside the family. It is confirmed that the company has adequate distributable reserves and cash to do so.

Andrew's original investment in the company shares was £75,000 in £1 ordinary shares when the company was incorporated in 1991. There was no share premium account. Andrew has been an employee and director of the company throughout this period. The firm has recently valued Andrew's shares at £13 each.

Requirement

Write a letter to Andrew in December 2021 setting out the following:

(a) The conditions that must be met in order for the proceeds received from a company acquiring its own shares to be treated as a share disposal for capital gains tax purposes.

(b) Assess whether the conditions are met and, if so, calculate Andrew's capital gains tax liability claiming any available reliefs.

(c) The consequences for Andrew if the conditions for capital treatment are not met. Include a calculation of the tax due.

(d) Outline the stamp duty consequences of the share buy-back, when any liability falls due for payment and who is responsible for payment of the liability.

Note: Andrew is UK resident for tax and has other income each year in the region of £200,000 and receives dividends annually in excess of £10,000.

Question 21.2

It is early March 2022. Peter Maddley, a relatively new client of your practice, called you a few weeks back in early February with some bad news. One of his fellow directors in Maddon Engineering Limited ("Maddon"), Aaron Donaldson, was tragically killed in a car crash.

Peter and his two friends, Aaron and Jeremy, set up Maddon, a successful engineering company, when they left university in the early 1990s. In 1991 each of them subscribed for 10,000 £1 ordinary shares each.

Peter, Aaron and Jeremy were full-time directors of the company until Aaron's untimely death. Just before his death, Aaron gifted his shares to his wife Sarah. However, Sarah does not wish to keep the shares now as they remind her of Aaron. Therefore, under the terms of the shareholder's agreement that was entered into when the company started, Maddon is going to buy back all of Sarah's shares for £150 a share on 4 April 2022.

Sarah is also a client of your practice. She has advised you that the transaction will only proceed if the "capital treatment" can be obtained. No one remembers what this actually means as the agreement was made so long ago. Sarah has done some research and would like to know what difference it would make if the 'income' treatment was adopted instead.

Sarah has also been in contact with you separately about her late husband's estate. She mentioned to you that in December 2018 Aaron set up a discretionary trust using £500,000 in cash from the sale of a property in California, USA. All UK and US capital gains tax liabilities on the sale of the property have been paid. However, no inheritance tax was paid at the time as the solicitor involved stated that it was not an issue and Aaron had no other transactions in his lifetime.

Sarah has asked you whether this is now required to be included in Aaron's death estate because "it was set up using cash that the tax has been paid on". She also suggested that, if it is required to be included, she would like to think you would be willing to turn a blind eye and forget she ever told you about this as she thinks HMRC have no way of finding out about it. In any case, she tells you Aaron would have delegated responsibility for paying any inheritance tax arising to the trust.

All parties are UK tax resident and additional rate taxpayers. Maddon should be treated as a trading company with no investment assets on its statement of financial position. Sarah should be treated as not owning any other shares aside from those gifted to her by her late husband, Aaron.

Note to students: part (b) of this question should be attempted after you have completed the chapters on inheritance tax and stamp taxes (**Chapters 22–32**).

Requirement

(a) Draft a letter to Peter, Jeremy and Sarah to include:

(i) An explanation, together with calculations, of how Sarah will be taxed on the repurchase of the inherited shares. Include a comparison between the income and capital treatments and detail the conditions that must be met for capital treatment to be available for the share buy-back. Assess if the capital treatment will be available for this transaction and calculate the tax payable as a result of your assessment.

(ii) A calculation of the stamp duty payable (if any) on the share buy-back and outline who is responsible for payment of the liability (if any).

(b) Write a briefing note for the partner to discuss with Sarah on the following matters:

(i) Comment on the availability of business property relief for the shares in Maddon held by Aaron at the date of his death. Calculate the value of the shares to be included in Aaron's death estate after any relief that may be available.

(ii) Discuss the lifetime inheritance tax (IHT) implications of setting up the trust and support your analysis with calculations. Advise on the due date for payment of any lifetime IHT. Consider whether the transaction is required to be included in Aaron's death estate and calculate the amount of IHT payable (if any) on death.

(iii) Outline what action you would take in relation to Sarah's suggestion that, if the lifetime gift is to be included in Aaron's estate, you should leave it out entirely.

Part Four

Inheritance Tax

Introduction to Inheritance Tax

Chartered Accountants Ireland's *Code of Ethics* applies to all aspects of a Chartered Accountant's professional life, including dealing with inheritance tax issues. As outlined at the beginning of this book, further information regarding the principles in the *Code of Ethics* is set out in **Appendix 2**.

In addition, **Appendix 3** examines the distinction between tax planning, tax avoidance and tax evasion, which can arise in relation to all taxes, including inheritance tax.

22.1 Introduction

The bulk of inheritance tax (IHT) legislation is contained in the Inheritance Tax Act 1984 (IHTA 1984). The legislation has been relatively unchanged since then, with the majority of changes coming in the form of anti-avoidance measures being introduced to tackle abuse and IHT avoidance.

All legislative references in this part are to the IHTA 1984 unless otherwise stated.

22.2 Meaning of Gift and Inheritance

22.2.1 Meaning of "Gift", "Inheritance", "Transfer of Value" and "Related Property"

Section 1 IHTA 1984 states that IHT is charged "on the value transferred by a chargeable transfer". The value transferred by an individual is measured using the loss to the donor principle. The amount that is subject to IHT is basically the value of the donor's estate before the gift, less the value of the donor's estate after the gift, i.e. the transfer of value. Generally, assets will potentially be subject to IHT unless they are classed as excluded property (see **Chapter 24, Section 24.8**).

One important point to note, particularly in relation to gifts of shares, is that the value received by the donee may not necessarily equate to the value transferred from the donor.

When measuring the loss to the donor, it is necessary to include the value of any related property. However the property should only be valued using the related property rule if this produces a higher value for IHT purposes.

Related property includes that owned by an individual's spouse/civil partner, plus any assets owned by a charity that were transferred by the donor/spouse, and which is either still held by the charity or was held at any time in the last five years.

Example 22.1: Calculation of transfer of value including related property
Tinky owns 6,000 shares in Spartan Ltd. Tinky's husband and her brother each own 2,000 shares in Spartan Ltd. The company has 10,000 shares in issue.

Tinky wants to give 2,000 shares to her son Po, and would like to know what value would be relevant for IHT. The values of the different sizes of shareholdings are as follows:

0–50% shareholding	£10 a share
51%–74% shareholding	£15 a share
75%–100% shareholding	£20 a share

Value transferred for inheritance tax purposes:

	£
Before (6,000/8,000)* £20 × 8,000	120,000
After (4,000/6,000)* £15 × 6,000	(60,000)
Value transferred	60,000

* The shares owned by Tinky's husband must be included to determine the relevant share price as these are related property. Tinky is then treated as owning a proportion of the enlarged shareholding.

Note: assuming Tinky does not make a claim for gift relief under section 165 TCGA 1992 (see **Chapter 16, Section 16.11.4**), for CGT purposes Po's base cost is only 2,000 × £10 = £20,000, being the market value of a stand-alone 20% shareholding!

'Inheritance' is not defined in IHTA 1984, but its common law meaning is the passing on of property following the death of an individual. Where the deceased has written a will, the recipients of property are generally referred to as beneficiaries, legatees or devisees.

When an individual dies, whether it be intestate (i.e. not having left a will) or having left a will, the person is treated as making a transfer of value equal to the value of their estate for IHT purposes on death – but one must not forget that IHT can also arise during their lifetime.

A liability to IHT can arise in the following circumstances:

- making a chargeable lifetime gift,
- on a lifetime gift (both chargeable lifetime transfers and potentially exempt transfers) following the death of the donor within seven years of the date of the gift, and
- on the value of the deceased's estate following death.

"Gift" is defined in section 42, which effectively says that a gift is any instance where property has been transferred from one person to another and the value of the donor's estate has been reduced as a result of the gift.

The scope of IHT is further restricted by stating that a gift must include a "gratuitous intent" on the part of the donor for the transfer of value to potentially fall within the charge to IHT. This allows for some important exceptions from the scope of IHT as follows:

▩ **Genuine "arm's length" transactions between parties (section 10)** If market value has been received for the transfer of any property, then there will be no loss of value to the estate to the donor.

A 'bad bargain' does not in itself mean that a transaction has been carried out on a non-arm's length basis. However, if the parties are connected then there would need to be clear commercial evidence to support the price agreed.

▩ **Maintenance of an individual's family (section 11)** In this case, the value of the donor's estate will be reduced but there is no associated "gratuitous intent". Examples would be the payment of school fees for a child, paying for medical or specialist care for a dependent relative or for the maintenance of an ex-spouse following divorce.

There are a number of other exceptions which are beyond the scope of this textbook.

22.3 Domicile and Deemed Domicile Rules for IHT

IHT in the UK is also subject to territorial limits. The UK does not seek to tax a transfer where neither the transferor nor the property transferred has a sufficient connection with the UK. Hence, it is important to consider both the domicile and the deemed domicile of the person and where the asset is located (situs).

Under UK law, every individual has a domicile and an individual cannot have more than one domicile at a time unless they are classed as deemed UK domiciled for IHT purposes (see **Sections 22.3.1** and **22.3.2**). Individuals who are either UK domiciled or deemed UK domiciled (for IHT purposes) are liable to IHT on their **worldwide estate**, wherever the assets are situated.

Individuals who are not UK domiciled or deemed UK domiciled for IHT purposes are only liable to UK IHT to the extent that their assets are situated in the UK or that their non-UK assets are not classed as excluded property (see **Chapter 24, Section 24.8** for more details).

An individual's domicile will depend on their specific circumstances. The concepts of domicile of origin, choice and dependency also apply for IHT purposes. An individual's residence status (as determined by the statutory residence test, however, is only significant for the purposes of IHT with regard to some of the deemed domicile tests outlined below. (See **Chapter 2** for details on domicile, deemed domcile and the SRT.)

22.3.1 Deemed UK Domicile

There are four ways that an individual can be deemed UK domiciled for IHT purposes:

1. If the individual:
   ● has been resident in the UK for at least 15 of the 20 tax years immediately before the relevant tax year; and
   ● the individual was UK resident in at least one of the four tax years ending with the relevant tax year.
2. For three years after they cease to be UK domiciled.
3. If the individual:
   ● was born in the UK and the UK is also their domicile of origin;
   ● has acquired another non-UK domicile of choice;
   ● was resident in the UK in the relevant tax year; and
   ● was resident in the UK for at least one of the two tax years immediately preceding that tax year.

This is known as the "formerly domiciled resident" rule.

4. The individual elects to be deemed UK domiciled under the non-domicile spousal election provisions (see **Section 22.3.2**).

An individual who is deemed UK domiciled for IHT purposes under one of these four categories is subject to UK IHT on the worldwide basis. Where someone is subject to IHT on the worldwide basis and foreign IHT arises in respect of a non-UK situs asset, double tax relief may be available (see **Chapter 28, Section 28.2**).

Example 22.2: Relationship between domicile and UK IHT
Ronaldo is Portuguese domiciled (and not UK deemed domiciled for IHT purposes) and owns a £7.5 million mansion in Cheshire. He also owns a £3 million apartment in Madrid. As he is non-UK-domiciled, he will only be subject to IHT in respect of the Cheshire mansion. The apartment in Madrid is not subject to UK IHT as it is excluded property.

However, should Ronaldo become UK-domiciled or become deemed UK domicile for IHT purposes through any of the four ways that this can be achieved, then the worldwide estate of Ronaldo will fall within the UK IHT net and the Madrid mansion would no longer be excluded property.

If Ronaldo is not UK domiciled or deemed UK domiciled for IHT purposes, his estate cannot claim tax relief in the UK for any IHT paid (or equivalent) in any other country in respect of the Madrid mansion.

Example 22.3: Deemed domicile: three-year rule
Paula has a UK domicile of origin and lives in England. She retires from work and decides that she wants to live for the rest of her life in Spain. She leaves the UK for Spain and acquires Spanish domicile of choice on 31 January 2019. She dies on 1 January 2022 still living in Spain.

Because of the deemed domicile "three-year rule" she is deemed domiciled in the UK at her death and her worldwide estate is chargeable to IHT. Her estate can claim tax relief for any IHT paid (or equivalent) in any other country.

If Paula had died after 31 January 2022 she would not meet the three-year rule and only UK situs assets contained in her estate would be subject to UK IHT in addition to any foreign situs assets not classed as excluded property.

Example 22.4: Deemed domicile: long-term UK resident rule
Bronislaw has a Polish domicile of origin although he works in the UK and is UK tax resident. He has lived and worked in the UK since 2 February 1998, but he has always intended to return home to Poland. He starts to feel ill and returns home to Poland to be with his family on 2 February 2021, and unfortunately dies on 2 February 2022.

Because of his common law domicile his worldwide estate would not be chargeable to IHT. However, the "15 out of 20" tax year deemed domicile rule means that he is deemed to be domiciled in the UK at his death and his entire worldwide estate is chargeable to IHT. His estate can claim tax relief for any IHT paid (or equivalent) in any other country.

Example 22.5: Deemed domicile: "formerly domiciled resident" rule
Steven was born in the UK and had a UK domicile of origin. In 2006 he acquired a Canadian domicile of choice when he emigrated to Canada to marry his long-term Canadian partner. Steven's employer seconded him to the UK on 6 April 2021 for a two-year period. As a result, Steven is UK resident in each of the tax years 2021/22 and 2022/23. On 31 March 2023, Steven was tragically killed in an accident crossing the street.

As Steven was born in the UK, has a UK domicile of origin, was resident in the UK in 2022/23 and was resident in the UK for at least one of the two tax years immediately preceding 2022/23 (being 2021/22), he is deemed UK domiciled at the date of his death and his entire worldwide estate is chargeable to IHT. His estate can claim tax relief for any IHT paid (or equivalent) in any other country.

22.3.2 *Deemed Domicile: Election by Non-UK Domiciled Spouse or Civil Partner*

Provisions within IHTA 1984 allow a person not domiciled in the UK and who is not already deemed UK domiciled for IHT purposes as set out in rules 1–3 of **Section 22.3.1**, but who is, or has been, married to/in a civil partnership with a UK domiciled person to elect to be treated as UK domiciled. This election applies for IHT purposes only. All references to "spouse" or "spousal" hereafter should be taken to include civil partners/civil partnerships. Where the election is not made, the spousal non-domicile exemption in respect of a gift by their spouse (who is UK domiciled or deemed UK domicile for IHT purposes) is £325,000 (see **Chapter 23**).

If a transfer of value has already been made as a result of the death of the UK spouse, the election can be made by the surviving spouse within two years of that death.

A person can make an election provided that during the period of seven years ending with the date on which the election is made/the date of death, the person had a spouse who was UK domiciled. At the time the election is made, the person making the election does not need to be married or in a civil partnership or resident in the UK.

Once an election is made, it cannot be revoked, although it is possible for the election to cease to have effect (see later).

In all cases, an election must be made by the non-domiciled person or their personal representative(s) in writing and sent to HMRC, and it must contain the date from which the election is to take effect. This election operates independently from the main IHT-deemed domicile provisions outlined previously. Someone who has elected to be treated as UK domiciled may, while the election is in force, become deemed UK domiciled by meeting the relevant conditions outlined in rules 1–3 (see **Section 22.3.1**).

When an election is made, the person making the election will be treated as domiciled in the UK for all IHT purposes from the date stated in the election, meaning that they are subject to UK IHT on the worldwide basis with double tax relief available for IHT (or equivalent) paid in any other country. Whether to make an election and the date it is take effect from requires careful consideration as it could mean that a transfer that did not give rise to a charge at the time is was made because it was excluded property, proves to be chargeable.

If a person has elected to be domiciled in the UK and as a consequence of that election an earlier disposition now gives rise to a transfer of value, clearly it would be not be reasonable for the original due dates for delivery of the IHT account and its payment to be satisfied.

Section 267B(8) provides that the due date for the delivery of such an account is 12 months from the end of the month in which the election is made. For the payment of the relevant tax and to establish the date from which interest is charged, the transfer is treated as if it was made at the date of the election.

Example 22.6: Deemed domicile – spousal election

Susan is domiciled in the UK and transfers an investment property worth £2m in 2021 to her spouse, Rocco. This is Susan's only lifetime transfer. Rocco is not domiciled in the UK nor is he deemed UK domiciled for IHT purposes. Subsequently, in 2023, Rocco transfers some Italian shares to the trustees of an offshore trust, which are excluded property for IHT purposes. Susan dies in 2025. At the time of the 2021 lifetime transfer, the value transferred is exempt to the extent of £325,000 and a potentially exempt transfer (PET) to the extent of £1,675,000. Following Susan's death, the failed PET is chargeable and after deducting the nil rate band, £1,350,000 is subject to tax.

Rocco's transfer in 2023 was a transfer of excluded property. Following Susan's death, Rocco has the choice of electing to be treated as deemed domiciled in the UK for IHT purposes. If he does so, the gift from Susan in 2021 will become fully exempt as a transfer where both spouses are domiciled in the UK. However, Rocco will then be treated as domiciled in the UK from 2021 for all IHT purposes. This means that his transfer to the trustees in 2023 is no longer one of excluded property and will be subject to IHT. As a transfer to a trust, it will be immediately chargeable to tax, though reliefs should be considered in addition to double tax relief, if applicable.

Rocco will need to consider all the consequences of making an election.

Questions

Review Questions

(See Suggested Solution to Review Questions at the end of this textbook.)

Question 22.1

Grey Properties Ltd, an investment company, has 100,000 issued £1 ordinary shares. The shares are valued as follows:

76%–100% = £35 per share
51%–75% = £25 per share
26%–50% = £14 per share
25% or less = £8 per share

Mr Grey owns 50,000 shares and his wife owns 28,000. He makes a gift of 30,000 shares to his daughter Anne.

Requirement
(a) Calculate the transfer of value made by Mr Grey for inheritance tax purposes.
(b) What is the base cost of the shares for Anne for CGT purposes, assuming no reliefs are claimed?
(c) If Mr Grey were to die in 38 months' time, explain the IHT implications of the gift (calculations are not required). Assume the company is wholly an investment company.

Question 22.2

On the occasion of their wedding in 2005, Walter gave his daughter Stephanie and his new son-in-law Martin a unique set of six antique chairs as a wedding gift. Stephanie received four and Martin received two. Stephanie's son James is an avid antique fan, so in December 2021 she gave one of her chairs to him when he turned 21.
The value of the chairs at the date of the gift was as follows:

	£
1 chair	50,000
2 chairs	110,000
3 chairs	250,000
4 chairs	375,000
5 chairs	500,000
6 chairs	800,000

Requirement
Calculate Stephanie's transfer of value for IHT purposes.

Question 22.3

Which of the following transactions are treated as a transfer of value for IHT purposes? Give explanations for your answers.

(a) Gift of shares in a family company to a daughter.
(b) Sale of a painting to a local art dealer.

(c)   Payment of a daughter's school fees.
(d)   Purchase of a Lamborghini from a local car dealership.
(e)   Gift of an investment property to a family trust.

Question 22.4

Three wealthy clients of your practice, Zelda, Willem and Cerys, have valuable assets located both in the UK and overseas. They are currently considering making a transfer of value of these assets in February 2022, which would be classed as a chargeable lifetime transfers for UK IHT purposes. Details are as follows:

(a)   Zelda has been living and working in the UK since July 2007. Before that she lived in Hong Kong where she was born and which is her domicile of origin. Zelda has not and does not intend to make the UK her domicile of choice.
(b)   Willem, who was German domiciled, settled in the UK many years ago and has taken all necessary steps to make the UK his domicile of choice.
(c)   Cerys was born in and brought up in the UK by her UK-domiciled parents. Cerys was resident in Ireland until she returned to the UK in 2014. In November 2020 she emigrated to Canada and, having broken all ties with the UK, has become non-UK domiciled.

Requirement
Briefly explain whether each of the above clients will be subject to inheritance tax on the transfers of their UK and overseas assets to a UK discretionary trust in March 2022.

Question 22.5

Pauline died from a long illness on 29 July 2020, leaving her whole estate (comprising her London home and a property in Italy) to her only daughter, Penny. Pauline had never married and was born in, and always lived in, the UK. Penny too was born in, and lived in, the UK. For several years while her mother had been ill, Penny lived and cared for her mother at the family home in London, which Pauline owned when she died.

Penny now plans to fulfil a lifetime ambition to emigrate to Australia and cut off all ties with the UK, as she has no living relatives left and all of her close friends have emigrated to Sydney over the last 10 years. She has no intention of ever returning to the UK and plans to leave before the end of 2021.

Her mother's death has got Penny thinking about her own mortality and she has recently spoken to a solicitor, who mentioned the concept of "domicile" and "deemed domicile" for inheritance tax.

Requirement
Explain the concept of "domicile" and "deemed domicile" for inheritance tax in the context of Penny's circumstances. How do these concepts affect her inheritance tax position both before and after her planned emigration?

Exemptions

There are a number of exemptions from the scope of IHT. The main conditions to be met in relation to each of the main exemptions are considered in turn below.

23.1 Inter-spouse Transfers (section 18)

Transfers to a UK domiciled/deemed UK domiciled (for IHT purposes) spouse, either during lifetime or on death, are completely exempt from IHT.

Where the donor is UK domiciled or deemed UK domiciled (for IHT purposes) but their spouse/civil partner is non-UK-domiciled, only the first £325,000 of the transfer is exempt from IHT, unless the non-UK domiciled recipient is deemed UK domiciled for IHT (see **Chapter 22, Section 22.3.1**). The reason for this is to prevent a UK domiciled person transferring their assets to a non-UK domiciled spouse, effectively taking the assets outside of the UK IHT net by virtue of the excluded property rules. Essentially, this makes most foreign situs assets excluded property.

In addition, non-UK domiciled individuals can, in certain circumstances, elect to be treated as deemed UK domiciled solely for IHT purposes (see **Chapter 22, Section 22.3.2**). A non-UK-domiciled individual can also become deemed domiciled in the UK under the rules for deemed domicile (see **Section 22.3.1**).

23.2 Small Gifts (section 20)

Lifetime gifts of up to £250 per donee may be made in any one tax year and be completely exempt from IHT. If a gift exceeds £250, then the whole amount is treated as a transfer of value (although it may be covered by some of the other lifetime exemptions), and not merely the excess over £250.

23.3 Normal Expenditure Out of Income (section 21)

A lifetime gift will not be treated as a transfer of value if the donor can evidence that it represents "normal expenditure out of income". This means that the expenditure must be of a habitual nature, year on year. The gift will be treated as being made out of income if the individual can show that they are left with sufficient income to maintain their normal standard of living. Examples would include the regular payment of life assurance premiums, school tuition fees or regular birthday/ Christmas presents.

23.4 Gifts in Consideration of Marriage/Civil Partnership (section 22)

Lifetime gifts on the occasion of a marriage/civil partnership are also exempt up to certain limits. The gift must be made, or promised, on or shortly before the date of the wedding or civil partnership ceremony. The limit depends on the relationship between the donor and donee. The limits are as follows:

> £5,000 – From a parent
>
> £2,500 – From a grandparent or remoter ancestor (or between the persons getting married)
>
> £1,000 – From any other person

These exemptions apply per marriage/civil partnership and not per donee. Any excess over the exempt limit is treated as a transfer of value, again subject to deduction of other lifetime exemptions. Note the difference between this and the small gifts exemption – the gift on marriage exemption is not an 'all or nothing' exemption and only the excess over the relevant limit is a potential transfer of value for IHT.

23.5 Gifts to Charities or Registered Clubs (section 23)

Gifts to charities or registered clubs, whether during lifetime or on death, are wholly exempt if certain conditions are met. The charity must be a "qualifying" charity established in the UK, EU or another specified country in the EEA (i.e. Iceland and Norway).

23.6 Gifts to Political Parties (section 24)

Gifts to political parties, whether during lifetime or on death, are wholly exempt if one of two conditions are met. To qualify for exemption, the party must have obtained, at the last general election, either two members elected to the House of Commons or one member and not less than 150,000 votes were given to candidates who were members of that party.

23.7 Maintenance Funds and Gifts to Housing Associations (section 24A and section 27)

Gifts to maintenance funds, whether during lifetime or on death, are wholly exempt if the funds are to be used for the maintenance, repair or preservation of historic buildings.

Gifts of UK land to housing associations are similarly exempt, whether during lifetime or on death. The gift must be made to a registered housing association.

23.8 Gifts for National Purposes (section 25)

Gifts to some national institutions such as museums, universities and the National Trust are wholly exempt, whether made during lifetime or on death.

23.9 Annual Exemption (section 19)

The annual exemption reduces the value of lifetime transfers of value. The annual exemption is £3,000 per tax year, and must be used against gifts in the chronological order in which they are made in the tax year.

Any unused annual exemption for a tax year may be carried forward for **one year only**. The current period annual exemption must be used first before taking relief for any unused brought forward exemption from the prior year.

Where two or more transfers of value are made on the same day, the annual exemption should be apportioned between the transfers in proportion to the value transferred.

There are a number of other exemptions, but these are beyond the scope of this textbook.

Questions

Review Questions
(See Suggested Solution to Review Questions at the end of this textbook.)

Question 23.1

Sean, who is domiciled in the UK, transfers property worth £1.5 million in July 2021 to his spouse, Gita, who is not domiciled in the UK and who he married in 2013. Gita had never been UK resident prior to 2013, she has a non-UK domicile of origin and is not deemed UK domiciled (for IHT purposes). In January 2023, Gita transfers some German shares valued at £200,000 to the trustees of a non-resident trust. The trust does not own any UK residential property; therefore this transfer is a transfer of excluded property. Sean dies in June 2024.

Requirement
What are the IHT consequences of the gift in July 2021? Would you advise Gita to elect to be treated as deemed UK domiciled for IHT at the time of her husband's death in 2024? Assume the nil rate band remains at £325,000 at all times.

Question 23.2

Annette, who is UK domiciled and has made no previous transfers, made the following gifts in 2021/22:

- 20 September 2021 – a plot of land, with a market value of £80,000, to her daughter Ana as a present for her forthcoming wedding.
- 20 December 2021 – cash gifts totalling £5,000 to her five grandchildren. Annette saved this cash from her surplus income over the year. She always gives her grandchildren cash as Christmas presents.
- 20 January 2022 – shares in an investment company, worth £380,000, to her husband Stefan, who is non-UK domiciled and is not deemed UK domiciled (for IHT purposes).

Requirement
Briefly explain the availability and amount of any immediate inheritance tax exemptions in relation to each of the above gifts.

Calculation of IHT Liabilities for Dispositions in Lifetime and on Death

Learning Objectives

After studying this chapter you will understand:

■ The computation of IHT liabilities and the scope of the charge, including, *inter alia*:
  ● potentially exempt transfers;
  ● chargeable lifetime transfers;
  ● the death estate;
  ● the nil rate band and the residence nil rate band;
  ● rates of IHT, including when the 36% rate is available;
  ● excluded property rules; and
  ● valuation rules.

24.1 Potentially Exempt Transfers

A potentially exempt transfer (PET) is a lifetime transfer made by an individual that will become fully exempt from IHT if the donor (i.e. the individual) survives seven years from the date of the gift. Therefore, a PET will only become a chargeable transfer if the donor dies within seven years of making the gift. This is referred to as a 'failed PET' and becomes potentially subject to IHT. If the donor dies between three and seven years after the date of the gift, then taper relief may be applied to reduce any IHT charge. PETs can also arise where an individual makes a gift to certain special types of trusts (these are beyond the scope of this textbook).

All gifts between individuals are PETs for IHT purposes. However, if the donor gives an asset away at any time but keeps an interest in it, e.g. a property in which they continue to reside rent-free, then the gift will be a PET **and** will also be a gift with reservation of benefit (see **Chapter 26**).

24.2 Chargeable Lifetime Transfers

Any transfer of value that is neither exempt nor a PET is a chargeable lifetime transfer (CLT). This includes gifts to most trusts (except certain special trust types and gifts to and from companies). Some trusts attract special tax treatment, which is beyond the scope of this textbook.

CLTs are the only occasion that can give rise to an IHT charge during the lifetime of a donor. IHT is effectively a cumulative tax and has a nil rate band (£325,000 in 2021/22 and up to 2025/26) applicable for cumulative transfers up to this limit. Therefore, IHT only becomes payable once chargeable transfers over a seven-year period exceed this threshold. The relevant nil rate band to consider is that applicable to the tax year in which the CLT is made.

Note that PETs do not affect the lifetime IHT payable, save to the extent that they use up annual exemptions that could otherwise be set against CLTs. This is because annual exemptions are used in the chronological order in which lifetime gifts are made.

The rate of IHT on any CLT in excess of the nil rate band is 20%, i.e. half the 40% rate applied to transfers on death, if the donee agrees to pay the IHT.

If responsibility is not expressly delegated to the recipient of the gift to pay the IHT due on the CLT, meaning the responsibility falls on the donor, then this CLT must be grossed-up by 20/80ths (or 25%) as the tax paid will also represent a loss in value to the donor's estate. To gross-up a lifetime gift, first deduct any available annual exemption(s) and any other exemptions or reliefs from the value transferred. Any available nil rate band is then deducted to arrive at the net transfer. This is the amount that must be grossed-up.

By law, the primary responsibility to pay IHT rests with the donor. Therefore, if the donor does not expressly delegate this responsibility to the recipient of the gift, one must assume that the donor will pay the IHT. Where this is the case, the gross gift is the value transferred (after deducting any exemptions/reliefs, **but before** deducting the available nil rate band) plus the IHT paid by the donor. It is this value that is included in the seven-year cumulation period calculation. A key principle of calculating the IHT position on a CLT, therefore, is to look back seven years for any previous CLTs that have already used part of the current CLTs nil rate band.

Example 24.1: IHT treatment of lifetime gifts

Barry gave his daughter a house on the occasion of her marriage on 12 June 2021. The house was valued at £125,000. In the previous month he gave his son £2,000, and a Celtic artifact to the National Museum that was valued at £25,000. These are the first lifetime gifts Barry has ever made.

In August 2021, Barry settled £450,000 into a discretionary trust for the benefit of his grandchildren. Barry decided to pay any IHT that fell due personally.

The gift to his son is a PET, but it uses up part of the the annual exemption for 2021/22; the gift to the museum is exempt for IHT purposes.

The gift to his daughter is also a PET. Both PETs will be subject to IHT if Barry dies within seven years. The transfer of value is:

	£
Loss to donor's estate	125,000
Less: marriage exemption	(5,000)
Less: annual exemption 2021/22 (£2,000 used up)	(1,000)
Less: annual exemption 2020/21	(3,000)
PET	116,000

The gift to the trust is a CLT and an IHT charge will arise, applied at the lifetime rate. There are no annual exemptions available but the full nil rate band is available as there have been no CLTs in the previous seven years.

	£
Transfer to trust	450,000
Less: nil rate band	(325,000)
Chargeable transfer	125,000

The net transfer must be grossed up for the loss to Barry's estate caused by him paying the IHT himself.

	£
(£125,000 × 20/80) + £125,000	156,250
IHT due @ 20%	31,250
Gross transfer (£450,000 plus £31,250)	481,250

The gross gift is important for the purposes of the seven-year accumulation for future CLTs.

24.3   Implications for IHT on Death

When an individual dies, there are three types of transfer which are chargeable to IHT:

1. PETs made within the seven years prior to death (sometimes known as 'failed PETs').
2. CLTs made by the deceased in the seven years prior to death.
3. The transfer of the estate itself on death. i.e assets to which the deceased was beneficially entitled to at the date of death.

24.4   PETs becoming Chargeable and Additional IHT on Lifetime CLTs

24.4.1   PETs becoming Chargeable on Death

When calculating any IHT due on a PET made within the seven years prior to death, it is first necessary to consider all CLTs made in the **seven years before the date of the PET**. The cumulative total of all such CLTs are deducted from the relevant nil rate band (that is, using the nil rate band applicable to the tax year of death) to arrive at the residual amount that will be available to set against the PET, which has now become a chargeable transfer because it has failed.

There is a further measure of relief (known as taper relief) given on any IHT that crystallises on a death occurring within seven years of the date of the PET. This reduces the IHT **and not** the failed PET. The longer the period between the date of gift and the date of death, the greater the rate of relief:

Time between the date the gift was made and the date of death	Taper relief percentage applied to the IHT due
Less than 3 years	Nil
3–4 years	20%
4–5 years	40%
5–6 years	60%
6–7 years	80%

24.4.2   Additional IHT on CLTs at Death

Where a CLT is made within the seven years prior to the date of death, all or part of which has been charged at the relevant lifetime rate, additional IHT may be payable on death. If no lifetime IHT had arisen on the CLT within the seven years prior to the date of death, IHT may still arise on death. This is because the IHT charge on CLTs in the seven years prior to death is recalculated at the date of death, using the full scale rate (i.e. 40%) and the nil rate band applicable at that date. The recalculation takes into account:

- other CLTs and PETs within seven years before the date of the CLT (PETs in the seven years before the CLT may not be failed PETs themselves, thus their only impact may be to use annual exemptions); and
- any failed PETs falling in the seven years before death.

The nil rate band in the year of death is used against CLTs and failed PETs in the previous seven years in strict date order.

The 36% rate of IHT is only available on the deceased's death estate (see **Section 24.7**) and not in relation to failed PETs or additional tax on CLTs on death.

Taper relief is also available on any IHT that becomes payable on death in respect of a CLT made within the last seven years. Credit is also given for any lifetime IHT paid in respect of the CLT **after** taper relief has been deducted. Note that the credit for lifetime IHT paid may reduce the IHT payable on death to £nil but **cannot** result in a refund becoming due.

Example 24.2: Taper relief for lifetime gift between three and seven years of death
Mark made the following lifetime gifts before his death on 25 April 2021:

		£
March 2009	Gift to discretionary trust	132,000
August 2014	Gift to his brother	280,000

Calculate the lifetime tax and any tax payable by Mark's brother as a consequence of his death.

(i) March 2009 – CLT

	£
Gift to discretionary trust	132,000
Less: annual exemption 2008/09	(3,000)
Less: annual exemption 2007/08	(3,000)
CLT	126,000

No lifetime IHT due as below £312,000 (the then nil rate band)

(ii) August 2014 – PET

	£
Gift to brother	280,000
Less: annual exemption 2014/15	(3,000)
Less: annual exemption 2013/14	(3,000)
PET	274,000

No lifetime tax due as a PET.

(iii) On death, any transfers occurring within the previous seven years become chargeable.

Only the PET to the brother was made within seven years prior to the date of death. However, when calculating the IHT now due on that PET, we need to take into account the effect of the CLT that was made within the seven years prior to the date of the PET.

	£	£
PET		274,000
Nil rate band at death	325,000	
Less: CLT within seven years	(126,000)	
Nil rate band available to set against PET		(199,000)
Taxable on death		75,000
IHT @ 40%		30,000
Less: taper relief (six to seven years = 80%)		(24,000)
IHT due		6,000

24.5 IHT on Estate on Death

On death, the deceased is treated as having made a final transfer of the whole of their estate. The tax charged depends on the value of the estate (ignoring any "excluded property" – see **Section 24.8**), and the effect of any CLTs and PETs made within the seven years prior to the date of death (which will utilise the nil rate band at death first). The nil rate band applying to the tax year in which the death occurs that is not used by PETs or CLTs in the seven years prior to death will be available to reduce the value of the estate chargeable to IHT. Any unused NRB can be transferred to the estate of a surviving spouse/civil partner (see **Chapter 25, Section 25.4.1**).

Any gifts out of the death estate that are exempt transfers (e.g. gift to a spouse/civil partner or gifts to a qualifying charity) are also left out of account in determining the value of the estate chargeable on death to IHT.

Important points to note in valuing the death estate:

- Only assets to which the deceased was beneficially entitled are included in the death estate. For example, if the deceased was a beneficiary of an interest in possession trust then the trust forms part of the estate and is included, whereas the proceeds of a life assurance policy where the deceased was not the beneficiary is left out of account. Note also, in relation to life assurance policies, the value to be brought into account in the estate of the beneficiary if they pre-decease the life assured individual is the open market value of the policy and not the policy surrender value.
- Assets should generally be valued at open market value, i.e. the value between a willing buyer and a willing seller (subject to special valuation rules for certain assets, which are discussed at **Section 24.9**).
- Excluded property is left out of account (see **Section 24.8**).
- Debts and liabilities are deductible from the estate if they are owed by the deceased at the date of death. Where a debt is secured on a particular asset, it is deducted from the value of that asset, whereas other debts are deducted from the estate generally. Deductible debts include debts for goods or services, income tax or CGT; gambling debts are not deductible.
- Reasonable funeral costs, including the cost of a tombstone, funeral clothes and mourning expenses are allowable.
- Executor costs of administering the estate are generally not deductible.
- The cost of administering or realising overseas assets is allowable but is limited to 5% of the asset value.

Any IHT payable on the death estate is borne by the executors and paid out of the estate. The person(s) who ultimately bears the IHT on the death estate depends on whether bequests made are 'tax-bearing' or 'tax-free'. The phrase 'tax-free' does not mean that the assets are not charged to IHT, but refers to the fact that the recipient is to receive the asset and someone else will effectively bear the IHT.

Recipients of specific gifts of non-UK assets bear the IHT unless an expression is made to the contrary in the deceased's will. Unless otherwise stated, specific gifts of UK assets out of the estate are tax-free gifts and any IHT due is to be borne out of the residue of the estate. The residue of the estate is what is left over after all specific bequests have been taken into account. It is normal practice to have a residuary beneficiary who is entitled to the residue of the estate.

The residue of the estate is, therefore, calculated after all tax-free bequests have been made. The tax on the residue of the estate is also effectively borne by the residuary legatee where the beneficiary is chargeable. This will not be the case, however, where the residuary beneficiary is non-chargeable, e.g. the residuary beneficiary is a charity or trust, or where the spouse/civil partner exemption is available.

One specific scenario requires consideration in relation to the **residue of an estate**. This is where the deceased makes tax-free specific legacies and the residue of the estate is wholly exempt. In this case the tax-free gift must be grossed-up by adding the death rate of IHT, i.e. by 40/60ths (40/100 – 40). The IHT is then computed on this gross gift and the IHT is borne out of the residue of the estate.

Note that no IHT is payable on the exempt residue; the residue available for the exempt residuary beneficiary is only being reduced by the tax payable on the tax-free specific legacy.

The total IHT borne by an estate over the total chargeable assets of the estate is a percentage, referred to as the "estate rate".

Example 24.3

Jennifer dies on 31 August 2021 leaving an estate valued at £825,000. Included in this is a UK investment property valued at £425,000, which she never lived in and leaves to her daughter. Jennifer leaves the residue of the estate to her husband. Jennifer made no lifetime transfers.

The IHT arising on Jennifer's estate is as follows:

	£
Estate on death	825,000
Less: transfer to husband – exempt	(400,000)
Transfer to daughter – chargeable	425,000
Less: nil rate band	(325,000)
Taxable estate	100,000
IHT grossed up × 40/60	66,667

Jennifer's gift to her daughter is a specific legacy, hence her daughter is deemed to receive the gift of the property plus the IHT thereon, which requires the gift to be grossed up using the 40% rate on death (i.e. × 40/100 – 40).

The gross gift to her daughter, including the IHT, is £100,000 plus £66,667 = £166,667. To check, the IHT of £66,667 should be 40% of £166,667, which it is.

Jennifer's death estate is distributed as follows:

	£
Property – to her daughter	425,000
IHT thereon – to HMRC	66,667
Remainder to residuary legatee – husband	333,333
Total estate	825,000

In this example the residuary legatee is exempt; however, the residuary legatee bears the IHT on the specific legacy to Jennifer's daughter as this is a gift of UK property and as such is tax-free.

Note that no IHT is payable by Jennifer's husband on the exempt residue; the residue available to him is only being reduced by the tax payable on the tax-free specific legacy of the property to her daughter.

Example 24.4: IHT treatment of death estate with prior lifetime gifts

Greg died on 19 October 2021 and left his estate of £750,000 to be divided equally between his wife and two children.

His only lifetime gift had been when he settled £350,000 into a discretionary trust in December 2014. Greg paid the IHT due on the gift so that the full value of the gift was available for the purposes of the trust's objectives.

continued overleaf

Calculate the IHT payable on the death of Greg.

(i) CLT (in lifetime)

	£
Gift to discretionary trust	350,000
Less: annual exemption 2014/15	(3,000)
Less: annual exemption 2013/14	(3,000)
CLT	344,000
Less: nil rate band for 2014/15	(325,000)
Taxable transfer	19,000
IHT on grossed-up transfer £19,000 + (19,000 × (20/80))	23,750
IHT @ 20%	4,750

CLT for cumulation = £344,000 + £4,750 = £348,750

(ii) Additional tax due on CLT at death

	£
CLT	348,750
Less: nil rate band for 2021/22	(325,000)
Taxable transfer	23,750
IHT @ 40%	9,500
Less: taper relief at 80% (six to seven years)	(7,600)
IHT due	1,900
Less: tax paid on lifetime gift	(4,750)
IHT due on CLT at death	NIL

No refund can be obtained of lifetime tax paid on CLT.

(iii) Tax on death estate

		£
Death estate		750,000
Less: exempt transfer (one-third to spouse)		(250,000)
Chargeable estate		500,000
Nil rate band 2021/22	325,000	
Less: CLTs within seven years	(348,750)	
Remaining nil rate band		NIL
Taxable estate		500,000
IHT @ 40%		200,000

24.6   Main Residence Nil Rate Band

The residence nil rate band (RNRB) is available for interests in a residential property, which has been the deceased's residence at some point, and which is included in their estate and left to one or more direct descendants on death. A direct descendant is a child (including a step-child, adopted child or foster child) of the deceased and their lineal descendants (e.g. grandchildren). The qualifying residential interest is limited to one residential property, but personal representatives can nominate which residential property should qualify if there is more than one in the estate.

The value of the RNRB for an estate is the lower of:

- the net value of the interest in the residential property (after deducting any liabilities, such as a mortgage); or
- the maximum amount of the RNRB, depending on the tax year of death.

The applicable value of the RNRB should be deducted before the nil rate band.

The RNRB is available for qualifying transfers on death on or after 6 April 2017. It reduces the tax payable by an estate on death only and therefore is generally not available to reduce IHT payable on lifetime transfers that are chargeable as a result of death because of the seven-year look-back rule, either for failed PETs or CLTs. However, the RNRB may be available against a single residence gifted in lifetime that is part of the deceased's estate on death by virtue of the 'gift with reservation of benefit' rules (see **Chapter 26, Section 26.3**), subject to the remaining conditions for accessing the RNRB being met.

Any unused RNRB can be transferred to the estate of a surviving spouse/civil partner where that spouse/civil partner dies on or after 6 April 2017, irrespective of when the first spouse/civil partner died (see **Chapter 25, Section 25.4.2**).

The maximum level of the RNRB was phased in as follows:

- 2017/2018 – £100,000
- 2018/2019 – £125,000
- 2019/2020 – £150,000
- 2020/2021 – £175,000

The legislation also includes a tapered withdrawal of the RNRB for estates with a net value of more than £2 million. If the net value of the estate (defined as after deduction of any liabilities but before reliefs and exemptions) is above £2 million, then for every £2 over the £2 million threshold, £1 of the RNRB is withdrawn.

Example 24.5
John dies on 29 June 2021 leaving an estate worth £1 million, including the home he owned and lived in all his life. At the date of his death, his home is worth £435,000. He leaves the home to his daughter, Zoe, and the remainder of his estate to his wife, Margot. John made no lifetime gifts.

John's inheritance tax position is as follows:

	£
Estate	1,000,000
Less: exempt legacy to spouse	(565,000)
	435,000
Less: residence nil rate band 2021/22	175,000
Less: nil rate band 2021/22	260,000
Chargeable estate	Nil

£65,000 of John's NRB has not been used. This represents 20% of his NRB, which can be transferred to his wife's estate on her death (see **Chapter 25, Section 25.4.1**).

The RNRB rules also provide that, where part of the RNRB might be lost because the deceased downsized to a less valuable residence before their death or ceased to own a residence on or after 8 July 2015, the "lost" part will still be available provided the deceased left that smaller residence, or assets of an equivalent value, to direct descendants. The "lost" part reinstated is known as the additional RNRB. However, the total amount available cannot exceed the maximum RNRB in the tax year of death (see **Chapter 25**, **Section 25.4.1**).

The qualifying conditions for the additional RNRB are broadly the same as those for the RNRB. These are as follows:

- the individual dies on or after 6 April 2017;
- the property disposed of must have been owned by the individual and it would have qualified for the RNRB had the individual retained it;
- less valuable property, or other assets of an equivalent value if the property has been disposed of, are in the deceased's estate; and
- less valuable property, and any other assets of an equivalent value, are inherited by the individual's direct descendants on that person's death.

24.7   36% Rate of Inheritance Tax

A reduced rate of IHT is available on death estates where a minimum level of legacy has been left by the deceased to a qualifying charity. 'Charity' has the normal meaning for IHT purposes, and includes registered community amateur sports clubs and organisations in the European Economic Area that are recognised by HMRC as being a charity for tax purposes. The 36% reduced rate of IHT only applies to charges that arise on death. The actual legacy to charity remains exempt from IHT and, subject to meeting the qualifying conditions, the rate of IHT payable in respect of the remainder of the estate is reduced from 40% to 36%.

In order to qualify for the reduced rate, at least 10% of the net value of the estate must be left to the charity. For the purposes of the 36% rate, the net value of the estate is the sum of all the assets after deducting any debts, liabilities, reliefs, exemptions and the nil rate band, but **excluding** relief for the charitable legacy itself.

Example 24.6
Hugo died on 30 April 2021 leaving an estate valued at £600,000 after the deduction of liabilities. He leaves £35,000 to the National Trust in his will.

	£
Estate (net of liabilities)	600,000
Less: nil rate band	(325,000)
Baseline amount	275,000
Baseline amount @10%	27,500

Legacy qualifies as it exceeds 10% of baseline amount.

Inheritance tax payable:

Baseline amount from above	275,000
Less: exempt gift to National Trust	(35,000)
Taxable estate	240,000
Inheritance tax @ 36%	86,400

Example 24.7

John died on 31 August 2021 leaving an estate valued at £850,000 after deduction of liabilities. He leaves £65,000 to the NSPCC in his will. His only lifetime gift was a gift of £250,000 cash to his daughter in July 2015. Because this gift had been made less than seven years before he died it must be taken into account in working out the IHT payable on his estate.

July 2015 – PET

	£
Gift to daughter	250,000
Less: annual exemption 2015/16	(3,000)
Less: annual exemption 2014/15	(3,000)
PET	244,000

	£	£
Estate (net of liabilities)		850,000
Less: nil rate band	325,000	
PET	(244,000)	
Available nil rate band		(81,000)
Baseline amount		769,000
Baseline amount @ 10%		76,900

The legacy does not qualify as it is less than 10% of the baseline amount.

Inheritance tax payable:

	£
Baseline amount (from above)	769,000
Less: exempt gift to NSPCC	(65,000)
Taxable estate	704,000
IHT @ 40%	281,600

Can anything be done to take advantage of the 36% rate?

The beneficiaries of this estate could choose to increase the charitable donation by another £11,900 by making an "Instrument of Variation" (see **Chapter 28**) so that the 10% baseline amount test is passed. This would mean IHT could be paid at the 36% reduced rate resulting in IHT of £249,156 ((£769,000 − £76,900) × 36%) rather than £281,600. This is a tax saving of £32,444, which will cover the additional payment to charity.

24.8 Excluded Property

The term "excluded property" is a technical term used to refer to certain types of property that are, subject to certain conditions, outside the scope of IHT. The most common examples of excluded property are:

1. Property situated outside the UK, where the person beneficially entitled to the property is domiciled outside the UK and is not deemed UK domiciled for IHT purposes.
2. Settled property, where the settlor was domiciled outside the UK when the settlement was made. However, where the settlor of property in a trust is not UK domiciled at the time the settlement is made, the property will not be excluded property at any time in the tax year if the settlor is a formerly domiciled resident in that tax year. This means that the trust property is not excluded property and is therefore subject to UK IHT. As a result, trusts established when non-UK domi-

ciled are not protected from UK IHT while the settlor is classed as a formerly domiciled resident (see **Chapter 22, Section 22.3.1**, point 4).

Property situated outside the UK is not excluded property if it is UK residential property owned indirectly (e.g. via a company or partnership) by the non-UK domiciled individual (who is not deemed UK domiciled for IHT purposes), or by the trustees of trusts that they have created. Therefore IHT on such assets may arise for non-UK domiciled or deemed domiciled individuals.

The calculation of the value of property that is not excluded property under this rule is the extent to which the open market value of an interest in either:

- a foreign close company (same definition as for corporation tax, see **Chapter 9**), or
- a foreign partnership,

is directly or indirectly attributable to the value of UK residential property.

For these purposes, UK residential property is defined as an interest in UK land that consists of or includes a dwelling, and replicates the definition under the non-UK resident capital gains regime (see **Chapter 17, Section 17.10**).

The property will remain excluded property if:

1. the value of the interest in the close company is less than 5% of the total value; or
2. the value of the interest in the partnership is less than 5% of the total value.

In determining whether the 'less than 5%' test is met, the value of the person's interest is increased by the value of any connected person's interest in the close company or partnership.

Assets added to a trust by individuals domiciled in the UK to trusts made when they were not UK domiciled are not excluded property.

Where property is transferred between trusts, its status depends on the current domicile of the settlor (or other person) that caused the property to move to the other trust. Should the settlor still be non-UK domiciled or not deemed domiciled for IHT purposes, the property will remain excluded property.

Example 24.8

Claude has been UK resident since July 2014. His domicile of origin is France where he was also born. Claude made a gift of an investment property in Bordeaux to his daughter Elaine in July 2015. He made no use of the property after the date of the gift. Claude became UK domiciled in January 2016 and died in March 2022.

As Claude was not UK domiciled/deemed domiciled at the date of the transfer, the property is excluded from IHT and consequently there is no PET in July 2015 and, even though death was within seven years of the date of the gift, the property is not included in valuing Claude's death estate in March 2022. In addition, the property is not a UK residential property in which he holds an indirect interest, it thus remains an excluded property.

Example 24.9

Leon and his two friends, Saoirse and Peter, are domiciled and resident in Ireland where they were born and have always lived and worked. Together they own the entire share capital of an Irish resident company currently valued at £2 million. Leon owns 51% of the shares, Peter owns 45% and Saoirse owns the remaining 4%.

The company owns a valuable freehold residential property in London, which currently has an open market value of £1 million.

On 20 June 2022, while attending a business conference, Peter and Saoirse are both killed in an accident.

continued overleaf

Despite being a non-UK domicile, the value of Peter's shares in the non-resident company is not wholly excluded property – 50% (£1 million/£2 million) of the value of his 45% shareholding is indirectly derived from UK residential property. Therefore £450,000 of the £900,000 value of his shares (£2 million × 45%) will fall within his death estate and is potentially subject to IHT, subject to any available reliefs or exemptions. As Peter was not UK domiciled or deemed UK domiciled for IHT purposes, double tax relief would not be available in the UK for any IHT (or equivalent) that Peter may be required to pay in Ireland.

The entire value of Saoirse's 4% shareholding is excluded property as she holds less than 5% in the foreign close company, despite 50% of the value of her shares being attributed to UK residential property.

If Leon and Saoirse were married or in a civil partnership, the attribution of Leon's 51% shareholding would mean that she would fail the less than 5% test and £40,000 (50% of the value of her 4% shareholding (£2 million × 4%)) would fall within her death estate and be potentially subject to IHT, subject to any available reliefs or exemptions.

Again, as Saoirse is not UK domiciled or deemed UK domiciled for IHT purposes, double tax relief would not be available in the UK for any IHT (or equivalent) that Saoirse may be required to pay in Ireland.

24.9 Valuation of Certain Assets

24.9.1 Quoted Shares and Unit Trusts

The process for valuing quoted shares is relatively straightforward: the stock exchange official closing price for the shares on the date of transfer/death is used. If a range of closing prices is provided, then the lower of the two values is used. The first is calculated using the 'quarter up' rule – meaning that the lowest closing price is taken and added to a quarter of the difference between the lowest and highest closing price. The second value is the average of the highest and lowest normal marked bargains recorded on that day. The price used for the valuation of the quoted shares is the lower of these two values. Contrast this with the valuation rule for CGT purposes for quoted shares (see **Chapter 16**, **Section 16.3.4**).

The process for valuing unit trusts is to take the lower of the two prices provided by the fund managers for the relevant date, i.e. the date of transfer/death.

Example 24.10: Valuation of quoted shares and unit trusts
Blake has the following assets in his death estate:

> 100,000 shares in Aviva Plc

> 6,000 units in the Meridian Unit Trust

On the day Blake died, the *Financial Times* reported Aviva Plc's bid price as 23p, an offer price of 35p with marked bargains at 24p, 29p, and a special marked bargain at 33p.

The fund managers of Meridian Unit Trust provided the following information for the date of death:

Bid price 117p

Offer price 121p

The assets will be valued as follows in the death estate:

Aviva Plc shares at the lower of the quarter up rule and the average of highest and lowest marked bargains (ignoring any special bargains):

> Quarter up = $(23 + (35 - 23) \times ¼) = 26$

> Average of normal bargains = $(24 + 29)/2 = 26.50$

So value of Aviva shares = $100,000 \times 26p = £26,000$

Units in Meridian using the lower of the two prices: $6,000 \times 117p = £7,020$

24.9.2 Unquoted Shares

Unquoted shares, by their very nature, do not have a readily ascertainable market value. It is therefore often necessary to agree a value for unquoted shares with the Share Valuation Division of HMRC. It is important to note that the value of unquoted shares usually increases disproportionately as the number of shares held increases. This is due to the fact that the ability to influence and, eventually, to control decisions made by the company increases at certain percentage holdings in the company. For example, at:

- less than 20%
- 51% or more
- more than 75%
- more than 90%
- 100% total ownership.

The relevant price to be used will be given in examples and questions. However, it may also be necessary to consider how the value is affected by the percentage of the shareholding held by the donor's related property, in addition to the loss in value to the donor as a result of reducing their shareholding. The related property value should be used only if it produces a higher price (see **Chapter 22, Section 22.2.1**).

24.9.3 Life Insurance Policies

Lifetime transfers of life insurance policies are valued at the greater of the surrender value or the premiums paid. If someone takes out a policy on their own life and has it written in trust for the benefit of someone else, then each premium payment is a transfer of value and will be a PET unless it falls within an exemption (e.g. small gifts or normal expenditure out of income or the annual exemption).

When the life-assured individual dies, the proceeds of the policy is payable to the person who owns the policy or to some other person specified under its terms. The maturity value of a policy taken out by the deceased on his own life will be included in his estate. If a policy has been assigned to another person during the deceased's lifetime, this is treated as a lifetime transfer.

24.9.4 Jointly Owned Property

Where a property is owned jointly by a married couple/civil partners, the value of the property is equivalent to the proportion of ownership to the total value of the asset. So, if two spouses each own 50% of a property worth £200,000, then that property would have a value of £100,000 for each of them.

Where the joint owners are not married or in a civil partnership, then it is possible to make a deduction from the proportionate value based on the ownership percentage of between 5–15%. For the purposes of this textbook, assume a deduction of 10%. Using the example above, the value for each of the owners if not married would be £90,000 (i.e. £100,000 less 10%). The reason for this deduction is that the property must be valued on a standalone basis and a purchaser is less likely to buy a share in an asset that is part-owned by a third party.

24.9.5 Joint Tenants versus Tenants in Common

It is important to appreciate the distinction in holding property as joint tenants or as tenants in common. Property held by joint tenants automatically reverts to the fellow joint tenant (under the law of survivorship) whereas tenants in common can each gift their part of the property as they see fit. Joint tenants are always treated as having a joint and equal share to the whole property, whereas ownership between tenants in common does not have to be split equally.

24.10 Pro Forma Computation to Calculate Value of a Death Estate

Death estate of Mr X who died on …

	£	£	£
Stocks and shares			X
Insurance policy proceeds			X
Personal chattels			X
Cash (including accrued interest net of tax)			X
Accrued income from interest in possession trusts (net of tax), etc…			X
			X
Less:			
Debts due from deceased estate		(X)	
Funeral expenses		(X)	(X)
			X
UK property	X		
Less: mortgage	(X)	X	
Foreign property	X		
Less: mortgage	(X)		
Less: expenses of realisation (max. 5%)	(X)	X	X
Net estate			X
Gifts with reservation			X
Chargeable estate			X

All workings for reliefs, valuation calculations, etc. (e.g. business property relief (BPR), agricultural property relief (APR), post-mortem relief, etc., for which see **Chapter 25**) should be shown as separate workings and referenced to the pro forma computation with supporting explanations provided.

Questions

Review Questions
(See Suggested Solutions to Review Questions at the end of this textbook.)

Question 24.1

Fredrick gave £400,000 in cash to a discretionary trust on 6 April 2018. This was his first gift of any kind.

Requirement
What inheritance tax is due, and on whom does the liability fall? Would any additional inheritance tax be due on the gift if Fredrick died on 10 April 2021 without making any further gifts? If so, how much?

Reliefs

25.1 Business Property Relief (sections 103–114)

Business property relief (BPR) is available to reduce the amount chargeable to IHT on certain business assets for both lifetime and death transfers. This includes gifts to a trust. The relief is given before annual exemptions in the case of lifetime transfers so that these are not unnecessarily wasted.

BPR on lifetime transfers is calculated as follows:

	£
Value transferred	X
Less: **BPR @ 50%/100%***	(X)
	X
Less: annual exemptions	(X)
Transfer	X

* This may also be less than 100% if the excepted assets rules restricts BPR (see **Section 25.1.2**). For lifetime gifts, if 100% BPR is available, clearly the annual exemption(s) is not used.

If an individual dies and their estate includes relevant business property, BPR is also given as a deduction in the estate when calculating death tax.

There is no need to claim the relief if it is due, as it is given automatically if the relevant conditions are satisfied. The assets transferred must be **relevant business property** for BPR to be available. There are, however, no territorial restrictions, which means BPR is available on worldwide relevant business property. The relief is generally only available on the transfer of a business or an interest in a business/partnership and is generally not available on the transfer of a single business asset.

The following are relevant business properties together with the applicable rate of BPR:

1.	A business or an interest in a business.	100%
2.	Shares in an unquoted trading company (no minimum holding).	100%
3.	Securities (loan stock) in an unquoted company where the company is controlled by the donor (i.e. where the donor holds more than 50% of the voting rights). Securities for BPR purposes do therefore not include directors' loan accounts.	100%
4.	Shares and securities in a quoted company where the donor controls the company (i.e. more than 50% of the voting rights). It is very unusual for an individual to hold more than 50% of the shares of a quoted company, so in the majority of cases quoted shares will **not** qualify for BPR.	50%
5.	Any land or building, machinery or plant owned outside the business which, for the two years before the transfer, was used wholly or mainly for the purposes of a business carried on by a company of which the transferor then had control or by a partnership of which the individual then was a partner. Note that such assets used in a sole trade owned by the transferor do **not** qualify for BPR.	50%
6.	Land, buildings, plant and machinery owned outside of the business, where they are used in the donor's business and held in a trust that the donor has a right to benefit from (as a beneficiary of an interest in possession trust).	50%

AIM-listed shares are treated as unquoted for the purposes of BPR.

BPR is not available if:

- The business or company is involved wholly or mainly in dealing in shares, land or buildings, or in the making or holding investments.
- The business is not carried on with a view to making a profit.
- The business is the subject of a binding contract for sale, unless that sale is to a company that will continue the business, and the sale is made wholly or mainly in consideration of shares in the acquiring company, e.g. on incorporation where a sole trade or partnership is transferred to a company.

25.1.1 Ownership

General Rule

The general rule is that property is not relevant business property for the purposes of BPR unless it has been held for a minimum of two years at the date of the lifetime or death transfer. Generally, if the property has not been held for this minimum period, then no BPR is due.

Exceptions to the General Rule

There are a number of exceptions to the two-year general rule for specific circumstances.

1. Where the transfer occurs between spouses on death – if the transferor became entitled to the property on the death of a spouse or civil partner, then relief is available for any period during which the deceased spouse or civil partner also owned it. This has the effect of aggregating the period of ownership between spouses/civil partners where there has been a transfer on death and allows BPR where the combined ownership period meets the two-year test (section 108).

   However, section 108 allows the periods to be aggregated only if the donor and the donee are married, **and** the transfer by the donor to the donee was made on death. This is the only time that the ownership period of the donor and the donee can be added together.

Example 25.1

James owns 20% of the shares in Driver Ltd, an unquoted trading company, and has done so since 1 April 2017. James died on 1 April 2021, leaving his entire estate to his wife Jane. On 1 December 2021, Jane gifted the Driver Ltd shares to a discretionary trust when the shares were worth £400,000.

Even though the two-year ownership period is not met, BPR is still available on the CLT of the shares to the discretionary trust. Although Jane only owned the relevant business property in Driver Ltd for eight months, when this ownership period is combined with the ownership period of her husband, the combined ownership period meets the two-year test because Jane became entitled to the Driver Ltd shares on the death of her spouse.

---

2. Where there are successive transfers in a two-year period – if the transferred property was acquired by way of an earlier transfer within the two-year period, then relief will still be available if the following conditions are met:

   (a) The earlier transfer qualified for BPR.
   (b) The earlier transfer was made to the current transferor or spouse or civil partner.
   (c) At least one of the transfers was made on a death.
   (d) The property would, apart from the two-year rule, qualify for BPR.

Example 25.2: BPR and successive transfers

Brian received 60% of the shares in Zee Ltd, a qualifying unquoted company, under the will of Charles, who died on 1 December 2020 and had held the shares for 20 years. The 60% holding attracted 100% business property relief on Charles's death estate.

On 1 February 2022, Brian transfers the 60% holding in Zee Ltd to a discretionary trust.

In this instance, rule 2 applies as:

(a) The earlier transfer from Charles to Brian qualified for BPR.

(b) The earlier transfer was made to the current transferor, Brian.

(c) At least one of the transfers was made on a death, being the earlier transfer from Charles to Brian.

(d) Except for the two-year test, the property would qualify for BPR.

BPR is therefore still available on this CLT.

---

3. Where old business property is sold and replaced with new business property. This applies if a donor sells business property and replaces it with other business property within three years, BPR will be available if the replacement asset is subsequently transferred and the aggregated ownership periods, i.e. the period of time during which both the old and new property was owned totals at least two of the five years immediately preceding the transfer. However, BPR on the replacement asset cannot exceed the BPR that would have been available on the original asset. In addition, only the relevant proportion of the proceeds from the sale of the first business property reinvested in the replacement business property will qualify.

Example 25.3: BPR and replacement property

On 1 March 2020, Sarah sold her shareholding (which she had held for 10 years) in Brandon Ltd, a qualifying unquoted company. On 1 February 2021, using the total proceeds from the sale of these shares, she bought a holding of shares in Tritan Ltd, another qualifying unquoted trading company.

Sarah died on 1 October 2021.

Business property relief is still available on the Tritan Ltd shares included in Sarah's death estate even though the two-year period is not met. Although she only owned the replacement business property in Tritan Ltd for eight months, when this ownership period is combined with the ownership period of her Brandon Ltd shares, the combined ownership period is two years out of the previous five. Sarah also purchased the replacement business property within three years.

If Sarah had only reinvested 50% of the proceeds from the sale of her Brandon Ltd shares in the Tritan Ltd shares, then only 50% business property relief would be available.

25.1.2 Excepted Assets

The BPR available on shares is restricted where the company holds "**excepted assets**" on its statement of financial position.

An excepted asset is one not used for business purposes throughout the two-year period preceding a transfer, or is not intended to be used in the future for the purposes of the business (i.e. a trading business or trading activity). Items that are held for investment purposes, e.g. investment properties and share investments, are excepted assets for BPR purposes, as are assets used wholly or mainly for the personal benefit of the transferor or a person connected with the transferor. A large cash deposit held for investment purposes and not required for future use in the business would also be classed as an excepted asset.

BPR is restricted to that proportion of the total assets of a company that the relevant business assets represent, i.e.:

$$\text{BPR} = \text{Gift} \times \frac{\text{Total assets} - \text{Excepted assets}}{\text{Total assets}}$$

Example 25.4: BPR and shares

Jack owned all of the shares in Gravy Ltd, an unlisted company mainly engaged in a catering trade, since 2002. He died on 4 August 2021 and left the shares, worth £620,000, to his nephew Willis. He has held the shares for a number of years and the statement of financial position of the company is as follows:

	£
Factory	350,000
Plant	75,000
Investments	45,000
Quoted shares	15,000
Net assets	485,000

As the investments and the quoted shares are excepted assets, BPR relief is calculated as follows, assuming that the balance of the value relates to the trading goodwill:

100% × £620,000 × ((£620,000 − £45,000 − £15,000)/£620,000) = £560,000 BPR available

---

It should be noted that if the excepted assets represent more than 50% of the total assets, HMRC may completely deny BPR on the grounds that the business is mainly an investment business. This is on the basis that the business must be wholly (i.e. 100%) or mainly (i.e. at least 51%) carrying on a business that is not an investment business and is not of the type excluded.

25.1.3 BPR on Lifetime Gifts Following Death

Chargeable Lifetime Transfers

Where BPR is given on a chargeable lifetime transfer (CLT) of value, it is not always the case that the relief continues to be available where the donor dies within seven years of the gift. In certain circumstances, normally where the donee has either sold or given away the business property, the relief may be withdrawn. The relief will also be withdrawn if the property no longer qualifies as business property.

The relief will **not be** withdrawn if the business property has been sold but has been replaced by other qualifying business property. As set out earlier, the replacement business property must be purchased within three years of the disposal of the old business property and the whole of the original proceeds of sale of the old property must be reinvested.

Where BPR is withdrawn, it increases the tax payable by the donee as a consequence of the donor's death within seven years of the gift. It does not alter the IHT position at the point of the actual lifetime transfer. Similarly, it does not affect the calculation of the donor's cumulative lifetime transfers for the purposes of using up the nil rate band available at the date of death, i.e. BPR remains available on the original CLT.

Potentially Exempt Transfers

There can be no withdrawal of BPR on a potentially exempt transfers (PETs) as there is no lifetime tax charge on a PET, hence BPR will not have been claimed.

If a PET becomes chargeable as a result of the death of the donor within seven years of the date of the PET, then BPR will be a consideration.

If the donee still owns the business property at the date of death, then BPR may be available if the other conditions were met at the date of the gift. If the donee has sold the business property before the death of the donor, then no BPR will be available to reduce the IHT charge, unless the proceeds of the sale have been reinvested into replacement business property. If the property no longer qualifies as relevant business property at the date of death, then BPR will not be available. An example would be on the transfer of unquoted shares in a company that become listed on a stock exchange before the date of death.

Example 25.5

Barney gave his shares in an unquoted trading company to his sister Eileen in July 2015 when they were worth £400,000. This was his only lifetime gift. Eileen sold the shares on 1 July 2016 and used the proceeds to buy a holiday home in Florida. Barney died in September 2021.

Calculate the IHT payable by Eileen in respect of the shares on the death of Barney.

	£
Gift in July 2015	400,000
Less: annual exemption 2015/16	(3,000)
Less: annual exemption 2014/15	(3,000)
	394,000

continued overleaf

Less: nil rate band applying at date of death	(325,000)
Chargeable to IHT	69,000
IHT @ 40%	27,600
Less: taper relief (80% 6–7 years)	(22,080)
IHT payable	5,520

BPR cannot be claimed as the property no longer qualified at the date of Barney's death (because Eileen had disposed of it and not replaced it with relevant business property at Barney's date of death). As the original gift was a PET and no lifetime tax was due, the annual exemptions are not displaced by the BPR that might otherwise have been available.

Example 25.6

Using the same facts from **Example 25.5**, but assuming that instead of selling the shares in July 2015, Eileen still owns them at the date of Barney's death. The company is now wholly an investment company and the shares are worth £900,000.

The IHT payable by Eileen in respect of the shares on the death of Barney is.

	£
Gift in July 2015	400,000
Less: annual exemption 2015/16	(3,000)
Less: annual exemption 2014/15	(3,000)
	394,000
Less: nil rate band applying at date of death	(325,000)
Chargeable to IHT	69,000
IHT @ 40%	27,600
Less: taper relief (80% 6–7 years)	(22,080)
IHT payable	5,520

BPR cannot be claimed as the property no longer qualifies as relevant business property at the date of Barney's death (because the company is wholly an investment company). As the original gift was a PET and no lifetime tax was due, the annual exemptions are not displaced by the BPR that might otherwise have been available.

Although the shares are now worth £900,000, the failed PET is still valued at £400,000. This would also have been the case if the shares had instead been gifted to trust and was no longer a relevant business property.

Gifts of Assets Used in an Individual's Company or Partnership

BPR is always withdrawn where the transfer qualifying for BPR was of an asset used in an individual's business. This is because the fall in value of the individual's estate is attributable to the fall in value of the business as a result of the transfer of the asset, and therefore the fall in value is attributable to relevant business property. However, on the death of the transferor, the individual asset is not by itself relevant business property of the transferee and BPR is therefore no longer available.

Example 25.7

Peter, a sole trader, transfers a property used in his trade to a trust in July 2019 when the property is worth £750,000. This is his only lifetime gift. Peter dies in April 2024 when the property is worth £1,100,000.

On Peter's death, no tax is payable on this CLT in lifetime, as the value of the transfer is attributable to relevant business property, it being his sole trade. Therefore 100% BPR is available.

The IHT payable by the trust in respect of the property on the death of Peter is.

	£
Gift in July 2019	750,000
Less: annual exemption 2019/20	(3,000)
Less: annual exemption 2018/19	(3,000)
	744,000
Less: nil rate band applying at date of death	(325,000)
Chargeable to IHT	419,000
IHT @ 40%	167,600
Less: taper relief (40% 4–5 years)	(67,040)
IHT payable	100,560

BPR cannot be claimed as the property no longer qualifies as relevant business property at the date of Peter's death.

As Peter dies within seven years, BPR will not be available as the property by itself is not relevant business property.

As the original gift was a PET and no lifetime tax was due, the annual exemptions are not displaced by the BPR that might otherwise have been available.

Although the property is now worth £1,100,000, the failed PET is still valued at £750,000. This would also have been the case if the shares had instead been gifted to trust.

25.2 Agricultural Property Relief (sections 115–124C)

Agricultural property relief (APR) works in a similar manner to BPR. It is available for gifts of farmland and farm buildings (including farmhouses) during lifetime or on death. This includes gifts to a trust. Farm machinery and farm animals are not qualifying APR assets; however these may qualify instead for BPR. The relief is again given before the annual exemptions but before BPR is applied for lifetime transfers. For assets that qualify for both reliefs, APR again takes precedence over BPR.

APR on lifetime transfers is calculated as follows:

	£
Value transferred	X
Less: **APR @ 50%/100%** *	(X)
	X
Less: BPR	(X)
	X
Less: annual exemptions	(X)
Transfer	X

* For lifetime gifts, if 100% APR is available and the remaining element is covered by BPR, clearly the annual exemption(s) is not used.

If an individual dies and their estate includes agricultural property, APR is also given as a deduction in the estate when calculating death tax. The relief is also automatic where the relevant conditions are met and no formal claim is required.

APR is available where the farm is situated in the UK, Channel Islands, Isle of Man or the European Economic Area (i.e. all EU countries plus Norway, Iceland and Liechtenstein).

The relief is available to shelter the **agricultural** value of the property which is **normally less than its market value or development value**. The agricultural value is the value of the land on the basis that it can only be used for farming.

The relief is available to a farmer who owns farmland and uses it in a farming business, or to a landowner who lets the land to a farmer who uses it for farming purposes.

APR is given at the rate of 100% of the agricultural value of the land, except in one very precise circumstance. APR is given at the rate of 50% where all of the following conditions are met:

- the land is let to a farmer;
- the lease was signed before 1 September 1995; and
- there is still more than two years left to run on the lease at the date of the lifetime/death transfer.

If any one of these conditions is not met, then 100% APR is due on the agricultural value, even if the land is let to a farmer.

25.2.1 Ownership

Generally, the land must be owned for the two years immediately preceding the transfer for APR to be available. This is increased to seven years where the land is let to a farmer.

As with BPR, if the land is sold and replaced by other qualifying land, then the combined period of ownership must be at least two out of the last five years for APR to be available. Where the land is let, the relevant period is seven out of the last 10 years.

The BPR rule that allows ownership periods to be aggregated where property passes from one spouse to another on death, similarly applies for APR purposes. Likewise, APR is also available in respect of successive transfers (see **Section 25.1.1,** point 2.).

Where a farmer runs a farming business, BPR may be available to cover any market value not otherwise covered by APR. This is often the case where the farmland has clear development value.

APR is also available to the controlling shareholder in a company that owns agricultural land. The relief is calculated with reference to the percentage of the agricultural value of the land to the total value of the company. BPR should then be considered in relation to the remaining value.

APR is also available for farmhouses/farm cottages as long as they are of an appropriate character in relation to the property. The occupation of the property must be in connection with the farming business and it should be normal for the land to include a dwelling of the type concerned.

The rules on withdrawal of BPR following the death of the donor noted above are also applicable to APR lifetime transfers falling into the death estate.

Example 25.8

The Viscount of Antrim owns a significant holding of farmland, which he lets to a local farmer who uses it mainly for growing potatoes. The lease on the property was granted in 1985 for a term of 40 years.

continued overleaf

In June 2018 he gave his daughter, Lady Penelope, 150 acres on the occasion of her marriage. The land had a market value of £2,400,000 and an agricultural value of £2,250,000.

The Viscount died in October 2021 and had made no other gifts in the seven years preceding his death.

Calculate the IHT payable by Lady Penelope on the Viscount's death on the basis that she still holds the land.

	£
Gift	2,400,000
Less: APR @ 50% (£2.25m × 50%)	(1,125,000)
	1,275,000
Less: marriage exemption	(5,000)
Less: annual exemption 2018/19	(3,000)
Less: annual exemption 2017/18	(3,000)
PET	1,264,000
Less: nil rate band at death	(325,000)
Taxable transfer	939,000
IHT @ 40%	375,600
Less: taper relief (3 to 4 years = 20%)	(75,120)
IHT payable	300,480

The APR was 50% in this example as:

▦ it was tenanted land;
▦ the lease was granted pre-1 September 1995; and
▦ the lease still had more than two years left to run.

BPR is not available on the remainder as the land was let and not farmed by its owner.

25.3 Quick Succession Relief (section 141)

Quick succession relief (QSR) is intended to alleviate situations where the same assets are subject to IHT twice within a relatively short period of time (five years). Where a donee dies after their estate has been increased by a chargeable transfer, tax may be due on the increased estate and may have already been charged on the earlier transfer. Where the death of the donee occurs within five years of the earlier transfer, QSR may be claimed. QSR is available for a transfer on death or for a PET that becomes chargeable due to the death of the original donor within seven years of the earlier transfer. If the time period is less than one year, 100% QSR will be available and this reduces by 20% for each additional year that passes between the date of the first and second death.

Years between transfer and death	Percentage relief
Up to 1 year	100%
More than 1 but no more than 2	80%
More than 2 but not more than 3	60%
More than 3 but not more than 4	40%
More than 4 but not more than 5	20%

The formula for calculating the available QSR is as follows:

$$\frac{\text{Previous transfer net of tax}}{\text{Previous gross transfer}} \times \text{Tax paid on previous transfer} \times \text{QSR \%}$$

The reason for the "tax paid on previous transfer" part of the formula is to take account of whether the gift had to bear its own tax or whether it was "tax-free". Unless specified to the contrary, gifts of UK assets do not bear their own tax whilst gifts of non-UK assets do bear their own tax. Where gifts do not bear their own tax, any IHT due is paid out of the residue of the estate (see **Chapter 24, Section 24.5**).

It is also important to note that QSR is available even if the donee has sold or disposed of the asset prior to death. This is because QSR is available if an individual's estate has been increased by a chargeable transfer in any of the five preceding years.

Example 25.9

Frank died on 3 April 2019 and left his entire estate valued at £554,000 to his cousin Vinny. Frank had made a gift of £126,000 to his best friend in the month before he died.

Vinny died in July 2021 leaving an estate of £625,000.

Step 1: Calculate the IHT due on Frank's estate

	£
Death estate	554,000
Less: nil rate band (Note)	(205,000)
Net taxable estate	349,000
IHT due @ 40%	139,600

Note: Nil-rate band

	£
Lifetime gift	126,000
Less: annual exemption 2018/19	(3,000)
annual exemption 2017/18	(3,000)
	120,000
Nil rate band	325,000
Utilised	(120,000)
Available	205,000

Step 2: Calculate the IHT due on Vinny's estate

	£
Death estate	625,000
Less: nil rate band	(325,000)
Chargeable estate	300,000
IHT @ 40%	120,000
Less: QSR: $\dfrac{£414,400^*}{£414,400 + £139,600} \times 139,600 \times 60\%$	(62,654)
IHT due	57,346

*Being £554,000 – £139,600.

Vinny received the value of Frank's estate less the IHT due on this. The increase to his own estate as a result of the transfer is therefore the net of these amounts.

25.4 Reliefs for Surviving Spouse of a Deceased Person

25.4.1 Transfer of Unused Nil Rate Band

This relief works by allowing the surviving spouse/civil partner to claim any unused nil rate band (NRB) of their deceased spouse/civil partner. It is available to all survivors of a marriage or civil partnership, no matter when the first partner died.

The NRB that is available to the surviving spouse or civil partner on their death will be increased by the proportion of the NRB unused on the first death. It is important that this is calculated on a proportionate basis as this takes into consideration changes in the NRB since the first death. The amount of the NRB that can be transferred is not reduced by the value of exempt transfers made on the death of the first spouse as these do not use up the NRB in the first place.

Example 25.10

Jackie died when her chargeable estate was £150,000 and the NRB was £300,000. She left her entire estate to her son. Her estate did not include a residence.

Jackie's husband has just died and his chargeable estate is £560,000. His son wants to know what NRB will be available in respect of his father's estate as the father had not made any transfers in the last seven years. His estate did not include a residence.

The NRB for 2021/22 is £325,000 and this is uplifted by 50% (i.e. the proportion of the NRB not used by Jackie at her death) to £487,500. Her husband's estate will be liable to IHT on the excess over the extended NRB of £72,500 (£560,000 − £487,500).

25.4.2 Transfer of Unused Residence Nil Rate Band

Any unused residence nil rate band (RNRB) can also be transferred to the estate of a surviving spouse/civil partner where that spouse/civil partner dies on or after 6 April 2017, irrespective of when the first spouse/civil partner died. There is no requirement that the first estate included a residence.

Again, the unused RNRB that is available is increased by the proportion of the RNRB unused on the first death.

A claim must be made on the death of the surviving spouse/civil partner to transfer any unused proportion of the first spouse's/civil partner's RNRB on their death, in the same way that the existing unused nil rate band of a spouse/civil partner can be transferred.

For deaths before 6 April 2017, as there was no RNRB at that time none can have been used. The brought-forward amount will be 100% of the residential enhancement in force at the later death of the surviving spouse or civil partner (subject to the tapering rules where the estate is worth more than £2 million (see **Chapter 24, Section 24.6**)).

Where the first death is on or after 6 April 2017, the transferable allowance is calculated as the unused percentage of the RNRB available to the first spouse or civil partner.

Example 25.11

Shane died on 15 September 2016 when his estate was £250,000. Shane left his entire estate to his wife, Denise, and he made no lifetime transfers.

Denise died on 31 December 2021 with a chargeable estate of £1,050,000, including her home, which is valued at £500,000. She left her entire estate to her daughter. Denise made no lifetime transfers.

continued overleaf

Denise's daughter wants to know what nil rate bands are available in respect of her mother's estate.

The NRB for 2021/22 is £325,000 and is uplifted by 100% (i.e. the proportion of the nil rate band not used by Shane at his death) to £650,000. Denise was also entitled to the RNRB in 2021/22 of £175,000. As Shane died before 6 April 2017, a further £175,000 (being a 100% uplift as none of her RNRB was used) RNRB is also available on Denise's death.

Denise's estate will be liable to IHT on the excess over the available nil rate bands of £50,000 (£1,000,000 – £650,000 – £350,000).

Example 25.12

Using the same facts from **Example 25.11**, except that Shane died in September 2020.

Denise's daughter wants to know what nil rate bands are available in respect of her mother's estate.

The NRB for 2021/22 is £325,000 and is uplifted by 100% (i.e. the proportion of the nil rate band not used by Shane at his death) to £650,000. Denise was also entitled to the 2021/22 RNRB of £175,000. As Shane died in 2020/21, 100% of his unused RNRB is also available on Denise's death, i.e. another £175,000.

The position is therefore the same as in **Example 25.11**.

25.5 Fall in Value of Gift Before Death (section 131)

An IHT relief is available, known as a "section 131 claim", where the value of an asset has fallen between the date of the original gift and the date of death of the donor. The claim reduces the further tax payable by a donee on a lifetime gift that comes into charge on the death of the donor within seven years. It is possible to make this claim if the donee no longer owns the property. In this case, the fall in value relief is determined by reference to the proceeds received for the disposal rather than the current market value at death. Relief is given by reducing the lifetime transfer by an amount equal to the fall in value, and it should be noted that this relief is calculated by reference to the loss in value to the donee, not by reference to the loss in value to the donor (which is used to calculate the value transferred by the donor).

Example 25.13

Ryan gave a painting to Sandra in January 2015. It was part of a set of two paintings which together were worth £750,000. Each painting on its own was worth £200,000 both before and after the gift. Ryan made no other lifetime gifts.

Ryan died in November 2021. At that date, the painting given to Sandra was only worth £80,000 as it had been damaged. Therefore, the value of the asset has gone down between the date of gift and the date of the donor's death.

The painting will be valued as follows in calculating any IHT due on death.

	£
Value of two paintings before transfer	750,000
Value of one painting after transfer	(200,000)
Value transferred by donor	550,000
Less: annual exemptions for 2014/15 and 2013/14	(6,000)
Less: fall in value relief (£200,000 − £80,000)	(120,000)
Chargeable on death	424,000
Less: NRB	(325,000)
Chargeable to IHT	99,000

continued overleaf

> The fall in value claim only affects the additional tax now payable by Sandra (on the failed PET) as a result of Ryan's death. It does not affect the value of the PET for accumulation purposes for Ryan. Therefore, the original PET (after annual exemptions) of £544,000 remains for the purposes of the seven year accumulation period. So for example, for the purposes of calculating the IHT on Ryan's death estate, when determining how much of the NRB at death is reduced by the chargeable transfers in the past seven years, the gift in 2015 would have a chargeable value of £544,000 not £424,000.

25.6   Post-mortem Relief

The general rule that IHT is calculated on the value of the death estate at the date of death is relaxed in certain circumstances. It may be possible to substitute a lower value for certain assets if they are sold after the date of death and realise a lower value than that which applied at the date of death. There are three common cases where this IHT relief can apply and the conditions and bases of valuation are considered below.

25.6.1   Sale of Quoted Shares/Securities within 12 Months of Death (section 179)

If the proceeds realised on the sale of quoted shares or securities within 12 months of the date of death of the donor are lower than the value included in their estate, it is possible to make a claim to substitute the lower value for the purposes of calculating the IHT due on the estate.

When calculating the claim that may be made, it is a requirement to determine the net effect of all disposals of such assets that take place within 12 months of the death. Thus any relevant assets sold for an amount higher than the value included in the estate valuation will reduce the benefit of making the post-mortem claim.

There is an important planning point here, in that it may be possible to delay sales that would achieve a higher sales price until after 12 months from the date of death, this would maximise the value of any claim.

Obviously, if the relevant sales that took place within 12 months of death would produce a higher value than originally included in the death estate, then no claim should be made.

In evaluating the possible benefit of making a claim, it is the gross sales figures that are compared to the original probate value included in the death estate.

There is also an anti-avoidance measure that must be considered. This is designed to stop shares being sold to realise post-mortem relief and then immediately reinvesting the proceeds (whether into the same shares/securities or not). The anti-avoidance legislation restricts the loss in value that can be claimed where there are any investments purchased between the date of death and the end of two months from the last sale of relevant assets within the 12-month period from the date of death. Where this restriction applies, the restriction is calculated as:

$$\text{Loss} \times \frac{\text{Amount invested}}{\text{Total gross proceeds}}$$

Example 25.14

Darina died on 12 August 2021 and left her estate of £725,000 to her three children. The estate included shares in AIG plc, valued at £50,000.

The executors sold the shares in September 2021, realising proceeds of £12,250 after deducting sales costs of £250. In November 2021, the executors purchased £10,000 of shares in Centrica plc.

Calculate any post-mortem relief available.

	£
Probate value	50,000
Less: gross proceeds	(12,500)
Loss in value	37,500
Less: restriction	
$\dfrac{10,000}{12,500} \times £37,500$	(30,000)
Section 179 claim	7,500

Therefore the shares would be included in the death estate at a value of £42,500 (£50,000 – £7,500).

25.6.2 Sale of Land or Buildings within Three Years of Death (section 191)

This relief works in a similar fashion to that for sales of quoted shares, etc. but with a few significant differences. The time period is three years from the date of death rather than one. The aggregation of profits and losses rule still applies but is modified in that it also includes sales that take place at a loss in the **fourth** year after death (sales at a profit in the fourth year are completely ignored).

When calculating the relief, differences in value between the date of death and the date of sale are ignored if they are less than the lower of £1,000 or 5% of the probate value.

A similar anti-avoidance rule on reinvestment also applies and covers the period from death to four months after the last sale in the three-year period. The relevant formula for calculating the restriction is:

$$\text{Loss} \times \frac{\text{Amount invested}}{\text{Total gross proceeds}}$$

Example 25.15

Justin's death estate included the following assets at the date of his death on 5 May 2021:

	£
House in Bristol	165,000
Cottage in Donegal	185,000
Apartment in Benidorm	95,000

In administering Justin's estate the following transactions took place:

- Sold house in Bristol on 12 August 2021 for £160,000
- Sold cottage in Donegal on 9 September 2021 for £164,500
- Sold apartment in Benidorm on 3 December 2021 for £94,500
- Bought farmland in Fermanagh for £35,000 on 2 February 2022

continued overleaf

Calculate any post-mortem relief that may be due.

The losses on the Bristol and Donegal properties are relevant to the section 191 claim. The loss of £500 on disposal of Benidorm must be ignored as it is below the lower of £1,000 and 5% of probate value.

The effect of ignoring the Benidorm disposal is that the last relevant sale took place on 9 September 2021 and only purchases taking place between death and four months from 9 September 2021 are relevant for restricting the claim. Therefore, the purchase of farmland in Fermanagh will not restrict the post-mortem relief.

The section 191 loss claim is £25,500, i.e. (£165,000 – £160,000) + (£185,000 – £164,500). Therefore the properties would be included in the death estate at a value of £160,000 and £164,500 for the Bristol and Donegal properties, respectively.

25.6.3 Sale of Related Property to an Unconnected Party within Three Years of Death (section 176)

A claim for this relief will be possible where the death estate included related property which is sold within three years of death to an unconnected party for a value less than that included in the death estate. This relief works differently from the other post-mortem reliefs referred to above in that the relief is obtained by substituting the standalone value applicable at the date of death (rather than by reference to the proceeds received at the date of disposal), i.e the higher related property value is not included in the death estate.

Example 25.16

Rosie died on 3 May 2021 and her death estate included 40% of the shares in Arkle Investments Ltd, a property investment company. Her husband owns a further 30% of the shares in the company. At the date of death, a 40% shareholding is worth £250,000, while a 70% holding is worth £525,000.

As no BPR is due because the activity of the company is an excluded activity, the shares were included in the death estate as 40/70 × £525,000 = £300,000.

The executors sold Rosie's shares for £280,000 six months after her death to a third party.

Calculate any post-mortem relief due.

All the conditions necessary to qualify for post-mortem relief have been satisfied as:

- the asset was related property in the death estate as the related property value was higher;
- it has been sold to an unconnected third party within three years of death; and
- the proceeds realised (£280,000) are less than the amount included in the death estate (£300,000).

The relief is claimed by substituting the standalone value of £250,000 (note that this is not the sale price of £280,000!) for the original related property value of £300,000. Therefore, relief of £50,000 is effectively obtained.

Questions

Review Questions
(See Suggested Solution to Review Questions at the end of this textbook.)

Question 25.1

Relief from inheritance tax is available on relevant business property.

Requirement
(a) What is "relevant business property"?
(b) What types of business do not qualify for this relief?
(c) What is the nature of the relief and at what rates is it given?

Question 25.2

Relief from inheritance tax is also available for agricultural property.

Requirement
(a) Under what circumstances is a transferor entitled to inheritance tax relief when transferring agricultural property and what is the nature of the relief?
(b) Is the relief available to a transferor of shares or debentures in a farming company?

Question 25.3

Chris Adams is a wealthy individual whose grandmother died on 13 November 2021. His grandmother was born, and always lived, in the UK. Chris is an executor of her estate, and of the discretionary trust noted below, and is keen to finalise the inheritance tax issues associated with her death as soon as possible.

Chris realises that he does not have the necessary knowledge to calculate the inheritance tax that is due and does not want to miss out on any relief which could be claimed to reduce the IHT liability and so increase the funds available to the beneficiaries of his grandmother's will.

Chris has given you the following information:

1. His grandmother gave £500,000 to a discretionary trust in June 2018, and paid any IHT due. He can't find the papers showing how much inheritance tax was paid, but he does know that the correct amount of IHT was paid.
2. Chris had been given the family home by his grandmother in May 2020, when it was worth £600,000.
3. His grandmother owned three rental properties on the Lisburn Road, Belfast. He has obtained an independent valuation of the three properties which indicates that the value at the date of death was £560,000. However, as his grandmother's will states that the properties are to be sold and the proceeds divided between her four grandchildren, he placed them on the market in February 2022. At this point the estate agent recommended an asking price of £550,000, but due to the state of the property market, the highest offer received to date (which Chris has just accepted) is £525,000.
4. His grandmother had credit card debt of £15,000 at the date of her death.
5. She owed £50,000 to Bank of Ireland, secured on her collection of art. The loan was used by her to travel all around the country and display her art at various exhibitions and will be repaid from her estate. The art is worth £250,000.
6. His grandmother owned a holiday home in Iceland worth £78,000.

7. At the date of death she had cash of £250,000 in a UK bank account and cash of £40,000 in an account in the Isle of Man.
8. Chris has incurred the following costs in his role as executor, which have been paid for out of his grandmother's estate: solicitor's fees of £5,000 in administering the estate, £2,000 on a headstone, £550 on mourning clothes for his family for the funeral and £14,500 in obtaining probate on the holiday home his grandmother owned in Iceland.

Requirement
(a) Calculate the inheritance tax due as a result of the death of Chris's grandmother.
(b) State who has to pay any additional inheritance tax due on the lifetime gifts.

Question 25.4

You work in the trusts and estates division of a local mid-sized practice. Your client, Fionn O'Shea, died on 31 March 2022. During your review of Fionn's tax file, you note that, during his lifetime, he had made the following gifts:

1. £9,000 to his son Shay on the occasion of his marriage on 10 March 2016.
2. £300,000 to a discretionary trust on 28 December 2016. You note that the trustees agreed to pay any tax due.
3. 100,000 Angel Bank plc £1 ordinary shares valued at £175,000 to the same discretionary trust on 25 November 2017. Again, the trustees agreed to pay any tax due. The shares had fallen in value to £75,000 at the date of Fionn's death.

Fionn also owned the following assets when he died: his home valued at £225,000, cash and investments valued totalling £85,000 and chattels valued at £15,000.

Fionn was also the life tenant of a qualifying interest in possession trust created by his brother's will following his death in 1988. The value of the trust fund at Fionn's death was £276,000.

Fionn was married to Alanna, who died in 2016 with no assets. He never remarried and left his estate to his son.

Requirement
Prepare a memo to the partner in your practice dealing with the following:

(a) Calculation of the lifetime inheritance tax payable, if any, in respect of the lifetime gifts.
(b) Calculation of the inheritance tax due on Fionn's death estate, making any appropriate claims or reliefs available to reduce the liability arising (if any).

Question 25.5

James Quinn died on 20 November 2021. His brother Andrew predeceased him on 31 March 2018, leaving his entire estate, valued at £575,000, to James. The month before Andrew died, Andrew made a gift of £156,000 to their only sister Laura.

At the time of his death, James's estate was valued at £1.5 million, including the assets left to him by Andrew in 2018. James left his estate to his favourite nephew.

Requirement
Calculate the inheritance tax payable due to James's death, making any appropriate claims or reliefs available to reduce the liability arising (if any). Assume James made no lifetime gifts. Outline the rationale for any claims or reliefs.

Question 25.6

It is 18 June 2021 and you are meeting Alexander Johnston, a new client of your office. Alexander's wife died earlier this year on 14 February and all of her estate (which did not include a residence) passed to him. Shocked at her sudden death, it has made him think about the large number of assets he owns and the gifts he has made, and the inheritance tax that might be payable on them.

Alexander has requested a calculation of the amount of inheritance tax that would be payable if he died today as a prelude to considering what inheritance tax planning could be implemented to reduce any liabilities that might arise. He provides you with the following information:

1. He has cash of £82,000 in a French bank account. He owes £10,000 in credit card debt.
2. He owns a house that he inherited from his brother in August 2018. This house was a specific gift of UK property left to him in his brother's will. His brother's estate paid inheritance tax of £75,000 that related to the value of the property in the death estate. The property had cost his brother £340,000 and was worth £525,000 at the date of his brother's death. The property is currently worth £590,000.
3. He owns 6,000 of the 10,000 shares in issue in AJ Ltd, an unquoted trading company, acquired in 2010. The following share values are relevant:

	£
Value – 40% interest in the company	275,000
Value – 60% interest in the company	625,000
Value – 100% interest in the company	1,400,000

4. He gave his son £220,000 cash in May 2017.
5. He owns an investment property in Stranmillis which is worth £280,000. However, due to the recent fall in property prices, the outstanding mortgage on the property is £290,000. The bank has a charge over his general assets.
6. He owns a ski chalet in Switzerland. The property is worth £120,000 and it is estimated that the cost of obtaining probate of the chalet would be £12,000.
7. He gifted his Aston Martin DB9 to his son in May 2018 when it was worth £65,000. He and his son both work in the same office block in Belfast and his son lives in Bangor. As Alexander lives in Holywood, his son picks him up in the DB9 three days a week and gives him a lift to work. The Aston Martin is currently worth £90,000.

Requirement

Prepare a report to Alexander dealing with the following:

(a) Calculate the inheritance tax that would be payable on his death if he were to die today. Claim all available reliefs.
(b) Outline the due date for payment of any inheritance tax arising, and advise what date the inheritance tax return would need to be filed with HMRC.

Question 25.7

Portia di Rossi died on 29 July 2021. She is survived by her four children and six grandchildren.

During her life, Portia was always very generous. She turned 80 in October 2015 and, every Christmas from then on, she gave £200 to each of her grandchildren. For Christmas 2015 only, she also gave £4,500 to each of her children. When her godson was married on 19 March 2017, Portia gave him £6,000. She made no gifts of any sort in any tax years prior to 2015/16.

A sum of £25,000 was donated by her in July 2016 to an American charity established in New York for fire-fighters injured in 9/11 as her brother was a long-time resident of New York and had been rescued from the street that day by a passing fire crew.

Keen to also provide for her children, five months before her death, in February 2021, Portia gifted £380,000 cash to create a discretionary trust which she established for her children. Portia made it clear at that time that any tax that arose on the gift was to be taken care of by the trustees.

At the time of her death, Portia owned the following assets:

1. Her home in Armagh, valued at £725,000 for probate purposes, but sold after her death in December 2021 for £645,000. She left this to her favourite nephew in her will.
2. The contents of the Armagh house, valued at £48,500.
3. A villa in Portugal, valued at £225,000.
4. 18,000 shares in Belfast Ceramics Plc. The closing bid and offer prices quoted in the Stock Exchange Daily Official List for the company at the date of death were £2.72 and £2.76. The shares were sold six months later for £1.45 each. Portia did not hold a controlling interest in this company.
5. 3,500 shares in British Meats Plc. The closing bid and offer prices quoted in the Stock Exchange Daily Official List for the company at the date of death were £12.35 and £12.95. The shares were sold three months later for £13.60 each. Portia did not hold a controlling interest in this company.
6. 390 of the 1,000 issued shares in Italiana Wine SA, a successful Italian trading company established by Portia's son, Paolo, which produces wine in Sicily mainly for the export market. Paolo owns the remaining 610 shares. Portia acquired the shares in January 2016. The shareholding is estimated to have a value of £180,000.
7. £69,000 in bank and building society accounts in Belfast.
8. £228,000 in a Guernsey bank account.

For tax purposes, Portia was domiciled in the UK at the time of her death.

Requirement

Calculate the IHT payable as a result of Portia's death, split between amounts payable in respect of her estate on death, and the amount(s), if any, payable on death in respect of Portia's lifetime gifts. Explain your treatment of each item and claim any reliefs possible to minimise tax which may be due. You may assume that Portia's husband predeceased her and fully used his NRB.

Interaction between IHT and CGT

Learning Objectives

After studying this chapter you will understand:

■ The interaction between IHT and CGT.
■ The IHT treatment of "gifts with reservation of benefit".

26.1 Overview

IHT and CGT are very different taxes, each with their own exemptions and reliefs and different methods of calculating the value of the asset and the tax due. So, having dealt with the rules of each of them separately, it can seem like a step too far to deal with both of them in respect of the same transaction. However, once it is appreciated that the taxes should be addressed one at a time (and not simultaneously), it becomes clear that all that is necessary is a clear knowledge of the rules together with an orderly approach to the situation in question.

Always try to deal with the CGT and IHT implications of a transaction separately before considering any interaction elements. Strictly, it does not matter which of the taxes is addressed first, but it is likely to be helpful to consider IHT initially as its implications may be useful when considering whether or not gift holdover relief for CGT is available under section 260 TCGA 1992.

Overall, there will only be a true interaction in three circumstances:

1. Where there is potentially an immediate charge to IHT in lifetime on the transaction (i.e. because the transaction is a CLT such as a gift to a trust), meaning section 260 TCGA 1992 gift relief can be claimed to relieve any CGT that arises on the transaction.
2. In circumstances where the donee pays the IHT on a gift. This will also form part of the base cost of the asset for CGT purposes on a later disposal by them.
3. The market value of the asset at the date of death, for IHT purposes, becomes the legatee's base cost for CGT. This is despite there being no CGT implications if a donee receives an asset from the deceased's death estate. In other words, the legatee receives the uplift to market value CGT-free.

26.2 Interaction of IHT and CGT

A gift can have both IHT and CGT consequences at the same time. The base cost for CGT purposes of a lifetime gift in the hands of the donee (for both PETs and CLTs) is the market value at the date of transfer unless gift relief is claimed. Remember also that the value of the transaction may be different for IHT purposes under the loss to the donor rule. The donor will be subject to CGT if the gift is a chargeable asset for CGT purposes. Any tax charge will be based on the market value of the asset at the date of gift. This will be the case unless the asset is exempt from CGT or if it is possible to make a holdover election under section 165 (mainly for business assets) or section 260 TCGA 1992 (see **Chapter 20, Section 20.1.3**). It may be possible to make a section 260 claim if the transfer is immediately chargeable to IHT, e.g. on a gift into a trust. The claim can be made even if the IHT charge is at 0%, i.e. within the nil rate band, or covered by a relief. Section 260 gift relief can be used on any type of asset, including non-business assets, so is a useful relief in situations where section 165 gift relief is not available or is restricted (for example where the transaction is a gift of shares that would otherwise be restricted by virtue of the level of chargeable non-business assets on the statement of financial position of the company).

If both section 165 and section 260 reliefs are potentially available, section 260 has priority. In most instances, gift relief is a joint claim to be made by the donor and the donee. This is not the case when the donee is a trust and section 260 relief applies. Therefore if the settlor transfers assets to a trust and wishes to defer the gain under section 260, the claim will be made by the settlor only and the consent of the trustees is not required. As we saw earlier, a gift relief claim must be made within four years after the end of the tax year in which the assets were transferred. Therefore, for gifts in 2021/22, a gift relief claim must be made no later than 5 April 2026.

Where there is a gift of an asset and it is possible to make a CGT holdover election, the base cost for the recipient becomes the market value at the date of transfer less the amount of gift relief claimed. The effect of this is that the gain is effectively passed on to the donee.

When an asset has been acquired following the death of the donor, the probate value becomes the CGT base cost. This can be particularly valuable where 100% BPR or APR is available. There will be no IHT due on a transfer on death and the donee will receive the property at its current market value.

Where post-mortem relief is claimed, this lower value becomes the CGT base cost rather than the original probate value.

Example 26.1

Jonathan Williamson is 70 years old and a widower. He has one child, his son Peter, to whom he intends to leave the whole of his estate on his death. Both Jonathan and Peter were born in the UK and have always lived and worked here.

Peter is currently planning to buy a house and so Jonathan would like to make a lifetime gift to him of one of his assets to fund the property purchase. Peter needs around £425,000 after deducting any tax payable, either by himself or his father. He will sell whatever gift he receives from his father immediately in order to buy the house

Jonathan owns two assets valued at £425,000 (see below) and would like advice on which he should gift (and why), factoring in all the relevant tax consequences. He would also like to know if he is better to gift the assets now or wait to pass them on to his son in his will.

1. 15,000 shares in Williamson Holidays Ltd

This is an unquoted trading company. Jonathan currently owns 30,000 shares in the company, representing a 75% holding. The 15,000 shares have an estimated market value of £425,000 and they cost him £325,000 in 2014.

The company owns a plot of land that it holds as an investment. The land comprises 6% of the value of its total assets and 10% of the value of its chargeable assets.

continued overleaf

2. A sailing boat known as "William and Son"
The boat is also worth £425,000 but cost £200,000 in June 2008. Jonathan took it on as project and spent a further £125,000 the next year installing a more powerful engine and satellite navigation equipment.

The tax implications of the two proposed gifts are considered below.

Gift of shares
(a) CGT implications

Lifetime gift
Jonathan would make a capital gain by reference to the deemed sales proceeds equal to the market value of the shares – i.e. a gain of £100,000 (£425,000 – £325,000) as Peter is a connected party under section 286 TCGA 1992.

Jonathan owns more than 5% of Williamson Holidays Ltd and has owned the shares for more than 12 months. In addition, Williamson Holidays Ltd is a trading company. However, business asset disposal relief (see **Chapter 19**) will only be available if Jonathan is a director or employee of the company in the two years prior to the gift of the shares to his son.

Gift holdover relief would also be available as the shares are unquoted and Williamson Holidays Ltd is a trading company. However, the relief would be restricted to 90% only because the company owns chargeable non-business assets (the plot of land held as an investment comprises 10% of the company's chargeable assets).

If Jonathan is an employee of Williamson Holidays Ltd, gift holdover relief should not be claimed unless Peter has significant capital losses to use because gift holdover will create a sizeable gain for Peter when he sells the shares immediately after receiving them.

Business asset disposal relief is a better option. Jonathan's gain of £100,000 would be reduced by any available annual exempt amount; assuming he has none remaining, the maximum capital gains tax would be £10,000 (£100,000 × 10%). Peter's base cost in the shares would be their market value at the time of the gift being £425,000. Accordingly, there would be no gain on the immediate sale of the shares by Peter following the gift, as his sales proceeds would equal his base cost, assuming he can sell them immediately for the same price. This would mean that Peter would have a clear £425,000 of cash available for the property purchase.

If Jonathan is not an employee of Williamson Holidays Ltd, he and Peter can claim gift holdover relief as both could then benefit from their CGT annual exemption. Jonathan would make a maximum gain of £10,000 (£100,000 × 10%) due to the non-business chargeable assets, which would then be reduced by any available annual exempt amount.

The maximum CGT liability for Jonathan would be £2,000 (£10,000 × 20% maximum) depending on the level of his income and the existence of any other capital gains. The remainder of the gain of £90,000 would be held over and would reduce Peter's base cost of the shares to £335,000 (£425,000 − £90,000).

Accordingly, Peter's gain on an onward immediate sale for £425,000 would be £90,000 (£425,000 − £335,000) as reduced by any available annual exempt amount. The maximum CGT liability would be £18,000 (£90,000 × 20%). The total CGT due would be a maximum of £20,000 between Jonathan and Peter (£2,000 + £18,000). Peter would only have £408,000 to fund the property purchase.

Gift via Jonathan's will
Gifts on death are exempt from CGT. Hence Peter's base cost would be the market value of the shares at the time of death. However he would not be able to fund the property purchase at the time he wants to and would be forced to wait, assuming he has no other way of funding the purchase.

(b) IHT implications

Lifetime gift
The gift would be a potentially exempt transfer that would only be subject to IHT if Jonathan were to die within seven years. If the gift became chargeable, business property relief would not be available as Peter would not own the shares at the time of Jonathan's death and he would not have replaced the shares with equivalent business property.

continued overleaf

In addition, Jonathan will still hold 15,000 shares in Williamson Holidays Ltd. Accordingly, the value of the transfer for IHT would be calculated under the loss to the donor principle representing the fall in value of Jonathan's estate at the time of the gift. This is likely to differ from the market value of the shares gifted as Jonathan's holding would be reduced from 75% to 37.5%, such that he would no longer control the company.

The fall in value in Jonathan's estate would be reduced by any available annual exemptions. If Jonathan dies, IHT would then be due on the excess of this amount over the nil rate band at the date of death (as reduced by any chargeable transfers in the seven years prior to the gift of the shares). Taper relief would be available if Jonathan were to survive the gift by at least three years. The maximum IHT liability would be 40% of the fall in value.

Gift via Jonathan's will
100% business property relief would be available on the non-excepted assets. Accordingly, only 6% of the value of the shares as at the time of death would be subject to IHT (on the assumption that the proportion of the company's assets held in the form of investments has not changed).

The shares would be included in Jonathan's death estate. The excess of the death estate over the available nil rate band (as reduced by any chargeable transfers in the seven years prior to death) would be subject to IHT at 40%. The maximum liability would be 2.4% (6% × 40%) of the value of the shares.

Gift of sailing boat
(a) CGT implications

Lifetime gift or via Jonathan's will
The sailing boat is a wasting chattel (tangible, moveable property with a useful life of no more than 50 years) and, as such, is an exempt asset for the purposes of capital gains tax. So Peter would have £425,000 cash in hand from the sale. Gifting the boat via his will would result in the same outcome, however, Peter's ownership would be delayed and he would not have the cash to fund the property purchase when he needs it.

(b) IHT implications

Lifetime gift
The gift would be a potentially exempt transfer and would only be subject to IHT if Jonathan were to die within seven years. IHT would be due on the excess of the value of the sailing boat at the time of the gift (as reduced by any available annual exemptions) over the available nil rate band at death (as reduced by any chargeable transfers in the seven years prior to the gift). Taper relief would be available if Jonathan were to survive the gift by at least three years.

Gift via Jonathan's will
The sailing boat would be included in Jonathan's death estate at its value on death. The excess of the death estate over the available nil-rate band (as reduced by any chargeable transfers in the seven years prior to death) would be subject to IHT at 40%.

Recommendation
It is clear that, purely from a tax point of view, Jonathan should give Peter the sailing boat rather than the shares.

There will be no tax at the time of the gift, either CGT or IHT. In addition, there will be no tax at the time of death, provided Jonathan survives the gift by seven years. Even if Jonathan were to die within seven years of the gift, the amount of IHT due on death is likely to be less than the amount due if the sailing boat were held by Jonathan until death due to the availability of taper relief. Before concluding on this, it would be necessary to consider the chargeable transfers made by Jonathan during the seven years prior to the proposed gift and the likelihood of the sailing boat increasing or falling in value.

The situation regarding a gift of the shares is not so straightforward. A lifetime gift will result in a CGT liability of up to £20,000. There is also the possibility of an IHT liability of 40% of the fall in value of Jonathan's estate if Jonathan were to die within three years of the gift. However, there would be no IHT liability if he were to survive the gift by at least seven years.

continued overleaf

Retaining the shares until death would avoid the CGT liability, but would guarantee an IHT liability up to a maximum of 2.4% of the value of the shares. Accordingly, a lifetime gift of the shares would be a gamble by Jonathan. If he were to survive the gift by seven years, the total tax due would be CGT of either £10,000 or £20,000, depending on whether or not he is an employee of Williamson Holidays Ltd (and the availability of business asset disposal relief). If he were to die within three years of the gift, the total tax due is likely to be considerable due to the IHT payable. His alternative is to hold on to the shares and pay a relatively small amount of IHT out of his death estate. Finally, Jonathan could be advised that an insurance policy could be taken out on his life in order to satisfy any future IHT liability arising in respect of a lifetime gift.

The following general conclusions can be drawn from the above.

1. IHT – assets that are subject to IHT but not CGT (i.e. those that are exempt from CGT) can be planned for by reference to IHT only. From an IHT point of view, it is advantageous to give away assets as soon as possible as this opens up the possibility of surviving the gift by seven years or, failing that, the possibility of taper relief. It is particularly important to gift assets that are expected to increase in value as the value on which IHT is calculated is frozen at the time of the gift.

2. IHT – care must be taken when advising on assets that qualify for business property relief or agricultural property relief due to the need for the recipient to hold the assets until the death of the donor in order for the relief to be available on the donor's death. If it is clear from the facts that the recipient intends to sell the assets gifted, there is likely to be a significant difference between the IHT due on death within seven years of the lifetime gift and that due on the asset when comprised within the death estate.

3. CGT – it is not always advantageous to claim gift holdover relief. Also, the relief is not always available; in particular, unless the gift is to a trust (in which case it will qualify under section 260 TCGA 1992), the assets must qualify for the relief under the conditions set out in section 165 TCGA 1992 (see **Chapter 16, Section 16.11.4**).

26.3   Consideration of the Impact of "Gifts with Reservation"

The "gifts with reservation" (GWR) rules were introduced as an anti-avoidance measure to prevent individuals gifting assets but continuing to derive some benefit from those assets after the gift had been made. Without the rules, the assets could fall outside the taxable estate if the donor survived seven years from the date of making the PET, even where they continue to derive a benefit from the assets.

The rules operate by treating the asset as continuing to form part of the donor's estate for IHT purposes, i.e. the gift is ignored. The most common asset to be affected by this legislation is the main residence of the donor, where it is gifted to someone (e.g. the donor's son or daughter) but the donor continues to derive a benefit from the property by continuing to live there.

This anti-avoidance legislation does not apply where the donor pays full market value for the use of the property gifted or if the donor is virtually excluded from benefiting from the property.

If a donor makes a GWR and dies within seven years, there is a potential double charge, with tax becoming due both on the original lifetime gift of the property (being a 'failed PET') and on the property being included in the death estate as a consequence of the reservation of benefit. HMRC acknowledges that there could be a double charge and deals with the matter by requiring two IHT computations – one showing the tax charge on the original PET, and one showing the tax charge if the asset is included in the death estate. Rather than imposing a double IHT charge, HMRC accepts the computation that produces the higher IHT charge, including taking into consideration the availability of the residence nil rate band/unused spouse's residence nil rate on the GWR (not available on the failed PET). In carrying out this comparison, credit for any tax previously paid on a lifetime transfer is limited to the amount of tax payable on the death in respect of the GWR property.

The residence nil rate band, which came into operation for deaths on or after 6 April 2017 (see **Chapter 24, Section 24.6**), will be available against a single residence that is part of the deceased's estate on death, whether owned directly by the deceased, or to which they are beneficially entitled through a qualifying interest in possession or a GWR, subject to the remaining conditions for accessing the residence nil rate band being met (see **Chapter 24, Section 24.6**).

Example 26.2

Luke gave his daughter his holiday cottage in Portrush in January 2007. Luke continued to spend three months of each year in the cottage between the date of the gift and his death in July 2021. This is a GWR and the value of the property at the date of his death will be included in Luke's death estate for IHT purposes, even though the original PET succeeded. Luke will be entitled to deduct the applicable residence nil rate band in the tax year of his death against the GWR.

NB: The value of the property in January 2007 is his daughter's base cost for CGT purposes.

Example 26.3

In July 2014, Anne gives a holiday home worth £450,000 (after annual exemptions) to her daughter, Betty, but continues to use the home on a regular basis. Anne's husband is still alive. The PET that arises at that time is also a GWR for IHT.

Anne dies in June 2021, having continued to use the holiday home up the date of her death.

At the date of her death it is worth £550,000, and is therefore treated as part of her estate under the GWR rules. Her remaining death estate is valued at £600,000. Anne made no other lifetime gifts.

Two calculations are required – one on the basis of only including the GWR, and one on the basis of only including the failed PET. HMRC take the calculation that produces the highest liability.

First calculation

Ignore the lifetime charge and charge the holiday home as part of Anne's death estate.

July 2014 – gift ignored, tax nil

June 2021 – tax on death estate, as follows:

	£
Holiday home	550,000
Remaining estate	600,000
Chargeable estate	1,150,000
Less: residence NRB	(175,000)
Less: NRB	(325,000)
Chargeable	650,000
IHT @ 40%	260,000

Total tax is therefore £260,000.

Second calculation

Charge the lifetime gift and ignore the holiday home as part of the death estate.

continued overleaf

July 2014 – tax on £450,000 gift, as follows:

	£
Holiday home	450,000
Less: NRB	(325,000)
Chargeable	125,000
IHT @ 40%	50,000

June 2021 – tax on death estate, as follows:

	£
Remaining estate	600,000
Chargeable estate	600,000
IHT @ 40%	240,000

Total tax is therefore £290,000 (£50,000 on the failed PET and £240,000 on the death estate).

The second calculation results in the greater amount of tax being payable; IHT is therefore charged on the basis of the second calculation, with the value of the GWR being reduced to nil.

It is possible to release a GWR before death by relinquishing any benefit retained. However, this is treated as a deemed PET at the date of the release of the benefit (and at the value at the date of release). As this is a deemed PET it is not possible to claim the annual exemption(s) against it. To avoid the double IHT charge on the original gift and the subsequent release of the benefit, HMRC again accepts the IHT computation that produces the higher IHT liability.

Questions

Review Questions
(See Suggested Solution to Review Questions at the end of this textbook.)

Question 26.1

Sean has gathered substantial wealth in his lifetime and is considering disposing some of it to his son, Shay. He is considering gifting his home to Shay but continuing to live in the house until his death. Sadly, Sean has recently been diagnosed with a terminal illness and his life expectancy is no more than three years. Sean has lived in the house all his life. He would not intend to pay any rent to Shay.

Requirement
Briefly explain the capital gains tax and inheritance tax implications of this proposal.

27

Administration of IHT

Learning Objectives

After studying this chapter you will understand:

- The administration of IHT.
- The deadlines for payment of IHT and the filing of IHT returns.
- The penalties and interest charges for late payment, late filing and errors in IHT returns.

27.1 Payment of IHT on Lifetime Gifts

Primary responsibility for the payment of any IHT due on lifetime gifts rests with the donor. The donor may delegate responsibility for payment of IHT to the donee. Where a donor makes a chargeable lifetime gift and does not delegate the responsibility for payment to the donee, the gift must be grossed up for the IHT that the donor has paid (see **Chapter 24**, **Section 24.2**). The reason for this is that the donor's estate has also been reduced by the IHT due.

The actual gift, in the hand's of the donee, is deemed to be net of any IHT due (see **Chapter 24** for the tax treatment of chargeable lifetime transfers and potentially exempt transfers). The due date for payment of the relevant IHT and filing of the relevant return is six months from the end of the month in which the transfer is made.

27.2 Payment of IHT on Lifetime Gifts Following Death within Seven Years

The due date for payment of IHT on a CLT or a failed PET is six months from the end of the month in which the death occurs.

27.3 Payment of IHT on Death Estate

The due date for payment of IHT on the death estate is payable on the earlier of:

1. six months from the end of the month in which the transfer takes place on death, or
2. the date of delivery of the IHT400 return.

Interest will accrue for any IHT paid late (with the exception that no interest will accrue for the first six months if the IHT400 is filed before the six-month date).

27.4 IHT Instalments

27.4.1 General Conditions

Any IHT payable on certain qualifying assets (referred to as qualifying property) may be paid in instalments if a claim is made to HMRC. If a claim is made, the IHT is payable in 10 equal instalments with the first instalment falling due on the normal due date.

No claim for the instalment option may be made if the donor pays any IHT due on the lifetime gift. Furthermore, if there is IHT due in respect of a lifetime gift that becomes payable following the death of the donor, the instalment option will only be available if the donee still owns the asset. The only exception to this rule is that, where the donee has sold business property that does not qualify for full BPR and reinvests the proceeds in acquiring replacement business property, then the right to pay IHT in instalments is preserved.

27.4.2 Interest Position

Depending on the type of property transferred, the instalments may be either 'interest-bearing' or 'interest-free'. As the name suggests, interest-free instalments are more attractive as interest only accrues from each instalment date if the IHT is paid after this date, whereas interest accrues from the normal due date for interest-bearing instalments. For interest-bearing instalments an interest charge is added at each instalment date based on the balance of unpaid IHT at the time.

Generally, the interest-free instalment option is available for transfers of land qualifying for APR, shares in trading companies and for a business or partnership share.

27.4.3 Qualifying Property

Qualifying property for the purposes of paying IHT by instalments is restricted to land or buildings, certain shareholdings, and a business or partnership share.

The instalment option is available in respect of all land and buildings, wherever situated. Generally, if BPR is available the instalment option is not relevant to the transfer of a business or partnership share. However, it may be relevant where the minimum period of ownership test has not been satisfied for BPR.

27.4.4 Cases where Instalments may Apply

The rules to determine whether or not shares are qualifying property are considered below. There are four cases in which the instalment option may be available:

1. Quoted or unquoted shareholdings that gave the owner control of a company (and, for this purpose, related property is also taken into account to determine whether the company is under control of the donor) are qualifying property.
2. Unquoted shares where the IHT payable on their transfer represents more than 20% of the total IHT payable on the estate.
3. Unquoted shares with a value for IHT purposes of greater than £20,000 and which represent at least 10% of the voting rights of the company.

4. Unquoted shares where the executors have insufficient funds with which to settle the IHT due (known as a hardship claim). This is a subjective test and is normally only considered as a last resort if cases 1. to 3. above are not viable.

Whether the instalments are interest-free or interest-bearing will depend on whether the shares are in a trading company as noted above.

Example 27.1

Frank left his home in his will to his nephew, Rick, following his death on 2 February 2021. £25,000 of IHT was payable.

Explain the IHT payments to be made and advise what will happen if the house is sold in December 2021.

The IHT may be paid in 10 equal interest-bearing instalments commencing 31 August 2021. Ten instalments of £2,500 may be paid and interest will be due on the unpaid balance of IHT due at each instalment date.

If the house is sold in December 2021, the balance of IHT plus any accrued interest becomes immediately due.

27.5 Filing of Returns

The filing date of the IHT100 for lifetime gifts is six months from the end of the month in which the transfer is made.

An IHT400 should be filed by the executors of the estate for any CLT and failed PETs together with details of the death estate within 12 months from the end of the month in which the death occurs. The executors may also include details of any GWR but there is no statutory obligation to do so.

There are provisions which allow for small estates, referred to as "excepted estates", to be exempted from the obligation to file an IHT400.

27.6 Penalties

The late filing penalty regime is:

- an initial £100 penalty;
- if the account is more than six months late, the penalty is £200;
- if the account is more than 12 months late the penalty increases to a maximum of £3,000;
- if the actual tax liability is less than these figures, the penalty cannot be more than the amount of the tax due.

Errors in IHT returns are subject to the same penalty regime that applies to other taxes (see **Chapter 1, Section 1.8**).

Questions

Review Questions

(See Suggested Solution to Review Questions at the end of this textbook.)

Question 27.1

Please refer to **Question 25.4** (Fionn O'Shea) in **Chapter 25**.

Requirement

In relation to the gift made on 25 November 2017:

(a) What is the due date for payment of IHT on this lifetime CLT and filing of the relevant IHT 100?
(b) If there had been additional IHT payable on death in respect of that gift, what would the due date have been?
(c) Assuming the executors of the estate deliver the IHT 400 on 29 July 2022, on what date is payment of IHT on Fionn's death estate due? What is the due date for filing an IHT400?

Question 27.2

Trevor Smyth inherited Smyth Farm from his father in 1993. In 1992, Trevor's father granted a 40-year tenancy over the whole of the farm to the family-owned company, Smyth Farms Ltd, which has carried on a mixed farming business there ever since.

In 2012 Trevor gave cash of £226,000 to a discretionary trust for his children, David and Sarah. In 2015 Trevor bought Windy Farm and Primrose Farmhouse. At the same time, he retired from any active part in the farm business in order to live in Primrose Farmhouse with his long-term partner, Eileen, whom he married in 2017.

On 14 June 2017, as an engagement present for Eileen, Trevor transferred Primrose Farmhouse into his and Eileen's joint names. At that time Primrose Farmhouse was worth £900,000. Valuers have advised that a half share owned by either party should be discounted by 15%.

Trevor died on 1 January 2022. At the time of his death his assets were:

1. His half share as beneficial joint tenant of Primrose Farmhouse – the whole was valued at £1,000,000.
2. Smyth Farm valued at £1,900,000, of which £700,000 is the value of the farmhouse and £300,000 is the value of Smyth Farm Stables (see below).
3. Windy Farm valued at £950,000.
4. 50% of the shares in Smyth Farms Ltd valued at £425,000.
5. Personal bank accounts and investments (net of funeral expenses and other debts owing at death) worth a total of £240,000.
6. A collection of shotguns and other shooting equipment with a value of £48,000.

Smyth Farm Stables, which comprises a riding school, stables, and some 30 acres used for horse grazing, was released from the agricultural tenancy some years ago. Sarah has since run Smyth Farm Stables as a riding school and horse livery business and paid her father rent.

The rest of Smyth Farm (comprising the farmhouse, farmland and a number of farm buildings used for storage and for shelter of farm animals) has remained within the tenancy granted in 1990 and has continued to be used for the Smyth Farms Ltd farming business. Since his father's move to

Primrose Farmhouse, David has lived at the farmhouse on Smyth Farm, from where he has run Smyth Farms Ltd.

The executors' valuer has advised that HMRC is likely to successfully argue that, although the market value of the farmhouse at Smyth Farm is £700,000, its agricultural value is £600,000, but that the agricultural value of the rest of Smyth Farm is equal to its market value.

Windy Farm, which comprises only agricultural land and does not include any buildings, has also been occupied and farmed by Smyth Farms Ltd since Trevor's purchase. In this case there is no formal tenancy agreement. The valuer has advised that its agricultural value is the same as its market value.

Requirement

Calculate the inheritance tax payable as a result of Trevor's death, with comments explaining reliefs or exemptions available, if any.

Question 27.3

Your very wealthy client, Mary, was recently diagnosed with a serious illness and while her long-term prognosis is excellent she is concerned that there will be a significant IHT liability when she dies. She is therefore keen to explore opportunities to reduce the potential IHT liability on her estate.

Mary has been approached by a local boutique tax firm who are marketing a convoluted IHT avoidance scheme (that falls under the Disclosure of Tax Avoidance Schemes regime) which, according to them, would completely remove any liability to IHT.

Mary tells you that she is seriously considering meeting them to discuss using the scheme as it "just sounds like good tax planning – which isn't illegal". In the local community, Mary has an excellent reputation and would not want to damage it.

Requirement

Set out for Mary your view on whether or not she should use the IHT avoidance scheme and what the consequences might be if she does.

Other Sundry Matters

Learning Objectives

After studying this chapter you will understand:

- The IHT treatment of gifts from companies.
- The impact of deeds of disclaimer/variations.
- Overseas aspects of IHT.

28.1   IHT Treatment of Gifts from Companies

Where a close company (as defined in **Chapter 9**) makes a transfer of value, that value may be apportioned among the participators according to their interests in the company and treated as a transfer of value by each individual for the purposes of IHT.

There is no apportionment of any value that is treated as the participator's income, for the purposes of corporation tax or income tax. There is also no charge in respect of excluded property, i.e. an amount that would be apportioned to a non-UK domiciled individual and which is attributable to property outside the UK. There is also no apportionment to shareholders who hold 5% or less of the company.

Any transfers of value caught by this legislation are treated as an immediate chargeable lifetime transfer (CLT) and not as a potentially exempt transfer (PET). As they are "deemed" transfers, the lifetime exemptions are generally not available. However, the legislation specifically provides that the annual exemption is available against such transfers, as is the spousal exemption to the extent that the estate of the spouse/civil partner is increased.

A change in the rights or number of shares held by a participator in a close company will also be considered to be a transfer of value. This is a deemed disposition and will also be treated as an immediate CLT and not as a PET. As the transfer is a deemed disposition rather than a deemed transfer of value, all the exemptions are available against the resulting transfer of value.

Example 28.1

Delta Ltd has an issued share capital of 100 shares, Richard owns 60 shares and Sean owns 40.

60 shares are issued to Richard's daughter and 40 to Sean's son.

Richard now has 60 shares out of 200 and has lost control of the company. Sean now has a "non-influential" 20% holding compared to his "influential" 40% holding. The values of both Richard and Sean's shareholding in the company have substantially diminished and each has made a transfer of value.

28.2 Double Tax Relief for Overseas Taxes Suffered

Relief for any overseas IHT is generally given under the provisions of a tax treaty, or more commonly by way of unilateral relief. Double tax relief is most commonly available where a UK domiciled or deemed UK domiciled individual, for IHT purposes, dies owning foreign property.

Unilateral relief is available in the UK for the overseas tax suffered, and will be given as the lower of the overseas tax payable or the UK IHT due on the foreign asset. For this purpose it will be necessary to calculate the "estate rate" to determine the UK IHT payable in respect of the foreign asset. The "estate rate" is the total IHT borne by an estate over the total chargeable assets of the estate as a percentage. Any unrelieved foreign tax is effectively wasted.

28.3 Deed of Disclaimer/Variation

If a beneficiary is entitled to receive assets on the death of the donor, the potential recipient is under no legal obligation to accept the gift. Instead, the beneficiary may disclaim the gift. If this is done by way of formal written deed, the asset passes to the residuary beneficiary of the estate.

The potential beneficiary must have received no benefit from the property before it is disclaimed. For example, if the potential recipient has received some dividend income from shares, then the gift cannot be disclaimed

If the potential recipient would prefer the gift to pass to a nominated person or some other body, then they may use a deed of variation to achieve this objective.

If a valid deed is made, the gift is treated as passing directly from the original donor to the revised beneficiary for IHT purposes. The original potential donor is not treated as having made a transfer of value for IHT purposes.

In order to make a valid deed of disclaimer/variation, all of the following conditions must be made:

- it must be made in writing, normally in the form of a deed;
- it must be signed by the person making the variation/disclaimer;
- it should include a statement that section 142 IHTA 1984 and section 62 TCGA 1992 apply to the variation/disclaimer; and
- it must be made within two years from the date of death of the original donor.

Normally, no consent is required to enter into a disclaimer/variation; the only exception is where the amount of IHT payable by the estate is increased by the disclaimer/variation.

Deeds of variation and disclaimer are very useful post-death planning tools. They can be used to derive the maximum benefit from any unused spousal NRBs. This is now less important with the surviving spouse's ability to transfer unused NRBs.

They are also useful for transferring bequests to the surviving spouse for later transfer as a PET. For example, where the entire estate would be immediately chargeable and the surviving spouse may survive for more than seven years (or three to benefit from taper relief).

They can also be useful in circumstances where an exempt charitable legacy has been insufficient to meet the 10% limit for accessing the 36% rate of IHT. In some situations, a deed to vary the legacy to meet the limit should be considered where the IHT saved more than covers the additional charitable legacy.

Questions

Review Questions
(See Suggested Solution to Review Questions at the end of this textbook.)

Question 28.1

You recently meet with the client of a new company you act for. Stewart Desmond is the sole shareholder of Desmond Engineering Limited and he wishes to discuss the tax implications of a transaction he is contemplating. He acquired his 100% shareholding in 1995 at a cost of £10,000. The company has a 31 March period end. The following is an extract of the discussion:

"As you know, the company has a plot of land that I would like to take out of the company in order to sell it on to an interested third party. The sale should be concluded by the end of April 2021. I recently obtained an independent valuation of the property in the amount of £625,000, but I would like to transfer the warehouse out of the company to myself for £350,000. The company only paid £100,000 for the plot in June 2001."

Requirement
Outline the corporation tax, inheritance tax and capital gains tax implications of the above proposed transaction.

Part Five
Stamp Taxes

Stamp Duty

Chartered Accountants Ireland's *Code of Ethics* applies to all aspects of a Chartered Accountant's professional life, including dealing with stamp taxes. As outlined at the beginning of this book, further information regarding the principles in the *Code of Ethics* is set out in **Appendix 2**.

In addition, **Appendix 3** examines the distinction between tax planning, tax avoidance and tax evasion, which can arise in relation to all taxes, including the various stamp taxes.

29.1 Background

Stamp duty, stamp duty land tax (SDLT) and stamp duty reserve tax (SDRT) are the liability of the purchaser or acquirer of the relevant asset.

29.2 Charges to Stamp Duty

Stamp duty applies to transfers of stock/shares and marketable securities that are transferred by a stock transfer form. Stamp duty is therefore charged on instruments, i.e. written documents. It applies to acquisitions of:

1. shares, stocks or marketable securities in a UK company;
2. shares, stocks or marketable securities in an overseas company with a share register in the UK;
3. an option to buy shares, stocks or marketable securities.

The transfer of shares, stocks or marketable securities is charged to stamp duty at 0.5% of the consideration, unless the transaction falls within one of the specific exemptions mentioned below. This duty is rounded up to the nearest £5.

The purchase of shares, stocks or marketable securities for a consideration of £1,000 or less is not subject to stamp duty and the purchaser does not have to notify HMRC of the transaction. If the purchase is for more than £1,000, the purchaser will have to send HMRC the stock transfer form for stamping and pay the appropriate stamp duty.

Example 29.1

On 31 July 2021, Steven purchases his brother, Paul's, shares in their UK family trading company for £75,000.

As this is above the £1,000 consideration threshold Steven will pay stamp duty of £375 (£75,000 × 0.5%) on the share acquisition.

29.3 Exemptions

The exemptions from stamp duty are primarily for transfers where there is no consideration; these include:

1. transactions where there is no chargeable consideration, i.e. gifts, except where there is a gift to a connected company (although stamp duty group relief may be available in company-to-company situations; see **Chapter 31, Section 31.8**).
2. divorce arrangements or dissolution of civil partnership;
3. transfers of shares, stocks and marketable securities acquired through a will or variation of a will;
4. changes in trustees;
5. transfers of shares, stocks and marketable securities acquired on entering into marriage or a civil partnership acquired from a spouse or civil partner;
6. government securities and most company loan stock; and
7. transfers to charities if the shares, etc. are to be used for charitable purposes.

The above exemptions also apply to stamp duty reserve tax (see **Chapter 30**).

Example 29.2

If, in **Example 29.1**, Paul gifted his shareholding to Steven, what would the stamp duty consequences be?

Steven would not be subject a stamp duty charge as the shares were gifted to him; this is one of the exemptions from stamp duty. However, the CGT and IHT consequences of the gift should be addressed.

29.4 Administration

Stamp duty is payable by the purchaser. A document must be stamped within 30 days of its execution. Penalties can be imposed for late submission as follows:

Length of delay	Amount of penalty
Documents late by up to 12 months	10% of the duty, capped at £300
Documents late by 12 to 24 months	20% of the duty
Documents late by more than 24 months	30% of the duty

The late submission penalties apply in addition to any stamp duty due. The minimum penalty charge is £20, rounded down to the nearest multiple of £5. A penalty will not be levied by HMRC where it is less than £20.

HMRC will only cancel a late submission penalty if there is a "reasonable excuse" for submitting the documents late.

The civil penalty regime that applies for incorrect returns also applies to the various stamp taxes, including stamp duty (see **Chapter 1, Section 1.8**).

As stamp duty, SDRT and SDLT are considered to be "duties", rather than "taxes", and much of the legislation requires a knowledge of UK law (e.g. land law for SDLT), it is advisable for a solicitor or a stamp taxes specialist to be involved in preparing the necessary returns.

A taxpayer has the right to appeal against any stamp taxes (including stamp duty) penalty that they disagree with. They must do this in writing within 30 days of receiving the formal adjudication notice.

If paid late, interest is chargeable from 30 days after the date of execution, whether or not the document was executed in the UK. Interest is charged at a rate of 2.6% per annum for each day, or part day, that the payment is late.

Example 29.3

Taking **Example 29.1**, when is the stamp duty liability payable by Steven due for payment?

Steven acquired the shares on 31 July 2021. Therefore the document transferring the shares and the stamp duty thereon (£375) must be submitted for stamping within 30 days, i.e. by 30 August 2021, to avoid a late filing penalty and interest.

29.5 Consideration

The consideration subject to duty is any money or money's worth provided by the purchaser. Where the payment of the consideration is subject to a contingency, it is assumed that the contingency is satisfied. However, any contingency that would result in a reduction of the consideration is assumed not to occur. Where the consideration cannot be ascertained at the time of the transaction, it must be estimated. For example, the shares in a company may be sold for a fixed amount plus a contingent amount (typically based on the company reaching certain financial targets in the periods after the sale). At the time of the sale, the purchaser of the shares will be required to pay stamp duty at 0.5% on the fixed consideration plus the best estimate of the amount of the contingent consideration.

Any changes to the consideration caused by future events must be notified to HMRC, and duty will be paid or repaid as appropriate.

Example 29.4

Again, using **Example 29.1**, assume that Steven pays his brother £75,000 for the shares plus a contingent amount of an additional £75,000 payable in five years' time if the turnover of the company exceeds £10 million per annum for a continuous period of at least two years.

As this is still above the £1,000 consideration threshold, Steven will pay stamp duty of £375 (£75,000 × 0.5%) on the share acquisition. However, Steven would also be required to pay stamp duty on the best estimate of the amount of the contingent consideration – an additional stamp duty liability of £375 on the basis of the £75,000 contingent payment.

The total stamp duty of £750 would be due within 30 days. Should the contingent payment not be fulfilled, then any changes to the consideration as a result of future events should be notified to HMRC and the overpaid duty would be repaid as appropriate.

Questions

Review Questions

Questions on the material covered in Chapter 29 are included at the end of **Chapter 31**.

Stamp Duty Reserve Tax

Learning Objectives

After studying this chapter you will understand:

■ The liability to, and payment of, stamp duty reserve tax.

30.1 General Principles

Stamp duty reserve tax (SDRT) is a transaction tax, charged on "agreements to transfer chargeable securities", unlike stamp duty which is charged upon documents. This would generally be in situations where the stock/shares or marketable securities are acquired through the stock market or a stockbroker.

SDRT thus applies to paperless share transactions (including electronic transactions) instead of stamp duty and applies to agreements to transfer chargeable securities for consideration in money or money's worth.

30.2 Items Liable to SDRT

SDRT is payable on paperless transactions when a person buys:

1. shares, stocks or marketable securities in a UK company;
2. shares, stocks or marketable securities in a foreign company with a share register in the UK;
3. an option to buy shares, stocks or marketable securities.

SDRT is not payable on shares, stocks or marketable securities acquired via UK unit trust schemes and UK open-ended investment companies. SDRT and stamp duty are not payable on shares, stocks or marketable securities in companies admitted to trading on recognised growth markets (e.g. AIM), provided the shares, stocks or marketable securities are not also listed on a recognised stock exchange.

30.3 Rate Charged

SDRT is charged at 0.5% of the amount or value of the consideration for the sale. The tax charge arises on the date the agreement is made or becomes unconditional. Note, unlike paper transactions that attract stamp duty, there is no de *minimis* £1,000 threshold for SDRT.

Once again, the sale of government securities and most company loan stock is exempt as are paperless transactions covered by one of the exemptions set out in **Chapter 29, Section 29.3**.

Example 30.1

Steven trades on the stock exchange and holds an account online. All transactions are paperless and all could have been made through CREST (see **Section 30.4**). On 31 August 2021 he buys shares in three companies as follows:

Grow Limited – a company quoted (only) on the Alternative Investment Market – shares cost £100,000
Indelt Limited – a Germany company with a UK share register – shares cost £200,000
Partek Limited – a UK unquoted company – shares cost £5,000

The SDRT consideration for each transaction is:

Grow Limited – as these shares are quoted on AIM, no SDRT is payable.
Indelt Limited – although this is a foreign company, SDRT is payable as the company has a UK share register. SDRT of £1,000 arises (£200,000 × 0.5%).
Partek Limited – SDRT of £25 arises (£5,000 × 0.5%).

30.4 Payment of SDRT

Many paperless share transactions that SDRT arises on are carried out electronically through CREST, the electronic settlement and registration system administered by Euroclear. CREST automatically deducts the SDRT and sends it to HMRC. CREST is then paid by the stockbroker who bills the individual for the SDRT and their own fees.

If the transaction occurs "off-market" (e.g. shares transferred outside of CREST and held by a nominee like a bank), a stockbroker deals with this type of transaction and pays the SDRT direct to HMRC.

However, if the individual deals with it themselves, they must notify HMRC about the transaction and make the SDRT payment.

30.5 Deadline for Notifying and Paying HMRC

If someone makes a trade "off-market", i.e. not through CREST, HMRC must be notified in writing. If the payment could have been made through CREST but was not, the deadline for both the payment and the notice is 14 days from the date of the trade.

If the payment could not have been made through CREST, the deadline is the 7th day of the month after the calendar month in which the agreement took place. For example, if shares or units are bought on 18 April 2021, the purchaser must notify HMRC and pay the SDRT on or before 7 May 2021.

If payment is not made by the due date, interest will arise from the date the SDRT was due until the date when it is paid. Penalties may also apply, as detailed in **Chapter 29**.

Example 30.2

From **Example 30.1**, when is the SDRT liability payable by Steven due for payment?

As the shares in Indelt Limited and Partek Limited could have been bought through CREST, to avoid a late filing penalty and interest the due date for payment and written notice is 14 days from the date of the trade, i.e. by 14 September 2021.

Questions

Review Questions

Questions on the material covered in Chapter 30 are included at the end of **Chapter 31**.

Stamp Duty Land Tax

Learning Objectives

After studying this chapter you will understand:

- The operation of stamp duty land tax (SDLT), including:
  - when SDLT is chargeable;
  - the rates of SDLT applicable to different property types and acquisitions (freehold or leasehold);
  - the treatment of lease premiums;
  - stamp duty/SDLT group relief; and
  - the interaction of SDLT with VAT on property.

31.1 General Principles and Background

Stamp duty land tax (SDLT) is a modern transaction tax on land transactions involving any estate, interest, right or power in or over land in England and Northern Ireland. Scotland and Wales have their own devolved regimes, which are beyond the scope of this textbook. It should be noted that documents evidencing land transactions and chargeable to SDLT are not physically stamped.

31.2 What and Who is Chargeable

SDLT applies to land transactions and is payable by the purchaser. An acquisition can take the form of the creation, surrender, release or variation of a "chargeable interest".

A "chargeable interest" means:

1. an estate, interest, right or power in or over land or property in England or Northern Ireland; or
2. the benefit of an obligation, restriction or condition affecting the value of any such estate, interest, right or power, other than an "exempt interest".

The "chargeable consideration", for the purpose of SDLT, comprises anything given for the transaction that is money or money's worth, of which cash is by far the most common form. However, chargeable consideration can also be non-monetary, such as:

1. the release or assumption of a debt;
2. works or services; and
3. the transfer of other property.

As a general rule, any non-monetary consideration should be valued at its market value, unless otherwise provided.

31.3   Exemptions

Certain interests in land are exempt interests and as a result are not chargeable to SDLT. The following land transactions are exempt:

1. Transactions where there is no chargeable consideration, except where there is a gift to a connected company (although SDLT group relief may be available in company-to-company situations).
2. Certain transactions following a person's death (variations of a will or intestacy within two years of death, for no consideration).
3. Certain transactions on the ending of a marriage or a civil partnership (divorce, annulment or judicial separation) or on the entering into a marriage or civil partnership.
4. Transfers to charities if the land is to be used for charitable purposes.
5. The grant of a lease by a registered social landlord in certain specific situations.
6. Changes in trustees.

Example 31.1

Steven and his wife divorce on 29 December 2021. In the divorce agreement they agree that she will live in the family home for the foreseeable future and it will be under her sole ownership. The family home is valued at £750,000. Steven will live in their London flat, which will be under his ownership. The flat is worth £850,000.

No SDLT is payable on either transaction, despite each being an acquisition of land and property by Steven and his wife. This is because a transaction is exempt from SDLT for couples divorcing, separating or dissolving a civil partnership where they agree either to split the property and land between them or the property is split under the terms of a court order.

31.4   When SDLT is Chargeable

The fact that a purchaser enters into a contract for a land transaction does not automatically crystallise a liability to SDLT.

Generally, a contract governing a land transaction that is to be completed by a conveyance will be chargeable on completion. However, where such a contract is "substantially performed" before it is formally completed, the contract is treated as if it were itself the transaction provided for in the contract. In this case, the date of substantial performance is the effective date.

Broadly, substantial performance is the point at which:

1. any payment of rent is made;
2. payment of most of the consideration other than rent is made; or
3. the purchaser is entitled to possession of the subject matter of the transaction.

31.5   The Charge to SDLT

The charge to SDLT depends on whether the land in question is entirely residential or if it is wholly or partly non-residential; and by the amount of the chargeable consideration, the amount being rounded down to the nearest pound.

A mixed use property is one that incorporates both residential and non-residential elements. Non-residential property includes:

- commercial property such as shops or offices;
- agricultural land;
- forests;
- any other land or property which is not used as a dwelling;
- six or more residential properties bought in a single transaction.

31.5.1 Residential Rates

The rates of SDLT for residential land transactions in England and Northern Ireland are:

Chargeable consideration	SDLT rate
Up to £125,000	Zero
The next £125,000 (the portion from £125,001 to £250,000)	2%
The next £675,000 (the portion from £250,001 to £925,000)	5%
The next £575,000 (the portion from £925,001 to £1.5 million)	10%
The remaining amount (the portion above £1.5 million)	12%

A flat 15% rate of SDLT applies if the purchase is of a high-value residential property in England and Northern Ireland, costing £500,000 or more, by a company (or by a partnership including a company) or collective investment scheme enveloping the property. There are a number of reliefs available from this 15% rate but these are beyond the scope of this textbook.

A relief for first-time buyers of residential land and property is available if certain conditions are met (see **Section 31.5.2**).

Example 31.2

Paula and her partner exchange contracts for the purchase of a house for £375,000 on 5 December 2021, with completion expected in March 2022. This is their first purchase of a house but they do not intend to live in it as their only or main residence.

The SDLT on the property is calculated as:

Charge	Amount
0% on the first £125,000 (a)	£0
2% on the next £125,000 (b)	£2,500
5% on the final £125,000 (c)	£6,250
Total SDLT (a + b + c)	£8,750

Example 31.3

Using **Example 31.1**, if instead Steven's wife agreed to buy him out of his share of the family home at a cost of £450,000 and this was not under the terms of a court order, a SDLT liability would arise as follows:

The SDLT on the property is calculated as:

Charge	Amount £
0% on the first £125,000	0
2% on the next £125,000	2,500
5% on the final £200,000	10,000
Total SDLT	12,500

31.5.2 First-time Buyers Relief

First-time buyers purchasing a residential property for £500,000 or less can avail of first-time buyers relief, provided that they intend to occupy the property as their only or main residence.

Where the purchase price is £300,000 or less, no SDLT will be due. Where the purchase price is over £300,000 but does not exceed £500,000, SDLT is due at 5% on the 'slice' above £300,000.

31.5.3 Higher Rates for Purchases of Additional Residential Property

The rates for each 'slice' in **Section 31.5.1** are each subject to an additional 3% surcharge where the property is classed as an additional residential property acquisition. Broadly, the acquisition will be treated as an additional residential property acquisition where someone acquires a residential property (or a part of one) for £40,000 or more and the following apply:

- it is not the only residential property worth £40,000 or more owned (or part-owned) anywhere in the world;
- the person has not sold or given away their previous main home; and
- no one else has a lease on the additional property, which has more than 21 years left to run.

The rates of SDLT for additional residential property transactions are therefore:

Chargeable consideration	SDLT rate
Up to £125,000	3%
The next £125,000 (the portion from £125,001 to £250,000)	5%
The next £675,000 (the portion from £250,001 to £925,000)	8%
The next £575,000 (the portion from £925,001 to £1.5 million)	13%
The remaining amount (the portion above £1.5 million)	15%

Note that the 15% rate of SDLT that applies to purchases of high-value residential property costing £500,000 or more by a company (or by a partnership including a company) or collective investment scheme enveloping the property is not subject to the higher rates, i.e. the rate for such properties remains a flat rate of 15% and not 18%.

There are different rules for determining whether a property acquisition is an additional residential property acquisition depending on whether the purchaser is an individual or a company. There are also special rules for joint purchasers, married couples and civil partners. These rules are beyond the scope of this textbook.

31.5.4 Surcharge for Purchases of Residential Property by Non-residents

For purchases with an effective date on or after 1 April 2021, a 2% SDLT surcharge applies on purchases of dwellings in England and Northern Ireland made by non-UK resident purchasers, including certain UK resident companies controlled by non-residents. In most cases the effective date is the completion date of the purchase.

The surcharge applies to purchases of both freehold and leasehold property, as well as to SDLT payable on rents on the grant of a new lease. It is charged in addition to all other residential rates of SDLT, including the rates which apply to first-time buyers and purchases of additional dwellings. It is only applicable to residential property purchases; purchases of non-residential property and mixed transactions (except in limited cases) are excluded.

Example 31.4

Petra is resident in Germany (under the SDLT residence test, see below) and purchases an apartment in London for £750,000 on 9 November 2021. She already owns another apartment in Cambridge.

The SDLT on the property is calculated as:

Charge Amount	£
2% on the first £125,000	2,500
4% on the next £125,000	5,000
7% on the final £500,000	35,000
Total SDLT	42,500

Meaning of Residence for SDLT Purposes

The existing residence rules (see **Chapter 2**, **Section 2.2**) for other taxes do not apply for SDLT. Instead, a separate residence test applies.

An individual is treated as UK resident for SDLT if they are present in the UK at midnight on 183 or more days during a continuous 365-day period that falls within the "relevant period". If an individual does not meet this test, they are non-resident for SDLT purposes. Although SDLT applies to land transactions in England and Northern Ireland only, for the SDLT residence test, present in the UK means present at midnight anywhere in the UK, including Scotland or Wales.

The "relevant period" begins 364 days before the effective date of the transaction and ends 365 days after the effective date of the transaction. This means that the individual could be resident at the effective date of the property transaction but turn out to be non-resident due to actions taken in the year following the transaction. If the original SDLT return is filed on the basis that the purchaser is UK resident, but it later transpires that, due to circumstances in the year after completion, the individual is non-UK resident, an amended return would need to be submitted and the additional SDLT paid. Conversely, a refund of SDLT would be applied for where the residence status changes from non-resident at the date of original submission to resident in the year after completion.

Example 31.5

Andrew lives in Canada. He purchases a freehold residential property in England on 1 June 2025 for £800,000. Between 2 June 2024 and 1 June 2025, he spent 100 days in the UK. He is therefore non-UK resident for SDLT purposes in relation to the transaction and the 2% surcharge would apply to the transaction.

However, between 2 June 2025 and 1 June 2026 he spends 200 days in the UK living in the property in England. He is therefore UK resident for SDLT purposes and an amended SDLT return should be filed for a refund of the 2% surcharge applied for from HMRC.

Where an individual purchases a residential property as a partner in a partnership, the residence test for individuals discussed above applies, but the relevant period begins 364 days before the effective date of the transaction and ends on the effective date of the transaction, i.e. there is no future test. If any partner in the partnership is treated as non-resident under this rule, the entire transaction is a non-resident transaction and, as a result, is subject to the 2% surcharge.

A **company is non-resident** for the purposes of the non-resident surcharge if, on the effective date of the transaction, either:

1. the company is not UK resident for the purposes of the Corporation Tax Acts (under the tests detailed in **Chapter 8**, **Section 8.2**); or
2. the company is UK resident for the purposes of the Corporation Tax Acts, but:
   (a) is a close company (see **Chapter 9**, **Section 9.1**);

(b) meets the non-UK control test in relation to the transaction (essentially, this is where the company is controlled by one or more SDLT non-resident persons); and

(c) is not an excluded company (which excludes very specific types of companies and which is beyond the scope of this textbook).

There are more complex rules for joint purchasers which are beyond the scope of this textbook.

31.5.5 Non-residential/Mixed Use Rates

The rates of SDLT for non-residential and mixed use land transactions are:

Chargeable consideration	**SDLT rate**
Up to £150,000	Zero
The next £100,000 (the portion from £150,001 to £250,000)	2%
The remaining amount (the portion above £250,000)	5%

Example 31.6

A buyer exchanges contracts for the purchase of a commercial property for £375,000 on 5 April 2021, with completion expected in June 2021.

The SDLT on the property is calculated as follows:

Charge	Amount £
0% on the first £150,0000	0
2% on the next £100,000	2,000
5% on the final £125,000	6,250
Total SDLT	8,250

31.5.6 SDLT Rules for Bulk Purchases

Relief from SDLT for purchasers of residential property acquiring interests in more than one dwelling may be available. Where the relief is claimed, the rate of SDLT is determined not by the aggregate consideration but instead by the mean consideration (i.e. by the aggregate consideration divided by the number of dwellings), subject to a minimum rate of 1% overall.

The relief may be claimed in respect of a transaction that is a "relevant transaction", defined as either:

1. a transaction, the main subject matter of which includes interests in more than one dwelling; or
2. a transaction which is one of a number of linked transactions, the main subject matter of which includes interests in at least one dwelling and where one or more transactions linked to it includes interests in at least one other dwelling.

Example 31.7

Paula purchases the freehold of a new block of five flats for £1 million.

The transaction is a relevant transaction for the purposes of the new relief as it involves the acquisition of more than one dwelling – i.e. the five flats. Therefore, the freehold is treated as if it were interests in the individual dwellings and the chargeable consideration is divided by the number of dwellings to give a chargeable consideration of £200,000 per flat.

The amount of SDLT payable on £200,000 is £1,500 (0% of £125,000 + 2% of £75,000). £1,500 × 5 = £7,500. But this is less than 1% of £1 million (£10,000), so the total amount of SDLT payable is £10,000.

31.5.7 Interaction with VAT on Property

If output VAT is required to be charged on the supply of a commercial property, the purchaser of that commercial property will pay SDLT on the total consideration, including VAT, i.e. SDLT arises on the VAT-inclusive price (see **Chapter 35** for more detail.)

31.6 Lease Premiums

When someone buys a leasehold property, the SDLT they have to pay depends on whether it is an existing lease or a new one. If it is an existing lease (an "assigned lease"), they only have to pay SDLT on the purchase price as if they'd bought a freehold property. The same rates, thresholds and conditions for deciding whether to complete an SDLT return also apply.

How SDLT is calculated on the grant of a new lease depends on the "premium" (the lump sum paid to buy a new lease), the rent payable under the lease, and whether it is a residential or non-residential lease.

31.6.1 Residential Property

SDLT on the premium paid for a grant of a new lease of residential property is charged using the rates table in **Section 31.5.1**. The amount of any rental payments is not taken into account in determining the amount of tax payable on the premium. However, if the net present value (NPV) of the rent is more than the residential property SDLT threshold of £125,000, the buyer must pay SDLT on the rent as well as on the premium. In this case, the tax is calculated at a flat rate of 1% on the amount of the net present value that exceeds the SDLT threshold.

For example, if the NPV of the rent under a lease is £180,000 then the amount of the NPV that is over the £125,000 threshold is £55,000. SDLT has to be paid on this £55,000 at the rate of 1%. This is added to the amount of SDLT that is due on the premium.

Example 31.8

Parker Limited leases a residential property building for 15 years signing the lease on 15 September 2021. A premium of £190,000 is payable with the annual rent £20,000 per annum. The NPV of the rent is £250,000.

Calculate the SDLT arising and state the due date for payment.

Solution

SDLT arises on both the premium element of the lease and the rental element. The SDLT on the property is calculated as follows:

Charge	Amount £
Premium element:	
0% on the first £125,000	0
2% on the next £65,000	1,300
Rental element:	
£125,000 (£250,000 – £125,000) @ 1%	1,250
Total SDLT	2,550

This falls due for filing and payment 14 days later on 29 September 2021.

31.6.2 *Non-residential Property*

For non-residential properties, the amount of SDLT due when someone buys a new non-residential lease depends on the amounts of the premium and rent they pay under the lease.

The buyer pays SDLT on the premium at the same rate as they would pay on the purchase price of a freehold non-residential property using the rates table in **Section 31.5.3**, which means they will only have to pay SDLT if the premium is more than the £150,000 non-residential threshold.

Also, in respect of non-residential property, the lease rental payable during the term of a lease will also be charged to SDLT to the extent that the NPV of the rental exceeds the £150,000 threshold. The rate of charge is 1% of the excess above £150,000. A 2% rate for leasehold rent transactions applies where the NPV is above £5 million. Therefore rent transactions with a NPV between £150,001 and £5 million will pay 1% on that amount, with any amounts above £5 million charged at 2%.

Example 31.9
Assume the same facts as in **Example 31.6**, except that Parker Limited leases a commercial building. Calculate the SDLT arising.

Solution
SDLT arises on both the premium element of the lease and the rental element as follows:

Premium element:

0% on the first £150,000	0
2% on the next £40,000	800

Rental element:

£100,000 (£250,000–£150,000) @ 1%	£1,000
Total SDLT	£1,800

This falls due for filing and payment 14 days later on 29 September 2021.

31.7 Notification Threshold

The purchaser only needs to file a SDLT return when:

- buying a freehold property for £40,000 or more;
- buying a new or assigned lease of seven years or more, where the premium is £40,000 or more and the annual rent is £1,000 or more;
- buying a new or assigned lease of less than seven years, where the amount paid is more than the residential/non-residential SDLT thresholds.

31.8 Stamp Duty/SDLT Group Relief

There is potential relief from SDLT where land and buildings are transferred within a group of companies (or bodies corporate), provided certain conditions are met. This relief allows groups to move property for commercial reasons without having to consider the SDLT implications. The two group companies do not necessarily have to be resident in the UK, though there may be corporation tax consequences for the transaction. Group relief for stamp duty is also available where the inter-group transfer is of stocks, shares or marketable securities.

If the purchaser and vendor of a chargeable interest are companies and, at the effective date of the transaction, they are both members of the same group, relief from stamp duty/SDLT (which would otherwise be payable on the market value of the shares, land or property being transferred) may be claimed by the purchaser. This is so that stamp duty/SDLT is not paid on transfers within groups. The purchasing company **may** choose to pay the tax **by not claiming** the relief. However, stamp duty/ SDLT group relief is not available if the transaction is not effected for honest commercial reasons or the transaction forms part of arrangements of which the main purpose, or one of the main purposes, is the avoidance of tax. 'Tax' here means SDLT, stamp duty, income tax, corporation tax and CGT.

For the purposes of this relief, companies are members of the same group if one is the 75% subsidiary of the other or both are 75% subsidiaries of a third company. One company, B, is the 75% subsidiary of another company, A, if company A satisfies the following conditions:

1. it is the beneficial owner (either directly or through another company) of not less than 75% of the ordinary share capital of company B;
2. it is beneficially entitled to not less than 75% of the profits available for distribution to equity holders of company B; and
3. it would be beneficially entitled to not less than 75% of any assets of company B available for distribution to its equity holders on a winding up.

31.8.1 Restrictions on Availability of Stamp Duty/SDLT Group Relief

Where the purchasing company (purchaser) and selling company (vendor) are in the same group (as defined above), **no** group relief will be available to the purchaser in three situations, which are as follows:

1. Where arrangements are in existence which would mean that a person/persons, could obtain control of the purchaser **but** not the vendor. This restriction operates where the arrangements are in existence at the effective date of the land transaction. The arrangements must be such that a person/persons, could obtain control of the purchaser on/after the effective date of the transaction. It does not matter whether the arrangements are actually used to transfer control.
2. Where a non-group member, or person, is to provide/receive, directly/indirectly, all or part of the consideration for the transaction, and this is done in connection with, or in pursuance of, an arrangement.
3. Where, in connection with, or in pursuance of, an arrangement or arrangements, the purchaser ceases (or could cease) to be in the same group as the vendor, i.e. the 75% condition is no longer met.

31.8.2 Withdrawal of SDLT Group Relief

A new land transaction return should be submitted if the purchaser ceases to be a member of the same group as the vendor either:

1. before the end of a period of three years beginning with the effective date of the relevant land transaction; or
2. in pursuance of, or in connection with, arrangements made before the end of a period of three years beginning with the effective date of the relevant land transaction.

The term "arrangements" includes any scheme, agreement or understanding, whether or not legally enforceable, e.g. a memorandum of understanding.

This effectively results in clawback of the previous SDLT group relief. The clawback is calculated on the basis of the market value at the time of the original transfer and at the SDLT rates in place at that time. For the withdrawal of the relief to be considered at the time the purchaser ceases to be a member of the same group and SDLT group relief was previously claimed, the purchaser must hold either:

1. the chargeable interest that was acquired under the relevant transaction; **or**
2. a chargeable interest derived from the chargeable interest acquired under the relevant transaction; **and**
3. the chargeable interest has not subsequently been acquired at market value by means of a chargeable transaction where group relief was available **but** not claimed.

Where group relief from SDLT has been claimed on a land transaction, any subsequent withdrawal of the relief must be reported by the purchaser on a new land transaction return.

While there is no clawback of stamp duty group relief on shares, this relief is denied in the first place if at the time of the transfer, arrangements are in existence which mean that any other person can gain control of the transferee company, i.e. there are arrangements for the transferee company to leave the group (see **Section 31.8.1**).

Questions

Review Questions (Chapters 29–31)
(See Suggested Solutions to Review Questions at the end of this textbook.)

Question 31.1

A client, Mr Symon Cawell, has been involved in a number of transactions and approaches you in February 2022 for advice. Details of the transactions are as follows:

Transaction 1 (11 October 2021) Symon took on a newly executed lease on commercial property in a prime area with a premium payable of £575,000, and a net present value of the rent payable of £185,000.

Transaction 2 (31 October 2021) Symon's oldest son married in December having purchased a property on 31 October costing £225,000, in which he and his wife are living. It is their first home and they do not own any other residential properties.

Transaction 3 (12 December 2021) Symon purchased government securities valued at £325,000.

Transaction 4 (1 January 2022) Symon recently lent £1,750,000 interest-free to a friend's internet advertising company. The company is now proceeding with a reorganisation and, in order to settle the debt, Symon agreed to receive, as consideration for the debt, 1,750,000 10p shares issued by the company in full satisfaction of the original loan.

Transaction 5 (12 January 2022) Symon gifted shares in his trading company worth £565,000 to his only daughter who works alongside him and has helped him grow the business.

Transaction 6 (28 February 2022) Symon's youngest daughter is due to start university later this year. Symon has bought a second residential property near the university for her to live in at a cost of £182,000. Symon's own residence is worth £250,000.

Requirement
In letter format to Mr Cawell, calculate the relevant stamp tax arising on each transaction (if any). Provide explanations for your analysis and clearly state the applicable stamp tax.

Question 31.2

Armour Ltd owns 77.5% of Brent Ltd, and 82% of Destiny Ltd. Brent Ltd owns 51% of Gaston Ltd.

On 1 September 2021, Armour Ltd sold the freehold of two warehouses, one for £750,000 to Destiny Ltd, and one for £120,000 to Gaston Ltd.

On 1 January 2022, Armour Ltd sold 8% of its shares in Destiny Ltd to an unconnected third party. As of that date, both Destiny Ltd and Gaston Ltd continued to own the freeholds of the warehouses and to occupy them.

Requirement
Explain the SDLT implications of these transactions, together with supporting calculations where necessary.

Question 31.3

Owen owns a commercial property that has an open market value of £350,000. There is an outstanding mortgage on the property of £50,000.

Requirement
Calculate the SDLT due if he sells it to his son for £200,000 (both with and without the outstanding mortgage) or sells it to his son for full market value and uses the proceeds to pay off the mortgage.

Question 31.4

Please refer to Chapter 13, Question 13.2.

Requirement
What are the SDLT implications of transferring the freehold property from Solar to Neptune?

Question 31.5

Apple Ltd owns 77.5% of Banana Ltd, and 85% of Date Ltd. Banana Ltd owns 51% of Grape Ltd. On 1 July 2021, Apple Ltd sold the freehold of two warehouses, one for £750,000 to Date Ltd, and one for £120,000 to Grape Ltd. Both Date Ltd and Grape Ltd continue to own the freeholds and remain in occupation of the warehouses.

Requirement
Explain the SDLT implications of these transactions and calculate any SDLT payable.

Question 31.6

Recently your client company purchased a commercial property for a consideration of £760,000 plus VAT. The company incorrectly paid SDLT on the VAT-exclusive price.

The directors of the company have discussed the matter and agree that the finance director, who has since left the company, paid the SDLT in the mistaken belief that it was due on the VAT-exclusive price. As such, they believe the error was not deliberate and do not consider the need to disclose the error to HMRC.

Requirement
Calculate the underpaid SDLT as a result of this error. Recommend how the company should deal with the error identified and outline how the HMRC penalty regime operates, to include the different penalties potentially payable in respect of the error in the SDLT return.

Administration of SDLT

Learning Objectives

After studying this chapter you will understand:

- The payment of SDLT, including penalties and interest.
- The filing of SDLT returns.

32.1 Duty to Deliver Land Transaction Return Form

The relevant legislation requires that, for every notifiable SDLT transaction completed or effectively completed, a land transaction return form (LTR) SDLT1 must be delivered to HMRC within 14 days of the effective date of the transaction. If SDLT is due on a transaction, the payment deadline is the same as for the return, i.e. within 14 days of the effective date.

Interest is chargeable on unpaid tax from the relevant date until the date of payment at the current rate of 2.6% per annum for each day or part day the payment is late. As discussed in **Chapter 1** and **Chapter 29**, the civil penalty regime applies to stamp duty, SDLT and SDRT.

A return is also required for all notifiable transactions even where there is no SDLT to pay or where a relief is being claimed, e.g. group relief (see **Chapter 31, Section 31.8**).

32.2 Who is Chargeable?

The purchaser is responsible for submission of the SDLT return and payment of the SDLT due.

If there are joint purchasers, only a single SDLT return is required and this can be completed by any one of them. However, **each** purchaser must sign the declaration. If the purchaser is a partnership, the declaration must be signed by all of the partners or by a representative of the partnership nominated to HMRC.

Where there are joint purchasers, they are jointly liable for payment of the tax although that obligation can be discharged by any one of them.

32.3 Penalties

32.3.1 Flat-rate Penalties

A purchaser who fails to deliver the SDLT return by the filing date is liable to:

1. a flat-rate penalty of £100 if the LTR is delivered within three months after the filing date, or
2. £200 in any other case.

32.3.2 Tax-geared Penalties

A purchaser who is required to deliver a LTR in respect of a chargeable transaction and fails to do so within 12 months of the filing date is liable to a tax-geared penalty.

The penalty is an amount not exceeding the amount of tax chargeable in respect of the transaction (and this is in addition to the above flat-rate penalty).

Often the most appropriate way of encouraging the submission of a late LTR is for HMRC to make a determination. HMRC may also choose this option where it considers that a purchaser, from other information that it holds, should have made a LTR and the filing date has passed. In this situation, if the purchaser does not comply with the notice of determination within the specified period, HMRC may ask the Tax Tribunal to impose a daily penalty.

The SDLT regime gives purchasers clearly defined obligations and, accordingly, HMRC have clearly defined powers to ensure compliance with these obligations. SDLT is a 'process now–check later' regime, similar to self-assessment. The 'check later' aspect is supported by enquiry and information powers. The compliance checks regime, and the various powers available to HMRC as a result, apply equally to the various stamp taxes (see **Chapter 1, Section 1.8**).

Questions

Review Questions
(See Suggested Solution to Review Questions at the end of this textbook.)

Question 32.1

Adam purchased his first property on 31 October 2021 for £150,000, funded by a bank mortgage of £120,000 and a deposit of £30,000. Adam does not intend to live in the property and plans to rent the house out.

Requirement
(a) What SDLT was due and why?
(b) What is the threshold of chargeable consideration above which a SDLT return is required for a residential property transaction?
(c) On the basis that Adam's purchase completed on 31 October 2021, on what date is the associated SDLT return and payment due for filing?

Question 32.2

Please refer to Chapter 19, Question 19.10.

Requirement
Calculate the SDLT payable on the sale of the Dungannon building. State who is responsible for this liability, the due date for payment of any liability that may arise and the filing date of the relevant return.

Question 32.3

Shaun is due to undertake the following transactions on 30 April 2021:

- Purchase of shares in Apple plc, a British company, for £950.
- Purchase of shares in Peaches plc, a British company, for £6,725.
- Purchase of shares in Blackberry SA, an Italian company, for £1,600.

Shaun is old-fashioned. He likes to complete as much as possible on paper, so he will not use the electronic share trading systems and will therefore use hard copy share transfer forms for his purchases.

Requirement

Calculate the stamp duty due on the above transactions, providing explanations for your calculations. State the due date for payment of any liability that may arise and the filing date of the relevant stamp duty return.

Question 32.4

Outline the stamp duty payable (if any) on the following:

(a) A transfer of UK unlisted shares worth £90,000 on the divorce of husband to wife.
(b) A sale of shares in a UK unlisted company for £524,000 to a registered UK charity.
(c) A sale of shares in a UK unlisted company for £150,000 between unconnected individuals.
(d) A sale of UK shares worth £895 between unconnected parties.
(e) A sale of shares in a UK unlisted company for £60,000 in cash and an agreement to waive £20,000 debt owed by the seller to the purchaser.

Part Six
Value Added Tax

VAT: Recap

Learning Objectives

This chapter is an overview of the cumulative knowledge of VAT required at CA Proficiency 2.

Students should refer to their CA Proficiency 1 or other studies to understand the level of cumulative knowledge required and the necessary technical details. Students are reminded that it is their responsibility to ensure they have the necessary cumulative knowledge required at CA Proficiency 2 and that this chapter is **not a substitute for detailed revision** of that knowledge.

Chartered Accountants Ireland's *Code of Ethics* applies to all aspects of a Chartered Accountant's professional life, including dealing with VAT issues. Further information regarding the principles in the *Code of Ethics* is set out in **Appendix 2**.

In addition, **Appendix 3** examines the distinction between tax planning, tax avoidance and tax evasion, which can arise in relation to all taxes, including VAT.

33.1 Introduction and General Principle

VAT is essentially a tax on consumer spending. The basic principle of VAT is that it is charged at each stage in the supply chain of goods and services. VAT charged on sales is referred to as **output VAT**; VAT charged on purchase is referred to as **input VAT**.

"Taxable supplies" are goods or services that are liable to VAT, whether at the standard rate, reduced rate or zero rate. Exempt supplies are not considered as taxable supplies (see **Section 33.3**). Examples of taxable supplies include:

- the sale of goods (including capital items);
- the sale of services;
- the leasing or renting of goods or services; and
- the sale of land and buildings.

UK VAT legislation is consolidated in the Value Added Tax Act 1994 (VATA 1994).

The general principle of VAT is that each taxable person in the chain of supply, from manufacturer through to retailer collects and charges output VAT on **taxable supplies of goods and services** made to their customers. Each taxable person in this chain is entitled to deduct from this amount the **VAT paid on purchases** before paying the net VAT over to HMRC (or receiving a refund from HMRC). The effect of offsetting purchases against sales is therefore to impose the tax on the **value added** at each stage of production. Therefore, it is the final consumer, who is usually not registered for VAT, who absorbs VAT as part of the purchase price.

33.2   VAT Registration and De-registration

Broadly, registration for VAT is compulsory if you make:

(a)   taxable supplies,
(b)   as a taxable person,
(c)   "in the course or furtherance of any business carried on".

A **taxable** person is an individual, partnership, company or other trading entity that is either registered for VAT or required to be registered for VAT. A taxable person also includes someone who should have registered for VAT but has not yet notified HMRC.

The phrase "in the course or furtherance of any business carried on" is intended to be all-embracing. However, section 94 VATA 1994 states that the word "business" includes any trade, profession or vocation.

A trader can register for VAT by using either a paper Form VAT1 or through the HMRC's VAT Online service. The information required includes the business's turnover, activity and bank details. Once HMRC has processed the registration, the trader's VAT number will be received in writing.

33.2.1   Registration Thresholds

For 2021/22, the VAT registration limit is £85,000. Registration for VAT is necessary if:

1.   a trader's taxable supplies (excluding VAT) have exceeded the registration limit in the previous 12 calendar months (the **historical test**) – unless the trader can satisfy HMRC that their taxable supplies (excluding VAT) in the following 12 months will not exceed the de-registration limit (see **Section 33.2.4**);
2.   there are reasonable grounds for thinking that the trader's taxable supplies (excluding VAT) in the next 30 days alone will exceed the limit; or
3.   a trader takes over another business and either 1. or 2. above applies.

Hence a trader should check the cumulative total turnover at the end of each calendar month to determine if registration is necessary. In all cases, the trader must notify HMRC:

■   within 30 days of the end of the relevant month (where the threshold is exceeded as a result of past sales); or
■   within 30 days (in the case of expected sales, i.e. where the trader believes that the taxable supplies in the next 30 days alone will exceed the registration threshold).

Once notification has been submitted the trader will be registered from either:

1.   the **end of the month after that in which the annual limit was exceeded** (as a result of past sales); or
2.   **immediately** (for expected sales).

In addition to the main VAT registration tests (1–3 above), there are other situations where a business may be required to register for VAT in the UK. These are covered in further detail in **Chapter 34**, **Section 34.4**.

33.2.2   Voluntary Registration

A person can choose to voluntarily register for VAT even if their taxable turnover falls below the registration limit. The most common reason for voluntary registration is where the trader would be making taxable supplies which are zero-rated as voluntary registration enables them to recover input tax on purchases at no additional cost to their customers. Such businesses would be in a constant VAT refund position. Recap on the other reasons that voluntary registration may be considered from your CA Proficiency 1 or other studies.

33.2.3 Specific Requirements by Business Type

The type of "business" in operation affects the VAT-registration requirements, which include, but are not limited to:

- sole traders, who can only have one VAT registration for all the "business" activities they own. It is the person(s) or the entity that is VAT-registered. Form VAT1;
- partnerships – each partnership must register separately for VAT if the partners are different. In addition to Form VAT1, partnerships must submit Form VAT2, requiring details of all the partners;
- a limited company must register for VAT on its own unless it is part of a VAT group (see **Chapter 34, Section 34.2**).

33.2.4 De-registration

A person is eligible for **voluntary de-registration** if, in the upcoming 12 months, the taxable supplies (net of VAT and excluding capital assets) is not expected to exceed £83,000 (for 2021/22).

Traders may also be **compulsorily de-registered**. De-registration is compulsory if the trader ceases to trade and stops making taxable supplies, there is a change in legal status (e.g. incorporation of a sole trader/partnership to a limited company), the business is sold or the business joins a VAT group (see **Chapter 34**).

Failure to notify a requirement to de-register within 30 days may lead to a penalty (see **Section 33.8**).

On de-registration, VAT is chargeable on all stocks and capital assets on which input VAT has been claimed which are held at the date of de-registration. If VAT due is less than £1,000, it is disregarded. However, if it is £1,000 or more it must be paid to HMRC in line with the final VAT return.

33.3   VAT Supply Rates

The rate of VAT depends on the type of goods or services in question. In the UK there are three rates for taxable supplies:

	VAT rate*	VAT fraction**
Standard rate	20%	1/6
Reduced rate	5%	1/21
Zero rate	0%	0

* Used where the value of the supply/sale is quoted exclusive of VAT.

** Used where the value of the supply/sale is quoted inclusive of VAT.

In addition, goods or services can be categorised as exempt supplies, meaning they are not liable to VAT. **It is important not to confuse the two concepts of zero-rated and exempt supplies**, as a business that makes only exempt supplies is not eligible to register for VAT and therefore cannot reclaim VAT on business expenses. A business that makes zero-rated supplies can register for VAT and therefore is able to reclaim VAT on business expenses.

Appendix 1 includes examples of the types of goods in each rate. You should also recap on other examples of each type of supply from your CA Proficiency 1 or other studies.

Standard-rated supplies are those that do not fall into the other categories, i.e. are not zero-rated, reduced rate or exempt.

Zero-rated supplies are not more expensive to the end consumer; however, they are still taxable supplies (at 0%), which means a trader making zero-rated supplies can register for VAT and recover the input VAT incurred on making these supplies. A business that makes only zero-rated supplies and which is registered for VAT will therefore always be in a VAT recovery/refund position.

A trader making only exempt supplies cannot register for VAT. Therefore, such a trader will not be able to recover VAT on the costs associated with making them, i.e. no input VAT is recoverable (see **Section 33.7**).

A business that makes a mixture of taxable and exempt supplies is referred to as partially exempt (see **Chapter 34, Section 34.1**).

33.3.1 Supplies Outside the Scope of UK VAT

In addition to exempt supplies, there are other sales that are deemed to be outside the scope of UK VAT, including:

1. sales/services for which the place of supply is outside the UK (see **Chapter 34**);
2. transfer of a business that is a going concern (see **Chapter 34**).

33.4 Amount on which VAT is Chargeable

The general rule for the supply of goods or services is that the amount on which VAT is chargeable is normally the **total sum** paid or payable for the supply of the goods or services, including all taxes, commissions, costs and charges, but **not including** the VAT chargeable in respect of the transaction.

In some instances, HMRC may determine that the **value** on which VAT is charged in relation to certain transactions **between connected persons is the open market value**.

There are also a number of specific rules for imports, credit card transactions, packaging and containers and mixed and composite supplies. Recap on these specific rules from your CA Proficiency 1 or other studies.

33.5 Supply of Goods or Services

33.5.1 Supply of Goods

A taxable **supply of goods** means the **normal transfer of ownership** of goods from one person to another and includes the supply of zero-rated goods. This includes, but is not limited to:

- the transfer of ownership of goods by agreement;
- the grant, assignment or surrender of a major interest (the freehold or a lease for over 21 years) in land (see **Chapter 35** for the VAT on property rules);
- taking goods permanently out of the business for the non-business use of a taxable person (known as **self-supply of goods**) or for other private purposes; and

- transfers under an agreement contemplating a transfer of ownership, such as a hire-purchase agreement.

There are specific rules for gifts of goods and self-supply of goods which students should review from their CA Proficiency 1 or other studies.

33.5.2 Supply of Services

For VAT purposes, a "service" is any commercial activity, **other than** a supply of goods (apart from a few specific examples), which is carried out in return for consideration (any form of payment, in money or in kind).

Typical services and supplies of services include, but are not limited to:

- caterers, mechanics, plumbers, accountants, solicitors, consultants, etc.;
- hiring or leasing of goods;
- restaurants – regarded as a supply of services not goods;
- goods lent to someone outside the business; and
- goods hired to someone.

33.6 Time and Place of Supply of Goods or Services

33.6.1 Time of Supply

VAT becomes due, or a liability for VAT arises, at the time when a **supply of goods or services takes place**. This is called the **tax point**. VAT must normally be accounted for in the VAT period in which the tax point occurs and at the rate of VAT in force at that time (unless the cash accounting scheme is being used, see **Section 33.9.2**).

Review the rules for the basic tax point and the actual tax point from your CA Proficiency 1 or other studies.

33.6.2 Place of Supply

The place of supply rules are very important for VAT as goods and services are liable to VAT **in the place where they are supplied**, or are deemed to be supplied, e.g. a supply in the UK applies UK VAT rates. A supply in a foreign country would be outside the scope of UK VAT.

The rules dealing with the supply of goods and services internationally are dealt with in detail in **Chapter 34**.

Place of Supply of Goods
The place of supply of goods is deemed to be as follows:

1. If the supply requires the transportation of goods, the place where the transportation begins is deemed to be the place of supply.
2. In all other cases, the location of the goods at the time of supply determines the place of supply.

Generally, when goods leave the UK (i.e. Great Britain and Northern Ireland) the place of supply will be treated as the UK. Conversely, where goods arrive from outside the UK, then the place of supply will typically be the supplier's country.

Place of Supply of Services
The general rule for the place of supply of services is generally deemed to be:

1. the country where the recipient of the service is located (if the recipient is in business). These are known as business-to-business (B2B) supplies.
2. the country where the supplier is located (if the recipient is not in business). These are known as business-to-consumer (B2C) supplies.

However, services relating to land are always treated as being supplied in the country where the land is located.

33.7 Recovery of VAT – Input VAT

Under the VAT rules, there is no distinction between capital and revenue expenditure for VAT (in contrast to the position for income tax and corporation tax as covered in your CA Proficiency 1 studies). When calculating the amount of VAT payable/reclaimable in respect of a taxable period, a registered person may **deduct** the VAT paid by them on the purchase of goods and services, which are used for the purposes of the **taxable business**. To be entitled to the deduction, the trader must have a proper VAT invoice or relevant customs receipt as appropriate.

While a deduction of VAT is allowable only on purchases that are for the purposes of a taxable business, a situation may arise where a **portion** of a trader's purchases may be for the purposes of the taxable business and the remaining portion for the trader's **private use**. It may also arise that inputs may be used for **both taxable and non-taxable** activities. In such cases, **only the amount of VAT that is attributable to the taxable business is deductible**.

Similarly, where a trader engages in both taxable and exempt activities (partially exempt), the input VAT must be **apportioned** on a "just and reasonable" basis (see **Chapter 34, Section 34.1**).

UK VAT legislation treats VAT paid on certain expenditure as non-deductible VAT. Specific rules also apply for VAT reclaims in respect of fuel, and pre-registration input tax. If certain conditions are met, relief for output VAT previously paid on bad debts is allowed. Recap on these from your CA Proficiency 1 or other studies.

Where input VAT is not recoverable, it forms part of the cost of the asset for income tax, CGT, corporation tax and capital allowance purposes.

33.8 Administration of VAT

VAT, like all the other major taxes in the UK, is a self-assessed tax. The trader must recognise when they need to register for VAT and report their VAT position to HMRC by making regular VAT returns. The records of the calculations and back-up documents used in the preparation of VAT returns must be retained in case HMRC need to verify the calculations.

33.8.1 VAT Returns and Payment of VAT

All VAT-registered businesses are required to submit their VAT returns and to pay any VAT amounts due to HMRC online in respect of the relevant 'stagger period' of the relevant VAT year. A VAT year depends on the trader's VAT stagger group: the year ended 31 March (stagger 1), 30 April (stagger 2) or 31 May (stagger 3).

HMRC recognises limited exemptions whereby a business does not have to submit its VAT return online (including under the Making Tax Digital rules; see below) or pay their VAT electronically. Recap on these from your CA Proficiency 1 or other studies.

A VAT-registered person normally accounts for VAT on a quarterly basis in respect of the relevant VAT. A VAT period is the inclusive dates covered by a VAT return. VAT returns submitted online must be filed, and any VAT due paid, within one month and seven days of the end of the relevant quarter, e.g. a return for the quarter ended 31 March 2022 is due by 7 May 2022. Where a trader is constantly in a VAT refund situation (for example, a trader that makes zero-rated supplies), they may instead elect for monthly VAT returns so that their refund is processed quicker.

UK VAT legislation also contains detailed rules on the maintenance and retention of records (including purchases and sales records). Recap on these from your CA Proficiency 1 or other studies.

Making Tax Digital (MTD)

Making Tax Digital (MTD) is a Government initiative to implement a digital tax system in the UK. Under the MTD for VAT rules, for VAT periods starting on or after 1 April 2019, businesses with a turnover above the VAT threshold (currently £85,000) are required to:

- keep their VAT records digitally; and
- provide their VAT return information to HMRC through MTD-compatible software.

VAT Notice 700/22 sets out examples of VAT records that must be kept digitally within the MTD-compatible software. HMRC allowed businesses until 31 March 2021 to ensure there were digital links between software products; 'cut and paste' is threfore no longer an acceptable way to transfer information. From April 2022, the MTD for VAT requirement is extended to all VAT-registered businesses, including those trading below the £85,000 VAT threshold (i.e. voluntarily registered businesses). Recap on the MTD for VAT rules from your CA Proficiency 1 or other studies

33.8.2 Penalties

Late Registration/Deregistration Penalties

If a trader fails to register (or de-register) for VAT by the relevant date, the total penalty depends on how late the registration is, how much VAT is due and whether the disclosure was prompted or unprompted (see **Chapter 1, Section 1.8**).

Penalties and Interest on Late Payments of VAT

HMRC record a 'default' for VAT if a VAT return is not received by the deadline or if full payment for the VAT due on a VAT return is not paid by the deadline.

Default Surcharges

Where a trader has defaulted, they may enter a 12-month "surcharge period". If the trader defaults again during this time:

- the surcharge period is extended for a further 12 months; and
- the trader may have to pay an extra amount (a surcharge) in addition to the VAT owed.

The surcharge is a percentage of the VAT outstanding on the due date for the accounting period that is in default. The surcharge rate increases every time the trader defaults again in a surcharge period. No surcharge is payable on a first default. Recap on the surcharge rates in a 12-month surcharge period from your CA Proficiency 1 or other studies.

A trader will not be subject to a surcharge where a VAT return is submitted late and:

- the VAT is paid in full by the due date;
- no VAT is due;
- or where a VAT repayment is due.

In addition to a surcharge, HMRC may also charge a penalty of up to:

- 100% of any VAT under-stated or over-claimed if a return contains a careless or deliberate inaccuracy;

- 30% of an assessment if HMRC issues an under-assessment and the taxpayer does not inform HMRC it is wrong within 30 days; or
- £400 if a trader submits a paper VAT return, unless HMRC has advised that this is acceptable.

The position is slightly different for small businesses with a turnover below £150,000. Recap on this from your CA Proficiency 1 or other studies.

HMRC may charge interest if the correct amount of VAT is not reported and paid; and may also pay interest to a trader who has overpaid VAT. The relevant rates of interest charged on late or unpaid VAT and on repayments of overpaid VAT are set out in **Appendix 1**. A new, points-based penalty regime is to be introduced from April 2022 for late payment and late filing for VAT.

Amending Errors

Errors can be corrected on the VAT return if the net value of errors found in the relevant period is **less** than the **greater** of £10,000 or 1% of turnover (excluding VAT) (subject to a maximum of £50,000). Errors above this limit must be disclosed separately in writing to HMRC.

HMRC can only raise an assessment to correct errors retrospectively for four years. The four-year cap works both ways. Although one cannot correct an overpayment made more than four years ago, in general one would not have to correct underpayments made more than four years ago either.

HMRC can refuse a repayment of overpaid output VAT/under-reclaimed input VAT if it would unjustly enrich the claimant.

33.9   Special VAT Schemes

HMRC operates several special schemes in relation to specific business size, industry or sector. Review the detailed rules for each from your CA Proficiency 1 or other studies.

33.9.1   Flat Rate Scheme

A trader can choose to avail of the flat rate scheme, in which VAT is charged at a flat percentage of turnover, with the percentage being aligned to the particular sector in which the trader operates. There are various conditions that apply before a business can join the scheme.

The purpose of the scheme is to ease administration for small businesses, and HMRC promote it on the basis that it is quicker, easier and less onerous for small businesses.

33.9.2   Cash Accounting Scheme

VAT-registered traders normally become liable for VAT at the time of the **issue** of the invoice to their customers, **regardless** of whether they have received payment for the supplies made. For example, a trader must include in his or her VAT return for quarter ended 31 March 2022 all invoices issued during January, February and March 2022. This is known as the **invoice basis of accounting** for VAT.

Alternatively, small businesses can operate a cash receipts basis when accounting for VAT, whereby traders do not become liable for VAT until they have actually **received payment for goods or services supplied**. Likewise, they can only claim input VAT **when payment has been made for purchases** and not, as under the invoice basis, when the invoice for purchases is received.

33.9.3   Annual Accounting Scheme

Small businesses can choose to submit one return annually. In the meantime, they pay fixed sums to HMRC based on their previous year's VAT liability.

VAT – Additional Aspects

Learning Objectives

After this chapter you will be able to:

- Deal with the VAT treatment of partially exempt businesses including the *de minimis* partial exemption rules.
- Describe the concept of group VAT registration and its consequences.
- Apply the transfer of going concern provisions to appropriate transactions.
- Describe the VAT treatment of Intra-EU and NI-EU acquisitions and supplies of goods, and be able to compute the VAT liability arising on these supplies and acquisitions.
- Apply the regulations with regard to the Protocol on Ireland/Northern Ireland.
- Describe the VAT treatment of the supply of services to and from the UK.
- Apply the regulations with regards to imports/exports.

This chapter focuses on the additional VAT knowledge required at CA Proficiency 2 and builds on the cumulative VAT knowledge from CA Proficiency 1 (covered in overview in **Chapter 33**). It is therefore highly recommended that you read and understand the principles outlined in **Chapter 33** and are comfortable that your cumulative knowledge of VAT required at CA Proficiency 2 level is sufficient before studying this chapter.

34.1 Partially Exempt Supplies

Some businesses make both taxable and exempt supplies. A dentist, for example, for whom normal dentistry work is exempt while cosmetic procedures are standard rated, would be a partially exempt business. Another example is a firm of business advisors providing consultancy services (standard rated) and insurance services (exempt). In such cases, where the business is a taxable person, the business is partially exempt.

The issue for partially exempt VAT-registered businesses is how much input VAT can be recovered from HMRC. Where purchases can be directly attributed to taxable supplies, the input VAT on these is fully recoverable. Similarly, where purchases can be directly attributed to exempt supplies, VAT cannot be reclaimed. Some business purchases cannot be so easily attributed, e.g. overheads such as electricity or telephone bills. How would our dentist, who provides both exempt and standard-rated supplies, go about attributing electricity costs between the two supplies?

This issue is known as "residual" input VAT and special rules apply to determine how it is allocated. Only the portion of this input tax that relates to taxable supplies can be recovered by a partially exempt, VAT-registered business.

There are two prescribed methods for calculating the amount of residual input tax that can be recovered:

1. HMRC's standard method; or
2. a special method, determined by the business itself, which is "fair and reasonable" and subject to HMRC approval before it can be used.

34.1.1 Standard Method

The standard method is commonly used by smaller businesses as it is relatively simple to apply. There are three different calculation bases under the standard method: value-based; use-based; and use of previous year's recovery percentage.

The relevant percentage arrived at is usually rounded up to the nearest whole number. This is then applied to the residual input tax to determine the amount that is recoverable.

Value-based

The value-based standard method of apportionment of residual input VAT is:

$$\frac{\text{Total taxable supplies (excluding VAT)}}{\text{Total supplies (excluding VAT)}} \times 100 = \% \text{ of VAT recovery}$$

Self-supplies or supplies of capital goods used for the business are excluded from the calculation.

Use-based

A use-based recovery means that residual input VAT is attributed in accordance with the use or intended use of input-VAT-bearing costs in making supplies. A new partially exempt business has the option of recovering residual input VAT on the basis of use only in the following situations:

- During its registration period – the period running from the date the business first registered for VAT to the day before the start of its first tax year (normally 31 March, 30 April or 31 May depending on the periods covered by the VAT returns).
- During its first tax year (usually the first period of 12 months commencing on 1 April, 1 May or 1 June following the end of the registration period), provided it did not incur input VAT relating to exempt supplies during the registration period.
- During any tax year, provided it did not incur input VAT relating to exempt supplies in its previous tax year.

HMRC guidance sets out that businesses should use the financial forecasts in their business plan to arrive at the use or intended use of input-VAT-bearing costs. The guidance further states that provided the business plan is "logical, objective and transparent it will invariably form an ideal basis for recovery of input tax under the use-based method".

A business might therefore decide to adopt the use-based method if it leads to higher residual input VAT recovery because it gives a higher recovery rate than the value-based method. For example, a business plan might reflect 85% taxable supplies whereas the value-based calculation would give 75% taxable activity.

Use of Previous Year's Recovery Percentage

A business can use its previous VAT year's overall residual input VAT recovery percentage to determine the provisional recovery of residual input tax in each VAT return. This is then finalised by way of an annual adjustment. The finalised annual recovery percentage is then used as the provisional recovery percentage for the next year, etc.

34.1.2 De minimis *Input VAT*

Normally the input VAT on exempt supplies is not recoverable; however, HMRC relaxes this restriction for partially exempt businesses where the total input VAT on exempt supplies is below a certain limit and it meets the following conditions:

- ▪ it is less than, or equal to, £625 per month on average; and
- ▪ it is less than 50% of total input tax.

Where a partially exempt business meets both of these stipulations, it is said to be *de minimis* and is allowed to reclaim the input VAT on exempt supplies in full, even though it relates to exempt supplies. The total input VAT on exempt supplies includes both the input VAT on purchases directly attributable to exempt supplies, and the portion of the residual input VAT that relates to exempt supplies (as identified using the above methods).

There are also two simplified *de minimis* tests that make it easier for smaller businesses to determine if they can fully recover input VAT on exempt supplies without having to perform the full calculations required under the normal *de minimis* test.

Test 1: total input VAT incurred is no more than £625 per month on average and the value of exempt supplies is not more than 50% of the value of all supplies.

Test 2: total input VAT incurred less input tax directly attributable to taxable supplies is no more than £625 per month on average and the value of exempt supplies is not more than 50% of the value of all supplies.

These simplified tests should always be considered before the normal *de minimis* test.

Example 34.1

In the quarter to 30 June 2021, a sole trader incurred the following VAT-related costs:

	£
Taxable supplies (excluding VAT)	190,000
Exempt supplies	30,000
Input VAT relating entirely to taxable supplies	6,000
Input VAT relating entirely to exempt supplies	5,000
Input VAT relating to both taxable and exempt supplies	10,000

Taxable supplies include £10,000 (excluding VAT) for the sale of equipment during the three months to 30 June 2021.

What input VAT can the business recover?

Solution

The input VAT is equal to the input VAT on the purchases directly attributable to taxable supplies (£6,000) plus the portion of the input VAT relating to both taxable and exempt supplies (this business uses the value-based standard method).

The portion is calculated as:

$$\frac{\text{Taxable supplies (excl. VAT)}}{\text{Total supplies (excl. VAT)}}$$

continued overleaf

Capital goods are excluded from the calculation, so the £10,000 in relation to the sale of equipment must be excluded. The calculation is therefore:

$$\frac{£180,000}{£210,000*}$$

* i.e. £190,000 + £30,000 – £10,000.

The recovery % is therefore 85.7% (which is rounded up to 86%). This is applied to the residual input VAT of £10,000 to give the amount of input VAT that is recoverable (i.e. £8,600). The balance of residual input VAT is exempt, i.e. £1,400.

The sole trade can therefore claim £14,600 (i.e. £6,000 + £8,600) of input VAT and the other £6,400 (£5,000 + £1,400) is not recoverable.

Simplified *de minimis* Test 1 is not met as the total input VAT for the quarter of £21,000 (i.e. £10,000 + £5,000 + £6,000) exceeds £625 per month (i.e. £1,875 for the quarter).

Simplified *de minimis* Test 2 is not met as total input VAT less input VAT directly attributable to taxable supplies is £15,000 (i.e. £21,000 – £6,000) and therefore greater than £625 per month on average.

The normal *de minimis* test is also failed as the total exempt tax (£6,400) is more than £1,875 (i.e. £625 per month).

34.1.3 Annual Adjustment

Partial exemption calculations are carried out each time a trader submits a VAT return and input tax is recovered every return period accordingly. These calculations are, however, not final. The residual input calculations are carried out for each VAT period and, at the end of the trader's VAT year, an annual adjustment must be made. The same calculation must again be applied, e.g. the value-based standard method if this was used, but this time it is the annual supplies and input tax that are used in the relevant calculations.

The *de minimis* calculation is also performed again using the annual limit: total exempt input tax is less than £7,500 (£625 × 12) and 50% of total annual input tax. The simplified de minimis tests can also be used for the annual adjustment review.

The trader compares the annual calculations to the sum of the ones for each VAT period and any difference is put through as an annual adjustment. The annual adjustment is accounted for on the first VAT return of the new VAT year. For example, a trader preparing returns on a quarterly basis under VAT stagger 1 would make the annual adjustment for the VAT year to 31 March 2022 in the quarter to 30 June 2022, i.e. the quarter following the VAT year end of 31 March 2022.

Where a business passed the *de minimis* test in a given VAT year, it can provisionally treat itself as *de minimis* in each quarter of the following year. This means it can provisionally recover input tax relating to exempt supplies in each VAT period, saving the need for partial exemption calculations in every period. However, it must still carry out the annual adjustment and review calculation at the end of the VAT year. If the *de minimis* test is failed at this point, then input tax relating to exempt supplies that was previously recovered must be repaid to HMRC.

There is a cap of £1 million of input tax. If a business expects input tax to exceed this in the next year, it cannot apply the simplified annual *de minimis* tests.

34.2 Group VAT Registration

Two or more "eligible persons" under common control, such as a number of interlinked companies, sole trades and partnerships may apply for group VAT registration, subject to certain conditions being met. A VAT group is treated as a **single** taxable "person" (as if it was registered for VAT on its own).

In these circumstances, one member of the VAT group acts as the "representative member" of the group. All inputs and outputs of the group are treated as being those of the representative member. However, all parties to the group are **jointly and severally liable** for all the VAT obligations of the other group members.

34.2.1 Conditions

"Eligible persons" are bodies corporate, individuals and partnerships.

Bodies corporate

Bodies corporate includes companies of all types as well as limited liability partnerships. Bodies corporate can form a VAT group if each:

- is established or has a fixed establishment in the UK; and
- is under common "control".

"Control" for these purposes means an ability to control more than 50% of the company's share capital, distributable income or assets on a winding up.

Certain bodies corporate, called "specified bodies" must satisfy two extra conditions to be members of a VAT group. These are beyond the scope of this text.

Individuals and Partnerships

Non-corporate entities, such as individuals and partnerships, can join a VAT group if they:

- control the UK body corporate or all UK bodies corporate in the VAT group; and
- are carrying on a business by making supplies; and
- are established or have a fixed establishment in the UK in relation to that business.

An individual/partnership controls a UK body corporate if it would be the UK body corporate's holding company (if it were a company). A partnership for this purpose means two or more individuals or bodies corporate carrying on a business in partnership.

The control condition is that all members of the group are controlled either by one member of the group, which can be a body corporate, an individual, or a partnership, or a single other 'person' who is not one of the members of the group.

34.2.2 Applications for Group VAT Registration

There is complete discretion and free choice over which "eligible persons" are included in the group VAT registration. Group registration is entirely the option of the eligible persons, it is therefore possible to not include some eligible persons, or even to form more than one VAT group within the same overall group of eligible persons.

A business making exempt supplies cannot register for VAT on its own, but it can be included in a VAT group with other eligible persons making taxable supplies. By including an exempt business in the group, the group overall becomes partially exempt, which could impact on overall input VAT recovery. The consequences may be advantageous or disadvantageous depending on the specific details of the group (see below).

When an application is made to form or alter a group registration, the application is normally accepted on the day on which it is made. However, HMRC do have the power to refuse the application within 90 days of it being made where the eligibility requirements are breached or "for the protection of the revenue".

Group VAT registration can be applied for retrospectively, but this is only allowed in very exceptional circumstances. A group registration can be amended at any time. Again, the amendment is normally accepted on the date on which it is made. If any member of a VAT group ceases to satisfy the criteria for group treatment, HMRC must be notified within 30 days of the change in circumstances.

UK VAT legislation gives HMRC extensive powers to refuse to allow an otherwise eligible person to be grouped and/or to compulsorily de-group it.

34.2.3 Advantages of Group VAT Registration

The advantages of VAT group registration include:

1. offers simpler VAT accounting from a compliance perspective – only one VAT return for the whole VAT group must be filed per VAT period rather individual VAT returns, payments/repayment claims for each member of the VAT group.
2. Centralises the VAT affairs of the group – meaning the group will have much greater central control over VAT transactions.
3. Supplies between group members are completely disregarded for VAT purposes – meaning that for inter-group transactions on which VAT would otherwise arise, output VAT does not need to be charged and paid over to HMRC. Nor is the recipient of the supply required to pay the relevant input VAT to the other group member and reclaim it from HMRC. There is a cash flow advantage in respect of inter-company transactions.
4. The inclusion of an exempt business in the VAT group may enable recovery of input tax that would otherwise be irrecoverable (but see also the disadvantages below).

34.2.4 Disadvantages of Group VAT Registration

The disadvantages of group registration include:

1. Every member of the group is responsible for the entire VAT debt of the group (e.g. a group member could become insolvent. In the case of a company, this could disadvantage minority shareholders).
2. Although there is only a single VAT return for the whole group, the same time limit still applies to submit that VAT return, even though there may be many different businesses providing the required information. It may therefore be difficult to collect all the information necessary to make that single VAT return complete and to file it by the relevant deadline. This could lead to default surcharge liabilities and interest if returns are and payments persistently late.
3. As the VAT return reflects all the supplies of the VAT group, if the VAT return is late the default surcharge, which is a percentage of the VAT that is late, is much higher. It only takes one business to be late getting its information to the representative member for the group's VAT return to be late. Default surcharges (see **Section 33.8.2**) are based on the VAT due on the VAT return for the group, not the VAT shown as due from the individual business responsible for not getting its VAT information to the representative member on time.
4. Liability for past VAT errors may take time to materialise, but can still have an effect on past or present group members, e.g. if the VAT debt relates to a member that is no longer in the group, the current group members will still be liable.
5. If a group member is due a repayment of VAT, it cannot move to monthly returns therefore any refunds are received up to two months later than would have been the case if it had not been a member of the VAT group and was able to file its individual returns on a monthly basis.
6. Where the total VAT payable by a VAT group exceeds £2.3 million a year, the group must enter the Payments on Account Scheme. This will affect cash flow as payments for a quarter will be

due during the relevant VAT quarter (i.e. monthly payments of VAT are required, as opposed to quarterly payments). The £2.3 million threshold includes VAT on imports and moving goods into and out of excise warehouses.

7. If a business making exempt supplies is within the VAT group, this will restrict the VAT input recovery for the group and could lead to irrecoverable VAT where there was none previously (see the partially exempt rules at **Section 34.1**).

34.3   Transfer of Going Concern

Normally the sale or transfer of the assets of a UK VAT-registered business will be subject to VAT at the relevant rate. However, if a business is transferred as a going concern (TOGC), the supply is not chargeable and it is considered to be outside the scope of VAT, i.e. it is not treated as a supply of goods or services. As such it is not subject to VAT and no output tax is due to be accounted for on the supply of that business. TOGC should therefore be considered when a sole trade or partnership incorporates (as the trade will transfer to a new company) or when a company/sole trade sells a trade and its related assets.

The TOGC provisions are intended to simplify accounting for VAT when a business changes hands. They have the following main purposes:

■   to relieve the buyer of a business from the burden of funding any VAT on the purchase, thereby helping businesses by improving their cash flow and avoiding the need to separately value assets that may be liable at different rates, or are exempt and which have been sold as a whole; and

■   to protect government revenue by removing a charge to tax and entitlement to input tax where the output tax may not be paid to HMRC.

Where a business is transferred under the TOGC rules, the purchaser/transferee must take into account the vendor/transferor's turnover when examining the VAT registration threshold. This means that if the vendor/transferor is compulsorily registered, the buyer/transferee is also treated as compulsorily registered from the date of transfer.

34.3.1   Conditions

Where the relevant conditions are met, the TOGC rules are mandatory and not optional. Therefore, it is important to establish from the outset whether or not the sale is a TOGC.

For the TOGC provisions to apply, the following conditions must be met:

1. the assets must be sold as part of the transfer of a "business" as a "going concern",
2. the assets are to be used by the purchaser with the intention of carrying on the same kind of business as the seller (but not necessarily identical);
3. where the seller is a taxable person, the purchaser must already be a taxable person or become one as the result of the transfer, i.e. be VAT-registered;
4. where only part of the business is sold, it must be capable of operating separately;
5. there must not be a series of immediately consecutive transfers of "business";
6. there should be no significant break in the normal trading pattern before or immediately after the transfer. A short period of closure that does not significantly disrupt the existing trading pattern will usually be ignored.

34.3.2   If Output VAT is Wrongly Charged

If output VAT is wrongly charged when it should not have been, because TOGC automatically applies, the following rules apply:

1. The vendor is required to cancel any VAT invoice already issued and provide the new owner of the business/transferee with a refund of the VAT charged if this has already been paid. This is normally done via the issue of a credit note or document giving similar effect.
2. If any VAT is incorrectly shown on a VAT invoice which is not cancelled, this is able to be recovered by HMRC from the vendor.
3. The new owner is not able to reclaim this amount as input tax (even if this has been paid to the vendor in good faith) because the supply is outside the scope of VAT and there was no taxable supply to begin with. However, if HMRC are wholly satisfied that the amount of VAT wrongly charged has been both declared and paid to them by the vendor, it may at its discretion allow the new owner to recover this as if it were properly recoverable input tax.

34.4   Supplies of Goods between Northern Ireland and the EU

Prior to 1 January 2021, the UK was part of the EU-wide VAT regime. From 1 January 2021, following the end of the Brexit transition period, significant changes have been made to the VAT rules for sales and acquisitions of goods with the EU. The VAT position post-EU exit is now not consistent across the UK. Special rules apply to the movement of goods between NI and the EU due to the provisions of the Protocol on Ireland/Northern Ireland.

Essentially, the Protocol maintains alignment to EU VAT rules in relation to supplies of goods involving NI. The Protocol, however, only applies to goods and does not impact the rules for supplies of services (see **Section 34.5**).

From 1 January 2021, businesses in Great Britain (England, Scotland and Wales) ceased to apply the EU-wide VAT regime. Instead, the VAT rules applying to movements of goods between Great Britain and the EU are generally the same as those for transactions with countries outside the EU (with some exceptions). This means that goods leaving Great Britain for the EU are treated as exports and zero-rated, provided they meet certain conditions; while goods arriving from the EU to Great Britain are regarded as imports and will typically be subject to import VAT (see **Section 34.7**).

The rules for supplies between NI and GB businesses are essentially unchanged and are generally treated as a UK domestic supply (see **Section 34.4.7**).

When considering the VAT position on intra-EU/NI supply of goods to and from the EU, specific terms are used:

- ■ "acquisition" – when a business customer in NI makes a 'purchase' from an EU Member State. For example, a VAT-registered business established in NI buying goods from an Irish VAT-registered supplier (and vice versa); and
- ■ "dispatch" – when a 'sale' is made by a VAT-registered business established in NI to another EU Member State. For example, a VAT-registered business established in NI selling goods to an Irish VAT-registered customer (and vice versa).

Note: the EU comprises the following Member States: Austria, Belgium, Bulgaria, Croatia, Czech Republic, Cyprus, Denmark, Estonia, Finland, France, Germany, Greece, Hungary, Ireland, Italy, Latvia, Lithuania, Luxembourg, Malta, the Netherlands, Poland, Portugal, Romania, Slovakia, Slovenia, Spain and Sweden.

34.4.1   Acquisitions (Purchases) from EU Member States to Northern Ireland

An 'acquisition' occurs when there is a supply of goods from an EU Member State into NI. The VAT treatment of acquisitions from an EU Member State depends on whether or not the customer (i.e. the recipient) is VAT-registered in NI.

Acquisitions of Goods by an NI Customer

The treatment for VAT on acquisitions from VAT-registered suppliers in an EU Member State depends on the **taxable status** of the purchaser, i.e. whether or not they are VAT-registered. For example, a German VAT-registered company may sell to VAT-registered businesses established in NI as well as to private individuals in NI who are not registered for VAT. German VAT will not be applied to the sales to VAT-registered businesses established in NI, but it will be applied to sales to private individuals in NI and to businesses established in NI which are not VAT-registered (though subject to the impact of the distance selling rules (see **Section 34.4.4**)).

Of course, if the German company were not VAT-registered in Germany there would be no German or NI VAT implications for either the business or the private customer in NI.

When a VAT-registered trader established in NI purchases goods from a VAT-registered supplier in an EU Member State and these goods are dispatched to NI, the trader must provide the EU supplier with their VAT number (and denote that they are established in NI by putting an 'XI' prefix in front of their VAT number). Upon receipt and verification of this number and confirmation of the goods being dispatched to NI, which is still treated as being part of the EU for supplies of goods, the EU supplier, if satisfied it is an EU–NI acquisition, will zero-rate the supply of goods.

The VAT-registered NI purchaser must then account for acquisition VAT, in accordance with what is known as the 'reverse charge rule'. The reverse charge rule refers to the method by which the purchaser must account for the VAT. So, a NI VAT-registered purchaser must:

1. declare a liability for the VAT as a sale (i.e. treat it as output VAT) in their VAT return using the appropriate UK VAT rate for the goods, which may be the zero, reduced or standard rate;
2. simultaneously claim the acquisition VAT as input tax (assuming the trader is entitled to full deductibility and is not partially exempt; see **Section 34.1**); and
3. account for VAT on any subsequent supply of the goods in the normal manner.

As the transaction is entered as both an output and an input on the relevant VAT return, the effect for the trader should be tax neutral (subject to the partial exemption provisions). Thus, the trader is in the same position they would have been had they acquired the goods from a UK supplier.

Example 34.2

If a VAT-registered grocery business established in NI purchases goods from Ireland for use in its NI business, which only makes taxable supplies, the business will have full VAT recovery.

If the purchased goods have a cost of £5,000 and are standard rated, the business's VAT position is summarised as follows:

Output VAT	Ireland acquisition (reverse charge)	£1,000
Input VAT	Ireland acquisition (reverse charge)	(£1,000)
VAT due to HMRC		Nil

If the grocery business had purchased the goods from a NI VAT-registered supplier, £6,000 (£5,000 + £1,000 VAT) would have been paid to the NI supplier for the goods and then the £1,000 VAT would have been claimed back in the VAT return.

The overall net position for the grocery business is zero VAT cost under each scenario.

Partially Exempt Supplies

Where a NI purchaser is registered for VAT but makes both taxable and exempt supplies, full VAT recovery will not be available. However, the NI purchaser will still be in a similar position as if they had bought the goods from a NI supplier.

Example 34.3

If a VAT-registered dentist established in NI purchases goods from Ireland for use in her NI business, which makes exempt (routine dentist work) and taxable (cosmetic procedures) supplies, the business will be partially exempt.

If the VAT-recovery percentage (see **Section 34.1**) is 25% and the purchased goods have a cost of £10,000 and are standard-rated, her VAT position is summarised as follows:

Output VAT	Ireland acquisition (reverse charge)	£2,000
Input VAT	Ireland acquisition (reverse charge)	
	VAT recovery @ 25%	(£500)
VAT due to HMRC		£1,500

If the dentist had purchased the goods from a NI VAT-registered supplier, she would have paid £12,000 (£10,000 + £2,000 VAT) for the goods and then reclaimed £500 in her VAT return.

The overall net position for the dentist is still a VAT cost of £1,500.

Place of Supply and Time of Supply

The place of supply for acquisitions will generally be NI if the goods are either removed to NI or are acquired using the VAT number of a business established in NI (where the value of acquisitions exceeds the UK VAT registration threshold of £85,000).

The time of supply for the acquisition of goods from a VAT registered supplier in an EU Member State by a VAT registered customer established in NI is:

- the 15th day of the month following the month of acquisition; or
- the date of issue of the invoice.

Acquisitions of Goods by a NI Customer who is Not VAT-registered

If a NI trader who is not VAT-registered (or a private individual) purchases goods from a VAT-registered supplier in an EU Member State, VAT is charged in accordance with the rates and rules in the EU Member State. The VAT treatment in NI depends on the value of the goods received.

Where a non-VAT-registered business customer established in NI (or a NI private individual) purchases goods from an EU supplier, the NI customer pays the VAT charged by the supplier from the relevant EU Member State and no additional UK VAT liability arises. The place of supply is the country where the supplier is established, i.e. the relevant EU Member State. This is subject to the rules on distance selling (see **Section 34.4.4**).

However, where a non-VAT-registered business customer established in NI purchases goods from an EU supplier and the value of the purchases exceeds £85,000 in a year (i.e. the UK VAT-registration threshold), the NI customer must register and account for VAT in the UK at the relevant rate. When an acquisition is made, VAT becomes due when the goods are acquired and should be accounted on the relevant VAT return. However, VAT cannot be reclaimed on any purchases for the business as it is not making any taxable supplies.

34.4.2 Dispatches (Sales) to EU Countries from Northern Ireland

A 'dispatch' is the term used to refer to a supply of goods from NI to an EU Member State. The VAT treatment of dispatches from NI depends on whether or not the customer (i.e. the recipient) is VAT-registered in the EU Member State.

Dispatches of Goods to VAT-registered Customers in an EU Member State

Where a VAT-registered supplier established in NI supplies goods to a VAT-registered customer within the EU, the transaction will be zero rated in NI but will be liable to VAT in the EU Member State of the purchaser. Essentially, the place of supply for dispatches will be the EU Member State of the customer.

A VAT-registered trader in NI may zero rate the supply of goods to a business customer in another EU Member State, but only if:

1. the business customer is registered for VAT in the EU Member State;
2. the customer's VAT registration number (including country prefix) is obtained and retained in the supplier's records;
3. this number, together with the supplier's VAT registration number, is quoted on the sales invoice; and
4. the goods are dispatched or transported to that EU Member State (and evidence is retained to show this dispatch).

If any of the above four conditions are not satisfied, the NI supplier must charge UK VAT at the appropriate rate, i.e. the transaction is treated as if it had taken place between an NI supplier and an NI customer. If the conditions for zero-rating are subsequently established, the purchaser (i.e. the EU VAT-registered customer) is entitled to recover the VAT paid from the VAT-registered supplier established in NI. The VAT-registered supplier established in NI can then make an adjustment in their VAT return for the period.

Dispatches of Goods to Non-VAT-registered Customers in an EU Member State

Generally, supplies made by a VAT-registered supplier established in NI to a non-VAT-registered person in an EU Member State are treated as taking place in NI. Therefore, UK VAT must be charged accordingly. However, where the combined values of sales made to the non-VAT registered EU customer exceeds the pan-EU distance selling threshold, the seller will be required to account for VAT in the relevant EU Member State (see **Section 34.4.4**).

Example 34.4

Soft Sofas Ltd, a UK resident and VAT-registered company based in NI, completes two sales to two customers. The first customer is a VAT-registered company in France; the second is a non-VAT-registered business in Portugal. The VAT treatment of each transaction will be as follows:

■ The French customer (EU company and VAT-registered) – Soft Sofas Ltd will zero rate the supply, provided the customer has given its VAT registration number. The customer must account for VAT under the reverse charge rules (output VAT and input VAT) in France, using the French VAT rate.

■ The Portuguese customer (EU company but not VAT-registered) – Soft Sofas Ltd will have to charge VAT at the UK rate. The customer cannot reclaim any VAT as it is not VAT-registered.

34.4.3 Distance Selling

Distance selling refers to the supply of goods by a business in Northern Ireland to a customer in an EU country, where the customer is not VAT-registered and the NI business is responsible for the delivery of the goods. It also refers to the reverse situation, where an EU supplier sells to a non-VAT registered person in NI. The most common types of distance selling are mail order or internet sales to private individuals, unregistered businesses, charities or public bodies. The distance-selling rules only apply to goods and not to services.

EU Suppliers Selling to non-VAT-registered NI Persons

Usually, an EU supplier who sells goods to a non-VAT-registered NI person will charge VAT in accordance with the VAT rates in their own country (i.e. an EU Member State). Prior to 1 July 2021, if the value of such sales exceeded £70,000 per annum, the EU supplier became liable to register for VAT in the UK and account for VAT on these sales.

From 1 July 2021, a threshold of €10,000 (£8,818) applies to the total cross-border sales made by an EU business to non-VAT registered customers, both in NI and in other EU countries. Once the threshold is breached, VAT in the country in which the customer is established will be due. To ease the administrative burden of businesses having to register in each EU Member State where they have customers, the EU supplier can use the new One Stop Shop (OSS) quarterly VAT reporting and payment system. This means that businesses falling in scope of the new rules will no longer be required to register for VAT in each EU Member States where they have customers. A business opting to register for OSS will be able to do so once in any EU Member State or in the UK, provided that it is VAT-registered in the EU Member State or is trading with the EU under the Northern Ireland Protocol.

Once registered for OSS, the business must account for VAT on all its distance sales through that OSS. Businesses exceeding the £8,818 threshold that wish to use the UK's OSS will be required to register for VAT in the UK if they are not already registered and will require an 'XI' indicator. The requirement to VAT-register will apply even if the overall turnover is below the normal UK VAT-registration threshold of £85,000.

For example, if a French company, which operates a catalogue selling adult clothing, makes sales in excess of €10,000 (£8,818) a year to non-VAT-registered customers in other EU Member States and NI, the French company will have to register for VAT in each EU Member State in which sales are made. The VAT OSS procedure can however be used as a simplification.

NI VAT-registered Suppliers Selling to Non-VAT-registered Persons in the EU

NI suppliers selling to EU non-VAT-registered customers had to be conscious of the distance-selling threshold in the various EU countries where their non-VAT-registered customers were located. Each EU Member State applied its own distance-selling threshold. For example, the Republic of Ireland's threshold was set at €35,000, whereas Germany's threshold was €100,000.

Prior to 1 July 2021, where a NI supplier breached another Member State's distance-selling threshold, they were required to register for VAT in that Member State and charge VAT in accordance with the local rates in that Member State. From 1 July 2021, the same system that applies to EU suppliers making sales to non-VAT-registered persons in NI will also apply where an NI VAT-registered business sells goods to non-VAT-registered customers in the EU (i.e. the threshold of €10,000 (£8,818) applies). For example, if an NI business sells £3,000 of goods to France, Italy and Bulgaria, the NI supplier would be required to account for VAT in each of these EU Member States as the combined value (£9,000) exceeds the £8,818 pan-EU threshold. The default requirement is to register for VAT in each EU Member State. However, the NI seller can register for the OSS in the UK and make one declaration for all three sales.

34.4.4 Summary of VAT Treatment of EU–NI Supply of Goods

The various permutations of the VAT treatment of EU–NI supply of goods are summarised in **Table 34.1**.

TABLE 34.1: VAT TREATMENT OF EU–NI SUPPLY OF GOODS

Country of establishment of supplier	Country in which customer is established	Status of customer	Place of supply	Person liable to charge and collect UK VAT
Dispatches (sales from NI)				
NI	NI	Business (VAT-registered) or private (non-VAT-registered)	UK	NI supplier will charge UK VAT at the appropriate rate depending on the type of goods.
NI	EU Member State	Business (VAT-registered)	EU Member State	NI supplier will zero-rate the supply where the conditions are satisfied (reverse charge may be applied by the EU customer under their local VAT rules).
NI	EU Member State	Private or business (non-VAT-registered)	NI	NI supplier will charge UK VAT at the appropriate rate depending on the type of goods, unless the supplier's sales to the EU exceed the distance-selling threshold.
Acquisitions (purchases brought to NI)				
EU Member State	NI	Business (VAT-registered)	NI	EU supplier will zero-rate the supply in their own country where the conditions for zero-rating apply (reverse charge to be applied by the NI customer).
EU Member State	NI	Private or business (non-VAT-registered)	EU Member State	EU supplier will charge VAT at local rate in their country. Customer does not have to account for UK acquisition VAT, unless the supplier's sales to the UK exceed the distance-selling threshold. However, if the NI business customer acquires goods worth £85,000 or more, they may have to register for VAT in the UK.

34.4.5 *Administrative Aspects of EU–NI Supplies of Goods*

EC Sales List

When a VAT-registered trader, including one established in NI, makes **zero-rated supplies** of goods to a trader in an EU Member State, summary details of those **sales** must be returned to

HMRC on a quarterly or monthly basis. This return, known as an EC Sales List (ESL), is to enable the authorities in NI and the EU Member State to ensure these transactions are properly recorded and accounted for. The return is made to the VAT authorities in the **country of the supplier** and should include:

- the VAT number of the foreign Member State purchaser (this can be verified with HMRC); and
- the total value (in Sterling) of sales to that purchaser in the quarterly period.

For online ESL submissions the return must be submitted **within** 21 days, or within 14 days for paper ESLs, of the end of the period covered by the return.

Intrastat VAT Return

The Intrastat system is designed to ensure that all **statistical data** relating to purchases and sales of goods between NI and EU Member States is available to the relevant authorities in each country and to the EU Commission. Certain thresholds of intra-NI/EU sales and purchases are required before an Intrastat return is required. The threshold for EU sales (dispatches) is currently £250,000, and for EU purchases (acquisitions) it is £1,500,000. Services are excluded from Intrastat.

Until 31 December 2021, businesses importing goods (arrivals) into Great Britain from the EU must also prepare monthly Intrastat reports if over the £1.5 million reporting threshold. This temporary measure only applies to purchases; there is no equivalent obligation on GB businesses exporting goods (dispatches) to the EU to report these on an Intrastat return.

XI VAT Prefix

Supplies of goods between NI and an EU country continue to be recorded in the UK VAT return (in boxes 2, 8 and 9) as EU transactions, i.e. as acquisitions and dispatches. However, invoices for such supplies must include a prefix 'XI' rather than GB before the business's VAT number, e.g. XI 123456789 instead of GB 123456789. This is to distinguish the transactions from supplies between GB businesses and the EU.

34.5 Supplies of Goods between Great Britain and the EU

From 1 January 2021, the VAT rules applying to movements of goods between Great Britain and the EU are generally the same as those for transactions with countries outside the EU, i.e as exports (for goods sold to the EU) and imports (for goods purchased from the EU) (see **Section 34.7**). There are some limited exceptions to this general rule which are beyond the scope of this textbook.

Example 34.5

Sweet Chestnut Ltd, a VAT-registered business based and established in London, makes the following transactions:

- sale of furniture to a VAT-registered company based in France; and
- purchase of raw materials from a VAT-registered company based in Spain.

The VAT treatment of each transaction is as follows:

- Sale to France – as this is an export, the place of supply is Great Britain and the supply will be zero rated. This would be the case regardless of whether or not the customer is VAT-registered.
- Purchase from Spain – as the place of supply is outside GB, Sweet Chestnut Ltd must account for UK import VAT at the appropriate UK rate for those goods. Sweet Chestnut Ltd can postpone payment of the import VAT and account for it in its VAT return (i.e. the VAT is accounted for as input and output VAT on the same return). The VAT should therefore be reclaimable in full (provided Sweet Chestnut Ltd is not partially exempt).

34.6   Goods between Great Britain and Northern Ireland

34.6.1   Supplies of Goods between Great Britain and Northern Ireland

As set out earlier, the Northern Ireland Protocol means that NI maintains alignment with the EU VAT rules for goods, including on goods moving to, from and within Northern Ireland. However, Northern Ireland is also part of the UK's VAT system.

Technically then, movements of goods between Great Britain and NI are imports/exports. However, for VAT accounting purposes they are essentially treated as UK domestic supplies. This means that the supplier will charge VAT as normal and the customer will recover VAT subject to the normal input tax recovery rules.

34.6.2   Movement of Goods between Great Britain and Northern Ireland

If a VAT-registered business moves its **own goods from Great Britain to Northern Ireland**, this will be seen as vatable and the business will need to account for VAT on the movement. It should be included as output VAT on the VAT return.

Where the goods are being used for taxable sales, the VAT may also be reclaimed as input VAT on its UK VAT return, subject to the normal rules.

Where the goods are used for exempt or partially exempt activities, the business may be required to make an adjustment to its partial exemption calculations.

A business will not be required to account for VAT when it moves its goods from Northern Ireland to Great Britain unless these goods have been subject to a sale or supply.

34.7   Cross-border Reclaims of VAT by NI Businesses

If a business that is registered for VAT in Northern Ireland incurs VAT on goods and services purchased in another country, it may be able to reclaim the VAT incurred. Prior to 1 January 2021, a UK business (i.e. businesses in both Great Britain and Northern Ireland) could recover VAT incurred in EU Member States using an electronic system. However, from 1 January 2021, this system is only available to NI businesses and only in prescribed circumstances. To use the EU electronic system, the following conditions need to be met:

- the claim is by a VAT-registered business in Northern Ireland;
- the VAT is incurred in an EU Member State;
- the VAT is incurred on goods, i.e. VAT on services is not reclaimable under the system.

Under the system, businesses established in NI can submit claims for EU VAT electronically, on a standardised form, to HMRC. Businesses can submit claims up to nine months from the end of the calendar year in which the VAT was incurred. The tax authorities in the EU Member State of refund have four months to make repayments, unless further information is requested, in which case the deadline extends up to a maximum of eight months. The Member State of refund pays interest in cases where the business meets all its obligations but deadlines are not met by the tax authorities. All EU Member States are required to afford a right of appeal against non-payment in accordance with the procedures of the Member State of refund.

Similarly, non-EU businesses that incur UK VAT while temporarily visiting NI can claim to recover UK VAT by filing Form VAT65A electronically. Claims must be submitted within six months after the end of the 'prescribed year' when the VAT was charged. The prescribed year runs from 1 July to 30 June, so it is necessary to make a claim by 31 December.

34.8   Imports/Exports of Goods from/to the UK

For VAT purposes, imports are goods arriving from non-EU countries into any part of the UK (i.e. Great Britain and NI) and, from 1 January 2021, goods arriving from EU countries into Great Britain. Exports are goods that are sold and transported to a customer based outside the EU from any part of the UK and, from 1 January 2021, for goods sold and transported to a customer in the EU from a business in Great Britain. The movement of goods between the EU and NI are not imports/exports but are instead dealt with as EU acquisitions and dispatches (see **Section 34.4**).

Essentially, the place of supply for exports is the UK; and for imports the place of supply is the overseas country.

34.8.1 Imports of Goods

Although the import of goods as defined above is not a UK supply, VAT will be due on the import and it will be the customer's obligation to account for this import VAT. The fact that the place of supply is not the UK means that the overseas supplier will not have any UK VAT obligations. Imports are chargeable to VAT at whatever rate would have been applied if the goods had been bought in the UK.

An importer of goods (i.e. someone buying goods from outside the EU to any part of the UK or, from 1 January 2021, from the EU to Great Britain) must calculate VAT on the value of the goods imported and account for it at the point of entry into the UK. The importer can then deduct the VAT payable as input tax on their next VAT return if they are VAT-registered. HMRC issues monthly certificates to importers showing the VAT paid on imports.

If security can be provided, the deferred payment system can be used, whereby payment is automatically debited from the importer's bank account each month rather than being made for each import when the goods arrive in the UK. All incidental expenses (e.g. packing, transport and insurance costs) incurred up to the first destination of the goods in the UK should be included in the value of imported goods.

Postponed Accounting for Import VAT

From 1 January 2021, most goods arriving from an EU Member State to Great Britain will be treated as an import and will be subject to import VAT. This change had the potential to create significant cash flow issues for many GB businesses as import VAT was generally paid at the point the goods entered the UK (although it could be deferred) and was later recovered only once a VAT return had been submitted. This caused a time lag between paying the import VAT upfront and the subsequent VAT reclaim. Goods arriving into the UK from a non-EU country were also subject to this treatment.

To alleviate this, 'postponed accounting' was introduced for all imports (both EU and non-EU into Great Britain, and non-EU into NI) from 1 January 2021. Businesses importing goods can now account for the VAT on their next VAT return, allowing the goods to be released from customs without the need for VAT payment. In effect, this means that the VAT is accounted for as input and output VAT on the same return, similar to the reverse charge procedure (see **Section 34.4.1**). As a result, the VAT should be reclaimable in full, unless the business is partially exempt.

There are special rules for consignments of goods worth £135 or less. Where these rules apply, UK supply VAT is charged at the point of sale rather than as import VAT.

34.8.2 Exports of Goods

All exports (as defined above) irrespective of the type of goods, are zero-rated for VAT purposes. To be zero-rated, HMRC must be satisfied that the export has taken place and require evidence from the exporter to that effect. The evidence must take the form specified by HMRC and be submitted to it within three months of the date of supply.

Example 34.6
GJA Pens Ltd, a UK resident and VAT-registered company established in Belfast, makes the following transactions:

(a)   sale of pen pots to Desktop Circus Inc., a VAT-registered company based in America; and
(b)   purchase of pen cases from Canadian Cases Corp., a VAT-registered company based in Canada.

What is the VAT treatment of each transaction? If the supplier in transaction (b) had been a VAT-registered EU business set out how the transaction would have been treated.

(a)   The customer is outside the EU. The supply will be zero-rated (export), regardless of whether the customer is VAT-registered or not.
(b)   The supplier, Canadian Cases Corp., is outside the EU. Although the place of supply is outside the UK, the UK customer (i.e. GJA Pens Ltd) must account for UK import VAT – but this should be reclaimable in full, unless GJA Pens Ltd is partially exempt.

If the supplier had been based in the EU, the supplier would have zero-rated the supply in their own country (when provided with the VAT number of GJA Pens Ltd). GJA Pens Ltd (the customer) would have accounted for UK output VAT on acquisition, which would then be fully reclaimable as input VAT (provided the business is not partially exempt).

34.8.3   Summary of VAT Treatment of Imports and Exports

The VAT treatment of imports and exports (i.e. any goods arriving or leaving the UK unless they relate to goods supplied between Northern Ireland and an EU country) of goods is summarised in **Table 34.2**.

TABLE 34.2: VAT TREATMENT OF SUPPLIES OF IMPORTS AND EXPORTS

Country of establishment of supplier	Country in which customer is established	Status of customer	Place of supply	Person liable to charge and collect UK VAT
GB or NI business (exporting goods)	Outside EU	Business or private	UK	UK supplier (zero rated).
GB business (exporting goods)	Inside EU			
Outside EU (importing goods)	GB or NI	Business	Outside EU	Although place of supply is outside UK, UK customer must account for UK import VAT (should be fully reclaimable if business is not exempt or partially exempt). Postponed accounting for import VAT can apply (see **Section 34.7.1**).
Inside EU (importing goods)	GB	Business	Inside EU	
Outside EU (importing goods)	GB or NI	Private	Outside EU	Although place of supply is outside UK, UK customer must pay UK import VAT (but it will not be reclaimable).
Inside EU (importing goods)	GB	Private	Inside EU	

34.9 Cross-border Supplies of Services

Businesses involved in cross-border supplies of services must be very careful to establish in which country the place of supply is. As mentioned in **Chapter 33, Section 33.6.2**, the place of supply rules determine where a supply of services is made, and where any VAT is payable. They also determine whether, if VAT is due on a supply, it should be accounted for by the supplier of a service or their business customer. It should be noted that the rules for services apply on a UK-wide basis, unlike the regime for goods where special rules apply to NI as a result of the Northern Ireland Protocol.

34.9.1 Place of Supply of Services

The general rules for the place of supply of services is (subject to a number of exceptions) deemed to be:

1. If the recipient is in business, in the country where the recipient of the service is located. These are known as business-to-business (B2B) supplies.
2. If the recipient is not in business, in the country where the supplier is located. These are known as business-to-consumer (B2C) supplies.

If the supply is in the UK it is subject to UK VAT; if the supply is in a different country it is said to be 'outside the scope' of UK VAT.

B2B Supplies (under the General Rule)
Where a UK business is the recipient of a B2B supply of services, the reverse charge basis applies, i.e. the UK business customer acts as if they are both the supplier and the recipient of the services (see **Section 34.4.1**). It is important to note that a customer does not need to be registered for VAT to be categorised as a business customer receiving a B2B supply of services (i.e. both VAT-registered and non-VAT-registered businesses are included).

If a UK business which is not already UK VAT-registered receives supplies of B2B general rule services from overseas suppliers, the value of those supplies must be taken into account when determining whether the UK business exceeds the VAT registration threshold and thus needs to be registered for UK VAT.

Conversely, where the UK business is the supplier and there is a B2B supply, the service is outside the scope of UK VAT (as the place of supply is deemed to be in the overseas country, i.e. where the recipient of the service is based). If the overseas country is in the EU, a similar reverse charge mechanism applies and the EU customer will account for the VAT. For non-EU countries the rules vary considerably and depend on local rules.

For a cross-border B2B supply of services, because the scope of these supplies is more extensive than it is for supplies of goods (where VAT registration of the customer is required), it is important to confirm that the customer is genuinely in business. If a business customer is based in the EU, the simplest way to check this is to ask for their VAT registration number. If the business is based outside of the EU or is a business customer that is not VAT registered (perhaps because they only make exempt supplies), other evidence may be obtained to confirm that the customer is in business, such as a letter from the local tax authority or the local Chamber of Commerce.

Example 34.7

A UK VAT-registered company charges a fee for services supplied to a French business and receives a supply of services from a Canadian business customer. Both types of services fall under the general rules for B2B supplies.

The VAT treatment for each is as follows:

▪ As a B2B supply of services, the place of supply is where the customer is established, i.e. France. The French business should provide the UK supplier with its VAT registration number or, if not VAT registered, an alternative form of commercial evidence to confirm that it is in business. No UK VAT will be charged, but the French customer will account for French VAT using the reverse charge mechanism.

▪ As a B2B supply, the place of supply is where the customer is established, i.e. the UK. The UK customer should provide its VAT number to the Canadian supplier. No Canadian tax should be charged on the transaction. The UK business will instead account for UK VAT on the transaction using the reverse charge mechanism. The UK VAT should be fully recoverable, provided the business is not exempt or partially exempt.

B2C Supplies (under the General Rule)

For B2C supplies, the general rule is that the place of supply is where the supplier is based. Therefore, if it is a UK supplier the place of supply is the UK and UK VAT would be charged to the customer. This applies regardless of where the customer is based.

Where a UK customer (which is not in business) receives services from a non-UK supplier, the supply is outside the scope of UK VAT and is dealt with in the overseas country.

Example 34.8

Xylem Ltd, a company based in Belfast, supplies a service to Peter, a non-business customer in Germany. The service falls within the general place of supply rules for services.

As this is a B2C supply of services, the place of supply is where the supplier is based, i.e. the UK. Xylem Ltd must therefore charge and account for UK VAT on its supply to the German customer.

Example 34.9

Alasdair, a private customer based in Edinburgh, receives a supply of services from a VAT-registered business in Belgium. The service falls within the general place of supply rules for services.

This is a B2C supply of services. As the supplier is based in Belgium, it must charge and account for VAT in Belgium (at the relevant rate for the type of service) on its supply to Alasdair. No UK VAT is charged.

Example 34.10

A UK VAT-registered business provides services to the following:

(a) a Danish company, registered for VAT; and
(b) a private Italian customer.

Who is liable to pay UK VAT in each case?

(a) The customer is a business and so it is a B2B supply and the place of supply is therefore Denmark. Therefore, there is no UK VAT (but reverse charge will apply to the Danish customer under its local VAT rules).
(b) The customer is not a business. The place of supply is therefore the UK, the UK supplier will therefore charge output VAT at the relevant UK rate.

34.9.2 Time of Supply of Reverse Charge Services

The rules regarding the tax point for reverse charge services are governed primarily by when a service is complete, if this is earlier than when payment is made. A distinction is also made between single and continuous supplies. As noted previously, for single supplies, the tax point occurs when the service is completed or when it is paid for, if this is earlier. In the case of continuous supplies, the tax point is the end of each billing or payment period.

For example, if leasing charges are billed monthly or the customer is required to pay a monthly amount, the tax point is the end of the month to which the bill or payment relates. Again, if a payment is made before the end of the period to which it relates or before the end of the billing period, then that payment date, rather than the end of the period, is treated as the tax point.

For continuous supplies that are not subject to billing or payment periods, the tax point is 31 December each year, unless a payment has been made beforehand. In that case the payment created a tax point.

34.9.3 Summary of the VAT Treatment of Cross-border Supplies of Services

A summary of the permutations of the general rule on the cross-border supply of services is shown in **Table 34.3**.

TABLE 34.3: VAT TREATMENT OF CROSS-BORDER SUPPLY OF SERVICES (GENERAL RULE)

Country of establishment of supplier	Country in which customer is established	Status of customer	Place of supply	Person liable to charge and collect UK VAT
UK	UK	Business or non-business/ private	UK	Supplier
UK	Outside the UK	Business	Outside the UK	No UK VAT (reverse charge will likely be applied if the customer is based in the EU. If based outside the EU it will depend on the country's local VAT rules)
UK	Outside the UK	Non-business/ private	UK	Supplier
Outside the UK	UK	Business	UK	Customer (reverse charge to be applied by the UK customer if VAT registered; if not may need to register for UK VAT)
Outside the UK	UK	Non-business/ private	Outside the UK	No UK VAT (the supplier will account for any local taxes and charge these to the UK customer)

Questions

Review Questions
(See Suggested Solutions to Review Questions at the end of this textbook.)

Question 34.1

Happy Pets Ltd is VAT registered and established in Northern Ireland and distributes pet food to home and foreign markets. The following transactions were undertaken by the company during the VAT period March–May 2021:

Sales invoiced to customers within the UK	£250,000
Sales invoiced to customers in the US	£10,000

The above amounts are stated net of VAT. The VAT rate applicable to the company's sales is 20%. During the same period, purchase invoices were received in respect of the following:

	Gross Invoice Value £	VAT Rate Applicable %
Stock purchased from suppliers in the UK	223,260	20
Stock purchased from suppliers in Ireland	50,000	20
Professional fees	5,880	20
Oil	1,050	20
Computer	8,934	20

The amounts stated include VAT where appropriate.

Requirement
Calculate the VAT due/(repayable) for the period March–May 2021.

Question 34.2

Elixir Ltd operates a NI-based, VAT-registered business selling materials for the repair and maintenance of yachts and small boats. During the VAT period of three months ended 31 October 2021, it recorded the following transactions.

	VAT Rate	£
Sales of Services (exclusive of VAT)		
Sales in UK		950,000
Sales to Spain (to Spanish VAT-registered customers)		320,000
Sales to non-VAT-registered customers in Ireland		25,000
Sales to VAT-registered customers in Ireland		135,000
Sales to customers located in Singapore		46,000
Costs (inclusive of VAT where applicable)		
Purchase of materials from UK suppliers	20%	423,000
Purchase (acquisitions) of equipment from German supplier	20%	200,000
Purchase of machinery locally	20%	235,020

continued overleaf

Legal fees	20%	11,748
Repairs and maintenance of office and equipment	20%	16,212
Audit and accountancy fees	20%	12,924
Electricity and gas	20%	2,520
Salaries and wages	n/a	167,000
Advertising costs	20%	35,250

Notes:
All of the above purchases of goods and services (except for wages, salaries and acquisitions) are supplied by businesses that are registered for VAT in the UK. The acquisitions are purchased from a VAT-registered business in Germany.

Requirement
Calculate the VAT payable by, or repayable to, Elixir Ltd for the VAT period ended 31 October 2021.

Question 34.3

You are a newly qualified Chartered Accountant working for Interserv Group Ltd (IGL), a large corporate group based in Belfast. The group structure is set out below. IGL provides services to distinct markets and is run through three separate companies with the head office costs being invoiced to the subsidiaries on a cost-plus basis. All the administration for the IGL group is done centrally and there is some overlap in activities.

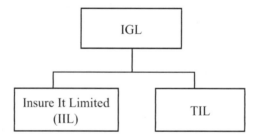

Each company in the group is UK registered, tax resident and has an establishment in the UK. Each of the two subsidiaries is 100% owned. IGL is the holding company of the group and its only income is from the provision of services to the two subsidiaries. IIL provides insurance underwriting services to the freight industry; TIL organises delivery of freight for customers.

The VAT figures from the last two quarters were as follows:

	IGL	IIL	TIL
Period 12/21	£	£	£
Total sales before VAT	*180,000	978,000	946,000
Input VAT incurred	35,086	60,334	71,345
Period 09/21			
Total sales before VAT	*180,000	834,000	828,000
Input VAT incurred	37,301	67,129	76,847

* IGL services are charged 50:50 to IIL:TIL. Only IGL and TIL are VAT registered as IIL provides exempt services to its customers (insurance).

Requirement

The finance director has asked you to consider whether it would be possible to simplify the VAT administration process by forming a VAT group. He asks you to prepare a note on this using the figures from the last two VAT quarters to illustrate any implications

Question 34.4

You are a junior in a small firm of accountants. You are currently preparing the VAT return for a client, Hayley Reid, who runs a number of successful beauty salons in the local area. The VAT return is for the quarter ending 31 December 2021, the busiest quarter for the business in the run up to Christmas.

You review the VAT file and note that gross sales receipts reported on the December 2020 return were much higher than the sales figures Hayley has provided you with for the 31 December 2021 quarter end. You would expect that sales in the current quarter to 31 December 2021 would be higher as Hayley opened a new salon in October 2021, which she tells you has been very busy since it opened. In addition, turnover in the previous quarters in 2021 exceeded the comparable turnover figure for the equivalent quarter in 2020.

When you mention this to Hayley she seems edgy and doesn't offer to provide till receipts to substantiate the cash takings nor any other explanation for the lower sales for the quarter to 31 December 2021. You are convinced that she has deliberately understated her true sales figure to reduce her VAT liability because she had previously mentioned that cash flow is tight after her husband lost his job late October.

Requirement

Explain what action you should take given your suspicions about Hayley's understated sales figures.

VAT on Property

Learning Objectives

After studying this chapter you will understand:

■ The VAT treatment of the supply of land and buildings in the UK.
■ The 'option to tax' election, which converts an exempt supply of commercial land and buildings to the standard rate of VAT.
■ The interaction of VAT with of stamp duty land tax.

35.1 Introduction

The final chapter of this Part introduces the basic principles associated with VAT on property. The relevant legislation that establishes the VAT treatment of property is the Value Added Tax Act 1994 (VATA 1994), while several HM Revenue & Custom's *VAT Notices* set out the treatment of VAT on property in more detail.

35.2 The Basic Rule

VAT on property is a specialised area of tax law and expert advice should always be sought before a transaction is completed. The basic rule is that transactions in land may be taxable supplies (i.e. subject to VAT at zero-rate (0%), reduced rate (5%), standard rate (20%)) or exempt supplies (no VAT is chargeable). Reduced rate supplies of property are beyond the scope of this text and are not addressed further.

Note that the word 'supplies' includes an outright sale or the grant of a lease in relation to the property. In respect of the grant of a lease, the lease must be a long lease, which is defined as one being for a period of more than 21 years.

The VAT classification of a property supply is important because, for the supplier, it not only dictates if output VAT is chargeable on the supply and at what rate (0%, 5% or 20%) but also if they are able to reclaim input VAT incurred on any purchases or expenses incurred by them that relate to that supply. For any taxable supplies of property, output VAT must be charged at the appropriate rate. Input VAT, however, can be recovered on any purchases used to make that taxable supply but only where VAT is charged at 0%, 5% or 20%. For exempt supplies of property, no output VAT is charged, therefore there can be no recovery of any input VAT on related purchases or expenses.

35.1.1 Zero-rated Supplies

Group 5 Schedule 8 VATA 1994 sets out those supplies of land and buildings that are zero-rated supplies of property. The following are the main categories:

1. the construction or renovation of new dwellings or buildings for **residential** purposes;
2. the construction or renovation of new dwellings or buildings for **charitable** purposes;
3. the sale of, or grant of a lease in, new dwellings or buildings for **residential** purposes;
4. the sale of, or grant of a lease in, new dwellings or buildings for **charitable** purposes;
5. the sale of, or grant of a lease in, non-residential buildings converted to residential use.

Note, this is not an exhaustive list.

35.1.2 Standard-rated Supplies

The following are the main categories of standard-rated supplies of property:

1. the construction or renovation of commercial buildings;
2. the sale of the freehold of a "new" commercial building ("new" is less than three years old);
3. the sale of the freehold of a commercial building that has not yet been completed;
4. the provision of accommodation in a hotel, inn, boarding house or similar establishment of sleeping accommodation.

Note, this is not an exhaustive list.

It is important to appreciate that the lease of a commercial property is **not** within the list of standard-rated items. Consequently, any premium and/or rental income in respect of a commercial property will be an exempt supply, unless an option to tax has been excercised.

35.1.3 Exempt Supplies

Group 1 Schedule 9 VATA 1994 sets out those supplies of land and buildings that are exempt from VAT. The following are the main categories:

1. the sale of the freehold of a commercial building which is not "new" (unless an 'option to tax' has been made, see **Section 35.3**);
2. the grant of a lease in a commercial building, including the grant of a lease in a "new" commercial building (unless an 'option to tax' has been made, see **Section 35.3**);
3. supplies of residential property that are not standard-rated, e.g. the sale of an old dwelling used for residential or charitable purposes.

This list is not exhaustive. It should be noted, therefore, that if a property supply is neither standard-rated nor zero-rated its supply will be exempt.

As previously outlined, where an exempt supply is made (and in the absence of an 'option to tax') any VAT suffered on costs relating to that supply are non-deductible. For example, an individual purchases a commercial unit for £500,000, on which VAT of £100,000 was charged by the vendor, with the intention of leasing the unit out to a tenant. If the purchaser (i.e. the prospective landlord) does not opt to tax the lease, they will not be able to recover the VAT charged on the purchase (£100,000). Such an individual may therefore become partially exempt as a result of their decision to lease commercial property (which has not been opted to tax) to a tenant. Partially exempt businesses are covered in **Chapter 34, Section 34.1**).

35.3 Option to Tax – Commercial Buildings

Exempt supplies of land and buildings often cause problems because any input tax related to that exempt supply is irrecoverable, unless the partial exemption *de minimis* test applies (see **Chapter 34**, **Section 34.2**). However, owners of property may elect to treat sales and leases of land and **commercial** buildings as taxable instead of exempt. This election is known as the 'option to tax'. There are certain specific circumstances in which the option can be revoked.

The option to tax replaces an exempt supply with a standard-rated supply, which means that any related input tax may be recovered in full by its owner because the supply being made is now a taxable supply. Once the option is made, it will **apply to all future supplies** that are then made in respect of that building by that taxable person. Thus, if a landlord makes the option to tax, this will affect all supplies relating to that building, e.g. rent charged to existing tenants, any premium or rent charged on a subsequent lease, any proceeds from the sale of the freehold, etc.

The owner must become registered for VAT (if not already registered) in order to make the option to tax. Once an option to tax has been made, it has to be notified to HMRC within 30 days of being made.

The option is made on a **building-by-building basis**. This means that if an owner of several different buildings wants to make an option to tax, they can choose to do so for some buildings and not others – it is entirely at their discretion. The option to tax may be revoked on a particular property under certain conditions, called the "cooling-off" provisions. The option to tax can be revoked in the following three situations:

1. **Within the first six months** after making it, provided that no supplies have been made that are affected by the option. Any input tax repayable as a result of the change from taxable to exempt supplies will need to be repaid.
2. Where no interest has been held in the property for over six years the option to tax will automatically lapse.
3. **20 years after it was made**.

There are some supplies that an option to tax does not affect and which remain exempt, even though the option has been exercised on the property in question. These include:

- dwellings – any grant in relation to a building, or part of a building, designed, adapted or intended for use as a dwelling or for a relevant residential purpose. The most common example would be a shop with a flat above it where an option to tax would make any rent from the shop standard-rated but any rent from the flat would remain exempt.
- Buildings for conversion into dwellings, etc. – when a business sells its commercial property, any option to tax can be disapplied if the buyer confirms their intent to convert the building into dwellings or relevant residential purposes.
- Charitable use – a supply in relation to a building intended for use solely for a relevant charitable purpose, other than as an office.

To sum up, the option to tax is therefore a useful planning tool for commercial properties – it can change the status of a supply in such a way that a trader is protected from suffering irrecoverable input tax.

35.4 Interaction with Stamp Duty Land Tax

If output VAT is required to be charged on a commercial property supply, the purchaser of that commercial property will pay stamp duty land tax (SDLT) on the total consideration, **including** VAT, i.e. SDLT arises on the VAT-inclusive price (see **Chapter 32**).

Example 35.1

On 31 July 2021, Devenish Limited bought a commercial property that was built in June 2019. The company agreed to pay £625,000 for the property. As the property is less than three years old it is "new" and 20% standard rate VAT is chargeable by the vendor. The total consideration is therefore £750,000 (£625,000 + (20% × £625,000)). The SDLT liability of Devenish Limited arises on the VAT-inclusive price and is as follows:

	£
0–£150,000 @ 0%	0
Next £100,000 @ 2%	2,000
Remaining £500,000 @ 5%	25,000
Total SDLT	<u>27,000</u>

Devenish Limited will pay an extra £6,250 (£125,000 output VAT × 5%) in SDLT as a result of the output VAT charged because the property is new.

Questions

Review Questions

(See Suggested Solutions to Review Questions at the end of this textbook.)

Question 35.1

Assume today's date is 31 December 2021. Classify the following property supplies as standard-rated, zero-rated or exempt. Provide explanations for your answers.

(a) The sale of the freehold of an office block constructed in November 2019.
(b) The grant of a 99-year lease in a brand new factory.
(c) The sale of the freehold of a factory first constructed in January 2017.

Question 35.2

Assume today's date is 31 December 2021. Classify the following property supplies as standard-rated, zero-rated or exempt. Provide explanations for your answers.

(a) A factory owner grants a 30-year lease over half his factory to another business that will be using the space for its partially exempt business. The factory was first constructed in June 2019.
(b) A property development company sells the freehold of a 25-year-old house it bought in a part-exchange deal with a customer.
(c) A property investment company sells the freehold of an office block first constructed in August 2019.
(d) A property investment company sells the freehold of an office block first constructed in August 2018 and which has been opted to tax.

Question 35.3

EyeSpy Ltd runs a chain of opticians in different towns across Northern Ireland. The company is partially exempt for VAT and in the year ending 31 March 2022 its partial exemption recovery percentage was 70%.

In January 2021, the company expanded to a new location in Enniskillen and bought an office building for £450,000 excluding VAT, if any. The office building was built in June 2019.

Requirement
Explain if EyeSpy Ltd incurred VAT on the building and, if so, calculate how much it is able to recover.

Question 35.4

Consider each of these supplies and decide whether or not the option to tax would be effective on the supply. Provide explanations for your answers.

(a) Sale of commercial land.
(b) Sale of a 75-year-old terraced house.
(c) Lease of a 15-year-old factory.
(d) Freehold sale of a two-year-old office block.
(e) 99-year lease of a one-year-old shop.

Question 35.5

Decide whether each of the different supplies below is standard-rated, zero-rated or exempt. If a supply is exempt, outline whether an option to tax can be made in respect of that supply. Provide explanations for your answers.

(a) Freehold sale of two-year-old factory.
(b) Grant of a 30-year lease in a brand new office block.
(c) A farmer rents out a plot of land to another farmer.
(d) A landlord leases out four floors of a building to an insurance company tenant (making exempt supplies).
(e) A landlord leases out a flat in a brand new luxury residential development for five years to an individual using it for their business.

Question 35.6

Paul James owns an office block in Belfast that is currently let out to two tenants, an insurance company (making exempt supplies) and a firm of accountants (making taxable supplies). The building needs some renovation, costing £800,000 plus VAT.

Requirement
(a) Explain the VAT treatment and implications for Paul of renovating the property.
(b) What would be the VAT implications, for both Paul and his tenants, if Paul were to opt to tax the property?

Question 35.7

Spidey Enterprises Ltd sold a commercial property built in July 2017 to Iron Man Developments Ltd for £1,250,000. The company had opted to tax the property in May 2020.

Requirement
Explain if Iron Man Developments Ltd incurred VAT on the building. Calculate how much stamp duty land tax the company paid on the acquisition of the building.

Appendices

Taxation Reference Material for Tax Year 2021/22 (Finance Act 2021)

Table of Contents

Inheritance Tax

Rates
Nil Rate Bands
Main Residence Nil Rate Bands
Taper Relief
Quick Succession Relief

VAT

Registration and Deregistration Limits
Rates

GENERAL

Beneficial Loans

Official rate of interest is 2%.

HMRC Late Payment and Repayment Interest Rates

The current late payment and repayment interest rates applied to income tax, national insurance, VAT, corporation tax* and inheritance tax are:

- Underpayments: late payment interest rate – 2.60%
- Overpayments: repayment interest rate – 0.5%

*Only applies to companies not paying corporation tax in instalments.

Sufficient Ties Table – Statutory Residence Test

Days spent in the UK	Arrivers	Leavers
Fewer than 16 days	Always non-resident	Always non-resident
16–45 days	Always non-resident	Resident if at least 4 ties apply
46–90 days	Resident if 4 ties apply	Resident if at least 3 ties apply
91–120 days	Resident if at least 3 ties apply	Resident if at least 2 ties apply
121–182 days	Resident if at least 2 ties apply	Resident if at least 1 tie applies
183 days or more	Always resident	Always resident

INCOME TAX

Income Tax Rates*

	Rate%
Starting rate for non-dividend savings income up to £5,000	0
First £37,700	20 (Basic rate)
£37,701–£150,000	40 (Higher rate)
Over £150,000	45 (Additional rate)
Basic rate for dividends	7.5
Higher rate for dividends	32.5
Additional rate for dividends	38.1

Income Tax Allowances*

	£
Personal allowance (1)	12,570
Income limit for personal allowance (1)	100,000
Marriage allowance (2)	1,260
Blind person's allowance	2,520
Dividend allowance (3)	2,000
Personal savings allowance (4):	
Basic rate taxpayers	1,000
Higher rate taxpayers	500
Property allowance (5)	1,000
Trading allowance (5)	1,000

* The rates and allowances in Scotland and Wales may differ.

(1) All individuals are entitled to the same personal allowance, regardless of the individuals' date of birth. This allowance is subject to the £100,000 income limit, which applies regardless of the individual's date of birth. The individual's personal allowance is reduced where their income is above this limit. The allowance is reduced by £1 for every £2 above the limit.

(2) A spouse or civil partner who is not liable to income tax; or not liable at the higher or additional rate, can claim to transfer this amount of their personal allowance to their spouse or civil partner. The recipient must not be liable to income tax at the higher or additional rate. The relief for this allowance is given at 20%.

(3) The dividend allowance means that individuals do not have to pay tax on the first £2,000 (2020/21 £2,000) of dividend income they receive.

(4) The personal savings allowance means that basic rate taxpayers do not have to pay tax on the first £1,000 of savings income they receive and higher rate taxpayers will not have tax to pay on their first £500 of savings income.

(5) The first £1,000 of trading income is not subject to income tax. The trading allowance also applies to certain miscellaneous income from providing assets or services. A £1,000 allowance is also available for property income.

Tax Credits

	2021/22 £ per year (unless stated)
Working Tax Credit	
Basic element	2,005
Couple and lone parent element	2,060
30-hour element	830
Disabled worker element	3,240
Severe disability element	1,400
Childcare Element of Working Tax Credit	
Maximum eligible cost for one child	£175 per week
Maximum eligible cost for two or more children	£300 per week
Percentage of eligible costs covered	70%
Child Tax Credit	
Family element	545
Child element	2,845
Disabled child element	3,435
Severely disabled child element	1,390
Income Thresholds and Withdrawal Rates	
First income threshold	6,565
First withdrawal rate	41%
First threshold for those entitled to child tax credit	16,480
Only income rise disregard	2,500
Income fall disregard	2,500

Car Benefits Charges

Car Benefit Percentage

The percentage rates applying to petrol and electric cars (first registered **before 6 April 2020**) with CO_2 emissions up to 55g/km:

0g/km	1%
1–50g/km (electric range >130 miles)	2%
1–50g/km (electric range 70–129 miles)	5%
1–50g/km (electric range 40–69 miles)	8%
1–50g/km (electric range 30–39 miles)	12%
1–50g/km (electric range <30 miles)	14%
51–54g/km	15%
55g/km	16%

For each 5g/km that a car is above 55g/km, an additional 1% is added to the percentage rate.

The percentage rates applying to petrol and electric cars (first registered on or **after 6 April 2020**) with CO_2 emissions up to 55g/km:

0g/km	1%
1–50g/km (electric range >130 miles)	1%
1–50g/km (electric range 70–129 miles)	4%
1–50g/km (electric range 40–69 miles)	7%
1–50g/km (electric range 30-39 miles)	11%
1–50g/km (electric range <30 miles)	13%
51–54g/km	14%
55g/km	15%

For each 5g/km that a car is above 55g/km, an additional 1% is added to the percentage rate.

For diesel cars, a 4% diesel supplement is added. Diesel cars that meet the Real Driving Emissions test are exempt from the supplement.

The maximum percentage charge is 37% and applies to petrol cars that have CO_2 emissions of 165g/km or more and diesel cars with emissions of 145g/km or more.

Fuel Benefit Charge

The same percentage figure used to calculate the car benefit charge, as above, is used to calculate the fuel benefit charge. The relevant percentage figure is multiplied by £24,600 for 2021/22 (£24,500 in 2020/21).

Van Benefits Charges

Van benefit	£3,500
Fuel benefit	£669

The charges will not apply if a "restricted private use condition" is met throughout the year.

There is no van benefit charge for zero-emission vans (for 2020/21 the van benefit charge was 80% of the main rate).

Authorised Mileage Allowance Rates

Use of own vehicle:

Vehicle	Flat rate per mile with simplified expenses
Cars and goods vehicles – first 10,000 miles	45p
Cars and goods vehicles – after 10,000 miles	25p
Motorcycles (all miles)	24p
Bicycles (all miles)	20p

Use of company car (rates from 1 June 2021):

Engine size	Petrol	LPG
1400cc or less	11p	8p
1401cc to 2000cc	13p	9p
Over 2000cc	19p	14p

Engine size	Diesel
1600cc or less	9p
1601cc to 2000cc	11p
Over 2000cc	13p

Simplified Expenses

Motor Expenses

Vehicle	Flat rate per mile
Cars and goods vehicles:	
first 10,000 miles	45p
after 10,000 miles	25p
Motorcycles	24p

Working from Home

Hours of business use per month	Flat rate per month
25 to 50	£10
51 to 100	£18
101 and more	£26

Living at Business Premises

Number of people	Flat rate per month
1	£350
2	£500
3+	£650

Pension Scheme Limits

Annual allowance	£40,000*
Lifetime allowance	£1,073,100
Maximum contribution without earnings	£3,600
Lifetime allowance charge – if excess drawn as cash	55%
Lifetime allowance charge – if excess drawn as income	25%
Annual allowance charge on excess – linked to individual's marginal tax rate	20%/40%/45%

* The annual allowance for certain high earners is reduced on a tapering basis. For every £2 of adjusted income over £240,000 an individual's annual allowance will reduce by £1 but is not reduced below £4,000 (also £4,000 in 2020/21).

Individual Savings Accounts (ISAs)

Overall annual investment limit: 2021/22   £20,000

(split any way between cash and stocks/shares)

Cap on Certain Income Tax Reliefs

Unless otherwise restricted, income tax reliefs are capped at the higher of:

1. £50,000; or
2. 25% of the individual's adjusted net income.

High-income Child Benefit Charge

Where income is between £50,000 and £60,000, the charge is 1% of the amount of child benefit received for every £100 of income over £50,000.

Capital Allowances

	2021/22 %	2020/21 %
Main pool (Note)	18	18
Motor cars – CO_2 emissions:		
0g/km (2021/22); < 50g/km (2020/21)	100	100
1–50g/km (2021/22); 51–110g/km (2020/21) (Note)	18	18
>50g/km (2021/22); >10g/km (2020/21) (Note)	6	6
New and unused zero-emission goods vehicles	100	100
Special rate pool (long-life assets and integral features of a building) (Note)	6	6
Research and development	100	100
Structures and buildings allowance	3%	3%

Note: Allowances are given on a writing down allowance reducing balance basis.

From 1 January 2019 to 31 December 2021, there is a 100% annual investment allowance on the first £1,000,0000 tranche per annum of capital expenditure incurred per group of companies or related entities on plant and machinery, including long-life assets and integral features but excluding cars. The limit is £200,000 from 1 January 2022.

Super-deduction and Special Rate Allowance

From 1 April 2021 to 31 March 2023, where a company incurs qualifying expenditure on new plant or machinery it may be able to claim the super-deduction and special rate first-year allowance (SR allowance).

The super-deduction provides an allowance equal to 130% of the qualifying spend and applies to new plant or machinery that would ordinarily qualify for the 18% main rate writing down allowance.

The SR allowance provides a first-year allowance of 50% on new plant or machinery that would ordinarily qualify for the 6% rate writing down allowance.

The two reliefs are not available to unincorporated businesses (such as sole traders or partnerships).

Specific Reliefs

Relief	Rate	Amount
Venture Capital Trust	30%	Max. £200,000
Enterprise Investment Scheme	30%	Max. £1,000,000
Seed Enterprise Investment Scheme	50%	Max. £100,000
Remittance basis charge	Resident in UK in 7 or more of previous 9 years. Resident in UK in 12 or more of previous 14 years.	Annual amount of £30,000 Annual amount of £60,000

NATIONAL INSURANCE CONTRIBUTIONS

Limit/Threshold	Frequency	£
Lower earnings limit:	Weekly	120
	Monthly	520
	Yearly	6,240
Upper earnings limit:	Weekly	967
	Monthly	4,189
	Yearly	50,270
Primary threshold (employee):	Weekly	184
	Monthly	797
	Yearly	9,568

Secondary threshold (employer):	Weekly	170
	Monthly	737
	Yearly	8,840
Upper secondary threshold (under 21) (employer):	Weekly	967
	Monthly	4,189
	Yearly	50,270
Upper secondary threshold (apprentice under 25) (employer):	Weekly	967
	Monthly	4,189
	Yearly	50,270

Employee's Contributions

■ Rate:
  ● on weekly earnings between £184 and £967   12%
  ● on weekly earnings above £967   2%

Employer's Contributions

■ Rate: on weekly earnings over £170   13.8%
■ Employer's allowance   £4,000

Other Classes

Classes 1A and 1B   13.8%
Class 2:
   Self-employed per week   £3.05
   Small profits threshold   £6,515
Class 3:
   Voluntary per week   £15.40
Class 4:
   Self-employment (rate on profits):
      on annual profits between £9,569 and £50,270   9%
      on annual profits above £50,270   2%

CORPORATION TAX

Rates

	Main rate
1 April 2020–31 March 2021	19%
1 April 2021–31 March 2022	19%

SME Definition for R&D Tax Relief

The company must have fewer than 500 staff and either:

1. less than €100 million turnover; or
2. balance sheet total less than €86 million.

CAPITAL GAINS TAX

Annual Exemption

Annual exemption for individuals...£12,300
Annual exemption for trustees..£6,150

Rates

General

The following rates apply to gains (except for residential land and property gains):

- 10% for individual basic rate taxpayers*
- 20% for individual higher rate/additional rate taxpayers
- 10% for gains qualifying for business asset disposal relief and investors' relief up to the lifetime cap (see below)

Gains on residential land and property disposals are taxed as follows:

- 18% for individual basic rate taxpayers and
- 28% for individual higher rate/additional rate taxpayers.

*Personal representatives of deceased taxpayers are not entitled to the basic rate of CGT.

Non-resident Capital Gains Tax on Direct Disposals of UK Land and Property

The following rates apply to gains on non-residential land and property disposals:

- 10% for individual basic rate taxpayers
- 20% for individual higher rate taxpayers
- 20% for personal representatives of a non-resident who has died

Gains on residential land and property are taxed as follows:

- 18% for basic rate taxpayers
- 28% for higher rate/additional rate taxpayers
- 28% for personal representatives of someone who has died.

Non-resident Capital Gains Tax on Indirect Disposals of UK Land and Property

The following rates apply:

- 10% for individual basic rate taxpayers
- 20% for individual higher rate taxpayers
- 20% for personal representatives of a non-resident who has died

Reliefs

Relief	Rate	Lifetime Cap
Business asset disposal relief	10%	£1 million
Investors' relief	10%	£10 million

STAMP TAXES

Stamp Duty and Stamp Duty Reserve Tax

	Rate
Stamp duty	0.5% on amounts exceeding £1,000
Stamp duty reserve tax	0.5%

Stamp Duty Land Tax

Residential Rates

The rates for stamp duty land tax (SDLT) on purchases and lease premiums are:

Chargeable consideration	Percentage
Up to £125,000	0%
The next £125,000 (the portion from £125,001 to £250,000)	2%
The next £675,000 (the portion from £250,001 to £925,000)	5%
The next £575,000 (the portion from £925,001 to £1.5 million)	10%
The remaining amount (the portion above £1.5 million)	12%

The above rates are each increased by 3% where the property is classed as an additional residential property acquisition.

A higher rate of 15% SDLT applies if the purchase is of a high-value residential property costing £500,000 or more by a company (or by a partnership including a company) or collective investment scheme.

A 2% surcharge applies to the purchase of residential property in England and Wales by non-residents. The surcharge applies in addition to various other rates, including the additional residential 3% supplement and the 15% higher rate.

Non-Residential/Mixed Use Rates

The rates for stamp duty land tax (SDLT) on purchases and lease premiums are:

Chargeable consideration	Percentage
Up to £150,000	0%
The next £100,000 (the portion from £150,001 to £250,000)	2%
The remaining amount (the portion above £250,000)	5%

New Leases – SDLT on Lease Rentals

Rate	Net Present Value of Rent	
	Residential	Non-residential
Zero	Up to £125,000	Up to £150,000
1%	Excess over £125,000	£150,001–£5 million
2%	N/A	Over £5 million

INHERITANCE TAX

Rates

Lifetime	20%
Death*	40%

* 36% where 10% or more of the net estate is left to charity.

Nil Rate Bands

Tax Year	Nil Rate Band £
2007/08	0–300,000
2008/09	0–312,000
2009/10 to 2021/22	0–325,000

Main Residence Nil Rate Bands

Tax Year	Main Residence Nil Rate Band
2017/18	£100,000
2018/19	£125,000
2019/20	£150,000
2020/21	£175,000

Taper Relief

Period before death:

3 years or less	0%
3–4 years	20%
4–5 years	40%
5–6 years	60%
6–7 years	80%

Quick Succession Relief

Period between earlier transfer and death:

1 year or less	100%
1–2 years	80%
2–3 years	60%
3–4 years	40%
4–5 years	20%

VAT

Registration and Deregistration Limits

	Annual value of taxable supplies
Registration limit for years 2019, 2020 and 2021 (from 1 April)	£85,000
Deregistration limit for years 2019, 2020 and 2021 (from 1 April)	£83,000

Rates

Rate	Examples
Exempt	■ Insurance ■ Postal services ■ Finance ■ Education ■ Health and welfare ■ Professional subscriptions
Zero rate (0%)	■ Food ■ Water and sewage services ■ Books (printed) and certain electronic publications ■ Transport ■ Charities ■ Children's clothing ■ International services ■ Women's sanitary products
Standard rate (20%)	All supplies of goods and services by taxable persons that are not exempt, zero rated or subject to reduced rate. Includes: ■ Adult clothing and footwear ■ Office equipment and stationery ■ Drinks and certain foods
Reduced rate (5%)	■ Domestic fuel or power ■ Installation of energy-saving materials for residential properties ■ Children's car seats

UK Retail Price Indices (as adjusted to base 100 in January 1987)

	1982	1983	1984	1985	1986	1987	1988	1989	1990	1991	1992	1993	1994	1995	1996	1997	1998	1999	2000
January	-	82.6	86.8	91.2	96.2	100.0	103.3	111.0	119.5	130.2	135.6	137.9	141.3	146.3	150.2	154.4	159.5	163.4	166.6
February	-	83.0	87.2	91.9	96.6	100.4	103.7	111.8	120.2	130.9	136.3	138.8	142.1	146.9	150.9	155.0	160.3	163.7	167.5
March	79.4	83.1	87.5	92.8	96.7	100.6	104.1	112.3	121.4	131.4	136.7	139.3	142.5	147.5	151.5	155.4	160.8	164.4	168.4
April	81.0	84.3	88.6	94.8	97.7	101.8	105.8	114.3	125.1	133.1	138.8	140.6	144.2	149.0	152.6	156.3	162.6	165.2	170.1
May	81.6	84.6	89.0	95.2	97.8	101.9	106.2	115.0	126.2	133.5	139.3	141.1	144.7	149.6	152.9	156.9	163.5	165.6	170.7
June	81.9	84.8	89.2	95.4	97.8	101.9	106.6	115.4	126.7	134.1	139.3	141.0	144.7	149.8	153.0	157.5	163.4	165.6	171.1
July	81.9	85.3	89.1	95.2	97.5	101.8	106.7	115.5	126.8	133.8	138.8	140.7	144.0	149.1	152.4	157.5	163.0	165.1	170.5
August	81.9	85.7	89.9	95.5	97.8	102.4	107.9	115.8	128.1	134.1	138.9	141.3	144.7	149.9	153.1	158.5	163.7	165.5	170.5
September	81.9	86.1	90.1	95.4	98.3	102.4	108.4	116.6	129.3	134.6	139.4	141.9	145.0	150.6	153.8	159.3	164.4	166.2	171.7
October	82.3	86.4	90.7	95.6	98.5	102.9	109.5	117.5	130.3	135.1	139.9	141.8	145.2	149.8	153.8	159.5	164.5	166.5	171.6
November	82.7	86.7	91.0	95.9	99.3	103.4	110.0	118.5	130.0	135.6	139.7	141.6	145.3	149.8	153.9	159.6	164.4	166.7	172.1
December	82.5	86.9	90.9	96.0	99.6	103.3	110.3	118.8	129.9	135.7	139.2	141.9	146.0	150.7	154.4	160.0	164.4	167.3	172.2

	2001	2002	2003	2004	2005	2006	2007	2008	2009	2010	2011	2012	2013	2014	2015	2016	2017
January	171.1	173.3	178.4	183.1	188.9	193.4	201.6	209.8	210.1	217.9	229.0	238.0	245.8	252.6	255.4	258.8	265.5
February	172.0	173.8	179.3	183.8	189.6	194.2	203.1	211.4	211.4	219.2	231.3	239.9	247.6	254.2	256.7	260.0	268.4
March	172.2	174.5	179.9	184.6	190.5	195.0	204.4	212.1	211.3	220.7	232.5	240.8	248.7	254.8	257.1	261.1	269.3
April	173.1	175.7	181.2	185.7	191.6	196.5	205.4	214.0	211.5	222.8	234.4	242.1	249.5	255.7	258.0	261.4	270.6
May	174.2	176.2	181.5	186.5	192.0	197.7	206.2	215.1	212.8	223.6	235.2	242.4	250.0	255.9	258.5	262.1	271.7
June	174.4	176.2	181.3	186.8	192.2	198.5	207.3	216.8	213.4	224.1	235.2	241.8	249.7	256.3	258.9	263.1	272.3
July	173.3	175.9	181.3	186.8	192.2	198.5	206.1	216.5	213.4	223.6	234.7	242.1	249.7	256.0	258.6	263.4	272.9
August	174.0	176.4	181.6	187.4	192.6	199.2	207.3	217.2	214.4	224.5	236.1	243.0	251.0	257.0	259.8	264.4	274.7
September	174.6	177.6	182.5	188.1	193.1	200.1	208.0	218.4	215.3	225.3	237.9	244.2	251.9	257.6	259.6	264.9	275.1
October	174.3	177.9	182.6	188.6	193.3	200.4	208.9	217.7	216.0	225.8	238.0	245.6	251.9	257.7	259.5	264.8	275.3
November	173.6	178.2	182.7	189.0	193.3	201.1	209.7	216.0	216.6	226.8	238.5	245.6	252.1	257.1	259.8	265.5	275.8
December	173.4	178.5	183.5	189.9	194.1	202.7	210.9	212.9	218.0	228.4	239.4	246.8	253.4	257.5	260.6	267.1	278.1

Taxation and the *Code of Ethics*

Under Chartered Accountants Ireland's *Code of Ethics*, a Chartered Accountant shall comply with the following fundamental principles:

1. **Integrity** – to be straightforward and honest in all professional and business relationships.
2. **Objectivity** – to not compromise professional or business judgements because of bias, conflict of interest or undue influence of others.
3. **Professional Competence and Due Care** – to attain and maintain professional knowledge and skill at the level required to ensure that a client or employing organisation receives competent professional services based on current technical and professional standards and relevant legislation; and to act diligently and in accordance with applicable technical and professional standards.
4. **Confidentiality** – to respect the confidentiality of information acquired as a result of professional and business relationships and, therefore, not disclose any such information to third parties without proper and specific authority, unless there is a legal or professional right or duty to disclose, nor use the information for the personal advantage of the Chartered Accountant or third parties.
5. **Professional Behaviour** – to comply with relevant laws and regulations and avoid any action that discredits the profession.

The Institute's "Five Fundamental Principles, Five Practical Steps" is a useful resource for members and students and is available at www.charteredaccountants.ie. As a Chartered Accountant, you will have to ensure that your dealings with the tax aspects of your professional life are also in compliance with these fundamental principles. You may be asked to define or list the principles as well as be able to identify where these ethical issues arise and how you would deal with them.

Examples of situations that could arise where these principles are challenged in the context of tax are outlined below:

Example 2.1

You are working in the Tax Department of ABC & Co and your manager is Jack Wilson. He comes over to your desk after his meeting with Peter Foley. He gives you all the papers that Peter has left with him. He asks you to draft Peter's tax return. You know who Peter is as you are now living in a house that your friend Ann leased from Peter. As you complete the return, you note that there is no information regarding property income. What should you do?

Action

As a person with integrity, you should explain to your manager that your friend Ann has leased a property from Peter and that he has forgotten to send details of his property income and expenses. As Peter sent the information to Jack, it is appropriate for Jack to contact Peter for details regarding property income and related expenses.

Example 2.2

You are working in the tax department of the Irish subsidiary of a US-owned multinational. You are preparing the corporation tax computation, including the R&D tax credit due. You have not received some information from your colleagues dealing with R&D and cannot finalise the claim for R&D tax credit until you receive this information. Your manager is under pressure and tells you to just file the claim on the basis of what will maximise the claim. He says, "It is self-assessment, and the chance of this ever being audited or enquired into is zero." What should you do?

Action

You should act in a professional and objective manner. This means that you cannot do as your manager wants. You should explain to him that you will contact the person in R&D again and finalise the claim as quickly as possible.

Example 2.3

Anna O'Shea, financial controller of Great Client Ltd, rings you regarding a VAT issue. You have great respect for Anna and are delighted that she is ringing you directly instead of your manager. She says that it is a very straightforward query. However, as you listen to her, you realise that you are pretty sure of the answer but would need to check a point before answering. What should you do?

Action

Where you do not know the answer, it is professionally competent to explain that you need to check a point before you give an answer. If you like, you can explain which aspect you need to check. Your client will appreciate you acting professionally rather than giving incorrect information or advice.

Example 2.4

The phone rings, and it is Darren O'Brien, your best friend, who works for Just-do-it Ltd. After discussing the match you both watched on the television last night, Darren explains why he is ringing you. He has heard that Success Ltd, a client of your tax department, has made R&D tax credit claims. Therefore, you must have details regarding its R&D. Darren's relationship with his boss is not great at present, and he knows that if he could get certain data about Success Ltd, his relationship with his boss would improve. He explains that he does not want any financial information, just some small details regarding R&D. What should you do?

Action

You should not give him the information. No matter how good a friend he is, it is unethical to give confidential information about your client to him.

Example 2.5

It is the Friday morning before a bank holiday weekend, and you are due to travel from Dublin to west Cork after work for the weekend. Your manager has been on annual leave for the last week. He left you work to do for the week, including researching a tax issue for a client. He had advised you that you were to have an answer to the issue by the time he returned, no matter how long it took. It actually took you a very short time and you have it all documented for him.

Your friend who is travelling with you asks if you could leave at 11am to beat the traffic and have a longer weekend. You have no annual leave left, so you cannot take leave. You know that if you leave, nobody will notice, but you have to complete a timesheet. Your friend reminds you that the research for the client could have taken a lot longer and that you could code the five hours to the client. What should you do?

Action

It would constitute unprofessional behaviour and would show a lack of integrity if you were to charge your client for those five hours.

Appendix 3

Tax Planning, Tax Avoidance and Tax Evasion

The global financial and economic crash of 2008 and the ensuing worldwide recession led to a fall in tax collected by many governments and moved tax and tax transparency higher up the agenda. Subsequent events further increased the focus and attention of the wider public – as well as governments – on both tax avoidance and the evasion of taxes: revelations in the 'Paradise Papers' and the 'Panama Papers', the EU's state aid decision against Ireland and Apple Inc., coupled with the 'tax-shaming' of many multinational brand names and famous people has led to tax, and tax ethics, appearing in media headlines almost on a daily basis. As a result, a number of international and domestic initiatives have dramatically changed the tax planning and tax compliance landscape and brought tax transparency to the fore in many businesses and boardrooms.

The tax liability of an individual, partnership, trust or company can be reduced by tax planning, tax avoidance or tax evasion. Although the overriding objective of each is to reduce the taxpayer's tax bill, the method each adopts to do so is different. Each is also vastly different from an ethical and technical perspective.

Tax receipts are used to fund public services such as education, hospitals and roads. Individuals and businesses in a country benefit from these services directly and indirectly and it is therefore seen as a social and ethical responsibility for them to pay their fair share of taxes. Evading or avoiding paying your taxes is viewed as unacceptable as a result.

Tax Planning

Tax planning is used by taxpayers to reduce their tax bill by making use of provisions within domestic tax legislation. For example, any company with good tax governance will seek to minimise its tax liability by using the tools and mechanisms – allowances, deductions, reliefs and exemptions for example – made available to them by the government.

Planning can also take the form of simple decisions, such as delaying sales when a fall in the rate of corporation tax is expected so that the company pays a lower rate of corporation tax on its taxable profits. Or a taxpayer may consider what type of assets to buy to maximise capital allowances. Any tax planning decision should work, not just from a tax planning and legislative perspective, but it should also be commercially feasible.

The UK government accepts that all taxpayers are entitled to organise their affairs in such a way as to mitigate their tax liability – as long as they do so within the law and within the spirit in which Parliament intended when setting the law. Tax planning is both legally and ethically acceptable.

Tax Avoidance

Tax avoidance is often viewed as a grey area because it is regularly confused with tax planning. Tax avoidance is the use of loopholes within tax legislation to reduce the taxpayer's tax liability. Although tax avoidance may seem similar to tax planning, as the taxpayer is using tax law to reduce their overall tax burden, the taxpayer is using tax legislation in a way not intended, or anticipated, by Parliament.

In 2004, the UK government launched the Disclosure of Tax Avoidance Schemes (DOTAS) regime, which covers most taxes in the UK including income tax, national insurance, VAT, capital gains tax, corporation tax, inheritance tax and stamp duty land tax. DOTAS was designed to provide early information to HMRC about tax avoidance schemes that had been developed and the users of those schemes.

The regime has been amended a number of times to ensure it remains up to date and that it identifies tax avoidance schemes as the tax avoidance market changes. The DOTAS regime requires schemes that contain certain 'hallmarks' of tax avoidance to be notified to HMRC. HMRC then take action to close down the scheme, usually by legislation as part of the annual Budget process.

The users of such schemes are also required to notify HMRC that they have used a particular scheme by including the scheme notification number on the relevant tax return or submission made to HMRC. HMRC will thereafter pursue the scheme user by opening an enquiry that challenges the avoidance scheme.

Avoidance behaviour is also challenged by the UK's General Anti-Abuse Rule (GAAR), which took effect from 17 July 2013 and is intended to counteract "tax advantages arising from tax arrangements that are abusive" and applies across a number of taxes.

Tax arrangements exist where obtaining a tax advantage is "one of the main purposes". To date, the opinions given by the GAAR advisory panel have all been in HMRC's favour. The GAAR counteracts the abusive behaviour and in effect reverses the tax saving.

The *Ramsay* principle (or doctrine) refers to an approach to statutory interpretation developed by the courts in cases involving tax avoidance. It began with the landmark decision by the House of Lords in *W. T. Ramsay Ltd. v. Inland Revenue Commissioners* (1981). The *Ramsay* principle can be summarised as:

1. look at the legislation – what did Parliament intend when it chose those words?
2. look at the particular facts of the transaction – should an individual transaction be considered in a wider context?
3. in light of 1. and 2., how does the law apply to these facts?

While tax avoidance is arguably legal, it is generally viewed as ethically unacceptable behaviour. Tax avoidance behaviour that is successfully challenged by HMRC will lead to the original tax saving being paid, in addition to penalties and interest on the error. The error will generally fall into the deliberate behaviour without concealment category (see **Chapter 1, Section 1.8**).

Tax Evasion

At the extreme end of the spectrum is tax evasion. Tax evasion involves breaking the law deliberately and either not paying any of the taxes that fall due or underpaying the taxes that fall due when the law clearly states that they must be paid. Tax evaders intend to deliberately break rules surrounding their tax position in order to avoid paying the correct amount of tax they owe.

A tax evader illegally reduces their tax burden, either by a misrepresentation to HMRC or by not filing tax returns at all, thereby concealing the true state of their tax affairs. Tax evasion can include onshore (within the UK) and offshore deliberate behaviour.

Examples of tax evasion include, *inter alia*:

- failure to file a tax return and pay the relevant tax arising;
- failure to declare the correct income;
- deliberately inflating expenses, which reduces taxable profits or increases a loss;
- hiding taxable assets;
- wrongly claiming a tax refund or repayment by being dishonest;
- not telling HMRC about a source of income;
- not operating a PAYE scheme for employees/pensioners;
- not registering for VAT when required to do so; and
- deliberate submission of incorrect or false information.

In all cases the Exchequer suffers a loss of tax. This is known as tax fraud. Tax evasion, and the tax fraud that flows from this behavior, is a criminal offence prosecutable by HMRC. It is viewed as ethically unacceptable behaviour. The error will generally fall into the deliberate behaviour with concealment category (see **Chapter 1, Section 1.8**).

As Chartered Accountants, we must be cognisant of the activities of clients and potential clients, particularly in cases of both avoidance and evasion.

Suggested Solutions to Review Questions

Chapter 1

Question 1.1

HMRC can issue an enquiry into any income tax return that is made. No reasons need to be given as to why the return has been selected for enquiry – it may be due to a risk assessment, or merely chosen at random from all the returns that have been filed. However, it is more likely than not that the return has been selected for enquiry due to a risk assessment.

1. HMRC must give written notice to the taxpayer when opening an enquiry, which must be sent within 12 months of the date the tax return was filed; or
2. If the tax return was filed late, by the next 31 January, 30 April, 31 July or 31 October following the anniversary of the date the return was actually filed or amended.

If the return is amended by the taxpayer, then an enquiry into the amendment can be raised by HMRC by the next 31 January, 30 April, 31 July or 31 October following the anniversary of the date the amended return was filed.

If an enquiry is not raised within these time limits, then the return is treated as final except for exceptional circumstances. If the returns filed give rise to a deliberate understatement, HMRC can seek to amend them under the discovery assessment provisions up to 20 years later.

Once an enquiry is completed, HMRC will issue a final assessment to the taxpayer. If the taxpayer feels this is incorrect, they may request, within 30 days, that HMRC conduct an "internal review". If after the internal review the taxpayer still disagrees with the decision, they can send a "notice of appeal" to the Tribunal within 30 days. However, once a return is final, it cannot be the subject of a further enquiry (except in the case of "careless" or "deliberate" underestimates).

If the taxpayer appeals to the Tribunal, the appeal may be heard by the First-tier Tribunal or the Upper Tribunal, depending on the complexity of the case. If either the taxpayer or HMRC consider that the Tribunals have erred on a point of law, then they can proceed with the case to the Court of Appeal, and finally to the Supreme Court. However, this is very expensive.

Question 1.2

Anytown Tax Advisors
Anytown

Ms Petra Mirren
Mirren Marketing Consultancy Ltd

10 July 2022

Corporation tax computation – 31 March 2021

Dear Petra,

Further to your recent instructions, please find set out below the information and advice you requested.

I have reviewed the 2021 corporation tax computation for the accounting period ended 31 March 2021 submitted by your previous agent. Unfortunately, the corporation tax liability for 2021, which was due for payment on 1 January 2022, has been underpaid by £22,000.

As a result of this, interest of 2.6% per annum applies. At the time of writing, interest of approximately £298 has accrued. Please note that if paid in the 2022 accounting period of the company, this will be initially added back in the corporation tax computation as non-trade interest but will be deductible later under the loan relationship rules.

The company is also likely to be subject to a penalty as a result of the underpayment. The penalty is likely to fall into the "careless" category as the company did not deliberately seek to underpay (the computation had been prepared by an accountant). Penalties in the careless category can be mitigated to 0% if an unprompted disclosure is made. However, because HMRC have already opened an enquiry into the 2021 period, the company cannot avail of the 0% category and thus the penalty will be either 15% for a prompted disclosure (£3,300) or, if the company does not make a prompted disclosure, 30% (£6,600).

In light of the potential to mitigate the penalty by some 15%, i.e. £3,300, we would recommend a full disclosure is made to HMRC as soon as possible. This can be done either by letter or by amending the 2021 corporation tax return, the deadline for which is 31 March 2023.

The net underpaid tax of £22,000 should also be paid at the same time. The letter submitting the amended return should clearly outline all adjustments. Paying the underpaid tax at the same time that the amended return is submitted also has the benefit of 'stopping the interest clock'.

You should also note that a £100 late filing penalty will also arise – it is irrelevant that this is the first time the company has filed a late corporation tax return.

If we can be of further assistance in this regard, or if you have any questions, please do not hesitate to contact me.

Yours sincerely,

Question 1.3

Paragraph 2 of Schedule 36 Finance Act 2008 does give HMRC the power to obtain information or a document from a third party, including a customer, if the information or document is reasonably required for the purpose of checking O'Connor & Co's tax position. HMRC must give notice in writing to the third party; the exercise of this power is known as a 'third party notice'.

However, under Paragraph 3 of Schedule 36 Finance Act 2008, HMRC may not issue a third-party notice without your agreement (as the taxpayer) or the approval of the First-tier Tribunal (Tax). If the approval of the Tribunal is granted, you must be given a summary of the reasons for the third-party notice, unless the Tribunal rules that this could prejudice the assessment or collection of tax.

I would not recommend that you give permission to the Inspector of Taxes to obtain information or documents from your customers at this stage. You are right to be concerned about HMRC taking this course of action. Your customers may assume that there are serious irregularities with your taxes if they are asked to provide information in connection with O'Connor & Co. to HMRC, which could be damaging to your, and the business's, professional reputation.

As the visit has not yet taken place, it is highly unlikely that HMRC would incur the time and expense required to seek approval from the First-tier Tribunal for a third-party notice. In addition, unless there are circumstances of which I am not aware, it does not seem that HMRC would have sufficient grounds for seeking such approval. I recommend that we contact the Inspector of Taxes as soon as possible on your behalf to advise that you do not agree to this.

Furthermore, it should be noted that HMRC have no right to inspect private premises. I would recommend again that we contact HMRC and remind them of this safeguard.

Chapter 2

Question 2.1

2020/21

Hank is eligible for SYT for 2020/21 as:

- he is UK resident for the current tax year (2020/21) (first automatic UK test – spends at least 183 days in the UK in 2020/21);
- he is not UK resident for the previous tax year (2019/20);
- he arrives part way through the tax year; and
- he started full-time work in the UK during the tax year 2020/21 for a continuous period of at least 365 days; and he had no UK ties from 6 April 2020 to 18 May 2020.

Hank is therefore UK resident only from 19 May 2020.

2021/22

Hank spent more than 183 days in the UK in the 2021/22 tax year, therefore he is UK resident for the 2021/22 tax year under the first automatic UK test.

2022/23

Hank is resident in the UK having spent more than 183 days there in the tax year. However, as he is leaving to work full time overseas, he may be able to qualify for SYT.

Note, if Hank had not been resident in the UK in 2022/23, then SYT would not be relevant, i.e. you only ever consider split year treatment when the person is UK resident in the tax year under review. (For example, if Hank had left on 15 April 2021 and had not returned, he would be non-UK resident in 2021/22 due to the first automatic overseas test (i.e. spends less than 16 days in the UK in the 2021/22 tax year). If this had been the case, his status would be non-resident for 2021/22 and split year treatment would not even be considered.)

Hank is eligible for SYT for 2022/23 as:

- he is UK resident in the current tax year (i.e. 2022/23);
- he was UK resident in the previous tax year (i.e. 2021/22);
- he is not UK resident in the following tax year as he meets the third automatic overseas test;
- he leaves part way through the current tax year; and
- from 11 October 2022 to 5 April 2023 he:
  - works full time overseas, and

- spends 16 days in the UK, which is less than the permitted 45 days (being 91 days pro-rated for the tax year of departure, i.e. 6/12 months × 91 = 45 days (the month of departure is treated as a whole month)).

Question 2.2

As none of the automatic tests apply to Sheila, we need to consider if there are sufficient UK ties that will result in her being treated as UK resident.

Sheila has not been UK resident in any of the three previous tax years prior to 2021/22 and has spent 98 days in the UK, therefore she must have at least three UK ties to be UK resident. Her ties are:

- the family tie (as her husband is UK resident); and
- the accommodation tie (as her brother is a "close relative" for these purposes and she stays with him for more than 16 days).

With only two ties (the accommodation tie is not applicable as the number of days is less than 91), Sheila will not be considered UK resident in 2021/22.

Question 2.3

As none of the automatic tests apply to Sean, we need to consider the sufficient ties test.

Sean was resident in one of the three previous tax years and spent 52 days in the UK, in which case there must be at least three UK ties for him to be UK resident. Therefore, he will remain UK resident for 2021/22 as he meets the necessary three UK ties:

- family tie (wife and children are UK resident);
- accommodation tie (his time spent at the family home in Belfast); and
- 90-day tie (he spent more than 90 days in the UK in the previous tax year).

Question 2.4

As Mr Harris is neither resident nor domiciled, he is liable to UK tax only on income arising in the UK as follows.

Income tax computations – Mr Harris for income tax year 2021/22 as a US citizen

	£
UK property business (Note 1)	45,000
Total income	45,000
Less: personal allowance	0
Taxable income	45,000
Tax payable:	
£37,700 @ 20%	7,540
£7,300 @ 40%	2,920
Total tax liability	10,460
Less: tax deducted at source	(9,000)
Tax due for 2021/22	1,460

Note:

1. Always include the gross amount in the income tax computation: £36,000 + £9,000 = £45,000.

In general, non-resident individuals are not entitled to allowances, including the personal allowance. There are exceptions, for example, citizens of the EEA. A French citizen therefore would be entitled to a personal allowance, but a US citizen would not. The impact of this is shown in the calculation below.

Income tax computations – Mr Harris for income tax year 2021/22 as a French citizen

	£
UK property business	45,000
Total income	45,000
Less: personal allowance	(12,570)
Taxable income	32,430
Tax payable:	
£32,430 @ 20%	6,486
Total tax liability	6,486
Less: tax deducted at source	(9,000)
Tax refund due for 2021/22	(2,514)

Question 2.5

(a) Janet is not resident in 2021/22 as she meets an automatic overseas test, in that she was resident in one or more of the previous three tax years and visits the UK for fewer than 16 days in the current tax year.

(b) Paul is resident in 2021/22 as he does not meet an automatic overseas test but does meet an automatic UK test in that he is present in the UK for at least 183 days in the tax year.

(c) Victor is not resident in 2021/22 as he meets an automatic overseas test, in that he works full time overseas and visits the UK for fewer than 91 days, with the number of days in the tax year on which he works for more than three hours in the UK being less than 31.

(d) Christine is resident in 2021/22 as she does not meet an automatic overseas test but does meet an automatic UK test, in that she has a home in the UK for more than 90 consecutive days (of which at least 30 days fall in the tax year), more than 30 days are spent there in the tax year and she has no home overseas.

(e) Terry is not resident in 2021/22 as he meets an automatic overseas test, in that he was non-resident in all of the previous three tax years and visits the UK for fewer than 46 days in the current tax year.

(f) Margaret is resident in 2021/22 as she does not meet an automatic overseas test but does meet an automatic UK test. This is because:

▪ she carries out full-time work in the UK for a period of 365 days with no significant break (i.e. at least 31 days) and all or part of that 365-day period falls within the tax year;

▪ more than 75% of the total number of days in the 365-day period when more than three hours per day are worked in the UK; and

■ at least one day in the tax year is a day on which she works more than three hours in the UK.
Margaret may be entitled to split-year basis in her year of arrival to the UK (2021/22) and
the year of departure (2022/23).

(g) As Ned does not meet any of the automatic overseas tests nor any of the automatic UK tests,
residence will depend upon his number of UK ties and the number of days spent in the UK.
Ned is resident in the UK in the tax year 2021/22 by meeting the sufficient ties test in that:

■ he spent between 121 and 182 days in the UK; and
■ he has a sufficient UK tie (90-day tie), having spent more than 90 days in the UK in one or
both of the previous two tax years.

As a leaver, Ned only required one tie to be resident in 2021/22.

Chapter 4

Question 4.1

As Jenna's adjusted net income is over £240,000, her annual allowance in 2021/22 is reduced by
£10,000 ((£260,000 – £240,000)/2) to £30,000. However, as Jenna has unused annual allowance
carried forward from earlier years of £35,000 her total annual allowance limit in 2021/22 is
£65,000.

Jenna has made excess pension contributions of £5,000 in 2021/22, which will mean she will
be required to pay an annual allowance charge. As an additional rate taxpayer this will be at the 45%
rate, i.e.£5,000 × 45% = £2,250.

Question 4.2

Cathy's adjusted total income is £610,000 (i.e. £650,000 less the gross personal pension contributions
of £40,000). Therefore, her total loss relief claim cannot exceed the greater of:

1. £50,000; or
2. £610,000 × 25% = £152,500.

Cathy is therefore able to set £152,500 of the trading loss in 2021/22 against her trading income,
which will result in a tax saving of £68,625 (£152,500 × 45%). The remaining unused trading loss
of £47,500 could be carried back to the 2020/21 tax year (subject again to her cap) or, under the
temporary loss extension rules, carried back and offset against trading profits in 2019/20 and then
(if still not fully relieved) to 2018/19. This carry back to the two earlier years is not subject to the
same cap. Alternatively, the losses could be carried forward for use against future trading profits
(not capped).

Question 4.3

Jonathan is entitled to income tax relief of £30,000 (£100,000 investment × 30%), therefore his
£50,000 tax liability will be reduced to £20,000.

If his tax liability in the 2021/22 tax year was £20,000 before his VCT investment was taken
into consideration, then his tax liability would be reduced to nil. The surplus tax reducer of £30,000
would be wasted as it cannot be carried back or carried forward.

Chapter 5

Question 5.1

Income tax computation for Laura for 2021/22

	Non-savings	Savings	Total
	£	£	£
UK trading income	165,000		165,000
UK bank interest		500	500
Overseas bank interest		1,000	1,000
Total income	165,000	1,500	166,500
Personal allowance	(12,570)		(12,570)
Taxable income	152,430	1,500	153,930

Income tax:	£
Non-savings:	
£37,700 × 20%	7,540
£112,300 × 40%	44,920
£2,430 × 45%	1,094
Savings:	
£1,500 × 45%	675
	54,229
Less: double taxation relief (Note 1)	(150)
Income tax payable	54,079

Note:

1. Double taxation relief is given as credit/unilateral relief. It is the lower of the overseas tax or the UK tax on that source of income. In this case:
   - ▪ overseas tax = £1,000 × 15% = £150
   - ▪ UK tax on that source of income =

UK tax including the foreign source	£54,229
UK tax without the foreign source	£53,779
	£450

Therefore, double taxation relief is £150 and full double tax relief is available.

Question 5.2

(a)
Income tax computation for Sarah for 2021/22

	£
Profit on apartment in New York	20,000
Less: loss on villa in Tuscany	(5,500)
Overseas property business profit	14,500
Less: personal allowance	(12,570)
Taxable income	1,930

Taxed @ 20% = £386

The £2,000 loss on the flat in London is carried forward against Sarah's future UK property business income.

(b) To qualify as an FHH, the property must be **furnished** accommodation and run on a **commercial basis with a view to the realisation of profit**. It must also satisfy the three conditions:
   1. *Availability* – be available for commercial letting as holiday accommodation for at least 210 days in the year.
   2. *Letting* – be commercially let as holiday accommodation to the public for at least 105 days in the year.
   3. *Pattern of occupation* – during a 12-month period, not more than 155 days fall during periods of longer-term occupation.

Income tax computation for Sarah for 2021/22

	£
Profit on apartment in New York	20,000
Overseas property business profit	20,000
Less: personal allowance	(12,570)
Taxable income	7,430

Taxed @ 20% = £1,486

The loss on the flat in London of £2,000 is carried forward against Sarah's future UK property business income.

The loss on the Tuscan villa of £4,500 is from a FHH letting and is thus carried forward against future overseas FHH letting profits. Overall, Sarah would have paid more tax in 2021/22 if the Tuscan property was a FHH due to relief for this loss being ring-fenced.

Question 5.3

Income tax computation for Marc for 2021/22

	Non-savings	Savings	Total
	£	£	£
UK trading income	65,000		65,000
UK bank interest		2,500	2,500
Overseas trading income	20,000		20,000
Total income	85,000	2,500	87,500
Personal allowance	(12,570)		(12,570)
Taxable income	72,430	2,500	74,930

Income tax:
Non-savings:

£37,700 × 20%	7,540
£34,730 × 40%	13,892

Savings:

£500 × 0%	0
£2,000 × 40%	800
	22,232
Less: double taxation relief (Note 1)	(8,000)
Income tax payable	14,232

Notes:
1. Double taxation relief is given as credit/unilateral relief. It is the lower of the overseas tax or the UK tax on that source of income. In this case:
   - overseas tax = £9,000
   - UK tax on that source of income =

UK tax including the foreign source	£22,232
UK tax without the foreign source	£14,232
	£8,000

Therefore, double taxation relief is £8,000. Marc has unrelieved foreign tax of £1,000 which, upon the making of a claim within four years of the end of the accounting period in which the excess foreign tax arises, can either be carried forward without limit or carried back to the previous three accounting periods on a LIFO basis.

Chapter 6

Question 6.1

(a) £70,000 – first £30,000 of genuinely ex-gratia termination payments is tax-free.
(b) None – specific exemption applies.
(c) None – specific exemption applies for payments on permanent disability leading to inability to work.
(d) Full £2,400 is taxable.
(e) Not taxable – specifically exempt.

Question 6.2

Income tax computation for Nuala Casey for tax year 2021/22

		£
Taxable element of termination payment (Note 1)		60,500
Salary		<u>33,750</u>
Total income		94,250
Less: personal allowance		<u>(12,570)</u>
Taxable income		81,680

	£	
Tax payable:		
£37,700 @ 20%	7,540	
£43,980 @ 40%	<u>17,592</u>	
Total tax liability	25,132	
PAYE	<u>(7,300)</u>	
Tax due for 2021/22	<u>17,832</u>	

Notes:
1. First £30,000 of termination payment exempt as non-contractual and entirely ex-gratia.
2. No income tax liability arose when the EMI option was exercised, nor did any income tax arise on the grant of the options under the EMI scheme. There is no charge to income tax on either the grant or exercise of the shares, provided that the exercise takes place within 10 years of the grant and the exercise price is the market value of the shares at the date of the grant. Nuala will have capital gains tax implications to address – see **Chapter 18, Section 18.3**.

Question 6.3

Income tax computation for Mr Houghton for tax year 2021/22

	£
	£
Taxable element of termination payment (Note 1)	65,500
Salary	20,000

continued overleaf

Share option income (Note 2)	5,000
Total income	90,500
Less: personal allowance	(12,570)
Taxable income	77,930

Tax payable:	£
£37,700 @ 20%	7,540
£40,230 @ 40%	16,092
	23,632
Less: tax deducted at source (PAYE)	(7,000)
Tax liability for 2021/22	£16,632

Notes:

1. Under general principles, the first £30,000 of a non-contractual, ex-gratia payment on termination would be tax-free. However, in this case the board of the company have created a general expectation amongst employees that they will receive a termination payment of this nature when they retire after a long period of service. This precedent has the effect of making the termination payment "deemed contractual" and so wholly taxable.

2. Gains on exercise of tax-advantaged/approved share options are generally tax-free, provided the options exercised have been held for at least three years. If the share option scheme rules allow "good leavers" to exercise their share options within three years of grant when they leave the company, then the gain on exercise will be subject to income tax. Thus the £30,000 gain arising on the options held for four years is tax-free, but the £5,000 gain arising on the options that are only 18 months old is taxable.

Question 6.4

Income tax computation for Gráinne Foley for the tax year 2021/22

	£
Taxable element of redundancy package (Note 1)	34,700
Less: personal allowance	(12,570)
Taxable income	22,130

Taxed @ 20% = £4,426

Note:

1. Lump sums from approved pension schemes are tax-free. The gift of a car from an employer, however, is treated as taxable income equivalent to the market value of the car at the date received. The total income from the termination payment that is taxable is, therefore, £64,700 (£1,200 + £22,500 + £41,000). However, it is then necessary to consider if the £30,000 ex-gratia payment rules may apply.

It is not mentioned whether the redundancy payment was contractual – but the fact that there is a £41,000 compensation payment implies it was not. There is also no mention of it being a habitual payment for all leavers. On that basis it would be appropriate to claim the £30,000 exemption, although HMRC may challenge this. HMRC approval should have been sought in advance of the package being agreed. The taxable income is £34,700 (i.e. £64,700 – £30,000).

Dividends on shares in the SIP are tax-free, provided the dividends are used to acquire additional shares in the company, which are then held in the SIP for a further three years. There is no limit on the amount of dividend that can be reinvested.

Chapter 8

Question 8.1

If the new company is incorporated in the UK, it will be UK resident. If it is incorporated overseas, and if the central management and control of the company is exercised in the UK, it will also be UK resident. The central management and control of a company is exercised where the highest level of control is exercised, i.e. major not operational decisions. Therefore, as Peter and Angela will make all the strategic decisions in the UK, the new company will be UK resident.

A company that has not received a company tax return or notice to file must tell HMRC if it becomes chargeable to tax within 12 months from the end of the relevant accounting period. Penalties can arise for failure to notify and these are chargeable on a behaviour basis.

Question 8.2

To: Finance director
From: Financial controller
Re: Proposed claim for tax relief on R&D expenditure

I refer to our recent meeting in relation to my review of the draft corporation tax computation, which identified that no claim for R&D expenditure has been included therein. By way of background and as requested, relief in the UK is available for capital R&D expenditure through the capital allowances regime; and for revenue R&D expenditure through the various tax regimes.

Revenue expenditure
The enhanced tax relief for revenue R&D can only be claimed on "relevant" R&D, i.e. R&D that is related to the trade carried on by the company. As the work carried out by the R&D department directly relates to the trade of Comtech this condition of the regime is not an issue.

Qualifying R&D expenditure
While the definition of R&D follows that in UK GAAP and IAS 38 *Intangible Assets*, HMRC recommends that the Department of Business Enterprise and Industrial Strategy guidance tests must be applied. In essence, a project will qualify as an R&D project if it is carried on in the field of science or technology and is undertaken to extend knowledge and to address scientific or technology uncertainties. The projects of our R&D department clearly qualify in this regard.

There are two R&D tax relief regimes in the UK – one for the SME sector (giving a further 130% tax deduction on qualifying revenue expenditure); and the large company regime, which provides for a taxable 13% R&D expenditure credit on qualifying expenditure.

An SME is defined as a company with no more than 500 employees and either not more than €100 million turnover or a balance sheet total of not more than €86 million. Comtech would therefore qualify as an SME and can avail of the 130% tax deduction.

To qualify for the relief expenditure must, *inter alia*, meet the following conditions:

1. must not be capital in nature;
2. must be attributable to relevant R&D that is either directly undertaken by the company or on its behalf; and
3. must be incurred on qualifying costs.

The qualifying expenditure must be such that it would have been allowable as a deduction in computing the taxable profits of a trade carried on by the company. The tax relief is claimed as an adjustment to the trading income computation. The expenditure on which I propose to submit a claim on behalf of Comtech Ltd meets all of the above conditions.

Under the SME scheme, where a company claims SME R&D tax relief and has a trading loss in the accounting period, the company can choose to surrender the loss for a cash payment of 14.5% of the loss for the chargeable period, though this can be restricted depending on the PAYE and NIC owed for the period. An SME may also make a claim under the large company rules if it fails to meet the specific criteria for that regime, but in so doing will be restricted to the limits for such companies.

Tax saving

See Appendix 1 for my calculations of the relief available to Comtech Ltd for qualifying expenditure in the 2022 period. Overall, a corporation tax saving of £73,818 is available to the company.

I would be pleased to meet with you to discuss this claim in more detail and would also suggest we conduct a review to establish if Comtech Ltd would still be within time to submit claims for any prior periods. I suggest we implement procedures to easily capture R&D costs in future periods given the significant cash flow benefits and savings available. Please also note that a claim for the year to 31 March 2021 would be possible until 31 March 2023. I would suggest that this is reviewed as soon as possible given the upcoming deadline for making the claim.

APPENDIX 1

Proposed claim for R&D relief for the accounting period ended 31 March 2022

	£
Qualifying revenue expenditure:	
Gross wages	212,567
Redundancy payments (Note 1)	0
Employer's NIC	27,209
Pension scheme contributions	15,000
Company car benefit in kind (Note 1)	0
Consumable items	22,425
Power, water, and fuel	8,762
Software	4,933
Rates (Note 1)	0
Subcontracted costs (Note 2)	7,963
	298,859
R&D relief @ 130%	388,517

continued overleaf

Corporation tax computation:

Taxable total profits before R&D relief	1,828,925
R&D relief	(388,517)
Amended taxable total profits	1,440,408
Tax payable: £1,440,408 @ 19%	273,678

Tax saved as a result of the R&D claim above:	
Draft tax liability: £1,828,925 @ 19%	347,496
Amended liability	273,678
Tax saving	73,818

Notes:
1. Redundancy payments, non-cash benefits in kind (in this case, company car benefits) and rates do not qualify for the R&D relief.
2. Subcontracted costs payable to a non-connected third party are a qualifying cost. The amount that qualifies is restricted to 65%, i.e. £12,250 × 65% = £7,963.

Question 8.3

(a) This is an ethical question for Peter and Annette. They have become aware of an error in the 31 March 2021 corporation tax return that has resulted in an underpayment of tax for the period but because the enquiry window has closed they are considering not disclosing the error to HMRC. It should be noted that even though the enquiry window has closed HMRC has a six-year time limit for discovery of careless errors and longer for deliberate errors.

The underpayment is £166,725, calculated as follows:

	£
R&D expenditure claimed	750,000
Correct R&D expenditure	(75,000)
Overclaimed R&D expenditure	675,000
Additional 130% claimed incorrectly thereon	877,500
Corporation tax underpaid thereon × 19%	166,725

As directors of FSNI, they have a duty to disclose the error to HMRC and thus it is recommended that they contact HMRC accordingly to advise same, and pay the tax and interest thereon and any penalties arising.

(b) HMRC's penalty regime focuses on the behaviour of the taxpayer, i.e. the company acting through its directors and officers. Where a company has made a mistake in a return submitted to HMRC, but has taken reasonable care in preparation of that return, no penalty will be levied by HMRC.

The categories of behaviour where penalties will be imposed are:

- careless (failure to take reasonable care);
- deliberate and not concealed (the inaccuracy is deliberate but there are no attempts made to conceal it);
- deliberate and concealed (the inaccuracy is deliberate and there are arrangements to conceal it).

Once HMRC has categorised the behaviour of the taxpayer, potential lost revenue (PLR) is computed. In this case the PLR (which is the additional amount of tax due or payable as a result of correcting the inaccuracy) is the underpaid corporation tax of £166,725. The potential penalty is based on a % of the PLR. However, HMRC may apply reductions to the proposed penalty where the company has disclosed the inaccuracy. There are two types of potential disclosure – prompted and unprompted. A disclosure is unprompted if it is made at a time when the person making it has no reason to believe that HMRC has discovered or is about to discover the inaccuracy.

As HMRC did not issue an enquiry notice by 31 March 2022 into any aspect of the return, the disclosure can be an unprompted disclosure. Therefore, should HMRC argue reasonable care was not taken in preparing the 31 March 2021 return, and levy a penalty accordingly, the unprompted percentages in the table would potentially be applicable to FSNI.

	Careless	**Deliberate but not concealed**	**Deliberate and concealed**
Maximum penalty	30%	70%	100%
Min penalty (unprompted)	0%	20%	30%
Min penalty (prompted)	15%	35%	50%

It is likely HMRC would view the behaviour as 'careless'. This would mean a maximum penalty of £50,018 and, potentially, a 0% penalty should the company make a full unprompted disclosure. It is recommended that this be submitted as soon as possible to achieve the maximum possible penalty reduction.

Question 8.4

(a) Solar Heating Ltd meets the conditions for SME and large company R&D relief. The £50,000 offer from Invest NI is notified as state aid. SMEs are able to claim R&D tax relief under the large company scheme in respect of expenditure that is not allowed under the SME scheme if the expenditure does not qualify under the SME scheme only because it was subsidised (including notified state aid).

Therefore, if Solar Heating signs the letter of offer and accepts the grant, R&D relief on the £525,000 expenditure would be available under the large company regime (as RDEC) instead. If it declines to accept the grant, it would be able to claim under the SME R&D regime.

The calculations of the net cost to the company after R&D tax relief both with and without the grant is shown below.

(i) Grant accepted – Claim under the large company regime

	£
Qualifying revenue expenditure	525,000
Taxable 13% RDEC	68,250
Less: corporation tax @ 19%	(12,968)
Net relief	55,282

continued overleaf

Cost to the company:

Expenditure	525,000
Less:	
Net R&D relief	(55,282)
Grant receive	(50,000)
Net cost	419,718

(ii) Grant declined – Claim under the SME regime

	£
Qualifying revenue expenditure	525,000
R&D relief @ 130%	682,500
Corporation tax saving @ 19%	129,675

Cost to the company:	
Expenditure	525,000
Less: Corporation tax saved	(129,675)
Net cost	395,325

(b) Recommendations

A claim under the SME regime (declining the grant from Invest NI) results in a net cost to the company of £395,325; while accepting the grant and thus claiming under the large company regime gives a net cost of £419,718. The SME claim would mean net cost of £24,393 less.

A claim under the SME regime would also have the additional commercial benefit of not being tied to any specific conditions regarding the grant set out by Invest NI in its letter of offer. Therefore, it is recommended that the Invest NI grant is not accepted in its current form. The company would be required to receive a grant of at least £75,000 for it to be considered seriously. Future grant applications should be similarly assessed.

The company would be required to make a claim for R&D relief in its corporation tax return for the accounting period ended 30 September 2021 and it has a two-year time limit from that accounting period end to make the R&D claim i.e. until 30 September 2023.

Question 8.5

BRIEFING NOTE

To: Tax Partner
From: Tax Senior
Date: March 2022

Subject: Purchase and disposal of intangible fixed assets

(a) Disposal of patent in June 2021
- The disposal falls within the corporate intangibles regime. This means that a trading profit will arise on sale. This profit is calculated as:

Proceeds	£200,000
TWDV	(£90,000)
Taxable trading profit arising	£110,000

- ▣ Under the regime, part of this gain can be sheltered using intangibles rollover relief so long as the entire £200,000 proceeds of sale of the patent is reinvested in a qualifying intangible asset used in the company's trade and the reinvestment takes place in the period 12 months before the disposal of the old intangible to three years after.
- ▣ Partial intangibles rollover relief may also be possible if the entire proceeds are not reinvested.
- ▣ A qualifying asset for these purposes would be the patent associated with the acquisition of the trade and assets of Warp Ltd's business.
- ▣ As the proposed expenditure on patent is £240,000, full rollover relief is available on the sale of the patent.
- ▣ Maximum profit rolled over is proceeds less original cost, not written down cost, i.e., £200,000 – £150,000 = £50,000
- ▣ This will mean that a claim for rollover relief of £50,000 can be made.
- ▣ The remaining taxable trading profit on the patent disposal of £60,000 (£110,000 – £50,000 rollover relief) will be subject to corporation tax of 19% in the accounting period ended 31 March 2022. Corporation tax of £11,400 will arise.

(b) Calculate annual writing down allowance
- ▣ The cost of the patent acquired for tax relief purposes will be £190,000 being its cost of £240,000 reduced by the £50,000 rollover relief claimed.
- ▣ The tax cost of the patent on which the 4% fixed rate election can be made will be £190,000.
- ▣ Therefore, the annual allowance on which tax relief will be available is therefore £7,600 (£190,000 × 4%).

(c) If the new patent is valued at £170,000 rather than £240,000
- ▣ If the full £200,000 proceeds received from the disposal of the old patent is not fully reinvested in qualifying corporate intangible assets, then rollover relief is partially available
- ▣ If the new patent costs £170,000, the maximum rollover relief would be restricted to £20,000 (£170,000 reinvested – £150,000 original cost) and the £30,000 of the £200,000 proceeds received that was not re-invested will be immediately taxable.
- ▣ In this case the taxable trading profit arising on the sale of the patent will be £90,000 (£110,000 – £20,000 rollover relief) which will be subject to corporation tax of 19% in the accounting period ended 31 March 2022. Corporation tax of £17,100 will arise.
- ▣ As £20,000 of rollover relief will be claimed, the base cost of the patent on which the 4% election would be available would be reduced to £150,000 (£170,000 less £20,000) – giving an annual allowance of £6,000.

Question 8.6

The tax computation of Investco Ltd for the accounting period ended 31 March 2022 will be as follows:

	£	£
Surplus non-trade loan relationship credits		3,000
Property income		12,000

continued overleaf

Chargeable gain		5,000
Total taxable gross income		20,000
Less: management expenses:		
Shareholder meeting costs	2,240	
Directors' remuneration (Note 2)	12,000	
Office rent	3,000	
Repairs	500	
Total management expenses		(17,740)
Taxable total profits		2,260
Corporation tax @ 19%		429

Notes:
1. The company is not subject to corporation tax on the dividend as it is a small company under the dividend exemption rules.
2. The full amount will be deductible provided the directors can demonstrate that the amount charged is reasonable for the work carried out. This is not necessarily a measure against the company's income but is more likely to be considered in the context of the director's activities, e.g. the director may spend significant time monitoring the company's shareholdings in listed companies.
3. Appraisal costs would be deductible if they were in respect of an overall appraisal of the market; however, when a specific target is identified, any appraisal costs associated with a decision to go ahead with the acquisition would no longer be allowable. In this case, the appraisal costs do not qualify as management expenses but as a capital cost of acquiring the asset.

Chapter 9

Question 9.1

The trustees of A's settlement are associates of Mrs A by virtue of section 448(1) CTA 2010 and their rights and powers may be attributed to Mrs A, who therefore controls the company. Company X is therefore a close company as it is under the control of Mrs A, being five or fewer participators.

Question 9.2

Control by voting rights is determined under section 450(3) CTA 2010.
   The associates of A are:

- his wife and his brother; and
- the trustees of A's settlement (section 448(1) CTA 2010).

The rights and powers attributable to A are:

- the rights and powers of his associates (section 451(4) CTA 2010); and
- the rights and powers of Company X (section 451(4) CTA 2010).

As a total of 510 votes are thus possessed by A or attributable to him, the company is a close company controlled by one person.

Question 9.3

Control – the rights in the shares held by Company Z in Company Y may be attributed to F, who controls that company (section 451(4) CTA 2010).

F is an associate of E but the rights attributed to F cannot be further attributed to E (section 451(4) CTA 2010).

No group of five participators or fewer can control Company Y, nor do the director/participators control it, and nor would the winding up test be of assistance here.

Therefore company Y is not a close company.

Chapter 10

Question 10.1

(a) Tax law provides that the company must account for tax as if the loan were a net annual payment after deduction of tax. If the loan amounted to £8,000 in the accounts to 31 March 2022, the company must self-assess tax liabilities in respect of any loans and this can mean that it will have to pay tax to HMRC equal to 32.5% of the outstanding loan made during the accounting period, i.e. £2,600. This will be the case where the loan remains unpaid and has not been released or written off within nine months and one day following the end of the relevant accounting period (the effective due date for payment of corporation tax for all but large companies).
If and when the loan is repaid, the company may claim a refund of £2,600. Exemption from this tax charge is, however, available:

- where the business of the company is or includes the lending of money and the loan is made in the ordinary course of that business, or
- where a debt is incurred for the supply of goods or services in the ordinary course of the business of the close company, unless the credit given exceeds six months or is longer than the period normally given to the company's customers, or
- the borrower satisfies the following conditions:
  - total loans to borrower or spouse do not exceed £15,000, and
  - the borrower works full-time for the close company or any of its associated companies (companies under common control), and
  - the borrower and/or his or her associates is not the beneficial owner of or able to control more than 5% of the ordinary shares of the company.

(b) Corporation tax liability – year ended 31/03/2022

	£
Taxable total profits: £133,000 @ 19%	25,270

Corporation tax payable on or before 1 January 2023.

Question 10.2

(a) Corporation tax computation for year ended 31/03/2022

		£	£
Net profit per accounts			32,900
Add:	Depreciation	15,000	
	Disallowed sundry (see (b) below)	800	15,800
			48,700
Less:	Interest	8,500	
	Capital grants	1,500	(10,000)
			38,700
Less:	capital allowances		(4,000)
Trading income			34,700
Net credit from loan relationships			8,500
Taxable total profits			43,200
Corporation tax payable			
£43,200 @ 19%			8,208

(b) Specific items – the expense payment is treated as a "distribution" in the hands of Y's brother and added back in the trading income computation.

Question 10.3

Corporation Tax Computation for y/e 31/03/2022

		£	£
Net profit per accounts			1,870,000
Add: Entertainment	W1	11,900	
Depreciation		100,000	
Loss on sale of plant		20,000	
			131,900
Less:			
Profit on sale of building		1,480,000	
Rents		200,000	(1,680,000)
			321,900
Capital allowances			(50,000)
Trading income			271,900
Trading losses forward – section 45 CTA 2010*			(210,000)
			61,900
Property income	W2		181,000
			242,900
Chargeable gain	W3		1,377,000

continued overleaf

Taxable total profits	1,619,900
Corporation tax:	
£1,619,900 @ 19%	307,781
Tax on loan £550,000 @ 32.5%**	178,750

* Section 45 claims are subject to the restriction rule. However, the company's deductions allowance for losses carried forward is £5 million, meaning 100% relief is available for these losses.
** If the loan is not repaid within nine months and one day of the year end.

Workings

1. Entertainment disallowed £

	£
Entertaining customers	6,000
Entertaining suppliers	5,000
Christmas gifts for suppliers	900
	11,900

2. Property income £

	£
Portion of premium subject to corporation tax:	
£50,000 × (50−19)/50	31,000
Property income (£200,000 − £50,000)	150,000
Property income	181,000

3. Chargeable gain – sale of building

		£
Proceeds from building		1,500,000
Legal fees		(18,000)
		1,482,000
Market value at 31/3/1982	50,000	
Indexation: 1.10	55,000	(105,000)
Gain		1,377,000

Question 10.4

Servisco Ltd Corporation Tax Computation year ended 31 March 2022

	£
Trading income	430,000
Less: loss forward under section 45*	(9,000)
	421,000
Net credits from loan relationships	50,000
Property income	100,000
	571,000
Chargeable gains	86,400
Taxable total profits	657,400

continued overleaf

Corporation tax

£657,400 @ 19%   124,906

* Section 45 claims are subject to the restriction rule. However, the company's deductions allowance for losses carried forward is £5 million, meaning 100% relief is available for these losses.

Servisco Ltd's dividend income would be exempt from UK corporation tax.

Question 10.5

Machinery Ltd Corporation Tax Computation year ended 31 March 2022

	£	£
Net profit per accounts		686,700
Add:		
Depreciation	59,790	
Loan interest treated as a distribution (Note 1)	2,731	
		62,521
Deduct:		
Bank deposit interest	(10,000)	
Property income	(50,000)	
		(60,000)
		689,221
Less: capital allowances		(10,700)
Trading income		678,521
Net credits from loan relationships		10,000
Property income		50,000
Taxable total profits		738,521
Corporation tax payable:		
£738,521 @ 19%		140,318.99

Note:

1. Loans from directors (and/or associates) with material interest.

	Loan £	Interest paid £	Interest at 6%	Deemed distribution
V. Duffy	4,000	600	240	360
Mrs J. Duffy	5,000	600	300	300
Trustees	5,000	750	300	450
Executors	5,000	750	300	450
D. O'Connell	5,000	750	300	450
L.T. Smith	10,000	1,321	600	721
	34,000	4,771	2,040	2,731

Neither Louise or Paul Hare are classed as having received excessive interest as each of their interest rates is 6% or less.

Question 10.6

Tax Advisors Ltd

Corporation Tax Computation for the year ended 31 March 2022

	£
Trading income	100,000
Net credits from loan relationships	100,000
Total profits	200,000
Qualifying charitable donations	(60,000)
Taxable total profits	140,000

Total corporation tax payable is £140,000 @ 19% = £26,600.

Chapter 11

Question 11.1

Anytown Tax Advisors
Anytown

Stephanie Adams
Finance Director
Shed-It Ltd
Any Road
Newry

Dear Stephanie,

With reference to your telephone call I outline the corporation tax implications of the potential expansion of Shed-It Ltd into the Republic of Ireland, together with other relevant tax considerations.

The company is considering expanding its trading activities into the Republic of Ireland and is looking at establishing either a branch of Shed-It Ltd or a wholly owned Irish subsidiary company, Shed-It (Ireland) Ltd.

The corporation tax and other relevant tax considerations of each option are addressed below.

(a) Branch operation
A UK resident company is subject to corporation tax on its worldwide profits. Therefore should the activities of the Irish operation be structured through a branch of the existing company, the profits of the Irish branch will be subject to UK corporation tax at the rate of 19%. However, it should be noted that rate is set to increase from 1 April 2023 and may be as much as 25% depending on the company's overall profits.

The profits of the Irish branch will also be subject to Irish corporation tax at 12.5%. Double taxation relief (DTR) would be available in respect of the Irish corporation tax suffered, up to a maximum of the equivalent UK corporation tax liability. DTR is limited to the lower of the UK corporation tax paid or the Irish corporation tax paid. In this case, full relief would be obtained for the 12.5% Irish corporation tax as this would be lower than the 19% UK rate. An additional 6.5% UK corporation tax (19% – 12.5%) would be paid by Shed-It Ltd on any Irish profits arising.

Shed-It Ltd can make a permanent irrevocable election that the results from its overseas branches are exempt from UK corporation tax, this would mean that corporation tax would only be payable in Ireland on any branch profits – saving corporation tax of 6.5%. However, any branch losses would not be relievable in the UK as a result.

In a situation where the branch is loss-making and a branch exemption has not been entered into, any losses of the Irish branch are relievable against UK profits and vice versa. In this scenario, Irish losses would attract relief in Ireland at 12.5% but an additional 6.5% (19% – 12.5%) UK corporation tax relief would be achieved against any UK trading profits.

As the initial activities are projected to be loss-making it would be recommended that Shed-It Ltd does not enter into a branch exemption election, allowing it to enable the Irish losses to be relieved in the UK. An election could then be considered once the branch is projected to make profits; any election should be made in advance of the beginning of the accounting period in which profits are projected.

(b) Subsidiary operation

The profits of a non-UK resident subsidiary of a UK resident parent should not be subject to UK corporation tax, but they will be subject to Irish corporation tax at 12.5%.

Shed-It Ltd will not be subject to UK corporation tax on any dividends it receives from Shed-It (Ireland) Ltd as it is likely to meet the distribution exemption rules either as a small company or as a distribution from a controlled company.

Any losses sustained by the Irish subsidiary will not be available for group relief in the UK under the normal rules. However, UK legislation does provide for relief under the specific rules that apply for EEA/EU group relief, subject to certain conditions being met.

While an overseas subsidiary will increase the number of related 51% group companies for UK corporation tax purposes, this is not relevant to Shed-It Ltd as it does not pay corporation tax in instalments.

Should Shed-It Ltd sell the shares in Shed-It Ltd in the future, this would potentially benefit from the substantial shareholdings exemption, subject to the relevant conditions being met. The sale of a branch operation by Shed-It Ltd would not benefit from this exemption.

Yours sincerely,

Question 11.2

With an irrevocable election, no charge to UK tax arises on the foreign branch profits. The computation is as follows:

Corporation tax computation: year ended 31 March 2022

	£
Trading profits	1,400,000
Corporation tax @ 19%	266,000

£79,412 (£450,000 × 100/85 – £450,000) withholding tax was paid on the exempt foreign income and this will not be relievable in the UK due to the election. However, tax of 4% has been saved on the foreign branch profits.

Without an irrevocable election, the computation would be as follows:

Corporation tax computation: year ended 31 March 2022

	£	£
Trading profits		1,400,000
Foreign income:		
$\dfrac{£450,000 \times 100}{85}$		529,412
Taxable total profits		1,929,412
Corporation tax @ 19%		366,588
Less: DTR – lower of:		
Foreign tax	79,412	
or		
UK tax on foreign income: £529,412 @ 19%	100,588	
		(79,412)
Corporation tax due		287,176

Chapter 12

Question 12.1

Corporation Tax Computation Period Ended 31 March 2022 – Z Ltd

	£
Trading income	NIL
Net credit from loan relationships	20,000
Total profits	20,000
Loss (under section 37(3)(a))	(20,000)
Taxable total profits	NIL

Corporation Tax Computation Period Ended 31 March 2022 – B Ltd

	£
Trading income	170,000
Deduct: losses forward under section 45	(16,000)
	154,000
Net credit from loan relationships	4,000
Property income	20,000
Total profits	178,000
Deduct: group relief surrendered by Z Ltd	(76,000)
Taxable total profits	102,000
Corporation tax £102,000 @ 19%	19,380

Loss memo

	£
Loss	96,000
Used against other income of current year	(20,000)

Surrendered under section 99 CTA 2010	(76,000)
Loss available	Nil

Note: it would also have been possible to group-relieve the full £96,000 from Z Ltd as it is not necessary to offset a current-year trading loss against the company's own profits before surrender. As both companies are subject to tax at 19% and are not quarterly payers, there would be no difference to the amount of tax or timing of payments.

Question 12.2

A Ltd – Corporation Tax Computation Period to 31 March 2022

	£
Net credit from loan relationships	1,000
Property income	20,000
	21,000
Loss set-off	(21,000)
Taxable total profits	NIL

B Ltd – Corporation Tax Computation Period to 31 March 2022

	£
Trading income	56,000
Net credit from loan relationships	2,000
Property income	25,000
	83,000
Less: group loss surrendered by A Ltd	(69,000)
Taxable total profits	14,000
Corporation tax £14,000 @ 19%	2,660

C Ltd – Corporation Tax Computation Period to 31 March 2022

	£
Trading income	48,000
Less: losses forward	(26,000)
	22,000
Net credit from loan relationships	3,000
Property income	2,000
Taxable total profits	27,000
Corporation tax £27,000 @ 19%	5,130

Loss memo of A Ltd

Trading losses brought forward	4,000
Loss – current year	90,000
Used against other income of current year	(21,000)
Claim section 99 balance of loss to B Ltd	(69,000)
Loss available to carry forward*	4,000

*The brought-forward trading loss of £4,000 can only be carried forward to set against future profits of the same trade as this is a trading loss pre-1 April 2017. Alternatively, part of the current-year loss of A Ltd could instead have been surrendered to C Ltd to reduce its total trading income to nil, or all of the losses could have been surrendered without utilising £21,000 against current year first.

Note that, as each company is paying corporation tax at 19% and none are quarterly payers, alternative group relief solutions would yield similar results.

Question 12.3

	Queen Ltd	Rook Ltd	Pawn Ltd
	£	£	£
Profit/loss per accounts	199,313	(80,586)	(2,030)
Disallow:			
Depreciation	12,000	16,000	10,000
Entertainment	1,350	1,650	1,200
Interest (Note 1)	400	–	10,720
	213,063	(62,936)	19,890
Capital allowances	(7,375)	(5,627)	(3,000)
	205,688	(68,563)	16,890
Trading losses brought forward			(16,890)
	205,688	(68,563)	–
Net credit/(deficit) from loan relationships (Note 2)	23,846		(10,720)
	229,534	(68,563)	(10,720)
Group relief re. trading losses carried forward	(63,110)		
Group relief re. LR deficit	(10,720)		10,720
Group relief re. current-period trading losses (Note 3)	(68,563)	68,563	–
Taxable total profits	87,141	NIL	NIL

Corporation tax payable:

	£
Pawn Ltd	Nil
Rook Ltd	Nil
Queen Ltd	Nil

Taxable total profits = £ 87,141 @ 19% = £16,556.79 payable on or before 1 January 2023 (as none of the companies are paying corporation tax in instalments).

Notes:
1. The PAYE interest is not tax deductible.
2. The interest payable by Pawn Ltd is for a non-trading purpose and is, therefore, deductible as a loan relationship, rather than a trading expense. This deficit can be group-relieved to Queen Ltd.
3. The trading loss of Rook Ltd is available via group relief to be offset against the trading income of Queen Ltd.
4. It is assumed that the dividend received from the French company qualifies for one of the exemptions and is not therefore taxable.
5. The group has an overall deductions allowance of £5 million that can be used in any way. Hence there is no restriction in the use of the losses carried forward by any company as the total is below £5 million.

Chapter 13

Question 13.1

Sale in June 2021
The conditions to qualify for substantial shareholding exemption (SSE) are as follows:

Shareholding requirements

■ The holding must have been substantial (i.e. at least 10%). This condition was met as at that time the holding was 100%.

■ The substantial shareholding must have been held throughout a 12-month period in the six years before disposal. This conditions was also met as the shares have been held since 2005.

Investee condition

■ Must have been a sole trading company or member of a trading group in the qualifying period (generally 12 months before disposal).

This condition was met as Kelly Luxury Cars GmbH was a trading company at the time of the disposal. As the disposal is not to a connected person, it does not matter that the company will be an investment company after the sale. Therefore SSE was available and the entire gain in June 2021 was exempt, saving corporation tax at the main rate of 19%. It should also be noted that the substantial shareholding does not have to be held in a UK resident company, so the German residence of the company is not an issue. There may also be foreign tax payable in Germany on the disposal and any tax thereon would not be available for double taxation relief in the UK as the gain is entirely exempt in the UK.

Proposed sale in May 2026
The 5% shareholding appears not to meet the substantial shareholding test as it is less than the 10% requirement.

However, as long as the 10% requirement is met throughout a 12-month period in the six years prior to the proposed disposal, then the disposal will qualify.

Hence the 5% disposal in May 2026 will also qualify for SSE, because in the six-year period prior to this (i.e. from 1 June 2020 to 31 May 2026) there was a 12-month period where the company held at least 10% of the shares in the subsidiary (i.e. it held 100% of the shares from 26 June 2020 until 25 June 2021).

If the remaining 5% shares are to be sold at a loss, no capital loss will arise as the loss is also subject to the SSE.

We would recommend delaying the transaction until after 25 June 2027, when the substantial shareholding requirement required for SSE will not be meet and a capital loss will crystallise, which can be used by the company against any current period chargeable gains or carried forward to be utilised in the future (carry back is not possible).

Question 13.2

REPORT TO THE BOARD OF DIRECTORS

Solar Group Corporation Tax Position – Accounting Period Ended 31 March 2022

Introduction

(a) The group's corporation tax liability for the year ended 31 March 2022 is £35,110 and is payable to HMRC by 1 January 2023. None of the companies in the group have taxable total profits in 2022 in excess of £300,000 (£1,500,000/5), hence corporation tax was not due on an instalment basis. The computation of the group's corporation tax liability for the year ended 31 March 2022 is included below.

(b) (i) The calculation of the chargeable gain on the disposal of Solar's investment in Saturn is included below. The gain after indexation allowance is £335,750. Ordinarily, Solar would have been assessed to tax on this gain at the main rate of corporation tax, being 19%.

However, under the substantial shareholdings exemption (SSE) legislation, there is an exemption from tax on gains and losses made by companies on the disposal of shares. There are a number of conditions that must be satisfied to qualify for the relief.

The main exemption will apply where a company makes a disposal of all or part of a substantial shareholding of shares in a trading company or member of a trading group. For this purpose, substantial means at least 10% of the ordinary shares of the company concerned, together with an entitlement to at least 10% of:

- the profits available for distribution to equity holders; and
- the assets available to equity holders in a winding up.

Trading company means a company carrying on trading activities whose activities do not include, to a substantial extent, activities other than trading activities. Substantial in this context is not defined, although in common with other tax reliefs, 20% is typically taken as the benchmark. The shares must have been held for a continuous 12-month period in the previous six years prior to the disposal.

Based on the above, Solar would appear to satisfy the conditions so that the gain on the sale of the shares in Saturn will be exempt from corporation tax on the potential capital gain arising of £335,750.

(ii) *Degrouping charge*

The calculation of the chargeable gain arising from the transfer of the property from Solar to Saturn, as a result of Saturn leaving the group is included below. When Saturn ceases to be subsidiary of Solar, it will be deemed to have sold the freehold property acquired from Solar at the date it was originally acquired from that company (i.e. March 2017). The deemed sale proceeds will be the market value at that time.

A gain of £126,500 will be deemed to have been made by Solar in March 2017 under TCGA 1992 section 179 (referred to as a degrouping charge) by virtue of the fact that where a company leaves a group and has, within the six years ending at the time, acquired an asset from another group member, the company leaving is treated as having sold the asset when it was acquired from the other group member at its market value at that time and immediately reacquired it.

Although computed as if the asset had been disposed of in March 2017, the gain is regarded as arising at the start of the accounting period in which Saturn leaves the group and would ordinarily be charged corporation tax at the rate applicable to that accounting period.

Under the legislation, where a degrouping event takes place, the degrouping charge arising is treated as deemed proceeds on the disposal of the relevant shares for calculating the gain or loss on the disposal of the shares. A consequence of this is that SSE is also available on the degrouping charge, meaning both the chargeable gain on the share sale and on the £126,500 degrouping charge are fully exempt from corporation tax.

(c) (i) *Proposed property transfer*

The proposed transfer of the property from Solar to Neptune will not give rise to a chargeable gain arising for Solar even though the sale to an independent third party would result in a capital gain of £100,000 by virtue of the fact that Neptune is a wholly-owned subsidiary of Solar and assets transferred between both companies are treated as transferred on a no gain, no loss basis under section 171 TCGA 1992 (i.e. no gain will be deemed to have arisen).

Corporation tax on the capital gain will therefore be deferred until such time as the asset is sold outside the group or if Neptune leaves the groups within six years, subject to the rules for degrouping charges.

(ii) *Sale of Neptune property*

The disposal of the property currently occupied by Neptune will be a disposal outside the group giving rise to a chargeable gain in Neptune. To mitigate the gain arising, advantage can be taken of TCGA 1992 section 171A. Neptune can jointly elect with Solar, within two years of the disposal, that the property is deemed to be transferred on a no gain, no loss basis to Solar with Solar being deemed to make the disposal. This enables the group to use the £200,000 capital losses of Solar against the capital gains of Neptune without having to physically transfer ownership of the asset intragroup before making the disposal outside the group. The use of the carried-forward capital losses is not restricted as the amount of carried-forward losses being claimed (both income and capital carried-forward losses) is below the £5 million threshold.

Alternatively, if advantage of capital loss relief available from say Solar is not taken, the chargeable gain may be rolled over or held over against a qualifying acquisition by Neptune or a qualifying acquisition by another group company. The usual 12 months before and three years after rules relating to rollover relief would apply.

(d) *Acquisition of Mars*

The group should be aware that anti-avoidance legislation is in place to prevent companies buying other companies and taking advantage of existing trading losses. These provisions disallow the carrying forward of trading losses incurred before a substantial change in ownership of the company's shares. The disallowance will apply if there is a change in the ownership of the company and either:

- there is a major change in the nature or conduct of trade carried on by the company within five years (beginning no more than three years before the change in ownership); or
- at any time after the change in ownership, the scale of activities of the trade carried on by the company has become small or negligible.

Given that the board of directors intends to make significant changes to the products sold, customers and markets, it is possible that (b) above would apply and the £500,000 losses would not be available to carry forward. These would be effectively wasted. We would recommend that the exact changes proposed are reviewed in more detail, taking into account HMRC guidance in this area before a decision to purchase Mars is made, as the availability of these losses should be factored in to the price paid for the company. We would also stress that even if the acquisition of Mars does not fall foul of this specific anti-avoidance rule, if there is any suggestion that the Mars acquisition is being undertaken to access these losses, then relief will also be denied. If this anti-avoidance rule does not apply, note that pre-acquisition losses cannot be group-relieved until a five-year period has elapsed.

SOLAR GROUP

Computation of corporation tax liability year ended 31 March 2022

	Solar	Neptune	Venus	Saturn	Mercury
	£	£	£	£	£
Trading profits	67,550	47,087	72,680	82,793	0
Chargeable gains			8,260		
Current year loss offset		(47,087)			
Profits before group relief	67,550	0	80,940	82,793	0
Less: group relief	(2,760)	0	(20,940)	(22,793)	0
Taxable total profits	64,790	0	60,000	60,000	0
Corporation tax @ 19%	12,310		11,400	11,400	**Total £35,110**

Workings
Working 1: Trading profits – Saturn

	£
Profits before capital allowances	112,559
Capital allowances	(29,766)
	82,793

Working 2: Trading loss – Neptune

	£
Loss b/f	75,000
Current year offset	(47,087)
Loss c/f	27,913

Neptune's trading loss is pre-1 April 2017 and can only be offset against future trading profits from the same trade. The group has a £5 million deductions allowance to utilise losses carried forward – the amount to be potentially offset is below the allowance and so can be fully used.

Working 3: Loss memorandum – Mercury

	£
Adjusted loss	46,493
Group relief:	
Solar	(2,760)
Venus	(20,940)
Saturn	(22,793)
Remaining	Nil

Working 4: Capital gain – Venus

The capital gain of Venus (£55,260) will be reduced by capital losses brought forward (£47,000), leaving an amount assessable to corporation tax of £8,260. (Note that treating the capital gain in Venus as reallocated to Solar under the rules for chargeable gains relating to groups of companies would have been correct also. It does not matter how the losses are group relieved as each company is paying corporation tax at 19%.)

SOLAR GROUP
Chargeable gain on sale of Solar's shares in Saturn

	£
Proceeds	300,000
Deemed proceeds: degrouping charge	126,500
Cost	(55,000)
Gain before indexation allowance	371,500
Indexation allowance: £55,000 @ 65%	(35,750)
	335,750

Chargeable gain arising on property transferred to Saturn as a result of Saturn leaving the group within six years – degrouping charge

	£
Deemed proceeds – March 2017	230,000
March 1982 market value	(50,000)
Gain before indexation allowance	180,000
Indexation allowance: £50,000 @ 107%	(53,500)
Gain after indexation allowance	126,500

Chapter 14

Question 14.1

(a)

DELANEY ELECTRICS (UK) LIMITED
Corporation Tax Computation for Accounting Period Ended 31 March 2022

	Notes	£	£
Profit/(loss) before tax			968,825
Add back:			
Depreciation		155,250	
Amortisation	4	12,000	
Legal and professional fees	3	3,559	
Repairs and maintenance	5	20,000	
Insurance	6	6,200	
Corporation tax penalty and interest	8(a)	6,000	
Customer entertaining	8(b)	1,000	
Leased car restriction	8(c)	1,148	
Management charge – transfer pricing adjustment	12	100,000	
			305,157
Deduct:			
Movement in general provision for bad debts	7		(10,000)
Rental profit	9		(29,160)
Dividend income	10		(60,000)
Profit on disposal of patent rights	11		(110,000)
Capital allowances			(92,324)
Adjusted trading profit			972,498
Taxable Total Profits:			
Trading profits			972,498
Property business profits	9		29,160
Total profits			1,001,658
Less: surplus NTLRD	8(a)		(2,500)
Taxable total profits			999,158

Notes:

1. Depreciation on finance-leased assets is deductible for corporation tax.
2. Statutory redundancy payments are always deductible. The ex gratia payment of £17,000 is also allowable, as this does not bring the total payment of £23,000 to more than four times the statutory amount (£6,000 × 4 = £24,000).
3. Legal fees in relation to the HMRC corporation tax enquiry are not tax deductible as the enquiry outcome was not in the company's favour and thus the cost is not wholly and exclusively for the purposes of the trade of the company. Legal fees re. the case against the supplier are wholly and exclusively for the purposes of the trade and so are deductible. Legal fees re. issue with tenants of leased property are not trading expenses but expenses of the rental business. The required adjustment is taken account of in the rental profit deduction line in the computation.
4. As the goodwill was acquired after 8 July 2015 but before 1 April 2019, the company is not entitled to a deduction for the £12,000 amortised in the period.
5. Repairs of the leased-out commercial premises are not trading expenses but expenses of the rental business. The required adjustment is taken account of in the rental profit deduction line in the computation. The extension to the trading premises is capital and not revenue and must be added back, but it should be considered if any of the expenditure qualifies for capital allowances.
6. As the keyman policy is not wholly and exclusively for the purposes of the trade, the premiums must be added back. Insurance in respect of the rented portion of the property is not a trading expense but a rental expense. The required adjustment is taken account of in the rental profit deduction line in the computation. Public liability and directors' leased car insurance are incurred wholly and exclusively for the purpose of the trade and are thus tax deductible.
7. Increase in bad debt provision calculated in accordance with IFRS is tax deductible. However, the general provision has decreased by £10,000 and as this would have been added back previously a deduction is available.
8. Sundry expenses:
    (a) Penalties and interest in relation to the HMRC enquiry are not wholly and exclusively for the purpose of the trade and thus not deductible for trade purposes. However, the corporation tax interest is allowed later as a non-trade debit.
    (b) Drinks, food and entertainment at the party is entertaining customers and suppliers and is therefore disallowed.
         The branded top is allowed for corporation tax as each:

         ● individually cost under £50; and
         ● bears the business name, logo or a clear advertisement; and
         ● does not consist of food, drink or tobacco.

    (c) A restriction is applied to the cost of leased cars where CO_2 emissions are > 5g/km for leases entered into on or after 1 April 2021 until 31 March 2021, and 50g/km for leases entered into on or after 1 April 2021.
         The restriction re. the BMW 6 Series is £7,650 × 15% = £1,148

9. Rental profit

	£
Rental income	40,000
Less expenses:	
Professional fees	(5,000)
Repairs and maintenance – rented building	(3,465)
Insurance – rented building	(2,375)
Rental profit	29,160

10. As we do not have sufficient information to determine if the company is small under the dividend exemption rules, the dividend income is exempt from corporation tax as it was received in respect of ordinary shares.

11. Under the corporate intangibles regime, the profit on the sale of patent rights would usually be taxed as trading income. However, as the entire proceeds on the sale of intangible fixed assets (patent rights) have been reinvested in other intangible fixed assets (copyrights) for use in the trade within a three-year period after the disposal, £110,000 (£260,000 – £150,000) can be rolled over/deferred until sale of the new copyrights. Therefore only £75,000 (£150,000 – £75,000) is taxed as trading income now and the remaining £110,000 profit is deducted.

12. As the arm's length price is £200,000 an additional amount of £100,000 arises under the transfer pricing rules because Delaney UK has received a tax advantage and Delaney UK and Delaney Ireland are under common control.

13. Bank interest payable in relation to an overdraft to fund working capital requirements is trading in nature and therefore a deductible expense in the calculation of trading profits.

(b) Corporation tax – loss in 2024

The company will cease to trade in the 2024 accounting period and is projected to make a trading loss of £1,792,000 that will be extinguished on cessation of the trade as it has no current-year income in 2024 to offset it against, and it is not possible to carry the loss forward as there will be no future profits (and no future trade).

Under the terminal loss relief rules, the trading loss of the final 12 months of the trade in 2024 can be carried back against the total profits of the previous three years. Losses are relieved first against total profits of the year ended 31 March 2023, followed by the year ended 31 March 2022 and then against 12 of the 18 months results for the accounting period ended 31 March 2021.

The table below summarises how Delaney (UK) may claim terminal loss relief to reduce its taxable total profits for the years ended 31 March 2021–2023 inclusive.

	Accounting Periods		
	31 March 2023	**31 March 2022**	**18 months ended 31 March 2021**
	£	£	£
Trading profit	60,000		500,000
Property income	75,000		67,000
Surplus NTLRC	70,000		

continued overleaf

Chargeable gains	175,000		
Taxable total profits	380,000	999,158	567,000
Less: terminal loss relief	(380,000)	(999,158)	(378,000)
Revised taxable total profits	Nil	Nil	189,000

Loss Memo

	£
Loss y/e 31/03/2024	1,792,000
Less: terminal loss relief against	
31 March 2023	(380,000)
31 March 2022	(999,158)
12 months ended 31 March 2021 (£567,000 × 12/18)	(378,000)
Unused – extinguished on cessation	34,842

Chapter 15

Question 15.1

Salary versus Dividend
Company perspective

Payment of a gross bonus of £100,000	£
Bonus	100,000
Add: employer's NIC @ 13.8%	13,800
	113,800
Less: corporation tax saved @ 19%	21,622
Cash cost to the company	92,178

Payment of a gross dividend of £100,000
The payment of a dividend by a company is from after-tax profits. Therefore there is no further tax cost or saving on the payment of dividend and the cash cost to the company is £100,000.

Tax position of Clara

Receipt of a gross bonus of £100,000		£
Bonus		100,000
Less: income tax:	£20,000 @ 40%	(8,000)
	£80,000 @ 45%	(36,000)
Employee's NICs @ 2%		(2,000)
Net cash received by Clara		54,000

Receipt of a gross dividend of £100,000			
Gross dividend			100,000
Income tax	£2,000 @ 0%	£0	
	£18,000* @ 32.5%	£5,850	
	£80,000 @ 38.1%	£30,480	
			36,330
Net cash received by Clara			63,670

* Gross remuneration £130,000, therefore £20,000 left of higher rate band. However, when Clara receives a dividend, £2,000 of the dividend she receives is deemed to use up £2,000 of her remaining £20,000 higher rate band, hence only £18,000 is available against the £100,000 dividend.

Overall
Dividend

	£
Cost to the company	100,000
Tax cost to the company	–
Net receipt by Clara	(63,670)
Net cost	36,330

Bonus

Cost to the company	100,000
Tax cost to the company	13,800
Tax saved on the bonus	(21,622)
Net receipt by Clara	(54,000)
Net cost	38,178

Payment of a dividend is more tax-efficient by £1,848.

Question 15.2

Mr and Mrs Andrews
Andrews Transport Limited
Any Road
Any Town
15 March 2022

Dear Mr and Mrs Andrews,

Remuneration Strategy

Further to our meeting of last week, please find attached my analysis of the current remuneration structure of Andrews Transport Limited (ATL) and my proposed changes to it under the following headings:

- Salary
- Dividends
- Pension planning
- Recommendations

When planning to benefit from tax-free payments in the future, it is important to bear in mind that that tax law can change and impact the rules and benefits in these areas.

When you have considered the opportunities outlined in the attached, please contact me so that we can decide how you will proceed with implementing any changes.

Changes to the remuneration structure of ATL – improving tax efficiency

1. *Salary Payments*
   - At present you, Mr Andrews, are the sole member of your family to be paid a salary by ATL, despite the fact that Mrs Andrews and the Andrews children also work in the business.
   - At present you receive a salary of £100,000 per annum from ATL. As Mrs Andrews does not receive a salary from the company, you can only avail of one personal allowance and

one basic rate band of £37,700. I would recommend considering making salary payments to Mrs Andrews and possibly reducing your own salary. Making salary payments to Mrs Andrews will allow you to avail of another personal allowance and another basic rate band of up to £37,700.

- I also recommend making salary payments to your children to reward them for their part-time work in the business. Payments up to the personal allowance of £12,570 in 2021/22 would represent tax-efficient remuneration for your children. But you must be aware of national minimum wage legislation and that details of the salary should be reported to HMRC under Real Time Information. The national insurance implications should also be addressed.
- ATL could receive a corporation tax deduction at 19% for the gross salary payments plus employer's NIC to both Mrs Andrews and your children.

2   Dividends

- As shareholders in ATL, both you and Mrs Andrews are entitled to receive dividend payments from the company. Assuming that both of you are receiving the maximum salary payments possible from ATL, you will be liable to income tax at 32.5% on the dividend received from ATL (or 38.1% if your taxable income was greater than £150,000). You are also each entitled to a £2,000 dividend allowance, meaning the first £2,000 of dividend income is tax-free.
- Unlike with salary extraction, there is no NIC on dividend payments.
- ATL will not receive a corporation tax deduction for the dividends paid to you.
- Dividends tend to be more tax efficient than salary/bonus, but there are other non-tax considerations to be addressed.

3   Pension Planning

- I would also recommend increasing the pension contributions to your pension fund. This could be done by you or ATL. The funding by you personally could be up to the level of your salary. You can contribute up to £40,000 per year to your pension scheme (known as your 'annual allowance') and receive tax relief on the contribution. The annual allowance for those earning above £240,000 reduces on a tapering basis so that it reduces to £4,000 for those earning above £312,000. For every £2 of income above £240,000, an individual's annual allowance reduces by £1.
- It may also be possible to use any unused annual allowance from the past three financial years. This is likely to be relevant in your case as only low pensions contributions have been made to date through your company pension. It is possible to contribute more than the allowance but no tax relief will be given on the contributions and you may be subject to the annual allowance charge.
- Alternatively, ATL could make the contribution. If this is done, then this limit does not apply. The limit on the contributions by the company is the funding required to pay your pension, subject to an overall fund limit of approximately £1,073,100.
- As your pension is underfunded there should not be an issue of a limit on the contributions that ATL can make. Your pension advisor could advise regarding this issue. ATL should receive a corporation tax deduction for the contributions it makes to your occupational pension fund (subject to the spreading provisions). Also, contributions are only deductible if paid.

■ In addition, the pension scheme is exempt from income tax and capital gains tax in respect of assets held in the fund.

■ On retirement you can take a tax-free lump sum from the pension fund equal to 25% of the pension fund. Withdrawals from the pension scheme are taxed as emoluments and are subject to tax at your marginal rate.

■ An associated benefit of the pension contributions is that they extract cash out of the company to you/your pension fund. This should prove to be tax efficient for you from a capital gains tax perspective if you wish to sell the business in the future, as the company's available cash will have been extracted by you at a minimum tax cost and the value for CGT purposes on a sale will reflect the value of the business and assets only and therefore could qualify in full for business asset disposal relief.

4 *Recommendations*

■ There are opportunities for you to save tax by rewarding yourself and your family adequately for the work that you do for the company. ATL should pay your two children for their work. This will lead to a saving for you as you will not need to fund them because of their earnings from ATL, i.e. instead of you funding them from income taxed at 40% they will fund themselves from income not taxed if kept within their personal allowances.

■ Mrs Andrews should be paid for the work she does for ATL. This will allow her to use the full basic rate band and possibly benefit from termination payment relief at a later time.

■ Consideration needs to be given to whether dividends should be paid.

■ Consideration should be given to increasing your salary to maximise any pension contributions. If a large pension contribution is envisaged, it would be more tax efficient for ATL to make the payment rather than you personally.

Chapter 17

Question 17.1

Jessica states that she left the UK in June 2018 and intends to return by December 2022.

As Jessica had always lived in the UK before June 2018, she would have been resident in the UK for four out of the seven tax years prior to the tax year of departure. This means that, unless she remains outside of the UK for a period of more than five complete years commencing from her date of departure, she will be treated as if she had remained resident in the UK for CGT purposes under section 10A TCGA 1992 under the temporary non-residence rules.

The period between June 2018 and December 2022 includes only four complete years.

If Jessica returns when she intends to later this year, she will be charged to UK CGT on the gain made on the disposal of the painting she inherited from her aunt in 2014. She will be treated as if the gain arose in the 2022/23 tax year and the CGT will be payable by 31 January 2024. The CGT liability could be as high as £46,000 ((£750,000 − £520,000) × 20%, assuming the current rates of CGT remain the same), though the CGT annual exemption will be available in the year of her return. Jessica will be responsible for advising HMRC of the gain by either contacting the self-assessment helpline or completing and submitting a form SA1 and submitting her 2022/23 tax return by 31 January 2024.

These rules do not apply to assets acquired whilst overseas, so the gain on the disposal of the Australian flat will not be caught under section 10A TCGA 1992. However, if Jessica were to become tax resident in the UK before she disposes of the flat, the gain will fall within the UK CGT net though principal private residence relief may be available under section 222 TCGA 1992. As the residential property is not based in the UK, any tax on the property would be due under the normal CGT payment deadlines and reporting on her tax return. The "90-day" test would have to be met in relation to the Australian property. Jessica could avoid this and a CGT liability on the painting sold during her time in Australia by simply delaying her return to the UK until after June 2023, at which point she will have been non-resident for more than five complete years.

Question 17.2

(a)

Capital gains tax position under the arising basis

	£
Foreign chargeable gain	220,600
Less: annual exempt amount	(12,300)
Chargeable gain	208,300
CGT @ 28%	58,324

Under the arising basis of taxation, an individual who is UK resident is taxed on the arising basis on their worldwide income, hence Sophia would be taxable on the foreign chargeable gains in full in addition to her employment income.

Capital gains tax position under the remittance basis

	£
Remitted foreign chargeable gain	25,000
CGT @ 28%	7,000
Remittance basis charge	60,000
Total CGT	67,000
Additional income tax on employment income	5,028
Overall tax bill under remittance basis	72,028

As Sophia is not UK domiciled, she can elect to be taxed on the remittance basis. However, as she is a long-term UK resident (resident in more than 12 out of the last 14 tax years), she is required to pay £60,000 as a remittance basis charge. Under the remittance basis, Sophia loses entitlement to both the CGT annual exempt amount and the £12,570 personal allowance for 2021/22 (resulting in additional income tax of £5,028 (i.e. £12,570 × 40%)). Therefore it would be more beneficial for Sophia to be taxed on the arising basis as the tax payable would be £13,704 lower.

(b) If Sophia was UK resident since 6 April 2001, in 2021/22 she will have been UK resident for 15 of the previous 20 tax years. She would therefore be deemed UK domiciled for UK CGT purposes and would only be taxable under the arising basis. The remittance basis would not be available. As calculated above, the UK CGT arising would be £58,324.

Question 17.3

Anytown Tax Advisors
Anytown

Catarine Martinique
Anyplace
Anytown

Dear Catarine,

Capital gains tax

This letter addresses the issues requested and is based on the information provided to us.

First, you are UK resident in 2021/22 under the statutory residence test as you meet the first automatic UK test, i.e. you are present in the UK for 183 days, you also do not meet any of the automatic overseas tests. As you are UK resident you are automatically taxed on the arising basis in respect of the foreign capital gain. A calculation of this is included below. CGT under the arising basis amounts to £128,884.

As you are French domiciled, and not deemed UK domiciled for UK CGT purposes, you can elect instead to be taxed on the remittance basis in 2021/22. This would mean only the £240,000 of the foreign gain remitted to the UK would be subject to UK capital gains tax (CGT). However, you would forgo both your UK personal allowance and UK CGT annual exemption in 2021/22 as a result.

As you are also classed as long-term UK resident, you would also be required to pay the £60,000 remittance basis charge having been resident in the UK for 12 out of the 14 tax years prior to 2021/22. A calculation of CGT under the remittance basis is also included below. Overall a CGT liability of £127,200 would arise in addition to additional income tax of £5,657 as a result of the lost personal allowance.

Consequently, you should not elect to be taxed on the remittance basis as you would pay additional UK tax of £3,973. Under the arising basis you will be free to remit the remaining proceeds to the UK at your leisure.

I look forward to discussing the above matters in more detail when we next meet, please give me a call at your convenience to arrange a meeting.

Yours sincerely,

A.N. Accountant

CATARINE – 2021/22 ARISING BASIS OF TAXATION

Capital gains tax

	£
Gain on Parisian apartment	472,600
Less: annual exemption	(12,300)
Taxable gain	460,300
Capital gains tax @ 28%	128,884

CATARINE – 2021/22 REMITTANCE BASIS OF TAXATION

Capital gains tax

	£
Remitted gain on Parisian apartment	240,000
Less: annual exemption	(Nil)
Taxable gain	240,000
Capital gains tax @ 28%	67,200
Remittance basis charge	60,000

continued overleaf

Capital gains tax liability	127,200
Plus additional income tax	
£12,570 @ 45%	5,657
Total tax payable	132,857

Question 17.4

Anytown Tax Advisors
Newry

Annette Stewart
Anyplace,
Anytown

Dear Annette,

This letter addresses the UK capital gains tax position of the Lough Erne property disposal by you and is based on the information provided to us.

Broadly, an individual who is UK tax resident is taxed on the arising basis of taxation, which would mean that the disposal of the Lough Erne property would be subject to UK capital gains tax (CGT) of up to 28% on any chargeable gain arising.

Under Section 2(1) TCGA 1992, residence in the UK drives chargeability to UK CGT. Therefore we first need to establish if you are UK resident for tax purposes in 2021/22, the tax year of the disposal.

As you live in Australia and have not been in the UK for six years it is likely that you will meet the second of the automatic overseas tests (non-resident in all of the previous three tax years and spends fewer than 46 days the UK in current tax year) and are thus not UK resident in 2021/22. Therefore, on first review, it would appear that you are not subject to UK CGT on this disposal.

However, a non-resident person disposing of UK residential property is subject to UK CGT. Thus this disposal by you as a non-resident person is caught, the Lough Erne property clearly being residential.

There are three possible approaches to the NRCGT calculation. Non-resident persons are free to choose whatever is the most tax-efficient calculation for them. The different methods of calculation are outlined below.

Method 2 would result in the lowest NRCGT gain, of £167,738. Clearly, this method should be chosen to report the gain. After the 2021/22 CGT annual exemption of £12,300 is deducted, the remaining gain of £155,438 is taxable at 28% as you use up all of your basic rate band every year. The resultant CGT liability is therefore £43,523.

I look forward to discussing the above matter in more detail when we next meet. Please give me a call at your convenience to arrange a meeting.

Yours sincerely,

A. N. Accountant

CHARGEABLE GAINS CALCULATIONS
Method 1 – rebasing

	£
Net proceeds	650,000
Less: market value at 5 April 2015	(360,000)
NRCGT chargeable gain	290,000

Method 2 – straight-line time apportionment

	£
Net proceeds	650,000
Less: cost	(425,000)
NRCGT gain over period of ownership	225,000
Time-apportioned post-5 April 2015 gain @ 74.55%*	167,738

* Total ownership is 110 months, period from 6 April 2015 to disposal was 82 months, 74.55% (82/110 × 100) of ownership relates to period from 6 April 2015 to disposal on 6 February 2022.

Method 3 – calculation over whole period of ownership

	£
Net proceeds	650,000
Less: cost	(425,000)
NRCGT gain over period of ownership	225,000

Question 17.5

(a) As Stefan is UK resident he is subject to UK CGT on the arising basis. Therefore, the full gain of £125,000 would be subject to CGT in the UK at 28% after deducting the £12,300 CGT annual exemption.

As Stefan is French domiciled he can elect to use the remittance basis in 2021/22 in respect of this foreign gain. If the £50,000 lodgement to his sole trade bank account is from the sale of the Dordogne property, this constitutes a taxable remittance.

As Stefan wishes to claim the remittance basis, he would be subject to UK CGT on this remittance of £50,000, again taxable at 28%. Stefan would also lose his CGT annual exemption in addition to the £12,570 personal allowance in 2021/22. This would result in additional income tax payable at 40%.

(b) If your suspicions are correct, the remittance of £50,000 falls to be included as a chargeable gain in Stefan's 2021/22 self-assessment return. It would be unethical to either omit this (which would be tax evasion) or to ignore your concerns (which would be a breach of the *Code of Ethics* of Chartered Accountants Ireland).

As Stefan's tax advisor, you should discuss the issue first with your manager and then discuss with Stefan the importance of ensuring that self-assessment returns are complete and the potential penalties that could arise for failure to include all relevant items.

Deliberately omitting a chargeable gain is tax evasion, which is a criminal offence. You may be required to report this to your firm's Money Laundering Reporting Officer (MLRO), who will decide whether or not a report should be made to the Serious Organised Crime Agency.

Note to students: in respect of any ethical scenario, marks will always be awarded for any other reasonable points made not included in the suggested solution.

Chapter 18

Question 18.1

	£
Sales proceeds re: 2,500 shares	30,000
Cost: 2,500/6,450 × £21,225	(8,227)
Taxable gain	21,773

continued overleaf

CGT @ 20%   4,354.60

Due for payment on 31 January 2023.

Note: as the disposal cannot be matched with any acquisition on the same day or the following 30 days, it must be matched with the section 104 holding, which is as follows:

Date

		No. of shares acquired	Cost £
5/10/2001	Purchase	1,500	8,000
10/4/2004	Purchase	2,800	10,000
18/3/2006	Rights issue, 1 for 2 held at £1.50 per share	2,150	3,225
Section 104 holding		6,450	21,225

The average allowable cost per share is therefore £3.29.

Chapter 19

Question 19.1

	£
Meets Condition (1)	
Gain	900,000
CGT payable @ 10%	90,000

Question 19.2

Business asset disposal relief not available – Condition (1) is not met, as she did not own business for at least two years prior to the disposal. The gain arising will be taxed at 20%.

Question 19.3

	£
Meets Condition (1)	
Gain	1,030,000
CGT:	
£1,000,000 @ 10%	100,000
£30,000 @ 20%	6,000
Total CGT	106,000

Note: gain exceeds lifetime limit of £1 million.

Question 19.4

Business asset disposal relief not available – Condition (1) is not met as it is not a qualifying business, i.e. not a trade, profession or vocation. A letting of unfurnished property is not a furnished holiday let; therefore, it is a property letting under rental provisions and is not a trade. The gain arising of £240,000 will be subject to CGT at 28%; the liability will be £67,200.

Question 19.5

Meets Condition (2)	£
Net qualifying gain (£360,000 − £90,000) 2021/22	270,000
CGT @ 10%	27,000

Gain (on subsequent disposal) 2022/23	£
Condition (2) is met	72,000
CGT @ 10%	7,200

Question 19.6

Business asset disposal relief not available as Condition (3) is not met. Must have at least a 5% interest. The gain arising of £300,000 will be subject to CGT at a rate of 20%, resulting in a liability of £60,000.

Question 19.7

Meets Condition (1)	£
Gain	630,000
CGT @ 10% (2020/21)	63,000

Gain on second disposal (2022/23)	1,000,000
CGT @ 10% on £370,000 (i.e. £1m − £630,000 = £370,000)	37,000
CGT @ 20% on £630,000 (i.e. excess over lifetime allowance)	126,000
Total CGT 2022/23	163,000

Question 19.8

No chargeable gains arise on cessation as there is no disposal at that time. The actual disposal will qualify for business asset disposal relief as Patricia meets the criteria of Condition (2). If Patricia sold the property after 30 April 2024 instead, then no BADR would be available.

Question 19.9

Meets Condition (1)	£
Gain	190,000
CGT @ 10%	19,000

Question 19.10

Report to James Devlin – Tax Implications of Recent Transactions
April 2022

Introduction

This report outlines the tax consequences of the disposal of both your shares in Devlin Communications Ltd and the Dungannon property. Both transactions constitute chargeable gains; therefore we have also considered reliefs available and outlined our recommendation that capital gains tax business asset disposal relief (BADR) is claimed as this is available on both transactions (although only partially available on the Dungannon property disposal). BADR reduces the rate of capital gains tax from the maximum rate for businesses from 20% to 10% and applies on a lifetime cap of £1 million for qualifying gains. Your full lifetime limit of £1 million is available as these are the only assets you have ever owned.

Details of the timing of tax payments and of available elections and detailed calculations are also included.

Devlin Communications Ltd share disposal

To qualify for BADR on a disposal of shares in a trading company or holding company of a trading group, the company must be your 'personal company', which means that you must be an officer or employee and must hold a 'material interest' of at least 5% of the ordinary share capital and voting rights in addition to holding 5% of the company's distributable profits and 5% of the assets on a winding up. These conditions must be fulfilled for a period of two years prior to the disposal.

You appear to meet all of these conditions as the company is a trading company, you were a director at the time of the disposal, you held 40% of the shares and you did so for a period of over two years prior to disposal. Therefore BADR is available on this transaction.

Dungannon property disposal

BADR is also available for the disposal of an asset owned personally by an individual if it can be 'associated' with a relevant 'material disposal'. Three conditions must be satisfied:

1. The individual makes a 'material disposal' of either the whole or part of their interest in the assets of a partnership or the shares in a company. Your disposal of your entire shareholding in Devlin Communications Ltd fulfils this condition.
2. The associated disposal is made as part of the withdrawal of the individual from participation in the partnership or the company. This condition is also clearly fulfilled as the Dungannon property disposal is tied into the share disposal.
3. The assets are in use in the business for two years ending with the earlier date of material disposal of (in this case) the shares in Devlin Communications Ltd. As the property was used and rented by Devlin Communications Ltd since 2011, this condition is also met.
4. The 5% condition is also met as you have disposed of your entire 40% shareholding in Devlin Communications Limited.

Therefore BADR is available, however the amount of BADR is restricted because the shop was not used throughout its entire period of ownership by Devlin Communications Limited, and is further restricted because a rent was payable by Devlin Communications Ltd – see Notes 2 and 3 of the calculation for further explanation.

Conclusion

As noted above, we recommend that BADR is claimed. This represents a saving of £17,384 (i.e. (£435,000 − £12,300) × 20% less £67,156). You should note that BADR is not automatic and must be claimed by the first anniversary of the 31 January following the tax year in which the gain arose. As both transactions happened in the 2021/22 tax year, the claims for BADR on each must both be made by 31 January 2024.

The capital gains tax that arises on the gains, which totals £67,156, must be paid on or before 31 January following the end of the relevant tax year. Therefore the liability must be paid by 31 January 2023.

James Devlin
CGT position

	Shares	**Shop**
	£	£
Proceeds	85,100	475,000
Less: cost	(100)	(125,000)
Gains before relief	85,000	350,000
Less: gains on shop not eligible for BADR £350,000 × 2/13ths (Note 2)		(53,846)
		296,154
Less: restriction to BADR for rent charged £296,154 × 70% (Note 3)		(207,308)
Gains eligible for BADR	85,000	88,846
Total eligible gains (£85,000 + £88,846)	173,846	
Total gains not eligible for BADR	261,154	
	435,000	
Less: annual exemption (Note 1)	(12,300)	
Chargeable gains	422,700	
Capital gains tax liability:	£	
£173,846 @ 10%	17,385	
£248,854 @ 20%	49,771	
Total CGT liability	67,156	

Notes

1. The annual exemption should be set against the gain subject to the highest tax (i.e. the gain not qualifying for BADR (20%), rather than those qualifying for gains (i.e. 10%). This reduces the non-qualifying gains to £248,854.

2.   The shop was only used in the business for 11 out of the 13 years of James' ownership. Therefore only 11/13ths of the gain on this associated disposal will qualify for BADR and 2/13ths will not.
3.   James received rent on the shop, which represented 70% of the market rent (£1,575/£2,250). Therefore the gain eligible for BADR is further restricted by 70%.

Chapter 20

Question 20.1

Áine Taylor
Belfast

26 November 2021

Dear Áine,

I refer to our recent meeting in relation to the proposed factory disposal. I have outlined the information requested below:

(a) Tax due

UK capital gains tax will be payable on the sale of the factory. The calculation below indicates that, in the absence of suitable reliefs, capital gains tax of £197,540 will be payable.

As you are trading as a sole trader, this tax will be payable by you personally. As the disposal will be made in the 2021/22 tax year, the capital gains tax will be payable on or before 31 January 2023. As you are an additional rate taxpayer, the rate of capital gains tax is 20% before any reliefs. This is calculated as follows

	£
Proceeds	1,500,000
Less: base cost	(500,000)
Taxable gain	1,000,000
Less: annual exemption	(12,300)
Taxable gain	987,700
Tax @ 20%	197,540

(b) Rollover relief

Rollover relief is available when a sole trader such as yourself sells a capital asset which is in their trade and uses the sales proceeds to acquire one of a number of specified assets that is immediately brought into use in the trade.

Qualifying assets include:

- Land and buildings.
- Goodwill.
- Fixed plant and machinery.
- Ships, aircraft, hovercraft, satellites, space stations, spacecraft, milk/potato/fish/ewe quotas, suckler cow premiums and payment entitlements under the agricultural subsidy Basic Payment Scheme.

However, the asset acquired does not have to be the same as the asset sold.

Rollover relief is only available if the new asset is acquired in the period twelve months before and three years after the date the factory is sold. If you are unsure when the new investment will be made, as long as it is within the three years from disposal (i.e. by 8 November 2024) a provisional claim for relief can be made. In addition, it would be recommended that you review expenditure in the year prior to disposal (i.e. from 9 November 2020 to 8 November 2021) to check if any qualifying spend was incurred in that period.

In order for full rollover relief to be available, the entire proceeds of sale of the first asset must be reinvested in the second asset.

If all of the proceeds on the sale of the factory (i.e. £1,500,000) are not fully reinvested, a gain equal to the lower of:

- the full gain (i.e. £1,000,000); or
- the cash retained

is left chargeable. If the amount of cash retained exceeds £1,000,000, then no rollover relief may be claimed. So for every £1 of cash that is not reinvested (up to £1,000,000 not reinvested), £1 of the gain is subject to capital gains tax. Therefore, rollover relief will only be available in respect of every pound reinvested over £1,000,000.

The gain rolled over reduces the capital gains base cost of the new asset by the amount of that gain.

Rollover relief must be claimed in writing to HMRC within four years after the **later** of:

- the end of the tax year in which *disposal of the old asset* took place (i.e. by 5 April 2026); or
- the end of the tax year in which *acquisition of the new asset* took place.

In your case, if reinvestment did not occur until 8 November 2024, the date for the claim for relief would be 5 April 2029. The earliest date a claim would be due will always be 5 April 2026 even if you had reinvested in sufficient qualifying assets in the period 9 November 2020–8 November 2021.

You should note that holdover relief is another form of deferral relief that may be available should you decide instead to lease property instead of purchasing a freehold investment.

(c) Enterprise Investment Scheme relief

On the basis that Shoe Manufacturer Ltd is a qualifying company, it may be possible to claim Enterprise Investment Scheme (EIS) deferral relief on the gain on disposal of the factory if you subscribe for shares in this company.

Relief given under EIS deferral is the lower of:

- the gain itself (i.e. £1,000,000);
- the amount specified in the claim (compared to rollover relief which cannot be tailored); or
- the amount subscribed for new shares in the EIS company.

This is a significant difference from rollover relief as only £1,000,000 would need to be subscribed for shares in the company for the capital gains tax on the gain to be fully deferred. Under rollover relief, the entire £1,500,000 would need to be reinvested to fully rollover the gain.

However, whereas rollover relief reduces the base cost of the new asset, under EIS relief the capital gain is merely deferred and will crystallise when certain specified events occur (normally on the sale of the shares). Rollover relief does significantly reduce the base cost of the new asset when disposed of in future, unless it is again replaced with a further qualifying asset.

Again, the relief will only be available if the shares are subscribed for within the period 12 months before to three years after the date the factory is sold.

EIS deferral relief must be claimed in writing to HMRC within five years from the tax filing deadline for the tax year in which the shares were issued. So if you reinvested £1,000,000 in Shoe Manufacturers Ltd shares in 2021/22, the claim should be made on or before 31 January 2028.

There are also a number of other valuable reliefs available under the EIS, including income tax relief at 30% on the initial investment (assuming you will not hold 30% or more of the shares) and capital gains tax relief on their eventual disposal if they are held for a minimum three-year period.

I hope this is helpful. However, if you have any queries please give me a call.

Yours sincerely,

Question 20.2

(a) EIS reinvestment relief allows the taxpayer to defer the capital gain to a later time. The amount of deferred gain is not rolled over against the base cost of the new EIS shares but instead is 'frozen'. This frozen gain will crystallise and become chargeable in the year of a "chargeable event". The amount of the gain that can be deferred is the lower of three amounts:

- the gain itself;
- the amount reinvested into EIS shares; and
- the specific amount claimed.

(b) Mark may specify the amount of the claim (which will be less than £88,300) to take advantage of his unused annual exemption and his capital loss carried forward.

	£
Gain	88,300
Less:	
EIS deferral relief	(48,000)
Capital losses c/fwd	(28,000)
Annual exemption	(12,300)
Chargeable gain	Nil

Therefore, Mark should invest a maximum of £48,000 in EIS shares, which will reduce the chargeable gain on sale to £Nil via claiming relief for his £28,000 capital losses carried forward and his 2021/22 annual exemption. This will also manage Mark's risk as he is investing a lower amount in shares in the EIS company.

Question 20.3

Denise may specify the amount of the claim (which will be less than 50% of the gain arising, i.e. £42,000) to take advantage of any unused annual exemption and capital losses.

	£
Gain	84,000
Less:	
SEIS reinvestment relief	(42,000)
Current-year capital loss	(10,000)
Capital losses c/fwd	(19,700)
Annual exemption	(12,300)
Chargeable gain	Nil

Therefore, Denise should invest the maximum of £84,000 into new SEIS shares as 50% of the amount subscribed, i.e. £42,000, would be exempted. This would reduce the chargeable gain to £42,000 for which her capital losses carried forward can be used to reduce the gain down to an amount equal to the CGT annual exemption. The remaining capital loss carried forward is £15,300.

Question 20.4

(a) As James sold the EIS shares within three years of their original acquisition, the upfront income tax relief obtained and not withdrawn restricts the capital loss on the disposal of the shares as follows:

	£
Proceeds	10,000
Less: base cost	(35,000)
Loss	(25,000)
Adjustment for EIS income tax	
Relief not withdrawn*	10,500
Capital loss	(14,500)

*Income tax relief: £35,000 × 30% = £10,500.

(b) If James had instead sold the shares on 31 March 2023, he will have sold them outside the three-year relevant period (meaning there would be no withdrawal of income tax relief). The allowable loss would instead be:

	£
Proceeds	10,000
Less: base cost	(35,000)
Capital loss	(25,000)

(c) Both capital losses can be used in the usual way in 2021/22 against gains in the same tax year or carried forward to use against future gains. As this is a disposal of EIS shares in an unquoted trading company, this is also eligible for income tax relief as an alternative to CGT relief. This would allow James to set the capital loss against income, which might otherwise be taxed at a maximum of 45% (if he was an additional rate taxpayer), compared to the maximum 28% CGT saving available by setting the loss against a chargeable gain on a residential property disposal.

Question 20.5

Simone is automatically entitled to incorporation relief on the incorporation of her sole trade as the following conditions are met:

- her sole trade business is transferred as a going concern;
- all of the assets (except cash) of the business were transferred to the company;
- Simone received shares in the new company as consideration.

However, as Simone received non-share consideration in the form of the £50,000 she is only entitled to partial relief. The CGT payable by Simone on the incorporation of her sole trade is therefore as follows:

	£
Gains	80,000
Less: incorporation relief (Note 1)	(32,000)
	48,000
Less: annual exemption	12,300
Taxable gain	35,700

CGT is payable as follows:

	£
Building gain:	
£50,000/£80,000 × £48,000	30,000
BADR thereon at 10% (Note 2)	3,000
Goodwill gain:	
£30,000/£80,000 × £48,000	18,000
Less: annual exemption	(12,300)
Taxable gain	5,700
CGT thereon at 20% (Note 3)	1,140

Total CGT payable is £4,140.

Notes:
1. Incorporation relief:

$$\text{Gains } £80,000 \times \frac{\text{Value of shares } £100,000}{\text{Total consideration } £250,000} = £32,000$$

2. BADR is available as this is a material disposal of business assets used in her sole trade to the company. Simone's full lifetime limit of £1 million is available as she owns no other assets.
3. BADR is not available on goodwill transferred to a connected company. As Simone is a higher rate taxpayer, the rate of CGT on the disposal of the goodwill is 20%, after deducting the annual exemption from this gain.

Base cost of shares

	£
Market value	100,000
Less: Incorporation relief	(32,000)
	68,000

Chapter 21

Question 21.1

Mr Andrew Jameson
Andrewstones Limited

11 December 2021

Dear Andrew,
As requested, we have set out below the tax consequences of the proposed purchase by the company of your shares in Andrewstones Ltd.

(a) Conditions for capital gains treatment
If the following conditions are met, the share buy-back of an unquoted trading company (which Andrewstones Ltd is) will be treated as a capital transaction taxable as a capital gain on you. We have also assessed whether, in the case of the proposed transaction, each of the conditions below is met:

- *Wholly or mainly for the benefit of the trade and not in the course of a scheme whose main purpose is the avoidance of tax.*
  In Statement of Practice 2/82, HMRC accepts the circumstances in which the trade benefit test will be met. The company's sole or main purpose in making the payment must be to benefit a trade carried on by it or by its 75% subsidiary. If the purpose is to ensure that an unwilling shareholder who wishes to end his association with the company does not sell his shares to someone who might not be acceptable to the other shareholders, the purchase will normally be regarded as benefiting the company's trade. Included within the examples of unwilling share-holders are a controlling shareholder who is retiring as a director and wishes to make way for new management. Therefore the trade benefit test should be met in this case. In addition, there is no suggestion that the transaction is being undertaken for a tax avoidance motive.
- *Vendor must be UK resident when the shares are bought back.*
  You have always been UK resident and there is no suggestion that this will change in any respect, hence this condition will be met.
- *Vendor must have owned the shares for the preceding five years (three years if acquired on death).*
  You have held the shares since 1991, clearly satisfying the five-year ownership test.
- *Must make a substantial reduction in shareholding: after-sale vendor and associate's interest must be reduced to 75% or less of interest before disposal.*
  You are disposing of 100% of your shareholding and thus clearly meet this condition. We do not count your son John's 25% shareholding as the shareholding of an associate in this case because John is not a minor.
- *After the transaction the vendor must not be connected with the company (or any company in the same 51% group). Connected means one can control more than 30% of the ordinary share capital, issued share capital and loan capital or voting rights in the company or is entitled to 30% of the assets of the company if it were to be wound up.*
  You will no longer hold any shares in the company, hence this condition will be met.

OR
- *If the buy-back facilitates the payment of an IHT charge within two years of the death of the individual whose death gave rise to the liability crystallizing.*
  This does not apply in this case.

On the basis of the above, it would appear that each of the necessary conditions are met in order to obtain capital treatment. However, please be advised that it is possible to obtain HMRC advance clearance that capital treatment will apply to the transaction. We would recommend that this clearance procedure is availed of to provide more certainty given the significant tax saving to be achieved (£88,770 capital gains tax versus £342,990 income tax distribution ignoring the dividend allowance).

(b) Anticipated CGT liability

It is expected that business asset disposal (BADR) relief is available to reduce the rate of CGT on the gain from 20% to 10% because you have disposed of a 75% shareholding in a personal trading company. The company is a trading company and you have held a shareholding of more than 5% for a two-year period (75% shareholding since 1991). You also meet the director/officer condition, thereby enabling a 10% rate of CGT. We are not aware of you having used your lifetime limit for BADR and assume the full lifetime limit of £1 million is available. On this basis, you will have CGT liability of £88,770. The full calculation is given below.

	£
Proceeds: 75,000 × £13	975,000
Less: original cost	(75,000)
	900,000
Less: annual exemption	(12,300)
Chargeable gain	887,700
CGT @ 10%	88,770

(c) Consequences if capital treatment is not obtained

If capital treatment is not obtained, any payment the company makes in respect of its shares will be treated as an income distribution (i.e. a dividend), apart from the amount that represents repayment of the nominal value of the shares.

We understand that you originally subscribed £75,000 for 75,000 £1 shares in 1991. As such, if the company paid you £975,000 in exchange for these shares and capital gains tax treatment was not obtained, then you would be treated as in receipt of a cash dividend of £900,000. As you are an additional rate taxpayer (because your income is over £150,000), tax of £342,900 (dividend additional rate of 38.1%; your £2,000 dividend allowance is assumed to have already been used by the £10,000 dividends you receive annually from other sources) would be payable. No capital gain/allowable loss arises on the £75,000 that is treated as the repayment of the nominal value of the shares as this would already have been taxed under the income tax rules as a distribution.

(d) Stamp duty

Please also be aware that the company (Andrewstones Limited) will be subject to stamp duty tax on the share buy-back in the amount of £4,875, being 0.5% of the £975,000 proceeds that the company will pay for the shares. There is a 30-day time limit after execution (when the share transfer documents are dated and signed by all parties) for getting the document stamped and paying the required stamp duty. If the share transfer document is not presented to the Stamp Office until after 30 days from the date the transaction is executed, then a late filing penalty and interest may be charged.

I hope the above is helpful, however if you have any questions, please do not hesitate to contact us.

Question 21.2

(a)

The Directors and Mrs Sarah Donaldson
Maddon Engineering Limited

11 March 2022

Gentlemen and Mrs Donaldson,

Re: Company buy-back of shares

First, may I once again extend my condolences on the recent death of Aaron.

I refer to our recent discussions in relation to the forthcoming share buyback by Maddon Engineering Limited ("Maddon"). You also requested information explaining the tax treatment, together with an explanation (with associated calculations) of how Sarah will be taxed and whether the capital treatment is available.

Tax legislation specifies that if the consideration payable by Maddon for the shares exceeds the amount of capital originally subscribed for them, the excess will constitute an income distribution unless the capital treatment applies. In this case, the consideration for the shares clearly exceeds the original consideration, as Maddon will be paying £1,500,000 to Sarah for the shares (10,000 shares × £150 per share). As Sarah received the shares from her husband before his death, her base cost is the original base cost when Aaron bought them and not their market value.

From Sarah's perspective, the buy-back is a taxable disposal. Essentially there are two possible tax treatments i.e. taxable as a capital gain or taxable as an income distribution. Calculations for each treatment are outlined below. As and as you can see the capital treatment is more favourable due to the lower rate of tax – 20% compared to an effective rate of 38.1% under the income treatment.

The remainder of this letter therefore assesses whether the capital treatment is available as Sarah has indicated the transaction will not proceed unless this is available.

Share buy-back – capital treatment

The capital treatment only applies where:

- *The repurchase is by an unquoted trading company whose trade does not consist of dealing in shares, securities, land or futures.*
  Maddon is a trading company, therefore this condition is met.
- *The repurchase is wholly or mainly for the benefit of the trade.*
  Sarah does not wish to retain the shares she received from Aaron just before his death – HMRC is likely to accept this scenario as meeting the wholly or mainly for the benefit of the trade test.
- *The shares must be bought back from a UK resident vendor who has held the shares for at least five years (three years if acquired on a death).*
  On 4 April 2022, Sarah will not have held the shares for three years; however Aaron's ownership period can also be taken into account. As he acquired the shares in the 1990s, this test is clearly met. Sarah is also UK resident; therefore the residence test is also met.
- *The vendor must, as a result of the buy-back, reduce his or her interest in the company by at least 25%.*
  Sarah is disposing of the entire shareholding, hence this condition is met.

■ *The vendor must not be connected with the company following the buy-back. The vendor will be treated as connected with the company if they either possess, or are entitled to possess, more than 30% of the issued ordinary share capital, loan capital, or voting power, or are entitled to receive more than 30 % of the assets on a winding up of the company.*

Sarah will no longer be connected with the company as she will hold no shares after the transaction is completed, therefore this condition is met.

■ *The share buy-back is not undertaken solely for tax avoidance reasons.*

There does not appear to be any tax avoidance motive and hence this condition appears to be fulfilled.

Based on all of the above, the capital treatment will be available for the transaction and will provide a tax saving for Sarah of £271,388. More certainty can be obtained by applying to HMRC in advance for clearance.

Stamp duty

Please also be aware that the company, Maddon Engineering Limited, will be subject to stamp duty on the share buyback in the amount of £7,500, being 0.5% of the £1,500,000 proceeds that the company will pay for the shares. If the buy-back occurs on 4 April 2022, the stamp duty payment and filing deadline will be 4 May 2022.

If you have any further questions, do not hesitate to contact me.

Yours sincerely,

Calculation of CGT /income tax liability re: share buy-back

Income treatment

	£
Amount received on share buy-back (10,000 × £150)	1,500,000
Less: original subscription price	(10,000)
Gross dividend received	1,490,000
Gross dividend	1,490,000
Less: dividend allowance	(2,000)
Taxable dividend credit	1,488,000
Income tax due at 38.1%*	**566,928**

*Sarah is an additional rate taxpayer so the dividend additional rate applies.

Under the income treatment, Sarah will also have a capital gains disposal as follows:

CGT calculation

	£
Proceeds	1,500,000
Less: cost	(10,000)
Capital gain	1,490,000
Less: amount subject to income tax as a distribution	(1,490,000)
Chargeable gain	Nil

continued overleaf

Capital treatment

Sale proceeds (10,000 × £150)	1,500,000
Less: cost	(10,000)
Chargeable gain	1,490,000
Less: annual exemption (2021/22)	(12,300)
Taxable gain	1,477,700
CGT payable @ 20%	**295,540**

Sarah is not an employee or director, therefore business asset disposal relief is not available to reduce the gain arising.

(b)

BRIEFING NOTE

To: Any Partner
From: A.N. Accountant
Date: 25 March 2022
Subject: Shares in Maddon Engineering Limited

Further to my recent conversations with Sarah, this briefing note addresses the IHT and ethical implications in respect of the chargeable lifetime transfer.

1.   Availability of BPR for the Maddon shares
BPR will be available at the rate of 100% on the 10,000 shares held by Aaron at the date of his death. This is due to the fact that they qualify as shares in an unquoted trading company. There is no minimum holding requirement, so the fact that Aaron only held one-third of the shares has no impact. As the shares have been held since the 1990s, the two-year holding period requirement is also met. BPR is also fully available as there are no excepted assets on Maddon's statement of financial position.

However, even if BPR was not available it should be noted that no inheritance tax (IHT) liability would arise as the shares are being transferred to Sarah on Aaron's death and are thus fully exempt from IHT under the spousal exemption.

The value of the shares to be included in Aaron's estate is therefore calculated as follows:

10,000 shares × £150 per share	£1,500,000
Less: 100% business property relief	(£1,500,000)
Value in death estate	£NIL

2.   IHT and ethical implications re. the chargeable lifetime transfer
The transfer of cash to the discretionary trust comes within the relevant property regime and IHT should have been paid thereon in lifetime as follows:

Lifetime IHT

December 2018	£	£
Gift to discretionary trust		500,000
Annual exemption – 2017/18		(3,000)

continued overleaf

Annual exemption – 2018/19		(3,000)
Chargeable lifetime transfer		494,000
Inheritance tax threshold – 2018/19	325,000	
Less: cumulative chargeable transfers		
in the previous seven years	0	
Available inheritance tax threshold	325,000	
Less: nil rate band		(325,000)
Chargeable lifetime transfer		169,000
Lifetime IHT thereon @ 20%		33,800

On lifetime transfers, the primary liability for payment lies with the donor (unless the donee agrees to pay tax), though Andrew would have delegated responsibility of this to the trust. In such a scenario the lifetime IHT is 25%.

As the gift was made in December 2018, the liability was due for payment on or before 30 June 2019. Interest and penalties may arise for failure to pay this liability.

The gift is also required to be included in Aaron's death estate as it was made in the previous seven years. IHT arises as follows:

Death estate

December 2018 £

Gift to discretionary trust		500,000
Annual exemption – 2017/18		(3,000)
Annual exemption – 2018/19		(3,000)
		494,000
Inheritance tax threshold – 2021/22	325,000	
Less: cumulative chargeable transfers		
in the previous seven years	Nil	
Less: available inheritance tax threshold		(325,000)
		169,000
Inheritance tax:		
£169,000 @ 40%		67,600
Taper relief @ 20%		(13,520)
Lifetime tax paid		(33,800)
Additional IHT payable on death		20,280

Please note that Sarah has suggested that if the transfer to the trust fails to be included in Aaron's estate, she would like us to turn a blind eye to this as she believes HMRC have no way of finding out about this. On the basis of the foregoing, the transfer to the trust is required to be included. As you know, it would be unethical to omit this from the inheritance tax return and, under the *Code of Ethics* of Chartered Accountants Ireland, we cannot do as Sarah wishes.

Could I suggest that when we next meet we agree how best to approach this with Sarah. I would also suggest that we take the opportunity to discuss with Sarah the importance of ensuring that the inheritance tax return is complete and the potential penalties that could arise for failure to include all relevant items.

Chapter 22

Question 22.1

(a) The transfer of value made by Mr Grey for IHT under the related property rules is calculated as follows:

Value of shares before transfer (78,000 × £35) × 50,000/78,000	£1,750,000
Value of shares after transfer (48,000 × £14) × 20,000/48,000	£(280,000)
Value transferred	£1,470,000

The unrelated value should be used if this produces a higher figure. In this case the unrelated value is lower and is calculated as follows:

Value of shares before transfer 50,000 × £14	£700,000
Value of shares after transfer 20,000 × £8	£160,000
Value transferred	£540,000

Thus the transfer of value for inheritance tax is £1,470,000.

(b) Anne has received the shares by way of gift from her father. Anne is treated as a connected person under section 286 TCGA 1992, hence Anne's base cost of the shares in Grey Properties Ltd is deemed to be their open market value. On the basis of receiving a 30% shareholding which is valued at £14 per share, Anne has a base cost for capital gains tax of £420,000 (30,000 shares × £14). A claim for gift relief is not possible as the company is an investment company.

(c) If Mr Grey dies within 38 months, the gift valued at £1,470,000 (which was originally a PET) after deduction of exemptions will fall within his death estate as he has survived less than seven years. However, taper relief of 20% would be available.

Question 22.2

In cases where assets (other than shares) are owned jointly by husband and wife, and one spouse makes a transfer of value for inheritance tax purposes, the value transferred is calculated as below.

	£
Value before transfer:	
£800,000 × [£375,000/(£375,000 + £110,000)] (Note 1)	618,557
Value after transfer:	
£500,000 × [£250,000/(250,000 + £110,000)] (Note 2)	(347,222)
Transfer of value	271,335

Notes:
1. Six chairs are worth £800,000, Stephanie has four of these. Four chairs are worth £375,000. Martin's two chairs are worth £110,000.

2. Five chairs are worth £500,000. Stephanie has three of these. Three chairs are worth £250,000. Martin's two chairs are worth £110,000.
The unrelated value of one chair is £50,000, which is lower; hence the related value is used for IHT purposes.

Question 22.3

(a) Gift of shares in family company to daughter
Yes, this is a transfer of value because it is a gift. The transaction would also have capital gains tax implications as a transaction with a connected person. Gift relief may be available.
(b) Sale of a painting to a local art dealer
No, this would not be a transfer of value because it is a genuine arm's length transaction between the parties, there is no gratuitous intent and there is no loss to the original donor as cash has replaced the asset.
(c) Payment of daughter's school fees
No, this would not be a transfer of value. While the donor's estate would be reduced, there is no associated gratuitous intent as this constitute's maintenance of the individual's family.
(d) Purchase of Lamborghini from a local car dealership
No, this would not be a transfer of value because it is a genuine arm's length transaction between the parties and there is no loss to the original donor as a car has replaced the money paid for it.
(e) Gift of an investment property to a family trust
Yes, this is a transfer of value because it is a gift. The transaction would also have capital gains tax implications.

Question 22.4

(a) Zelda's domicile of origin is outside the UK. As she has not been resident in the UK for at least 15 of the 20 tax years immediately before the relevant tax year, being 2021/22 (she has been UK resident for 14 tax years (2007/08 to 2020/21)), she remains non-UK domiciled and is only subject to inheritance tax on a transfer of any UK assets.
(b) Willem has acquired a UK domicile of choice and is therefore subject to inheritance tax on transfer of both his UK and overseas assets.
(c) Cerys is no longer UK domiciled but she remains UK deemed domicile for three years after changing her domicile status in November 2020 and is therefore subject to inheritance tax on transfer of both her UK and overseas assets. It may be advisable to delay transferring her foreign assets into the UK resident trust until after November 2023, at which point she will be not be deemed UK domiciled. However, at that point Cerys would still be subject to IHT on the transfer of any UK assets and any foreign assets not classed as excluded property.

Question 22.5

Currently Penny's domicile is a domicile of origin in the United Kingdom, as an individual acquires their mother's domicile at birth where their parents are unmarried. This means that should Penny die before she leaves the UK, she will be UK domiciled for IHT purposes at that time and subject to inheritance tax on all her worldwide assets, including the London property and the Italian property inherited from her mother. This would also apply to any gifts in lifetime. This is the most robust form of domicile and can only be displaced by acquiring a domicile of choice.

Penny plans to emigrate to Australia before the end of 2021; she plans to cut off all remaining ties with the UK. This is suggestive that Penny intends to acquire a domicile of choice in Australia by being both physically present there **and** sufficiently evidencing the intention of staying there permanently. There will be a heavy burden of proof on Penny to demonstrate to HMRC that she has displaced her domicile of origin in the UK with a domicile of choice in Australia.

This is because if Penny is not UK domiciled she will only be subject to UK IHT on her UK assets (including the London property if she still owns it at the time) with relief available for any inheritance tax she might pay on her UK assets in Australia. However, the deemed domicile rules are also relevant. These mean that any individual previously UK domiciled will be considered to be UK domiciled for UK IHT purposes (only) for three years after they cease to be UK domiciled. So if Penny permanently leaves the UK for her new domicile of choice in Australia in December 2021, she will remain UK deemed domicile for IHT until December 2024. Once again, all of her worldwide assets will be caught.

In addition, where a non-UK domiciled individual has been resident in the UK for 15 of the previous 20 tax years immediately before the relevant tax year and the individual was UK resident in at least one of the four tax years ending with the relevant tax year, deemed domicile will again apply. At the point that Penny becomes non-UK domiciled in December 2024, she will only have been non-UK resident for two complete tax years (2023/24 and 2022/23 as in 2021/22 she will have been UK resident until the date of her departure), meaning she will have been UK resident for 15 of the previous 20 years of assessment and she was UK resident in 2021/22, one of the four tax years ending with 2024/25. Penny remains deemed domicile under this rule until 5 April 2026. Four complete tax years of non-residence are therefore required to shake off deemed domicile. Thereafter, Penny will be non-UK domiciled for IHT purposes and only subject to UK IHT on any UK situs property with credit available for any IHT she may also pay on those assets in Australia.

Should Penny become resident in the UK after acquiring her domicile of choice in Australia, she is also at the risk of becoming deemed domicile under the formerly domiciled resident rule. This would catch her worldwide assets and the assets of any non-UK trust established while she is non-UK domiciled.

Chapter 23

Question 23.1

At the time of the transfer by Sean in July 2021, the value transferred of £1,500,000 is exempt to the extent of £325,000 only as Gita is non-UK domiciled and a PET to the extent of £1,175,000. Sean dies less than seven years later in June 2024, meaning the failed PET is chargeable and, after deducting the nil rate band, £850,000 is subject to tax. No taper relief is available because Sean died less than three years after the original gift.

The £200,000 transfer by Gita in January 2023 was a transfer of excluded property under section 6(1) IHTA 1984 by a non-UK domiciled individual holding non-UK property. Following Sean's death, Gita has the choice of electing to be treated as deemed domiciled in the UK. If she does so, the gift from Sean in 2021 will become fully exempt as a transfer where both spouses are domiciled in the UK. This would result in an IHT saving of £340,000 (£850,000 × 40%).

However, Gita will then be treated as deemed domiciled in the UK from 2021 for all IHT purposes. This means that the £200,000 transfer to the trustees would no longer be one of excluded property and will be subject to UK IHT. As a transfer to a trust, it will be immediately chargeable to tax as a chargeable lifetime transfer at the date of the deemed spousal election. The relevant IHT return will be due for filing within 12 months from the end of the month of the election and the IHT payment due (if any) within six months of the end of the month of the election. However, it will be fully covered by the nil rate band.

It seems that an election would be worthwhile given the tax saving of £340,000, however Gita will need to consider all the consequences of making an election in the context of her entire asset portfolio.

Question 23.2

■ The land valued at £80,000 gifted to her daughter Ana is reduced to £69,000 by applying the marriage exemption of £5,000 for a marriage gift to a child and annual exemptions of £3,000 for each of 2020/21 and 2021/22.

■ The gifts to her grandchildren are likely to be fully exempt as 'normal expenditure out of income', as they are habitual, paid out of surplus income and presumably Annette is able to maintain her usual standard of living.

■ The first £325,000 of the gift from Annette to Stefan is exempt as it is from a UK domiciled to a non-UK domiciled spouse. Stefan may wish to consider electing to be deemed domicile as £55,000 constitutes a transfer of value by his wife.

Chapter 24

Question 24.1

Lifetime IHT arises as follows:

	£
Cash gift – 6 April 2018	400,000
Less: annual exemption:	
2018/19	(3,000)
2017/18	(3,000)
Net gift	394,000
Less: 2018/19 NRB	(325,000)
Chargeable transfer	69,000

Primary responsibility for any lifetime IHT rests with the donor unless Frederick specifically requests as a term of the gift that the donee bears the IHT. Thus IHT due in lifetime is 20/80 × £69,000 = £17,250. The value for cumulative purposes is therefore £411,250 (i.e. £394,000 + £17,250).

Should Frederick die on 10 April 2021, additional IHT falls due on the gift on death as follows:

	£
Gross gift including lifetime tax	411,250
Less: 2021/22 NRB	(325,000)
	86,250
IHT @ 40%	34,500
Less: taper relief (3–4 years) @ 20%	(6,900)
	27,600
Less: lifetime IHT paid	(17,250)
Additional IHT on death	10,350

Chapter 25

Question 25.1

(a) Relevant business property means:
   (i) A sole trader's business, or a partnership share, including professions and vocations.
   (ii) Unquoted securities of a company which, together with any unquoted shares of the company (including related property in both instances), give the transferor control immediately before the transfer.
   (iii) Any unquoted shares in a company.
   (iv) Quoted shares and/or securities of a company that, together with any related property, give the transferor control immediately before the transfer.
   (v) Any land or building, machinery or plant owned outside the business which, for the two years before the transfer, was used wholly or mainly for the purposes of a business carried on by a company of which the transferor then had control or by a partnership of which the individual then was a partner.
   (vi) Any land, buildings, machinery or plant that, immediately before the transfer, were used wholly or mainly for the purposes of a business carried on by the transferor and were settled property in which he was then beneficially entitled to an interest in possession.
   Shares on the Alternative Investment Market (AIM) are treated as unquoted.

(b) A business, or an interest in a business, or shares in or securities of a company, are not relevant business property if the business, or as the case may be, the business of the company, consists wholly or mainly of:
   (i) Dealing in securities, stocks or shares.
   (ii) Dealing in land or buildings.
   (iii) Making or holding investments.

(c) The relief applies to transfers of value in lifetime or on death, the value attributable to relevant business property being reduced by 100% in respect of (a) (i) to (iii) above and 50% in respect of (a) (iv) to (vi).

Question 25.2

(a) Agricultural property relief is available on the transfer of agricultural property within the UK, EU or EEA. This includes agricultural land or pasture; woodland and any building used in the intensive rearing of livestock or fish if the occupation of the woodland or building is ancillary to that of the agricultural land or pasture; and also such cottages, farm buildings and farmhouses occupied with the agricultural land as are of a character appropriate to the property.

   The provisions for agricultural property relief are very similar to the rules for business property relief, in that the agricultural value is reduced by 100%. Agricultural property relief is given at the rate of 50% where the land is let to a farmer and the lease was signed before 1 September 1995 and there is still more than two years left to run on the lease. If any of these conditions are not met, then 100% relief is due. Where a farmer runs a farming business, business property relief may be available to cover any market value not otherwise covered by agricultural property relief. Therefore agricultural property relief should be applied first.

(b) Agricultural property relief is available on the transfer of shares or debentures in a farming company, provided that the holding gave the transferor control of the company immediately before the transfer and the agricultural property forms part of the company's assets. Relief is given only on that part of the value of the holding that reflects the agricultural value of the underlying property. The rate of relief is 100%.

Business property relief is available on the non-agricultural value of a holding where the relevant conditions are satisfied at 100% on holdings in unquoted farming companies and at 50% on quoted controlling holdings.

Question 25.3

Transfer to Discretionary Trust

Tax due on gift in June 2018

	£
Gift	500,000
Less: two annual exemptions (2018/19 and 2017/18)	(6,000)
Less: nil rate band for 2018/19	(325,000)
Taxable	169,000

	£
Taxable @ 25% (as grandmother paid the tax due to presumption in law)	42,250
Total value transferred as a result of gift	536,250

Additional tax now due on death

	£
Initial transfer of value	536,250
Less: nil rate band for 2021/22	(325,000)
Chargeable on death	211,250
Inheritance tax due @ 40%	84,500
Less: taper relief (20% as 3–4 years between gift and death)	(16,900)
Tax due	67,600
Less: lifetime tax paid	(42,250)
Tax now due	25,350

Payable by trustees of estate

Gift of family home is now a failed PET and is chargeable to IHT

	£
Value of gift	600,000
Less: two annual exemptions of £3,000 (2020/21 and 2019/20)	(6,000)
Value now chargeable (no nil rate band remains)	594,000

	£
Inheritance tax due @ 40%	237,600

Payable by Chris personally

The residence nil rate band is not available as this is a lifetime and not a death transfer.

Death Estate

	£	£
Rental properties (Note 1)		525,000
Cash – UK bank account		250,000
Cash – IoM bank account		40,000

Art	250,000	
Less: associated debt (Note 2)	(50,000)	
		200,000
Holiday home in Iceland	78,000	
Less: allowable probate costs (max. 5% so restricted)	(3,900)	
		74,100
Total		1,089,100
Less debts of estate		(15,000)
Less: funeral costs – headstone		(2,000)
Less: funeral costs – clothes		(550)
Death estate		1,071,550
Inheritance tax due @ 40%		428,620

Nil rate band all used by lifetime gifts.

Costs incurred by executors in administering the estate and in respect of obtaining probate are not allowable.

Notes
1. As the buildings will have been sold by the executors within three years of death and the sales price is lower than market value at the date of death by more than 5% of that value and £1,000, the sales price can be used in the death estate.
2. The loan secured against the art collection is deductible in full.

Question 25.4

MEMO

To: Any Partner
From: A.N. Accountant
Date: 30 April 2022
Subject: Fionn O'Shea estate

This briefing note deals with the following matters:

(a) Calculating the lifetime inheritance tax (IHT) payable for lifetime gifts.
(b) Calculating the inheritance tax due on Fionn's death estate, making any appropriate claims or reliefs available to reduce the liability arising.

Each of these matters is considered in turn below.

(a) Lifetime IHT on gifts

10 March 2016 – gift to Shay

	£	£
Gift to Shay		9,000
Marriage exemption		(5,000)
Annual exemption – 2015/16		(3,000)

Annual exemption – 2014/15		(1,000)
		NIL

No inheritance tax due.

28 December 2016 – gift to a discretionary trust

		£
Gift to discretionary trust		300,000
Annual exemption – 2016/17		(3,000)
Annual exemption – 2015/16 (already used)		0
Chargeable lifetime transfer		297,000
Inheritance tax threshold – 2016/17	325,000	
Less: cumulative chargeable transfers in the previous seven years	0	
Available inheritance tax threshold	325,000	
Less: nil rate band		(297,000)
		NIL

No inheritance tax due.

25 November 2017 – gift to a discretionary trust

		£
Gift to discretionary trust		175,000
Annual exemption – 2017/18		(3,000)
Annual exemption – 2016/17 (already used)		0
Chargeable lifetime transfer		172,000
Inheritance tax threshold – 2017/18	325,000	
Less: cumulative chargeable transfers in the previous seven years	(297,000)	
Less: available inheritance tax threshold		(28,000)
Amount liable to inheritance tax		144,000
£144,000 @ 20%		28,800

BPR is not available on the gift of shares to the discretionary trust as it is assumed that the holding was less than 51% and was thus not a controlling interest.

(b) Death Estate

10 March 2016 – gift to Shay

Exempt transfer due to marriage exemption and annual exemptions.

No inheritance tax due.

28 December 2016 – gift to a discretionary trust

		£
Chargeable lifetime transfer		297,000
Inheritance tax threshold – 2021/22	325,000	

Less: cumulative chargeable transfers in the previous seven years	NIL	
Less: available nil rate band		(297,000)
		NIL

No inheritance tax due.

25 November 2017 – gift to a discretionary trust

		£
Gift to discretionary trust – fall in value relief applied*		75,000
Annual exemption – 2017/18		(3,000)
Annual exemption – 2016/17		0
Revised chargeable lifetime transfer		72,000
Inheritance tax threshold – 2021/22	325,000	
Less: cumulative chargeable transfers in the previous seven years	(297,000)	
Less: available inheritance tax threshold		(28,000)
Amount liable to inheritance tax		44,000
£44,000 @ 40%		17,600
Less: taper relief 40% (4–5 years)		(7,040)
Less: lifetime tax paid		(28,800)
Additional IHT payable on death		NIL

* When death tax is payable on a gift because the transferor has died, but the value of the gift has fallen between the date the gift was originally made and the date of death, then the fall in value relief allows a claim to be made to have death tax charged on the reduced value of the gift.

31 March 2022 – death estate		£
Main residence		225,000
Cash and investments		85,000
Chattels		15,000
Value of interest in possession trust		276,000
Gross value		601,000
Inheritance tax threshold – 2021/22	325,000	
Less: cumulative chargeable transfers in the previous seven years		
Chargeable lifetime transfer – 28/12/2016	(297,000)	
Chargeable lifetime transfer – 25/11/2017	(172,000)*	
Available inheritance tax threshold		NIL
Amount liable to inheritance tax		601,000
Less: RNRB (including wife's unused amount)**		(225,000)
Less: claim to use wife's NRB		(325,000)
		51,000
Inheritance tax payable @ 40%		20,400

* Where a lifetime gift has fallen in value, relief is only available against IHT payable in respect of the gift itself. The reduced value does not get cumulated or carried forward to the death estate. The original transfer value is still included in the death estate calculations for the purpose of calculating the available nil rate band.

**The RNRB in 2021/22 is £175,000. This is uplifted by the unused percentage of his wife (in this case 100% was unused), which gives a total potential RNRB to use of £350,000. However, the RNRB is the lower of the value of the residence or the total RNRB including any unused spousal amount. As his residence was valued at £225,000, this is the maximum amount that can be used. The remaining RNRB cannot be used against other assets in the estate and is therefore lost.

Question 25.5

IHT due on Andrew's death estate:

	£
Death estate	575,000
Less: remaining NRB*	(175,000)
Taxable estate	400,000
IHT @ 40%	160,000

NRB*:	
Lifetime gift	156,000
Annual exemption 2017/18	(3,000)
Annual exemption 2016/17	(3,000)
	150,000

NRB	325,000
Utilised	(150,000)
Remaining NRB	175,000

James's death estate	£
Value of death estate	1,500,000
Less: NRB	(325,000)
Chargeable estate	1,175,000

IHT payable @ 40%	470,000

Less: quick succession relief

$$\frac{415,000^*}{415,000 + 160,000} \times £160,000 \times 40\%$$

	(46,191)
IHT due	423,809

* Estate of £575,000 − IHT £160,000 = £415,000.

Question 25.6

Report to Alexander Johnston – Inheritance Tax

June 2021

Introduction

This report outlines the inheritance tax (IHT) consequences if you were, unfortunately, to die on today's date (18 June 2021) on the basis of your current wealth, assets and various gifts made.

IHT of £132,625 would arise on your estate based on the information provided to us. Detailed calculations are outlined below.

The due date for payment of IHT is six months from the end of the month of death or, if earlier, the date the IHT return is filed. Using 18 June 2021 as a reference point for these calculations would leave the IHT liability due for payment on or before 31 December 2021. The relevant inheritance tax return would be due for filing 12 months from the end of the month of death, i.e. 30 June 2022.

Conclusion

As this work is a prelude to IHT planning, please read the information herein carefully and we will be in touch to arrange a time to meet to discuss in more detail and to consider any queries you may have.

Calculation of potential inheritance tax liability – assumed date of death 18 June 2021

Potential Death Estate

	£	£
House inherited from brother		590,000
Cash		82,000
Shares in AJ Ltd	625,000	
Less: available BPR		
(100% for unquoted shares in a trading company)	(625,000)	
		0
Investment property	280,000	
Less: associated debt	(280,000)	
		0
Chalet in France	120,000	
Less: allowable probate costs – 5%	(6,000)	
		114,000
Aston Martin (Note 1)		90,000
Total		876,000
Less: debts of estate		(10,000)
Less: nil rate band (Note 3)		(436,000)
Death estate		430,000
Inheritance tax @ 40%		172,000
Less: quick succession relief (Note 2)		(39,375)
Inheritance tax due		132,625

Notes:

1. Aston Martin is a gift with reservation. Therefore the higher of the value at the date of gift and the value at the date of death is included in the death estate.
2. Quick succession relief is available, calculated as:

IHT paid on previous transfer × relevant % × (increase in donee's estate as a result of first transfer / (increase in donee's estate as a result of first transfer + IHT paid on thereon))

i.e. $£75,000 \times 60\% \times \dfrac{£525,000}{£525,000 + £75,000} = £39,375$

3. Calculation of available nil rate band:

	£
Nil rate band at death	325,000
Less: gifts in previous 7 years (cash to son)	(214,000)
Available own nil rate band	111,000
Nil rate band from wife's death	325,000
Total available nil rate band	436,000

The gift of cash to Alexander's son in May 2017 was a PET, however, as Alexander hypothetically dies within 7 years on 18 June 2021, this is chargeable as follows:

	£
Gift of cash	220,000
Less: annual exemption	
2017/18	(3,000)
2016/17	(3,000)
	214,000

If Alexander leaves the house he lived in to a direct descendant, which can include his son, the RNRB will also be available.

Question 25.7

Portia di Rossi – Inheritance tax calculations 2021/22

Lifetime Gifts

Portia has made a number of lifetime gifts which need to be assessed from an IHT perspective to establish tax payable in lifetime and potential additional IHT payable thereon on death.

None of the gifts qualify as a PET as Portia died less than seven years after making the earliest transfer of value.

The following failed PETs and CLTs arise during Portia's lifetime:

2015/16 Tax year	£	£
Failed PET – Gifts to children	18,000	
Less:		
Annual exemption 2015/16	(3,000)	

continued overleaf

B/f annual exemption 2014/15	(3,000)	
		12,000*
2016/17 Tax year		
Failed PET – Gift to USA charity	25,000	
Wedding gift to godson	6,000	
	31,000	
Less:		
Annual exemption 2016/17	(3,000)	
Marriage exemption	(1,000)	
		27,000*
2020/21 Tax year		
Discretionary trust	380,000	
Less:		
Annual exemption 2020/21	(3,000)	
Annual exemption 2019/20	(3,000)	
		374,000
Total chargeable		413,000

* No tax in lifetime as it was then a PET nor on death as both are covered by the IHT NRB.

Tax payable on death by trustees of discretionary trust

	£	
Value liable to tax		374,000
NRB at death	325,000	
Utilised by PETs now chargeable on death	(39,000)	
		(286,000)
Liable on death		88,000
IHT thereon @ 40% on death		35,200
Less: IHT @ 20% paid on CLT of £49,000 (CLT £374,000 less NRB £325,000)		(9,800)
Additional IHT on death		25,400

IHT treatment of assets at date of death

Calculation of taxable estate on death

	Notes	£
Armagh house	2	645,000
House contents	2	48,500
Villa in Portugal	3	225,000

continued overleaf

Belfast Ceramics Plc shares – 18,000 × £1.45	4		26,100
British Meats Plc shares – 3,500 × £13.60	4		47,600
Belfast bank accounts			69,000
Guernsey bank account	3		228,000
Italiana Wine SA shares	5	180,000	
Less: business property relief	5	(180,000)	
			0
Taxable estate			1,289,200

IHT payable by Portia's executors on her estate at death:

As Portia's £325,000 NRB has been exhausted by lifetime transfers, the whole of the taxable estate is chargeable to IHT at 40%, being £515,680.

Notes

1. Lifetime Gifts

   The annual Christmas gifts to Portia's grandchildren are covered by the £250 small gifts exemption and are therefore exempt from IHT.

   As only gifts to UK or EU charities are exempt from IHT, the gift to the US charity is not exempt.

   The first £1,000 of the gift to her godson is exempt as a gift in consideration of marriage, with the remainder being a transfer of value.

2. House in Armagh

   The property was sold for less than its probate value. Under post-mortem relief, where an interest in land is sold within four years of the date of death, a claim may be made that the sale price is treated as the date of death value for IHT purposes. The sale value has been included in the estate tax calculation on the basis that such a claim would be made. The value of the contents of Portia's Armagh house also falls into her estate.

3. Overseas assets

   As Portia died domiciled in the UK, her worldwide assets are liable to UK IHT. Therefore, both the Portuguese villa and the Guernsey bank account are part of her estate on death.

4. Quoted shares

   Post-mortem relief also allows, where quoted shares are sold within 12 months of the date of death for less than their probate value, a claim to be made to substitute the gross sale price for the probate value.

   However, the change in value of all investments sold within 12 months of death must be taken into account.

   The Belfast Ceramics Plc shares were sold at a loss, whereas the British Meats Plc share sale produced a gain.

   Overall, as a claim would be beneficial, the actual sale proceeds after death have been included in the calculation, on the basis that a claim would be made.

5. Company assets

   Business property relief (BPR) is not limited to UK situated business property.

   Since Portia held shares in an unquoted trading company and meets the two-year ownership test (having acquired the shares in 2016), BPR is available in respect of these shares.

Chapter 26

Question 26.1

Capital Gains Tax

As Shay is Sean's son, he is treated as a connected party under section 286 TCGA 1992, hence market value is imposed on any transactions between them that are gifts or at undervalue.

The gift of his residence is a deemed disposal at market value for capital gains tax purposes. However, as Sean has lived in the property all his life, the entire gain will be exempt by virtue of principle private residence relief.

Inheritance Tax

The gift of his house will be treated as a gift with reservation of benefit, and as such is treated as follows:

    (i) as a PET at the time of the gift (using the valuation at the time of the gift); and

    (ii) as part of Sean's death estate (using the valuation at the time of death) because it is assumed Sean will die within seven years of making the gift.

This results in a potential double charge should Sean die within seven years of the gift. HMRC will select the treatment giving rise to the higher total tax payable and will require two computations as denoted above. When calculating the inheritance tax arising under the GWR rules, Sean will be able to claim the available residence nil rate band in the year of death together with any residence nil rate band unused by his spouse/civil partner. This, however, is not available when calculating inheritance tax on the failed PET.

Chapter 27

Question 27.1

(a) The due date for payment of the lifetime IHT and the filing of the IHT 100 is six months from the end of the month in which the transfer takes place (i.e. 31 May 2018).

(b) The due date for additional IHT payable on the lifetime gift as a result of Fionn's death on 31 March 2022 is six months from the end of the month in which death occurs (i.e. 30 September 2022).

(c) Payment of IHT on the death estate is due on the earlier of:

    ▪ six months from the end of month in which the transfer takes place, assuming this occurs on 31 March 2022 (i.e. 30 September 2022); or

    ▪ the date of delivery of the IHT400 return (i.e. 29 July 2022).

In this case IHT on the death estate is due on 29 July 2022. The due date for filing the IHT400 for any CLTs, failed PETS and details of the death estate is within 12 months from the end of the month of death (i.e. 31 March 2023).

Question 27.2

Calculation of IHT on failed PET to Eileen – 14 June 2017

No spouse exemption is available despite the subsequent marriage.

The value is the loss to the donor which will be more than half of the total value of £900,000.

Peter's 50% retained is worth less than 50% of the whole. Using a 15% discount the value is £382,500

	£
Value of PET (loss to estate)	517,500
Less: annual exemptions 2017/18 and 2016/17	(6,000)
Net chargeable transfer	511,500
Available nil rate band (Note 1)	(105,000)
Taxable amount	406,500

	£
Tax @ 40%	162,600
Less: taper relief at 40% (gift more than 4 but less than 5 years before)	(65,040)
Tax payable	97,560

Note:

1. The chargeable transfer in 2012 (less £6,000 for two annual exemptions) used £220,000 of the nil rate band, so the nil rate band for calculating IHT on the failed PET reduced from £325,000 to £105,000.

Tax on estate at death – 1 January 2022

	£
Bank accounts, investments, etc. net	240,000
Shotguns, etc.	48,000
Smyth Farm	1,900,000
Windy Farm	950,000
Smyth Farm Ltd shares	425,000
Total	3,563,000
Less: agricultural relief and business property relief (Note 2)	(1,175,000)
Total value of estate net of reliefs	2,388,000
Less: nil rate band (nil due to all used by failed PET in 2017)	Nil
Net taxable value	2,388,000
Inheritance tax @ 40%	£955,200

Notes:

1. The half share of Primrose Farmhouse passing to Eileen, as the surviving beneficial joint tenant, is exempt by virtue of the spouse exemption. Thus it is ignored.
2. Business property and agricultural property relief

   Business property relief (BPR)

   Total value of Smyth Farm Ltd shares (seemingly a trading company, so 100% BPR available) is £425,000.

   Agricultural property relief (APR)

   Windy Farm: no APR available as Trevor has never occupied it for farming – seven years of ownership would have been needed for APR to apply.

Smyth Farm:

- No APR available for stables (£300,000) as they are not occupied for agriculture.
- APR is only available on £600,000 (agricultural value) of £700,000 (market value) of the farmhouse.
- As the tenancy is prior to 1995 and has more than two years left to run, APR is only available on 50% of £1,500,000 (£1,900,000 less £300,000 for stables and £100,000 of farmhouse value) i.e. £750,000.

Total value of reliefs £1,175,000.

Question 27.3

The UK government accepts that all taxpayers are entitled to organise their affairs in such a way that mitigates their tax liability, as long as they do so within the law and within the spirit in which Parliament intended. Tax planning is both legally and ethically acceptable.

However, the same cannot be said about the IHT avoidance scheme being marketed by the boutique tax firm. Tax avoidance is often viewed as a grey area because it is regularly confused with tax planning. Tax avoidance is the use of loopholes within tax legislation to reduce a taxpayer's tax liability. Although tax avoidance may seem similar to tax planning, as the taxpayer is using tax law to reduce their overall tax burden, tax avoidance means that the taxpayer is using the legislation in a way not intended or anticipated by Parliament.

The scheme being marketed falls within the Disclosure of Tax Avoidance Schemes (DOTAS) regime, which requires schemes that contain certain hallmarks of tax avoidance to be notified to HMRC. HMRC then take action to close down the scheme via tax legislation, usually as part of the annual budget process.

The users of such schemes are also required to notify HMRC by including the scheme notification number on the relevant tax return or submission. HMRC will then pursue the scheme user by opening an enquiry to challenge the avoidance scheme. Tax avoidance behaviour that is successfully challenged by HMRC will lead to the original tax saving having to be paid in addition to penalties and interest on the error. The error will generally fall into the deliberate behaviour without concealment category.

So, while the scheme may seem attractive, it would result in Mary's estate being on HMRC's 'radar' and the likelihood is that any IHT saved by the scheme would have to be paid anyway, together with interest and penalties. As the penalty will be classed as deliberate and the tax underpaid is likely to exceed £25,000. It is also likely to lead to publication on HMRC's website.

Given Mary's excellent reputation, it would be strongly recommended that she not contact the boutique firm and that instead she discuss acceptable forms of IHT planning, such as the use of reliefs, that may be available to mitigate the potential IHT arising. The use of reliefs, subject to the relevant conditions being satisfied, would be viewed as good tax planning and ethically acceptable.

Chapter 28

Question 28.1

There are several tax consequences of the proposed transfer of the warehouse from the company at undervalue.

Corporation tax

The transfer of the plot of land from the company to Stewart is a disposal of a chargeable asset; any gains arising on the disposal are liable to corporation tax for the company. Stewart is connected to the company under section 286 TCGA 1992 as he controls the company through his ownership of the majority of the company's share capital. As a result, section 18 TCGA 1992 imposes market value on any capital transaction between Stewart and the company. The market value imposed by section 18 forms the base cost for any future disposal by Stewart of the warehouse.

The corporation tax payable by the company will be as follows:

	£
Deemed proceeds – market value	625,000
Less: original base cost	(100,000)
Indexation allowance*:	
$\dfrac{278.1 - 174.4}{174.4} \times 100,000$	(59,500)
Chargeable gain	465,500
Corporation tax thereon @ 19%	88,445

*Indexation factor up to 31 December 2017 only.

Close company implications

Furthermore, there are, potentially, both IHT and CGT implications if the transaction is proceeded with as a transfer at undervalue. The company is a close company under section 439 CTA 2010 as it is controlled by five or fewer participators as Stewart holds 100% of the shares.

CGT

The provisions of section 125 TCGA 1992 mean that a transfer at undervalue by a close company can result in the reduction in the base cost of the company's shares for its shareholders by the amount by which the asset is undervalued, thereby reducing the base cost Stewart can use in the calculation of CGT arising on a future disposal of the his shares in the company.

However, section 125(4) TCGA 1992 provides an exception from this legislation in several cases, including where the transferee is a participator, or an associate of a participator, in the company and an amount equal to the undervalue amount is treated as a distribution or a capital distribution; or in cases where the transferee is an employee of the company and an amount equal to the undervalue amount is treated as the employee's employment income.

In these circumstances, it is likely that the transfer at undervalue would be treated as an income distribution under section 385(1) ITTOIA 2005, unless Stewart is an employee. This works by treating the amount by which the asset is undervalued as a dividend liable to income tax. Therefore, if Stewart only pays £350,000 to the company for the land plot, he will be treated as receiving a dividend of £275,000. A distribution of this size would be subject to income tax at an effective rate of 38.1%, resulting in an income tax liability of £104,775 (ignoring the £2,000 tax-free dividend allowance).

IHT

There are also potential IHT implications to consider. Sections 94–102 IHTA 1984 contain anti-avoidance rules applying to transfers of value (e.g. sales at undervalue) by close companies. The transfer of value is apportioned between the close company's participators for IHT purposes. In Stewart's case, the entire transfer of value of £275,000 would be apportioned to Stewart for IHT purposes as he holds 100% of the shares.

Assuming Stewart made no other transfers of value in the same tax year, or in the previous seven years, the entire amount would be covered by his nil rate band (£325,000) and annual exemption (£3,000 plus a potential £3,000 from the previous tax year if it remains unused). Though there would be no IHT payable in lifetime, this chargeable lifetime transfer could affect the level of IHT on Stewart's death estate if he died within seven years. However, as it is likely that the transfer at under-value would be treated as an income distribution under section 385(1) ITTOIA 2005, unless Stewart is an employee, no CLT will arise for IHT purposes.

Chapter 31

Question 31.1

Private and Confidential
Mr Symon Cawell,
Grove House,
2 Maybury,
Belfast

1 March 2022

Dear Symon,

First, may I start by thanking you for your time at our recent meeting.

You asked me to consider the stamp duty implications of the various transactions, to which please see below.

Stamp taxes on transactions

Rental of property
Stamp duty land tax (SDLT) is chargeable on the premium at the rates applicable for non-residential property. This is calculated as follows:

	£
£0–£150,000 @ 0%	0
Next £100,000 @ 2%	2,000
Remaining £325,000 @ 5%	16,250
Total SDLT payable on premium	18,250

However, SDLT is also chargeable on 1% of the net present value of the rent exceeding £150,000. The SDLT on the rent is, therefore, 1% of £35,000 which comes to £350. Therefore, the total SDLT payable amounts to £18,600.

Purchase of house by son
No SDLT is payable as first-time buyer's relief is available because the consideration is less than £300,000 and they intend to live in the property as their only or main residence.

Sale of Government securities
No stamp duty arises on this purchase as the purchase of Government securities and loan stock is an exempt transaction.

Shares received in satisfaction of debt

You received shares worth £175,000 in lieu of repayment of the loan originally provided. Consideration subject to stamp duty is any money or money's worth provided by the purchaser. Therefore, the loan provided constitutes consideration and is thus chargeable to stamp duty as being consideration for the purchase of shares at a rate of 0.5% which comes to £875.

Gift of shares to daughter

No stamp duty arises on this as it is a gift for no consideration.

Purchase of property for daughter

As you are not replacing your main residence with this acquisition and your main residence is worth more than £40,000, this will be classed as an additional residential property acquisition. A 3% surcharge applies to each 'slice' of the consideration, thus SDLT is payable as follows:

	£
£0–£125,000 @ 3%	3,750
Remaining £57,000 @ 5%	2,850
Total SDLT payable	6,600

Should you require anything further, do not hesitate to contact me.

Yours sincerely,

An Accountant

Question 31.2

For the purpose of claiming group relief for SDLT on the transfer of the two warehouses by Armour Ltd, Armour's ownership of Destiny Ltd was 82% at the time of the transaction and thus no SDLT was payable on the sale of the warehouse to Destiny Ltd for £750,000 due to SDLT group relief. However, within a three-year period, and by 1 January 2022, Destiny is no longer a member of the group as Armour's ownership has fallen to 74%. As this is below the 75% ownership threshold, group relief will be withdrawn. SDLT of £27,000 is now payable (being the total of the first £150,000 at 0%, plus the next £100,000 at 2% and the remaining £500,000 at 5%).

Gaston Ltd did not qualify for group relief for SDLT purposes at the time it acquired the warehouse from Armour Ltd as its ownership by Armour Limited is less than 75%. However, as the chargeable consideration of £120,000 is below the non-residential threshold of £150,000, no SDLT is payable.

Question 31.3

If it is sold for £200,000 after the mortgage is paid off, the consideration is £200,000. The SDLT on the property is 0% on the first £125,000 and 2% on the next £75,000. Therefore the charge is £1,500. If it is sold for £200,000 with the son taking over the mortgage, the consideration is £250,000 (as assumption of a debt is viewed as consideration). The SDLT on the property is 0% on the first £125,000 and 2% on the next £125,000. Therefore the charge is £2,500.

The sale for £350,000 means consideration is £350,000. The SDLT on the property is 0% on the first £125,000, 2% on the next £125,000 and 5% on the next £100,000. Therefore, the charge is £7,500. The mortgage is not taken on by his son and so has no impact on the SDLT due.

Question 31.4

Assets subject to stamp duty land tax (SDLT), typically land and property, can be transferred between 75% group companies without any stamp duty liability, provided the transfer is not part of arrangements for the transferee company to leave the group or consideration for the transfer is not being provided directly or indirectly by a third party.

In this situation, no SDLT liability will arise due to the availability of SDLT group relief. However, relief from SDLT will be withdrawn if Neptune was to leave the group within three years of the execution of the instrument of transfer while still holding an interest in the freehold property. Relief would also be withdrawn if Solar's ownership of Neptune fell below 75%.

Question 31.5

Apple, Banana, and Date form a group for SDLT group relief purposes, as Banana and Date meet the 75% subsidiary test. The sale to Date Ltd was eligible for SDLT relief and one condition for that relief is that Date Ltd must remain within the SDLT group for three years after buying the warehouse.

Grape Ltd was never in the same SDLT Group as Apple Ltd, but no SDLT was due as the consideration is less than £150,000.

Question 31.6

The underpaid SDLT is as follows:

£760,000 × 20% = £152,000 (VAT)
£152,000 × 5% = £7,600 underpaid SDLT

This is an ethical question for the directors. They have become aware of an error in the SDLT return that has resulted in an underpayment of tax for the period but they are considering not disclosing the error to HMRC. As directors of the company, they have a duty to disclose the error to HMRC and thus it is recommended that they contact HMRC accordingly to make a full disclosure and pay the SDLT, any interest thereon and any penalties arising.

The penalty regime for errors focuses on the behaviour of the taxpayer, i.e. the company acting through its directors and officers. Where a company has made a mistake in a return submitted to HMRC, but has taken reasonable care in preparation of that return, no penalty will be levied by HMRC.

The categories of behaviour where penalties will be imposed are:
- careless (failure to take reasonable care);
- deliberate and not concealed (the inaccuracy is deliberate but there are no attempts made to conceal it); and
- deliberate and concealed (the inaccuracy is deliberate and there are arrangements to conceal it).

It is likely HMRC would view the behaviour as careless. The potential lost revenue (PLR) is then computed. This is the additional amount of tax due or payable as a result of correcting the inaccuracy The PLR in this case is the underpaid SDLT of £7,600.

The penalty for an error in a return is based on a % of PLR. However, HMRC may apply reductions to the proposed penalty where the company has disclosed the inaccuracy.

There are two types of disclosure – prompted and unprompted. An unprompted disclosure is made when the person making it has no reason to believe that HMRC has discovered or is about to discover the inaccuracy.

As HMRC have not opened an enquiry or contacted the company in respect of the SDLT return, the company can make an unprompted disclosure. Therefore, should HMRC argue reasonable care was not taken in preparing the return, and levy a penalty, the unprompted percentages in the table will be potentially applicable.

The maximum % penalty for a careless error is 30%. This is reduced to 15% for a prompted disclosure and 0% for an unprompted disclosure. The penalty is therefore likely to be nil.

Chapter 32

Question 32.1

(a) First-time buyer's relief is not available as Adam does not intend to live in the house as his only or main residence. The chargeable consideration is £150,000; it is irrelevant that a £30,000 deposit was paid first followed by the balance of £120,000.This is subject to SDLT at 0% on the first £125,000 and 2% on the next £25,000. Therefore SDLT of £500 is due.
(b) A SDLT return is required if the chargeable consideration is more £40,000.
(c) The SDLT return and payment are both due 14 days after completion (i.e. 14 November 2021).

Question 32.2

SDLT will be payable by the purchaser of the Dungannon Property in the amount of £13,250 (being the total of the first £150,000 at 0%, plus the next £100,000 at 2% and the remaining £225,000 at 5%). There is a 14-day time limit after execution for getting the document stamped and paying the required stamp duty. Therefore, as the transaction occurred on 31 March 2022, the SDLT and associated return must be presented to HMRC by 14 April 2022, otherwise a penalty and interest may be charged. The SDLT is a liability of the purchaser and not the vendor of thte property.

Question 32.3

Apple
As the amount being paid for the shares is below the "nil duty rate" of £1,000, no stamp duty is payable.

Peaches
As the amount being paid for the shares is above the "nil duty rate" of £1,000, the rate of stamp duty payable on the purchase of the shares is 0.5%.

Therefore, the stamp duty payable is 0.5% of £6,725 = £33.62. Stamp duty is rounded up to the nearest £5, so the actual amount payable is £35.

There is a 30-day time limit after execution (when the share transfer documents are dated and signed) for getting the document stamped and paying the required stamp duty.

Therefore, assuming the Peaches transaction proceeds on 30 April 2021, the share transfer document must be presented to HMRC by 30 May 2021 with the correct duty payment of £35 to avoid a penalty and interest being charged.

Blackberry
There is no duty payable on foreign shares, so the stamp duty here is nil.

Question 32.4

(a) A transfer of UK unlisted shares worth £90,000 on divorce from husband to wife is exempt from stamp duty.

(b) A sale of shares in a UK listed company for £524,000 to a registered UK charity is exempt from stamp duty (subject to being adjudicated).
(c) A sale of shares in a UK unlisted company for £150,000 between unconnected individuals is stampable at 0.5% × £150,000 = £750.
(d) A sale of UK shares worth £895 between unconnected parties does not attract a stamp duty liability because the consideration is less than £1,000.
(e) A sale of shares in a UK unlisted company for £60,000 in cash and an agreement to waive £20,000 of debt owed by seller to purchaser attracts stamp duty at 0.5% on £80,000, being £400, as the debt waiver counts towards consideration.

Chapter 34

Question 34.1

Calculation of Happy Pets Ltd VAT liability for March–May 2021:

	Net of VAT	VAT Payable
	£	£
VAT on Sales		
Supplies in UK	250,000	50,000
Supplies to US (Note 1)	10,000	0
Purchases from Ireland (Note 2)		10,000
VAT on sales		60,000

	Net of VAT	VAT Recoverable
VAT on Purchases		
Purchase of stock from UK suppliers (£223,260 × 1/6)	186,050	37,210
Purchase of stock from Ireland (Note 2)	50,000	10,000
Professional fees (£5,880 × 1/6)	4,900	980
Oil (£1,050 × 1/6)	875	175
Computer (£8,934 × 1/6)	7,445	1,489
		49,854

VAT on sales	60,000
VAT on purchases	(49,854)
VAT payable	10,346

Notes:
1. An export, therefore the supply is zero-rated irrespective of the type of goods sold.
2. Where goods are purchased for business purposes from an EU country by a business in Northern Ireland, the supply is zero rated and the supplier will not charge VAT, provided they are given the VAT number of the EU purchaser. The purchaser must account for VAT on the reverse charge basis in their VAT return (assume 100% VAT recovery and partial exemption rules do not apply).

Question 34.2

	Net of VAT	Output VAT
	£	£
VAT on sales (output VAT)		
Sales in UK (£950,000 × 20%)	950,000	190,000
Sales to Spain (to Spanish registered customers)	320,000	0
Sales to non-VAT-registered customers in Ireland (£25,000 × 20%)	25,000	5,000
Sales to VAT-registered customers in Ireland	135,000	0
Sales to customers located in Singapore	46,000	0
VAT on sales		195,000
VAT on EU acquisitions (£200,000 × 20%)	200,000	40,000
Total VAT on sales		235,000

	VAT-inc	VAT Content	Total VAT Content
	£	£	£
VAT on costs (input VAT):			
Purchase of materials from UK suppliers (£423,000 × 1/6)	423,000	70,500	
Purchase of machinery locally (£235,020 × 1/6)	235,020	39,170	
Legal fees (£11,748 × 1/6)	11,748	1,958	
Repairs and maintenance of office and equipment (£16,212 ×1/6)	16,212	2,702	
Audit and accountancy fees (£12,924 × 20%)	12,924	2,154	
Electricity and gas (£2,520 × 1/6)	2,520	420	
Salaries and wages	167,000	0	
Advertising costs (£35,250 × 1/6)	35,250	5,875	
			122,779
EU acquisitions	200,000	40,000	40,000
VAT on costs			162,779

VAT on sales	235,000	
VAT on purchases	(162,779)	
VAT payable	73,000	

Question 34.3

IGL, IIL and TIL operate within the UK. Their VAT profiles can be summarised as follows:

- IIL provides a VAT-exempt service (insurance). Therefore, no input VAT is currently recoverable in respect of its purchases.
- The services provided by IGL and TIL are liable to VAT and thus they can recover VAT on purchases subject to the normal rules.

In the last two quarters the group incurred input VAT of £348,042 and recovered £220,579 or 63.4% (full input VAT recovery by IGL and TIL) of that.

A VAT group is treated in the same way as a single company registered for VAT on its own. In a VAT group, the "representative member" is responsible for all VAT accounting, including the completion and submission of the VAT return. IGL, IIL and TIL qualify to apply for group VAT registration as they are all bodies corporate and each:

- is established or has a fixed establishment in the UK; and
- is under common "control".

All the companies within a VAT group are jointly and severally liable for any VAT due. Thus, they are not liable for only their share of the VAT, but for the whole VAT due from the group. The main effect of VAT registration is that any supplies made between members of the VAT group are disregarded. All that is considered is what is coming into the group and what is going out of the group as a whole. What is happening within the group is irrelevant.

In this case, this would have meant that the output VAT in respect of the charges from IGL would have been eliminated as follows:

	IIL	TIL
Period 12/21	**£**	**£**
Amount charged from IGL	90,000	90,000
Output VAT eliminated thereon	18,000	18,000
Period 9/21		
Amount charged from IGL	90,000	90,000
Output VAT eliminated thereon	18,000	18,000

Irrecoverable output VAT saved for IIL would have amounted to £36,000. However, the group would have been deemed to be partially exempt, which would have had the following impact:

1. Input VAT of £112,192 (i.e. £71,345 + £76,847 − £36,000) would arise on purchases used solely for the VAT-liable business of TIL.
2. Input VAT of £91,663 (i.e. £60,334 + £67,129 − £36,000) on purchases used solely for the VAT-exempt business of IIL.
3. Input VAT of £72,387 (i.e. £35,086 + £37,301) on purchases of IGL relating to the general operation of the business (i.e. dual use inputs) that will need to be split on an agreed recovery basis.

Items 1. and 2. do not represent any change from the current recovery position. The recovery basis for 3. would need to be chosen by considering the most reasonable way to split the VAT, e.g. turnover, number of employees, square footage used, etc. For illustration purposes, I have used turnover but further work would be required before this method is agreed as most appropriate for the group.

The IIL to TIL turnover split is 50.5 to 49.5 (i.e. £1,812,000 to £1,774,000) and so 50.5% of IGL's dual use input VAT (£36,555) would be irrecoverable. The balance of £35,832 is recoverable.

In the last six-month period, IGL has charged IIL and TIL £288,000 for its services. IIL's portion of that VAT is £36,000, which was not recoverable. As outlined above, the irrecoverable amount in that six-month period would be increased to £36,193 if all activities had been consolidated into the one VAT group in that period. Therefore, if the companies had been in a VAT group, additional irrecoverable VAT would have arisen over and above the amount of irrecoverable output VAT saved.

A six-month period is a very limited timeframe to analyse and I recommend we look at a 12-month period or perhaps longer to conclude if the companies should form a VAT group.

Question 34.4

If the suspicions are correct, the omitted turnover falls to be included in the 31 December 2020 VAT return. It would be unethical to either omit this (which would constitute tax evasion) or to ignore your concerns (which would be a breach of the *Code of Ethics* of Chartered Accountants Ireland).

As Hayley's tax advisor, you should discuss the issue first with your manager before emphasising to Hayley the importance of ensuring that VAT returns are complete and the potential penalties that could arise for failure to include all relevant items.

Deliberately understating turnover to reduce the VAT payable is tax evasion, which is a criminal offence. You may be required to report this to your firm's Money Laundering Reporting Officer (MLRO) who will decide whether or not a report should be made to the Serious Organised Crime Agency.

Note to students: in respect of any ethical scenario, marks will always be awarded for any other reasonable points made not included in the suggested solution.

Chapter 35

Question 35.1

(a) The sale of the freehold of an office block constructed in November 2019 is the sale of a new commercial property (under three years old) therefore this is a standard-rated supply on which 20% output VAT must be charged.
(b) The grant of a 99-year lease in a brand new factory is the grant of a lease. This is not a standard-rated supply and because it is commercial property it is therefore an exempt supply as the option to tax has not been elected for.
(c) The sale of the freehold of a factory first constructed in January 2017 is the sale of a commercial property that is not new and is therefore an exempt supply as the option to tax has not been elected for.

Question 35.2

(a) A factory is a commercial property and the word "lease" means it is an exempt supply as the option to tax has not been elected for.

(b) Some domestic property is zero-rated, i.e. residential property that is brand new and is being sold by the constructor – this property does not meet either of these criteria, therefore it is not a zero-rated supply. It cannot be standard-rated as it is not commercial property, therefore it is an exempt supply.

(c) As this is a sale of a new commercial freehold, it is standard-rated and 20% output VAT must be charged.

(d) As this is the sale of a commercial freehold that has been opted to tax, despite the property not being new, this is a standard-rated supply and 20% output VAT must be charged.

Question 35.3

As the building is a new commercial building less than three years old, the sale of the building will have been standard-rated. VAT charged thereon would have been £90,000 (£450,000 × 20%).

As EyeSpy Ltd is partially exempt, it would have been entitled to recover input tax of £63,000 (£90,000 × 70%) in the year ending 31 March 2022.

Question 35.4

(a) The sale of land is an exempt supply and the option to tax can be made on this supply.

(b) The sale of a 75-year-old terraced house is an exempt supply, but it is a dwelling and residential building rather than a commercial building, so the option to tax can be made but will not be effective.

(c) The lease of a 15-year-old factory is an exempt supply – because it is a commercial building, the option to tax can be made.

(d) The freehold sale of a two-year-old office block – the sale of a new, commercial freehold is a standard-rated supply. It is therefore not exempt so the option to tax is not relevant.

(e) A 99-year lease on a one-year-old shop – this is not the sale of a new commercial freehold, so it is an exempt supply. An option to tax can therefore be made.

Question 35.5

(a) The freehold sale of a two-year-old factory is freehold, new and commercial and hence a standard-rated supply. An option to tax could be made but would not have any effect.

(b) The grant of a 30-year lease in a brand new office block is an exempt supply. As it is an exempt supply of a commercial building, the option to tax will be effective.

(c) A farmer rents out a plot of land to another farmer. This is not residential so it is not zero-rated. It is not the sale of new commercial property and is thus not standard-rated. Therefore this must be an exempt supply. The option to tax can be made because it can be effective over an exempt supply of any sort of land.

(d) A landlord leases out four floors of a building to an insurance company – it is a lease, it is a commercial building so it is an exempt supply. The exempt supply of a commercial building means the option to tax can be made and effective. It does not matter that the tenant is making exempt supplies. The option will mean standard-rate VAT at 20% will be charged on any supplies in relation to this property, including rents. As the tenant is exempt they will not be able to recover the related input VAT.

(e) This is a lease of residential property, so it is an exempt supply. It does not matter that the tenant is using the property for business purposes. Zero-rating does not apply as no major interest has been granted. The option to tax is not effective over a domestic property.

Question 35.6

(a) Renovating and building services are standard-rated supplies, so VAT will be charged to Mr Jones on these costs.
(b) Since Mr James is leasing a commercial property, he is making an exempt supply so the input tax on the renovation costs will relate to the exempt supply of that office block and will be irrecoverable. If Mr James were to opt to tax the building, he would then be making a taxable supply. Thus, when the renovation occurs, the input tax he pays will relate to a taxable supply and hence will be recoverable in full.

The option to tax means that any future supply he makes in connection with the office block will be a standard-rated supply. The next time he sends an invoice for rent to his tenants, he will have to add 20% VAT on top. For the tenants, they will receive an invoice for rent that has gone up by 20%.

One of those tenants is an accountant making fully taxable supplies. Therefore, the extra 20% is input tax for the accountant and because the accountant makes taxable supplies, the input tax charged on the rent is recoverable in full. The most that the accountant tenant will 'suffer' from the 20% increase is a cash-flow disadvantage.

The other tenant is an insurance company, which makes exempt supplies. When the rent goes up by 20% that increase is input tax, which is irrecoverable as it relates to exempt supplies. This will be a direct cost to the insurance company.

When the landlord makes an option to tax, he does not have to seek permission from the tenants before doing so. However, the landlord should check the lease agreement because some lease agreements do not allow the rent to be increased (even by VAT). In such cases, the irrecoverable VAT must be met out of the landlord's rental profits. If the lease agreement is silent, the landlord can make an option to tax without any permission being given by the tenants.

Question 35.7

Even though the property is not less than three years old it has been opted to tax by its owner, therefore 20% standard-rate VAT of £250,000 (£1,250,000 × 20%) is chargeable by the vendor, Spidey Enterprises Ltd. The total consideration is therefore £1,500,000 (£1,250,000 + £250,000). The SDLT liability of Iron Man Developments Ltd that arises on the VAT-inclusive price is as follows:

	£
0–£150,000 @ 0%	0
Next £100,000 @ 2%	2,000
Remaining £1,250,000 @ 5%	62,500
Total SDLT	64,500

Index